Women in the Modern World

Women
in the Modern World

EDITED AND WITH AN INTRODUCTION BY

Raphael Patai

The Free Press, New York
Collier-Macmillan Limited, London

Contents

Women in the Modern World

Introduction

By Raphael Patai

THE BOOK AND ITS AUTHORS

This book attempts to present a survey of the changes that have taken place in the status of women in recent decades, and, particularly, since World War II.

In general terms, these changes can be summarized briefly: throughout the world women have moved toward greater freedom and have achieved greater equality with men both within and outside the family, in the legal, sexual, social, occupational, economic, political, and cultural realms. The old order, which confined women to the home as servants, and helpers to their menfolk, has been, or is in the process of being, replaced by a new one in which women increasingly undertake to fill many roles, within the home, as wives, mothers, and homemakers, and outside it, as partners and coworkers of men in all types of enterprises.

Most of the twenty-four contributors to this volume are natives or residents of the countries or geographical areas they discuss. They include professors of sociology or other social sciences at various universities, and authors who for years have been thoughtful and critical observers of the local scene. Only two are "outsiders," in the sense of being neither natives nor residents of the areas they describe, but they have been lifelong students of these areas. Eighteen of the articles were written by women; three by men, and one by a team of two men and one woman. Yet the tenor of all twenty-two articles is unmistakably one of emphatic approval of change; they all endorse an equalization of the position of the two sexes; they all consider moves in this direction an advance; and they all envisage a future in which these processes of change will become accomplished facts.

In view of this unanimity, which reflects the actual prevailing mood and endeavor of the younger generation of women in most of the world, it is a noteworthy fact that the closer women are to equality with men in any given country the less they seem to wish to make use of this achievement by devoting their lives to professional careers. It is as if, having started out from a base line representing the traditional position of legal and social disability and a life confined in its entirety to home and family, the developments in the most advanced Western countries had described a full circle and reached a goal that, at least in its practical connotations, is found to lie very close to the start. A discussion of the various stages of this circular development will help in viewing the local variants, described in the twenty-two articles, against the background of this world-wide trend.

THE BASE LINE OF CHANGE

In order to trace the base line of the changes, we must go far back into history. Students of prehistory have not yet agreed whether, at the dawn of civilization, there was a "matriarchal age" characterized by female domination over males. But by the time the earliest sources of human history began to flow in sufficient abundance to give us an intelligible picture of the relationship between men and women, a patriarchal society was the prevalent form of social organization. This, at least, was the case in the Near East which boasts of the oldest recorded history of mankind. There were six outstanding characteristics of the man–woman relationship in these societies: 1) They were headed by a male ruler; 2) Men dominated women and considered them property; 3) Men were entitled to several wives as well as concubines whereas women were restricted to premarital chastity and marital fidelity; 4) All or most occupations were male preroga- tives and women were confined to housework and to helping their menfolk in agricultural tasks; 5) Temple and secular prostitutes were available to men, but the average woman was supposed to have little or no contact with men except for members of her family; and 6) The value of a woman was correlated with her ability to bear children (especially male children), yet women were regarded as ritually impure during their procreative period and, in particular, during and after their menses and delivery. There were, of course, many local variations of this picture, but its traits can easily be recognized in ancient Egypt, Babylonia, Palestine, Greece, and Rome, to mention only the major classical fountainheads of modern Western culture, and essentially identical conditions could be found in many, if not most, parts of the world up to the beginning of the twentieth century.

The demand for marital fidelity was carried to its extreme in India in the institution of *sati* (the burning of widows upon the death of their husbands). Also from India come the term and concept of *purdah* (the complete segregation of women), although this practice was, and to some extent still is, equally prevalent in parts of the Muslim world as well as several other world areas.

It is significant that, dissatisfied as European man was with most aspects of his cultural patrimony, he found nothing to be changed or improved in connection with the traditional status of women. Consequently, while he devoted prodigious energy to introducing successive improvements into practically all of the cultural realms bequeathed to him by preceding generations—art, architecture, astronomy, mathematics, geometry, mechanics, medicine, chemistry, physics, law, ethics, and even religion—he left untouched the ancient rules that governed the position of women and the relationship between women and men. This reluctance to tamper with what were considered ultimate and permanent solutions involving unalterable and delicate balances meant that the status of women in Europe and America as recently as the nineteenth century differed only in insignificant detail from that of Near Eastern women of four or five thousand years earlier. Exactly how remarkable this persistence of ancient sex mores was becomes apparent only if we consider that in all other areas of social relationships new developments had made the old ways obsolete and even unlawful. The subordination of certain groups of human beings to others had come to be regarded with abhorrence as incompatible with humane principles. But even after the abolition of serfdom and slavery, men felt no shame at keeping women in a state of subjugation. Even in the early years of the twentieth century, women did not have the suffrage. It was not granted them until 1913 in Norway, 1915 in Denmark, 1918 in England, 1920 in the United States, and 1921 in Sweden, and was granted even more recently in other European, American, and certain Asian and African countries. Whatever property women owned was controlled by their fathers or husbands; their marriages were arranged by their parents; and restrictions of varying severity were put upon their activities, interests, and even their use of language.

The West of Yesterday

The actual position of women in various countries of the world before the onset of what could be called the feminine revolution is described in the opening sections of the articles contained in this volume. The emerging picture has two dissimilar sides. In the Western World, the well-to-do middle- and upper-class women lived lives of idleness, were closely guarded and chaperoned, and were educated to become empty-headed but refined, shallow but charming ornaments of a man's world. These women lacked the training, the need, and the desire to work. That they did not have the right either, bothered them as little as the knowledge (if it ever reached them) of their disability in practically all fields, and the fact that they were permanently under the guardianship of a male: father, husband, or other relative. If circumstances pulled the economic rug from under their feet, and they remained without the financial support of a relative, they usually went under. Just as it was considered improper for a lady to earn a living, so too was it difficult for her even to know how to earn one.

These middle- and upper-class women, however, were only a small minority in every country. Most of the women (like most of the men) belonged to the lower class, and their circumstances represented the other side of the picture. Prior to the industrial revolution, the lower- or working-class woman usually belonged to a farming family, or, in cities, to a family of shopkeepers, small artisans, or service people. Following the industrial revolution, she was, with increasing frequency, the daughter or wife of a factory worker or miner. As far as her legal rights were concerned, she had as few as the middle- or upper-class members of her sex. As to domination by males, again her situation was largely the same. Yet if she lived in a cage, it was certainly not gilded, nor could it be kept constantly locked, for the simple reason that the working-class woman often had to undertake work outside her home in order to supplement the income of her menfolk. The peasant woman helped her husband on the farm, the wife of the shopkeeper in the shop, the artisan's wife in the workshop. The industrial revolution, which, in most places, preceded the feminine revolution by a few decades, placed an ever-increasing number of girls and women in factory jobs. The working-class woman was thus an economic asset, first to her father and later to her husband, and this single factor made all the difference in her status. A woman who contributed to the income of the family could not be dominated or controlled by the man to the same extent as the woman kept idle all day in her husband's house. Shared responsibilities inevitably brought about a certain sharing of prerogatives as well.

TRADITIONAL WESTERN SEX MORES

An important aspect of the difference between the position of the middle- and upper-class women, on the one hand, and that of the lower- or working-class women, on the other, manifested itself in the sensitive area of sex mores. Middle- and upper-class sex mores in the nineteenth century were characterized by the double standard which can be traced back to the ancient Near East and which holds that everything is permitted to man while everything is forbidden to woman. To enforce women's conformity to what Levy Cruz calls the complexes of virginity and matrimonial fidelity, the middle and upper class resorted to an array of preventive measures that made it extremely difficult if not impossible for a woman to talk to or to be alone with a man not directly related to her. Under these circumstances a girl had few opportunities to fall in love, and she had neither the maturity of judgment nor the will power to object to the spouse chosen for her by her parents.

In both sectors of society, it was taken for granted that men and women see each other primarily as sex objects. Consequently, a man and a woman would wish to remain alone together for one aim only: sexual intercourse. The ideals of premarital chastity for girls and marital fidelity for women were upheld more or less equally by all classes throughout the Western world, with the exception of the Scandinavian countries in which premarital sex relations by girls were countenanced by the peasants and the birth of a child to an unmarried girl was regarded as a sign of her ability to bear children. However, even in countries where premarital chastity was the generally accepted ideal, there were considerable differences in the degree of actual adherence to it. Among the middle and upper classes, most girls and women could be kept apart from men, and by careful chaperonage and restrictive measures it was, in most cases, possible to enforce upon them both premarital chastity and marital fidelity. A woman who allowed herself to be manipulated into a position where there was even the faintest possibility of her being seduced was therefore fair game. The assumption was that a "lady" would know how to avoid anything that even remotely resembled a risky situation. Since, however, considerable latitude in sex was granted to men, the two contradictory moralities could be maintained only by providing men with sexual objects outside of their own class. This contradiction caused the middle and upper classes to consider prostitution an indispensable institution.

The lower or working class was prevented by its living conditions from realizing the ideals of female chastity and fidelity to any degree comparable to middle- and upper-class mores. Girls working in the fields, fetching water or brushwood, or employed in factories could not be chaperoned and kept from meeting young men. Fortuitous encounters could not be prevented from leading to planned meetings, and these, in turn, from developing into assignations. Nineteenth-century statistics on the subject are not available, but it can be assumed that they would not differ materially from what present-day returns tell us about rural areas in Latin countries which have as yet barely been touched by the social changes of the last two generations, and which show a relatively high frequency of premarital sex experience among girls (for instance, as high as 20 per cent in a Sicilian small town).

The Change Sets In

Such, in brief, was the position of women in the Western world up to the end of the nineteenth century. Within each country there was a deep cleavage between the position of middle- or upper-class women and the position of lower- or working-class women. Differences between one country and the other, however, were neither numerous nor significant. In fact, the changes which have resulted in the present pronounced variations in the position of women in various parts of the Western world are of very recent vintage.

How these variations arose is an intriguing question. Many of the details are given in the articles in this book. Generally speaking, the last few decades have seen changes that have moved each country in the same direction — improving the position of women. Some countries started on this road earlier than others. Again, the rate of change was not identical everywhere; some countries moved ahead briskly and resolutely, others only yielded their old attitudes and mores inch-by-inch. The result today is that the social position of women, especially of those of the middle class, differs greatly among the countries of the Western world.

The emancipation of woman, as a rule, proceeded hand in hand with a lessening of class differences. Simultaneously the gap between the once wealthy middle class and the poor working class narrowed, and both classes moved toward a median position in which their differences tended to become blurred.

As far as values and mores are concerned, Soviet Russia and Communist China are the only countries treated in this volume that have deliberately attempted to make those of the working class be accepted by society as a whole. In the non-Communist Western world, on the other hand, middle-class values and aspirations are generally upheld, and have become increasingly dominant in all sectors of society. With regard to the position of women, however, middle-class mores and values have given way, even in the free world, to those of the lower or working class. For it cannot be denied that what modern socioeconomic developments have brought about has been an extension upward into the middle class of certain features that for a long time were characteristic only of lower or working-class women.

One of these features is the entrance of middle-class women into all types of gainful employment. As recently as World War I, the simplest and surest means of distinguishing between a middle-class and a lower-class family was to take a look at their women. If they did not work, the chances were that the family belonged to the middle class; if they did, it was, in all probability, a lower-class family. Obviously, this distinction no longer holds true. Only two generations ago, a middle-class woman engaged in a gainful occupation outside her home was viewed with suspicion, ridicule, or pity. Today, she is an accepted part of the social order. Moreover, the degree of participation of women in the labor force can be used as an index to the "advanced" status of a country, in the same manner as its per capita income, literacy, newsprint consumption, transportation, communications, life expectancy, morbidity, and so on. This, of course, is a generalized statement, which must be qualified in the light of the data contained in the various articles in this book.

THE NEW SEX MORES

Another characteristic of lower- or working-class women, which in recent decades has been extended upward into the middle class, is their greater sexual freedom. In this area, the middle class has not only followed the lead of the lower class (unawares, of course, for consciously the middle class would not dream of emulating a class beneath it in status, and the general trend is for the lower class to adopt as many middle-class traits as feasible), but in many places it has outdistanced it and given to its women (or allowed them to acquire) a freedom of sexual behavior equaling that of men. This, however, is an area in which there are still considerable differences among the various countries of the Western world.

Closest to the traditional situation are the Latin countries and Greece, in which the gap between the very strict sexual mores of the middle and upper classes and the relatively lax ones of the lower class has barely begun to narrow. The traditional concept of family honor, highly vulnerable to any, even the slightest, sexual transgression by its women members, is still a dominant concern of both the middle and upper classes, and still leads, especially in the middle class, to a jealous guarding of girls and women.

On the other hand, there are those countries (such as the Scandinavian countries, Soviet Russia, and, to a lesser extent, Germany, France, England, and the United States) in which the double standard of sexual morality has by and large disappeared, and the degree of freedom in sexual conduct, though dependent in each case on the social class, is the same for both sexes. It would be tempting to speculate on the factors responsible for this difference between the Latin and the Mediterranean countries and those of Central and Northern Europe and North America. Climate, race, cultural traditions, economic circumstances, religion — any or all of these may, and probably do enter the picture. Whatever the causes, it is significant that there is a variable that places the Mediterranean countries of Europe (as well as their cultural heirs in America) in an intermediate position between the rest of the Western world and the Middle East.

Closely connected with the development of new sex mores in the Western countries are the rapid advances in the field of women's rights. Vestiges of the old disabilities still survive here and there (for instance, the British law providing that the proceeds from the joint efforts of husband and wife belong to the former, or the Argentinian law, which makes the husband the administrator of his wife's property). But on the whole, the legal position has changed more in the last five decades than during the previous five millennia, and has reached the stage throughout the Western world where the principle of equality of men and women before the law has not only been accepted theoretically, but approximated in actual reality. The leader in these developments is Scandinavia, where the legal equality of women and men has reached a level unique in the entire Western world. What this means, and how great has been the distance traversed in all countries in a relatively short period, is shown in each article of this book in sections that deal with the traditional situation and the legal position of women.

FEMALE SPECIALIZATIONS IN THE WEST

As far as the legal, economic, and social aspects of their existence are concerned, women of the Western world, or at least an ever-increasing number of them, have achieved the bold dream of the early suffragettes: equality with men. Yet there are certain biologically determined factors that make complete "equality" of the sexes impossible. For one thing, women, generally, have smaller frames than men, weigh less, and wield less muscle power. Those who become mothers are, temporarily, incapacitated by childbearing. These differences make it difficult, if not impossible, for them to engage in all types of work on an equal footing with men.

In the past, in various societies around the world, there have been isolated examples of women undertaking activities that are usually considered the preserves of men. The Amazon army of the King of Dahomey and the women pearl divers of Japan are examples that readily come to mind. The only example that can be found today of a disregard for women's lesser muscular strength is Soviet Russia's practice of employing women for such work as road-building, construction work, mining, porterage, street-cleaning, and the like. In all other countries (including the other Communist countries of Europe), equality of women in employment means that they encounter no legal obstacle or social prejudice in seeking work of their own choice in accordance with their skills, inclinations, and physical ability.

These factors seem to be responsible for the concentration of women in occupations that are closely related to the tasks they have fulfilled in the past as part of their traditionally-defined scope of activities within the family. It has always been the mother who taught her children in their early years, and teaching has long been one of the few professions open to women. Today, when informal socialization has everywhere become supplemented by formal schooling, this extension of the mother's original educational task is mostly taken care of by women, who constitute the majority (75 to 80 per cent in some countries) of the teachers in the lower grades of the elementary schools.

Another traditional female task has been caring for the sick, whether child, husband, sibling, or elderly parent. With the increase in hospital facilities, the importance of this household role has diminished, although it has by no means disappeared. And because of this tradition, women have turned to nursing as a profession so intensively that it has become an almost exclusively female specialization.

There are several other female specializations as well, related to teaching and nursing in the sense that they too, essentially consist of rendering personal services to people in need of help. Social work and counseling are among these, although in some Western countries they are only now being introduced and therefore the number of women employed in them is quite small.

Somewhat more remotely related to the realm of personal services is the work of secretaries, typists, stenographers, and other office personnel, most of whom are women, who generally work for male bosses. All in all, it appears that even in the most emancipated and equalized society many (or, perhaps, most) women work at tasks that have some relationship to the roles they always have played within the family. Thus in the modern Western world there remains a considerable division of labor according to sex. Even where there is no legal obstacle that would prevent women from occupying equal positions in all work branches, there are nevertheless certain occupations staffed solely or mostly by women, while others remain male domains.

On the other hand, there is one handicap under which women still suffer in most countries of the Western world: where men and women perform the same work, women are usually paid less than men. In spite of this much decried social injustice, women in general take a relatively small interest in labor-union activities.

"But We Prefer the Home"

A different question is whether women are happy with their recent achievements. This question arises only after the "liberation" of women has become an accomplished fact and, more than that, a normal part of the social order. Once it has become taken for granted that women have all the freedom men have, that they can earn a living in all or most occupations just as easily, or with as much difficulty as men, the status of being a breadwinner is apt to lose its challenge and assume the character of daily drudgery. When this stage is reached, most women begin to have second thoughts and, with the exception of a relatively few career women, come to the conclusion that to marry, bear children, raise them, and be a homemaker is preferable to working outside the home. In societies which allow their women sufficient leeway to play simultaneously, or to shuttle back and forth between, "women's two roles," to use Alva Myrdal's and Viola Klein's phrase, they tend more and more to concentrate on the role within the home of wife, mother, and homemaker, rather than that of the career woman working or competing with men on various occupational and professional levels. These societies are all part of the Western world, or, to be even more precise, of the most Westernized part within it, the one which spearheads the achievements of modern Western civilization. The most outspoken female utterances voicing this latest feminine attitude come from the United States, Great Britain, Scandinavia, and Soviet Russia. In these countries, having to a large extent achieved what they wanted, women now are saying in effect: "Now that we have won the right to take an equal place in a man's world, we prefer to return to the home, to our own places in our women's world. It is good to know that we can play both roles, that we have a right to both worlds, but we shall be satisfied with relatively brief excursions into the world of men before taking up, or after having fulfilled, the role to which nature has predestined us, of being wife, mother, and home maker."

The Afro-Asian Majority of Mankind

Asia and Africa contain two thirds of the world population — well over two billion out of a total of three in 1967 — and it is estimated that before the end of this century they will be the home of more than three fourths of mankind, which by that time will have passed the six billion mark. Whatever happens to the people of Asia and Africa is, therefore, happening to most of the world and should also be of concern to the non-Afro-Asian minority of the human race.

On several other counts, too, Asia and Africa can claim the interest of the rest of the world. They offer a unique and fascinating variety of cultures—varying from those of the most primitive tribes, technologically still in the stone age, to those of highly sophisticated societies which produced literary masterpieces centuries and even millennia before the Romans learned how to read and write. All the races of mankind originated in Asia and Africa. In these areas can be found the tallest and the shortest people in the world, and those possessing the longest and the shortest life-spans. The oldest nations and the newest ones are located in these two continents.

Yet with all this variety and extreme range, there are a number of common features characterizing Afro-Asia in contradistinction to Europe and America. The most significant of these is undoubtedly the tradition-bound orientation which has been, until the recent onset (or, should one say, onslaught?) of Westernization, the predominant Afro-Asian mood and outlook on life, and which has had a profound effect on social order in general and on the position of the Afro-Asian woman in particular.

Of the two continents, Africa is the home of the newest nations, those that have been independent for only the last few years. Sub-Saharan Africa is also the "dark" continent in the sense that little is known about its history prior to its penetration by European or Arab travelers, missionaries, and conquerors. This, however, does not mean that the unrecorded antecedents of these peoples are of a lesser antiquity than those of their neighbors to the north and the east. The paradox, that the peoples with both the longest and shortest histories—the Egyptians and the Negroes—are next-door neighbors in Africa, is only apparent. Some six thousand years ago, when the recorded history of Egypt began, the Negroid peoples were as much part of the African scene as they are today, and it is only because they, in contrast to the ancient Egyptians, left few historical records that their present-day descendants appear to us as "historyless." What the course of their history was, we do not and cannot know, but that their present socio-cultural order is the end result of a historical development as long as that of Egypt cannot be doubted.

These considerations, together with the observed facts of the traditional nature of all Afro-Asian cultures, allow us to make the generalization that the position of women in both continents had remained largely unchanged for millennia until their relatively recent contacts with the West. As a general rule, woman was regarded as a lower kind of creature, made periodically impure by her menses and by childbirth—in which state man must not touch her. She was considered mentally inferior to man, suspected of having no soul, and excluded from religious teachings and most religious ritual.

Traditional Freedoms in Afro-Asia

And yet, by a peculiar quirk of ancient Near Eastern outlook, still dominant in many parts of Afro-Asia, this lowly creature, whose every step must be directed and controlled by men, was (and is) in a position to either uphold or utterly destroy the honor of her family. No crime committed by a son could bring such devastating disgrace upon the entire gens or even clan, as the slightest infringement of the sex mores by a daughter. Apprehension of this danger, which does not pass even with the daughter's marriage, is one of the reasons for the birth of a girl being an unwelcome event in most parts of Africa and Asia.

It is remarkable, to say the least, that in a world in which this was the institutionally embedded position of women, there should nevertheless have developed notions of romantic love, and individual women should have achieved positions of prominence and even leadership. This, however, does not change the fact that, in general, the situation of women in most cultures of Africa and Asia was one of oppression, subjugation, and subservience to men.

An example of an ancient and tradition-bound culture, in which women nevertheless enjoyed a high degree of freedom, is presented in the article on Burma. Since women already had freedom, all that had to be done following Burma's emergence as a modern state was to incorporate into its new constitution the traditional claims of Burmese women to equal consideration with men. The exceptional character of this situation becomes evident if one moves across the border into Vietnam. There, until the enactment of the 1958 Family Law, women were classed with infants and the insane as incompetent.

The denial of rights to women and a double standard of morality are almost inevitably companion phenomena. Thus, the oppression of women, as well as the emphasis on premarital chastity of girls and marital fidelity of wives—while men are allowed the greatest latitude in matters of sex— is a general characteristic of the sex mores in most cultures of Africa and Asia. One of the notable exceptions is sub-Saharan Africa where, in many cases, the indigenous cultural development gives equal sexual freedom to men and women. Rituals for the sexual initiation of girls, institutionalized or patterned premarital relations, men who will offer services to a husband in exchange for the privilege of enjoying his wife's favors are some of the peculiarly African expressions of the sexual freedom of women. As soon as Islam intrudes upon the traditional African scene, however, these indigenous institutions tend to become replaced by the familiar Muslim double standard of sexual mores.

The "Purdah" System

For one who has not directly observed how female seclusion, veiling, harem, or purdah function, it is difficult to visualize what their effect is on the daily lives of not only the women themselves, but the family and the society as a whole. That the women, including small girls approaching puberty, are extremely limited in their movements, and that no man outside the male members of their immediate families must ever see them, are the most widely-known features of this system. Less publicized and appreciated is the meaning of the purdah system to the family and society.

As far as family life is concerned—and the typical purdah-observing family is usually an extended or joint family consisting of three generations with collateral relatives added—within the home, men and women form two separate groups, with little contact between them. The women's world, which centers around the home, is of no concern to the men. The men's world, which comprises everything outside the home (often to the extent of the men even taking care of the purchase of foodstuffs in the market), is of no concern to the women. The women are kept in ignorance of all the things that occupy their menfolk throughout the day. However, since the women are uneducated and often illiterate, in all probability, they would not be capable of understanding the men's affairs, even if they were given accounts of them. A result of this situation is that the men and women of the same family have literally nothing in common except the small day-to-day events that take place within the home. It is inevitable that under these circumstances sex should play an inordinately important role as the only tie between husband and wife, and that the relationship between the two should be dominated by the husband's possessive, often obsessive, jealousy.

For the younger generation, whose early socialization is in the hands of the mother, the purdah system means that the first influences which decisively mold their personalities for their entire lives are absorbed from individuals who are ignorant, limited, and superstitious, and who feel insecure outside their narrowest family circle. A socialization process emanating from such a source cannot fail to produce tradition-bound, over-conservative personalities lacking imagination, enterprise, and initiative.

In society, the purdah system simply means that there is no social life as is known and enjoyed in the Western world. The men meet in cafes, in the bazaar, in places of worship and business, at sports and entertainments, and more recently, in political groups. Women are excluded from all these activities, with the exception of those few women who are present as entertainers or in some related professional capacity. The most frequently encountered Western form of social intercourse—that of a group of young men and girls, or married couples, getting together in each others' homes to chat, eat, drink, and dance—does not exist in purdah society; does not, because it cannot.

This type of family and social life is the breeding ground of the well-known attitude characteristic of most, if not all, individuals produced by it. These individuals see members of the opposite sex primarily as sex objects and take it for granted that if a man and woman are alone, it must inevitably lead to one outcome—sexual intercourse. This inbred assumption motivates men to insist on a strict enforcement of the purdah rules upon all women under their jurisdiction: daughters, wives, and sisters. In this manner, a vicious circle is created, whereby the purdah system produces men who insist on its continuation.

WESTERNIZATION AND WOMEN

The winds of Westernization, which tear at some Afro-Asian countries like a mighty storm while caressing others like a gentle breeze, never leave the position of women untouched. In Negro African societies this usually means the elimination of both their traditional sexual freedom and the venerable socioeconomic institution of polygamy. In Muslim countries, Westernization has had varied effects. In Turkey and Tunisia, polygamy was officially outlawed. In Syria, Lebanon, Egypt, Jordan, and Iran it remained legal, but has almost completely disappeared from the upper and middle reaches of society. In Pakistan, modern-minded women have gone counter to the centuries-old *ijma'*, the consensus of opinion of Muslim religio-legal experts, that, in traditional circles, has in itself the force of a binding law, and declared that the true intent of the Koranic passage upon which the legality of polygamy had been based for thirteen centuries is, in fact, to prohibit plural marriages except for a few specific cases. In Muslim Indonesia, the complaint of women is much more modest: it is directed against those men who, in disobedience to the Koranic law, marry two or more wives when their income is barely sufficient to support one. In Saudi Arabia, Yemen, and other parts of the Arabian Peninsula, traditional patriarchal polygamy has not yet changed even to the extent of allowing the women's opinion about it to become audible.

In non-Muslim Asia the changes have been equally indecisive and varying in extent and rate. Polygamy and child marriage were outlawed in India, but to what extent the law is obeyed is unknown. In Burma, polygamy is still legal but rarely practiced, and if it occurs, the husband is obliged to maintain a separate home for each of his wives. In China, where concubinage was the traditional form of polygamy, it has been abolished, and men and women have been made equal before the law. In Japan, the great attraction Western culture holds for the cities has resulted in a sharp dichotomy between the rural population in which traditions still dominate family life, and the urban young generation characterized by an almost frantic attempt to be "modern" at all costs.

WHAT OF THE "TEEMING MILLIONS"?

It is no longer fashionable to use the phrase "teeming millions" when speaking of the peoples of India or China. Yet the fact remains that these two countries are not only the most populous in the world (India, the smaller of the two, has about twice as many inhabitants as the Soviet Union, the next largest by population), but that between them the two constitute an increasing percentage of the world population: by 1967 they comprised some twelve hundred million people, or more than one third of all mankind. To be the most densely populated nations, however, carries with it the onus of being the most inadequately fed, and it means to be threatened more imminently than others by the specter of starvation. For lack of any other alternative, first India, and more recently China, have adopted official policies of birth control, flying in the face of age-old religious and socio-cultural traditions. This single step in itself is enough to radically change the total life pattern of the Indian and Chinese woman. This submissive, downtrodden creature, who barely dared to show herself, let alone speak up, in the presence of the masterful males, who was the passive recipient of their lust and contempt, who bore them their annual litter like any patient farm animal, is now suddenly addressed by the great ones of the land, asked to decide whether a child should be born to her, and made to feel that in this most vital area of her and her husband's life she is the master of her own destiny! Never again can a woman who has learned birth-control techniques and, more importantly, has acquired the mentality and outlook necessary for their actual practice, be her old self again.

But the problem of how to reach those "teeming millions" with the technological messages of modern times remains to be solved. In Communist China, in "neutralist" India, and in "capitalist" Arabia, the majority of the people—the women to an even greater extent than the men—are illiterate. Although this circumstance does not make mass communication impossible, it does make it very difficult. Where the printed word cannot penetrate, the radio must be used. But here, too, there are barriers such as mutually unintelligible local dialects. Then the battle begins against age-old tradition, venerable custom, ingrained values, and sacrosanct mores. At stake is much more than family planning: the liberation of women from their slave-like existence, and a total reshaping of the man-woman relationship, along with a general improvement of the living conditions of the underprivileged masses who form the vast majority in both Asia and Africa.

Efforts are being made, but not everywhere are they wholehearted. In some places the ruling class shies away from facing the problem of how to improve the lot of the lower-class majority, because this, they feel, would damage upper-class interests which are conceived in short-range terms from a selfish standpoint. Characteristically, in countries that have not yet come to grips with this larger issue, the lot of women in relation to that of men has not been improved either, their problems have not been tackled, and their status remains largely as it was in the past. In view of this general observation it would be most interesting to investigate whether substantiation could be found for the following tentative hypothesis: the greater the distance between the status of the lower and the higher classes, the greater the inequalities between men and women, and vice versa.

THE LIBERATION OF AFRO-ASIAN WOMEN

Whatever the impediments, however great the conservative opposition, the movement for the emancipation of women is not only well under way, it is gathering momentum. In the second half of the twentieth century, no country in the world remains isolated. None can afford for long to lag behind its immediate or more remote neighbors. All must, therefore, face up to the problem of how to introduce certain features from the modern Western world before which some of their old, traditional mores and values sooner or later must give way. All these changes, whether in technology, industrialization, urbanization, labor relations, political organization, or social structure, bring with them concomitant changes in the position of women. The rate of change differs from country to country, but its general direction is identical everywhere. The women emerge from their purdah, they shed their veils, in some areas decisively and defiantly, in others hesitantly and shamefacedly. The liberation movement begins in the big cities, primarily in the capitals, and spreads from there into the countryside. Where the purdah and the veil are not present physically, their figurative counterparts are broken through instead, and the processes of women's emancipation differ in detail, but remain similar in substance and trend.

A huge process of change is thus under way. When completed, that is, when the position of women in all Afro-Asia will be one of equality with the men, in the sense, at least, in which this has been achieved in several countries of the modern Western world, it will signify a transformation of human life unparalleled in magnitude in all history. For what was the abolition of serfdom and slavery, and even the liberation of some peoples from colonial rule, compared to the emancipation of a billion women, the female contingent of two thirds of all mankind? There were, and are, many people who had been slaves, and had been set free and barely noticed the difference in their lives. The fact that India, for example, has ceased to be a British colony, has had little bearing on the everyday lives of most Indians. But the emancipation of women directly and immediately affects the lives of all, of the women, their husbands, their parents, and their children. Not since Prometheus brought down fire from heaven to enrich the life of man, has there been an innovation which has thus transformed the lives of all men.

Although the attention of the women themselves, as manifested by their feminist leadership, may be focused on the immediate issues of their emancipation and acquisition of equal rights, from the point of view of the men the problem is not an isolated one, but an integral part of a much larger and complex problem caused by Western cultural influences. Very generally speaking, one can distinguish between two types of reactions: one which favors the admission of Western influences into the traditional culture, and one which opposes it. Exponents of the former are for the emancipation of women, because they consider freedom and equality of women part and parcel of advancement, understood as movement toward the West; those of the latter oppose it, for precisely the same reason: because they, too, see in it a manifestation of the intrusion, which, however, they decry, of Western values into their cherished traditional culture.

Both sides are, of course, right in regarding the emancipation of women as part of the Westernizing movement. A woman who discards the veil and steps out of purdah in order to take her place beside the men of her society can find such a place for herself only in a social milieu which is, at least partly, Westernized. For one must realize that in a traditional African or Asian socio-economic structure there is simply no place for women outside their age-old, custom-determined roles. Traditional society, in most parts of Asia and Africa, is one that defines very closely the roles of men and women. For women to break out of their circumscribed roles, therefore, means that they must break out of the old cultural framework. To give a single illustration: if a girl in an old-fashioned Indian or Japanese village does not want to live out her life as determined by the age-old local mores, what can she do? In the village, there is no alternative way of life which she could adopt; therefore, she must leave and go to the city, where Westernization has made headway and where "modern" occupations and roles are available. Every step women take in the direction of emancipation, of equal rights and other improvements in their position, must inevitably lead them away from the traditional culture of their society and toward a Westernized or partly-Westernized, cultural configuration. In this sense, all women who fight for emancipation fight for modernism and Westernism.

The Full Circle

It is evident that the problem of how to reconcile the duties of wife and mother with the new role of breadwinner away from the home does not yet loom as large on the Afro-Asian horizon as it does in the Western world. And in the case of those relatively few women who have been confronted with it, the attraction of a career seems to prove stronger than that of the home, in contrast to the West, where in similar situations the decision is being made with increasing frequency for the home, for wifehood, and motherhood. The situation reminds one of the famous story about the Point Four social workers engaged in sincere efforts to persuade the nursing mothers of a Kurdish mountain tribe to give up old-fashioned demand feeding for rational schedule feeding, while at the same time back in the United States mothers were encouraged, on the basis of the latest research results, to return to demand feeding. The difference is that while the suckling habits of centuries can easily be left unchanged once studies confirm that they are best, no such short cut from traditional to neo-traditional, with the omission of the intervening "modern" phase, seems possible in the realm of the position of women. The "modern" phase, then, must come about. We can, therefore, go along with the confident or hopeful look into the future with which most of the contributors to this book close, and expect with them a considerable liberation of women, and a replacement of their traditional role with new, modern ones throughout the two continents of Asia and Africa.

But one should like to look beyond this phase, however great an achievement it will represent. In view of the voices raised and the trends observed in countries where women have achieved full emancipation, rights and equality, one should be inclined to envisage this stage in Afro-Asia as merely a temporary or transitional one, which will be closely followed by the next, the "neo-traditional" phase, characterized by the voluntary return of the, by then, fully liberated women to a position somewhat resembling that from which today they so eagerly wish to break away. Having seen the sometimes doubtful advantages of working with men, of competing with men in most fields, and outdoing men in some, it can be anticipated that they will recognize, like their Euro-American sisters who preceded them on the same road, that the role which was woman's throughout history by necessity is the one they prefer by choice. Then, and only then, will the process of the emancipation of women be truly completed.

I

The Indian Sub-Continent

INDIA AND PAKISTAN

In this first of the seven parts into which the material of this volume is grouped, two countries are discussed whose traditional cultures assigned the most restricted and confined positions to their women. Both India and Pakistan have, moreover, thus far proved quite resistant to any change in the position of their women, and can thus serve as case histories illustrating, on the one hand, the traditional situation which can no longer be found in most other parts of the world, and, on the other, the odds that the movement for the emancipation of women has to face as it begins its work in an overwhelmingly conservative society.

India

By Vatsala Narain

*I*ndia is the heir to a culture almost as old as that of the ancient Near East. Yet she is one of the youngest nations in the world. She is also one of the most populous—in 1963 her estimated population was 461.3 million.

India is one of the few countries in the world where there are more men than women. In 1961, there were 941 females to every 1,000 males. The life expectancy of women at birth was 40.60 years, as against 41.90 for men. In 1911-1920 it was 20.90 and 19.42 respectively. This single factor, the doubling of the average human life span within 40 years, illustrates the revolutionary changes that have taken place, and are still continuing, in the second largest country in the world.

ANCIENT VEDIC SOCIETY

In an ancient and traditional society such as the Hindu, the legal and social position of women is inextricably linked to religion and caste and is the result of a social, political, and religious development of several centuries, beginning with the Vedic period (4000 to 300 B.C.).

Vedic society was patriarchal. However, although the father was the head of the family, the mother too enjoyed high status. The central position of women in domestic life is well expressed in the Rigvedic term, *Jayedastam*, "the wife is the home." Aryan seers were so accustomed to thinking of a man constantly accompanied by his wife, that they could not imagine their gods as standing alone. And all invocations of divinities were addressed to the gods and their wives, the goddesses.

In those early days, the birth of a daughter, which in later Hindu society came to be considered a curse, seems to have been almost as welcome as that of a son, though generally a son was preferred. Moreover, the Vedic daughter appears to have enjoyed many of the rights and privileges of a son.* Like him, she underwent the ceremonial initiation, *Upanayana*, and like him, she studied the holy scriptures until she married. The scholarship of women was so outstanding that the Rigveda includes twenty women among its compilers. Women's education continued even during the post-Vedic age though it was confined to the three upper castes, the *dwijas*. The Kamasutra not only upholds the education of women but assigns a prominent place to the study of the fine arts, such as drawing and music. There are even references to women of the ruling class being trained in military and administrative fields. Legally, however, whether married or single, women were never independent. A woman could not inherit, unless she was an only child.

During the Vedic age, the presence of the wife was essential to all sacrifices and ceremonies. Man alone was not regarded as spiritually complete; oblations offered to the gods by a single man would be refused. Certain sacrifices, however, were performed exclusively by women.

Vedic Marriage Pattern—Marriage in the Vedic age was a social and religious duty, required of everyone. The Avestian idea of bachelors being spiritually impure was shared by the Vedic Aryans. Marriage enabled a man to become a householder, to offer sacrifices to the gods, and to procreate sons. But although considered extremely necessary, marriage was not made compulsory until about 300 B.C., and then only for girls.

---

* Affection and concern for children continue to be traits of the Hindus today. In Vedic literature there are frequent references to daughters being fondly caressed and affectionately brought up by their parents. As they grew older, they played an important part in the management of their parents' household.

Women in Vedic society appear to have enjoyed greater freedom than their descendants in India today. At festivals men and women mingled freely and were afforded opportunities for seeking life partners and for premarital sex relations. There was also greater freedom from the marriage barriers of caste. *Anuloma*, marriage of higher caste men with lower-caste women, was more frequent than *pratiloma*, marriage of higher-caste women with lower-caste men.

Rakshasa, or *khsatra*, obtaining a bride by capture, appears to have been practiced as a knightly feat throughout Indian history. *Paisacha*, the duping or overpowering of the bride by the bridegroom, appears to be of the greatest antiquity, but was not completely approved even by the Vedic texts. *Gandharva*, marriage following a period of courtship, is mentioned in all Vedic texts and seems to have continued well into the post-Vedic age. From the description of the festivals at which sexual license was allowed and of the *gandharva* form of marriage, it may be assumed that the practice of postpuberty marriage was current. The whole array of marriage hymns was intended for sexually mature girls.

Child Marriage—Some of the Dharmashastra writers, who flourished from 400 B.C. to A.D. 100, began to advise that girls should be married soon after puberty. Following sharp conflicts of opinion, prepuberty marriages became customary by about A.D. 100, and India remained the land of child marriage for many centuries.

Though monogamy was considered ideal, polygamy was widely practiced in Vedic society, especially by the wealthy ruling castes. Among royalty, a man's first four wives occupied recognized positions, designated by special names. Wives who wanted to get rid of their rivals said hymns and performed certain rites to achieve their purpose. Polyandry was also practiced, but sporadically.

Post Vedic Society

The post-Vedic period (from 300 B.C. on) was crucial in determining the present status of women in India. This age saw the systematic compilation of Hindu law. Among the lawgivers, Manu (ca. 2nd century B.C.) was the most influential.

Manu's Code, says Das, forged "unbreakable shackles on Indian women for countless succeeding generations. Even today, it is his laws which keep Indians helpless in the prison of Hindu orthodoxy. Manu for the first time legally assigned to woman her definite place in society. But his laws reflect a conflict. . . . a mother is more to be revered than a thousand fathers, yet his laws place women socially on a level with the lowest of all groups in Aryan society, the Sudra."

Lowered Position of Women—In the post-Vedic period the aim and purpose of offerings at the great sacrifices became concentrated around the birth of a son. Women, who had previously shared in the intellectual and religious life, were considered to have no purpose in life except to bear sons. Daughters were looked upon as a misfortune. According to Manu, for women marriage was equivalent to the religious initiation ceremonies required of men. To serve a husband was parallel to a man's residing in a teacher's home for religious instruction; and to perform household duties served the same purpose as a man's daily worship and lighting of sacred fires. Strict discipline and fidelity to the husband were also demanded of the wife. The highest duty, *dharma*, of a woman, according to Manu, is to obey and serve her husband.

Although a wife was considered indispensable in the religious field along with her husband, she was dependent in all matters upon men. In childhood, marriage, and old age she was to be governed by father, husband, and son, respectively. Women were excluded from the intellectual world, ineligible even to hear the Vedas, and restricted to the study of the Puranas alone.

The scope of marriage was further limited by the introduction of strict endogamous and exogamous rules which defined whom a man was allowed and whom he was forbidden to marry. By the beginning of the Christian era, these had hardened into inflexible laws, any breach of which came to be regarded as unthinkable sin.

Divorce and widowhood—Up to the beginning of the post-Vedic period, divorce was allowed and practiced by all sections of the community. Even some of the medieval digest writers permitted divorce and described the circumstances under which the wife could initiate it. The husband was allowed to take a second wife, after a prescribed waiting period, if the first was barren.

Widowhood, too, had presented few problems, and widows were regarded sympathetically. The marriage of a widow to the brother of her dead husband was well regarded. By the beginning of the Christian era, however, asceticism swept through India, and the lawgivers became more hostile to women, forbidding them to remarry. The attitude toward widows became so harsh that by around A.D. 1200, their complete disfigurement by tonsure was ordained and the wearing of colorful clothes was prohibited. These practices, more common in south India than in north India, were first confined to the Brahmin caste and later extended to other castes. Even today, many orthodox Brahmin widows observe them.

Rise of Sati—Early in the post-Vedic period appeared the first scattered cases of *sati*, self-immolation of widows. From about A.D. 700, ardent advocates of *sati* arose in the two lawgivers Angiras and Harita. The practice came to be regarded as ideal for a widow, her highest religious duty, replacing a lifelong asceticism. She thereby elevated, not only herself but also her husband, if he were in hell, to heavenly bliss. *Sati* was further intensified with the advent of foreign invaders. Moghul rulers, like Humayun and Akbar, tried to restrict it but without success. By the time the British came to India, *sati* had become general, and was even practiced by child widows. Although it was legally banned in 1829, stray cases occurred as recently as September, 1952.

Introduction of Purdah—All historians agree that *purdah* did not come into vogue until Muslim rule in India. The participation of women in social life during the Vedic age ruled out purdah. But by the time of the Epics (about 100 B.C.) some seclusion was practiced by ladies of royal and aristocratic circles. The general adoption of purdah in such circles started in the fifteenth century, both as protection for women, and as a prestige measure in imitation of the Muslim rulers. The lawgivers of this period heartily endorsed it on the basis of the old Vedic injunction of keeping a close watch on women. Unknown in south and western India, it was, and is to this day, practiced in the states of Uttar Pradesh, Bihar, and Bengal, despite the rising level of education for women.

WOMEN'S PROPERTY RIGHTS

Following the Vedic age, the right of women to inherit property steadily diminished. Manu deprived even the daughter who was an only child, of her patrimony, allowing her only marriage expenses, and making her son the heir of her father's property. Nor was a widow recognized as her husband's heir. During the age of the legislators and the Puranas (A.D. 100-900), the right of the widow even to her personal belongings was made conditional upon her chastity.

Under Muslim rule in the post-Puranic age, the Indian woman's position deteriorated further, partly because of the need for more stringent security measures and the consequent limitations on her freedom. Attempts made by both Muslim rulers and Hindu legislators to improve her status by giving her definite property rights had little if any effect on her servile position.

Despite their long contact with the Muslims, the Hindus did not assimilate some of the more liberal rights accorded to women by the Islamic Shari'a law but continued to adhere to the theoretical basis of the legal subordination of women as laid down by Manu.

HINDU WOMEN IN THE 1800'S

The British began to gain power in India during the eighteenth century at a time when the Hindu woman's position had reached its lowest depth. Ideologically, legally, socially, and morally, woman was considered of no significance. Polygamy, child marriage, illiteracy, *sati*, permanent widowhood, and the complete subordination of woman through the denial of legal rights were prevalent throughout Hindu society. The caste system and the joint family (consisting of three or more generations sharing a common home, hearth, and property) also contributed toward keeping women in a lowly position. They were virtually slaves, having lost even their urge for freedom and their awareness of possessing an independent personality. In the words of Pandita Ramabai, "She [was] forbidden to read the Sacred Scriptures, she [had] no right to pronounce a single syllable out of them. To appeal to her uncultivated low kind of desire by giving her ornaments to adorn her person and by giving her dainty food together with an occasional bow which costs nothing [were] the highest honours to which Hindu woman was entitled." Women's only function was, as Abbé Dubois put it, "to minister to men's physical pleasures and wants; they were considered incapable of developing any of those higher mental qualities which would make them more worthy of consideration and also more capable of playing a useful part in life."

LEGAL STATUS OF WOMEN

Once the British reign was consolidated, the need for uniform legislation became apparent. Inspired by the efforts of Indian social reformers, the British government of India proceeded to enact a series of laws directly affecting many aspects of women's lives.

Legal steps were taken as early as 1860 for the abolition of child marriage, with its frequent sexual abuse of child brides by their adult husbands. The rulers of some of the princely states, such as Mysore, Baroda, and Indore, had independently raised the legal age of marriage many years prior to the enactment of the British law. The Indian Penal Code declared that consummating marriage with a girl younger than ten was rape, punishable by life imprisonment. Despite the bitter opposition of orthodox elements, the age of consent was raised to twelve years. However, for want of initiative and propaganda, the law remained on paper only. In 1925 an act was passed distinguishing between marital and extramarital sexual consummation, and raising the age of consent to thirteen in the former case, and to sixteen in the latter.

The Child Marriage and Restraint Act of 1929, popularly known as the Sarada Act, prohibited throughout India the marriage of girls under fourteen and of boys under eighteen years of age. Knowledge of the law did not reach the villages, however, for lack of an adequate communications system. Moreover, the law could be enforced only after a complaint against a violator had been lodged in court. The tight social structure of the village made it practically impossible for any member of the community to lodge such a complaint; and, consequently, the practice of child marriage continued in most villages. To evade the British law, some parents went to French and Portuguese territories and had their underage children married there. Another serious flaw of the act was that it imposed only a fine on the offender; the fine was paid and considered simply an added item of the wedding expense.

Secularizing Marriage—As a result of Western influence, the secularization of marriage began in India in 1872 with a law providing for divorce and giving the right of inheritance to women. The Special Marriage Act of 1954 provided that marriages can be contracted by registration; that persons of different faiths can marry without having to renounce their faiths; that neither party can have a living spouse at the time of marriage; that the bridegroom must be at least twenty-one and the bride eighteen; that marriage cannot be contracted with a lunatic or an idiot; and that the parties must not be within the prohibited degrees of relationship.

Persons marrying under this act were presumed to have separated from the joint family, and their share in the family property was regulated according to the Indian Succession Act of 1925. These two provisions rendered this form of marriage most unpopular, so that even the educated strata of society have refrained from marrying under the act.

Marriage Reforms

The Hindu Marriage Act of 1955 introduced some long-awaited reforms. It put an end to polygamy and made monogamy universal. (This law was preceded by the act passed by the princely state of Baroda in 1942 prohibiting bigamous marriages, and by the Hindu Bigamous Marriage Act passed by Bombay in 1946.) The minimum age of marriage was reduced to fifteen for girls and eighteen for boys. The act provided for both judicial separation and divorce. If a spouse remained absent for seven years, the deserted partner could contract another marriage. The marriage was declared void in cases of impotence or lunacy, in cases where the consent of the parent or guardian was obtained by force or fraud, or in cases where the woman had been impregnated at the time of her marriage by a person other than the bridegroom.

The introduction of divorce was the greatest departure from traditional custom. Among the higher castes, marriage was considered a sacrament that could not be dissolved. In most of the lower castes, divorce and remarriage were customarily permitted. The new law named as grounds for divorce adultery, conversion to another religion, lunacy, incurable disease, renunciation of the world by entering a religious order, failure to resume cohabitation after the expiration of a decree for judicial separation, and bigamy. If, after marriage, the husband committed rape, sodomy, or bestiality, this too constituted grounds for divorce.

With regard to alimony and maintenance, a legally specified sum is to be paid regularly to the applicant as long as she or he remains chaste and unmarried. In contrast to the laws of other countries, not only the wife but the husband, too, can obtain alimony, if the court considers a claim just.

After the abolition of *sati* (1829), lifelong widowhood posed a problem. The Widow Remarriage Act of 1856 permitted the remarriage of widows. It also gave them rights to their deceased husband's property. These rights, however, were lost upon remarriage.

The dowry, which in earlier days was given to the bridegroom as a token of affection, had assumed scandalous proportions and some states passed laws to eliminate the abuses. The state of Indore limited the sum, and Andhra made it culpable to accept dowry; but no restrictions were placed on gifts made at the time of marriage. The Dowry Bill of 1960 applied to all of India, but again lacked provisions restricting gifts and hence fell short of its intended results. Dowry continues to be paid in the form of gifts, which create an almost unbearable financial burden for many middle-class families.

Some states, such as Madras and Mysore, outlawed prostitution as early as the 1920's. In Delhi and in Andhra it has been banned only very recently. The Andhra Bill even goes so far as to prohibit women from dancing in marriage processions, since such dances were traditionally performed by prostitutes.

WOMEN'S RIGHTS TO PROPERTY

One of the first property laws enacted by the British was the Married Women's Property Act of 1874. An amendment of 1929 recognized women's right to property not held in joint ownership. By the Act of 1937, which applied to the entire country, a widow was entitled to the same share a son received in the estate of a man who died intestate.

The Succession Act of 1956 was a landmark in the history of Hindu law. It provides that a daughter and a widow inherit property as well as a son, and gives full rights of disposal to any woman who inherits property. As Mrs. Desai comments, this act "has placed woman on an equal footing with man with regard to the right of use of property."

The Hindu Adoption and Maintenance Bill of 1956 accords the right of adoption to unmarried women, divorcées, and widows. Under this act, both male and female children can be adopted (traditional Hindu adoption was confined to male children). This act also enables a woman who leaves the bed and board of her husband to claim maintenance even without legal separation or divorce, a provision of great benefit to women who wish to leave their husbands but fear the social stigma still attaching to divorce.

The same act requires both men and women to be financially responsible for their aged and infirm parents and for unmarried and widowed daughters.

GIRLS' EDUCATION

In spite of the enthusiastic social reforms of the 1920's and 1930's, the education of girls continued to be mostly confined to elementary schools, with their number dropping sharply in secondary schools, and becoming almost infinitesimal in colleges and universities. According to the 1941 census, the literacy rate for women was as low as 6.0, against 22.6 for men. Within ten years, female literacy rose to 7.8, and by 1961 to 12.9 per cent. In the same year the male literacy rate rose to 34.4 per cent.

In 1947, the proportion of girls to boys in educational institutions was 30 to 100. The disparity was widest in higher education, with only 7 girls for every 100 boys. Of a total of 4,297,725 girl students in 1947, 3,475,165 were in primary schools, 602,280 in secondary schools, and 23,207 in colleges. In addition, there were 56,090 in special schools, and 141,043 in unorganized institutions. Out of a total of 218,165 educational institutions in that year, 28,196 were girls' schools. In 1957-1958, a decade later, the total number of schools increased to 383,755, but girls' schools to only 29,901. Preprimary education (ages three–six) still remains rudimentary. The few nursery schools and kindergartens are mostly in urban areas and run by private organizations.

Primary Education—As noted in the preceding paragraphs, the extension of girls' education has been largely on the primary level (ages six to eleven). In 1949-1950, there were 13,978 primary schools for girls, attended by over 5 million out of an estimated 22.29 million girls. In 1957-1958, the number of girls' primary schools had increased by 2,815 and the number of girl students by over 2 million. The 1965-66 "target" in elementary education was to have 61.6 per cent of all girls aged six to eleven attend elementary schools, as against 90.4 per cent of the boys.

Primary education in India is based on the principle of "learning by doing," generally known as Basic Education. While the curricula in both basic schools and primary schools are very similar, in the former, each subject is taught in close correlation with a basic craft, making productive work the core of education, thus rendering the entire curriculum more practical, realistic, and interesting. Girls study such courses as domestic work, hygiene, child care, home nursing, and needle craft.

Secondary Education—Secondary schools (ages eleven to seventeen) are divided into two levels, each to be attended for three years. In 1957-1958, out of a total of 51,844 secondary schools, 5,828 were for girls, attended by 4 million pupils. In a decade the number of girls schools had doubled, and the number of pupils increased 5½ times. The 1965-1966 "target" for the eleven to fourteen age group was to have 16.5 per cent of the girls attend schools, as compared to 39.9 per cent of the boys.

The secondary-school curriculum prepares the pupils either for university studies or for immediate employment. Physical education is emphasized and extracurricular activities are encouraged under the National Plan of Physical Education and Recreation. Special facilities for the study of dance, music, and the fine arts are also provided, with scholarships to deserving students.

Higher Education—The expansion of higher education following independence has been striking. Today there are forty universities, with a total of over one and a half million students. One of them, the Shremathi Nathibai Damodar Thackersey (SNDT) Women's University in Bombay and in Poona, admits only girls. However, women attend all universities and institutions of higher education, as shown in Table 1.

TABLE 1—University and College Students in 1958–1959 by Sex and Type of Institution

Type of Institution	Number of Institutions	Number of Students Enrolled		
		Total	Men	Women
Arts and Science Colleges	920	734,616	609,937	124,679
Technical, Professional and Other Special Educational Colleges	706	222,805	200,969	21,836
Total	1,626	957,521	810,906	146,515

Urban and Rural Education—Although in urban areas the education of girls is gaining wide acceptance, especially among middle-class families, in rural district girls' education still lags considerably behind that of boys.

In 1957-1958, of the total primary schools for girls, 11,274 were rural, with 5,242,158 pupils; of the secondary schools for girls, 1,311 were rural, with 1,093,600 pupils; five rural universities and colleges had 19,819 women students registered; and 3,341 technical and professional institutions on the upper secondary level had 131,271 girls. From 1950 to 1957, the government contributed 50 per cent of the total expenditure involved to a plan for the development of women's education in various types of colleges.

In 1955, with the help of the U.S. Technical Cooperation Mission, training facilities were made available to women in home economics. Other expansion programs sponsored by the Government of India, with the aid of American foundations and the British Council, include the India Wheat Loan Educational Exchange Program and the Village Apprenticeship Scheme, both intended to develop a realistic spirit of social service and responsible understanding of problems of rural reconstruction in India through selected university students and teachers.

Following World War II, as a result of the rising cost of living, women were forced to seek employment, and, in order to earn better salaries, they needed better education. Economic changes thus affected the educational picture, and developments in education enabled Indian women to occupy economic positions formerly reserved for men.

WOMEN'S OCCUPATIONS

The number of new jobs now available to women is significant of the emerging new India. Today, woman's economic horizon, once limited to household chores and farm labor, has widened considerably. The status of urban middle-class women has been bettered and the urge toward economic independence has been awakened. Economic necessity has led women into all types of employment, where their presence has been accepted by men. They move about freely, and have quickly learned to work side by side with men.

Numerically, agriculture is by far the most common occupation for women. Most women work the fields as a part of the family unit, and the generally very low economic standards of the farmers allow women no choice but to work as unpaid helpers of their menfolk. In recent years, women have sometimes been left behind with a double load of work on the farm and in the home because of the migration of men to urban areas. But, even apart from these cases, there is no limit to their working hours. Those who get paid are generally paid in produce. Official regulation of wages and working hours means nothing to a rural woman, whose work in most cases is part of the family burden she must shoulder. The economic independence achieved by many urban middle-class women is still entirely beyond the ken of her rural sister. Several rural welfare programs are now under way to improve the status of agricultural laborers. For example, the Village Welfare Services, under the Social Board's wide programs, are trying to provide employment for women by training them in various village and cottage industries.

In urban areas, most employed women work in industry, at unskilled or semiskilled tasks. In 1947, 264,000 women were employed in factories; by 1956 their numbers increased to 301,000. Most of them worked in textiles (cotton and jute), tobacco, food, and chemical production. In 1961, of a total of 20 million persons employed in mining and manufactories, 5.5 million were women.

With the exception of piecework, where the pay is the same for men and women, the latter are paid lower wages than men doing the same work. The value of women's work is said to be less; the prices of goods produced are fixed at a low rate on the basis of women's lower wages, and the cost of employing women workers is higher because of special laws protecting them.

In recent years a trend toward eliminating women workers can be observed, especially in textiles. The most important causes for this have been plant modernization laws protecting women workers. The whole purpose of the protective laws appears to be defeated by this trend. A compensatory feature is increased employment of women in other industries. Industrial working women are little concerned with economic independence. In this respect, they closely resemble village women working on the land. As a rule, women tend to regard industrial employment as temporary.

Domestic service is sought by many village women in the towns, as cooks, kitchen helpers, children's nurses, and so on. As yet, no laws protect domestic servants, although a bill recommending an eight-hour working day, medical care, the provision of living quarters, and one month's vacation with full pay has been presented to Parliament. Should such a law be enacted, its actual effect would remain doubtful. In most households, especially in the smaller towns and villages, servants are part of the large, joint family and treated as such, and would dislike being treated on an impersonal basis, feeling they would lose some of the advantages and satisfactions gained in the long service of a household.

Women are also employed in small trades, such as lacemaking and the selling of vegetables and flowers. Certain small enterprises, such as laundries, leather-cleaning, and tailoring also attract women.

Employment possibilities for lower-middle and upper-middle-class women were very scarce after independence. But soon new needs arose and new jobs were created. The first field to open to women was teaching, which even to the traditionally minded was a respectable occupation for woman.

In 1950 there were 77,877 women teachers, representing approximately 15 per cent of all teachers in the primary schools; in 1957-58, their number increased to 126, 980, representing 17 per cent. Women teach in both boys' and girls' schools. The salaries differ greatly from state to state as well as among the institutions, but not according to sex.

Some women occupy leading positions in education as inspectors, principals of schools and colleges, and specialists in various fields. One woman even became vice-chancellor of a university.

Medicine ranks second to teaching as an occupational choice. In 1957-58 there were 235 medical training institutions (medical schools and colleges, veterinary schools, and nursing schools). Women doctors and nurses, however, are still in short supply. In 1957, out of a total of 69,605 M.D.'s, 7,000 were women, employed in hospitals, in university teaching positions, in private practice, or in research; and there were 22,386 nurses, 26,823 midwives, and 70,000 public health nurses or health visitors. This is a marked increase over five years earlier, but still far short of the nation's needs.

Several professions allied with medicine have only recently opened to women. These include dentistry, in which women are needed for the treatment of women in conservative rural areas and of children in preventive and corrective work; physiotherapy, for children's hospitals; visiting service and care of the handicapped; pharmacy, for the filling of prescriptions and for chemical and analytical work in pharmaceutical factories and hospitals, and in the manufacture of cosmetics, confectionery, and plastics.

Women lawyers are increasing in number. In 1957 there were 8,959 women in legal and business services; of them, 185 were employers, 5,559 employees, and 3,178 independent workers. Women magistrates are quite common. Judicial appointments have also been made.

Among the newer professions, vocational guidance and social welfare are promising fields for women. Many opportunities are open in labor welfare, medical and psychiatric social work, educational organizational work in community development, child welfare, and administrative services. The remuneration in these occupations is comparable to that of a well-trained teacher.

Journalism is an expanding field. Several women work as editors and business managers of women's magazines. There are many women writers for the radio and for magazines in both English and Indian languages. Training in journalism is available in the School of Journalism sponsored by the United States Information Service. The All India Radio in New Delhi employs women feature writers, commentators, and even technicians. Women have been in charge of several important radio stations.

Architecture, commercial art, and advertising also attract women. Several private firms and agencies have highly-paid women on their staffs. The artistic skills of women find an outlet in interior decoration and textile design. In various handicrafts, including hand-looming, there is a revival of old skills, and the efficient marketing of the products both at home and abroad is entirely in the hands of women.

Few women have entered engineering, but women engage in white-collar jobs in increasing numbers. In government agencies, in the foreign service, and in the police department, all administrative posts are open to women. Many women have successfully competed with men in the examinations which are a prerequisite for these offices. The rapid increase of middle-class women who seek employment can be seen at the Employment Exchanges. The number of women applying for jobs rose from 1,500 in 1948 to 4,500 in 1951, and to 40,000 in 1957.

WORKING CONDITIONS

Numerous administrative and legislative measures have been introduced to improve the health, education, housing, and social welfare of the people, as in the Five Year Plans. Many laws regulating working conditions and labor relations, enacted following independence, have also affected the position of women.

Except for the tea plantations in Assam, there are no restrictions in India regarding the recruitment of women workers. But under the Factory Act of 1948, women are permitted to work only between 6:00 A.M. and 7:00 P.M., and not more than nine hours a day. The Mines Act prohibits the employment of women underground. Both the Factory and Mines Acts safeguard women against the hazards of lifting heavy weights, restricting the maximum load to 65 pounds for adults, 45 pounds for adolescents, and 30 pounds for girls. Employment of women in any dangerous operation is also prohibited.

Separate washroom facilities must be provided for women and men. Where eighty or more women are employed, nurseries must be maintained for children under six years of age, and the employers are required to supply them with milk. The law also provides for special rest periods for working mothers to enable them to feed their babies. Some states have passed laws providing maternity benefits to women employed in factories and plantations. The Mines Maternity Benefit Act was passed in 1941 by the government.

Other Benefits—The Employees' State Insurance Act of 1951 provides for sickness, maternity, disablement, and workmen's compensation. It covers laborers employed directly as well as clerical staffs; it excludes persons whose pay exceeds Rs. 400 (or $84.00) per month. The rate of maternity benefit has been fixed at 75 nP. (or $0.16) per day, to be paid to an expectant mother for a period of twelve weeks (six weeks preceding and six following confinement). Though the act is comprehensive, it has many shortcomings and touches only a fraction of the problem. Medical aid is expensive and is provided only as a maternity benefit. However, it does give some assistance to women who must work.

Disparity in Wages—Until recently, the principle of equal pay for equal work was not accepted even in large industries, and the wages of men and women were markedly unequal. In recent years, however, the same basic wages for men and women have been demanded on the grounds of equity and justice. In some states, under the standardized schemes, men and women do receive the same pay for the same type of work.

MODERN MARRIAGE PATTERNS

In tradition-bound Hindu society, caste has withstood the forces of urbanization and industrialization with amazing tenacity, sometimes even being strengthened by them. Some caste rules, however, such as the ban on interdining and intermixing, have been broken in most urban areas.

The marriage pattern, on the other hand, has remained unchanged. In both urban and rural areas, endogamous marriage is still the rule, though within a subcaste some of the rules have been relaxed. In most urban middle-class families, education has been accepted as an essential part of the girls' training, and their employment is often favored; but individual choice in marriage is still not accepted, and matchmaking is still regarded as the responsibility of the parents or guardians. In all marriage arrangements, the status and reputation of the family are important. In regions such as south India, where cross-cousin and maternal uncle-niece marriages are preferred, the consent of neither the man nor the girl is obtained. In other types of marriages, the boy's consent is obtained, but the girl's is only nominal. In very few families are the girl's wishes really considered, or the engaged couple permitted to exchange letters before the wedding.

In most cases, the traditional Vedic wedding is performed. Very few persons take advantage of the Special Marriage Act and have their marriages registered. Desai reports that of 805 literate, middle-class women interviewed, 63 per cent preferred the traditional Vedic marriage to the modern registered marriage. At the same time, the women indicated a preference for marriage by choice. Another researcher, too, found the younger generation to be more favorably inclined toward this new mode of marriage. Greater opportunities for meeting young people of the opposite sex, less traditional pressure, and more freedom of expression within the family would undoubtedly result in an increase of marriage by choice.

WOMAN'S ROLE IN THE FAMILY

The woman fills a dual role in the family: first, under the parental roof, second, in her husband's home.

As a daughter, although her position is not as favorable as that of a son, she is, nevertheless, brought up with care and affection. And in most families, today, she receives at least some formal education.

The unmarried girl is expected to help her mother with all the household chores and the social and religious ceremonies, in order to learn family and caste traditions. By helping her mother, she is oriented in all the procedures of the performance of *puja*, the religious ritual. She is also taught some prayers. Her entire upbringing aims, in most cases, at obtaining a good husband and preparing her to be a good, obedient daughter-in-law. A girl looks after her younger brothers and sisters and, if she is educated, is expected to guide the younger ones in their school work. Certain responsibilities of household management are also entrusted to her.

Marriage brings a transformation of her role and duties. Hindu marriage is essentially a marriage between families, and the honor of the bride's family depends upon her behavior in her new role as a wife. She is expected to follow all the customary practices and behavior patterns of her husband's family. Now it is her mother-in-law whom she helps with household duties. A bride's position in the new family may not be lower than that of her husband's younger sister, but she is not a full participant in many family affairs. At this period, she is more or less on probation. In the village, her duties primarily involve domestic and agricultural work.

In traditional homes, during the early years of marriage, no importance is attached to the personal life of the young couple, although in urban areas they are allowed to take an evening walk together or go to the cinema, and in the villages they may attend the village fair, and visit the temple together.

Motherhood—After she marries, whether a woman is educated or not, and in both rural and urban areas, obedience to her husband and respect for the authority of her father-in-law and mother-in-law are expected and enforced, although she is not actually in a servile position. Motherhood enhances her status, and she becomes a responsible young member of the family, at home with the traditions and customs of the household. She is given a voice in family matters and may sometimes exert her influence either directly or through her husband. She now has an important role to play in connection with the marriage of younger members of the household. The training of a younger daughter-in-law rests with the older one. A transformation takes place in a woman's life. In her paternal home she was an object of love and affection, although her status was only that of a visitor. But now in her husband's family, as the future mistress of the house, she is listened to and consulted on all important matters and thus becomes an integral part of the family.

The period until her children are grown is a difficult and delicate one for a woman. During this time, many problems in the family become acute and may cause the breakdown of the joint family. In striving to observe the old injunctions and *dharmas* of the household, a woman is under great pressure to sacrifice her personal comforts and desires. The greater her self-effacement, the higher is the acclaim accorded her in the traditional view.

Family Life Today—Today, even though changing economic conditions cause many families to break away from the husband's parental home, these families continue to form part of the joint family, if not structurally, at least in sentimental attachment.

To live alone as a small family in an urban area means a profound change for both man and woman. There is no father or elder brothers for the man to look up to, no mother-in-law for the woman to obey. Another aspect of this change is commented upon by K. M. Kapadia who points out that an educated young man is no longer satified with the prospect of a wife who is to be the acquiescent slave of his desire and the mother of his children, but looks to her for intellectual compatibility and participation in the pleasures and joys of life. Yet when such a couple returns to the village or to the joint family, either on periodic visits or permanently upon retirement from the city, they must again readjust to the old ways. In effect, the woman has to conform to two standards of behavior, and this puts severe strains upon her.

WOMEN'S POLITICAL RIGHTS

The political awakening of Indian women began in the early 1920's. It gained momentum under the leadership of veteran British champions of women's political rights. Moreover, as a part of the larger national movement for freedom and social reform, the women's rights movement had the support and encouragement of all the leading men of India. Thus, unlike their Western sisters, Indian women did not have to struggle for equal political rights. The women's movement in India has in no sphere—political, economic, social, or educational—demanded special rights for women as opposed to men. What the Indian women's organizations have asked for is *equal rights*. In all this, the All India Women's Conference played an important role.

The new constitution of independent India extended the franchise to all citizens twenty-one years of age and over. As Lakshmi Menon has observed, only a little over thirty years after the first agitation for suffrage, Indian women secured an equality of rights that had taken much longer to achieve in Western countries.

The general elections of 1952 were the first opportunity for the exercise of universal franchise. Although separate figures for men and women voters are not available, women participated with an enthusiasm that sometimes took the form of a religious ritual.

WOMEN IN LEADERSHIP

In spite of the nonalignment directives issued by the All India Women's Conference, women participated in all stages of the 1952 elections. They were party workers and election agents, and fifty-one women contested seats in the Lok Sabha, the national parliament. Of these, nineteen were elected. In the state assemblies, out of 15,573 contestants for 3,370 seats, 216 were women, winning eighty-two seats. In the second general elections, in 1957, twenty-seven women were elected to the Lok Sabha, and 195 to the state assemblies. This has not been phenomenal, but, as Professor Kogekar put it, the general elections have at last given women an opportunity to emerge from the comparative seclusion to which they had so long been condemned. The faint stirring of interest in public issues, a sense of importance and power, the assertion of equality at the ballot box—these are bound to give women greater confidence in their own ability to play their part in the life of the community.

Indian women political leaders are active in their parties. They have been presidents of the Congress, and members of the Congress Working Committee, the Communist Party, and of the National Executive of the Socialist Party. With the assumption by Mrs. Indira Ghandi of the office of the Prime Minister in 1966, India became the first major country in the world to have a woman at the head of its government.

Women participate in the building of the nation on all levels, including the Village Councils (the so-called *panchayats*, consisting of five members), local and district boards. One village in South India has an elected *panchayat* made up entirely of women. The Five Year Plans have greatly increased the political and economic consciousness of rural India, and the various village development projects and organizations are vitally stimulated by the participation of women.

WOMEN'S ORGANIZATIONS

The most important women's group is the All India Women's Conference (AIWC), considered by many the voice of the forward movement of Indian women. It has helped to develop friendship and understanding among women of widely differing backgrounds. Among other prominent women's groups are the Young Women's Christian Association, the Federation of University Women, and the National Council of Women.

Women also play an important role in voluntary social services. At first, such services were carried out exclusively for the benefit of women. The women's clubs, Mahila Mandal, Mahila Sabha, and Vikas Grahs, set up shelter homes for widows and destitute women. (These women's clubs also participated in the struggle for independence.) The Central Welfare Board, coordinating agency of voluntary services in both rural and urban areas, rendered valuable service during the Five Year Plans.

Under the Plans (1951-1961), women assisted the government at every level. In order to strengthen government efforts to secure funds for the implementation of the plans, they broadcast the message of thrift and investment of savings, which helped bring about a steady increase in the sale of National Savings Certificates (between October 1956 and May 1957, $4,263,000, were collected).

Family Welfare Organizations—In the field of family planning and counseling, valuable services have been rendered by women. The Family Planning Association of India has branches all over the country, and large sums were allotted in the Plans to birth control.

The Family Welfare Activity, aiming at the urban employment of women of the lower-income groups, was taken up with great vigor by the

Central Welfare Board. Experiments carried out in three centers, under the management of women social workers, revealed the potential of an organized family welfare scheme. Under the plan, maternity and child welfare centers, staffed by 26,000 midwives and 1,200 health visitors, were established.

Similarly, the Rural Welfare Extension programs began as a part of the community projects exclusively for women under the guidance of the Social Welfare Board. The Kasturba Gandhi National Memorial Trust gave its full cooperation in training women workers in rural areas. This work is expected to be carried out entirely by women organizers in home economics and social education and by village workers.

Under the Moral Hygiene programs, provisions are made for rehabilitation services at home. These are to be implemented on district and state levels. The Social Welfare Board has been instrumental in bringing together the social services into an integrated network.

IMPROVEMENTS STILL NEEDED

The position of Indian women today is the outcome of more than a hundred years of individual and collective efforts by Indian social reformers and educational pioneers. The most recent, and perhaps most decisive, contribution was made by the Indian constitution, which ushered in a new era not only for Indian women but for India as a whole, by making men and women legally equal partners in every respect.

However, inequalities and disabilities imposed by a tradition of centuries cannot easily be eradicated. The educational disparity between girls and boys is bound to continue for some time, especially in rural districts. Rapid advances in this area are greatly hampered by the extremely low teachers' salaries that make teaching one of the least desirable professions and result in a chronic shortage of teachers.

Women alone cannot bring about the changes still needed for achieving real equality with men, in their family status and in the economic and social spheres. The men of India must not merely tolerate changes, but actively support them. Basic modification of the traditional notion of male supremacy is needed as well as the education of women to shoulder new responsibilities.

The highly protective and proprietary attitude of the family toward an unmarried daughter must also change, and, simultaneously, adequate living accommodations must be provided for single girls in the cities.

The position of the married woman who must, or who wishes to, seek outside employment must be facilitated by providing day nurseries for small children and the means to reduce the burden of housework.

The average age of girls at marriage is tending to rise, indicating that laws long on the books are beginning to take effect. It is still too early to say whether there is a comparable rise in the number of women using divorce laws. The remarriage rate of widows has so far not increased. Traditional disapproval still seems too strong to be easily overcome.

Suffrage, too, is a right not exercised by most women. Illiteracy, ignorance, and inadequate communications have resulted in the general absence of village women from the polls.

Most changes so far are confined to the cities. The rural majority (about 90 per cent of the total population of India) has still barely been touched by them. "Village India," with its hundreds of millions, is the great challenge for the small, educated minority of city women and men who recognize that the tradition-bound, male-dominated system must give way to a broader, more liberal society in which Indian women and men can work side by side for the progress of the nation.

BIBLIOGRAPHY

Altekar, A. S., *The Position of Women in Hindu Civilization*, Benares (1956).
Appadorai, Angadipuram, *Status of Women in South Asia* (UNESCO), Bombay (1954).
Baig, Tara Ali, *Women of India*, New Delhi (1958).
Buhler, G., *Laws of Manu*, London (1886).
Cormack, Margaret, *Hindu Women*, New York (1953).
Das, Frieda Mathilda, *Purdah: The Status of Indian Women*, London (1932).
Desai, Neera, *Women in Modern India*, Bombay (1957).
Dubois, J. A., Abbé, *Hindu Manners, Customs and Ceremonies*, Oxford (1906).
Jolly, J., *Outlines of a History of Hindu Law on Partition, Inheritance and Adoption*, Calcutta (1885).
Kabir, Humayun (ed.), *Seven Years of Freedom*, New Delhi (1954).
Kane, P. V., *History of Dharmashastra*, Vol. II, Part I, Poona (1930).
Kapadia, K. M., *Marriage and Family*, Bombay (1955).
——, *Hindu Kinship*, Bombay (1947).
Karandikar, S., *Hindu Exogamy* (1929).
Macdoell, A. A., and A. B. Keith, *Vedic Index*, Vol. I, Part II, London (1912).
Mulla, D. F., *Principles of Hindu Law*, Bombay (1926).
Myrdal, Alva, and Viola Klein, *Women's Two Roles*, London (1958).
Pinkham, Mildreth Worth, *Women in Sacred Scriptures of Hinduism*, New York (1941).
Radhakrishnan, S., *Religion and Society*, London (1947).
Ramabai, Pandita Sarasvati, *The High Caste Hindu Women*, Philadelphia (1888).
Ross, A. D., *The Hindu Family in Urban Setting*, Toronto (1961).
Sarkar, S. C., *Some Aspects of Earliest Social History of India*, London (1928).
Shamashastry, R., *Kautilya—Arthasastra* (transl.), Mysore (1951).
Shastri, Shakuntala Rao, *Women in Vedic Age*, Bombay (1954).
——, *Women in Sacred Laws*, Bombay (1960).
Sengupta, Padmini, *Women Workers of India*, New York (1960).
Upadhaya, B. S., *Women in Rigveda*, Benares (1941).
Vora, Dhairyabala, *Evolution of Morals in the Epics*, Bombay (1959).
Woodsmall, Ruth Frances, *Women and the New East*, Washington (1960).

PERIODICALS AND REPORTS

Kennedy, Beth C., "Rural-Urban Contrasts in Parent-Child Relationships in India," *Indian Journal of Social Work*, Vol. XV, No. 3 (1954).

Planning Commission. *Review of First Five Year Plan* (1957).

——. *Second Five Year Plan:* A draft outline (1956).

——. *Second Five Year Plan.* Progress and Report, 1958–1959, 1960.

——, *The New India: Progress through Democracy*, New York (1958).

Government of India, *Women in Employment (1901–1956)*, New Delhi (1958).

All India Women's Conference, *Seminar on Careers of Women*, New Delhi (1956).

Times of India Directory and Year Book, 1961–1962.

Pakistan

By Shereen Aziz Ahmed

*D*ivided into two parts, Pakistan has an unusual geographic position. West Pakistan and East Pakistan are separated from each other by a thousand miles of Indian territory. West Pakistan abuts on the Middle East and has a common frontier with Iran, while East Pakistan borders on Burma and lies close to Southeast Asia.

And the women? shall we begin with the women of the plains or the mountains, the women of the rice lands or the tea gardens, the women of the cities—the bustling port of Karachi, verdant Dacca, or historic Lahore —or the women of the Chittagong Hill Tracts, or of Hunza, the Shangri-La of the world, that beautiful valley where women of eighty look like forty?

To understand the Pakistani woman, her aspirations, and her tenacious fight against outmoded social customs, poverty, and illiteracy, one must know her background. Her attitude toward life, her philosophy, her values are all tied in with her historical and cultural heritage. Her religion, Islam, is part and parcel of her thoughts, of her everyday life. It is a code of personal behavior, a complete social system, determining her attitude toward her parents, brothers and sisters, her husband and his relatives, toward elders and those younger than herself, toward orphans and the under-privileged. From it she gleans a knowledge of her inheritance, her place in the family and society, her attitude toward education, and all those little details which make Pakistani culture and religion so closely interwoven.

HISTORICAL AND CULTURAL BACKGROUND

For approximately eight centuries (even in historical perspective a period of time to be reckoned with) the Muslims ruled the subcontinent of India, with their power at its peak during the sixteenth century under the rule of Akbar the Great. Art, architecture, music, and poetry flourished. Persian was the court language. The world can still see the glories of those days in the exquisite Taj Mahal at Agra, the Badshahi Mosque, Shalimar Gardens, and Jehangir's Tomb at Lahore. But internal rivalries and jealousies weakened the entire structure so that when the British came to trade, they found a disunited people. From trade to conquest was not a big step; and for nearly two centuries, Britain ruled India as a colony. The Moghul rulers and their descendants, refusing to cooperate with the British, took little or no part in the administration of the country. The Sepoy Mutiny of 1857 finally sealed their fate. Sir Syed Ahmed Khan, a leading Muslim scholar who later founded the famous Aligarh University, awoke the slumbering Muslims who had wasted years nursing their grievances. The poet Iqbal chastised them for their inactivity:

> An infidel before his idol with waking heart
> Is better than the religious man asleep in his mosque

Separation from India—In 1906 the Muslim League was formed, a politi-cal party that was ultimately to wrest a part of India from the departing British as a homeland for the Muslims. Head and shoulders above other leaders was Qaid-i-Azam (the Great Leader) Mohammed Ali Jinnah. Educated in the West, yet steeped in the Eastern culture of the Moghul courts, a brilliant lawyer armed with the best of both worlds he made the dream of the poet-philosopher Iqbal come true when, in 1940, through the famous Lahore Resolution, he demanded a separate homeland for the Muslims of India.

When the British granted India independence, they carved a separate state out of that portion of the country where Muslims were in the majority. Sovereign since August 14, 1947, Pakistan, literally "Land of the Pure," has a population 88 per cent Muslim, with a minority of Hindus, Christians, and Buddhists.

WOMEN'S TRADITIONAL ROLE

Pakistan is essentially an agricultural country, gradually finding her feet industrially, as evidenced by these 1961 census figures:

Women of Pakistan

	Rural	Town
West Pakistan	15 million	4 million
East Pakistan	23 million	1 million
Total	38 million	5 million

Pakistani women work outside the home, but not far from it; helping in the fields, in the wheat lands of West Pakistan and the rice lands of East Pakistan, in sowing and harvesting, and all the smaller tasks shared by a farmer and his wife. The rest of their time is spent cooking, sewing, and taking part in numerous ceremonies, either in the immediate family, or in a neighbor's house, or even in a neighboring village. Cooking is an elaborate business, done at a leisurely pace. From a Western point of view the Pakistani woman's life might be dull, but to her a marriage, a birth, the circumcision ceremony of a son, or a religious festival are her whole life and she spends much time in preparing for and taking part in each. She controls the purse strings and arranges the marriages in the family. Her influence is particularly felt in her relationship with her sons, whether married or unmarried. A son always holds his mother in high esteem.

In the village home, where there is no money for education or luxuries, whatever is left after the bare necessities of life, such as food, clothing, and shelter, is spent on ceremonies. These are not conventions which can be done away with overnight, for on these ceremonies depends the *izzat*, or prestige, of the whole family.

When a girl is married she requires a decent trousseau, which includes household items and kitchen utensils; otherwise her in-laws will not respect her. When a child is expected, the daughter returns for the confinement to her parents' home where, at the birth of the child, she will be feted, given a new set of clothes and perhaps some jewelry, and with her new born child will return in triumph to her husband's house.

New clothes for the religious festival of Id-al-Fitr are a must for every member of the family. The wife prepares the traditional sweets for such an occasion—*sawayyan*, made of very fine vermicelli cooked with milk and sugar and decorated with slivered almonds and a touch of pure silver paper so thin that it can be blown off with one breath. Everything has to be correct. The etiquette surrounding these customs is well known by those who practise them. Any deviation would be frowned upon and considered bad taste. Handed down through the generations, many of them originated during the Moghul period.

Effect of Independence on Women—The achievement of independence was accompanied by dramatic events that brought about significant changes in the lives of many Pakistani women. Communal riots broke out immediately following independence, a massacre took place, and millions of women and children were engulfed by suffering. The impact of these tragic events was especially great in West Pakistan, into which streamed eight million refugees from India. What could women, with little initiative outside the home, do to help in this national calamity which threatened the very existence of the country, upsetting its economy and bringing in its wake hunger, disease, and death? Without hesitation, well-to-do women left the seclusion of their homes and helped in feeding, clothing, and housing these helpless multitudes. They worked in clinics and hospitals, helping the handful of doctors and the still smaller number of nurses to cope with infectious diseases, such as cholera and smallpox. They opened camps for the distribution of food, clothing, and medicines. Many women worked round the clock, not in air-conditioned hospitals but in improvised structures, in school buildings vacated for the purpose, and out in the open in the blazing sun.

What did this crisis do to the women of Pakistan? What did it do *for* them? The women who became refugees learned what it was like to lose the breadwinner of the family. The young girls among them realized how badly their mothers and they themselves were equipped to face such an emergency. They looked with admiration at their rescuers and helpers in whom they saw the embodiment of what women can do when put to the test.

Women's Organizations—All this was unpaid, volunteer work. Gradually, as aid for the stricken became more organized and women began to form themselves into groups, each group taking on a specific responsibility, the wife of the Prime Minister, Begum Liaqat Ali Khan, banded these women into one organization so as to channel their efforts, give them direction, and plan for the future. This organization was named the All Pakistan Women's Association, and today its members combine to form one of the largest bodies of voluntary workers in the world. Set up in February, 1949, with Begum Liaqat Ali Khan as its first President, this association has continued to help the underprivileged in every sphere of life.

The All Pakistan Women's Assocation has as its main objectives the informed and intelligent participation of the women of Pakistan in the growth and development of the country and the advancement of the welfare of Pakistani women through the improvement of their legal, political, social, and economic status.

Gratified and encouraged by what women could do if they worked together and with national goals of uplift in view, they chalked out a more ambitious program of setting up schools, clinics, hospitals, colonies for craftsmen, industrial homes for women engaged in cottage industries, and showrooms and shops to sell the finished articles. The All Pakistan Women's Association became known outside Pakistan for its active and valuable national program.

Today there are thirty-nine branches of the Association in West Pakistan and twenty in East Pakistan. The Karachi branch alone runs twelve educational institutions, including two secondary schools and one full-fledged college of science and arts, not to mention dispensaries, clinics, and a sixty-bed hospital. The work of APWA must be judged against the limited resources available to carry on these projects. Since the work kept expanding more rapidly than funds could be found to finance it, it was fitting that the government should step in and help financially, though even this was not enough.

EDUCATION

English is the official language of Pakistan, the language of the government, the high courts, business houses, and universities. The over-all percentage of literacy is 15 per cent, but among women much lower.

The old-fashioned idea of education for a girl was very limited. She attended a *maktab*, or school attached to the mosque, and learned to read the Koran in its original language, Arabic. Having mastered this, yet not trained either to speak Arabic or to write anything besides what the Koran contained, she would then be taught the feminine accomplishments, which would ensure her position as a good wife and mother. Included would be a certain amount of arithmetic.

Rural—The villager still has to be convinced of the value of education for girls, for the expense of being educated is considerable. Clean clothes, shoes, books, and equipment can be expensive when most of the budget is spent for food. Therefore, there has to be some obvious gain to a poor family from educating a girl. With a boy it is different; he will earn his living and be able to support his wife and children. But today the desire for change has spread to the villagers, not only to improve their own lot, but to improve the village itself.

People in remote and backward areas of the country are taking the initiative in effecting the necessary improvement in the educational, economic, and social spheres. The urge for more hospitals, schools, and welfare institutions in the country is a hopeful sign for the future.

However, it would be a great mistake to consider only those educated who know the mechanics of reading and writing. There is other knowledge — knowledge about things, about what goes on in the country, about foreign countries. In other words, there can be education without literacy. If you see a crowd of men and boys standing outside a tea shop, on the road, straining their ears so as not to miss a single word of the commentary coming over the radio about the cricket match between Pakistan and Australia, you will realize that *wanting* to know is also important. And the men who go to the tea shop at a certain time knowing exactly when the news will come on are adding to their store of knowledge and have their own information about the politics of the country and especially about such burning topics as Kashmir. Therefore, in spite of illiteracy, people are alive to what is going on around them.

In her excellent study of a Punjabi village, Dr. Zakiye Eglar writes: "The demand for educated girls has become widespread. In the villages people have already learned to inquire whether a marriageable girl has completed primary or high school. As people are coming to prefer an educated girl with a small dowry for a daughter-in-law to an uneducated girl with a large dowry, parents have become eager to educate their daughters."

Another welcome sign is that the villager is trying to cut down expenditure on ceremonies and give the money saved to a village fund that will be spent on community development, such as the building of schools and roads.

There is a special earnestness noticeable in all girls' schools and colleges in Pakistan. Rows and rows of shiny pigtails, heads bent low over notebooks, pens moving as fast as nimble fingers can make them. These are the lucky ones, the ones who managed to get seats in the overcrowded schools, and they are eager to learn.

Urban—The urge for education among women living in urban areas is remarkable. Neither government nor private agencies can cope with it. Everywhere there is a clamor for more schools and more colleges for women. The 1961 census showed that three times as many boys as girls attended school. This proportion is much higher at the university level. There, for every seven men only one woman has the privilege of obtaining a degree.

At the university level the most popular subject with women is medicine. There is always a waiting list to get into these institutions. There are four medical colleges for women, the best known being the Fatima Jinnah Medical College at Lahore. And women are free to enter men's colleges too.

Study Abroad—The number of girls who obtain scholarships and go to foreign countries to study is increasing slowly but is very small compared to the number of women who are educated at home. Among those who go to foreign countries, quite a number are unmarried. For these, life abroad can be quite difficult. It is very embarrassing for them, to say the least, to explain to boys who want to take them out on dates that in their society, girls do not go out alone with boys. Sometimes boys take it as a personal affront, and then the girl has to explain painstakingly what is and what is not accepted in her society and why.

BURQA AND PURDAH

A foreigner visiting a Pakistani city for the first time is startled to see a woman walking in the streets enveloped from head to foot in a cloaklike garment, which covers even the face, leaving only holes or a thin open-mesh net through which she can see. This woman is wearing the *burqa* because she observes *purdah*, or seclusion. How prevalent is this custom?

In the villages—and 85 per cent of the population of Pakistan lives in villages—women do not observe purdah. How would they live if they did? They have to work the fields with their menfolk, something they could not do wearing the *burqa*.

Urban women are a small minority and may be divided into two groups: upper- and middle-class women. At the top of the social ladder, living in the big cities, are the educated wives of men prominent in government, in business, in politics; they do not lead a secluded existence. There are also women prominent in their own right as doctors, lawyers, business women, and even ambassadors. None of them could possibly lead the active life they do and wear the *burqa*.

The women of the middle class may or may not wear the *burqa*. It is sometimes a case of on again, off again, depending on where they go, whom they are going to meet, and, above all, how many people who know them well will see them and gossip. Some middle-class women wear the *burqa* as a symbol of prestige. Historically, its origin is said to have been to shield women from conquering soldiery. A tradition grew up, therefore, that "nice" women do not display themselves to the public gaze but stay at home and devote themselves to home, husband, and children; and, if they are compelled to go out, they do so suitably covered.

Some scholars are of the opinion that the veiling of women was due to an ignorant and narrow-minded interpretation of the Koran which says: ". . . and tell the believing women to lower their gaze and be modest . . . and to draw their veils over their bosoms . . ." Obviously, this admonition could have been intended only for women who move outside the home.

In Pakistan, educated women feel that the word *purdah* should be taken in a metaphorical sense. They aver that the Koran has enjoined on Muslim women modesty in word and action, while fulfilling the feminine obligations of daughter, wife, and mother. However, the fact remains that in the twentieth century there are still women who wear the *burqa*. Education, and education alone, can lift the veil.

LEGAL POSITION

Islamic Basis—Non-Muslim delegates to the 16th Session of the United Nations were intrigued to hear a Pakistani delegate state during her speech that she was not sure she wanted equal rights with men, because in order to obtain these she would have to give up some of the rights that Islam gives to women. These delegates were interested to hear of the rights given to Muslim women thirteen centuries ago, long before Western women even started fighting for their rights.

The Koran recognizes the Muslim woman as a juridical person in her own right. As soon as she attains her majority she is able, according to law, to contract on her own behalf, to deal with her own property, to sell or retain her lands or houses, to do business according to her own wishes, without interference, her husband having no legal claim to any profits she makes. But where does a woman's private wealth come from? She can inherit it from her father, a daughter's share being half that of the share of the son. She can also inherit from her mother or her brother if he dies without children.

A woman need never assume her husband's name, and the majority of Pakistani women retain their own names even after marriage. Many women, however, especially those who travel abroad, adopt the Western practice. Women of the privileged class often use the Pakistani *Begum* instead of the English Mrs. or the French Madame. *Begum* is sometimes erroneously considered to be a title. The error arises from the fact that during Moghul rule it was the title of the ruler's wife.

Exercise of Rights—What Pakistani women have to fight for is the implementation of existing rights. Some of them are so ignorant that they are unaware of these advantages; or, if they are aware of them, they do not have the money to go to court or the inclination to make a public exhibition of themselves in a society that expects a woman to be modest and retiring. Obviously, the village woman suffers the most in this respect; this means, again, the majority of the women of Pakistan.

Women have had the right to vote since 1935 on the basis of adult franchise. They have turned out in large numbers, even the *burqa*-clad women. Since the introduction of the system of representation called Basic Democracies, in which a group of a thousand villagers elect one person as their spokesman, and so on in tier fashion, women have taken increasing interest in elections at all levels. It is claimed that in one rural constituency, 12 per cent more women than men cast their vote.

Controversy over Polygamy—To say that a spark can set off a conflagration is to state the obvious, but this is exactly what happened in 1955, when a highly placed political leader took a second wife. Throughout the country, women protested against this act which was in violation of the conditions under which a man can take a second wife as laid down in the Koran. Islam considered it permissible for a Muslim to marry two, three, or four wives only in such emergency situations. Most Muslims feel that the Koran's emphasis on "if ye fear that ye cannot do justice to so many wives, then one only" represents an attempt to abolish polygamy completely.

Reform of Marriage Laws—Women were therefore determined to fight for the reform of the marriage laws. Earlier, in May, 1954, a woman member of the Punjab Legislative Assembly presented a Marriage Reform Bill but failed to carry her point despite considerable feminine support. When matters came to a head in the following year, a national conference was held by the All Pakistan Women's Association on the "Status of Women," and some months later the government set up a Family Laws Commission to go into the question. Three of the members were women. Their findings were contained in a report submitted to the government in June, 1956. Following a two-year lull, in 1958, under the leadership of President Mohammed Ayyub Khan, things began to move rapidly ahead. The seven years' struggle of the women of Pakistan to reform the existing un-Islamic marriage and family laws culminated on March 2, 1961, with the promulgation of the Muslim Family Laws Ordinance. The news was received with great jubilation, especially by the All Pakistan Women's Association and other women's organizations all over the country.

The new ordinance prevents the abuse of polygamy by demanding that the husband satisfy the Arbitration Council in writing that the second marriage is necessary or just. It provides that in case of divorce the husband must give notice to the Chairman of the Union Council, who thereupon tries to bring about a reconciliation; failing this, the divorce takes effect after the lapse of three months, or, in the case of pregnancy, after delivery, whichever is later. Failure to notify the Chairman of the Union Council is punishable by imprisonment or a fine.

The ordinance also provides for the registration of marriages without undue inconvenience or expense. Evidence of the marriage and the terms of the marriage contract are preserved in this manner with the result of limiting unnecessary disputes.

The minimum age of marriage for girls is fixed at sixteen. The new law facilitates the claiming of maintenance by the wife through the Arbitration Council, and enables children of a predeceased son or daughter to secure their right of inheritance as recommended by the Family Laws Commission.

MARRIAGE PATTERNS

Marriage is the most important event in every woman's life, for in Pakistan marriage is universal; there is no monasticism in Islam. The Pakistani woman has no distinctive sign to show that she is married. Whether in the village or the city, a Pakistani mother plans well ahead for this happy event. In homes where there is not much money to spare, the bride's trousseau is painstakingly stitched by the mother, married sisters, and relations. Exquisite embroidery in gold, silver, or silk thread embellishes her brightly colored garments, and tiny round mirrors are sewn on the material to give a dazzling effect. In the bridegroom's house there is a good deal of preparation too, and very important indeed is the sewing which goes on there, for the wedding dress of the bride, usually of satin or silk, according to the means of the family, is made by the bridegroom's parents.

In Pakistan, most marriages are arranged by the parents. To those in favor of love marriages parents say, "Look at the fate of love marriages, how many of them do not last, but end up in divorce." On the other hand, to say that arranged marriages last *because* they are arranged is surely a fallacy. But in a society where the sexes do not mingle freely, it is natural that the parents, with their experience of life, should pick mates for their children. It is expected that parents will do the best for their children, and that, knowing their children well, they will make a suitable choice, keeping in mind the age, status, and temperament of the young people concerned. Because a girl has no alternative to marriage, she usually looks forward to her married life. She has been prepared beforehand to adjust herself to her new environment. She does not ask much of life, and so is willing to make sacrifices.

In a village wedding many of the old traditions are still preserved, including the arrival of the bridegroom at the bride's house on horseback. In the cities, the bridegroom comes in his own car or hires one. The band plays loud and long, and the guests, bedecked in their finery, enjoy themselves immensely. Watching the numerous ceremonies that precede the actual *nikah*, or marriage ceremony, one would expect a long and complicated service before the two young people become man and wife; but the *nikah* takes only ten minutes.

Marriage for the Pakistani Muslim is a contract, pure and simple, and is valid when both parties give consent. It is not a religious ceremony held in a mosque, but a civil contract. As such, each contracting person can make his or her own terms, which become part of the contract after mutual agreement. If the wife fears that her husband may take a second wife, she is at liberty to stipulate in the contract the right to divorce him if he does. She can also make sure that in the case of divorce he will support the children whose custody she has, according to law, until a boy is seven years old, and a girl has reached maturity.

A very important part of the marriage is the *mahr*. This is a sum of money, part of which is paid by the groom to the bride upon marriage, while the remainder is deferred and can be claimed by the wife either upon divorce or if the husband dies. This sum of money is very important. The amount paid to the bride enhances her *izzat*, and therefore the sum is usually commensurate with the position of the bride. But more significant still is the fact that the newlywed woman can do what she likes with the money, her husband having no further claim to it. If she is a good business woman she will invest it wisely. Therefore, the *mahr* aims at assuring the wife a certain amount of economic independence.

DIVORCE

Islamic law recognizes the right of both parties to dissolve the contract, but divorce has been declared by the Prophet to be "of all the lawful things the most disliked in the eyes of God." A divorced woman has the right of marrying again. Divorce initiated by the husband involves his handing over of the remainder of the *mahr* to the wife. If the divorce is iniated by the wife (*khola*) she must relinquish her claim to the *mahr*. The third kind of divorce (*mubarat*) is by mutual consent.

OCCUPATIONS

The largest number of working women are the unpaid workers in the rural areas. The thirty-eight million village women definitely earn their own living, although they are not paid wages. They contribute a large amount of time and labor to enhance the family budget. Agriculture is the mainstay of the country, and in it the woman's work is just as important as the man's. Methods of sowing and harvesting are changing slowly. Mechanical devices are being used, but they are not received with as much eagerness as in the West. There is no shortage of manpower, so that a change to a different way of farming would mean that alternative employment must be found for idle hands by seeking industrial jobs in the city. If large numbers of villagers flocked to the cities, it would cause unemployment and frustration.

The midwife of the village is the counterpart of the woman doctor of the city. Midwives do a thriving business and make good money.

Even before independence, two careers recognized as suitable for women who, bound by convention, did not wish to associate too freely with men were teaching (at all levels) and the medical profession. In the latter, women specialized in gynecology and pediatrics. A doctor's profession can be a very lucrative one. Few, if any, women would go to male doctors for their confinements, and it was felt that a woman doctor, who was usually a mother herself, would have more experience and be more sympathetic because she was a woman. Women doctors now also specialize in other fields, such as heart and skin diseases.

One of the most pressing needs in the country is being met by the large number of girls who are now entering the nursing profession. The need is so desperate as to be almost tragic. Again, age-old prejudices have to be overcome. Nurses have to live away from home. They have to be out all night when on duty. They have to do jobs that are unpleasant. Women leaders have appealed to society women to show respect for and appreciation of this profession by recognizing nurses socially and inviting them to their homes.

Women are now found even in jobs which bring them into close contact with men. They work as airline hostesses, in the pharmaceutical and packing industry, in the readymade garments industry, in banks and commercial houses. Women seem to be specially suited for jobs at information desks, as receptionists, and in travel and tourist offices. Women also work in the social-welfare branch of the Ministry of Health, Labor, and Social Welfare. Compared to the number of women in the labor force in industrialized countries, however, the proportion of women workers is very small. Those women who work do so mainly for financial reasons. The cost of living is rising and public opinion is conducive to women's employment. These two factors are attractive enough to tempt women to join the labor force in increasing numbers, but there must be enough jobs to absorb them. Government departments, social institutions, industrial and commercial unions, public opinion, all have to be geared to opening jobs to women. Women work not only in, but many of them own and run, such establishments as hairdressing salons, hotels, dress shops, cosmetic firms, and even concrete-pipe factories.

Often women are partners with their husbands, helping and advising in the business, especially where a woman's taste can be effective, as in interior decorating and cabinet making.

The Pakistani woman has a sensitive eye for beauty in all forms. Women artists, whether they paint in the style made familiar by the famous contemporary artists Abdur Rahman Chugtai and Zainul Abedin, or in an ultramodern individualistic style, are building national prestige in the world.

In literature, there are women writers of short stories and romances in the national languages as well as in English. These writers are a valuable source of information on the life led by Pakistani women in these days. Many of these writings depict the frustration felt before independence, others show how the enthusiasm generated by freedom is dampened by the pervading poverty and illiteracy.

Pakistani literature also has its women poets who are inspired by the poems of princesses of the Moghul Courts. The harvest songs of the villages and the boat songs of East Pakistan are the most popular forms of music. But the love songs of the films can be heard everywhere, on records, on the radio and in private homes.

Journalism, whether in English or in the national languages is a popular profession among women of the educated class, for it is a profession that can be carried on in the home. Since independence, two women's magazines in English—*The Mirror* and *Woman's World*—have been established, edited by women and run by an almost purely feminine staff. In a country where the number of national publications is minute compared with those in the West, such magazines are doing a national service in the interests of women. These magazines, although social in character, are also vehicles for political opinions. In recent elections, both women editors stood for election for the same seat, the editor of *Woman's World* winning this coveted position.

If women are available, if they have the necessary skills and if they are poor, they must be given facilities to earn their living. Among the most important needs are creches and day nurseries for working mothers with small children, and part-time jobs for women who cannot work full-time. As more and more women join the professions, they are organizing to protect their interests. The Business and Professional Women's Club, the Federation of University Women, the Home Economics Association, and many others are the outgrowth of this need.

Only recently have Muslim women in Pakistan accepted jobs as stenographers or private secretaries. Their hesitation was because the work brings them into too close an association with men. It is too early to tell but it would be interesting to know in what way the restrained behavior of the private secretary affects her efficiency.

A very lucrative profession, but one not looked on with much favor and even looked down upon in some circles, is that of the film star. Yet, strangely enough, women of good families have acted in films, and one of Pakistan's top stars is the daughter of a prominent businessman. For the common man with little money to spend on luxuries, the cinema is the cheapest and most popular of all entertainment. The majority of films are imported, but it is imperative to build up a national film industry to save foreign exchange. Obviously, too, the social life of Pakistan can only be depicted by its own people talking in the national languages, Urdu or Bengali.

In government services women get equal pay for equal work along with men, a benefit for which some advanced countries are still clamoring. Women in government service are also granted three months' maternity leave with full pay. These generous rules can cause some dislocation, to say the least, especially in educational institutions. Also, in the manner in which she is taxed, the wage-earning Pakistani woman is better off than women in some highly industrialized countries. Tax is deducted from her salary separately, and not from the combined salaries of herself and her husband.

POLITICS

Pakistani women are not only free to contest elections with men but also have seats reserved for them. So far, they have not contested the general seats, but there is a great deal of activity for the reserved seats.

In the past, women have requested representation in the Cabinet. What they actually had in mind was that the Ministry of Social Welfare should be headed by a woman. It was a fair enough demand. In a previous government, a woman was Deputy Minister of Social Welfare. And the Cabinet of the West Pakistan Governor has a full-fledged woman Minister who holds the portfolio of education.

With the promulgation of the new Constitution by President Mohammed Ayyub Khan, on June 8, 1962, five seats were reserved for women in each of the Provincial Assemblies, three seats for women from West Pakistan to the National Assembly, and an equal number of seats from East Pakistan. The election of women to the Assemblies was news. Photographs of the successful candidates had a place of honor on the front page of a leading Pakistani English daily with nationwide circulation.

Meetings were held in which each woman candidate had the opportunity to address the voters. Each candidate recalled her services in the field of social welfare and outlined her future program. All emphasized the need for adequate representation of women in public bodies and stressed the necessity for better educational facilities for women. Some promised that, if elected, they would strive to cut down unnecessary expenditure on ceremonies; others, that they would continue to work for the benefit of the underprivileged. The seats were keenly contested. In one constituency, twenty-eight women contested five seats.

WOMEN'S HOME INFLUENCE

Throughout the centuries, women have been the custodians and upholders of moral and religious standards. The more time woman spends in the home, the stronger is this influence. The home thus becomes the center of all cultural activities. All ceremonies originate here. It is the mother who teaches the children how to behave. The girls, especially, learn the niceties of deportment—how to dress, what to wear and when, how to be courteous to guests and how to behave toward others in whose company they will move as married women. It is the mother who teaches the children their duty towards God. When ceremonies are celebrated in the family, such as the Id-al-Fitr, the feast following the month of fasting, or the Id-al-Azha, commemorating the sacrifice of Abraham, all activities of the house revolve around the mother. It is she who decides every detail.

Thus, through her influence on the family she affects the life of the community and keeps alive the traditions of centuries.

JEWELRY

Pakistani women love jewelry. Bangles are probably the most popular —but, to a Pakistani, the word means many things since there are various forms, such as the *Kara, Kangan,* or the *Jehangiri* (the latter made by Emperor Jehangir for his wife, the Empress Nur Jehan, and designed by himself). The glass bangle, or *choori*, is a must for all celebrations, and nothing is more fascinating than the musical tinkle of several glass bangles as the wearer moves her hands. Teen-agers love to wear bangles matching or contrasting with their clothes.

The ornaments of Pakistani women are not mere frivolity. They serve an important purpose. For women who neither understand nor appreciate the saving of money by putting it in the bank, silver or gold ornaments are an important financial reserve which they can sell in times of need. Here is another occupation for the woman who spends much of her time in the home—the making of jewelry for herself and for giving to her daughter at her marriage.

DRESS

Western dress has been adopted almost universally by Pakistani men with a Western education. It is questionable whether the traditional dress of the Pakistani women will be preserved as it has been up till now. My impression is that the onus is on the Pakistani woman who travels abroad.

The sari has been accepted as the most beautiful and graceful dress in the world. The two other kinds of dress worn by Pakistani women are not so well known. They are the *shalwar* (baggy trousers narrowed at the ankles), the *camise* (a knee-length tunic with slits at the side) and the *dupatta*, or veil, which is draped over the shoulders or used to cover the head on certain occasions such as entering a mosque, reading the Koran, or entering the presence of elderly persons or those of high rank. The other is the *gharara*, a formal dress, originally worn by ladies of rank at the Moghul court. This, too, consists of a *camise* and a *dupatta*, but the place of the *shalwar* is taken by a divided skirt, very wide and flared, beautiful, but expensive to make. Soon after independence, it was suggested that the *gharara* should be recognized as the dress for women on formal occasions, state functions, and the like. But the idea was not pressed, as it was felt it would be unfair to insist on a dress which so few people could afford.

Even the village woman chooses her own clothes—her main considerations being color (the brighter it is the prettier), quality, and price. Women's magazines have started making suggestions, with the aid of beautiful models, for subtle changes in the dress of the Pakistani teen-ager: the *shalwar*—a bit tighter at the ankle; the *dupatta*—of thicker material and much narrower in width. But fashion is still left to the taste of the individual. A change in outlook, however, can affect the entire mode of dress, as for instance during the last war, when there was an urge toward all-round simplicity, and again now, when women are being urged by their leaders to adopt simplicity in dress.

RESPONSIBILITY OF EDUCATED WOMEN

It is the educated women who must shoulder the entire responsibility of taking an active part in the progress of the country. This tiny, privileged minority, barely one per cent of the population, acquit themselves very well by the recognized standards of progressive countries. They are represented in many professions. They are also on local bodies, on municipal committees, in Basic Democracies, in social service, in Parliament, on government commissions, and in government service. They represent Pakistan on international bodies; they have represented their country on the U.N. Commission on the Status of Women, a Pakistani women being the first Asian to be elected as its chairman. Every year the Pakistani delegation to the General Assembly of the United Nations has had a woman delegate on the Third Committee. Wives of ambassadors and officers serving in the Pakistan Foreign Service all over the world are proving an asset to their husbands, taking an active part in explaining their culture to the nationals of the country to which their husbands are accredited, each one in her own sphere, doing her bit. Outstanding among them are: Her Excellency Begum Liaqat Ali Khan, Pakistan's Ambassador to Italy and Tunisia; and Miss Fatima Jinnah, beloved and respected sister of the Qaid-i-Azam, affectionately known as Madar-i-Millat (the Mother of the People); and others.

The challenge is: will the educated, the privileged, those endowed with so many benefits and opportunities, live in their own little world or will they use their talents and advantages for the benefit of the have-nots, thus spreading the Islamic spirit of brotherhood and equal opportunity for all? The President of the All Pakistan Women's Association, Begum Liaqat Ali Khan, has pointed out that the only way in which the chosen few can hope to achieve real progress for the country is by cutting out all extravagance in house, dress, food, entertainment, luxuries, and ceremonies; by supporting national products, industries, savings plans, and bonds, and the family planning program; by encouraging professional training for all women; and by building up traditions of service and character. And lastly, the kernel of the whole problem, she said, was to "Place a premium on rural welfare work, for in the millions of fields and villages of Pakistan lie the seeds of success or failure."

Slowly but surely the signs of progress multiply. The screens that used to separate the girl students from the boy students in the classrooms of the University of Peshawar have disappeared. The most conservative area of all in the north, known as the Tribal Area, now boasts of ten girls in the medical college out of the fifty places reserved for girls.

Woman's role can never change. There can only be a shift of emphasis. The immutable role of the woman as mother shows that the home must always play an important part in her life.

Anchored to the past, Pakistan has not yet developed a new social system combining the best of the old and the new. Women leaders can help the nation find this healthy norm which will fit in with the conviction that women should engage in outside work and take an active part in national progress—but not at the expense of the home.

II

The Muslim Middle East

IRAN, TURKEY,

AND THE ARAB WORLD

The three articles of this part discuss countries that range from the extremely tradition-bound (Saudi Arabia and Yemen), in which the position of women is even more restricted than in the Indian subcontinent, through intermediate (Iran, Syria, Iraq, Egypt), in which the relative urban freedom of women sharply contrasts with the continuing restrictions in rural areas, to advanced (Turkey, Lebanon, Tunisia), in which the women have achieved a position approximating that of their sisters in the Latin countries. Yet Islam, which is the religion of the overwhelming majority in these countries (with the exception of Lebanon), is still so influential in determining the position of women in all of them that they can be conveniently grouped together.

Iran

By Latifeh Yarshater

INTRODUCTION

*I*n *considering the condition* of women in Iran, one must bear in mind that Iranian society is experiencing a period of transition. The old and the new exist side by side, and although Iran has been remarkably flexible and receptive in her efforts to modernize, the age-old customs and attitudes rooted in an ancient and venerable culture have acted as a partial deterrent to the process. This fact has given rise to the inevitable tensions and frictions attendant upon periods of social change.

While the Iranian upper classes and urban groups have been quick to adapt to the spirit of change, making rapid transformation possible, the rural and tribal peoples, as elsewhere, have remained relatively tradition-bound. The more progressive and liberal religious leaders generally have supported modernization, particularly in the days of the constitutional revolution, but most of the other religious leaders have adhered to the old customs and consider Westernization a threat to their authority.

Geography has also affected the rate of change. Persia is a country of widely varying climates and terrain, with great mountain ranges and deserts. Dwellers on mountain slopes, in narrow valleys, arable plains, or oases face many difficulties in communication with those in other parts of the country. Thus, patterns of custom and social behavior, as well as general outlook on life, vary widely. The sophisticated, Western-minded, skeptical intellectuals of the privileged classes, for example, are utterly different from the simple, pious, hard-working peasants of the remote villages.

No generalized picture of women in society is possible. Although the educated, fashionable urban women follow the trends of Western social life, rural women prefer the mores of a distant past. As new and old buildings are juxtaposed in a Persian city, so too in its streets women in the latest Paris fashions mingle with women wearing veils. Nevertheless, the trend for more than two decades has been toward greater prestige, freedom, and opportunities for women. Helped by the progressive intellectuals, they have become more and more conscious of their rights and responsibilities. The struggle to achieve equal opportunities with men, which began with the 1906 revolution, gained momentum in the course of time, and culminated in the so-called White Revolution of 1963 which was inspired and initiated by the enlightened reformer-king, Shah Mohammad Reza Pahlavi.

HISTORICAL BACKGROUND

Zoroastrian Society—Religion had a vital influence on the social institutions of pre-Islamic Iran. The position of women among the Zoroastrians is depicted in the Avesta, the sacred book of Zoroastrians, traditionally attributed to Zoroaster or Zarathustra (believed to have lived between the tenth and sixth centuries B.C.); in a large body of Zoroastrian literature, originating for the most part in late Sassanian times (third to seventh century A.D.); and in the practices of the Parsi community in India and the Zoroastrian minority in Persia, who refused to accept Islam and, with minor changes, maintained the ancient religion of Iran.

Judging from the Avesta, woman's position in Zoroastrian society was high. She was considered a companion for man, had important responsibilities at home, and could attend social and religious gatherings in a man's company. Zoroastrians regarded the institution of marriage as more than a civil arrangement; it had a profoundly religious character. It was a man's religious duty to marry a good woman and raise as many children as possible, thereby multiplying the forces of good in the world. According to Zoroaster's dualistic outlook, every man should contribute, by means of good thoughts, good words, and good deeds to the final defeat of evil. To raise a large family of righteous sons and daughters was considered a sure way of helping Ahura Mazda, the supreme God, against his opponent Ahriman. The greatest blessing that could be bestowed upon a man was a large number of worthy sons.

A man was considered a true citizen only after he married. Only a man with a family could occupy responsible civic positions. In such a society, the wife necessarily enjoyed an important position. This position is historically attested by the number of Sassanian princesses who ruled either independently or jointly with their husbands.

Nevertheless, the Iranian family was a patriarchal one. The father was considered the head of the family, its ultimate arbiter, and the controller of joint family property. A woman had no legal identity in the strict sense of the word. Her property and assets were handled by the male head of the family, whether father, brother, or husband. She could, however, conduct a legal plea in her husband's behalf and manage his affairs if he authorized her to do so, and she could act as guardian to a son disinherited by his father. And although a woman did not enjoy equal legal rights with her husband, she was respected and loved by her menfolk. The dignity of motherhood was reflected in many of the customs of the Persian people. Her sons, for example, would not sit in her presence without her permission.

Among the upper classes a man was allowed more than one wife. To be the father of many sons was a great achievement for a man, since male children remained in the family, while girls left home once they were married.

The property of a deceased husband was divided among his children and his wife. If he had had more than one wife, only the first, who was considered the mistress of the household, and her children received any inheritance. She shared equally with her sons, and received twice as much as her unmarried daughters; if the daughters were married, they did not inherit from their father. Other wives and their children had no legal right to inherit, unless the father had left a written will providing for them.

Zoroastrian Marriage—Marriages were usually arranged by the family, the bride's feelings being unimportant. Gradually, however, particularly during the Sassanian period, the rights of women were increased, and girls were allowed to refuse the man chosen for them. If a girl gave birth to an illegitimate child, her father was obligated to care for it and raise it.

The ideal marriage was considered to be based on mutual love and esteem, as exemplified in the Persian national epic, the *Shah-Nameh* (Book of Kings), in the love stories of Zal and Rudabeh, Rustam and Tahmineh, Bijan and Manijeh, and in many other writings.

The minimum age for marriage was fifteen for girls. They were expected to bring a dowry, since they could not inherit property from their father once they married. The bridegroom agreed to pay his wife a certain sum of money—specifically indicated in the marriage contract—if he divorced her, thus giving the woman a means of support if she were abandoned by her husband. This custom is still generally practiced in Iran.

A woman was permitted to dissolve the marriage legally if she had valid grounds, and to have her husband punished for abuse. There were no restrictions against remarriage for either widow or widower.

If a woman was unable to bear a child, the couple could adopt one, in order to secure the continuation of the family.

Marriage between brothers and sisters and between mothers and stepsons was not unknown among royal, aristocratic, and priestly families. Perhaps preservation of the purity of the family line and retention of family property accounted for this. In any event, the custom was apparently confined to a few circles, and had declined before the advent of Islam, which was totally opposed to it. Today, marriage between first-degree relatives is not practiced by either the Zoroastrians of Iran or the Parsis of India.

Manicheism—The Manichean attitude toward women, marriage, and the family is also worth noting. This religion was started by Mani, a Persian prophet who proclaimed his universal religion in the third century A.D. In the course of a few centuries, the religion spread from North Africa to China. Zoroaster regarded life as a gift of God, to be enjoyed and cherished; Mani looked upon the world as a demonic device to prevent the release of the heavenly light that was swallowed by the forces of darkness during the course of a primeval battle. Mani's pessimism was diametrically opposed to Zoroaster's optimistic view of life. According to Mani, man and woman were created by an archdemon who sought to fetter the light particles imprisoned by his forces within their bodies. Although made of demonic material, they were given the form of a heavenly god. The archdemon endowed man with a number of vices, but woman was given an even larger share. Thus, Manicheans were averse to anything that tended to perpetuate life, since life on this earth was merely a shackle to the particles of light which yearned to ascend to heaven, their original abode. It was with great reluctance that the Manicheans allowed the ordinary members of their church—though not the elite—to feed, clothe, and shelter themselves, enter into matrimony, and raise children.

In the fifth century A.D. Sassanian Persia witnessed the rise of still another religious movement. Mazdak, its leader, who had Manichean affinities, came to the conclusion that the basis of all evil—animosity and strife between men—was greed, greed to possess wealth and women. To destroy evil at its source, and so establish permanent peace, he advocated the communal possession of material goods. The relatively rapid spread of this teaching indicates the need for social reform toward the end of the Sassanian era.

The Islamic Conquest—The change was finally heralded in Iran, not by an indigenous religious movement, but by Islam. In 651, its small army of simple but faith-inspired and zealous Arabs was able to topple the great Sassanian empire, seize the wealthy provinces of Iran, and reach, within a short time, the borders of India and China. Islam, subsequently adopted by the masses of the Persian people, profoundly changed the social life of the country.

In Persia some Muslim laws represented a step backward for women who had already attained a higher status than Islam could offer. But in at least two areas Islam was effective in augmenting the rights of Persian women. It abolished the prevailing caste system, thus providing greater opportunities for the low-caste women; and it explicitly recognized the legal identity and economic freedom of woman.

During the Islamic period, a number of Persian women became prominent in politics and literature. Among the women writers were Rabea (tenth century), Mahsati (sixteenth century), Qorrat Al-Ain (nineteenth century), and Parvin (died 1940), a leading poet of contemporary Iran.

Among political leaders, mention should be made of the able Sayyideh Khatun (eleventh century) of the Buvayhid dynasty, who ruled for many years on behalf of her minor son; Torkan Khatun, the wife of Malekshah (twelfth century); and Gowharshad, the wife of the Timurid Shahrokh (fifteenth century) whose enlightened patronage of the arts and pious outlook culminated in the building of the Gowharshad mosque in Meshhed, one of the most fascinating architectural monuments in Persia.

Status of Women in Islamic Persia—The position of women suffered something of a reversal after the Safavid dynasty (sixteenth and seventeenth centuries), which supported an extreme form of Shi'ism and introduced a kind of theocracy. The general political and social decline of the past few centuries was scarcely helpful to the position of women. Coupled with the fanaticism advocated by some religious leaders, it even furthered the seclusion of women and restricted their education.

The situation of women in nineteenth-century Iran was, in fact, far from enviable. They were shrouded in the black *chador*, which covered the entire figure and was draped over the head to hide all of the face except the eyes. Women of the upper classes wore, in addition, a black visor which projected over the eyes.

Not only were women required to veil themselves in public, but every aspect of their personal lives was restricted by convention. The women's quarters in a house, the *andarun*, were separated from the rest of the house. No visitor, except relatives, saw them, nor was it considered good form to inquire about the women of a household. A woman's existence, except for her husband, was restricted to the company of members of her own sex.

It is said that the veil was never intended as a hindrance to women. In the beginning, it was assumed as a form of protection from the hungry eyes of invading conquerors. It was worn, too, as a symbol of dignity and class status, being forbidden to slaves and women of the lower classes. The veiling of women is unknown among tribes, and the peasants do not adhere rigidly to the custom. As time passed, however, it became common practice in the cities, and gradually came to be associated with the inferior position of women.

Awakening and Western Influence—With the awakening of Persia at the turn of the century, the growing contact with the West, and the spread of liberal ideas, a new consciousness arose among women about their rightful position in society. In 1906, a revolution of the liberals led to the establishment of a constitutional government in Iran that gave further impetus to progressive movements and to social and patriotic awareness on the part of women.

As the years went by, Iranian women slowly made advances. In 1925, General Reza Khan, a strong and popular military leader who had embraced the cause of reform and modernization, was proclaimed shah and the present dynasty was inaugurated. Social reforms gathered momentum under Reza Shah's leadership, and Iranian women moved forward in a noticeably more favorable atmosphere.

Abolition of the Veil—In 1935, after Reza Shah had paved the way and diminished the power of the clerical opposition, one of the most important steps in the history of modern Iran was taken, and a cherished dream of the progressive elements was put into practice: the institution of the veil was abolished, and women, now emancipated, were required to go unveiled. A new era was thus opened in the life of the Iranian woman. It was now possible for her to be trained, along with men, in the institutions of higher education, to assume social and administrative responsibilities, to contribute significantly to the advancement of society, and to press forward more effectively for further rights for herself. Although since the abdication of Reza Shah, following World War II, the veil has made a partial return among the less educated classes, subsequent events have contributed to woman's freedom.

The 1950's witnessed a rapid increase in the number of women's organizations and in women's active participation in political, social, and educational endeavors. In 1959, under the able leadership of Her Royal Highness Princess Ashraf Pahlavi, all voluntary women's organizations were federated in the High Council of Women's Associations of Iran in order to coordinate their activities and strengthen their position. This development inspired Iranian women to concerted efforts to gain further legal and political rights and equal opportunities with men. While progressive elements in government circles and outside them joined in the support of such efforts, legal and procedural requirements made the realization of the women's objectives difficult.

A real turning point, however, came about in 1963, when the Shah cut the Gordian knot by launching a revolutionary program of great social and political significance. Realizing the importance of the role of women in a society aiming at speedy progress and modernization, and after having obtained the overwhelming support of the Iranian people for his revolutionary program in the January 1963 referendum, the Shah announced his intention to grant the Iranian women complete political franchise. On March 3, 1963, the Iranian Council of Ministers adopted a decree modifying the electoral law with a view of allowing Iranian women to participate in the next elections. These took place in the same year, and six women were returned to Parliament while two women were among that half of the Senate which is appointed by the Shah.

The complete political franchise has opened the way for other reforms aimed at by Iranian women. Equal rights in legal and family matters, which often require fresh interpretation of religious customs and laws, are still to be achieved. Measures to mitigate the existing inequality in such matters are already being enforced by the government.

TOWN AND COUNTRY

Persia is largely agricultural. Almost three quarters of her 21 million people live in some 45,000 villages. Cities, however, play a leading role in the changing status of women.

Economic factors determine the position of women in town and country. In the country, women are not only responsible for running the household and bringing up the children but also take a hand in farm work and animal husbandry. In general, they have a fuller share in the life of their communities than women in urban areas. This is even more true of tribal women, who shoulder all kinds of responsibilities.

Restriction of Women to Home Tasks—In urban centers, the greater division of labor and the traditional customs and institutions have restricted the majority of women almost entirely to household tasks. In a typical urban, lower-middle-class family, a woman would be busy from dawn to dusk working around the house, preparing food and attending to her children. Since modern household conveniences are few, the home routine absorbs practically all of her time. There is little time or opportunity for social activities.

Among the more well-to-do families in the cities, the women are generally provided with servants and can afford to spend more time on their toilet, social activities, and enjoyment of the arts. Their power behind the scene can occasionally be felt in business and politics.

Emergence of Women in the Cities—In recent years, the position of women in rural and tribal areas has changed slightly, in the cities, significantly. This is especially apparent in Tehran, the capital, a city of some two million population and the economic, political, cultural, and administrative center of Persia. Among the more advanced groups the wife is now considered a friend and companion of her husband, and shares his social life to a great extent. The younger generation of women graduating from high schools and colleges have been quick to adopt the latest fashions, manners, and attitudes of Western women.

LEGAL AND POLITICAL STATUS

Property Rights—Under the civil law of the country, a woman has complete control over her personal property. Article 1118, Section 8, of the Marriage Law states, "A woman may use her property independently, in whatever manner she chooses." She can, therefore, transact business, sign contracts, open bank accounts, and make a will. She may sue or defend a case in courts of all levels and can appoint her own attorneys.

In marital and political matters, however, there is still no equality between the sexes. In accordance with Islamic law, a girl still receives half a share against the full share of a son in their father's estate. A woman is fined half as much as a man. If she is called to testify, she counts only as half a witness, except in the case of the birth of children, when the testimony of one woman alone suffices.

A man has the right to choose his wife's domicile (which, however, must not endanger her health, property, or good name), unless the contrary is provided for in the marriage contract. She must have the consent of her husband for traveling abroad, subject again to the marriage contract.

Divorce—According to Islamic law, divorce is a prerogative of the husband, who may divorce his wife at will and without a court verdict. To safeguard women against capricious divorces and to provide them with some means of maintenance, the Muslim law and customs provide for a sum of money to be paid by the husband to his wife, in case of divorce, and specified in the marriage contract. The wife has a legal right to claim this *mahr* payment any time she chooses, but in practice it is claimed only when the marriage is dissolved. On the other hand, a wife may forego her *mahr* in order to obtain her husband's consent to a divorce.

The inequity of the divorce laws has caused considerable concern among socially conscious Persian women. Amendments have been suggested by all women's organizations, and although men generally admit their desirability, the explicitness of the Muslim law has so far blocked any drastic change.

Nevertheless, women do have certain rights in matters of divorce. A woman may ask for and obtain a divorce: if the husband becomes insane or impotent; if he refuses to perform his basic marital duties; if he contracts a hard-to-cure infectious disease; if he refuses to support his wife, or is unable to do so; or if he is guilty of mental cruelty. The law also provides for a man and a woman to make such provisions in their marriage contract as may be agreed upon by both. In this manner, a woman may secure the right to choose her domicile, to divorce her husband with or without any condition, to bring up the children in case of divorce, or to bar her husband from polygamy. As women grow more conscious of their rights, and as their economic situation improves, they take greater advantage of these legal possibilities.

A woman cannot remarry for three months after her divorce. The custody of children is given to the husband. The wife can keep her sons until they are two years of age and her daughters up to the age of seven, after which their father can claim them. If the mother remarries or becomes insane before her children reach the stipulated ages, custody of the children reverts to their father.

Employment and Politics—Labor legislation, which is fairly recent, stipulates equal pay for equal work to men and women. This is carefully observed in the civil service, but less so in factories and small businesses. Women enjoy the same labor benefits and safeguards as do men.

Before 1963, women's political rights were insignificant. Following the traditional social patterns, the right to elect members of the legislature, or to be elected to it, was confined to men. Women could, on the other hand, participate in municipal elections, and technically they could be elected to municipal posts, although in practice such provisions remained on paper only.

After the White Revolution of 1963, the franchise granted to Iranian women completely changed the picture. Women were put on equal footing with men, and assured full political rights. As a result, women can now assume any job that men may have. (A notable exception to this general rule is the practical exclusion of women from the army and the police forces.)

EDUCATION

Traditional Pattern—In ancient and medieval Persia the curricula emphasized religious and literary disciplines. The traditional school was the one-room *maktab* where the pupils were taught to read and write and to recite the Koran, sitting cross-legged on the floor with wooden tablets to write on. There were special *maktabs* for girls, but only middle- and upper-class girls were sent to them. Some families had tutors for their girls.

Teaching at higher levels took place in *madrasas*, religious schools supported by charitable endowments and often attached to mosques. Training in sciences and professions was usually private. The master passed his knowledge and technique to the disciple, or father to son.

In the middle of the nineteenth century, forces of change and modernization began to transform the educational system. Vestiges of the old system, however, can still be seen in some rural areas.

Beginnings of Mission Schools—In 1859 the Persian government founded a Technical School *(Dar al-fonun)* in which modern sciences were taught side by side with traditional disciplines. American and European missionaries had started schools even earlier. The first American school, conducted by the Presbyterian Board of Foreign Missions, was founded in 1836 at Rezaieh in Azerbaijan. Schools of higher grades for both boys and girls were gradually established by this Board in other cities and attended by increasing numbers of students. A school for girls was first opened in Tehran in 1874, another in Hamadan in 1882. The last American school was opened in Meshhed in 1926. In 1933, 1,708 boys and 1,346 girls studied in American schools in Persia.

In Tehran, Alborz College for boys and Sage College for girls, run by the Presbyterian Missions, were responsible for the education of many capable young men and women who were to distinguish themselves among their contemporaries. Feminine leadership in modern Persia has drawn heavily upon the graduates of the American schools.

Modern Education for Girls—The necessity for better education for girls was stressed by progressive elements during the constitutional revolution early in this century. Effective measures, however, were taken only after 1923, when Reza Shah came to power. The number of elementary schools for girls increased considerably and girls were encouraged to enter secondary schools. The education of women, however, was seriously hampered by veiling and seclusion, which made free association between men and women impossible and barred coeducation at institutions of higher learning.

Following the emancipation of women in 1935, this barrier was removed. The University of Tehran became coeducational in 1940. In the same year, all foreign schools were taken over by the Iranian government (although in the last decade some of them were again returned to foreign supervision).

In 1947, the Public Education Act was passed by Parliament, providing for four years of free and compulsory elementary education for every Iranian child, boy or girl. Social and economic difficulties, however, continued to keep literacy at a low level (about 15 per cent, according to an estimate based on a partial 1961 census). But the number of Normal Schools for boys and girls (30 in 1948) increased, and even some ultraconservative elements began to realize the importance of giving equal educational opportunities to both boys and girls.

In the last thirty years, girls have received a better and more extensive education, and the gap between men and women in educational benefit has narrowed. The impressive increase in the number of women teachers —more than 14,000 in 1960—reflects both the need for the expansion of women's education, and the public response to it. There are now no important academic fields not open to women with the exception of theological and military schools.

Primary and Secondary Education—In primary education, the scope and content of the curriculum are the same for both sexes. Primary schools are either coeducational or separate, according to available facilities and circumstances.

In secondary education, boys and girls are separated, but the duration of studies and the curricula are the same for both, except that girls take lessons in handicrafts, such as needlework, and in domestic science. After the fourth year of the secondary school, girls have the choice either of following the general curricula preparing for university studies, or of preparing for a separate branch, specially designed for girls, which emphasizes home economics and trains girls for an enriched and cultivated home life. At the end of two years, the students receive a secondary-school diploma.

Higher Education—All universities in Persia are open on the same terms to both sexes. The University of Tehran provides higher education for women in liberal arts and professional fields, including law (since 1946), public administration, medicine, dentistry, pharmacy, veterinary science, agriculture (since 1958), engineering, and fine arts. The disciplines most popular with girls are those of letters and fine arts. In 1960, there were about 3,000 women and 9,000 men students at the University of Tehran, including the Teachers College.

Vocational and Professional Schools—A notable trend in the Persian educational system in recent years has been the expansion of vocational schools. Schools for cooking, tailoring, hairdressing, handicrafts, and secretarial skills are generally private establishments. But the Ministry of Education, which has embarked on a large program of expanding vocational schools since 1956, has also opened a number of schools to raise the standard and quality of these professions. The School of Social Welfare in Tehran, the first of its kind, was opened in 1958. A number of vocational schools sponsored by the Department of Fine Arts, such as the School of Painting and Sculpture, the Music Conservatory, the School of Dramatic Arts, and the School of Ballet, are popular with girls.

Nursing schools have been sponsored by various charitable organizations, such as the Red Lion and Sun (the Persian equivalent of the Red

Cross), the Royal Organization of Social Services, and the Iran Foundation. There are altogether fourteen nursing schools throughout the country. Although the standard and prestige of nursing have been considerably raised by the establishment of these schools, and by the many trained nurses who have studied abroad, an acute shortage of trained nurses remains.

The education of girls is also helped by extracurricular programs such as summer camps, athletic clubs, and summer courses. Educational camps for girls received special encouragement from the Ministry of Education, the Pahlavi Foundation, and various other organizations in 1953, when a new series of summer-camp programs was established.

Physical Education—Physical education of girls receives special attention not only in the schools but also through private athletic clubs and various organizations sponsored by the Physical Education Department. A Girl Scout Program was revived in 1958 under the sponsorship of the Ministry of Education.

Adult Education—In view of the low level of literacy, adult education has long been a concern of the Ministry of Education, but the results achieved in this field have fallen far short of the country's needs.

In 1965 a wide campaign was launched against illiteracy, and an increasing number of villages were being provided with young teachers who would teach for the duration of their military service. This program is accompanied by the opening of a number of literacy classes for adults. The High Council of Women and its affiliated organizations have a very active hand in the execution of this program and many women volunteers teach in classes set up for illiterate women.

Pressures for More Education—Naturally, advances through the education of women are more noticeable in urban centers and in the more prosperous communities. In some villages, and in highly conservative circles, prejudice against the education of women still exists. One of the main problems is how to cope with the increasing demand from rural as well as urban areas for better schools, more schools, and more teachers.

SOCIAL POSITION OF WOMEN

Before the abolition of the veil in 1935, women were greatly handicapped in exerting any significant influence except indirectly through their husbands and children. Now, however, it is possible for a woman to live by herself, administer her own affairs, choose a career, mix with professional colleagues and friends, and feel equal to men of her own status and ability. Small provincial communities are, of course, less broadminded.

Among the lower classes, and in religious circles, women are still subject to many prejudices. They are considered unequal to men, destined only to function as wives and mothers, within the home.

Family—The patriarchal family pattern continued, by and large, until the beginning of this century. The Civil Code reflects age-honored tradition when it states, "In relations between a married couple, the authority is a prerogative of the husband."

The old pattern requires a woman to obey her husband in all important matters, such as guiding the children's education and vocational choice, social relations, place of residence, and travel. This is still true in rural areas and in more conservative urban circles.

The young wife's only tasks are to bear children and keep house. Occasionally, her husband may become infuriated with her to the point of physical violence.

In general, however, and particularly in urban society, a wife is loved by her husband, who may go to great lengths to satisfy her wishes. In personal or family problems, the wife, the sister, or the mother may have considerable influence on a man's decisions. Not infrequently, a woman makes her views felt also in her husband's business affairs.

In middle-class families, the mother enjoys considerable affection and esteem. She, in turn, is a source of love and assurance to all members of her family, while the father is often distant and aloof. When the father becomes too strict or harsh with the children, it is usually the mother who tries to mollify him and save the children from his wrath. However, if the children become too unruly, she often asks the father to scold or punish them. In their early years, children are reared by the mother alone. The upbringing of her daughters is entirely in her hands. She also has control over the household and its management. Her real power is greater than the preceding statements suggest. By subtle persuasion, cajoling, and coaxing, she manages to have her way more often than is believed.

In the more advanced classes in contact with the Western world, a man and his wife discuss all important family matters and general issues. The wife's active and often dominant role in the family's social life is a far cry from her secluded position in the traditional Persian family.

The tension between wife and mother-in-law is proverbial in Persia. In the conservative families where the young couple lives with the husband's parents, his mother dominates his wife. But in the more modern families the wife asserts her rights with considerable success. It is being increasingly recognized that the husband's parents should allow the young couple as much freedom as possible in planning their life.

SEX MORES

Sex mores in present-day Persia derive partly from old Iranian traditions, as modified by Islam, and partly from developments of the last fifty
years, mainly under the influence of Western culture.

Muslim law allows men much greater sexual freedom than women.
Traditionally, great emphasis is placed on female purity and chastity. The
veiling and segregation of women are the entrenched manifestation of this
attitude in urban society. In many villages, and among the tribal people,
the working conditions of men and women prevented complete separation,
and even the veil was only infrequently used. The spread of coeducation to
rural areas and the elimination of the veil have greatly changed the traditional ways.

Even though the birth of a girl is not welcomed to the same extent as
that of a boy, the girl baby, too, enjoys much love and attention. She can
play with her brothers until she reaches the age of eight or nine. As a
teen-ager, she is not allowed to go out unaccompanied or to mix with men.
She is expected to dress simply and to use no makeup until she marries.
She does not appear before male visitors in her parents' home. She is
usually shy and aloof, and except for her girl friends, has no outside
contacts.

In the more progressive families, both boys and girls are brought up
much like their brothers and sisters in the Western world. They play together, go to the same school, and are at ease with each other. Girls attend
parties accompanied by parents, brothers, or family friends.

Dating—Dating is not a recognized practice. A young man and a girl
are generally not allowed to go out together unless they are engaged. But
there is no objection to their meeting in the presence of an elder member
of the family, or at parties. Since, however, the younger generation has
come to regard love as the basis for the choice of a marriage partner,
attempts at secret meetings without the knowledge of the parents are
frequent.

Girls are expected to remain virgins until they marry. The emphasis
tradition places on virginity has led to certain rites and observances among
the conservative groups, whose chief purpose is to ascertain the chastity
of the bride. If she is not found to be a virgin, and if there is no prior
understanding between bride and groom, the marriage is, as a rule,
dissolved, bringing utter disgrace upon the bride's family.

Adultery—As for adultery, the Iranian penal code, generally speaking,
prescribes the same penalty, whether the transgressor is a man or a woman.
If the parties involved are a man and a married woman, both are punishable; if the woman is unmarried, only the man is punished. If sexual

relations between unmarried persons result in the girl's pregnancy, the man must marry her. If a man catches his wife, sister, or daughter *in flagranti*, and kills either or both of the culprits, the law excuses him; a woman avenging herself by a similar crime of passion has no such legal protection. This discrimination has led to strong protests on the part of women's organizations, and the amendment of the law is still being demanded.

Prostitution—There is no penalty for prostitution as such, but the law provides severe penalties for aiding and abetting it. Municipal authorities generally overlook prostitution as long as it is not flagrant, and the prostitutes keep to their districts. The police periodically raid dubious hotels, and the Health Department inspects the red-light districts from time to time in its fight against venereal diseases.

The Penal Code protects women from being married off while still underage, from rape, and from attempts to prostitute them.

The dual sexual morality, embedded in Muslim tradition, assumes new forms with the advance of modernization. Today, as in the past, husbands expect unquestioning loyalty from their wives. Extramarital affairs of married men were not frequent in the past, because it was possible for them to have several wives. With the decline of polygamy, such affairs are becoming less rare, particularly among the urban upper classes.

MARRIAGE PATTERN

Traditionally, marriage is not only socially desirable, but also strongly encouraged by religion. Parents, therefore, regarded it as their duty to arrange for the marriage of their children when they reached marriageable age. This is still true among the conservative classes and in rural communities. Among the socially advanced groups marriage is becoming more and more a matter of the young people's own choice.

Legal Safeguards—A law of 1931 placed marriage on a civil rather than a religious basis. Another, passed in 1935, fixed the minimum age at sixteen for girls and eighteen for boys. In the cities, the longer period required for training for a profession, the two years of obligatory military training, and frequent economic difficulties tend to increase the average marriage age. In some rural and tribal districts, on the other hand, the legal minimum age for girls is felt to be too late and is disregarded. The engagement of very young children, to be married later, still occurs in tradition-bound communities, although it is rapidly dying out. Marriage among relatives of the first degree is prohibited in Islam, but marriage among cousins is considered particularly desirable.

The Marriage Contract—Whether the marriage is arranged by the relatives or by the young people themselves, basically the same customs and ceremonies are observed. Roughly, they consist of three phases: the betrothal, the marriage contract, and the wedding.

A "legally" married couple (that is, a man and a girl on whose behalf the marriage contract has been signed) may postpone the wedding for a period of time, occasionally for several years, until the husband establishes himself financially, or a house is built, or a family obstacle removed. In the meantime, the girl stays with her parents. Generally, among the younger generation the wedding immediately follows the signing of the legal contract.

Polygamy—The Islamic law permitting four wives remains valid, and though polygamy has become rare, all Persian women's organizations continue to fight for its legal abolition. Shi'ite Islam, the official religion of the country, also permits a number of "temporary" or "term" wives (*mut'a*). A man may take a wife for a predetermined period, after which the marriage is automatically terminated, unless the marriage contract is renewed. Children of a temporary wife have the same rights as those of a permanent wife. This institution is also rapidly declining and has practically disappeared among educated people.

HOME ROUTINE

In a Persian village, the main room, where all the members of the family live together, is usually covered with rugs made by the women of the house. Quilts, mattresses, and pillows are neatly piled near the walls. An oil lamp stands on a shelf, on which the family possessions are often displayed. A mirror and some religious pictures hang on the walls.

In the summer, most villagers sleep on the roof or in the courtyard; during the cold winters they keep themselves warm around the *korsi*, a low table covered by quilts, with mattresses spread around it and a brazier of charcoal under it to provide heat. The *korsi* is still used in the cities as well as by the lower middle classes.

The Village Household—Village women get up early, usually at sunrise, and after the ritual washing of hands and face and saying of prayers, they boil water for tea in a samovar and prepare breakfast, mostly bread and cheese, on a cloth spread on the floor. Daughters help with the work in the house and take care of the younger children.

The typical Persian village household is almost entirely self-sufficient, with the women baking bread, milking the cow, attending to the poultry, making cheese, butter, buttermilk, and yogurt, bringing water from the spring or well, washing clothes in the stream (or in a shallow basin if water is scarce), picking and drying fruits, and kneading dung loaves for fuel. If after all this work a woman finds herself with time on her hands, she uses it for spinning, knitting, and even weaving. In winter she attends to the *korsi*, keeping the fire going in the brazier, around the clock.

Lunch is very simple. The men eat their bread, cheese, fruit, or yogurt in the field. The evening meal, which is the main repast, is cooked in a saucepan supported by two stones, and may consist of a small piece of meat with some vegetables or cereals. The leftovers are often eaten at lunch the next day. Sometimes the family enjoys *pilau*, rice stewed with meat or vegetables.

In busy seasons the women and children help the men. The wives hold a large sheet under the fruit trees while the men shake down the fruits. In the Caspian provinces, women work in the rice and tea fields.

Tribal Life—Among the semi-nomadic tribes, women follow a similar routine, except that their daily work is much heavier, since flocks and herds are the main source of livelihood. When the tribe is on the move, the women do most of the packing and unpacking. The women also spin and weave tent cloths, bags, and rugs.

Urban Homes—In towns, the women of the working class do all the housework—cooking, washing, cleaning, marketing, and taking care of the children. For middle-class women, who can afford to have a more varied life, washing, cleaning, and cooking are sometimes done by a servant, under the wife's supervision. She herself may go out in the morning to shop or to meet friends but will return before the lunch hour to take lunch with her husband and children. In the afternoon, she sees to the preparation of dinner, but will also have time to visit friends, receive guests, and do some sewing or mending. In the evenings, the family may go to a motion picture theater, attend a party, receive friends, or stay at home listening to the radio or watching television.

Some seasonal household work, such as drying herbs, making pickles and cooking jam in quantities sufficient for a whole year, is common in many middle-class families, although decreasingly so in consequence of the development of food industries and the change of outlook of the younger generation.

Urban Home Life—In the more fashionable and well-to-do urban classes. particularly in Tehran, the women spend less time in household work and more in social, professional, recreational, and philanthropic activities. To go to the dressmaker or the hairdresser, to have morning coffee or lunch with friends, to shop and attend parties—these constitute the daily routine for such women. They also enjoy taking meals in restaurants, going on holidays, and engaging in sports. An increasing number of women of this class take an interest in cultural and charitable work.

Men help little, if at all, in the household, and the duties of women in both village and town are heavy and manifold. As servants become more and more difficult to obtain, the burden of the home routine becomes heavier. Thus, the introduction of household appliances and gadgets is welcomed by modern women.

WOMEN'S OCCUPATIONS

In rural communities women play an essential part in economic life, and in many cases work harder and show a keener sense of responsibility than the men. In the towns until recently, only the women of the poorer social strata (who, of course, constituted the overwhelming majority) worked outside their homes, mostly as domestic servants or in traditional industries, such as rug-making. Their working conditions were far from enviable: they worked long hours for little money, with few holidays, or none at all.

In recent years, both work opportunities and conditions have improved as a result of laws protecting women workers against long hours, under-age employment, poor sanitary conditions, underpayment, and possible abuses. The minimum age for a working girl is ten years.

The economic and industrial growth of the country has contributed its share to women's progress. City women are thereby enabled, and prefer, to work in factories, hotels, hospitals, and so forth, where they receive higher salaries and enjoy greater freedom than as domestics.

New Opportunities for Educated Women—Today, women are represented in almost all occupations. The Anglo-Iranian Oil Company and the National Bank of Iran were among the first to employ women typists and clerks. Other firms and government departments soon followed suit, and women began to compete with men in these occupations, as they do in the Western world.

The number of girls trained in Iranian and foreign universities is steadily increasing, and women gradually are penetrating professional fields and government services. Women stenographers and clerks have become a familiar sight in Iranian offices.

Nursing, a man's field only a few years ago, has become a woman's profession. Women are also numerous in laboratories, pharmacies, and medical research centers.

Since the establishment of the new School of Social Welfare in 1958, the number of women who have chosen social work as a profession is increasing, along with the growing number of social-welfare organizations. Women lawyers and, to a lesser extent, women doctors, find difficulty in being accepted, and their numbers, except in the case of gynecologists and dentists, still remain low.

In 1961, the Faculty of Letters of the University of Tehran had fourteen women professors. Considering that girls were enabled to enroll in the university only in 1940, this illustrates the rapid advances made by educated Persian women.

The Arts and Literature—In the arts, women are active in the Tehran Conservatory, both as students and as teachers. In traditional vocal music, both classical and popular, they have achieved spectacular success. In the performance of Western music, they have a good record of talent and achievement.

Painting has attracted a great many gifted Persian women, whose works are frequently exhibited. The dramatic arts are another field in which women have distinguished themselves. This is particularly interesting, since the theater in its Western form is a newly adopted genre in Persia and its world contrasts sharply with the sheltered and secluded life of women in traditional Persia. In traditional dancing, women have always had a leading position. The ballet, introduced recently, has found considerable popularity with girls, at least in Tehran.

A number of women have won recognition in literature, and some were well known as poets long before other fields were opened to women. Some of the best modern poets of Persia are women.

In short, there is today hardly any profession or trade which women have not found it possible to enter, with the exception of certain diplomatic, political, and juridical careers.

Although the law provides for equal pay for equal work, in practice women are generally paid somewhat less than men, with the notable exception of the Civil Service.

Married women are free, in principle, to embark upon a career, but the Civil Code enables the husband to object if he considers his wife's work incompatible with the interests or the dignity of his family.

WOMEN'S ORGANIZATIONS

Women's organizations, active since 1918, have done much to improve the status of women. The Society of Patriotic Women, founded in 1921, fought for the emancipation of women. The Women's Center was organized in 1935, with the support of the Ministry of Education, and has been active in adult education for women.

In 1942, the short-lived Iranian Women's Party was founded with the purpose of improving the position of women and gaining political rights for them. In 1943, the Communist Tudeh Party created an Organization of Iranian Women to fight for legal and political rights for women; when the Tudeh Party was outlawed, in 1953, this organization ceased to exist.

The twenty-four women's organizations now active in Persia are concentrated mainly in the fields of education, social work, hygiene, charity, and political enlightenment. Some are particularly interested in women's legal rights and have been able to persuade many key people to support their ideas.

To coordinate their efforts, the majority of these organizations, including the women's societies of the ethno-religious minorities, formed a federation in 1957. The High Council of Iranian Women, organized in 1959 and affiliated with the International Council of Women, has given a strong lead to its member organizations in many charitable and educational fields, and particularly in the campaign against illiteracy.

WOMEN AS CULTURAL TRANSMITTERS

The role of the Persian woman in transmitting culture derives from her position in the family. Traditionally, men had very little to do with the household or the upbringing of young children. The education of children and particularly of girls in their formative years was entrusted to women. It was mainly through them that the Persian cultural heritage (customs, folk medicine, etiquette, folk tales, folk songs, wedding and funeral rites and, to a lesser degree, religious beliefs and observances) was passed on from generation to generation.

Popular traditions are usually mixed with superstitious ideas and attitudes which are also an integral part of the cultural heritage of a people. Women in Persia had their full share in transmitting such ideas and attitudes to their children. In folk medicine, for example, the less enlightened women frequently combined valid medical practices with magic cures.

Women were the chief exponents of Persian cooking, a highly developed art, considered one of the great cuisines of the world. They were in charge of a number of home industries, such as spinning, knitting, weaving, and needlework, although the artistic and technical lead in these crafts generally was assumed by men.

The spread of modern education, the raising of the literacy level, and the development of mass media and communications expose the children of today to a large variety of cultural sources and influences. Nevertheless, the mother remains the most important single influence in laying down the earliest substratum in the child's mind and thereby determining the general direction of his later development as an exponent of Persian culture.

Progress Dependent on Overcoming Tradition and Inequalities—From a position of inequality and submission, Persian women have risen in a short time to near-equality with men and to enlightened self-assertion. The great majority of Persian women live in villages, however, where change has been much slower, and age-old customs, observances, and superstitions, coupled with a low level of literacy, hamper the adoption of progressive measures. Age-honored rules and regulations, based on religious traditions and defended by conservative elements, make the introduction of progressive measures difficult.

Through the endeavors of the socially conscious and active women of Persia both the legal and actual inequalities of Persian women will no doubt eventually disappear.

Despite the odds against her, the Persian woman has made great strides toward social progress and a more enriched and cultivated life. She has become socially and politically conscious and keenly aware of her rights as well as her responsibilities. The social conditions of the country have generally been favorable to these developments. Yet much remains to be done in educating and enlightening women in the villages and the conservative urban classes, and in surmounting the remaining barriers to their full legal rights.

Judging by the rapid advances and considerable achievements of Persian women in the last three decades, one can hope that a brighter and richer life, and greater social progress are in store for them in the future.

Turkey

By Nermin Abadan

As Bayard Dodge remarked, "The customs of two-thirds of the women of the world are changing to a greater extent in our lifetime than they have changed during the past two thousand years."[1] Political rights, economic necessities, the ravages of wars and revolutions, and the belief in the value of the liberation of women have induced the leaders and responsible citizens of more and more countries to insist upon a complete review of the functions and aspirations of women. This is particularly true in Turkey, due to the substantial reforms of Atatürk, founder of the Turkish Republic. But in other Middle Eastern countries, too, as Daniel Lerner expressed so well, the traditional society is passing, because relatively few Middle Easterners still want to live by its rules.[2]

---

1. Bayard Dodge, Foreword to Ruth Frances, Woodsmall, *Women and the New East* (Washington: The Middle East Institute, 1960), p. ii.
2. Daniel Lerner, *The Passing of Traditional Society: Modernizing the Middle East* (Glencoe, Illinois: The Free Press, 1958), p. 399.

The traditional rule, that age brings wisdom, worked well in immobile, isolated villages where change was slow and experience was the only teacher. Today, many young men have rejected tradition. Similarly, the traditional rule that woman is inferior by nature applied only as long as she was given no opportunities to try alternatives to her assigned sexual and work roles. The housewife often remains a conservative influence, but the daughter usually takes advantage of her new opportunities, and is no longer her mother's replica.

The reforms introduced under the inspiring leadership of Atatürk constituted a bold attempt to liberate women from their secondary, passive, and subdued role that consisted solely of being a commodity of exchange and a producer of offspring. Atatürk's goal was to enable the Turkish women to develop their abilities by granting them equal opportunities, free education, and full political rights. He said in March, 1923: "Our enemies claim that Turkey cannot be considered a civilized nation, because she consists of two separate parts: men and women. Can we shut our eyes to one portion of a group, while advancing the other, and still bring progress to the whole group? The road of progress must be trodden by both sexes together, marching arm in arm . . ."[3]

Two years later he said: "In some places I see women throwing a cloth or a towel or something of the sort over their heads, covering their faces and their eyes. When a man passes by, they turn away, or sit huddled on the ground. What is the sense of this behavior? Gentlemen, do the mothers and daughters of a civilized nation assume this curious attitude, this barbarous posture? It makes the nation look ridiculous: it must be rectified immediately!"[4]

THE TRADITIONAL SITUATION

The traditional status of Turkish women cannot be fully understood without considering the religious rules that governed their lives for more than a thousand years. A major characteristic of Islam is the special attention it pays to life on this earth. It also prepares the individual for the beyond *(akhira)*, but it teaches that that goal can only be achieved by a proper way of life in this world. This explains why Islam is so deeply concerned with regulating everyday life in its most minute details. The legal aspect of women's status within Islam is a most striking example of this socio-theological order.

The traditional Islamic Shari'a, valid in Turkey until 1926, determines the rights and obligations of women: 1) The mother is obliged to nurse her newly born baby. 2) Girls are in the custody of their father; when they

3. Enver Ziya Karal (ed.), *Atatürk'ten düsünceler* (Ankara: Is Bankasi, 1956), p. 52.
4. *Op. cit.* p. 55.

marry they pass under the tutelege of their husband. In some cases, a guardian may be designated by the *kadi* (judge). 3) Marriage is recognized only if it is consummated. 4) The husband has the privilege of divorcing his wife at will. The wife has the right to divorce only in exceptional cases, or if it is explicitly included in the marriage contract. 5) In matters of marital and extramarital relationship, men have almost absolute freedom, while complete submisssiön is required of women. 6) A wife can dispose of her property only with the husband's consent. 7) The wife's share in inheritance varies from one-eighth to one-sixteenth of the property left.[5]

In short, Islamic law never places women on an equal footing with men. Some of the countries that adopted Islam, Turkey among them, had in pre-Islamic times accorded their women greater rights and privileges, and in these countries the introduction of Islam meant a definite deterioration of the woman's position.

Even after the adoption of Islam by the Turks, some of their former customs survived, but disappeared later when the Caliphate was taken from the Abbasides by Sultan Selim I and merged with the Ottoman Sultanate. An exaggerated formal interpretation of the Koran, and especially its clauses relating to women, resulted in a large number of oppressive administrative edicts issued by sultans acting as caliphs, that is, religious heads of the Muslim world. Among them are found strange prohibitions barring women from entering dairy shops, going to picnic grounds, promenading on the streets on certain days of the week, leaving the house, walking with their fathers or sons on the street, using the same carriage, crossing certain squares, wearing tight face veils, and the like.[6]

The emancipation of women tied in historically with the general tendency toward modernization that began in Turkey in the first half of the nineteenth century. Those in favor of a radical Westernization of Turkish society asked for the introduction of monogamy into the imperial household, including the elimination of the Sultan's *odalik* (concubines); free choice of feminine garments; noninterference of the police in the private life of women; greater consideration toward women in general; freedom of choice in matters of marriage; the suppression of intermediaries; the creation of a medical school for girls; the adoption of a European civil code; the abolition of polygamy in general; and the outlawing of repudiation, that is, arbitrary and summary divorce.[7]

---

5. O. Pesle, *La femme musulmane dans le droit, la religion et les moeurs* (Rabat: Les editions la porte, 1946).
6. Hâmide Topçuoglu, *Kadınların çalısma saikleri ve kadın kazancının aile bütçesindeki rolü* (Ankara: Kültür matbaasi, 1957), p. XXI.
7. Pervin Esenkova, *La femme turque contemporaine, education et role social* (Tunis: Extrait de la Revue IBLA, 1951), p. 255.

Another group of intellectuals, preoccupied with the idea of the creation of a national state and deeply imbued with ideas of Turkish nationalism, did not attach much importance to the feminine problem. They were hostile to Westernization and said about the women's demands: "The call for European education for well-to-do Turkish girls is in reality nothing but Montmartrian immorality."[8] However, even these nationalist thinkers deplored polygamy, repudiation, and the veil.

The Islamic traditionalists were in favor of modernization in the Japanese manner; they stressed that Islam was not opposed to progress, but advocated the retention of the veil. They were, however, ready to concede women the right to dispose of their own property, to walk alone in the streets, to frequent women's organizations, and to attend primary and secondary schools.[9]

The aspirations articulated by a thin layer of Turkish society were not strong enough to carry these to fruition. Military defeats and domestic difficulties were used as justification for maintenance of the *status quo*. In 1889, after the disastrous end of the Turkish-Russian war, an edict of Sultan Abdulhamid II outlawed the wearing of the *yashmak* (transparent half-veil) and *ferace* (thin outer cloak) for all women except members of the imperial household. This strange decision resulted in the black veil (*çarsaf*) becoming the streetwear of Ottoman women toward the end of the nineteenth century. During World War I, when women began to work in public offices, they were forced by the police to return home if their black skirts were shorter than the officially prescribed length.[10]

Although women's life in the Ottoman Empire was hemmed in by innumerable restrictions, it would be erroneous to assume that they were completely passive sufferers. Their struggle for more and better education, equal rights, and the abolition of polygamy and repudiation, was carried on vigorously in the last quarter of the nineteenth century and the beginning of the twentieth, mainly in two Islamic magazines edited and written by women, both conservative and liberal.[11] Women's education, too, began in the nineteenth century. Unveiling, as a result of education, began prior to 1920.

However, the real turning point in the Turkish woman's emancipation came with the start of the national struggle. During the life and death

---

8. Celâl Nuri, *Kadınlarımız* (Istanbul, 1917).
9. Esenkova, *op. cit.*
10. Enise Yener, "Eski Ankara kiyafetleri ve giyiniş tarzlari," Ankara üniversitesi *Dil Tarih ve Coğrafya Fakültesi Dergisi, XIII, Vol. 3*, Eylül 1955; Celâl, Musahipzade, *Eski Istanbul yaşayışı*, Istanbul, 1946, pp. 121–41; Sermet Muhtar Alus, "Çarşaf," *Aylik Ansiklopedi*, No. 36, p. 1058.
11. Charlotte Lorenz, *Die Frauenfrage im Osmanischen Reiche* (Dissertation, Berlin 11.2.1919), p. 70.

conflict in Anatolia, educated women such as Halide Edip,[12] as well as peasant women, helped in the supply of arms and food. Six months before the end of the war, in his speech of February 3, 1923, Atatürk said of them: "Our women shall no longer be secluded, hidden, or veiled; this would cause the whole country additional suffering. The Turkish women have fought bravely for national independence. Today they should be free, enjoy education, and occupy a position equal to that of the men; they are entitled to it!"[13]

TOWN AND COUNTRY

It goes without saying that reform measures, great political and civic leadership, and dedication to Western ideas on the part of a sincere, progressively-minded ruling class, are still not sufficient to change completely the social structure of a patriarchal, traditional society. This becomes especially evident in the sharp discrepancy between rural and urban women. Even today, four decades after the emancipation of Turkish women, traditions and mores still have a strong hold on rural areas, and in particular in isolated, small villages in the southeastern parts of the country. However, even in the towns the old ways of life continue side by side with the new ones. This can be observed by simply looking at the women walking along any city street: some are veiled in black, others wear light-colored veils or are covered with a black or printed head scarf; some are dressed in a wide and heavy cloak, or in some thinner material; and both younger and older women can be seen wearing hats and low-cut dresses or blue jeans. Even one single family sometimes presents a picture of this striking evolution: the grandmother wearing low-heeled shoes and a scarf, the mother with uncovered head but wearing a high-necked dress, and the daughter copying the latest American or European fashions. However, in the larger cities, such as Ankara, Istanbul, Izmir, Eskişehir, Bursa, and Adana, one finds more and more adherents of Western style and behavior.

Research results on the subject of the growing mobility of the rural population, which is mainly due to the construction of new roads, invariably indicate that increasing contact with urban centers tends to weaken the hold of tradition and to induce change in clothes. The impact of radio, magazines, and newspapers is also felt in the villages. In several rural centers, such as the Aegean region and the Central Anatolian plateau,

---

12. Halide Edip Adivar served with the national armed forces during the War of Independence as a sergeant. She is a writer of international distinction, was a professor in the University of Istanbul and in universities in the USA.
13. Karal, *op. cit.*, p. 52.

traveling village teachers have put on fashion shows for women. The newly created "Woman's Hour," broadcast daily by Radio Ankara, has produced the largest audience response on record.

Nevertheless, outside the larger urban concentrations, the Republican reforms have so far touched only a minority of women. The visitor to Ankara, the capital, has only to walk to the older part of the city, up the hill, which rises behind the great equestrian statue of Ataturk, to see women shroud their faces from the stranger's eye as carefully as any of their Arab, Persian, or Pakistani sisters. There is one difference, however: a Turkish woman who decides to go unveiled is less criticized than a woman in other Muslim lands, and, as time passes, more and more of them avail themselves of this freedom.

POLITICAL RIGHTS

In 1930, even before the right to vote was granted to either men or women, women were appointed to municipal councils. This was followed in 1933 by the granting of other political rights to women. On December 5, 1934, Articles 10 and 11 of the Turkish Constitution of 1924 were amended so that every woman received the right to vote upon reaching the age of twenty-two, while women over thirty were made eligible for election to office. (At that time, all elections were still indirect, carried out in two stages.) As a result of this important innovation, eighteen women were elected to the Grand National Assembly in 1935.

The most important development in Turkish public life was the transition in 1946 from a one-party to a multi-party system. In that year for the first time elections were based on the right to express one's will at the polls, a right which was taken advantage of by the overwhelming majority of Turkey's eligible voters of both sexes. The fact that more than 80 per cent of the women were illiterate did not affect the voting pattern. The new Constitution of July 9, 1961, as well as the new electoral law of 1961, reaffirmed explicitly the right of both sexes, to vote and to run for office.

The transition to a multi-party system brought about a decline in the number of women representatives in parliament:

Parliamentary sessions	V	VI	VII	VIII	IX	X	XI	XIII
Year	1935	1939	1943	1946	1950	1954	1957	1961
Number of women representatives	18	15	16	9	3	4	8	5
Percentage of total	4.5	3.5	3.5	2	0.6	0.6	1.3	1.2

This, however, did not mean a curtailment of women's political rights, nor a change in the public attitude toward their full participation in parliament. Women in parliament were accepted as equal colleagues, appointed to major committees, and enabled to participate fully in political life. However, Turkish women had been spared the struggle for political rights and did not gain the experience that usually comes with such struggles.

The Turkish electoral law of 1961 required that candidates be designated through the secret votes of a relatively large number of party delegates. This can be considered one of the most serious obstacles to direct political activity. But eventually the number of women in parliament should increase.

The new bylaws of Turkey's major political parties require the setting up of women's auxiliaries and the election of at least one woman to the executive council of each party. As a result, the participation of women in political life has become greatly intensified. In the primaries that preceded the October 1965 general elections, the lists of the six major political parties included a total of seventy women candidates, one of whom headed the list of her party.

EDUCATION

The Çapa elementary school, the first for girls, dates from 1870. The first secondary school for girls was started in 1908; the University of Istanbul admitted women in a separate section in 1915, and began full coeducation in 1921, with the Faculty of Medicine acting as pioneers.

One of the important steps toward a radical educational reform was the promulgation of the Law of Unification of Instruction of March 3, 1942, which brought all the religious schools, including those of the non-Muslim minorities, under unified control. This enabled the leaders of the young republic to mold the new generation to the shape they envisaged for it.

The introduction of the Latin alphabet in 1928 made it possible for large masses to be taught to read and write in a relatively short time. The increase in the number of girl pupils and students in the post-war period was quite spectacular.

Number of Girl Pupils and Students

Year	Primary Schools	Middle Schools	Lycées	Vocational Schools	Universities
1927–28	119,689	2,408	383	456	590
1944–45	616,737	24,127	5,830	19,096	4,188
1954–55	858,090	37,791	8,388	38,914	4,193
1960–61	1,298,906	86,851	22,797	62,730	13,731

In 1960–61, 31.5 per cent of all the girls between seven and fourteen did not attend school. Although the law calls for free, coeducational and compulsory primary education, it cannot be enforced because of a shortage of both schools and teachers. Moreover, due to the indifference in some villages to girls' education, school attendance is not too regular. With an annual population increase of almost 900,000, a substantial number of school-age children, mostly girls, are left without the possibility of attending school. Following the May 27, 1960, revolution, the government tried to solve this problem by passing a law obliging reserve officers who did not graduate from a university to perform their military service as teachers in one of the many village schools of Anatolia. Insufficient preparation in pedagogical matters created problems in several places, although, in general, this "ersatz-teacher" army proved very valuable.

Secondary education, which, like all government education, is free, includes the middle school (junior high school) and lycée (senior high school), each with a three-year course. The general rule throughout Turkey is that the higher the age group, the lower the percentage of girls in relation to boys attending school. The following table indicates the seriousness of this problem:

Sex Distribution of Pupils and Students 1960–61

School	Total Number of Students	Percentage of Boys	Percentage of Girls
Primary	2,855,337	63	37
Middle	292,590	76	24
Technical and Vocational	108,217	70	30
High	75,625	74	26
University	65,088	80	20

Some of the junior and senior high schools are coeducational. But public opinion is strongly in favor of separate schools above the elementary level. Although educators, by and large, deplore separate schools, which they consider a break in the natural relations between the sexes and uneconomical for the nation, a change is not very probable because the public is predominantly in favor of separate schools. Data that has been gathered indicate that most of the emotional problems of Turkish teen-agers revolve around the frustration caused by a socially imposed, artificial segregation of the sexes, and by the lack of a uniform, approved code of behavior. This seems to bear out the feeling many educators have that the significance of coeducation in the Muslim world, and, in particular, in a secular state like Turkey, cannot be overemphasized.

A comparison of the value systems of boy and girl lycée students (carried out in 1959 but made public only several years later) showed that the boys were politically oriented to a much higher degree than the girls. The boys, for example, attached more importance to voting and were more interested in national affairs than in local.

Another interesting development in the field of public education, mainly in the postwar period, is the increased recognition that it is necessary to provide women with vocational and technical education as well as with training in home economics.

Vocational training for girls in Turkey began in 1864 when Mithat Pasha, a progressive statesman, founded a girls' home institute in Rusçuk; this was followed in 1869 by a second similar institution in Istanbul. As early as 1930, six additional such institutes were established. Their great popularity among the rising lower middle class, as well as in the rural areas, led in the last twenty years to the opening of more than 200 vocational-training centers for girls, with an enrollment of 90,000 full- or part-time students. To them are added evening courses for adults, teacher-training centers, and courses given by traveling teachers in the villages.

In 1960–61, 654 courses in sewing, cooking, embroidery, and so on, were conducted by 536 teachers, with a total enrollment of 15,171 students, mostly young mothers or elderly peasant women. In many cases these are for the first time in their lives exposed to new trends, new methods, and new ideas.

Of great importance for the future development of Turkey's rural population is the extension work carried out by the Ministry of Agriculture, which, in January 1957, set up the so-called "4-K" rural youth clubs. These clubs are the Turkish counterpart of the American 4-H clubs. (The Turkish equivalents of Hand, Head, Heart, and Health begin with the letter K.) The 4-K program is coeducational. The experiences of the last few years show that the enthusiastic response of the parents and the fitness of some girls to act as project leaders has induced the villagers to take a more modern view of women's clothes, child care, and health measures. However, this type of extension work cannot be applied everywhere with the same success, because it requires a certain amount of attitudinal preparation.

The potential importance of these centers for vocational education becomes more evident if one considers that only 75 per cent of all girls in Turkey are able to enroll in schools; only 31 per cent of these enrolled students graduate; only 10 per cent of all enrolled school children attend junior high school, and only 2 per cent of all girls attend senior high school, vocational, technical, or comparable institutions. In 1960–61, there were 102 Home Science Institutes for girls with 29,422 students. These institutes, located all over the country, give, in addition to the regular high school curriculum, supplementary training in home economics, with specialization in the later years in child care, sewing, fashion, artificial-flower making, embroidery, cooking, and household management. The program of these institutions, is, unfortunately, too narrowly confined to teaching modern style, developing the girls' taste and encouraging attention to children's clothes. The program should include a widening of the girls' outlook regarding career possibilities in keeping with the actual and potential social and economic conditions of the country.

A considerable number of so-called Girls' Evening Institutes offer courses in specific subjects, such as the making of gloves, lamp-shades, men's shirts, and so forth. Attendance is free and the only prerequisite is literacy. In 1960–61, 183 such Evening Institutes with 58,949 students were operating throughout Turkey.

In rural education, the Village Institutes have played a remarkable part. First opened in 1940 in various parts of Turkey, these coeducational rural training centers prepared village primary-school graduates for becoming teachers in villages. These students came from villages and, upon graduation after five years, either returned to their own village or went to another. This system partially solved the problem of emigration to the big cities. Twenty thousand teachers, with a proud feeling of their educational mission, graduated from these Institutes and took up the fight against illiteracy, traditionalism, and inertia. In 1951, coeducation was given up, and in 1954 the Village Institutes were closed down and merged with the forty-three Teachers Training Institutes. These measures caused the discontinuation of one of the most remarkable and bold educational experiments in the country. Since the 1960 Junta, spirited debates have taken place about the advisability of reopening the Village Institutes.

Adult education, which began in 1928 with the campaign for literacy following the adoption of the Latin alphabet, has not produced remarkable results. In 1955, 55 per cent of the male and 80 per cent of the female population of Turkey was still illiterate. This is the basic difficulty that has to be overcome before a still archaic social order can be changed. The most effective institutions for adult education, the so-called People's Houses and People's Rooms, in which all types of popular programs and courses were conducted, have also been abolished. Their libraries were dismantled and the books put in storage soon after the Democratic Party took over the Government.

In November, 1955, a new commercial-teachers training college was opened in which girls can receive secretarial training. This school is a cooperative enterprise of the Turkish Ministry of Education and the U.S. Technical Assistance Program, with the initial participation of the Graduate School of Administration of New York University. Secretarial training for girls is also given in the Atatürk Girls' Institute in Ankara, the Ankara College, the Istanbul College for Women (founded in 1890), the American Academy for Girls at Üsküdar, Istanbul (founded 1870), the Girls' College at Izmir, the French Dame de Sion, the Austrian St. Georg School, and the German Lycée.

The teaching profession, the first career to open to Turkish women, is still a substantial field for women's professional activities. One fourth of the teachers in primary schools, one third in the middle schools, and one half in the lycées are women.

Following World War II, instruction in many new fields specially suited for women was introduced with the opening of such institutions as the Institute of Librarianship, the Faculty of Nursing, the School for Social Welfare, and the Faculty of Home Economics, all in Ankara. Nursing in Turkey took its inspiration from Florence Nightingale's service in Üsküdar during the Crimean War, when Turkish women entered voluntary service. Later, in World War I, emergency training for women volunteers was given for the first time. But only after long years of perseverance and patience did social attitudes and adverse public opinion toward nursing change.

SEX MORES

One of the most delicate problems arising from the rapid social and cultural change which Turkey is undergoing at present is that of behavioral norms in interpersonal relationships. The transition from marriage by parental arrangement to one by individual choice, and from social segregation to an intermingling of the sexes, creates endless conflicts. Wherever the old and the new live side by side, the dilemma of the younger generation reveals itself in an acute form. The quick charge of promiscuity, so easily pronounced in Muslim countries, and the urge for more freedom, often produce severe emotional crises. Due to the absence of generally agreed-upon behavioral standards, the role of peer groups among young people is increasing, while the opposite influence of family bonds and parental authority diminishes. A study carried out by the author among university students indicates that the majority of men would refuse to marry a girl who "had had a friendship with a person of the opposite sex"—a form of social intercourse regarded as normal in almost all Western countries.

While premarital chastity is still expected of the girls in urban as well as in rural areas, social intercourse between the sexes follows no fixed or standardized forms. It varies largely according to the educational level of the parents, the atmosphere of the social environment, and the prevailing political mood. Customs may range from the approval of participation in a mixed excursion to a public beach in bikini bathing suits to the prohibition of greeting classmates of the opposite sex in a small coeducational Anatolian high school. The lip service paid to traditional social mores, the shunning of all open discussion of these problems in the press, and the traditional approach of almost all Parent-Teacher Associations result in a frustrated youth with a tendency to engage in clandestine dating. In small towns, only formally engaged girls are allowed to go out alone to take a walk or to attend a movie. A nationwide survey of attitudes among high school students has shown that almost 60 per cent of those emotionally upset and failing in schoolwork suffer from the problem of not being able to adjust their own relationships to members of the opposite sex to the indeterminate and unstable requirements, taboos, and expectations of the parental and school environment. As David Riesman pointed out most eloquently, the ingenuity needed to escape the all-too-evident impasses of the Middle East can be neither imported nor locally engendered without a lessening of the dominant male values. Men must learn to see each other not merely as sexual rivals, and sex roles must be changed instead of being reinforced by patterns of child-rearing.[14]

The upper strata is a relatively small part of Turkish society, consisting mostly of businessmen, members of the professions, and civil servants. They are imbued with Western thinking and are trying to work out an informal code of behavior for their own children that would grant them freedom and yet require a certain amount of self-control. The urban lower-middle class has adopted more rigid rules; they allow less freedom of association and social interplay. It was found in a recent study of two social classes in Ankara, for instance, that the concept of women as the weaker sex, unable to govern itself and therefore in need of unceasing control by the men of the family, has been internalized to a very high degree. Any infringement of the rules of chastity, whether real or symbolic, by a daughter, is of extreme importance to the family as a whole. The situation amounts to a veritable "virginity cult" that manifests itself in various forms but is clearly present in all strata of society. Male superiority, on the other hand, provides the basis and justification for double standards in sexual morality. Premarital or extramarital sex relations are strictly taboo for women, but tolerated in men.[14a]

In the rural areas, the traditional taboos on social contact between young girls and boys outside of their kinship relationships still retain their hold, except at weddings, circumcision and other festivities. In general, village girls are not even allowed to see their fiances until the day of the wedding. The status of women among the minority groups, such as the Greeks, Armenians, and Jews, is more permissive. Also among the Shi'ite Muslims in the Southeast, the so-called Alawites, the norms regulating sex mores are less severe.

The traditional outlook on the relationship between the sexes has created

14. Lerner, *op. cit.*, pp. 7–8.
14a. Serim Yurtören, *Fertility and Related Attitudes Among Two Social Classes in Ankara* (Unpublished Master's Thesis. Cornell University, 1965).

a number of specific problems, including opposition to girls' engaging in professions that require close contact between them and men, such as nursing or secretarial work. It has resulted in a relatively high percentage of unmarried girls, due to the lack of opportunity to meet suitable mates. And it has caused extremist behavior on the part of youthful gangs in public places, boys and girls letting themselves go under the influence of alcohol or trying to protest visibly against the rigid archaic facade of a crumbling social structure. However, the general trend is toward a more modern and normal consideration of these problems. The fast rate of urbanization and the imperative need to speed up industrialization will certainly cause a more rapid change in the near future in the standard sex mores, as well.

THE MARRIAGE PATTERN

The most important date for the advancement of Turkish women was the adoption of the Swiss Civil Code on October 4, 1926. It made polygamy illegal and gave the right of divorce to women as to men, thus insuring their freedom and equality. In one respect, however, the weight of custom has forced a change in the new code. The Swiss Civil Code has twenty years as the minimum age for marriage for men and eighteen for women. In Turkey, these figures were reduced to eighteen and seventeen, with the provision that in special cases a magistrate can give permission to marry to persons fifteen years of age, of either sex, with the consent of the parents. This was in recognition of the general early maturing in peasant communities. In June, 1938, the age limits were further reduced to seventeen and fifteen respectively, while the minimum age in special circumstances was kept at fifteen for men but was lowered to fourteen for women. Although the present legal provisions make civil marriage obligatory, many marriages are still solemnized in the villages by local Imams, especially in the east, simply by the pronouncement of a prayer, without any registration.

By its significant silence, the Turkish Civil Code allows marriage between Muslims and non-Muslims—a new situation that expresses the secularization of the Turkish state. With the growth of American military and economic aid, causing the presence of considerable American male personnel, marriages between urban Turkish girls and American men have increased remarkably.

A large number of mixed marriages between Turkish men and non-Turkish women resulted from the temporary employment of many Turkish laborers in West Germany, Holland, Switzerland, and Austria. In many cases, these "guest workers" (as they are called in West Germany), left wives behind when they set out on their journey, and subsequently divorced their Turkish wives in order to marry a Western girl who could be a companion to them instead of a submissive servant.

The Turkish Civil Code grants both sides the right to ask for divorce. The grounds for divorce can be classified into two groups: specifically stated ones, such as desertion, ill treatment, or adultery, and those of a general nature, such as incompatibility of character. Since the adoption of the Turkish Civil Code, divorces have rapidly increased, and are mostly sought by couples married from six to ten years. The great majority of the divorces are those of childless couples, and the most frequently quoted grounds are incompatibility of character, followed by desertion.

During the ten years' rule of the Democratic Party, religious marriage was silently approved, if not encouraged. This means that a large number of marriages probably remained unregistered. The Ministry of Justice, therefore, felt morally obliged to legitimatize children born to such couples. (The total number of children thus registered was close to eight million.) And the birth registrar was authorized to issue a regular birth certificate to all new-born babies without requesting that the normally obligatory civil marriage certificate of the parents be produced.

Another innovation of the Turkish Civil Code is a kind of trial divorce, that is a separation of husband and wife for one to three years. The Turkish Civil Code, in line with its Swiss prototype, does not admit absolute equality of husband and wife. The husband is the head of the family. The wife must follow the husband, who alone is entitled to choose a domicile. She is required to participate in the expenses of the household, by contributing financially or by assuming tasks in the household. If the wife wants to exercise a profession or work elsewhere, she has to obtain the consent of her husband. But she may dispose freely of her material goods and has unlimited rights of ownership over all her acquisitions.

Religious weddings are not recognized legally. They may, however, be carried out after the civil ceremony. In cities, a reception follows the civil marriage act. In villages, after the wedding there are festivities with folk songs, drums, dances, and separate feasts for men and women, usually lasting three days. In rural areas, marriages are still to a large extent planned by the parents, although the consent of the girl is obtained more often than before. The money received by the girl's family from the prospective groom is spent entirely on the trousseau. Various privileges, such as free medical treatment and discount purchases at governmental agencies are obtained only on the basis of regular birth or marriage certificates. This induces the villagers more and more to have civil weddings. Even so, many women in remote villages still have no knowledge of civil marriage, and often the couple cannot reach the civil authorities who are too remote.

In the cities, low salaries and economic difficulties frequently cause the postponement of marriage until the men are twenty-seven to twenty-nine years of age, and the girls twenty-three. In the villages, both girls and boys marry when they are sixteen to eighteen years old.

THE WOMAN'S POSITION IN THE FAMILY

Here again, one must differentiate between urban and rural family life. In the cities, the increasing number of small apartments in large housing developments replacing the old-fashioned large houses result in the growth in the number of nuclear families, consisting of father, mother and children (usually two), with an in-law or other relative, usually an elderly aunt or a younger unmarried sister or niece who lives in. This type of family is very different from the large, extended, patriarchal family still prevalent in the villages. However, the close kinship ties characteristic of the extended family have not yet completely disappeared. Even in large cities, where housing shortage and lack of accommodations do not permit extended-family-living, at least one person of the older generation, usually the mother of the husband, lives with the family. Although in the villages real authority comes to a woman when she acquires the status of mother-in-law, in the cities it is more or less customary that final authority remains with the wife, even if her widowed mother-in-law lives in the same apartment. Old people's homes are as yet unknown in Turkey. The latest development is for old parents to live very near their children, often in the same apartment house. But such solutions require a certain financial ease. In general, old people are taken care of by their own children or nearest relatives. But in spite of such joint living, in the city it is the mistress of the house, the young wife, who decides with the husband about financial matters, the education of children, new acquisitions, and so forth.

If the wife works outside the home, her earnings are contributed to the common family budget. According to a survey of the economic role of business women and clerical workers, 80 per cent of wage- and salary-earning women add their income to the family budget, and only 31 per cent handle the current expenses independently. This indicates a general absence of conflict between the interests of the family as a whole and those of the women individually. According to the well-established Turkish-Islamic pattern, women, as mothers and wives, have always devoted themselves physically and morally to the welfare of their families. After embarking on outside work, they still seem to be eager to give all their financial resources to their families.

In rural areas, the extended family is still the prevailing form, with each nuclear family living in two or more separate rooms with an extra kitchen within the farm grounds. In some, all members of the extended family eat together; in others, each nuclear family cooks for itself. In every case, however, authority is in the hands of the wife of the head of the family; she decides all questions related to the household: food, supplies, clothes, future marriages and purchases in the nearest city. Contact with the local authorities, registration of the children at school, and work division in the fields are usually left to the discretion of the father, who also handles all financial transactions outside the home, such as dealings with the bank and the tax collector. But even in these matters, the mother is usually consulted and her advice sought and followed.

Turkey has one of the highest birth rates in the world: 40 per 1,000, as against a death rate of 14 per 1,000. Thus the average population increase is about 26 per 1,000. A consequence of this population explosion is that 43 per cent of Turkey's population is under the age of fourteen. A survey carried out by the Population Council in 1963 found that most of the married couples in Turkey wished to have only two to four children; that is, considerably fewer than they actually had. In rural areas the average number of births for each mother is twelve or more, with eight to ten children surviving. Seventy-two per cent of the women surveyed and 65 per cent of the men wished to know more about birth control.

The Five-Year Plan announced in 1961 introduced for the first time new ideas on this topic, which was severely tabooed by the then-existing legal code. It stated that the "prohibition of the use of contraceptives will be abolished. Specialized personnel for the teaching of methods of family planning will be trained, a special program for large-scale education on family planning will be put in force, and medical supplies will be freely distributed." On April 1, 1965, the Turkish Parliament promulgated a new law, decreeing the creation of a special family-planning unit attached to the Ministry of Health. It was expected that one of the most important results of this new legislation would be a decrease in the number of secret abortions; according to reliable estimates, six out of one hundred such abortions at present result in death. The most popular contraceptive device is the intra-uterine spiral. The use of contraceptive pills seems to most women to require too many complicated calculations. The newly created family-planning clinics in Ankara and Istanbul are extremely popular and soon will be followed by additional mobile rural units.

An organization for maternity and child health, established in 1952, operates in large cities such as Ankara and Izmir, providing clinics for pregnant women and care for mothers and children. It distributes milk, layettes, and free medicine and gives health lectures and food demonstrations for women. In 1961, there were thirty-four maternity health centers with thirty-two branches throughout the country.

In addition, in the rural areas without access to hospital facilities, there are close to 300 health centers. Large or small, all render valuable services, teaching mothers the elements of child care and teaching the general public disease prevention, cleanliness, and sanitation.

The graduates of the Midwifery Schools in Istanbul and Ankara are scattered all over Turkey, numbering in 1960, 2,843. Nevertheless, the demand far exceeds the supply. In the villages, elderly women still usually function as midwives.

By and large, with respect to their position in their families, Turkish women fall into two major types. The first is the urban woman, married or unmarried, who leans towards a modern comprehension of her responsibilities and rights. She represents the "modern" type. The second is the conservative, tradition-bound village woman with little independence. The degree of her personal freedom depends largely upon the regional customs and her relationship with her in-laws. The more developed, dynamic rural areas have begun to display an increasing tendency toward more independence for women. The change in attitude comes mainly from the influence of the movies, exposure to radio, and the use of the growing transportation facilities.

THE HOME ROUTINE

Modern kitchen equipment, canned food, standardized merchandise, ready-made clothes, and all the other facilities and products at the disposal of women in highly industralized countries are still relatively rare and expensive in Turkey. They are available only to a small segment of the middle and upper classes. The newly established food industries have, however, begun to change the routine of the housewife. Margarine has partly replaced butter or animal fat, even in remote villages. Detergents, soap, toothpaste, insecticides, crackers, baby foods, fruit jellies, and packaged noodles are sold nowadays over the counters of the village groceries.

In cities, electric irons, ovens, refrigerators, and washing machines are the most widely used appliances. Here again, their use is a question of socioeconomic status, rather than of dislike of innovation. In rural areas, however, little or no electricity is available as yet. As fuel for cooking, lignite coal or woodcoal is used in the small towns, and dried cakes of dung on the Anatolian plateau. In this respect, a minor, though important, revolution is taking place at present in the remote rural areas of Turkey: it is brought about by the increasing availability of bottled gas that enables those peasant women whose husbands can afford this relatively expensive luxury, to improve considerably their entire household routine.

As far as food supply is concerned, the more isolated villages of eastern Turkey are still more or less self-sufficient. Vegetables and fruits are grown in accordance with the available water for irrigation. In general, the routine work of the peasant woman remains very hard and time-consuming.

The Social Position

Ataturk's own marriage at the very beginning of the national struggle, with Latife Hanim, one of the educated women in Izmir, gave concrete expression to his ideas and attitudes on the question of the social position of the educated Turkish woman. To this day, the significant class differences in Turkey, in addition to those between the urban and rural populations, are the ones that stratify society along educational levels. This holds true among Turkish women to the same extent as among men. Young girls and mothers who received a bilingual, modern education, take an active part in the country's struggle for social advancement. An increasing number of Turkish women—although still a minority—are making full use of their newly won position and work as community leaders, mainly in social welfare, education, and the promotion of the arts. Their accomplishments are fully acknowledged by their male counterparts. Equality between the sexes as far as work division in professional circles is concerned is now taken for granted.

In contrast, the great bulk of Turkish women still conform to the old image of the tradition-bound, obedient, submissive, religious female. Value judgments prevalent in the urban lower-middle class and in the rural areas still do not recognize women's rights to personal identity. They are resigned to a status devoid of legal rights, and many of them evince a fatalistic approach to questions of vital importance. However, even in the most traditional regions, women are never completely under male domination, nor condemned to complete seclusion. Their way of life, in comparison with conditions in the rural areas of other Muslim countries, can be termed moderate-traditional.

Women's Occupations

The participation of women in the economic life of Turkey has long ceased to have news value for the Turkish public. Here again, a fundamental distinction has to be made between different types of working women: the well-trained, qualified, efficient professional women; the unskilled factory workers; and the hard-working peasant women in agricultural sectors, who constitute the majority of all Turkish women. The accomplishments of women in this latter group in their dual role as workers and mothers are far from being sufficiently acknowledged. The fact that agricultural workers, whether male or female, are not included in Social Security makes their lot even more difficult.

Major Occupational Groups in 1959

	Male	Female
Liberal professions, technicians	138,000	29,000
Administrators, entrepreneurs, clerical staff	200,000	26,000
Salesmen	270,000	6,000
Transport & Communications	184,000	2,000
Mining	46,000	1,000
Artisanship, manufacturing workers	685,000	114,000
Unskilled workers	260,000	17,000
Services	237,000	25,000
Agriculture	4,738,000	5,062,000
Unclassifiable	1,829,000	2,024,000

Little reliable information is available about the economic independence of women in rural life. It is known, however, that they receive no wages, although in some places (for example, the Black Sea area where many men go to the big cities to work as waiters, painters, etcetera), it is often they who earn all the money at home and bring in the harvest all by themselves.

The numerical relationship between men and women in the population of various regions has a bearing on the woman's role as worker. In the Black Sea region, for instance, there are 140 women, in Trabzon 118, in Giresun 114, for every 100 men. (The country-wide average is 103 women for every 100 men.) This surplus of women explains the high percentage of female workers in the regions in question. The opposite is equally true. In the east, in Bitlis, for instance, there are 100 men to 97 women, and there the percentage of female workers is only 9 per cent. Other factors that influence women's participation in agriculture are the means and the techniques employed. Ploughs and tractors are monopolized by men; women usually do their work by hand. Finally, social mores, such as the confinement of women to the home, determine the scope of their work.

In industry, although women constitute an important labor potential for the future, at present, their participation is numerically insignificant. They are employed primarily in textile manufacturing; rug manufacturing; the tobacco industry; in the processing of nuts, raisins, and figs; and in workshops for military tailoring. A completely new trend is represented by a small number of women workers who, unable to find employment at home, emigrated to West Germany.

Labor legislation limits work to eight hours a day, six days per week. "Equal pay for equal work" is the norm and the principle, but in some cases women do not perform the same work as men and hence are paid less.

The Labor Law provides for maternity leaves, followed by forty days with shorter working hours, medical examination during and after pregnancy, time off allowed for the nursing of infants, and the establishment of nurseries and kindergartens. But since the Labor Law applies only to working places with more than ten employees, adequate facilities and good buildings are generally provided only in the state enterprises which account for 30 per cent of the national industrial output. Membership in labor unions is open to women; the participation of women in union work, however, is minimal, partly because of their fear of being accused of indecorous behavior. In the poorer sectors of the community women work in order to subsist; among the well-to-do their purpose is to earn more money for cultural activities, amusements, luxuries for the house, and to provide greater opportunities for their children.

In the professions, Turkish women have chalked up substantial achievement records.

Women Professional Workers in 1953

Schoolteachers	15,309
Medical profession	5,309
Lawyers	599
Judges	139
University professors	251
Fine arts (literature, music & the plastic arts)	2,080
Civil servants	22,287
Engineers & architects	610
Managers	680
Government supervisors and top administrators	350
Saleswomen	4,000

In addition, they have specialized in fields ranging from astronomy to nuclear physics, from chemical research to petroleum engineering. They own and manage enterprises such as chemical laboratories, factories, and stores. Some are agricultural experts, veterinarians, and police officers. Many work for the airlines, in railway offices, as tourist guides, as post-office clerks. The number of secretaries, librarians, and social workers is steadily increasing.

As might be expected, most professional women live in big urban centers, such as Istanbul, Ankara, Izmir. It is interesting to note that the social disapproval of women's work increases in ratio to their professional interest and career-mindedness. However, the social pressure on the working women is inversely proportional to the degree of economic need that induces them to seek work. Conservatism is evidently in the process of being eroded by economic necessity and the impact of modern life. Crises arise because of the gap between the traditional guiding images and the actual behavioral response to particular circumstances. It takes time for the new image of woman in society to become accepted and for the traditional outlook to adapt itself to the new times.

A new phenomenon in the field of women's occupations is the increase in the number of Turkish women workers going abroad to earn better wages and/or to acquire a foreign language and gather new experiences. In 1964, there were 8,905 Turkish women employed in West Germany alone. Of these, 43 per cent were in the twenty-five to thirty-five age bracket; the second largest contingent was the twenty-one to twenty-five age group. A survey carried out by this author on behalf of the Turkish State Planning Organization showed that about 45 per cent of the Turkish female workers abroad were married, and came from large cities such as Istanbul, Ankara, and Izmir. Their educational level was much higher than that of the men. About 52 per cent had a postprimary education, as against 42 per cent of the men. This educational gap between Turkish men and woman workers in West Germany creates a certain tension between the two sexes, since the women are disinclined to associate with their less educated countrymen.

Turkish women workers in West Germany are mostly employed in the electrical industry, clothing manufacturing, food industry, and services. Their skill and intelligence are highly appreciated, and they adjust to Western, advanced, highly-industrialized conditions more easily than the men. A considerable number of them, wishing to advance to secretarial jobs, take up evening studies. Their attitude toward the forms of family life and the status of women in Germany is mostly positive, although they deplore the lack of intrafamily solidarity. Interestingly, the least amount of resistance against eating pork (forbidden by Islam) comes from the women, whose efforts for adjustment in general are all-inclusive.[14b]

WOMEN IN LEADERSHIP

The dynamics of Turkish history in the recent turbulent years challenged Turkish women to participate more actively in social affairs. Their response came with a surprising readiness. The areas that attracted their most intense attention were politics, the welfare needs of women and children in the crowded slum areas of large urban centers, the promotion of education on all levels, voluntary aid, scholarships, training courses for adults, pediatrics and children's hospitals, and, finally, the molding of public opinion as members of the Turkish press. A few examples will suffice to illustrate this general trend.

Judge Melâhat Ruacan became the first woman member of the High Court of Cassation in 1954 (this, incidentally, was an international "first").

14b. Nermin Abadan, *Bati Almanya'daki Turk işçileri ve sorunları*. DPT, Ankara, 1964.

Since then, other distinguished Turkish women judges have been nominated to this position. Professor Nüzhet Gökdoğan, a woman, was elected Dean of the Faculty of Science at the University of Istanbul. Well-known women doctors, such as Müfide Küley (professor for internal diseases at the University of Istanbul), Kâmile Mutlu (professor for pathological anatomy at the University of Ankara), and Pakize Tarzı, a gynecologist with her own maternity hospital, set the pace for further specialization of women in various branches of medicine.

The active participation of women (Nimet Özgüç, Mebrure Tosun,.and Halet Çambel) in archaeology has attracted a new Turkish generation to this science. In journalism Mrs. Iffet Halim Oruz for many years has owned and published a weekly magazine called "Woman." Of the younger generation, Nilüfer Yalçin, a graduate of the Istanbul Girls' College and Faculty of Letters, founded a powerful political weekly "Forum." Following World War II, the diplomatic field, too, opened to young Turkish women. At present, several women occupy positions of responsibility in the Turkish embassies and legations in various countries.

The field in which both professional and lay women participate most frequently is that of social welfare and charity. These activities have increased tremendously since World War II. At one time, such functions were a matter of status and prestige, and were performed on an honorary basis; today, women of various educational levels find constructive outlet for their talents and energies in social work. The first national conference of Social Work in Turkey (Ankara, December 27–29, 1959) attracted more than 2,000 people, mostly women.

WOMEN AS CULTURAL TRANSMITTERS

In spite of the difficulty in distinguishing between the functions of the family as a whole and those of its female members, it is evident that the pre-school education of children, their religious indoctrination, and the teaching of handicrafts (mainly rug-making, embroidery of all kinds, and linen weaving), home management, interior decoration, and tailoring are areas monopolized by women. In the broader sense, Turkish women play a main role in cultivating the traditional arts. The Turkish Handicraft Society, whose purpose is to make Turkish handicraft known at home and abroad and to promote its sale, has a shop in Ankara completely directed by women.

Also, modern art is promoted by many women artists in Turkey. Women painters (Füreyya, Eren Eyüpoğlu, and Asuman Kılıç for example) have won international recognition. Women singers (Leyla Gencer, Ferham Onat, Belkıs Aran, and Suna Korat) perform on international stages. The ballet school, established in 1952 by the Turkish Government, has trained more than a hundred students, mostly young girls. Actresses (Yıldız Kenter, Melek Öktem, Muazzez, Melâhat Ars) play everything from Shakespeare to Ionesco. The world of literature has attracted a number of Turkish women, the best known of whom is the late president of the Turkish Pen Club, Halide Edib Adivar. In the present generation, Azra Erhat and Nezihe Meriç give expression to new phenomena and unknown aspects of Turkey's society.

THE OUTLOOK

Whether we are concerned with the transition from "closed" to "open" societies, from community to society, or from separate traditions to universalism, the appearance of new forms of culture which transcend the frontiers of closed human groups is undeniable.

It seems, however, that there is a deep truth in the thought of Ménie Grégoire who, analyzing the conditions of the working women, maintained that much as the "woman at home" will increasingly become a myth, so the assumption of the "woman worker equal with her male counterpart" is not likely to achieve reality.[15]

In Turkey, following the spectacular population explosion of the first decades of the Republic and the dynamic intrusion of a female vanguard into various domains of public life, it is possible to anticipate the awakening of the great majority of Turkish women, the peasant girls and mothers of Anatolia.

The newly adopted five-year plan for Turkey's economic development allocates an important role to Turkey's woman power. The development and activation of this still tradition-bound population segment will not only help accelerate industrialization but also affect significantly the whole way of life and the self-images of Turkey's womanhood.

As Alva Myrdal and Viola Klein put it, the problem for developed as well as under-developed countries is no longer "should the woman work outside the home?" but "what kind of work should the woman perform?"[16]

In contemporary Turkish fiction the Turkish woman is usually depicted as a hard-working, ardent creature, full of good will, brave, resistant, proud, ready to sacrifice her interests for her family; yet she is sometimes misunderstood by her own family and society; although working outside the home, she remains chaste; she frequently harbors idealistic sentiments; she displays endless patience; and she is able to stand up to her man.

This highly idealized and roughly sketched portrait will certainly not

---

15. Gregoire Ménie, "Mythes et réalites," *Esprit*, No. 295, Mai 1961, p. 759.
16. Alva Myrdal and Viola Klein, *Women's Two Roles: Home and Work* (London: Routledge and Kegan Paul Ltd., 1956).

fit completely the future Turkish woman. But some of its features may survive and help the Turkish woman of tomorrow face the new problems and hardships of the future.

BIBLIOGRAPHY

Abadan, Nermin, *Üniversite Öğrencilerinin serbest zaman faaliyetleri*, Ankara, 1961, S.B.F. Yayını.

Berkes, Mediha, "Elvan köyünde sosyal bir araştırma," *Ankara Üniverstesi Dil Tarih Coğrafya Fakültesi Dergisi*, C. II.

Boşanma istatistikleri, 1932–1968, Yayın No. 419, Sh. 1, 8–9.

Eldeniz, Perihan Naci, *Atatürk ve Türk Kadını*, Türk Tarih Kurumu, Ankara, 1956.

Esenkova, Pervin, "La femme turque contemporaine, éducation et rôle social," Extrait de la Revue *IBLA*, Tunis, 1951.

Gorvine, Elisabeth, ILO Home economic adviser, *Kız Teknik Öğretim programlarının değerlendirilmesi teklifleri*, Ankara, 1957, Maarif basımevi.

Karal, Enver Ziya (ed.), *Atatürk'ten düşünceler*, Iş Bankasi, Ankara, 1956.

Karpat, Kemal, "L'état de la famille turque," *Çağdas*, Istanbul, No. 6, 1946.

Keleş, Ruşen Y., "Türkiyede sehirlere akın ve planlama üzerine etkisi," *Planlama*, No. 2, 1962.

Lerner, Daniel, *The Passing of Traditional Society: Modernizing the Middle East*, Glencoe, Illinois: The Free Press, 1958.

Lewis, G. L., *Turkey*, London: Ernest Benn, 1957 (2nd ed.).

Lorenz, Charlotte, *Die Frauenfrage im Osmanischen Reiche*, Dissertation, Berlin, 11.2.1919.

Mansour, Fahmy, *La condition de la femme dans la tradition et l'évolution de l'islamisme*. Paris: Libr. Felix Alcan, 1913.

Meslekî ve Teknik Öğretim müesseseleriyle ilgili rakkamlar, Ankara, 1961.

Nuri, Celâl, *Kadınlarımız*, Istanbul, 1917.

Pesle, O., *La femme musulmane dans le droit, la religion et les moeurs*. Rabat: Les editions la porte, 1946.

Pritsch, Erich, "Das schweizerische ZGB in der Türkei," *Zeitschrift für auslaendisches u. internationales Privatrecht*, 24 Jhrg. Max-Plack Institut. Pp.686–718.

T. C. Evlenme Istatistikleri, 1932–1960, Nr. 418.

Teknik ve Meslekî Öğretim müesse cleriyle ilgili rakkamlar.

Topçuoglu, Hâmide, *Kadınlarin çalışma saikleri ve kadin kazancının aile bütçesindeki rolü*. Ankara: Kültür matbaasi, 1957.

Tümertekin, Erol, "Turkiye ziraatindeki kadin gücünün dağılışi, *Türkiye Coğrafya dergisi*, 1959, Nr. 18–19.

Tütengil, Cavit Orhan, *Içtimai e Iktisadî bakımdan Türkiye'nin Karayolları*, Istanbul, 1961.

Woodsmall, Ruth Frances, *Women and the New East*, Washington, D.C.: The Middle East Institute, 1960.

Yener, Enise, Eski Ankara kiyafetleri ve giyiniş tarzlari, Ankara Universitesi *Dil Tarih ve Coğrafya Fakültesi Dergisi*, XIII, Vol. 3, Eylül 1955.

The Arab World

By Charles W. Churchill

INTRODUCTION: SHARI'A AND SUNNA

The Arab world extends over southwest Asia and the northern half of Africa. In this world area there are thirteen major independent states (in addition to several smaller principalities) in which Arabic is the language of all or most inhabitants, and (with the exception of Lebanon) Islam is the dominant religion.

The Arab countries in North Africa are (from west to east) Morocco, Algeria, Tunisia, Libya, Egypt, and Sudan. Those in southwest Asia are Syria, Lebanon, Jordan, Iraq, Saudi Arabia, Yemen, and Kuwait. The Sheikdom of Muscat and Oman, and the Aden Protectorate, in the eastern and southern parts of the Arabian Peninsula, are at present on the verge of attaining complete independence. The land area of the Arab world comprises about 4.3 million square miles, with a population of ca. 100 million.

The status of women in the entire Arab world has been inextricably interwoven with religion, that is Islam, which spread over most of this area within a few decades after the death of Muhammad (570–632), founder and prophet of the Muslim faith.

The Shari'a, or Islamic Law, principally drawn from the Koran as revealed by God to Muhammad, would appear to leave no room for secular opinion. This, however, is not quite the case, because Islamic law has five categories, ranging from those things which are enjoined, through those recommended and those of which the religion takes no account, to those which God absolutely forbids. Between the two extremes of what must be done and what is forbidden lies a broad area for the development of schools of jurisprudence.

To the Muslim, man or woman, there is no divisiveness in the Shari'a. The law is the law and that is that. However, human fallibility being what it is, even in the traditional culture, variations of interpretation have arisen in the application of the Shari'a to specific cases.

To be sure, the Koran is supposed to be the font of revelations; but since it does not cover all contingencies of life, a second source, the Sunna, has entered into the development of the Shari'a. The Sunna are a set of traditions derived from the words and acts of Muhammad and were developed over a long period. Actually the Sunna are based in part on old Arab usages that gradually became woven into the Shari'a in the belief that Muhammad had associated himself with them.

The Sunnis, or orthodox Muslims, who comprise most of the Arab world, recognize four schools of jurisprudence, the Hanbalis, Malikis, Hanafis, and Shafi'is. The Shi'as, who represent dissenting groups from the Sunnis, also have a number of schools. The Sunni schools tend to respect each others' opinions. The Shi'as are more independent. Thus, generalizations about Islamic law, especially personal and family law, are subject to qualification from area to area and sect to sect within the Arab world.

THE TRADITIONAL PATTERN

The traditional Muslim pattern of marriage regulations allows both parties in a prospective marriage to withdraw from a betrothal. If the party who withdraws has received gifts, the gifts must be returned unless they are perishable or have been consumed, in which case there is no compensation. But practice has varied with different schools of law.

Once the marriage contract has been signed by representatives of both parties, the marriage is valid and requires no other sanction, religious or secular. Marriage is a contractual relationship, a special kind of contract in some ways, but nevertheless a contract.

The marriage contract, in order to be valid, must contain no limitation on the duration of the marriage (except in one Shi'ite sect that permits temporary marriages for those on journeys); must be witnessed by two male witnesses; and must not contravene the rules, regulations, and prohibitions to which a Muslim marriage is subject.

Barriers to Marriage—Three kinds of relationships form permanent barriers to marriage: blood relationships, marriage relationships, and so-called milk relationships. Blood relationships precluding marriage are those between parents, children, and grandchildren and between brothers and sisters. However, a man may marry his niece or his aunt, and first cousins are not only permitted but preferred as marriage partners. A marriage relationship precluding marriage is prior marriage to a relative of the prospective spouse in the direct line of ascent or descent; nor is a man allowed to marry his former daughter-in-law. Milk relationships are a unique feature of Islamic law. In general, suckling establishes a mother-child relationship just like a blood relationship, with most of the same prohibitions effective against natural relatives as marriage partners.

In addition to these permanent barriers to marriage there are temporary ones. Widowhood precludes remarriage for a period of four Muslim lunar months and ten days, while a divorced woman must not remarry for three months.

Muslim men may marry not only Muslim women, but also women belonging to the "Peoples of the Book" (Jews and Christians). Muslim women, on the other hand, may marry Muslim men only. These religious barriers, however, can be removed by conversion.

Polygamy—The pre-Islamic inhabitants of the Arabian Peninsula knew no limitation on the number of wives allowed. The restriction of plural marriages to four wives was a reform instituted by Muhammad, and actually signified a rise in the status of women. Islamic law does not encourage casual marriage and divorce. Polygamy is allowed but not recommended, and the husband is required to give equal treatment to all his wives both sexually and in the matter of support.

Choosing a Mate—Women have limited freedom in selecting a husband, but a man is limited only by immaturity, fifteen being generally agreed to be the age of maturity. A woman cannot be forced into marriage if she is a virgin. However, she must heed the advice of the male relative who is responsible for her, ordinarily her father or any male relative on her father's side who is *in loco parentis*. Should the woman and her guardian disagree, the case may be brought to a kadi (judge of the religious court). The Hanafi school of jurisprudence, however, accords to women complete freedom to make a choice, providing it is a suitable one. The guardian may, if he believes the choice unsuitable, ask the kadi for a nullification. On this point, Abu Hanifa (founder of the Hanafi school) has a general following in Syria, Lebanon, Iraq, Egypt, and the Sudan. But his definition of suitability is the strictest of any school.

Suitability of the Marriage Partner—Suitability of marriage partners is judged by lineage, membership in Islam, economic considerations, character, and occupation. Lineage rules differ from school to school, identification being with tribal groups. Rules concerning membership in Islam differ between those groups whose lineage is originally Arab and those descendants of non-Arabs, such as the north Africans, who have accepted Islam and subsequently became Arabicized. Among the Arabs, any Muslim man is suitable for any Muslim woman as far as membership in Islam is concerned. Among the originally non-Arab groups, current membership in Islam does not make a man suitable for a woman if his parents were not Muslims and hers were. In economic matters, the man must be able to provide a bride price and a standard of living as good as that to which the bride is accustomed. Lack of piety would be a barrier in a man whose intended bride comes from a pious family. Great disparity in occupational status between a man and his prospective father-in-law is an additional barrier. Often it is held that a man can raise a woman to his status, but she cannot do the same for him.

One prerogative that a Muslim Arab woman has, and which many Western nations do not grant their women, is the right to own property. Her property is not subject to the control of her husband.

The Bride Price—The dowry, or, more properly, "bride price," must be paid to the wife according to the terms of the marriage contract, and must be comparable to that received by other women in her family. The bride price may be paid in installments, but the terms must be clearly spelled out. If no bride price is specified, the contract may still be valid, provided the bride price actually offered is suitable for the woman's status. If the woman's guardian thinks the bride price is not suitable, he can take the case to the kadi and the marriage may be dissolved. The bride price may be altered at any time prior to the consummation of the marriage, but not thereafter. In general, if the man repudiates the woman before consummation but after signing the contract, he must pay half of the bride price. If the woman reneges, the man owes nothing.

Marriage Duties and Rights—The man is in theory responsible for furnishing the house but usually the woman's family does it instead. The husband alone is responsible for supporting his wife, as far as possible in her accustomed status.

In general, the wife is bound to obey her husband, unless compliance with his wishes might cause her physical injury.

In Islam the woman receives her legal rights only through the intermediacy of her guardian. She is considered inferior, as revealed in the Koran. There is intense anxiety on the part of the woman until she bears her first son, at which time both father and mother are accepted as mature and adult. When a first son is born, both his father's and mother's name are changed to *Abu* (father of) and *Umm* (mother of). Girls, although not valued as highly as boys, are not mistreated, and, in fact, sons often accuse their fathers of favoring the daughters. Affectional relations are the same for children of both sexes.

The legally recognized duration of pregnancy varies from school to school, ranging from nine months to five years. A man may be away for years, and, upon returning home, his wife may present him with a newborn baby. The belief is that the seed may be quiescent in the woman for years and then start to grow.

Rights of inheritance differ between males and females. A wife is entitled to one quarter of her husband's estate by right, if he leaves no male descendants, but only to one eighth if there are male heirs. In general, sons receive twice as much as daughters, and children are favored over adults.

Restrictions on a Wife — In the traditional situation, the only education to which a woman may aspire is memorization of the Koran and knowledge of the duties of Islam. She is considered inferior intellectually to man and unstable emotionally. Her sexual desires are such that she must be closely guarded. Any deviation from the sex mores is subject to punishment, even death. To mete out such punishment is a duty of father and brothers, usually the latter. Adulterers are to be stoned according to the Koran. However, adultery must be witnessed, which makes this form of punishment rare.

Love is something that grows with marriage and is thought of more as compatibility and respect than romance. The woman is expected to be at home when her husband returns from his daily chores, in order to serve him but not to be a companion. She is to mother his children in accordance with the will of God, but her recreational and social life is strictly drawn from the companionship of other women, as the husband's is with other men. Such situations are conducive to homosexuality. But what may seem an indication of homosexuality to a foreigner is merely custom in most cases. Thus men will kiss each other on meeting, or walk together hand in hand. No public display of affection would be tolerated between the sexes.

Home and Routine — Depending on the local culture, girls are segregated from men between the ages of six and eleven, and assume the garments of women. At the age of six, little girls are expected to help in household chores, and especially in the care of younger children. Afternoon gossip sessions are the normal pattern of female social life. One topic of absorbing interest is sex. Although girls receive no sex education, they are permitted to listen to the frank conversation of the older women.

The absence of the man of the house relaxes the atmosphere of the household. Formalities of interpersonal relationships are eased, and women may engage in singing or dancing. In some places, such as Fez, Morocco, there is an underground life of women complete with posted sentinels to watch for the master's return. This life is unsuspected or ignored by the men.

In the truly conservative parts of the Arab world, such as Saudi Arabia, the traditional household routine starts with early prayers at daybreak. The wife then serves her husband bitter coffee, followed by a breakfast consisting of tea, milk, and eggs with unleavened bread. After the husband has left for work, the wife eats her breakfast with the children. From the age of nine or ten, the male children eat with their father.

The wife and daughters do the housework while the very young children play in the neighborhood, with the older children taking care of the younger. At noon, the man returns and is served a lunch of rice and meat. After he has had his nap and leaves again, the wife may visit with the neighbors, but she must be home by late afternoon before her husband returns. Supper consists of wheat and meat, stew, and *laban* (cultured milk, similar to yogurt).

After supper the husband may visit with male friends or have male visitors, with whom he may engage in long discussions or play a kind of backgammon. Bedtime comes early.

Women do not go to the general markets. Such purchases are men's work. On Fridays there may be picnics to which people walk.

The woman's sole occupation is that of housewife. She is restricted to the home, and has only female contacts. Even in women's hospitals nursing is done by non-Arab women, often Indians, Pakistanis, and some Western women.

Divorce—Divorce in Islam is the unlimited right of the male, providing he follows the approved forms. He may twice remarry the same woman, but should he divorce her a third time, he is forbidden to remarry her unless in the meantime she has been married to and divorced by another man. If, however, the man pronounces the divorce formula, "I divorce you," three times on the same occasion, this counts as a triple divorce and remarriage follows the same rules as if there had been divorces at three separate times. As a result, it is rarely used.

Forbidding remarriage to a thrice-divorced couple follows the logic that, if they have divorced too often, they must be unable to get along. The circumvention of the ban through an intervening marriage is based on the theory that the woman may be matured by her marriage to a second partner. The implication is, of course, that women in general are immature.

If the husband cannot support his wife, she may return to her father's household, which then has a claim on future earnings of the man. A husband's refusal to support his wife is usually sufficient grounds for the kadi to grant her a divorce.

Women have the right to keep their young children in the event of divorce or separation until the child is seven to nine if a boy, and nine to eleven if a girl, depending on the school of jurisprudence. The child is then returned to its father. By agreement, girls can remain longer with their mothers, but boys must join their fathers to learn men's ways.

The Women Among the Bedouins—In addition to urbanites and villages, who have been considered so far, Arab society also comprises nomads, the so-called Bedouins, who live in tribal groups in the desert and its fringes, and wander with their camels, or goats and sheep, in search of pasture. While the urbanite looks down on the illiterate, unwashed nomads, he, somewhat paradoxically, takes pride in his own Bedouin origin, remembering that it was the Bedouins who carried the sword of Islam across North Africa to Spain and into the Asian continent as far as Pakistan.

The Bedouins have been traditionally slack in their observance of Islamic rules, which, in turn, has had its bearing on the position of the women among them. The relative freedom of movement of the Bedouins, and their less circumscribed way of life is reflected in the greater freedom of Bedouin women, who mostly go unveiled and are enabled by tribal mores to communicate with young men before marriage. In general, nomadic tribes have allowed considerably more interaction between the sexes, although with no less concern for the chastity of women, than settled society.

As a result of the emergence of Arab national states, and the victory of urban values, the Bedouins are everywhere increasingly becoming settled in villages and cities. Many of them seek and find employment with the oil companies, and these contacts with a Western or Westernized environment leave their mark on them in general and on their attitude to women in particular.

LEGAL REFORMS

Westernization—The change that can be observed since the beginning of the twentieth century, and, more particularly, since World War II, in the status of women in the Arab World, is everywhere a result of Westernization, the extent and intensity of which differs from country to country. A related factor is the size and influence of the new middle class, whose emergence is in itself an outcome of Westernization. With respect to modernization and socioeconomic development, the Arab countries range from most tradition-bound Saudi Arabia, Yemen, and the Sheikdoms of the Arabian Peninsula, to most Westernized Lebanon and Tunisia. Although the present analysis will concentrate on the Arabian Peninsula and Lebanon, as representative of the two extremes of this range, other countries will also be referred to at least occasionally.

Westernization proceeds everywhere from the major urban centers toward the surrounding countryside. Thus in the Arabian Peninsula, where the process is still in its early stages, the influence of Western culture is felt only in major cities or in complexes centering around such technological installations as oil refineries. In Lebanon, on the other hand, the more or less Westernized cities are surrounded by villages in which Western influences are quite marked.

New Legislation—Several Arab states have introduced modifications into the Shari'a law by legislation based on European precedents. The new laws may or may not be accompanied by statements referring to the Shari'a. Sometimes the Shari'a is simply ignored. Thus, in Egypt there has been since 1931 a requirement that marriages must be registered in order to allow a petition regarding the validity of a marriage to be heard in court. The tie to Islamic law in this case was a new interpretation of what constitutes publicity, a condition of the validity of marriage according to the traditional jurists. Publicity now came to mean an official document.

On the other hand, one must not minimize the opposition to changing the status of women by legislation. As late as 1952, el-Azhar University in Egypt, the recognized leader in Islamic interpretation, issued a *fatwa* or edict, concerning the status of women in Islam, which emphasized that: (1) women should not go about outside their homes; (2) women should preserve their chastity and reputation and should not be a temptation to men; (3) women should not attend public functions because their emotions overcome their reason; (4) women are created for one function, to become mothers; (5) women in general, due to their femininity, have a tendency to be emotional and forget their reason, which is why the Prophet Muhammad said that the testimony of a woman is worth only half that of a man; (6) men can divorce women because they have the right but women cannot do so; (7) God prefers men to women.

But it was not long after this that Gamal Abdul Nasser came to power, suppressed the reactionary Muslim Brotherhood, secularized family law, and advanced the modernization of Egypt considerably. Now, any educated Egyptian will agree emphatically that the veil is dead.

There has been a new development also in the method of paying the bride price. In Lebanon the bride price is now usually paid in two installments: one part at the time of the wedding, and the rest if and when a woman is divorced. This arrangement serves as a protection for the woman and represents a definite improvement in her status. Thus far, this new custom is followed only rarely in Saudi Arabia, usually in a marriage between a Saudi man and an Arab woman from a more Westernized country, such as Lebanon. Indeed, knowing the hazards of marrying a Saudi Arabian prince, most Lebanese women would not consider such a marriage without a substantial deferred bride price. Some marriages are even entered into with the expectation of divorce and a contingent substantial cash payment.

Liberalized Marriage Code in Tunisia—The tendency to liberalize divorce for the woman has gained ground steadily in most countries, especially Tunisia, where as early as 1930, Sheik Tahar el-Haddad published a book justifying the rights of Muslim women. His point was a daring one for a Muslim. He argued that the references to women in the Koran were not immutable but were intended only for women at the stage of development in the time of Muhammad; the abolition of slavery had not hurt the Koran, and the same could be said for the emancipation of women. He advocated education for both men and women, claiming the Koran as inspiration. He thought marriage should be the concern of the couple itself and divorce a matter for the state to govern through the judiciary.

In 1955, Habib Bourguiba, President of Tunisia, known among other titles as the emancipator of women in Tunisia, changed the laws regarding the family. Marriage was to be strictly by mutual consent, and the goal of marriage was to be *mutual* respect, with men and women sharing equally in family responsibilities. The bride price and the marriage contract were placed under the jurisdiction of the civil courts. The bride price became substantial, and the woman had the right to use it as she saw fit.

To be legal, marriage had to be contracted before a civil officer or a notary public. The legal age of marriage became fifteen for the girl and eighteen for the man, and the consent of parent or guardian was necessary only for those under twenty. Fathers could not force their daughters into marriage. Polygamy was forbidden under penalty of a prison sentence or a fine (this was justified by Koranic provisions that allow polygamy only if the wives are treated equally; since this was an obvious impossibility, polygamy could be banned). Divorce was obtainable only by judicial action, and the absolute right of the man to divorce his wife as he pleased was abolished; both parties had the right to sue for divorce; if the woman received the divorce and was in the right, she kept the children. The legal duration of pregnancy was limited to one year; women were given full political rights to vote and to hold office; and they were to obey their husbands only in respect to the latters' positions as heads of families.

Tunisia, therefore, has as modern a family code as any country in the world. But the stroke of a pen does not change the habits of centuries. Among the poorer and less educated classes, male domination is still the norm.

Lebanese Women's Legal Status—In Lebanon the present legal status of women, as everything else in that country, is a product of cross-cultural relations between East and West. Legally, women have progressed somewhat less than they have in other ways. Each religious community has, and can follow, its own law, provided that it does not conflict with

Lebanese state law. Since Lebanon is the only country in the Arab world without a clear Muslim majority, the Christian family law in it is not subject to Muslim authorization.

Most Catholics in Lebanon follow the Maronite rite, which, though it differs from Roman Catholicism, accepts the authority of the Pope. Maronite marriages must be solemnized by a priest. Intermarriage is possible, but is discouraged, and it is subject to Church rules regarding offspring.

The second largest Lebanese Christian community is the Greek Orthodox, among whom marriage requires the consent of both parties if they have reached majority, which is eighteen for the male and fifteen for the female. Otherwise, the guardians' consent must be obtained. Here too, marriage must be solemnized by a priest.

In the Muslim communities the Islamic codes are followed. These require that the consent of both parties be obtained before the marriage. The age of majority of males is eighteen, of females, seventeen. If both parties have not reached majority, the authorization of the kadi and the consent of the guardians must be obtained. In any event, no male may be married before the age of seventeen and no girl below the age of nine. Men have the usual right to have up to four wives.

A Lebanese woman does not lose her nationality upon marrying a foreigner unless she automatically acquires the nationality of her husband by the law of his country.

As to property rights, in general, all religions permit husband and wife to have separate estates. The wife has full control of her property and can mortgage it, sell it, lease it, or dispose of it by will or however she pleases, without the consent of her husband.

A Lebanese law of 1929 provides that a Lebanese non-Muslim male or female who is of age may dispose of property, personal or real, by transferring it to whomever he or she pleases, whether an heir or not, provided there is no surviving mother, father, husband, wife, or child, who cannot be deprived of their legal portions. Twenty per cent must go to the husband or wife, and 15 per cent to the mother or father if the testator leaves no surviving children. Male or female share and share alike, if the testator leaves no surviving father, mother, husband, or wife. If these survive, the legal distribution must be: 10 per cent to husband or wife, 5 per cent to a surviving mother and a surviving father, and 30 per cent to the children.

In the Muslim community the husband may dispose by will of no more than one third of this estate to others than heirs. Among the Druzes, however, complete freedom is given to the testator, male or female, to dispose of property by will. But if a person dies intestate, Muslim rules of inheritance apply.

A will executed outside of Lebanon is valid if it is in accordance with the laws of the country concerned, and if the testator is a non-Muslim.

EDUCATION

The variations in the educational norms and institutions between one Arab country and another are considerable. Again, a brief statement about the situation in the Arabian Peninsula and in Lebanon will serve to point up the two extremes.

In the Arabian Peninsula, education for women is still largely a matter of Koranic memorization. But increasingly, girls attend girls' schools where secular subjects are also taught, or they have private tutors if their families can afford them. During the rapprochement between Saudi Arabia and the United Arab Republic, a number of Saudi girls were sent to girls' schools in Egypt. The Saudi King subsequently ended this arrangement on the grounds that he wanted to save foreign exchange. The real reason might well have been the King's opposition to girls' education beyond the Koranic schools. Nevertheless, several new girls' schools have recently been established in Saudi Arabia, and the winds of change are blowing more vigorously under King Faisal.

The ruling family in Saudi Arabia is part of the Wahhabi tribe. Under the leadership of the late King Ibn Saud, the Wahhabis attempted to purify the practices of Islam by removing any recent undesirable outgrowth, and to reestablish a puritanical way of life. On the other hand, however, the Saudis have also been interested in the exploitation of their oil resources and the substitution, as far as possible, of Saudis for the foreign personnel employed by Aramco, the Arabian-American Oil Company. Because modern oil exploitation demands considerable specialized skills, the two purposes of the Saudis may well prove irreconcilable. Some prosperous Saudis send their daughters to schools in Lebanon, including the American University of Beirut, where in 1964–1965 six Saudi girls were studying. The Saudi government demands that girls over twelve years of age must veil in school.

While Saudi Arabia is feeling the beginning of change, in neighboring Yemen women are still in the Middle Ages as far as education goes. The *Imam* (King) of Yemen continued the policies of his father in a calculated attempt to isolate Yemen from the world, particularly the Western world. As a result, reform in education for women was still in the more or less distant future. The Yemeni revolution, still unresolved in 1967, can be expected to have effects which so far are incalculable.

Contrast the Arabian Peninsula with Lebanon, and, to a lesser extent, with Syria, Jordan, Iraq, Egypt, Tunisia, and even Libya. All are on the move toward improved education for girls. In Lebanon, Muslim and Christian, boy and girl, mingle in the American University of Beirut. Among its students are girls from all over the Arab world (except Egypt, which has its own university system). The female enrollment is about 15 per cent of the total and is increasing. Secondary education is still segregated and largely in the hands of private institutions. But in urban elementary schools, girls are coming into their own. In the past, education has tended to emphasize academic subjects, but the deficiencies of this type of schooling have been recognized by most Arab governments, and vocational schools are beginning to appear. Educational aspirations for girls of the lower classes are apt to be vocational, with the leading choices being still traditionally feminine occupations, such as dressmaking and midwifery.

In Lebanon, the education of women differs by generation, class, and religion. In the city of Beirut, in 1952, more than a third of the women of the older generation had had no education. For those who had been to school, the average duration of education was 3.9 years. Moving up the class and income scale, about 4 per cent of the wives of heads of households had higher education, that is, baccalaureate (the equivalent of one year of college in the American system) or higher. Nine tenths of these women had attended private schools. In comparison, the male heads of households had had an average education of 6.1 years, while 13 per cent had achieved at least the baccalaureate.

The French occupation introduced a large number of French schools into the country with the result that to this day twice as many people speak French as English. Among those who speak any foreign language, the men are roughly twice as numerous as the women. The men, evidently, felt an economic need for learning European languages which was not felt among women.

Lebanese Christians embraced Western-type education considerably earlier than did the Muslims. Recently, however, Muslim women have begun to seek education almost to the same extent as the Christians. In many, if not most, poor families, however, even today only the boys are sent to school.

Since achieving independence, most Arab governments have engaged in building schools for both boys and girls, although much fewer schools for girls than for boys have so far been constructed. A United Nations report from 1963 shows that in that year 29 per cent of school-age girls actually attended schools in Iraq and Syria, 37 per cent in Jordan, 44 per cent in Lebanon, and 39 per cent in Egypt.

In the Lebanese cities, the average duration of school attendance by girls has shown a marked increase in recent years. In the villages, and especially in the predominantly Muslim areas, there is a considerable lag in this respect. A recent study of parents in thirteen villages in the rural Beqa' Valley of Lebanon showed that the average duration of schooling for males was 2.6 years, while for females only 0.6 year. The girls and women of whole villages may be completely illiterate. The younger generation showed but little improvement as compared with the parents: 3.1 years of schooling for boys and 0.8 years for girls. An interesting sidelight on plural marriages is the fact that of a total of 39 second wives, all but one were illiterate. Although 90 per cent of the mothers were illiterate, the illiteracy rate fell to 75 per cent among their daughters — still hardly rapid progress.

Nevertheless it appears that the solid front against education for girls has been broken. While some still oppose it violently and openly, others justify themselves on some such ground as poverty. There is a steadily changing set of attitudes that will result in substantial improvement of female education in the villages. One problem is shortage of teachers. In the villages, teachers are men, because a woman teacher would not be allowed to leave her home in the city and go to work by herself in a village. Men, on the other hand, find little to attract them to the villages, because of the low teachers' salaries.

SEX MORES AND ATTITUDES

Relationships between the sexes differ widely, depending on religion, class and country.

Saudi Arabia — The ruling family of Saudi Arabia is extremely conservative in its attitude toward women, who are relegated to the harem (the women's quarters) and expected to behave strictly in the traditional way. The emerging middle class is beginning to show signs of the inevitable ferment characteristic of social change in the relations between the sexes. This is particularly true in the families of men with better jobs in the oil companies, whose women tend to become lax with regard to veiling. The men themselves often tell their wives not to bother about their veils in the presence of Western men.

Girls are beginning to discuss the wearing of the veil, and some have ceased wearing it on most occasions. There is general agreement in the middle class that discarding the veil will be a big step in improving the status of women.

On the other hand, premarital chastity remains a universal and unchallenged norm in all classes. Men and women do not mingle either before or after marriage, nor do women usually act as companions to men. Courtship is nonexistent.

Polygamy is becoming less respectable. Public opinion condemns the man who takes a second wife unless there is a good reason, such as the childlessness of the first wife. Rarely does a man have more than two wives. Divorce is resorted to instead, but this, too, is often condemned, especially when the couple have children. Women are still forbidden by law to ride alone in taxis. The life of the Bedouin women, both in Saudi Arabia and elsewhere, has remained unchanged. Increasingly, however, the Bedouin tribes are settling down to village life, and many tribesmen find jobs in the cities and begin to adapt to urban standards. The villages, too, remain almost entirely unchanged unless they are associated with oil companies.

Yemen—In Yemen, if an unmarried girl becomes pregnant, she may go to jail, or both she and the male relatives who are held responsible for her conduct may be killed. Dr. Fayien reports that many men and unknown number of women engage in homosexual practices, the men starting about the age of fifteen, usually with their fathers' friends. Homosexual women are beaten, but there is no penalty for men.

According to Attilio, in Yemen small girls are still bought and sold, and slave markets still exist. Sexual access to slave girls is part of their owners' rights.

In the rural areas of Yemen women do not veil, but on the whole there is little difference in the status of women between town and country. Only when a woman becomes a widow, or is divorced, or her husband is absent, does she enjoy greater freedom. Such a woman has nothing to lose for even if she should become pregnant the legal fiction of the "dormant seed" can be used to attribute to the husband any pregnancy occurring up to four years after separation. For young girls, on the other hand, the loss of virginity is nothing short of a catastrophe, even if a resulting pregnancy can be aborted by means of a powerful drug. For if, on her wedding night, a girl should be found lacking in virginity, she will be repudiated by her husband and cast out by her own family. The public viewing of the bedsheet following the wedding night is still practiced in the villages, although in the cities it has become quite rare.

As to polygamy, one observer, Dr. Fayien, believes that one man in two would be polygamous if he had the means. Marrying child brides is still a practice among the upper classes of Yemen. Sometimes, if the husband is over twenty, he may take another bride of his own age until his child bride matures.

In Sana, the capital of Yemen, Dr. Fayien found a good deal of extra-marital adventuring taking place in several houses of rendezvous. The assignations were accomplished by using two adjoining houses, one the home of a purported wise old man who would dispense wisdom to young men, the other a house occupied by an ostensibly respectable widow who liked to have young women around. There was a connecting door between the houses. Occasionally a woman, finding herself attracted to a man whom she would observe from behind the windows of her house, would find out who he was and where he lived, and then pay a visit to his harem where she would manage to let him catch a glimpse of her with her veil raised. Such behavior would inevitably prove titillating to the man, and the ensuing consequences could be foreseen. An important factor in such intrigues, whose general atmosphere reminds one of *The Arabian Nights*, is the help of a female relative who would in her turn also be helped. The penalty for being caught is severe, usually death.

Lebanon—In Lebanon, upper- and middle-class Muslim and Christian women have achieved considerable freedom, the Christians somewhat more than the Muslims. Nevertheless, all Lebanese girls, of whatever religion or class, are expected to be virgins at marriage or face repudiation by their husbands. However, premarital social relations between men and women have become prevalent. Usually these relationships are part of total family interaction or take place in groups of young men and girls. Quite likely, too, the girl's brother will be part of such social groupings.

In the upper class, groups of young couples, or, less frequently, pairs, visit nightclubs or gambling casinos. In the middle class, cinema dates are allowed, sometimes for a lone couple. But the young man will feel constrained to invite the family along too. The family, or some member of it, will usually accept the invitation.

Premarital petting, short of sexual relations, does occur, and respectable young girls will discuss with their close girl friends, but not with their families, the pleasures of being kissed. Considering the constrained pattern of courtship, the problem most often faced is how to be alone with a boy.

Many young or not so young bachelors are predatory in their habits and boast privately of their successes. Girls are extremely worried about their reputation and consequently are unlikely to succumb to anyone. Illegitimacy does occur, but rarely.

Girls must be exceedingly careful of gossip. Repeated dating with a young man is interpreted as serious interest, and, ordinarily, before long, it is expected that a declaration be made either personally, or, in more conservative circles, through the families. If the affair does not lead to a proposal, the girl's subsequent eligibility may be severely damaged by the suspicion of her loss of virginity, and the presumption of other defects. This being the situation, it would be unthinkable for a young girl secretary to travel with her employer. Traveling alone on a vacation, if it involves being alone overnight, is also reprehensible.

Marriage in Lebanon—Both Muslims and Christians are opposed to interreligious marriage, and such marriages are, in fact, very uncommon. Since intermarriage is taboo, interreligious courtship is also opposed, and practically non-existent.

Marriage is still a family affair in all classes and religions. The first meeting of two eligible young people is an occasion for endless family discussion about the suitability of the young man or young woman. Amateur matchmakers are always alert for the slightest signs of interest, and will speculate on the exact meaning of a simple phrase that would be considered a common pleasantry in the Western world. Prospective marriage partners are evaluated on two bases: their families' social status, and their families' income, the premise being that membership in a prosperous "good" family is the pathway to security whether the individual has much talent or not.

The traditional Arab pattern, calling for arranged marriages, is still strong in most places and most classes. Among the educated middle and upper classes, however, there has been a great increase in the Western type of relationship of romance and egalitarianism, with considerable freedom in the choice of a marriage partner, as long as both the girl and the young man are of the same religion and of similar family background.

Polygamy is declining very rapidly, especially in the urban middle and upper classes. A social survey of the city of Beirut showed that fewer than 0.5 per cent of the families were polygamous, and husbands in these had only two wives. Village surveys showed about 3 per cent of polygamous households. These figures are comparable to those from studies in Egypt and slightly lower than in Iraq.

Family Planning—The practice of birth control varies with class and religion. The spokesmen of Islam, formerly opposed, now permit family limitation. Indeed, large-scale attempts to limit population growth by contraception are common in overpopulated Muslim countries. Both the Greek Orthodox and the Catholic churches oppose birth-control practices and pressure is exerted to have large families. In Lebanon, this is effective to some extent among the Maronites, but much less so among the Orthodox. As people move up on the class scale, the size of the family tends to diminish.

Extramarital Relations in Lebanon—In Beirut and other cities, a loosening of the sexual code governing marital fidelity seems to have taken place. The extent or prevalence of extramarital relationship is, of course, extremely difficult to measure, but there seems to be substantial agreement among women that extramarital affairs occur quite frequently in the middle and upper classes, particularly in the latter.

For the young men of the poor or lower-middle class a sexual outlet is provided by legal prostitution. This institution is considered normal, and a safeguard facilitating the preservation of the virtue of respectable girls. However, middle-class young men are becoming increasingly ashamed of such sexual adventures. For men of more means, there are the *artistes*, who are mostly European girls arriving in Lebanon as members of traveling shows. Theoretically this is their sole function, but the label *artiste* carries with it an understanding of sexual availability for a price. Married and unmarried men visit the nightclubs and attend the shows in which the girls are featured. After the show, the girls change to evening dresses and sit at tables until they are approached by the men. What follows is then up to the girl. This is a common pattern in many Arab cities. Occasionally a puritanical Minister of State or a Head of State will issue orders to do away with this practice; orders which may or may not be obeyed.

THE WOMAN'S ROLE IN THE FAMILY

The home routine, though still unchanged in conservative, rural, and poorer groups, has become much less restrictive elsewhere.

In the cities of Lebanon the woman's position in the family has been improving steadily since World War I, with the increase of educational facilities particularly those introduced by the French. Since World War II, change has been more drastic, especially so in the last five years. Women are increasingly seen outside their homes. On Sundays there are as many women as men on the crowded beaches of Beirut, the younger generation, of course. Beach behavior is undoubtedly a symbol of the loosening of the bonds.

In the prosperous class, modern electrical appliances have entered the home. Servants, almost invariably women, release other women from the drudgery of housekeeping and child care. This enables them to spend more time in pursuing all kinds of interests. Some women broaden their horizon by reading or other forms of education. Such women are usually more interesting persons, and more capable of being companions to men instead of merely segregated sexual objects.

The mother of the household has increased her prestige in the eyes of her children. Indeed, this process has gone so far in some homes that some women exercise the prerogatives of American women and are genuinely in control of the family. This applies largely to the middle class and the less conservative part of the upper class. It applies also much more to Christians than to Muslims.

In Egypt, Iraq, Jordan, and Syria, the conditions of urban life have advanced along the same road as in Lebanon, differing only in degree. The segregated, illiterate woman, with her undeveloped mind, restricted to female gossip and having no chance to mature mentally, is being replaced by a woman who has some knowledge of world affairs, takes an interest in politics, and has a fairly full social life.

Dress—In the tradition-bound countries of the Arabian Peninsula the women dress today as they did two, three, or more generations ago. Whether they wear the veil or not, their heads are as a rule covered by a large and heavy headkerchief, and their bodies by fully-cut dresses of dark brown, dark blue or black cloth, with long wide sleeves and skirts that reach almost to the ground. Most women go barefoot, but they invariably have and wear some jewelry. In the cities, among the well-to-do, Western clothes, especially evening dresses are worn by the women in the harem.

Similarly in Baghdad, Iraq, the *abba*, or long black cloak, is still standard outdoor wear for women, although the veil is being progressively discarded.

Lebanon represents in this respect, too, the other end of the scale. Here the acceptance of Western dress styles has reached a stage where among the Westernized middle and upper classes there is little restraint even on those girls who wish to dress provocatively. In all social groups, girls display a tremendous preoccupation with clothes. Working girls, whose families can afford it, spend almost their entire pay on clothes, and they are not usually casual clothes except for beach wear or picnics. In the winter, suits are worn, but in the summer standard garb for the university student is a tight silk dress or skirt and a more or less transparent blouse. High heels and nylon stockings are standard, and makeup is elaborate. Some Muslim girls, not university students, dress in a chic French style but wear a completely transparent symbolical veil over their faces. A few years ago girls were shy about being seen on the beaches in bathing suits, especially in a bikini. Now they take it in their stride, and many wear scanty two-piece bathing suits.

Women as Educators — As in the rest of the world, women have the primary responsibility for the formative years of the children's lives. They inculcate in them attitudes that are shared by Arabs in general, and which characterize their own countries in particular. It is for this reason mainly that thoughtful Arabs are anxious to improve the education of women. Women with infantile minds cannot train children who will be capable of facing modern problems. To their daughters, women transmit knowledge of woman's role in society. Boys are usually anxious to associate with their fathers, who lead infinitely more interesting lives than do women of the traditional harem. Also, in the traditional culture, the respect due the father leads the child to think of him in an emergency; children who are hurt are more likely to call for their father than their mother. Men and women are exceedingly fond of children — all children, not just their own.

In some respects, women are the worst enemies of women's emancipation. They share the general desire for sons, and not merely in order to please their husbands and families. They watch the girls as they mature, and are always ready to gossip about them. Since their reputation is a constant source of fear to girls, this prevents them from moving faster to an egalitarian status.

Leisure Time — Young men are still following in their fathers' footsteps by spending a good deal of their leisure time with other young men in coffee shops. But coffee houses, which at one time were entirely filled with men, are being supplemented by shops that cater to family groups, couples, and mixed groups of men and women. There is much variety in this respect from city to city. In Baghdad, for instance, men still associate mostly in occupational clubs, and for recreation-with-entertainment there are nightclubs for men only. In a number of cities, however, private clubs have sprung up, where modernized families meet to dine and dance. Amman, the capital of Jordan, has several prospering clubs of this nature where young married couples and their children mingle, especially on holidays and weekends.

As to the social life in private homes, the same variations can be observed from country to country and from city to city. In Baghdad, while there has been much greater participation of women in all areas of life, even American-trained university professors still entertain men only, with no women visible. However, this practice continues not because of adherence to the principle of segregation, but merely because people are unwilling to breach a traditional custom. Moreover, wives in these circles no longer veil, and participate in family activities. Generally, in Baghdad homes the men still eat first. Cooking, incidentally, takes place once a day only, and the same food is eaten at lunch and dinner.

As to the women themselves, recreation no longer is restricted to the harem. Even heavily-veiled women attend the cinema, sitting usually in the more expensive and more secluded balcony seats. In many cities there are special ladies' matinees, but many women attend at all times. The cinema, incidentally, has had enormous influence in opening up the world to the Arabs, both men and women. Although a great deal of what they see is misleading, it at least widens horizons. The Egyptian film industry dominates the field in the Arab world with its Arabic-language pictures. The characters appearing in these films include Arab women who do not veil, are not segregated, participate in family affairs, and engage in romantic behavior. Motion pictures are not shown in Saudi Arabia, while in Yemen movies have been introduced only following the arrival of Egyptian armed forces in the country; this fact accounts in part for the slowness of change in these countries. In Saudi Arabia there are two television stations, which contribute to broadening the viewpoint of the more prosperous families in areas near oil installations.

Divorce—The Sunni majority of the Lebanese Muslims follows the Hanafi rite which provides that the husband may divorce at will, but the wife may do so only if this privilege is granted by the husband in the marriage contract. In the Maronite community, divorce is not permitted, annulment or separation, however, can be granted by an ecclesiastical court.

In the Greek Orthodox community, the husband may be granted a divorce if he discovers at marriage that his bride is not a virgin, or later, that his wife is practicing birth control. He may also receive a divorce if his wife commits any of the following acts without his permission: sleeps outside the conjugal home, attends banquets, bathes with men in mixed baths, or goes to the races, the theater, or gambling halls. Adultery or refusal to obey a court order to cohabit with her husband for three years are additional grounds, as is her refusal to obey his repeated orders not to visit a particular person or house.

The woman may be granted a divorce because of impotence in the man or if he brings but fails to prove, an adultery charge against her. Additional grounds include encouraging the wife to prostitution or neglecting her for three years. Adultery of the husband in the conjugal home and refusal to mend his ways are also causes for divorce. The consequences of adultery for the man are qualified by place and attitude, while no such privilege is granted to the woman.

Either party may be granted a divorce if the other spouse suffers from incurable insanity, joins a monastic order, is imprisoned for five years or more for a defamatory offense, makes an attempt on the life of the other, or adopts another religion. Both parties may remarry, but the woman must wait four months.

Foreigners are subject to their national laws in matters of divorce, separation, alimony, and the custody of children. Action by foreigners must be brought before the mixed courts, that is, courts which concern themselves with marriages of different religions or nationalities. In such cases, duly certified copies of the pertinent national law must be submitted to the courts.

WOMAN'S ROLE IN SOCIETY

Women's Occupations — In the economic life of the more modernized Arab countries, each year marks the opening up of new job opportunities to women. In Lebanon this holds true for many fields but has so far not included politics. Released at a relatively early date from the segregated life of the harem, Lebanese women first found an outlet for their energies in home industries, particularly in textiles. Subsequently, when modern textile factories were built, women were recruited to operate the machinery. They were mostly young girls who could be observed at work in attires varying from Muslim dress to veils on the head but not the faces.

In Damascus, female key-punch operators were hired in the early 1950's to punch cards for the statistical department of the Syrian government. Some wore no veils at all, some had veils covering their hair only. When a strange man entered, some of the girls went right on working, while others paused perceptibly, made a half motion to cover their faces but evidently decided that it was not worthwhile, and returned to their work.

Office jobs as clerks, typists, stenographers, and secretaries have been held by girls for some years and are increasingly so. Hospital-staff nurses and public-health nurses are usually women. However, there is a rapid turnover in many jobs as the girls leave to be married. Governments are still fairly conservative and government jobs are held by men overwhelmingly, but girls are being employed as social workers and more and more girls are entering the civil service.

In private enterprise, midwives survive from the traditional period and still deliver most of the children. But the number of women physicians is increasing, although they usually specialize in obstetrics, gynecology, and pediatrics.

Lebanese girls have been leaving their villages to work as maids in the cities for many years. They used to be very young girls contracted out by their parents and paid miserably for eighteen-hour days with an hour off to attend church on Sunday. In recent years, the age level of these household employees has increased substantially and the girls have been demanding and getting better pay for shorter hours. What is more, they want electrical appliances. They usually leave within a few years to get married, and are highly acceptable marriage partners. In some Arab countries servants are mostly male. In Egypt, for example, most of them are young men from the Sudan.

In general, women have entered occupations that are new to the area; they work as radio and television commentators, in the tourist trade, as airline hostesses, and as page girls. In the motion-picture industry they become performers, script girls, or office workers. In some cases they go into service industries as owner-operators. Traditionally they have been entertainers, and some of the most popular singers are women who have huge followings and are greatly admired for their renderings of sentimental Arabic songs. Girls increasingly study commerce in the universities and fill such jobs as press attachés and newspaper reporters. The United Nations has hired Arab girls not only as office workers but as experts who are sent to other Arab countries to aid in their progress.

An increasing percentage of schoolteachers in the cities are women. Teaching is considered a highly respectable occupation, even in Saudi Arabia where female participation in the working world is, as a rule, still taboo. In Yemen, however, there has been no progress in this respect, since girls still do not go to school. Indeed, in Yemen the only occupation of women other than farm work and household duties is needlework for merchants, which is done at home.

In the arts, women are gaining acceptance. Among painters, sculptors, pianists, and concert singers there is an increasing number of women. These are, however, exceptional cases, and as such are generally well publicized.

All that has been said about women's occupations pertains almost entirely to urban, and usually young, women. In the villages, change is agonizingly slow. But there is no question that urban changes are radiating out to the countryside with the increasing prosperity and with the spread of schooling into the rural areas. For example, one prosperous *mukhtar* (mayor) in a solidly traditional village in Lebanon has recently sent his young daughter to a university to major in mathematics.

In general, it is still true that the normal expectation for the educated girl is a short period of work followed by marriage and children. Career women are usually either relatively unattractive, or too particular in accepting a suitor, or else widows or divorcees. However, it is increasingly respectable for married women to return to work, which gives them the added status of wage earner in the family.

Women in Public Life—Egyptian women, perhaps, are exercising more leadership than the women in any other Arab country. They have fought, and with considerable success, for the recognition of women's rights. They have won political rights, such as the vote and the right to hold public office. They occupy relatively high political positions. In Iraq, a woman has held the rank of Cabinet Minister.

In Tunisia, the niece of Habib Bourguiba, Saida Bouzagrou, represents the new woman in the Arab world. She started demonstrating in favor of the Neo-Destour, Bourguiba's political party, at the age of seventeen. She married in 1945 and had six children. Her marriage, however, did not stop her social and political activities. In 1951 she was fighting by the side of her uncle for independence. She organized the women's section of the Neo-Destour party, and in 1952 was sent to prison for her efforts. Upon her release, she organized women's associations to aid terrorists who were fighting for freedom. In 1954, after independence had been achieved, she worked steadily for the rights of women. Subsequently, she occupied a government position and became the President of the Union of Tunisian Women and of many other associations.

In Lebanon, on the other hand, the political leadership of women is negligible. Women have the vote, but the nature of Lebanese politics is such that general leadership is impossible because of the fragmentation of the country into religious communities. Women in Lebanon have turned to welfare activities and are providing leadership in civic improvement and fund raising. Of 321 voluntary welfare societies in the country, 139 have women presidents. In the city of Beirut the proportion is even higher, with 77 women presidents out of a total of 140. Such leadership is common in many Arab countries. Even in Saudi Arabia some female leadership is being exercised in the founding and management of girls' schools.

Women like Saida Bouzagrou, although little known outside the Arab world, have contributed their share to the fight for independence. In Baghdad, women laid aside their *abbas* and donned uniforms to help Kassem during the revolution. Women have been very active in Algeria in the independence movement. Except in the Arabian Peninsula, Jordan, and Iraq, they have won the right to vote. There is no doubt that women are participating increasingly in the life of the modern Arab world.

BIBLIOGRAPHY

Arab Women's Congress in Cairo 1944. *The Moslem World*, 1945, pp. 316–323.

Churchill, Charles W., *The City of Beirut: A Socio-Economic Survey*, Beirut: Dar el-Kitab, 1954.

Daghestani, K., *La Famille Contemporaine en Syrie*, Paris: Laroux, 1932.

——, "The Evolution of the Moslem Family," *UNESCO International Social Science Bulletin*, 1953, pp. 681–691.

Fayien, Claudie, *A French Doctor in the Yemen*, London: R. Hale, 1957.

Granqvist, Hilma, *Birth and Childhood among the Arabs*, Helsingfors: Söderström, 1947.

——, *Child Problems among the Arabs*, Helsingfors: Söderström, 1950.

——, *Marriage Conditions in a Palestinian Village*, 2 vols., Helsingfors: Societas Scientiarum Fennica, 1932, 1935.

Joly, Gertrude, "The Woman of the Lebanon," *Journal of the Royal Central Asian Society*, London, 1951, vol. 38, pp. 177–184.

Patai, Raphael, *The Kingdom of Jordan*, Princeton: Princeton University Press, 1958, chapter "The Family" (pp. 136–155).

——, *Golden River to Golden Road: Society, Culture and Change in the Middle East*, Philadelphia: University of Pennsylvania Press, 1962.

——, (ed.), *The Republic of Lebanon*, New Haven, Conn.: Human Relations Area Files, Inc., 1956, chapters "The Family" (pp. 254–296), "The Position of Women" (pp. 474–478).

——, (ed.), *The Republic of Syria*, New Haven, Conn.: Human Relations Area Files, Inc., 1956, chapters "The Family" (pp. 373–414), "The Position of Women" (pp. 609–611).

Sakakini, Widad, "The Evolution of the Syrian Woman," *United Asia*, Bombay, 1949, vol. I, pp. 531–535.

III

The Latin-Mediterranean World

GREECE, ITALY, SPAIN,
SPANISH AMERICA, AND BRAZIL

These four Latin areas together with Greece form, as far as the position of women is concerned, an intermediate group between the basically conservative Middle East and South Asia and the more progressive central and west European countries. The double standards of sexual morality still prevalent in them tie these areas to their southeastern neighbors. On the other hand, the advancing penetration of women into many new occupations, as well as legislative improvements of their position, approximate those of their northern neighbors.

Greece

By Egly Psaltis

THE TRADITIONAL SITUATION

Despite the great regional variations in the population of modern Greece, the traditional situation of women was the same all over the country, its mainland and its isles. Everywhere women lived within the family and were dominated and protected by its male members. This situation is attested in Greece from early antiquity. In ancient Athens, the average woman was a housewife, excluded from public life (originally, even from the theater and the Olympic games), and her education was confined mainly to reading, writing, and music. "To woman, silence is an ornament" summed up her position. Brilliant, cultivated women were either rare exceptions, or they were *hetaerae*, members of a special class of prostitutes, who often attained a high degree of culture, knowledge, grace, and manners and deeply influenced the great men of classical Greece. The rule was for a decent woman to stay at home to serve and obey her husband, and, in turn, be respected and cherished as a wife and mother.

In the great, unified, powerful, and Christian Byzantine Empire, women were more active in public life. Several became empresses in their own name, and reigned with their spouses. They were active in church charities. But even in this period, the proper place for the average respectable woman was in the home. The husband was the head of the family, the woman's lord and protector.

During the four centuries of Ottoman rule (1453–1829), women shared the general lowering of standards of all Greeks who did not flee to the West. Most of them were uneducated. Fear of the "infidel" conqueror with his polygamy, harems, and view of women as instruments of pleasure kept Greek women confined to their homes more than ever before. At the same time, the great common aspiration of all Greeks to preserve the Christian religion and to achieve national liberty caused women to become companions to their husbands and, if the occasion demanded, even their comrades-in-arms. This capacity for being a companion earned Greek women the respect of their menfolk. When finally independence was achieved in 1829, the relationship of Greek women and men continued to exhibit a dual aspect: on the one hand, women remained submissive to father, brothers, husbands, sons; and, on the other, they received respect, as well as love as faithful helpmeets through good days and bad. This is the typical situation of women today in all the tradition-bound sectors of the population.

Town and Country

The population of Greece (8,388,553 in 1961) consists of about 60 per cent rural or semi-urban, and 40 per cent urban inhabitants. The number of women is 4,296,659 as against 4,091,894 men. The greatest surplus of women is found in the Greater Athens area where there are 108 women for every 100 men.

In the country, the position of women is still largely traditional. The difference between the most primitive mountain regions and the most developed urban center of Athens represents several decades of evolution. The standard of living and the social conditions of women vary accordingly. But even apart from these extremes, there is a considerable gap between the village and city woman, the former lacking education, social activity, and status, as compared to the latter.

The majority of the rural population in Greece is very poor. Much of the soil is arid and, for lack of funds, unimproved. Lack of comfort, monotony, and underemployment cause the ablest villagers to leave. As a rule, the peasant woman is uneducated and overworked. She helps the men in most agricultural tasks, is responsible for taking care of the household, and engages in various kinds of homecraft. Modern conveniences are totally lacking, social activities and voluntary or professional social work non-existent. Entertainment is confined to very special occasions, such as betrothals, weddings, christenings, namedays, funerals, church services, public festivals in honor of the local patron-saint, and the annual holidays, the most important of which is Easter, so dear to the Greek soul with its symbolism of resurrection.

Recent developments have introduced certain changes into this picture. They are mainly the result of the generally changing atmosphere, faster and cheaper means of transportation, closer contact between town and village people, and government-sponsored efforts to improve the general standards of rural life. During Greece's occupation by German, Italian, Albanian, and Bulgarian troops (1942–1944), while the countryside suffered more from oppression, the towns suffered primarily from lack of food and were dependent on the black-market supplied by certain rural areas. Thus the peasants of these areas obtained unusually large amounts of money which they used to buy furniture, clothing, and the like, up to that time used exclusively in the towns. At the same time, there was greater village-to-town movement for security reasons, especially during the guerilla-warfare phase of the resistance, when entire villages were burned down and a large section of their population exterminated as reprisal measures. World War II was followed by Communist guerilla warfare which ended only in 1950 and during which about 720,000 people were evacuated from rural areas—mainly the frontier regions—to centrally located towns. Many of these people remained permanently, and those who did return to their villages had had an opportunity to get acquainted with city life and the new possibilities it offered.

Thus, the trend towards urbanization, noticeable in many countries, is particularly strong in Greece. Many village girls obtain employment in the cities and become not only economically, but socially independent. In spite of the advantages, however, it is sometimes difficult for them to adjust to the new environment.

City women present a different picture: higher education, more intensive social activities, greater opportunities for employment, more comforts and diversions are open to them. In the urban center of Athens, upper-class women lead lives patterned after the general fashion of the West, while women of the middle and lower classes enjoy modern comforts and status combined, to a varying degree, with the main traditional characteristics of Greek family life.

LEGAL STATUS

Prior to World War II, Greek women could neither vote nor be elected to public office (except that, under certain conditions they were allowed to vote in municipal and communal elections in 1930). The law of 1949, ratified by Parliament in 1951, gave women the same rights to vote in municipal and communal elections as men enjoyed. This was followed by the law of June 7, 1952 that granted women full equality of political rights with men.

Before World War II, women were also excluded from most appointive public offices, such as the magistracy, the diplomatic and military services, and the archaeological inspectorate. Following the Universal Declaration of Human Rights at Lake Success on December 19, 1952, signed by Greece on April 1, 1953, a succession of laws has assured Greek women near-equality of rights in this field. From 1954 on, women have been admitted to the bar, to juries in criminal cases (where their number, however, is limited to three as against seven men, and they cannot preside over the jury, nor are they admitted to a jury for press affairs), to the office of notary public, and they have been permitted to act as witnesses in connection with contracts and other official declarations, except wills. The law of 1955 dealing with public functions declares: "Women can exercise all public functions, except the ecclesiastic ones, and be appointed to all positions of civil servants of the State or of legal entities of Public Law, on equal terms with men." It also enables women to undertake auxiliary work in the armed forces, for the police force, the port authority, fire brigade, forestry service, and customs service.

As for personal rights, Greek women acquire property, sell or dispose of it as they please, inherit and bequeath, make and receive grants and donations, sign and execute wills and contracts, form societies and associations, work as employees or in their own enterprises, sue, defend and testify in court — all on equal terms with men. There are no limitations on their rights so long as they are not yet, or are no longer, married.

Marriage brings women certain restrictions as far as family law is concerned, since, according to Greek law, the husband is the head of the family. Thus, in case of disagreement, it is the husband's will that prevails. He chooses the couple's place of residence (which in principle belongs to him), decides questions of the children's education, and can veto his wife's choice of work or profession. The wife can appeal to a court against her husband's decisions if she can prove that he exercises an "excess of power," but this is very difficult in practice.

The wife takes her husband's name and belongs to his municipality or community. However, the 1950 nationality law provides that a Greek woman who marries a foreigner can keep her nationality if she so desires. The same right is given to a foreign woman who marries a Greek.

Only the father has authority over minor children. The mother exercises it in his name only if, and as long as, he is absent or unable to exercise it himself. Should the father die, the mother becomes the children's guardian.

Until 1955, a woman could become guardian of only her own children or grandchildren. One of the main changes introduced by the law of 1955, already referred to, was to allow women to become guardians of any minors, on equal terms with men. The same law allowed women to act as witnesses at the drafting of wills.

An illegitimate child has legal ties only to his mother and her family, unless he is recognized, voluntarily or judicially, by the father, and he bears her name. But even in this case, the mother has no "paternal" or "maternal" authority over her child, only guardianship, which must be granted her by a court.

In principle, marriage introduces no changes in the wife's rights over her own property unless she willingly adopts the "dowry" system, which gives the husband, for the duration of the marriage, full rights to administer, and full use of the income of, the property of his wife. It reverts to her, should the marriage be dissolved. This system is generally practiced in Greece, although the new Civil Code of 1945 provides that, in the absence of other stipulations in the marriage contract, the assets of each spouse continue to constitute his or her own separate property. Both spouses inherit from each other on equal terms.

From the fiscal viewpoint, men and women are equals, and taxed equally. The law of 1955 provides for joint income-tax declarations of husband and wife, whether they follow the "dowry" system or that of separate property. In the latter case, the new tax law puts the woman at a disadvantage because she must declare her financial transactions to her husband, but, on the other hand, it puts the onus of sole responsibility for the veracity of the joint declaration on the husband.

In penal law, men and women are treated equally, with the sole exception of the delay of execution granted to a pregnant woman until after delivery of her child.

The laws of civil procedure are also the same for both sexes, with one exception: a woman is not liable, as a man is, to imprisonment for debt, unless she is engaged professionally in a business enterprise.

The system of retirement pensions is, in principle, the same for men and women, as far as percentages received for the number of years of service are concerned. However, there are certain differences, such as the following: women usually are entitled to retirement a few years earlier than men; widows are usually entitled to a certain percentage of their husband's pension as long as they do not remarry, while widowers are not entitled to any pension deriving from their wives' work. As to the children, they are always entitled to a pension deriving from their father, but from their mother only if their father is dead or unable to work. Another striking difference is that children's pensions (whether deriving from father or mother) are paid to boys only until they reach majority—unless they are unfit for any work, in which case they continue to receive it—while pensions are paid to girls indefinitely, as long as they do not marry.

EDUCATION

To a certain degree, the education of women in Greece follows the standards of general education throughout the country. Standards, which, after the brilliant periods of antiquity and Byzantium, fell to a low degree during the Ottoman occupation, with the exception of ·the famous Greek schools of Constantinople. Thus education became one of the first necessities of the young Greek state of 1830.

The permanent lack of sufficient public funds and a succession of wars and other catastrophes, which often necessitated the use of school buildings for purposes other than educational ones (as hospitals, refugee shelters) and sometimes resulted in their destruction by the occupants, and which left some regions without sufficient teachers, helped to retard general public education. Private schools, on the other hand, flourished, but they were expensive and available only in large cities for the most part. It was only in 1964 that education became free on all levels. This general situation was particularly detrimental to women.

The first royal decree pertaining to education (1834) introduced elementary public instruction for girls, although all degrees of instruction were provided for boys. Soon, however, private initiative as well as the state realized that education for girls was also important, and measures were taken to correct the situation. Although elementary education (six years until 1964 and eight since then) is obligatory for both boys and girls, women in the past have taken less advantage of existing educational opportunities than men, with resulting higher illiteracy among them. This situation was correlated with several factors. Women did not, as a rule, have to earn their livelihood; they had fewer opportunities to obtain paid positions with an educational background as a prerequisite; girls of the lower classes and of peasant families were required more often than boys to stay at home and help in the household or fields. Rural and even city families of very low income showed no interest in the education of their girls, although willing to make sacrifices for the education—even up to a university degree—of at least one of their sons, because this enhanced the prestige of the entire family. Until recently, greater emphasis was placed on the enforcement of the compulsory elementary education of boys than of girls, particularly in rural areas. Public secondary schools usually are located in a town, and it is more difficult for girls than for boys from rural areas to attend them since their living in town would cost the family money and would run counter to the traditional custom of keeping young girls at home. Boarding schools are not favored by Greek parents, and to let a girl live alone away from home would be regarded as morally reprehensible.

Finally, girls are not subject, as are boys, to military conscription, and hence miss the education that many illiterate boys gain during their period in the service.

All of these obstacles notwithstanding, progress has been made, especially since World War II. It is shown statistically in the steady increase of literacy among both men and women (see Table 1).

TABLE 1—Percentage of Illiterates Aged 10 Years and Over, 1907–1960.

Year	Total	Men	Women
1907	61	40	80
1920	52	34	70
1928	42	24	59
1951	24	11	35
1960	18	8	27

By the 1960–61 school year, the number of girls in elementary schools almost equalled that of boys (434,682 girls against 473,094 boys). In secondary schools, the discrepancy was somewhat greater (123,320 girls against 168,209 boys), while in higher education the girls lagged behind even more (11,990 girl students against 26,879 boys). In the faculties of philosophy, which train teachers, the number of girl students (2,057) was considerably greater than that of men students (788), as it was in the Schools of Architecture (303 girls, 299 boys). This reflects the traditional feeling that teaching is the most suitable profession for women.

Very few girls, if any, receive training in the practical technical schools, such as those for electricians, plumbers, carpenters, welders, shoemakers, and automobile mechanics. And, as one might expect, girls are almost the only pupils in schools for dressmaking, millinery, embroidery, lacemaking, home economics, cooking, and nursing. Thus, while boys are primarily trained in "masculine" trades, girls receive training in what are traditionally considered "feminine" occupations. This is clearly shown in Table 2.

**TABLE 2—Number of Men and Women Students
in Technical Schools, 1961–62**

Type of School	Men	Women
Agricultural	1,760	454
Technical	41,623	1,966
Commercial	3,162	954
Home Economics	—	2,560
Merchant Marine Officers	254	—
Personal Services	668	1,766
Religious	1,128	—
Arts	2,141	3,618

A new and important factor in rural education has been introduced by the establishment of numerous Children's Homes, with the help of the Queen's Fund. In these institutions, both boys and girls receive post-elementary education and are trained in various practical skills. The opportunities thus made available are especially valuable for girls who can receive training without having to leave their homes or villages.

SEX MORES

Sex mores in Greece are characterized by the double standard: men's premarital and extramarital sex experiences are regarded lightly, while the same behavior on the part of women is considered the gravest offense. In fact, the "honor" of the family very largely depends on the "honor" —that is, the sexual modesty—of its women. In the larger urban communities with the greater anonymity offered, there is a certain relaxation of these traditional principles. Among both the cosmopolitan upper class and the poor lower ones, which are less tradition-bound as a result of the demoralizing poverty and promiscuity occasioned by overcrowded living quarters, violent reaction to unsanctioned female sex activity is infrequent. But, even where tolerated, such behavior is socially condemned. Condemnation is strongest in the middle class which forms the bulk of the urban population and often leads to violent action on the part of the husband, father, or brothers of the offending woman. In village populations, in order to restore the "honor" of the family, the men feel themselves morally obliged to kill the offending woman. Although such extreme measures are strongly condemned by many, "crimes of honor" are still frequent, and the ensuing court procedures usually lead to rather lenient verdicts.

Even those who disapprove of such violence consider chastity one of the main female virtues. Consequently, loss of virginity not only makes it most difficult for a girl to marry, but, if discovered by the bridegroom during the wedding night, is recognized by the courts as grounds for divorce.

The average man veers easily from extreme respect for the virgin and, generally, the "honest" woman, to utter disrespect and impertinence toward the woman of easy virtue. This is one of the reasons why friendship between men and women has been very rare in Greece. Only very recently has this situation begun to change among the young generation, mainly as a result of the increase in the number of young women either studying or working professionally with men. However, all the limitations imposed upon women by the prevailing sex mores do not prevent them from being charming, gay, and chic.

Adultery, although met with much greater social tolerance if committed by the husband, is legally grounds for divorce for both spouses.

Once a man and woman are sentenced for having committed adultery with each other they cannot marry each other, even if their former marriage ties are dissolved.

Social disapproval of extramarital intercourse and social interest in the protection of the family are shown by the stigma attached to unmarried mothers and to children born out of wedlock. Although the law protects both to a certain extent, the child suffers from economic disadvantages compared to the legitimate children of the father.

Prostitution has been a part of Greek life since antiquity, as one would expect of a country jealously guarding its women's chastity and engaged in a far-flung sea trade, with practically every town a port-city. Up to the end of World War I, prostitution was strictly supervised by the police and those practising it were confined to licensed brothels. A law of 1922 provided for the gradual closing of the houses of prostitution, but during World War II and the agitated years that followed, the number of prostitutes again increased. The laws of 1955 and 1960 definitely outlawed brothels, but prostitutes, now living in their own private quarters, are still licenced, registered with the police, and obliged to undergo periodical medical examinations. However, the law and the courts do their best to wipe out procuring.

Homosexuality is not illegal, but is socially frowned upon. It is relatively limited and largely confined to men.

THE MARRIAGE PATTERN

The prevailing mode of marriage in Greece used to be the *synoikesion*, or marriage arranged by a relative or friend who would propose the match to the families of the boy and the girl, describing their assets in exaggerated terms. Although the increasing opportunities for social contact between men and women are causing arranged marriages gradually to lose ground, these are still frequent, and it would seem that they do not result in more unhappy or unstable unions than the hastily contracted "love marriages."

Where marriages are not arranged, the rule is that the man proposes to the woman. The most generally followed form is for the man's father or mother, or, if he is old enough and has a social position of his own, the man himself, to ask for the hand of the girl from her father or from the family. In most cases, the girl is aware of the proposal and has already given it her encouragement. If the woman is old enough and independent, the proposal is made to her directly. In the younger age group, the boy often proposes to the girl directly, and they tell their parents afterwards.

Whatever the form of the proposal, and whether the marriage is arranged or not, the father's consent is necessary if the future spouses are under age, and even if they are of age, propriety demands that it be obtained.

The personally and officially declared consent of the young man and the girl themselves is also a legal requirement. The minimum legal age for marriage is fourteen for girls and eighteen for boys.

When a couple intends to wed, they must first publicly announce their plans in the church of the village, or in two local city newspapers, so that anyone knowing of an impediment to the marriage may come forward.

The wedding itself is a typically Greek ceremony. Whether rich or poor, in the city or the village, with or without accompanying entertainment, the main ritual is the same religious ceremony. Since there is no separation between Church and State in Greece, and no possibility of contracting civil marriage, the couple must satisfy the Church as to the absence of any impediment to the marriage and be married at church. Subsequently, the marriage must be entered at the Public Registry. In Greek Orthodox canon law there are many restrictions on marriage: certain relatives cannot marry each other, and no one is allowed to marry more than three times. If a Christian and a non-Christian wish to marry, one of them must first convert to the religion of the other. This restriction does not apply to Christians of various denominations, because a common religious bond exists between them. Since about 90 per cent of all Greeks belong to the Greek Orthodox Church, there is rarely a problem. However, if a member of the Greek Orthodox Church marries a Roman Catholic or a Protestant, two wedding ceremonies are held, one in each church.

If a husband or wife wishes a divorce, he or she has to apply to the Church. The Church tries to effect a reconciliation, but if this fails, the case comes before the Civil Courts which are only competent to grant civil divorce to either spouse on one of the following grounds: adultery, bigamy, attempt on the life of the other spouse, desertion for a minimum of two years, incompatibility, mental illness for a minimum of four years, leprosy, sexual impotence at the time of the wedding and for at least three years thereafter, and officially declared disappearance. Following the civil divorce, the Greek Orthodox Church also grants its religious divorce. If Catholics obtain a civil divorce, their Church continues to consider them married. Socially, divorce is frowned upon, especially in traditional circles. Statistically, the frequency of divorces is low. In 1959, there were in Greece 74,213 marriages and 2,281 divorces. In 1961 there were in all Greece 3,665,893 married, and 45,815 divorced persons.

The question of the dowry is considered important. By custom, the bride brings her husband a dowry when she marries. This usually consists of household articles, land, shares, houses, cattle, and the like. Since, according to Greek law, the husband is the head of the family and bears its financial burdens, the dowry is considered a contribution of the bride to the new household.

To provide a dowry for each daughter is a legal obligation of parents.

The dowry must be commensurate with their wealth, the number of their children, and their social position, as well as that of the daughter's fiance. The girl's parents are exempted from this obligation only if they are destitute, or if the daughter has enough personal wealth to supply her own dowry, or if she marries for the second or third time and has received a dowry at the time of her first marriage, or if she marries without the legally required parental approval (being underage), or if she has committed any act that would entitle them to disinherit her.

The dowry is either handed over to the husband in full, or the wife retains title to it and the husband is given the right of administration and usufruct. Real estate as dowry is always given in usufruct only. The dowry is returned to the wife should the marriage be dissolved.

The dowry system has many opponents in Greece. It is considered incongruous with modern life, when women work and help to support the family. Besides, among the poor lack of a dowry is often the reason for girls not being able to marry, while girls of wealthy families often have the feeling that their dowry buys them husbands. More and more young couples disregard the dowry and base their future life on other considerations, such as common work and interests. But the time is still far off when this old institution will have disappeared completely.

WOMAN'S POSITION IN THE FAMILY

During the traditional wedding ceremony, the Church recommends to the bride to obey and even to "fear" her husband, who is considered as the wife's "head," just as Christ is the head of the Church. But this is immediately tempered by the corresponding recommendation to the husband "to love his wife like his own body," just as Christ loved the Church.

In practice, the woman is traditionally considered to be "queen of the home" and, in all classes of society, it is her responsibility to keep house and to bring up the children. Although the social position of a family is usually determined by that of the husband, it is widely held that a family is mainly what the wife makes of it.

This influential position of the women in the Greek family is not always apparent. Especially in the villages, where the woman bears a particularly heavy burden, she has no apparent or recognized prestige, nor does she seek it for herself. She is often shy, rarely participates in the discussion of general issues, which, in fact, she is not sufficiently educated to understand, practically never goes to a café, which is the usual place for social and political gatherings in the village. She can be seen on foot following her husband who is mounted on a donkey, or serving the men of her family at table and eating by herself afterwards. Yet, apart from the fact that such customs are on their way out, they indicate a desire to serve dear ones, rather than a status of enslavement. In fact, the village woman, who takes all this for granted, is a curious mixture of humility and dignity and is certainly far from considering herself an oppressed slave. On the contrary, she often greatly influences the men of her family in a quiet, unobtrusive way.

In the average urban family, the woman's position is more or less the same as in most Western European countries. Within the traditional limits of personal dignity and family honor, city women are becoming more and more emancipated. Yet in many families, the birth of a boy child is considered a great piece of good fortune while that of a girl is met with less enthusiasm. This is related to the financial obligation to provide the girl with a dowry, to the fact that formerly, and to a large extent to this day, women contributed nothing or little to the family's income, that they do not carry on the family name, and that the girl's conduct could, at any moment, bring disgrace to the family honor. These considerations are, to some extent, counterbalanced, particularly in the eyes of the mother, by the general expectation that a boy, when marrying, will be estranged from his home, while a girl will in all circumstances remain close to her parents.

In a country in which the men are accustomed to be proud of their manhood and ready to proclaim and assert their superiority over women, it is almost paradoxical that women nevertheless play such an important role in the family and are, generally, so cherished and loved by all of its male members. The explanation seems to lie in the long centuries of Turkish rule during which even the uneducated women were the main transmitters of culture, and in the women's close attachment to their children, for whom they are the greatest source of love, influence, and emotional security. The typical Greek woman constantly displays an attitude of tenderness, spontaneous self-denial, and self-sacrifice for her family, particularly for her children. Her husband and children are her life and her happiness. Her love is well understood and reciprocated in most cases. The two most spontaneous exclamations of any Greek in trouble, pain, or great joy, are "My mother!" and "My Virgin!"—showing a preoccupation with both the earthly and spiritual aspects of motherhood.

Another, contradictory feature of women's position in the family is a result of the old feeling that she is a feeble creature, unable to face life alone, who must be protected by the men of her family. This is why parents are not considered to have fully done their duty to their daughters if they have not managed to "establish" them, that is, marry them suitably. This is why state pensions are given to daughters of a pensioner as long as the girls are unmarried, and why one often meets examples of traditional families in which the sons, or at least one of them, do not marry until their sisters are safely married, so that they can be on hand to protect them. As the gainful employment of women becomes more common and they achieve greater economic independence, the male members of the family feel more relieved of responsibility for them. There are also touching examples of sisters who gladly sacrifice their dowry, their youth, and hopes of building a family of their own, in order to enable a talented brother to get a higher education or to bring up younger brothers and sisters after the parents' death.

The Home Routine

Good housekeeping has always been considered a necessity and the housewife's responsibility. It consists of maintaining perfectly clean and tidy living quarters, preparation of meals, upbringing of children, and fulfilling the family's social obligations according to its intellectual and professional interests and its financial resources—the latter constituting the man's responsibility for the most part.

Home routine in the country is more or less uniform and dull. Hard work is the rule, entertainment the exception. The first rule of living is early to bed, early to rise—and to work. The lack of electricity in most small villages (the vast electrification program is beginning to reach them only now), the absence of public evening entertainment or amusements, and the need to walk or ride an hour or more daily to the fields induces the peasants to start their day at sunrise and finish it at sundown.

The women usually get up before the men to prepare the family's frugal breakfast and the equally frugal noon meal which the men take to the fields. Then, either the men alone, or in certain seasons, both men and women, go to the fields. (The pattern is somewhat different in sailing or fishing villages, but the main lines of life are the same.) The wife usually stays at home to clean and tidy the living quarters; look after the youngsters and send them to school; tend the goats and poultry; cultivate the kitchen garden; cook (using primarily the family's own produce); make cheese and yogurt; and, above all, knead and bake bread, truly the staff of life for the Greek peasant. Then she washes, mends, irons, and, from time to time, whitewashes the house. Often, she has to fetch water from the village well or fountain, where there is usually an opportunity to gossip with the other local women. She also collects wild herbs, greatly appreciated as salads or seasonings, and wood for cooking and heating. When all this is done, she busies herself with various handcrafts (not usually intended for sale), such as weaving, including heavy woolen blankets as well as cotton and silk, according to the region and the family's means; and sewing, embroidery, or knitting, and her work often possesses aesthetic merit. The majority of the articles of a girl's dowry, and the finest, are made by herself with the help of the women of her family. At the wedding festivities, an important and picturesque ceremony is the exhibition of these articles (*proikia*) and their transportation to the bridegroom's house.

When the season requires it, the farmers work very hard at the agricultural chores and so do the women. In the slack seasons, the men spend much of their time in cafés where, for a pittance, they have an opportunity to discuss politics, read the newspapers, play games, and contract business.

The village women's work is never finished. Although the villagers in many areas form the poorest element in the population, they usually have many children. For peasant families, children are an economic asset, since they serve in place of hired hands in working the small family farm. In addition, the high birthrate is the result of social, ethical, and religious attitudes, all of which militate against birth control. The raising of her many children, with few modern conveniences, keeps the country woman fully occupied and generally exhausted.

In the cities, the home routine follows the same general lines, but is easier and more pleasant. The average middle- and upper-class families still employ domestic help, although this is gradually becoming more difficult to obtain. Women who used to work as servants now prefer to take other jobs, mainly in factories, where they earn more and enjoy greater personal freedom.

The use of modern appliances is growing, particularly in the large cities, but most middle-class homes still have only a few of them, such as a refrigerator and electric stove.

The urban housewife usually gets up in time to prepare her family's breakfast, or to share it with them if it is prepared by a servant. She then looks after the children, sends them to school or to work and, if she herself is employed, hurries off to her own job. If she does not hold a position outside the home, she stays in and does the housework. Food purchases may be made by the husband, but usually are made by the wife, and it is she, of course, who is responsible for preparation of the meals. Usually, she has not studied dietetics but knows how to cook tasty meals.

Very few husbands help with housework, and even fewer like to be seen doing it, for this is generally considered to detract from the dignity of both spouses and to be unsuitable for a man. However, household repair jobs, such as those involving electricity, plumbing, carpentry, etcetera, are usually the husband's responsibility. But in this area, too, a change is noticeable in the young generation, with husbands lending a hand at home to wives who are themselves engaged in outside work. The situation becomes difficult when a working woman has small children and must try to hold down what amounts to two full-time jobs.

Most urban families are fond of entertainment, much of which takes the form of parties given at home. Television does not exist as yet, but a radio and phonograph are usually the first appliances a family purchases.

The most popular entertainment is the cinema—not very expensive in Greece—followed by the theater, concerts, card-playing, meals at restaurants, and excursions. Spectator sports, hiking, and bathing are also popular.

THE SOCIAL POSITION

The social position of a woman is, as a rule, determined by that of her father and, if she is married, by that of her husband. In recent years, the number of women who have received recognition for their own professional work has increased with the result that more women are achieving social position independently of their menfolk.

As long as gainful employment for women was exceptional and men were the only breadwinners, women were considered social and economic dependents, despite any large personal patrimony or dowry they might have had. This is still the case in the villages, where women engaged in agricultural work have no cash income of their own, nor any social or economic position distinct from the family, traditionally represented by the men. Income from selling handcraft work in semi-rural areas is, as a rule, too small to give them any economic independence. Moreover, in rural and semi-rural areas and among the lower urban class, women work outside the home only if serious economic circumstances force them to, never because of an interest in the job, for their work is mostly of the most menial type and adds nothing to their social status. Naturally, women wish to be freed from such work by a good match, that is, by marrying someone who will enable them to stay at home and enjoy a better life and more prestige. Most lower-class men consider it a matter of personal prestige to be able to keep their wives at home. The ambition of many of these women, which has earned them the gratitude and respect of their menfolk, is to enable the talented young men in their families to advance themselves through education and become reputable scientists, civil servants, or politicians. This usually requires not only hard work but the strictest budgeting and much self-sacrifice on the part of the mother.

Among the middle and upper classes in the cities, many women make use of their improved circumstances by doing volunteer welfare and social work. The two World Wars, and especially World War II, with the shortage of man-power and, later, the hardships, famines, destruction of property, currency devaluation, and general economic unrest, made it necessary for women to engage in all types of administrative and other gainful employment. Today, paid occupations seem more natural for women and secure them the same social positions as those occupied by men. Above all, it has brought them economic independence with all its social consequences.

WOMEN'S OCCUPATIONS

"Housewife" is the official designation appearing on identity cards, documents, contract forms, and so on of a woman without a definite profession. In 1961, 66.49 per cent of all Greek women aged 10 years and over were thus classified. A partial explanation of this high percentage is the inclusion of village women in this category, although they share most agricultural tasks with the men.

Peasant women leaving the village to seek work in towns usually become servants, chambermaids, laundresses, or factory workers, chiefly in the textile and tobacco industries. Recently, they have tended to take up nursing, dressmaking, hairdressing, or typing, and many of them act as midwives. Very few village women go on to higher education, but when they do, it is usually to become teachers.

In the cities, there is a greater variety of occupations for women outside the home. In small towns, most women who rise above the status of servants, industrial workers, shop employees, or untrained nurses, are teachers, social and welfare workers and, occasionally, low-grade civil servants, bank employees, or, more rarely, dentists or physicians (chiefly pediatricians). In the large cities, and particularly in the Athens-Piraeus and Salonica areas, women are able to obtain more interesting employment with better remuneration.

The total civilian labor force, that is, the economically active population, constitutes 72.22 per cent of the men, and 21.37 per cent of the women aged 10 years and over. Within the economically active population, women represent 12 per cent of the employers; 25 per cent of the self-employed workers; 25 per cent of the salary and wage earners; and 65 per cent of the unpaid family workers. The first two categories consist mostly of women in the professional, artistic, scientific, or business fields. Most of the professional women are teachers. In 1954, there were 346 women lawyers, against 9,233 men, and 19 women public notaries.

In public service, women's salaries are equal to that of men. But women encounter much greater difficulties than men in trying to obtain high positions or to advance in their work, due primarily to their being newcomers in the field and to the still existing prejudice against the value of their work.

A few women are lecturers at the universities and colleges; some were recently admitted to the magistracy; and there are also a very few directors of ministerial services.

In 1956 26 per cent of the civil service employees were women. In the telephone and telegraph services their number was 20 per cent; in the electrical works, 4 per cent; in banks, 20 per cent.

In private enterprise, in 1960, the percentage of women employees varied greatly, from 63 per cent in the tobacco industry to 1 per cent in transport and communications. The percentage of women is high in the medical and public health services (60 per cent), in the textile industry (54 per cent), in education, religion, fine arts and science (48 per cent), in the service occupations (44 per cent), in the rubber and clothing industries (43 per cent), in farming, cattle breeding, fishing, logging, and the paper industry (41 per cent). Their average in all factories and industries is 40 per cent. It is remarkable that in 1960 no less than 14 per cent of those working in mines and quarries were women. Their percentage is low among administrative and managerial personnel (9 per cent) and commercial workers (4 per cent).

Greece has not yet signed the International Labor Organization's Convention providing equal wages to men and women for equal work. However, it is hoped that this will be achieved eventually, because Greece is linked to the European economic community whose Treaty of Rome, 1957, provides such equality. The General Federation of Greek Workers, composed mostly of men, has already declared itself in favor of the equality of salaries.

WOMEN IN POLITICS

Following the acquisition of full political rights by women, all political parties have organized women's sections, whose role and activities, however, are generally limited. So far, only one woman has become a cabinet member (Minister of Welfare). Out of 300 members of Parliament, elected in 1958, only four were women; in the 1961 elections, only two women were returned, while in both the 1963 and 1964 elections only one woman was returned. Women vote conscientiously, but show a lack of enthusiasm for becoming actively involved in politics, and the leading political parties are reluctant to include women candidates on their electoral lists. In local administration women are more active. In the first post-war municipal and communal elections of 1951, 127 women were elected as either ordinary or deputy councilors in the municipalities and communities of the country. In the 1959 elections, 215 women were elected as ordinary, and 140 as deputy councilors. One or two women were elected as municipal council presidents. In addition, several women are members of the administrative committees of various communal or municipal institutions (hospitals, foundling homes).

Three women have been appointed by the government as members of the Greek delegation to the Commission on the Status of Women and the General Assembly of the United Nations. Yet none has succeeded in passing the competitive entrance examination for the Diplomatic Service.

WOMEN'S ORGANIZATIONS

Real leadership is exercised by women in feminine and feministic organizations. The first women to raise the question of women's franchise (in 1912) were Kalliope Parren, President of the Greek Women's Lyceum Club, and Mrs. Avra Theodoropoulos, who in 1920 founded and was for more than 40 years President of the League for Women's Rights. Of the other women's organizations active today, the most important are the National Council of Greek Women, the YWCA, the League of University Women, the Association of Intellectual Women, and the Federation of Women's Clubs. Greek women also occupy important positions in various international organizations comprised of women and/or dedicated to advancing women's rights.

Modern Greek women have always shown leadership in social welfare. In the beginning, philanthropy was unorganized. Every wealthy or well-to-do family had its poor dependents, beginning with relatives, neighbors, former servants, invalids, and elderly people of the community. It was soon felt that this type of charity was insufficient. A cholera epidemic in 1855 gave the impetus to concerted action. Under the leadership of Queen Amalia, a group of women set up the Amaleion Orphanage for Girls. After each war, new orphanages were organized by Greek women: the National War Orphanage (Kallithea) in 1912; the "Ethniki Steghi" (Athens) in 1922; the Asylum for Orphan Girls (Salonica); the Children's Asylum (Volos); two homes for children war victims by the National Council of Greek Women, and others.

In addition, women took care of the poor in general. In 1872, the Ladies' Society of the Friends of the Poor was founded. Women also founded institutions for the aged, the asylum for incurables, and other similar charity institutions in Athens, Crete, Drama, Jannina, Kavalla, Mytilene, Nafpaktos, Patras, Salonica, Serres, Servia, and Xanthi.

Women's interest in child welfare and youth movements resulted in the creation of innumerable institutions such as the first kindergarten (1913), the Benakeion Children's Asylum (Kifissia); the Children's Nest (Holarghos); the day-nurseries and kindergartens of the National Children's Wardrobe (Athens); the Friends of the Pupil (Athens); the Metera (Mother) in Athens for assistance to unmarried mothers and illegitimate children; the first canteens for poor students (which later became a combined university-state project); the first summer camps. They initiated the first movement for the establishment of Juvenile Courts and the semi- or non-governmental care of juvenile delinquents. The Patriotic League of Greek Women, created in 1914 by Queen Sophia, became in 1922 the Patriotic Foundation of Social Welfare and Care, which, although an independent agency, has worked since 1928 as the official state institution for child and maternal welfare, with nearly 100 branches throughout the country. In the Greek Red Cross most of the volunteers are women.

Women worked heroically in helping the 1,500,000 Greek refugees from Asia Minor who had to be absorbed in 1922 by a nation of five million, and in aiding the victims of earthquakes and floods. What they did during World War II defies summarization in a few sentences.

The Civil War of 1947–1950 demanded new sacrifices of Greek women. They responded nobly, organizing Greek Care, The Friends of the Village, The Friends of the Army, and The Friends of the Police. The abduction of Greek children during this period and their transportation to countries behind the Iron Curtain required quick action. Upon the initiative of Queen Frederica the ladies of the Fund for Help to Northern Provinces (now called The Royal Fund), established fifty-two children's towns which, with the assistance of state and other organizations, and with funds raised throughout Greece, sheltered thousands of children aged from six to fourteen until they could be sent back home, after 1949–1950.

The same eagerness to help was expressed in sociomedical services. In 1884, the big hospital Evanghelismos, in Athens, and its school for hospital nurses was founded by Queen Olga. In recent years, women have set up and led societies for the Protection of Crippled Children, for the Blind, and others.

Social workers in the professional sense are of very recent vintage. The first school for their training was founded by the YWCA of Greece, in Kifissia, a suburb of Athens, in 1948. Since then, more than two hundred girls graduated and went to work in various provinces and villages. Later, other schools for social workers were founded under various auspices.

Volunteer work by women is tending to diminish among the younger generation, as a result of their wider employment in paid positions, and of the increase in the number of professional social workers. Nevertheless, private social and welfare work is still largely responsible for much that is done in Greece in this field.

Women play a leading part in private education. As early as 1872, a Workshop for Poor Women was set up by the Ladies Association for the Training of Women, followed by several other craft schools, also organized by women, such as the Greek Royal Schools of Handcraft, the Home of the Girl, the Handwork Section of the National Council of Greek Women, and so on. Other women's associations founded professional schools for girls and women, such as the school of the Union of Greek Women for Professional Housekeeping (1897), the Greek Home (1938), the Evening Secondary Commercial School for Girls (founded in 1925 by the League for Women's Rights), several schools for illiterate women set up by the Greek Women's Lyceum Club, the National Council of Greek Women, the League for Women's Rights, and others. Efforts are made also to assist girl students and working girls in special homes. Very extensive activity in the educational and social life is carried out by the Greek YWCA. Finally, the Greek Women's Lyceum Club has a wide program for the preservation of Greek costumes and dances.

WOMEN AS CULTURAL TRANSMITTERS

Women are undeniably the chief carriers of the special modern Greek culture with its three basic factors: the Greek-Orthodox religious feeling, national consciousness, and family tradition. They assumed this role during the centuries of Turkish domination when, together with the Church, they dedicated themselves to the great twofold ideal of preserving their religion and their national traditions.

The Greek Orthodox priests in that period conducted secret night schools, in which they implanted into the children the spirit of Greek independence. Side by side with the clergy, Greek women were the mainstay of Greek-Christian culture. During four centuries, and particularly toward the end of the eighteenth century and the beginning of the nineteenth, when the idea of the organized armed insurrection assumed concrete shape, women gave striking examples of courage. They participated in many battles, preferring to commit suicide rather than be captured or raped by the enemy. They were among the members of the Philiki Etaireia (Friends' Society), the secret movement that prepared the Greek War of Independence (1821–1828). In all the local uprisings that preceded the war, as well as during the war itself, women fought side by side with their men. As early as 1792, in Souli, a mountain village in Epirus, a corps of 400 women, under the woman captain Moscho Tzavella, fought regularly against the Turks, together with the men's corps. In Mani, a locality of the Peloponnesus, 2,000 women soldiers fought alongside of 5,000 men in the Battle of Mistra in 1770. Lascarina Bouboulina (1771–1825) from Hydra and Spetses Islands had her own ships and led them in several battles; Manto Mavroghenous (1796–1840), from the Island of Mykonos, started the insurrection on that island and fought, at the head of her own army corps, in various parts of Greece; Domna Visvitzi (1784–1850), from Ainos, fought as captain of her own ship; Constantina Zaharia fought mainly in the years 1821–1826; Assimo Goura distinguished herself at the siege of the Athens Acropolis in 1826–1827; Charikleia Daskalaki fought in Arkadi, Crete, during the Cretan insurrection of 1866. The classical example of heroic self-sacrifice is the "Dance of Zalonghon," where, on December 16, 1803, a group of sixty women, cut off from the others and closely followed by Ottoman soldiers, chose death rather than captivity. They performed a traditional Greek file dance on the edge of the Zalonghon precipice and at each round, one of them threw down her child and followed him with the cry, "Death before slavery!" Their example inspired many other women elsewhere, and was reechoed in many heroic deeds performed by Greek women in World War II. Such heroism and sacrifice are clearly a fruit of the deepest cultural conditioning that made these women not only the comrades-in-arms of their fighting men but also the mothers of heroes.

This tradition did not cease with the formation of the independent Greek state in 1829. The local insurrections continued. The Ionian Islands were returned to Greece in 1863; Thessaly and part of Epirus, in 1881; some of the Aegean Islands and Macedonia, in 1912–1913; the Dodecanese Islands after World War II. In all the struggles leading to the integration of these parts of Greece, the sole basis of the Greek claim to them, admitted by other countries, was the "ethnic" origin and feeling of their inhabitants, which was determined by their language and their Greek Orthodox faith, two factors in the preservation and transmission of which women played crucial roles.

The idea that women, as wives and mothers, are, in particular, the transmitters of Christian-Greek culture and constitute a more tradition-bound element in Greek life than do the men, is corroborated by observations in the field of emigration. In emigration, which has always been of the greatest importance for Greece, because of its poverty and the Greek tradition of travel and sea-trade, men predominate. In 1963, 61,966 men and 38,106 women emigrated. The differential is partly due to the fact that the requirements and skills necessary to emigrate are found mostly among men, but it is believed that it is also due to the greater reluctance of the women to be uprooted from their home and country. Those women who do emigrate often have difficulties with the language of their new country and when emigrating with their families sometimes hamper the men in integrating rapidly into their new cultural environment. This "braking" function of the women is usually considered a good thing by the male emigrants, for although the men love traveling and easily acquire a cosmopolitan attitude they eventually return to their own tradition and culture, particularly in familial and religious matters. And, knowing that the most powerful transmitters of their culture are women, they very often return to marry a girl from home, or, if this is not possible, an emigrant Greek girl in order to secure, through her, a basically Greek home culture for themselves and their children.

Future Outlook

The education of women should continue to spread at the high school, technical, and professional training levels. But it is not to be expected that women will soon reach full equality with men, either in absolute numbers or in advancement and working opportunities.

Social evolution progresses rapidly. The urbanization and industrialization of the country will bring women closer to full emancipation and to economic independence. The loosening of family ties will continue as the family gradually is reduced to smaller units comprising merely the closest relatives. Sexual mores will ease, but, at least in the near future, the outstanding characteristics of Greek women, even of the modern working women, will remain those of the good wife and mother, with charm tempered by restraint. For the rest, women, like men, will follow the general trends of the life of Western Europe.

Italy

By Tullio Tentori

THE TRADITIONAL STATUS

*T*he *status of Italian women* still suffers from the traditional concept of feminine submission to men. The situation of course varied with the period and region, and at times, within certain contexts, it was possible for women to gain control, in fact, if not in theory. But even today, a large part of the population, both male and female, have not yet accepted the cultural principles on which the new constitutional laws are based, nor have these new laws yet been carried out as decreed by the Italian Constitution of 1948. Hardly any distinction is made between femininity and submission, sacrifice, and economic disability. This is not a subjective statement, but one that can be documented easily by research, polls, and interviews.

Women have been excluded from holding public offices or taking on political responsibilities. They have been limited economically: although

---

Translated from the Italian by Larissa Bonfante Warren.

women could possess and transmit wealth, they could not accumulate it by earning money. They have been limited in individual competition: their right to education, for example, has been neglected or denied. They have been limited socially, especially in their contacts with people outside their own homes or outside close family ties. They have been urged to follow only those values concerned with domestic virtues. All this has made women not only incapable of competing with men, but unwilling to do so. Furthermore, man idealized woman and declared her to be the ruler of the household. Woman accepted the homage and the title, and took· as the model for her life the ideal of *domum mansit, lanam fecit* ("she stayed at home and made wool"), which had been assigned to her by man. Failing to see the hypocrisy of this ideal image, she willingly confined herself behind the walls of domesticity, circumscribing her whole world and all her interests, working and sacrificing to please the men in her life. Only occasionally was she able to make certain demands, and at times she even succeeded in dominating her master, on the psychological plane in particular.

Roman law had brought the position of women, in terms of the possibilities open to them, almost to an equal level with men; but in this too the Middle Ages marked a decline. It is true that in certain situations women could assume responsibilities, as in those cases foreseen by the institution of the *mundio*, according to which a widow could—as the faithful executor of her husband's wishes—govern the household in his stead, provide for her daughters' dowries, and keep her sons at her side. But it was only under extraordinary conditions that a woman freed herself from her dependent state and assumed a role as a leader in the internal and external affairs of the family, and for the most part these situations occurred only within the ruling class. Within this upper class the woman's position was strictly controlled, because the will of the individual had to be subordinated to the superior goal of the family's honor and power. Moreover, the man's important public role, his habit of authority and command, and the harshness of the wars between factions all served to strengthen his position at the same time that the woman's was debased by the restrictions and emptiness of her social role. Nevertheless, there did arise strong feminine personalities, during the medieval period and the Renaissance: Eleanor of Arborea, Giovanna la Pazza, Catherine of Siena, Rita da Cascia, Gaspara Stampa, Vittoria Colonna, Lucrezia Borgia, and others.

To be born a woman was to be condemned to serve a life sentence, the burden of which was in no way made lighter by the family. Laws and customs held a difficult existence in store for her. It is significant that moral precepts were thought necessary to remind parents of their duty, such as "Should our good Lord send you daughters instead of sons, guard yourselves as from fire lest you show your disappointment, since God does

not send children in accordance with the parents' wishes." Such warnings
bring to mind the harsh times of Alfonso d'Este, who—though a generous
ruler in other respects—forbade any celebration whatever at the birth of
his daughter Beatrice: he had wanted a son, and it was the custom to avoid
any rejoicing at the birth of a girl into a princely house. For the birth of a
female, in contrast to the appearance of a male heir, no debtors' books were
burned, no prison doors opened, no bonfires lit in the square, nor was food
and money distributed. The Renaissance might have led women to hope
they had become men's companions, their equals in heart and mind, worthy
to share that serene and perfect life which seemed to have been made
possible by the development of art, science, and philosophy; in reality, however, their condition was little changed from other times, when the Devil's
arts of reading and writing were still kept from them.

In the Italy of the nineteenth century, the middle-class woman could
only be mother, wife, daughter, or sister; in other words, her role was
in relation to the family, never to a political or economic organization. If
she left the family group, it was to enter a convent; and this was not always
by her own choice, but often because of family pressures, to gain prestige
or advantage, or out of respect for tradition. For similar reasons, the family
also reserved the right to decide on the marital state of its members,
determining whether the individual was to marry or not, and choosing his
or her marriage partner.

Marriage was definitely a family proposition, and the individual's will
had to give way to the family's economic interests and prestige. It was up
to the family to provide for those who were ready for marriage, and since
it was unthinkable that the wishes of the children could differ from those
of the parents, the latter often made plans for their children's future
without even informing them. There was not even any interest in finding
out whether the future couple was congenial. It was felt that love was a
mechanical consequence of marriage: "Love will come later," they thought
and said.

As a result of this attitude, the man's wishes and hopes were ignored
as much as those of the woman. He, however, could make up for this
later on. It was he who was to assume the formal function of head of the
family, and as such, he was allowed to take many liberties, both recognized
and tacitly assumed. He could visit his friends, and the various distractions
he could seek, including extramarital affairs, involved little risk other than
blackmail or revenge, a "crime of honor," on the part of the parents of his
mistress.

For the woman, the choice of husband was far more important because
her whole life was to take place within the home and family relationships.
She had been proclaimed ruler of the household: but in effect she was its
slave. She was not permitted to leave her realm without the protection and

control of her male subjects. A respectable middle-class woman or a member of the upper class could not even go to Mass by herself. It was among the urban poor that exceptions to this rule were found, because poverty forced them to live practically in the street. But even the street was full of neighbors with sharp eyes and tongues who effectively exercised the control of society. The limits of street and neighborhood were precisely determined and not to be overstepped. A woman's world rarely extended beyond the walls of her own home, where her interests were confined to her husband and sons on whom she depended completely. The Italian constitution of 1865 acknowledged this state of inferiority, thus confirming the Napoleonic code.

INDUSTRIALIZATION

This was the situation when industrialization began. This development was stronger in the north, and consequently affected northern women more than the women of the south. Industrialization employed women of the lower classes, thus affecting their life directly; indirectly, however, it changed the attitudes of the middle-class woman as well.

The textile industy was the first to employ women: it took male and female weavers from the country (not without a certain amount of opposition) where they had worked mostly at home, and regimented them into factories. By 1890, 12,386 women were working in the silk industry; in 1894, 15,503 women worked in the wool industry, and in 1901, 82,932 worked in the cotton industry.

Soon, other industries also took on female workers. The tobacco factories in the large cities absorbed them. Machine industries used women for marginal work such as cleaning. In Sicily, women went to work in the sulphur mines. The garment industry offered many opportunities, especially in the large cities which furnished the smaller centers with the newest fashions; it provided work, in factories and shops, for seamstresses, embroidery workers, pressers, milliners, and designers. Many sales girls were needed. Businesses and offices employed secretaries, clerks, and book-keepers. In certain areas women were hired for the first time as regular agricultural workers, especially in the rice fields of the Po Valley and the Vercellese, as well as for picking olives and for the cultivation of tobacco and hemp.

In Italy the movement for the independence and emancipation of women, encouraged by the spread of ideals which were gaining recognition in some countries of Europe and in North America, began as soon as the nineteenth-century movement for national independence had been successful in its main goals. The constitution of the new nation then called for important changes in the economic, political, and cultural organization of the country, changes that affected all institutions, whether dealing with politics or with the family. Now for the first time, the growing industry of the north offered employment for the women of the lower class, while the government, in order to fulfill its obligation to provide elementary education for everyone, was offering employment to lower-middle and middle-class women as *maestrine,* or elementary school teachers, with whose problems the Socialist Romantic novelist De Amicis sympathizes so deeply.

Women's entrance into the ranks of productive labor brought about greater changes in the urban bourgeois world than in the rural atmosphere. Peasant women were, in certain areas, well accustomed to working in the fields or as servants, and their change from agricultural to industrial work was accepted by the men without too many difficulties. Furthermore, the ruling class encouraged women going into factory work, just as it did child labor, because women could be paid lower wages, and female labor furnished an excuse for holding down the wages of the men. Such a situation did not, however, hold true for all regions; and it must also be remembered that, in the last century, industrialization took place only in certain areas. Even in the regions where women took part in farm work, it was mostly within the family property. Only in certain zones were women recruited for seasonal labor, to pick olives or work in the rice fields. Shepherds, woodsmen, fishermen, artisans, and others working outside the home were traditionally men only; the women were confined to the home just like middle-class, bourgeois women. The same thing was true of the small landholders who tried to imitate the middle-class way of life.

THE MIDDLE CLASS WOMAN

This state of affairs did not change the outlook of the middle-class woman, always ambitious to enter into a higher social class, who saw the family as an institution guaranteeing her economic security. Her home, her husband and her children absorbed all her interest. She only saw the worst aspects of the active dynamic development of the middle class. The female adjustment to the male ideal of "success" can be described as "putting up a good front for the family," and "saving money for the sake of the family," even at the cost of personal sacrifice. Often, too, says Paola Gaiotti de Biase in a searching study of Italian women, the intelligent and capable woman realized this goal by using the man's system of exploitation. The seamstress, the artisan and the maid, with their low wages, made it possible for a "lady" to make a more elegant, rich, and fashionable appearance, and to seem fortunate and happy in the eyes of her friends. The misfortune of these workers gave her no moral qualms, secure as she was in the knowledge that she had contributed to the family's wealth and prestige. The author rightly comes to the conclusion that such a woman needed these satisfactions in order to escape the painful awareness of her own uselessness, her husband's indifference, her boredom, and lack of relationship.

The new economic and technological conditions offered the middle-class woman more leisure time, but she did not use it to broaden her field of interests. Instead, the romantic ideal allowed her to escape from the limitations of her domesticity. Girls from "good families" absorbed this ideal in private schools and through more or less surreptitious reading of contemporary novels. This was a manner of dealing with the unhappy reality of having to live in a family where the highest value was propriety.

Charity Work—For a woman of social standing, only philanthropy and good works offered an acceptable activity outside of her own family. During the second half of the nineteenth century various new feminine religious orders dedicated to social work were established. Among them were the Marcelline and the Daughters of Maria Ausiliatrice, dedicated to young women's education; the Misericordine, which provides home care for the sick; the Sisters of the Good Shepherd, which helps fallen women; and the Sisters of the Poor, which assists the aged poor. The ladies of the nobility, who at the beginning of the Risorgimento in the first half of the nineteenth century, had been famous as wives and mothers of patriots, later gained fame through their good works. Princess Filangeri, for example, founded hospitals and shelters for homeless children, while other noble women dedicated themselves to other causes. Lay Catholic women organized the Pious Union of Catholic Women in 1870, and the Congregation of San Vincenzo.

Feminism—The feminist movement, important at this time in other countries, was represented in Italy by eccentric and isolated individuals. Not until 1900 was the National Council of Italian Women established as a member group of the International Council of Women, which had been founded in Washington in 1888. Among the founders of the National Council were intellectuals such as Ada Negri, and members of the nobility such as the Duchess of Aosta, Princess Letizia of Savoia, and the Countess Ruspoli Spalletti, who served as President for many years with the assistance of Dr. Teresita Sandewski Scelba, at first General Secretary and later Vice-President. Rather than deal with politics, the Council defended the role of the family according to the Italian tradition which held that the real duty of women was to bear children and educate the men. Socialist women opposed this point of view, and in 1906 founded the Lega Socialista per la Tutela degli Interessi Femminili (Socialist League for the Protection of Women's Rights), that had as its goals the improvement of professional education for women, the mitigation of the difficulties of childbirth and motherhood, and the protection of infants and children.

The first important international conference of the Council was held in Rome in 1908, and disappointed many of the delegates. Anna Kulishoff, the Socialist, commented in her party's magazine (*La Critica Sociale*, 1908) that what had been missed was "the overall declaration of the rights of women to economic and spiritual independence which necessarily depends on the question of work." Other criticisms included Angelica Balabanoff's complaint of the purely philosophical manner of dealing with the important problems of equality of wages and salaries, the economic plight of the private schools, and the inspection of women's working conditions in factories, at home, and in religious institutions.

The conference of 1908 did not even satisfy the Catholic women, who left the session when, in dealing with the problem of church and state in reference to the schools, the non-Catholic delegates approved a motion to support a completely secular school, and the introduction of an objective, impartial, comparative study of religions and their principles, goals and social consequences, into the curricula of both elementary and high schools. In July 1908, the Unione Donne Catholiche Italiane (Union of Italian Catholic Women) was organized.

In spite of all this, however, the National Council continued its work, under the leadership of Countess Spalletti and Dr. Sandewski Scelba, until 1924 when fascists took over the direction of the organization. Countess Daisy di Robillant became President. The political collaboration in which the Council now was involved lowered its prestige in the eyes of the world, and at the end of World War II it had to be reorganized according to democratic principles.

WOMEN'S VOTE

The question of women's vote was brought up in Parliament for the first time in 1873, then in 1880, 1884, 1900, and 1907 — always in vain. Finally in 1908, when the election law was being changed, the question was put to a vote: it was defeated, with 209 votes against, 48 in favor, and 6 abstaining. In 1916, the government planned to introduce a bill granting women the vote in governmental elections. In 1919, Deputy Gasparotto presented in the Chamber of Deputies a bill governing elections in which the right of women to vote was included. It was approved, with 74 in favor and 55 against, but never came up before the Senate. During the fascist period, which marked a decline in the field of women's rights, in general, their right to vote was ignored.

Only after the fall of fascism, in 1945, were women at last granted the right to vote. The first opportunity they had to exercise this right was in the municipal election of 1946, when 8,441,557 women, or 53 per cent of the total voters, took part. This represented 81 per cent of the women eligible.

The Northern regions—Piedmont, Lombardy, Emilia, and Tuscany— elected the largest number of women, two thousand, to the municipal governments.

In 1946, elections were held to form an assembly, the Constituent Assembly, to take charge of drafting the new Italian constitution. Out of a total of 556 delegates, the twenty-one women who took part contributed to the drafting of the new constitution which went into effect January 1, 1948, and which recognized many rights long denied to women. The new constitution declared that all citizens have equal dignity in society and are equal before the law, regardless of sex or race; that marriage is based on the moral and judicial equality of the spouses; that all citizens, men and women, over twenty-one have the right to vote; that citizens of either sex have equal rights to run for election to public offices; that the working woman has the same rights as working men and should earn equal wages for equal work; and that working conditions for a woman must allow her to fulfill her basic function in the family, and to protect mother and child adequately.

The principles of the constitution are being realized at the present time. Laws and regulations that do not conform to these principles are being modified, but there is still much work to be done. Many women hold important positions in the civil service and in politics (though more in the latter than in the former). In 1958, legalized prostitution was abolished.

EDUCATION

In the nineteenth century neither the men nor the women of the lower classes received any formal education, and most of them were illiterate.

The problem of education for women first came up among the middle class, probably as a result of the educational reform of 1860. The Casati law of November 18, 1859, provided for compulsory education, and stated that each municipality should have at least one school for boys and one for girls with a two-year course, starting at the age of six; teachers for the girls' school were to be women with the same qualifications as those required for men. As a result, the government and the private schools had to find and train these teachers; and it became necessary that at least part of the female population should go on to secondary schools, so the special teacher-training institutes, called first *normali* then *magistrali*, were started.

These schools were attended for the most part by girls of the middle class. Upper-class families felt that their daughters had to receive at least as good an education; boarding schools and finishing schools provided these girls with an education that had as its chief goal the imparting of "culture," and whose content conformed to the dominant point of view of woman's social role. At a later time the liberal middle- and upper-middle classes began to send their daughters to secondary schools and *licei* which had more prestige and a higher social standing than the normal schools, in addition to giving a less expensive and more liberal education than the private girls' schools.

The gradual entrance of women into the various types of schools is reflected in official statistics. The *scuola media*, roughly equivalent to the junior high school in America, for children ten to fifteen years old, where the bases of a liberal education are acquired, can be taken as an example.

In the year 1913–1914, the girls attending this type of school numbered 96,467; the number rose to 302,785 in 1938–1939 (the eve of World War II), and in 1962 it was 718,208. Table 1 compares the attendance of boys and girls. It includes also the relative number of male and female teachers and shows the tendency of the woman to avail herself of an education which prepares her for the teaching profession. This tendency is confirmed by Tables 2 and 3 which relate to the admissions to the various faculties of the

TABLE 1—Students and Teachers in the Scuole Medie, By Sex

Year	Students			Teachers		
	Male	Female	Total	Male	Female	Total
1913–14	185,675	96,467	282,142	15,341	4,959	20,300
1938–39	506,606	302,785	809,391	34,402	26,267	60,669
1958–59	1,094,952	718,208	1,813,160	64,709	83,524	148,233

TABLE 2—Students and Professors in the Universities, By Sex

Year	Students			Professors		
	Male	Female	Total	Male	Female	Total
1913–14	26,392	1,634	28,026			1,788
1926–27	37,217	5,647	42,864	2,370	31	2,401
1938–39	62,345	15,084	77,429	3,239	123	3,362
1958–59	118,659	45,286	163,945	5,160	368	5,528

TABLE 3—Students Attending Italian Universities in 1959–1960

Faculty	Men	Women
Sciences	13,880	8,641
Medicine	16,213	1,979
Engineering	19,397	800
Agriculture	2,760	66
Business & Economics	32,306	3,409
Law	24,317	6,485
Letters	7,683	22,605
Courses leading to diplomas in statistics, elementary school supervision, physical education	2,103	1,301
Total	118,659	45,286

universities; the only faculties where the women outnumber the men are those of letters and liberal arts, which qualify them to become teachers. The large number of women attending the faculties of science is also related to teaching qualifications, since such studies make it possible to teach science and mathematics in high school.

SEX MORES AND MARRIAGE PATTERNS

Since no data on the sex mores and marriage customs of Italy as a whole are available, these observations are based on research done in both northern and southern communities, on figures taken from the census, and on public opinion polls.

Age at Marriage—To begin with, both men and women now tend to marry later. Today the majority of men marries between the ages of twenty-five and thirty-five (more than two fifths between the ages of twenty-five and thirty, and one fifth between thirty and thirty-five). In the beginning of the twentieth century, however, seven out of ten men married when younger than thirty and half of these were extremely young. Brides younger than twenty-five once accounted for more than 67 per cent of the total. The percentage of those between twenty-five and thirty has risen from 18 to 26. Because more women work, they need a longer period of preparation and study when marriage is not their only immediate concern. Very recently (1960–1961), however, a tendency for the average marriage age in the country to go down has appeared; this can be related to better economic conditions with the resulting rise in employment and more available housing, as well as to the abolition of legalized prostitution and the closing down of brothels.

Marriage Rate—Next, there is a higher marriage rate. In the first decade of Italian unification (1861–1870), out of every 100 men who died 70 were unmarried, 23 married, and 7 were widowers; today, only 24 are unmarried, 53 are married, and 23 widowers. As for the women, 24 per cent died unmarried in the decade of 1951–1960 compared to 62 per cent in 1861–1870; those married make up 29 per cent compared to 20 per cent and, finally, the number of widows has gone up from 18 per cent a century ago to 47 today.

Birthrate—The birthrate, on the other hand, has gone down considerably; it is now down to half of what it was in 1860, from 37.6 to 17.8 per 1,000 of population. The number of illegitimate births, too, is greatly reduced. Today they make up only 3 per cent of total births, while in 1861 they constituted 7.5 per cent.

These facts, however, along with many other official statistics which could easily be added, have only a limited value. There are important cultural differences among the various regions, and the statistical facts need to be examined in the light of factors which cannot be measured statistically. The smaller proportion of illegitimate births, for example, cannot be explained simply by a tendency towards having fewer relationships out of wedlock, or a greater tendency to recognize children born out of wedlock; it could be related to a tendency to legalize extramarital unions wherever possible, or to a more widespread knowledge of birth-control techniques.

Divorce—There is no divorce in Italy, only legal separation.

THE SITUATION IN SICILY

A comparative survey of the problems of the woman was conducted by Gabriella Parca, in three towns of southern, central, and northern Italy. In the town of Gangi (10,943 inhabitants), in the mountainous interior of the province of Palermo in Sicily, she found that men and women belong to two different worlds; they look at each other, they desire or fear each other, but rarely can they love each other. The lack of an area in which they can work together heightens their fantasies and turns sex into a myth. During pre-adolescence (ten to eleven years), girls begin to think of love; for lack of any other interests or distractions to occupy their minds, love becomes an obsession, although it remains a dream and a fantasy. The boys watch the girls in church or follow them from afar in the street. On rare occasions, usually at family gatherings, the young people can meet and talk briefly together. On these meetings are based those long "secret engagements" which must not come to the parents' attention.

Isolation of Sexes—In this atmosphere of sex isolation, those rare opportunities for two young people to be together become "dangerous" moments for the woman; according to the author of the survey, the result is that as many as 20 per cent of the girls have premarital sexual relations. Often, when the girl becomes pregnant, she refuses to believe it even when the doctor or midwife tell her. "It's impossible. I didn't do anything. I didn't go all the way," she says, and this is not an excuse: it is true for her, since in giving herself she felt no pleasure, only a terrible fear that her family might find her out.

In such a situation, the girl feels that the man who has "compromised" her must make every effort to marry her, even if they were not officially engaged. In many cases a marriage does not take place, and the young man disappears—because he has no money, because he never really intended to marry the girl, or because he changed his mind. Such a situation leads to the "crime of honor"; this is not limited to this specific town, as anyone who reads the newspaper can ascertain. In the south, either the woman herself or her male relatives whose duty it is to protect the honor of the family, must take justice in hand. In certain cases the family encourage the betrayed girl to take revenge. Often the girls will punish themselves by committing suicide, especially those who had come to work in the large central or southern cities, or they may turn to prostitution.

Elopement—In certain areas, elopement is becoming almost an institution, either because of parental opposition to the marriage, or to overcome the economic problems of the dowry or wedding expenses. The young people leave home, or they get together secretly and then reveal what they have done to their parents, who are asked to approve and forgive a *fait accompli*. This custom is not easily analyzed statistically, although it is documented by fiction and neorealistic movies. It is the solution used by Castellani, the director of *Due Soldi de Speranza*: a girl of a town near Naples, faced with her father's opposition to her marriage, persuades the young man she loves to run away with her. The father, however, continues to withhold his approval which turns the whole village against him.

Changing Patterns—Even in the most culturally-backward areas, the old pattern, according to which the parents found and chose their daughter's husband, has disappeared. I often discussed this question with parents and daughters when I conducted surveys in isolated areas in the country, in order to see to what extent archaic customs persist. The parents would talk about how things used to be done, and remember what had happened to them when they found themselves suddenly tied to a person not of their own choosing—but their memories did not relate to any possibility of following the same customs today. The girls often would answer, "In these matters the parents should stand aside; I'm going to choose my own fiancé." This does not mean, however, especially in the south, that the girl does actually take the initiative. For the girls of Lucania, whom I interviewed, it meant that they had no intention of passively accepting the situation but claimed the freedom of accepting or refusing any proposal of marriage.

In effect, competition forces girls not to be too choosy and not to refuse a proposal too hastily. This competition also forces girls to exercise strict self-control, especially within the restricted atmosphere of the small towns where gossip, a tremendously important instrument of social control, enables people to know everyone's personal affairs. Each girl, therefore, tries to get the reputation of being a "catch": not only morally unexceptionable, but an active, hard-working girl, skilful in household tasks, sweet tempered, frugal and economical, not addicted to luxury or frivolities. She tries to lead people to understand that her family will be able to help her fiancé, either financially or through important connections; whenever possible, she makes it known that she is able to contribute her earnings to the family income. By means of gossip, she attempts to attack her rivals, and to reveal all their bad points. This is the reason for her restraint, her discretion about personal matters, even in cases where she might be acting against her own interests. She will try to avoid going to the doctor and getting medical care even if she needs it, because she is afraid it will be thought that she is not healthy, and this might lower her marriage value.

Gabriella Parca writes that in the Sicilian village, previously discussed, woman sees herself and is seen exclusively in relation to man from the time she is a little girl. Her ambition is to become a wife, and, consequently, she has no spiritual autonomy, nor does she have any desire for economic independence. The only women who work in town are the teachers. All the others are housewives and therefore completely dependent, first on their fathers and then on their husbands. They become submissive, obedient, passive. The same thing is true in various other southern communities.

Marriage: The Supreme Goal—Of the cultural outlook of Ragusa, a city in Sicily (where, following the discovery of oil, a significant industrialization is taking place), Madga Talamo writes that the only way for a woman to get settled is for her to marry; actually, what happens is that the woman automatically moves from her father's control to that of her husband. In order to reach this goal of marriage, a woman uses every available means. As one of the men of Ragusa said, "Sometimes the girl herself will go to any lengths to be seduced so that she can be sure she will get married; often the mother will give the young people the opportunity to meet, get engaged, and get married before the young man has a chance to change his mind."

Once a girl and her young man become lovers, the wedding must take place discreetly; the girl cannot wear a wedding dress with the veil, and the ceremony is conducted in the sacristy, in the presence of only a few close friends and relatives. It always takes place at about five or six in the morning, so that no one will notice, because the young couple is frowned upon by the townspeople. It would seem, too, that criticism is more severe in the lower classes, since it is more common for people of the middle class to "have to get married."

If the seducer refuses to marry the girl, the "code of honor" demands revenge. In such cases a killer can even become a hero, for he is defending the most sacred thing on earth, a woman's chastity—a value that is not just hers, but belongs to her entire family. The woman's weakness, which renders her incapable of defending herself, requires that the males prevent or avenge her dishonor if they wish to keep the family from being disgraced.

Once the woman is married, she gains a security she lacked. The home is in effect her kingdom, where she gains her own autonomy in relation to the man and thus, self-assurance. A part of this self-assurance is due to the fact that she has finally reached the status of a wife; it is toward this goal that she has exercised in the past a strict self-discipline in order to appear proper in the eyes of possible suitors and their families. In her new situation there are still moral and sexual limits that confine her behavior, but she has been freed from having to compete with possible rivals and can achieve independence in relation to herself and her husband. Within the home she can exercise her authority in the organization of the household and in the children's education.

Marital Problems—Married life becomes barren of affection, based as it is simply on the fulfillment of daily needs and on sexual relations. Living together, instead of bringing closeness, creates a distance between man and wife who have different goals for their lives. In such situations infidelities inevitably occur, but they are checked by both cultural mores and fear of the violent and scandalous revenge which the betrayed husband must take, if the infidelity should become publicly known.

Conjugal "faithfulness" has different meanings according to the sex of the one who must respect it. Anna Anfossi, basing herself on answers gathered in the previously mentioned research on Ragusa, points out that men and women look on adultery in a different light; each seems to refer it to his or her own sex, with the result that men do not consider it serious, while women feel it is much more important. Faithfulness does not therefore have a single value, but varies according to the sex and the social standing of husband and wife. The man has the authority, and so is allowed greater freedom. The woman, instead, represents obedience and is subject to all the obligations implied by the marriage ties. For this reason the seduction of a woman is not considered a serious breach for a man, nor is homicide for the sake of honor, often the consequence of a seduction, considered serious. The opposite is true of homicide for the sake of gain, which is considered almost as bad as the murder of a parent or brother. There is certainly an incongruity in the estimation of the two, seduction and homicide for the sake of honor, since they have a cause-and-effect relationship. The more lightly seduction is considered, the more serious a homicide of honor should be considered. But in effect, though a seduction is not serious from the man's point of view—he can even consider it a proof of virility, which in turn has a worth of its own—it is extremely serious for the woman, whose whole family shares in the disgrace and shame.

In Southern Italy

Female gossip is a dangerous social force. E. C. Banfield, in the course of his anthropological survey of Montegrano, found that a woman is more easily forgiven for faults like meanness and bad manners than for gossiping. Montegrano is the fictitious name of a real village in Lucania, with a culture quite typical of the south. Conditions in Montegrano are similar to those in the rest of Lucania, or in Abbruzzo, Calabria, the interior of Campania, and certain coastal regions in the vicinity of Catania, Messina, Palermo and Trapani.

The same study brings out the fact that parents expect their children to respect their wishes in the choice of a marriage partner. Girls who are stubborn about the man chosen for them are beaten. In one case a girl over twenty years old who was determined to marry a man her mother did not approve of was deprived of her dowry, kept without food, and frequently beaten.

The results of the Montegrano study confirm what already has been said about elopement as a means of getting past parental opposition to the marriage. Banfield quotes a story as typical of the situation in the town. A girl of fifteen fell in love, but her parents opposed the marriage. She resolved her situation by having relations with her lover until she became pregnant, her parents then consented to the wedding.

Premarital and Extramarital Relations—The principal goal of premarital sex relations is marriage: the woman gives in to the man when she knows she can fulfill this lifelong ambition. When she cannot look forward to such a goal, either because she is already married or because the man is married, she is not likely to surrender. This is demonstrated by the fact that there was little adultery in the town studied by Banfield. At the same time there was an obsession with the possibility of the woman's infidelity. In cases of marital infidelity, the solution was the immediate killing of the adulterous pair. This was the answer Banfield received to his poll questions; and this is the reaction generally accepted by the traditional south; thus adultery leads to murder. It is worth repeating, however, that these cases are not frequent.

The different value given to the "crime of honor" by northerners—the Turinese—and the southerners who have emigrated to Turin is well brought out by an inquiry conducted by Anna Anfossi in 1961. For the natives of Turin, both men and women, the crime of honor was one of the most serious crimes. On the other hand the men, and even more often the women, from the south considered that the crime of honor was a less serious crime than stealing, informing, being unfaithful to one's husband or wife, having an abortion, or killing for gain.

Banfield feels that the belief commonly held in the south, that the woman will of necessity "fall victim to temptation," brings about its own realization. In a society where everyone believes that a man or woman will inevitably make love unless prevented, a man who finds himself alone with a woman is practically forced to proposition her, since otherwise her attractiveness or his virility would be questioned. In such circumstances, the southern woman, knowing that women forget moral standards when confronted with temptation, easily gives in.

According to this point of view, whoever transgresses must be treated with the greatest severity, since blame and punishment are necessary pressures to prevent everyone else from sinning. This procedure, however, weakens moral judgment, since the person punished feels unfortunate rather than guilty.

This explains the idea, prevalent in the south, of the "fated" character of evil and the impossibility of avoiding sin. The commission of sin is attributed either to the specific situation, or the "hot southern blood," or even to biological heredity. This idea was encouraged at first by romantic ideals, then by the "love story" magazines. Actually, as indicated, the southern woman can avoid temptation perfectly well, and her love for her children compensates for the lack of affection in her relations with her husband.

Prostitution, too, is justified by this idea of the "hot southern blood," as a means of avoiding greater evils and protecting respectable girls, since it is regarded as impossible for a young man to exercise sexual continence. This reason is frequently given in criticizing the law of 1958 which closed down the brothels; but this criticism is not limited to southern Italy, and certain ideas go far beyond geographic boundaries.

IN TUSCANY

In certain zones of central Italy, especially in the countryside, ways of thinking agree quite closely with southern ideas. But things are very different whenever industrialization has begun to affect ways of life and traditional modes of thought.

Let us take Certaldo, for instance, a town in Tuscany, studied by Gabriella Parca. Certaldo, with a population of 8,500 is situated in the Chianti region, and the major occupation of its inhabitants was once agriculture. Today, industry employs half of the active population, while agriculture employs only 37 per cent.

Social Life—The division of the sexes is not as rigidly drawn at Certaldo as in the more southern regions. Boys and girls go walking together in the streets without parental control, they laugh and joke among themselves. To be alone, couples do not have to have recourse to subterfuges; one sees couples embracing in the lanes or at the movies, or going off to the countryside in a car. In school, some teachers are trying gradually to introduce sex education by pointing out to the students the life phases of little animals kept in cages in the classroom.

According to a local doctor, the age of puberty in girls is now ten to twelve, whereas it was formerly thirteen to sixteen; this is probably due to better nutrition. The girls of this town, too, begin to think of love when they enter adolescence. They do not encounter barriers set up between themselves and boys their own age, but can have dates without difficulty. At fifteen, many are engaged or have boy friends whom they would like to marry; but if the couple does not get along, they break off without great difficulty, an engagement is not an eternal bond.

Young people often go dancing, even in public places outside the town itself. Often the families are present, but only in order to enjoy themselves, to listen to the singing, and to look at the young people, not to check up on them. The families feel that girls should be able to look after themselves.

In Certaldo, it is as normal for a girl to go to work as it is for her to go to school. She likes to spend what she earns on herself, primarily on clothes. A girl can receive her fiancé at home, although her mother is always there at such times. If she goes out, she is free to go wherever she wants to, and she can return home from an important party even after midnight.

Marriage—The average age for marriage is twenty for the girl—once it was around twenty-five—and for the man around twenty-five, whereas it was once around thirty. The girl rarely gets pregnant before marriage; if she does, the wedding takes place sooner. If by chance she should get pregnant and not get married, the situation is not dramatized, and the girl remains at home with the child.

The parents do not interfere in the choice of husband, and pay little attention to the question of finances. The girls want very much to be married in a church wedding with a white dress and long veil carried by two bridesmaids. A procession of cars, a hotel reception, and a honeymoon are likewise part of the anticipated ceremonies.

In marriage they are quite frank; if something is wrong they say so, and, according to the men, the woman is often able to gain her point.

As far as conjugal unfaithfulness is concerned, in Certaldo, as in the south, a distinction is made between the man's and the woman's infidelity; this distinction is found in Italian law, which provides more severe punishment for the women than for the men. The man considers his own infidelity a slight wrong, while the same wrong done to him is a cause for a separation. There is, however, no question of avenging one's honor. As a matter of fact, if one hears gossip about one's wife, one prefers to believe her rather than what others say. In Certaldo fifteen couples were separated, almost all of them because of repeated "slight wrongs" on the part of the husband.

In Northern Italy

In northern Italy a study was recently carried out by Alessandro Pizzorno in R., a Lombard community of 7,550 inhabitants, fourteen miles from Milan. R. has industries, and all its inhabitants have the possibility of employment. Of the women, 1,462 are employed (as against 2,205 men), mostly in manufacturing.

The Role of the Factory—Previously girls of the lower class started to go to work very early, sometimes even as soon as they had finished elementary school, at the age of eleven or twelve. Today, the tendency is to remain in school longer (the management of the local industries encouraged this tendency by declaring that they gave preference, in their employment policy, to those who had finished the *scuole medie*), and as a result, there are girls of sixteen, seventeen, and even twenty, who have not yet started working.

The factory is an initiation into life. Here the young girl learns what her family avoided letting her know. An older married woman worker usually tells the younger girl about a number of things, especially those concerned with sexual relations. A girl of twenty-five, when interviewed, said, "of course, girls hear more vulgar talk from women than from men. There are no men at the place where I work. At work I learned all there is to know about what happens with men and women. They certainly don't spare you any details."

According to Pizzorno, this function of the factory continues a very ancient tradition of transmitting information learned through experience; once this was done through agricultural rites or performances, as well as by means of stories and legends.

The family is not concerned with this kind of knowledge, and limits itself to teaching the facts of physiology. Young people, however, feel that this should change, and that there should be a change also in the attitude towards women who have had sex experience before marriage. These women are judged more severely by the old than by the young, by the women than by the men, by housewives than by working women, by the lower classes than by those with more education.

Girl Meets Boy — Girls meet boys especially when they go dancing. Both boys and girls, usually in groups, go dancing outside the town, in places which can be reached by bicycle, or even on foot. In this way they avoid the control of the older people of the community, and can meet many people before becoming engaged, while still remaining within the area of the acceptable. If the girls do not follow this custom, it is because they want to go beyond the accepted limits. About twenty or thirty girls, who regularly go out of town or who are picked up in a car by dates from out of town, are actually called "whores" by the older members of the community. The young men are not sure of the fairness of this judgment, and some of them say that after they get married these girls can still make very good wives.

The young men themselves go out of town to have a good time, but when they want to get married they look for a girl from the town. The engagement has two phases: the first when the young man brings the girl home and introduces her to his parents; and the second, the official ceremony, when he gives her the ring. The engaged couple has a great deal of liberty. It sometimes happens that a boy or a girl becomes engaged several times before actually getting married; but since those who do this are not well thought of, repeated engagements are avoided.

According to many people, almost all engaged couples eventually have complete sex relations before marriage. At the time when this study was carried out (in 1960), two or three weddings were rushed because the girl was pregnant. The young people feel that having sex relationships helps them to get to know each other better.

Married Life—The married woman who works has to fulfill her duties both at work and at home, so that she has much less free time than the man. A mother who leaves her children alone will be sharply criticized by the community. To avoid this, the nursemaid has become an institution for working women. Each nursemaid takes care in her home of one to three preschool-age children, and is paid up to ten or fifteen thousand lire a month ($17–$25). The mother brings the children before going to work and picks them up in the evening.

Birth Control—Probably because of these problems, the question of planned parenthood is important, and the family is usually limited to three or four members. The responsibility for birth control is considered to be the man's, as can be gauged from typical statements by the inhabitants of R.: "Not all men are able to exercise self control . . ."; or "You have to be careful: it's more the man's job than the woman's. . . ."

Birth control is a fairly serious problem for Catholic women, as the following excerpt from an interview with a woman worker indicates:

"I would have liked to have more children, I don't know how many, but more. I have a little girl who's growing up and will leave. And we'll be left alone. My husband didn't want any more children, because he said he was too old. Usually, if you can, it's a good thing to have many children; they keep one another company. But if you can't afford it, you have to think about it: having lots of children is a problem. My mother-in-law had nine children and she raised them as best she could. But today children need more things, and more education. You can't be irresponsible about these things. . . . Of course, it's rather a sin for a good Catholic, having only one child or even only a few children. Certain priests (especially the parish priests, who know what life is) understand this problem. Others (those of the schools, and the friars) don't understand a thing. Once a priest refused to absolve me because I wouldn't promise I would go ahead and have as many children as God sent me. Then I went to the parish priest at ——— and he gave me absolution. To tell you the truth, I didn't want to make a fuss with my husband about this. I know some women who risked ruining their marriages on account of this. I didn't want to do this and I always said so clearly when I confessed. I tried to convince my husband, but since he didn't give in, I gave up. Marriage isn't just to have children. . . . Life is what it is and you can't be irresponsible."

Birth control is generally felt to be a proof of superiority in R. This can be seen from the attitude people have towards southerners, who are considered to be irresponsible because they have many children.

Social Life—The married woman, because her time is so limited, has few relations with the world outside of work or the close family circle.

The clubs are not open to women. Sometimes, in the evening, women go to the café to watch television. Even on Sunday, the woman remains at home while her husband goes out with friends. In the last few years this custom is changing, since husband and wife either remain at home to watch television, or go out together to watch it if they don't own a set.

Woman's lack of social life causes her to take less interest in the world around her. The difference between men and women in this respect is indicated by their respective interest in reading the newspaper: 37 per cent of the men read the newspaper daily or almost every day, but only 15 per cent of the women. More women than men read the weekly magazines, however. This could be interpreted as meaning that reading the newspaper implies a greater potential interest in social problems and social life, while the reading of magazines can, at least in part, be considered as an escape, and therefore emphasizes the woman's isolation.

The Home Routine

The woman really does have a greater number of problems and duties towards the family than the man. She contributes to the family budget with her work and she still has to keep the household functioning.

In 1960, I was conducting a sample study of the condition of women in Tivoli, a town of 33,197 inhabitants near Rome, where women had for years been accustomed to working according to their abilities and social class, in factories, offices or schools. I noticed that even though the woman was aware of the strain and of the double work load, outside and inside the home, it never occurred to her to ask her husband to help with either the household work or the care of the children, and husband and wife both considered it a dishonor to place the work of the household on a basis of equality and collaboration.

Women's Occupations

In Italy, more than in other countries, woman continues to enter the working world. The cold facts of statistics have lately revealed that in countries more advanced industrially the number of women gainfully employed tends to rise rather slowly, or even to become stabilized. In Italy the opposite is true, even taking into account the fact that the country is in a period of economic development, and that modernization and industrialization have taken place more recently here than elsewhere. From 1954 to 1961, the male working force was augmented by only 5.6 per cent, the female by 25 per cent. The data of the Central Institute of Italian

Statistics tell us that of an economically active total population of 20,923,000, women make up 5,715,000. The fact that the movement from agriculture to industry is even greater among women than men is especially remarkable. This statement becomes more meaningful if we remember that a century ago, at the beginning of the industrial revolution in Italy, 90 per cent of working women were in agriculture, while today only 33 per cent are engaged in it, as against 31 in industry, and 36 in other activities. It is also important to realize that 65 per cent of the working women are between the ages of fourteen and forty, while in other countries belonging to the European Common Market most female workers —taken on because of the lack of male workers—are older women. In Milan, the largest Italian industrial center, of 237,170 working women, 113,620 are factory workers, 76,140 office workers, 2,010 professional women, 20,240 self-employed, 23,790 assistants, 440 work in management, and 330 are entrepreneurs.

Women View Themselves

By way of integrating the foregoing data it seems opportune to summarize the results of an inquiry conducted in 1964 in northern Italy, which may be considered in its present phase of cultural transition as an indicator of the development which can be expected to take place in the rest of the country. The inquiry was conducted by A.C.L.I., a Catholic organization devoted to the advancement of the working classes. A sample group of 1,256 women of various social classes between the ages of fifteen and fifty-five, comprising working women and housewives, unmarried and married, with and without children, was interviewed. The interviewees were, besides, selected proportionately from three different social circles: (a) urban (the city of Milan, population 1,582,534; Turin, population 1,025,822; and Genoa, population 784,194); (b) intermediate communities with populations not over 5,000 located in the provinces of the three aforementioned cities); and (c) rural. The questions put to the interviewees concerned various problems. Let us examine a few answers.

About the issue of premarital virginity, only one third of the interviewees considered it a positive value for a man not to have sexual experience prior to marriage. That is to say, the majority adhered to the traditional outlook according to which it is not merely allowed, but desirable, that a man should have premarital experiences. On the other hand, as far as virginity in women is concerned, only 23.19 per cent of the urban interviewees answered that the women's premarital virginity had no positive significance for the future of the family. In the intermediate group the number of those who gave this answer was 11.02 per cent, and in the rural 8.5 per cent. Again, 64.77 per cent of the urban respondents considered premarital virginity in women desirable, while 35.23 per cent either did not regard it as preferable, or were uncertain, or did not answer the question. In the intermediate group, the corresponding figures were 70.06 per cent and 29.94 per cent; in the rural, 72.41 per cent and 27.59 per cent, respectively.

One of the most marked differences between the urban group and the two others was in the attitude toward divorce. In the cities, 46.61 per cent of the interviewees considered divorce acceptable, while 53.39 per cent were against it; in the intermediate group the figures were 26.20 per cent and 73.80 per cent; in the rural, 22.88 per cent and 77.12 per cent, respectively.

All three groups showed an overwhelming acceptance of family planning, again with a greater percentage favoring it in the urban than in the other two groups. In the urban group, 73.30 per cent of the interviewees approved of the modern family with two or three children; in the intermediate group 67.15 per cent, and in the rural 63.63 per cent took this position. As to parental authority over the children, a great majority of those interviewed in all three areas (81.18 per cent in the urban, 80.67 in the intermediate, and 79.31 in the rural) felt that this must be divided between both spouses. This indicates that the concept of the patriarchal family, hierarchically ordered and dependent on the father, is in the process of becoming obsolete, probably as a result of modern education and the great frequency of feminine labor. The woman can now assert herself, and can attain independence through her work. The economic crisis of 1965, with the consequent large-scale layoffs, has adversely affected the position of women workers as evidenced in numerous newspaper and television interviews. Nevertheless, women have a firmly established role in the world of production, science, and politics. They now want to be recognized in a new status in the family itself. This is indicated by a series of data in the same inquiry, which show that the percentage of women who dislike extra-domestic work is very high. 77.90 per cent of the urban women, 80.07 per cent of the intermediate, and 86.20 per cent of the rural, stated that they would prefer to stay at home, if they were in a position to do so. In evaluating the meaning of these responses one should, however, keep in mind that many men as well would, in all probability, prefer not to go to work if they could permit themselves to do so.

The questionnaire used in the interviews contained also the following question: "Do you believe that at the present time it is more of a duty than it was in the past for a woman to participate in political life and social activities, or do you believe that it is better that she should occupy herself more with the home and the family?" The following table shows the answers:

	Urban Zone	Intermediate Zone	Rural Zone
In favor of participating in political life and social activity	48.58%	35.97%	30.09%
In favor of women occupying themselves with the house and the family only	44.42%	54.47%	60.19%

The preceding figures show that Italian women are still uncertain as to their choice between the traditional role in the home and the new role in an outside occupation.

The Outlook

Woman, who is no longer only the sweet, humble queen of the household, the maid and childbearer, who can now support herself and play a role in the outside world, still has only superficially faced the problems connected with her new state. The practical goals she has gained give her the illusion of having attained an independence that has not yet been recognized or realized in the culture itself. The new condition of the woman now places before both men and women the problem of newly interpreting, within the culture, their respective positions, and it calls for a realization of moral, intellectual, and spiritual goals that will lead to a deeper and a more meaningful conception of human dignity.

Spain

By Mercedes Formica de Careaga

THE TRADITIONAL POSITION

*I*n the past the Spanish woman—whether urban or rural whether of the lower, middle, or upper class—always lived for her home. There she played an important role, based almost exclusively on her feminine accomplishments. The question of aspiring to any of the rights traditionally held by men could never have arisen in her mind. Whether consciously or not, she completely subordinated herself to the men who headed and dominated her family.

The legacy of nine centuries of Arab civilization, superimposed upon the old Roman cultural groundwork, and followed by Christian domination which, in turn, was permeated by subtle Jewish influences, endowed the Spanish woman with a rare complexity. Although she submitted to the limitations of usage and custom, she was not without enterprise and the ability to act. And beneath her diffident and impassive personality, was a character with many potentialities.

Translated from the Spanish by Judith Arnon.

Beneath her apparent indifference, she was awaiting emancipation. She concealed her reading, and when she wrote for publication, she generally used a masculine pseudonym to avoid being called *marisabidilla* (bluestocking), or *marimacho* (mannish woman).

Only widowhood permitted her to manifest her capacity for work, her efficiency, and her other abilities. Few families crumbled when the husband died; the widow usually managed to maintain the household, saw to it that her sons acquired professions and that her daughters married, even without benefit of a dowry. Under unfavorable economic conditions, she achieved this by means of improvised earning activities—dressmaking, ·teaching, taking care of other people's children, embroidering, making lampshades, painting fans, ironing, or making candy. This admirable character allowed the world to glimpse her hidden abilities only from time to time. During her husband's lifetime, she had seemed totally incapable of any initiative or independent action.

This subordination of woman to man was compensated for by a series of moral obligations incumbent upon the latter. The father, brother, or husband rarely abandoned the women of his family, and there were frequent cases of bachelors who did not marry so that they could continue to support their mothers and sisters. Nevertheless, in cases where this moral duty was not fulfilled, or where unmarried women without funds had no male relative to count on, the alternatives were few: the convent or poorly paid menial jobs.

The beginning of this century marked the period of "lady companions," girls of good families whose economic position had suffered. Having no professional training, they earned their livelihood by accompanying wealthy young ladies to theaters, and on promenades and excursions. Custom forbade a *señorita* to go out alone. From this milieu of genteel companions, called *doñas* in Andalusia, came the first female university students. As in every other place in the world, this economic problem primarily affected girls of the middle class. Rich unmarried women managed well. The poor working girl either married or remained a domestic.

After World War I, the first women doctors, university graduates in philosophy, the humanities, science, pharmacy, and law appeared. The first women teachers constituted the culmination of this breakthrough.

Women students first attended classes accompanied by a respectable chaperone, and, of course, with full parental consent. This development was an indication of progress in masculine attitudes, initiated and supported by men of liberal views, rather than that of an incipient feminist movement. The girls themselves, daughters of educated fathers—doctors, engineers, teachers, lawyers—were motivated not only by genuine intellectual interests, but also by a natural instinct for self-preservation, faced as they were by an uncertain future. By that time, few women entered convents without a real desire to do so, or permitted a brother to sacrifice his happiness in order to support them.

Full participation of women in university life, and subsequently in professional careers, began in the decade preceding the proclamation of the Republic in 1931. It was consolidated during the period of the Republic, and at present, after a slight reversal, it has begun once again with renewed vigor.

THE RURAL WOMAN

To this day vast differences separate women's lives in various parts of the country. The fruit pickers of Valencia, Castello, Alicante, or Murcia, the Galician or Basque peasant women, and those living on the huge, poorly cultivated landed estates of Andalusia and Extremadura, do not have the same standard of living or culture. One must distinguish, first of all, between women in irrigated rural zones, whether or not their husbands own the land they cultivate; peasant women of regions where the land is divided into small parcels, farmed by their owners (typical examples are the Galician and Basque provinces); and the large estates where the land, belonging to a few landowners, yields one product; such areas include the olive country, the flat or hilly pasture land, the wheat fields, the cattle grazing land.

In past centuries, rural women constituted, as in other countries, the most wretched class of the population. Hampered by illiteracy and ignorance, their living conditions were extremely difficult, with scant hygiene and medical care, and frequent promiscuity. Today, this is no longer the case. The Spanish rural woman in irrigated areas, whether or not she owns the land she tills, is the *huertana* (farm woman) par excellence. Her economic condition is prosperous; her pleasant, orderly work is carried on within the family orbit, whether she cultivates orange groves, almonds, vegetables, or flowers. She has more than enough to live on, and this material ease permits her to acquire education and culture. In irrigated zones, laws protecting the peasant who cultivates the land makes a virtual landowner of him.

It is in smallholders' regions that the peasant woman still leads a difficult existence. Galicia is a typical example; many of the women emigrate to South America, and it is the greatest source of domestic help in Spain. One cow, a few pigs, a bit of land on which to plant corn, constitute the entire wealth of the Galician woman, and those who do not leave have only the hope of employment in a nearby factory.

The Basque peasant, whose agricultural areas have so much in common with those of Galicia, has been liberated from poverty by recent industrial development. The Basque *cashera* of Vizcaya, Guipuzcuoa, or Alava, enjoys high cultural and material standards. Not only does she own some land, cattle, and the family house that is handed down from generation to generation, but the proximity of factories and industries offers her well-paid job opportunities. Thus, she may lead a life approximately on a level with that of a middle-class girl from Barcelona or Madrid.

After the Civil War, many landowners, spurred by a sense of social justice, built decent homes and schools for the workers on their property. In addition, the Seccion Femenina (Female Section), a state organization, initiated in 1940 the Hermandad (Sisterhood) of City and Country, whose main activities consist of maintaining farm schools, a traveling- teachers' program, and rural schools. Motorized and horse-drawn traveling schools make the rounds of villages and small towns for eight months every year. Women instructors, including physical-education teachers for children, give the peasant women courses in home crafts (sewing, cooking, home economics, family group relations, handiwork), rural industries (apiculture, aviculture, skin tanning, leather work, milk industries, pig breeding, and floriculture), general culture (religion, history, reading and writing, gymnastics and sports), as well as health and hygiene information.

The Badajoz and Jaen projects of the government were initiated in order to industrialize and electrify these two typical monoculture provinces. From 1952-1961 the Badajoz Plan brought 46,697 hectares under irrigation, settled 3,700 people on these lands, and gave work to 23,000 workers, including 3,400 in new industries. During the same period, 10 new agricultural industries were started in this region of Extremadura. The Jaen Plan in Upper Andalusia improved conditions similarly. A great deal remains to be done, but if such traditionally monocultural zones are improved as planned, the problem of the Spanish rural woman will disappear.

THE LEGAL POSITION

The Legal Position—The legal position of Spanish women may be considered from two points of view: that of the family, and that of society. On April 24, 1958, after a campaign initiated and carried on by the author, the Spanish Courts of Justice approved amendments to sixty-six articles of the Civil Code, which constituted the greatest change since the promulgation of that body of laws in 1888. Prior to this change, Spanish women suffered from many legal disabilities, dating back to Arab and Roman influences. Terms such as *Imbecilitas sexus*, indicated that a woman was regarded as an imbecile by her very nature. In the laws of Castille, women were classed with children, invalids, and delinquents.

A widow who remarried was deprived of the custody of her minor children, and the right to administer their property. The widower who remarried retained these rights.

Since the reform of April 24, 1958, a woman may act as a witness to all kinds of wills, have guardianship and custody, and, as a widow, she retains the right to administer the property of her minor children even though she remarries.

The law distinguishes between three kinds of matrimonial property: (1) *Parafernales*, the exclusive possessions of the wife; (2) the property of the husband; and (3) earnings or assets acquired during marriage called *gananciales*, which are divided equally between wife and husband if the marriage is dissolved by separation. According to the old Civil Code, the husband could dispose of his earnings or assets without the consent of his wife. Since the reform, he must obtain the consent of his spouse to dispose of assets he has invested in real estate or commercial enterprises.

Prior to the reform of 1958, a woman with legal grounds for separation, lost claim to the house, which was considered the property of the husband. She was obliged to leave it, to be "entrusted" to another domicile, under a guardian, who was always chosen with the consent of the husband. She also lost custody of her children over three years of age for the duration of the separation procedure which, with appeals and petitions, could take six years. The alimony she received was never sufficient, and she never, in practice, received her half share, since her husband could alienate it without her consent, sell it or mortgage it.

The 1958 reform abolished the placing of the wife under guardianship. The house is no longer considered the husband's, but the family's, and the judge decides who is to remain there. In most cases, the wife and children remain, while the husband moves to a hotel, and is obliged to pay adequate alimony. When separation dissolves the marriage, the woman's *parafernales* are transferred to her and she receives half of the *gananciales*. It is very rare for a Spanish woman to demand separation, for there is no divorce, and the position of a wife separated from her husband is not enviable. As a rule, the woman has serious grounds to ask for a separation, and uses the property she receives for the upbringing of her children.

Prior to 1958, a wife's adultery was treated differently from a husband's. The Civil Code considered a wife's infidelity as grounds for separation in any case, but a husband's only when it created a "public scandal" or a "disgrace for the wife." An adulterous wife was always prosecuted, and when condemned, sent to prison or a convent, as the husband decided. If a husband caught his wife *in flagranti* and killed her, he was condemned only to a short period of exile. A wife, under the same circumstances, was treated like any other criminal. Following the 1958 reforms, "adultery of either of the spouses" became grounds for separation.

The law of July 22, 1961, argued in the Spanish courts by State Attorney Doña Pilar Primo de Rivera, has put an end to another anomaly. Prior to it, a woman had, in theory, the same rights to a university career as a man.

She could, for instance, obtain her law degree, but would be unable to obtain a position as a magistrate, in the diplomatic corps, or as a state attorney. There was no legal basis for this, but in practice she was restricted to subordinates' or assistants' jobs. A group of women graduates at last took action to change this situation. They wrote articles, gave lectures, and, in 1951, participated in the first Ibero-American-Philippine Women's Congress, organized by the National Delegation of the Seccion Femenina. This was followed by a study of Spanish women in the professions, organized by the author. This study was the seed of the Law of July 22, 1961, in which women's rights to engage in all types of political, professional, and vocational activities were recognized to be equal to men's.

EDUCATION

Prior to the Civil War, with the exception of a few daughters of intellectuals who understood that in addition to running a home, women could acquire a cultural horizon, most Spanish women had only one aspiration: to get married. The aims of a woman's education were to prepare her to be a good wife, a devoted mother, and a fine homemaker. In the 1930's, things changed. Life became much more expensive in postwar Spain, and many women were faced with the necessity of going to work. Offices became filled with secretaries, stores with salesladies, tourist agencies with interpreters, airlines with hostesses. This situation, which was at variance with the traditional Spanish ideal, was imposed by the force of reality. In addition, city girls who no longer wanted to be maids sought professional training that would enable them to work as hairdressers, clerks, office workers, and the like. Domestic servants were recruited among country girls from poor agricultural areas.

This situation brought to the fore the problem of education of women. Should they study according to their intellectual ability? Or, should their education be limited to a minimum that would prepare them to fill subordinate positions only? Mediocre men feared female competition and supported the latter alternative. Intelligent men wished to give women absolute freedom. Certain traditional groups proposed a happy medium: the creation of special female professions, such as those of home economics teachers, social workers, nurses, and the like, considered appropriate for women. For twenty years this tendency prevailed. A group of women university graduates, however, fought incessantly for the right of every woman to fill any and all positions according to her abilities. The law of July 1961 was the fruit of this struggle.

Today, female education is open to all social classes. Scholarships and the will to achieve bring together former señoritas and the daughters of workers in university classrooms, laboratories and libraries.

The law provides that every girl upon reaching sixteen years of age must devote herself to the service of the state for a period of six months. Every year hundreds of thousands of girls are thus detailed to serve in offices, hospitals, nurseries, or charity kitchens, each in accordance with her training and ability. At the same time, they receive thorough home economics training, similar to the type offered to rural women by the Traveling Teachers of the Sisterhood of Town and Country. In this manner, every Spanish girl receives some basic training according to her ability and talent. On the other hand, the indispensable homemaking tasks are not neglected, since the desire of most women is still to stop working when they get married, in order to dedicate themselves fully to their husband, children, and home.

SEX MORES

In general, the sexual life of the Spanish woman begins with marriage. Given their moral and religious training, 95 per cent of all Spanish girls remain virgins until they marry. Birth control is not allowed; abortion is punishable by a light prison sentence for the pregnant woman who consents to it and by a heavy prison sentence for anyone who performs it.

No sexual education of any sort is given in schools. Mothers usually tell their small children either that they "brought them from Paris," or that the stork brought them. Only recently have modern mothers begun to give their inquisitive children valid information suitable to their understanding. One must add that the position of unwed mothers and of illegitimate children is extremely difficult (the magistrates of the office of Protection of Minors do not give the right of custody to the mother of an illegitimate child). All this is conducive to making the relationships between young people rather restrained and cautious.

Large families are frequent, and couples who limit the number of children, despite the orders of the Church, are excluded from the sacraments. This is understandably painful for men and women brought up in the Church whose character has been formed by its teachings. Only in special cases does the Catholic Church, to which 98 per cent of Spaniards belong, allow the use of the method developed by the Japanese gynecologist Dr Oggino and named after him. Public discussion of sex is not pleasing to the Spaniard, nor has there yet been a Spanish counterpart to the Kinsey Report, and thus little concrete information is available on the subject.

Elena Quiroga, who won the Nadal Literary Prize in 1950, reports that in some towns of Galicia, unwed mothers, instead of being scorned, are regarded with admiration. On Sundays, during the dance in the square, they remain standing, holding their children in their arms, as a sign of pride. These girls are admired, not because they are promiscuous, but because they are what the people call *mozas probadas*, that is, women who have proven their ability to bear children.

In past centuries, custom in this respect was more liberal. Thus, up to the beginning of the eighteenth century, a type of common-law marriage was practiced. It was called *la barragania*, and constituted an intermediate relationship between true marriage and a casual short-lived affair. The *barragana* or *manceba* (the woman living in barragania) was well treated and respected, and the children born of such unions succeeded to the titles and honors of their fathers, as was the case with Don Martin Cortés, son of Doña Marina and Hernán Cortés; Fernando Colón, son of Christopher Columbus and Doña Beatrice Enríques; and Francisca Pizarro, daughter of Hernando Pizarro and Doña Isabel Mercado, and heir to the titles, honors and riches of the Conquistador of Peru.

MARRIAGE

In Spain, marriage is a religious (Catholic) ceremony with civil consequences. There exists, however, civil marriage as well, for those not professing the official state religion. In either case, marriage is indissoluble. Bride and groom go to the wedding ceremony conscious of performing a tremendously important act, which will unite them until death. The Spanish family sets an example for permanence and solidity.

Head and master of the house is the husband, although the wife often manages to have her way while letting her husband think that it is his.

A Spaniard does not take kindly to the idea of a well-educated and intellectually gifted wife. He views suspiciously a wife who is his equal, and with real repugnance one who is his superior. Truly intelligent wives know how to appear mediocre. Successful marriages are those in which the wife is, or appears to be, "Good-looking, good-looking; silly, silly," as the saying goes.

The upper-middle class woman does not work outside the home. Those of the lower-middle class who worked before marriage try to keep their jobs, mostly because they have become accustomed to a higher standard of living that can only be maintained if both husband and wife work. Among the working class, too, the wife works, usually as a domestic paid by the hour.

The Spanish wife is obliged to follow her husband wherever he chooses to reside. The husband administers the couple's property and income, unless separation of property was stipulated at marriage. This, however, is done rarely because the husband considers it humiliating and damaging to his pride. Generally, the woman is in charge of only small daily or monthly household expenses.

Certain legal acts can be performed by the wife only if the husband permits her to do so. For example, she can testify in court, litigate concerning her *parafernales*, mortgage her property or practice business only if duly authorized by her husband. As to those juridical acts which the wife carries out without the husband's authorization, some jurists consider them null and void, others, among them Castan Tobeñas and some members of the Supreme Court, regard them as subject to annulment if the husband or his heirs are so inclined.

The Woman in the Family and in Society

The woman as mother has always had great influence in Spain. As a widow, her important role as supporter of her children has been discussed earlier. As a wife, her position is dependent upon that of her husband. In case of separation, the judges who determine the amount of her alimony, bear in mind not only her material needs but also the needs arising from her social position which, in turn, is a reflection of her husband's position.

The law regulating the family subsidy provides that every salaried employee shall receive an increment upon marrying. If the husband dies, his wife receives a widow's pension from the state if he was a state official, or from the private firm where he was employed. If he leaves an estate, the widow can claim a pension payable from the estate. The amount varies depending on whether or not there are children.

The Spanish woman lives with the men of the family — father, brothers, husband — in the same part of the house. Long past are the days of the harem and of those Christian houses in which the women were relegated to the *estrado*, a room set aside for them to receive their exclusively female friends.

With few exceptions, the Spaniard is not given to forming friendships with women. A relationship of this sort is hardly understood. He is either in love with a woman, or is completely indifferent. There is no Spanish counterpart of the "amorous friendship" *(amitié amoureuse)*, so popular among the French, nor to the friend-escort, the *cicisbeo*, frequently encountered in Italy up to the nineteenth century.

In social relations, there is an instinctive tendency for the sexes to separate into two groups. In one, the women talk about suitors, if they are single girls or married women with marriageable daughters, or about children and household matters. The male group talks about "work, business, soccer, bulls, and women." For, although they talk little to the women, they speak a great deal about them.

The separation of the two sexes is strictly observed, especially at gatherings occasioned by the death of a friend or relative, and no woman of any social class would dare enter the room reserved for male mourners. In Andalusia, whether in the large houses surrounded by courtyards and gardens, or in the simple habitats, this separation of the sexes is even more evident. In large cities, with their smaller homes containing only one living room, social mingling of the two sexes is inevitable. However, as much space as possible is always reserved for the head of the family; he has his study where he isolates himself and where, until recently, the library was located.

People with university background accustomed to coeducation, or artistic circles of writers, painters, newspapermen, and theatrical people, enjoy gatherings of both sexes, and they meet to chat in private homes or in cafés. Such groups are growing from day to day.

The single girl is still subject to considerable limitations. Although both men and women attain legal majority at the age of twenty-one, from twenty-one to twenty-five, girls may not leave their father's house without parental permission, except to marry, or to enter a convent.

THE HOME ROUTINE

Even women who work outside the home spend several hours a day with household tasks. Maids facilitate the care of the home, but it is always the lady of the house who selects the menu for the two daily meals, sees to it that the house is cleaned and that the laundry is done, as well as all the other chores. In upper-class households the latter include the daily changing of sheets, tablecloths, towels, and personal underwear. The linens are always starched. The floors are waxed, although recently some women have taken to varnishing them.

Maids in upper-class houses, and many in middle-class homes, have their own bathrooms and well-furnished bedrooms. Since 1957, with the founding of the Domestic Help Service, the position of maids has improved considerably. They have all kinds of social security, plus benefits for old age, accidents and sickness, the monthly fees for which are paid largely by their employers (90 per cent) with a small (10 per cent) contribution from the maids themselves. They are also given a dowry and a hopechest when they marry.

There is an old tradition in Spain of regarding servants as members of the family. In Andalusia, for example, a sick servant would be cared for at home, and not sent to the hospital. Aged servants were "retired," and lived on in the home until death. Today, crowded modern living conditions created the need to establish Homes for Retired Servants, under the state's Domestic Help Service.

Middle-class homes usually have maids coming in to work by the hour. If a family cannot afford a maid, the wife does all the work. Electric household appliances are not extensively used; washing machines are found here and there, refrigerators and vacuum cleaners very rarely. The best of husbands would find it humiliating to help his wife dry dishes, sweep the floor, or make the bed. The woman does everything, and many wives even take hot noon meals to their husbands at work. The custom of having a substantial breakfast, and taking along a sandwich for lunch, or going to a cafeteria, does not exist. The typical Spanish meal requires cooking, and its preparation is time-consuming. Even today, with so many social changes in progress, a mother could not conceive of her daughters going off to work or to school without leaving their rooms in good order; they would never dare expect the same of a son.

THE SOCIAL POSITION OF WOMEN

The social position of the women in Spain still depends on that of the family. The upper class in Spain consists of the nobility and the wealthy bourgeoisie—bankers, landowners, proprietors of factories and industries. The upper-middle class, composed of persons who owe their position to their education and skills and who live on their earnings, often in managerial jobs, includes doctors, engineers, lawyers, architects, writers, etcetera. The lower-middle class, made up partly of those of the aforementioned groups who have lost their wealth or position, include clerks, employees, and assistants. Beneath them in the social scale is the most numerous working class.

The upper-middle and lower-middle classes supplied women students to attend universities and the protagonists of the special Spanish brand of feminism. Unfortunately, the great masses of workers, obliged to face immediate and vital problems, cannot develop their inherent intellectual talents. In order to raise their cultural level, Workers' Universities and vocational schools have been founded which, at one and the same time, also train them in a skilled trade.

It is interesting to note that when women began to enter various occupations, this resulted in a levelling off of class differences. Thus, the daughter of a doctor may work as a secretary or a saleslady in a store, and her colleague may be the daughter of the superintendent of the apartment house in which they live, or of the chauffeur who drives her father's car. The son of the doctor, however, would be unlikely to meet the son of the superintendent or of the chauffeur as a colleague. It is not easy to rise from one social class to a higher one.

The explanation of the dependence of woman's social position on that of her family lies in the fact that a Spanish girl never leaves her father's house until she marries. In other countries, working girls live independently, sharing rooms with girl friends. In Spain this is almost unheard of.

WOMEN'S OCCUPATIONS

Women's occupations show great variations depending on family circumstances, economic status, and social position.

The mother of small children can hardly find time for other activities. The exception to this rule are the few who manage to write, as do three of the best modern Spanish novelists, Carmen Laforet, Ana-Maria Martin Gayte and Ana-Maria Matute, university graduates and winners of the Nadal Prize, who have written their books while taking care of their homes and bringing up their children.

In the cities, most working women are employed in secretarial work, as saleswomen, telephone operators, telegraphists, nurses, or in the textile industry, canneries, and factories of all types. Others work in private homes as dressmakers, laundresses, cooks, companions, nursemaids, or general maids.

In the regions of Lagartera, Almagro, Galicia, in the Canary Islands, and in the towns of the Alpujarras, embroidery and lacework constitute the main occupation and source of income of many families, within which the tradition of "stitches" and designs has been handed down from mother to daughter. On sunny days, one can see young and old women, as well as little girls, sitting in front of their houses, busy with their embroidery and crocheting.

Pottery, the decoration of china and glassware, mat making, basket weaving, rug making, as well as aviculture, apiculture and other important home industries, are specialties to which many women devote themselves.

Women who do not work outside the home devote some hours every day, or at least every week, to social work. The girl who completed her six-month period of Social Service and contributed to the effort to alleviate her country's problems in one field or another retains a sense of responsibility, and usually continues to do part-time volunteer work.

In the cities, the housing and employment problems have become more acute because of migration from the rural areas. Many Spanish women, some motivated by charity, others by a sense of social justice, try to provide these newcomers with work, help them adjust to the new situation and solve the new problems of city living. The wife of a worker may find employment for a few hours a day through the Domestic Service placement office, but she would have to leave her children alone or in the care of a neighbor. To relieve mothers of this problem, women's groups are trying to increase the number of free day nurseries. This work is pursued especially by the society of *Luisas de Marillac*.

The Seccion Femenina carries out its important activities through the Sisterhood of Town and Country, the Social Aid Benefits, the civic tasks of the Social Service, the Youth Front, the students' organizations, as well as the cultural and art organizations, such as the Choruses and Dances. All these are run by women. Here, too, should be mentioned the charities organized by women, the fight against cancer, and women's participation in the International Red Cross and in Caritas.

WOMEN IN LEADERSHIP

Bearing in mind the difficulties that Spanish women encountered in their struggle for the development and use of their intellectual faculties, it is not surprising that the number of women in leadership is small. Lack of opportunity, not of ability, is the reason. The law that ended their disabilities is dated July 22, 1961. As of this year, one can speak of the ability of women to fill positions of leadership, and discuss whether the legislature was justified in showing confidence in their talents.

Fifty years earlier, in 1910, the Minister of Education, Sr. Burrel, secured a variety of openings for the Spanish women, which crystallized in the following decades. By the time of the Republic of 1931–1936, several capable women had high positions. Maria de Maeztu, founder and first director of the residence for women university students, an authentic pioneer of Spanish feminism, was an outstanding member of the *Junta de Ampliacion de E.tudios* (Committee on Curriculum Development) which played a very important role in Spanish intellectual life. Her collaborators were Rafaela Ortega y Gasset, Jimena Menendez Pidal (today director of the pedagogical center "Estudio"), Africa Ramirez, Pilar Madariaga, Eulalia Lapresta, and Dolores Galvarriato.

In the field of law, Dr. Victoria Kent, the first woman director general of prisons, carried out important and humane reforms in the penal system.

Among women occupying positions of great responsibility, the following may be mentioned: Doña Margarita Salaverria de Arguelles, the first Spanish woman diplomat, today Minister Plenipotentiary of the First Class; Doña Pilar Careaga de Lequerica, engineer; Matilde Ucelay de Ruiz Castillo and Maria Juana Ontañon, architects; Doña Luisa Trigo, doctor of medicine.

Between 1939 and 1962, the positions of leadership held by women were largely of a political nature. Among them are Doña Pilar Primo de Rivera, chief of the National Delegation of the Seccion Femenina and Doña Mercedes Sanz Bachiller, founder of Social Aid, and expert in labor questions; these two women are Procurators of the Courts, a position similar to that of the former Provincial Deputies. To theirs should be added the name of Doña Josefina Sedeño, a telephone operator, who was elected Procurator by her Union in 1961. Doña Carmen Werner de Duran founded the Girls' Youth Front, the Homemaking Schools, and Youth Hostels. She was also instrumental in founding the Domestic Help Service, the Vocational Schools, and the Homes for the Aged. Doña Syra Manteola, an accountant, is one of the most capable Spanish women living today, and has a great sense of social justice. She devotes her energy to the elimination of illiteracy and the problem of housing for rural families that have migrated to the city. She is the Head of the Section of Family Social Work of the National Housing Institute. Carmen Herrero, president of *Luisas de Marillac*, has an extraordinary capacity for work, and great organizational ability. Carmen Cavestaeni, one of the best pilots in Spain, is the heart and soul of the Society for the Care of the Aged.

WOMEN AS CULTURAL TRANSMITTERS

Compared to the length of human history, the period granted to the Spanish woman for her cultural development has been extremely brief. Nevertheless, there have been women on the soil of the Iberian peninsula who have carried the torch of culture and art since the Middle Ages. The names of the Arab poetesses, Vallada and Romaiquia, come to mind first. Doña Beatriz Galindo, *La Latina*, with a solid background in the humanities, who studied at the University of Salamanca, was Queen Isabella's teacher. During the colonization of the Americas, Doña Mencia Calderon brought great culture and civilization to the Viceroyship of La Plata (Argentina). In the fine arts, the sculptress Luisa Roldan, known as *La Roldana*, was outstanding. Her works are still admired during the Holy Week processions in Seville. The poetess Teresa de Ahumada became Santa Teresa de Jesus.

In the eighteenth century, there were two great patronesses of painting, Countess-Duchess de Benavente, who patronized and "launched" Goya, and Doña Cayetana de Silva, the Duchess of Alba, who was Goya's favorite model and deepest love. Their contemporary was the Duchess of Arcos, Honorary Member of the Royal Academies of San Fernando of Madrid and of the Imperial Academy of Art of St. Petersburg. Towards the end of the nineteenth and beginning of the twentieth century lived the novelists Emilia Pardo Bazán, the best writer of her time, Cecilia Bohl de Faber who used the pseudonym Fernan Caballero, Concha Espina, another fine writer, and the poetesses Rosalia de Castro, Carolina Coronado, and Gertrudis Gomez de Avellaneda.

The great woman criminologist and author, Concepción Arenal, struggled against ridicule and indifference, but succeeded in improving the penitentiary system. Her slogan, still to be read over the entrances to some prisons, was "Hate the crime but pity the criminal." The contemporary historian, and only female member of the Historical Academy, Doña Mercedes Gaibrois de Ballesteros, has produced important works in collaboration with her husband, the historian Antonio Ballesteros. Doña Maria Goyri, wife of the present President of the Language Academy, Ramón

Menendez-Pidal, was a talented philologist who has collaborated with her husband in his research work on Sephardi themes.

Doña Maria Luisa Caturla, the only woman among the Patrons of the Prado Museum, an art historian, discovered several unknown works of Zurbarán, whose life and works are her field of specialization. Zenobia Camprubi, wife of Juan Ramón Jimenez, Nobel Prize winning poet, sacrificed her own literary ambitions in the interests of her husband's poetic talents. Doña Dolores Moya de Marañon, wife of the well-known doctor and writer Don Gregorio, and daughter of a cultured journalist, has for forty years worked as her husband's secretary and able collaborator.

The present Duchess of Alba, a young mother, follows the tradition of her family. A painter of note herself, she is a true patroness of the arts. The social-artistic gatherings of the Countesses de Yebes and Campoalange encourage the search for new values. In addition, both are talented writers.

But where the Spanish woman has had the most outstanding role is in the field of the novel, where Eulalia Galvarriato, Carmen Laforet, Elena Quiroga, Ana-Maria Matute, Carmen Martin-Gayte, Dolores Medio, Mercedes Ballesteros are outstanding. There are also talented journalists, such as Maria de la Mora, Josefina Carabias, Carmen Castro (who is also an art critic), Pilar Narvion, and Begoña Garcia-Diego. The outstanding women painters of our times are Menchu Gal, Maruja Mallo and Sofia Morales. In other fields are the industrial engineer and teacher of physical sciences, Doña Carmen Segura; the physician Doña Mercedes Mazas, and the lawyers Doña Pilar Villar, Doña Carmen Salinas, and Doña Josefina Bartomeu. Doña Lidia Falcon teaches at the University of Barcelona and is the author of several important volumes on the civil and labor rights of women.

THE OUTLOOK

As recently as two years ago, this paper would have ended with the statement that the greatest aspiration of the Spanish woman was to see enacted a law permitting her to obtain those positions to which her intelligence entitled her. Today, such a law is a fact, and its promulgation is the culmination of all our aspirations. It now remains to demonstrate concetely that the Spanish woman deserved the confidence the legislators placed in her.

Now that the quest for equal work opportunities has been satisfied, it is an opportune moment to restate that the Spanish woman has always had one ideal, namely, to have a family, and to devote her efforts to husband, home and children. This ideal often had to be reconciled with the pressing reality, that obliged many women to work outside the home in order to live decently; and to this the women have willingly adjusted. But the fact that women have adjusted to the demands of the times does not mean they have forgotten the old ideal which is part of their nature. Although they have clamored for equal rights because life has forced them to work outside the home, they also insist that these rights must be exercised prudently. Even if she becomes a good lawyer, engineer, or doctor, a woman must never forget that her ultimate *raison d'être* is to create a family, despite all risks, sacrifices, and renunciations that this vital endeavor entails. We should not like to live in a world of overly independent, overly gifted women if it would entail their putting aside the humble yet magnificent task of giving life the continuity it demands.

Satisfaction over our achievements, after a long struggle, does not mean that we have reached the final phase. The principle is good. It was just and human for the working woman—whether single, widowed or married—to work on the same level as the man. But the ideal remains to have a family. We therefore hope that the economic organization of the country will reach a stage in which the functions will be divided, the man going to work, and earning enough for the home, the woman remaining at home, caring for the children, preparing them for the future, making the home a pleasant place for the husband to return to. After all is said and done, how sad is the so-called continued "independence" of the woman. It is but the right to the most dismal solitude.

Spanish America

By Rosa Signorelli de Marti

THE TRADITIONAL POSITION

*B*efore discussing the present position of the Spanish-American woman, it is necessary to take a look, even if only a cursory one, at her position in the past. This will make the causes of the inequalities that are still operating today more understandable.

The circumstances of the past, together with present conditions are responsible for the different rates of progress in women's rights and position: in some countries they have advanced rapidly, in others, slowly, while in some, they have remained more or less unchanged since Colonial times.

Prior to the beginning of the movements for emancipation, the position of the woman in all of these countries was characterized by a lack of legal rights in private life and by the absence of any participation in public life. For all practical purposes, her entire life was confined to the home.

In matrimony, the old patriarchal pattern subordinated the woman to

Translated from the Spanish by Judith Arnon.

her husband both legally and socially. The husband was the owner of the family estate. Everything the woman brought into the marriage, everything she received later as a gift, or earned or inherited, became the property of her husband. Nor did she inherit from her husband. Only if his death left her in penury did she receive one fourth of his estate, but in no case more than one hundred gold pounds no matter how large a fortune the husband left.

A mother's rights in relation to her children were minimal compared to those of her husband, who was legally entitled to pawn or even sell his children, in case of necessity. The mother's rights were limited to giving her consent to the marriage of any of her children who were over twenty-five years of age, and only in the absence of the father.

Nevertheless, the woman was a decisive factor in the wellbeing of the home, for, in addition to taking charge of the housekeeping (which, in well-to-do families was carried out by slaves), she supervised all household crafts, such as spinning, securing food supplies, leather work, the preparation of remedies for family ailments, and so on, which in those times had great importance due to the high price of manufactured products. The poorer women carried out all the household tasks themselves and cared for their usually large families. In practice, they alone were often responsible for the management of the household, since the husband who usually worked in remote parts of the country remained absent from the home for long periods of time.

The social position of women was an organic part of the feudal type of social organization imposed on these colonies by the Spanish conquistadors. For many Central and South American peoples this constituted a marked retrogression. In Mexico until the fall of the great Tenochtitlan in 1521, Aztec women commanded great respect in the eyes of the law and of society. They possessed property, signed contracts, appeared before tribunals, and cemented intertribal alliances through matrimony.

A wife could ask for divorce if her husband mistreated her or was incapable of supporting her and their children. If the marriage was dissolved by divorce, she could remarry anyone she liked.

At the age of fifty, the woman was freed of submission to her husband, obtained the same rights he enjoyed, and was accorded great respect. She became part of the group of elders to whom people went for advice.

The dynastic lineage was transmitted through the woman. If her son was too young to act as *cacique* (chief), as well as in certain other circumstances, she acted as regent.

The Aztecs had great respect for pregnant women, treating them with great consideration and courtesy, for they considered them the fountain of life.

The position of Aztec women changed radically under Spanish domination. They became objects of exploitation for work and pleasure; their rights were abolished; their education, formerly so highly developed, no longer concerned anyone. Illiteracy was taken for granted with regard to women, and so deeply-rooted was this feeling that today it still exists among the native population throughout Latin America.

Following the triumph of the independence movements, when the various countries began to organize as nations in their own rights, with their own judicial systems, they took inspiration from two sources: the preexisting ruling institutions and customs, to which they gave legal form; and the provisions contained in the Napoleonic Code, which, in turn, is based on Roman Law.

As for legislation concerning women, the countries already freed from Spanish domination covered the old laws with a thin veneer of liberalism, preserving the outlook of ancient Roman Law that regarded women as suffering from *imbecilitas sexus*, that is to say, as imbeciles, due to their sex. In some Spanish-American countries, vestiges of these concepts are found to this day.

The characteristics of women's position during the colonial period survive in the different Spanish-American countries to the extent to which the economic and social conditions of that period still persist. On the other hand, the social and cultural differences between the women who were descendants of the Spanish immigrants and the native women were very sharp. The former belonged to the dominant group which, in the early days of colonization, exploited the country economically, and later, when its members came as immigrant working people, brought with it social, cultural, and technical achievements which gave it the advantage in the struggle for life. The opportunities of the women of this group were incomparably superior to those of the native women. The latter were pushed into obscure corners, confined to carrying out the rougher and low-paying jobs, without any legal or social protection, and deprived of all possibilities for education, hygiene, and similar advantages. Generally speaking, this is the situation in which the women of the poorer classes of the population in each country still find themselves.

As far as the development of institutions and society in Spanish America in general is concerned, it is not easy to find a dividing line between prewar and postwar conditions. For other continents, World War II had a tremendous importance, not only because of the destruction and loss of life it caused, but also because of the profound technological and social innovations it brought about. In South America the war was not felt directly, either for better or for worse. Far from the battlefields, playing no important role in any aspect of the dispute, the continent was reached only by a faint echo of the war. Nor have its economic, social, and political consequences affected South America except indirectly. Thus in Spanish America, World War II cannot serve as such a convenient dividing line between the old and the new, as it does in other parts of the world.

TOWN AND COUNTRY

The main differences between the position of the urban and rural Spanish-American woman are due to the character of the economy in those two sectors of each country. The basis of rural economy is agriculture or fishing, or a combination of the two. These factors shape the life of the society, the family and the woman. Underdevelopment was the common characteristic of all types of rural economy. Familial and social organization were, generally, semipatriarchal, with the woman subordinated to the man legally and socially. Her role in the rudimentary economy, on the other hand, was basic. Her tasks were many: to bring up her numerous children, to prepare meals for all the men who worked on the farm, to spin, to sow, to harvest, to care for the animals, and all this on a very low economic, social and cultural level.

In the underdeveloped regions, which abound in every Spanish-American country, most of the people lived in dire poverty. This was the prevalent life pattern of the Indians and *cholos* of Bolivia, of the indigenous populations of Ecuador, Peru, Chile, and other countries.

In the cities, where industry had begun to develop, the situation of women was better, since they enjoyed greater possibilities of work, higher wages, a certain hygienic standard, etcetera. The economic advances, attained by the Spanish-American countries in varying degrees, and felt mainly in the urban centers, brought with them a higher standard of living and placed within women's reach new opportunities for education, work and social welfare. This was parallelled by civil legislation which strengthened her position in the family and in society.

The young woman who lives in a poor village, far from railway stations, main roads, or ports, is still surrounded by approximately the same social and technological environment as her mother and grandmother before her. Her horizon is limited to the distance to which her feet can carry her, and she is tied to the animals and plants, to the river, the brook, the lagoon, or the hills that she knew as a child. But then the old dusty track is asphalted; automobiles and trucks begin to pass the old *rancho*, carrying people from other places or laden with fruits destined for a remote market. Soon the character of the place begins to change. Buildings rise, businesses open, a service station is built, a bus line appears, new sources of work are created; a dentist, a doctor move in; the house of a private teacher is turned into a school. . . . Primitive, uneconomic, unhygienic conditions are gradually transformed and the position of the country woman is improved.

LEGAL STATUS

The legal position of the woman has been developing in the direction of equality with man.[1] In the field of women's civil rights, progress is being made although inequalities have not yet disappeared completely. Thus, in Argentina, the husband retains certain privileges such as the right to mortgage and sell property belonging to the couple without requiring the wife's consent. He remains administrator of all their possessions, including those belonging to his wife. And he alone has custody of their children, which means, for example, that a mother cannot travel abroad with her children if her husband does not authorize her to do so.

This position of the Argentinian woman dates back to the law of 1926, called the Woman's Civil Rights law, which was a compromise between the older law and the new reality: the achievement by women of a position in society no longer compatible with the limitations imposed upon them by the Civil and Commercial Code. The law of 1926 did not modify the basis of the matrimonial situation. It retained the principle of community property, but it improved the legal position of the woman, especially that of the married woman, by abolishing a great part of the legal inabilities that were the concomitants of the married status with reference to the administration of the couple's property.

Prior to this law, the legal position of the married woman was completely subordinate to her husband. Moreover, she was severely limited in making use of the few laws that were in her favor. For example, the Civil Code authorized the husband to give his wife power of attorney to administer their property during his absence or illness; legal decisions, however, thwarted women in the exercise of this right by holding that the husband could not grant a general power of attorney to his wife, but only temporary and concretely-circumscribed ones to carry out a specific action.

The example of the status of married women in the United States was a weighty factor in the abolition of the legal inequalities that marriage imposed on women in Spanish-American countries. In Mexico, since the great legal reform that began with the Constitution of Queretaro of 1917, all the Codes in effect, and especially the Civil Code of 1928, follow the principle that men and women have identical rights. The Chilean Civil Code, which is very similar to the Argentinian, was modified by the law of 1934 by eliminating the restrictions on the woman; her position is the same in the Commercial Code. In Uruguay, where women achieved political equality before civil equality, legislative reforms concerning their rights were initiated in 1926.

---

1. In this connection, mention should be made of the U.N. Commission on the Status of Women whose aim is to obtain equality of rights for man and woman, and of the Inter-American Women's Commission which, since its creation 34 years ago, has worked intensively to achieve the same objective throughout the Americas.

There has been general progress, during recent years, in labor legislation, from which the working woman has benefited. The principle of "equal pay for equal work" has already been accepted in Argentina, Mexico, Costa Rica, Ecuador, El Salvador, Guatemala, Honduras, Nicaragua, Panama, Chile, the Dominican Republic, and Colombia.

As to political rights, the honor of having been the first country in Spanish America to grant voting rights to women belongs to the Republic of Ecuador. With the passage of the law of female suffrage in Paraguay on July 5, 1961, a chapter in the political development of the continent was closed: all women in all the American republics are now accorded the dignity of full citizenship.

EDUCATION

Education of women is fundamental for the achievement and full exercise of their legal and social independence. Consequently, as long as their education and professional training remain inferior to those of men, their economic, social and political opportunities inevitably suffer.

The women's educational level varies greatly with the general degree of development achieved in each country. The average female educational attainment in capital cities like Buenos Aires, Mexico City, or Lima, is much superior to that of the remote rural regions where the population lives on a subsistence level with very low standards of living and culture. In the latter regions, where illiteracy reaches 90 per cent, one can well imagine how low the educational level of the woman is. The first task is to raise the literacy level. All over Spanish America, there is a growing interest in making free and compulsory primary education available to all.

In the fight against illiteracy, most noteworthy is the work of the government of Colombia, with its energetic program of elementary education, and that of El Salvador, with its remarkable literacy campaign in the agricultural areas. A nationwide literacy campaign is being carried out in Argentina by the National Literacy and School Building Committee with the active cooperation of the Army.

The education of women in urban and industrial centers is being intensified in all countries. The old-fashioned curricula are being replaced by a more practical complement of subjects that will provide women with the necessary means for earning a living and becoming an important factor in the development of their countries.

This change is being carried out at varying rates of speed in the different countries. In general, on both the primary and secondary levels, the tendency to cram the pupils' heads full of book-learning is very widespread. The subjects taught have little bearing on the actual environment and conditions. These shortcomings are found also in university teaching, particularly in the humanities.

Attempts are being made to provide professional and technical education of a type that will enable women to find their places in the new industries. For this it is necessary, in all of Spanish America, to increase the number of professional and technical schools, and to adapt their study programs to the particular conditions and requirements of the region in which the students are going to live and work.

At present, in many countries, the industrial schools accept female students; the fact that not many women attend such schools must be attributed to the low demand for qualified women in the job market.

Labor unions make an important contribution to this field by maintaining schools and training courses in various trades. But the attendance of women in these courses is negligible, mainly because the participation of the woman in union activities in general is weak. This problem received special consideration in the National Seminar on the Participation of Women in Public Life, that took place in Argentina in 1960.[2] In it, the following resolutions were adopted: (1) To awaken the conscience of women toward the community in general and the trade-union in particular; (2) To favor their affiliation with unions, their active participation in their work, and their promotion to managerial jobs and union responsibilities; (3) To further women's direct participation in collective bargaining; (4) To ask that women union delegates be included in committees and legislative bodies.

Examples of the trend towards practical training of women are the vocational university of Uruguay; the establishment of the technical baccalaureate and the foundation of the coeducational Technical University in Ecuador; the Center of Studies for Development of the Central University of Venezuela; the courses and programs in industrial education offered by the government of Guatemala in collaboration with the country's industry and given at the Technical Vocational Institute. In Guatemala there are also courses in industrial training for women given at the centers of industrial studies connected with primary schools, private academies, vocational schools and schools for workers. Women attend industrial schools in greater numbers than business schools, and constitute a high percentage of the student body in both types of institutions.

It is fitting to point out that this increase in training facilities for women coincides with the opening of new opportunities and the social transformation that is taking place as a consequence of the strengthening of the Guatemalan national economy.

---

2. This Seminar was organized by the Direccion Nacional de la Mujer and inspired by the Regional Seminars of Bangkok (Thailand) in 1957 and of Bogota, Colombia, in 1959, under the auspices of the United Nations.

SEX MORES

The traditional female attitude towards the opposite sex in Spanish America is a heritage of the colonial period, during which Spanish customs, and particularly Castilian-Arab mores, were transplanted to America. In those days, women were restricted to their homes; girls were controlled by their mothers who brought them up in accordance with the Spanish standards of feminine restraint toward men which, in effect, meant the complete suppression of any spontaneous sentiment or emotion.

The separation of the sexes was strictly observed in primary and secondary schools and impressed upon the children by parental precept and example. In addition, two completely different standards of behavior, attitudes and outlook were applied to boys and girls, the former being given great latitude and many privileges, the latter being severely restricted in social contacts, studies, and movements. One of the consequences of this type of upbringing is that man and woman look upon each other almost exclusively as objects of potential sexual relations, either legitimate or clandestine.

The failure to establish relationships based on mutual interests is one of the factors that obstructs marital happiness. Husband and wife do not really know each other, and both suffer from prejudices of a sexual nature, that are as deeply rooted in the man as in the woman.

This situation emphatically points to the necessity of imparting pre-marital education to members of both sexes, in which the medical, social, juridical, and technical aspects of married life should be stressed. Unfortunately, this type of education is almost totally unknown even in the largest cities.

Another disastrous consequence of this old-fashioned relationship between the sexes is the prevalence of extramarital relations. The general feeling is that such liaisons are quite in order for men, while they involve great loss of dignity and status for women. In many cases, young women who leave their villages or small towns and go to the big city to find a better livelihood get entangled in such illegitimate relationships. What usually happens is that after a short while, the man who succeeded in seducing such a girl leaves her and then she easily falls victim to another who similarly takes advantage of her. The incidence of pregnancies resulting from such relationships is very high.

This is the story of almost all the unwed mothers in the cities. Like those in the country, they lack all legal and social protection. Their fate, and that which awaits their children, can easily be imagined. With rare exceptions, they do not wish to return home, where they could count on the support of their own mothers. In the overwhelming majority of cases, they sign away their babies before they are born, through one of the many intermediaries who do a prosperous business selling the babies to childless couples; occasionally, the mothers simply abandon the babies; in even more unfortunate cases, they do away with them. In any event, the unwed mother, now freed of her child, becomes emotionally crippled; as a rule, the next step that inevitably follows is prostitution. On the other hand, if the unwed mother keeps and supports her child, which is generally the case in rural areas, her sense of responsibility grows with the difficult role of playing both mother and father; thus, inadvertently, she acquires additional status in society. She can give full play to her maternal feelings and aspire to distinction through her child and the sacrifices she makes for it.

The picture painted above fits most closely the native women, whose lives are circumscribed by cultural and social backwardness. Women originating in more developed countries, poor as they may be, do not generally become victims of such situations.

It is a herald of change for the better that in recent years a reaction against the traditional separation of the sexes is noticeable in many parts of Spanish America. The new trend is for men and women to know and understand each other, to work together, and to develop sincerity in their relationships. An important outcome of this new development is the increase in the number of marriages based on mutual respect and consideration.

MARRIAGE

In general, modern laws regard marriage as a contract; in some cases, as in Argentina, it is a contract *sui generis*, for in contrast to the usual ones, it cannot be dissolved by the joint decision of the two parties, nor by that of one of them alone.

Generally speaking, the husband is the acknowledged head of the Spanish-American family. In Argentina, the law provides that the husband is the head of the family and that there exists only one matrimonial establishment: the conjugal partnership. That is, by virtue of matrimony, a conjugal contractual relationship or association is established that is governed by the rules laid down in the partnership contract, as long as they do not conflict with what is expressly determined by the Civil Code.

The capital of the association is the wealth, property, and profits of both spouses: whatever each of the two brings into the marriage, whatever they acquire through inheritance and in the form of gifts during the marriage, and whatever they earn from their work.

As the head of the family, the husband decides on the place of domicile, which the wife must accept (this is the law in Argentina, Uruguay, Chile, Peru, Venezuela), except in certain special cases.

As to the children, the husband enjoys greater rights than the wife. In most countries, he has custody over them. In Bolivia and Nicaragua he has, in addition, the right to administer and use his children's property, and in Chile, the right to punish them, direct their education and choose their profession.

But there is a trend in legislation to recognize the right of the mother to custody. In Peru, this right belongs to both parents, but in case of dissent, the father's decision prevails. In Mexico and Uruguay, both parents also have custody. In the former, the father is the administrator of the child's property and wealth, but the law limits this right by requiring consent of the wife for his most important administrative decisions. In Uruguay, by the law of 1946, the father and the mother decide jointly who of the two will administer the property of their minor children.

Generally, therefore, the husband controls and administers the property of the couple, with certain limitations. In Chile, for instance, he needs the court's permission if he wishes to transfer or sell real estate brought into the marriage by the wife.

As to the dissolution of the marriage bond through divorce, it is legally accepted in some countries, such as Mexico and Uruguay. In Argentina, divorce is not permitted, although numerous bills have been presented to Congress since the year 1888. In 1955, a divorce law was passed, but it was again abrogated in 1956. The Argentinian Civil Code speaks of "divorce" when, in fact, it refers to the separation of the couple and their property without dissolving the marriage bond. The term divorce is accepted in this sense only, as in Canon Law.

In addition to legal matrimony, other forms which are not legalized are very widespread in Spanish America. Thus, in rural areas, there are more common-law marriages than legitimate unions. In the remote and underdeveloped areas of many countries, the functions of the Civil Registration Office are unknown, and conjugal relationships are established simply through an agreement between the man and the woman, in many cases after he rapes or seduces her.

In these places, and in general among the very poor classes, there is also a high percentage of illegitimate births. Without means, without any kind of training, women in these circumstances must face life under the most difficult handicaps, often succumbing to misery and illness and the loss of their child.

WOMEN IN THE FAMILY

In the more modern regions of the continent, where to some extent, civilization has diffused uniform sentiments, ideas, actions, and reactions women generally are regarded by the members of their families with the same affection as in most other civilized countries. In the remote, isolated areas, inhabited by primitive natives, one finds less regard for women, perhaps because of different value standards and the vestiges of a basically different cultural outlook.

Scattered all over Spanish America one finds large, old families, the descendants of immigrants of the colonial period, whom past struggles, sacrifices, and achievements have knit into solid and united communities. These families had brought along from Spain the old concept of saint-mother, and in them, the woman is the focal personality around whom all the members of the family group themselves, tied to her by spiritual and sentimental bonds. She keeps alive traditions, preserves memories dear to the heart, encourages everything that strengthens family unity, rejects everything that might threaten to weaken it. She is, as it were, the family priestess, who watches over the life of its members from cradle to grave.

The average Spanish-American family falls into one of two distinct categories, urban and rural. The position of the women shows considerable differences between the two. In the villages, families engage in the production of practically everything they use and consume: not only do they produce all the food eaten, but in most cases also build their own houses and make their own furniture, textiles and leather goods.

The woman in this type of family shoulders numerous tasks: she takes care of the children, prepares meals for all, cleans the house, sews the clothes, bakes the bread, tends to the animals, harvests, irrigates, etcetera. In the province of Mendoza (Argentina), she takes part, in addition, in the grape harvesting; in Tucumán province, in sugar-making; in el Chaco, in the picking of cotton. Yet with all the joint efforts of husband and wife, life in rural areas is very hard, indeed so hard that the family often decides to leave and try its luck in the city. The constant stream of village-to-town migrants creates difficult social problems.

The established urban family, on the other hand, is part of the city's general economic texture. Instead of producing all or most of what they consume, the adult members of such families must concentrate on earning enough money to buy the necessities of life. The woman is liberated from the heavy burdens of the self-sufficient home and even the remaining housework is facilitated by the introduction of an increasing number of modern appliances. The time thus saved can, and in many cases is, used by the housewife to undertake outside employment to augment the family income.

THE HOME ROUTINE

The family in Spanish America is organized on the principle that the mistress of the house is responsible for all the tasks that are considered specifically feminine. These tasks, however essential for the well-being of the family, are in general considered inferior to paid work outside the home.

One often hears the opinion that the woman who is nothing but a housewife does not work; the correct way of putting it would be that she earns no salary. Furthermore, the domestic routine is considered intellectually limiting for the woman, for it narrows her horizon. This is not merely male opinion; in the large cities, especially, the housewives feel that a woman who has no other function is economically and intellectually inferior. Keeping house can be a full-time job where time- and work-saving appliances are not available, where there is a lack of ready-to-serve foods, where apparel is expensive, obliging the woman to sew her own clothes, and where the husband and male children refuse to help with the household chores because they are regarded as undignified for men. Another important factor, especially in the rural sector, is the lack of training opportunities for women in home economics and other practical subjects.

Nevertheless, even though the housewife may thus be confined to her home for most of the day, she is exposed to the impact of community problems which affect her either directly or indirectly through the members of her family. Examples of this are the cost of living and the real purchasing power of salaries and wages.

The Inter-American Seminar on the Strengthening of the Family, organized by the Inter-American Commission of Women with the cooperation of the government of Venezuela in Caracas in 1960, was the first inter-American attempt to study and understand the factors affecting the family as a basic social institution. It issued a Declaration of Principles that affirmed the democratic desire for social justice and upheld human rights as the basis of the common effort for the well-being of the family.

The conclusions reached by the Seminar pointed to the urgent need to raise the economic, social, cultural, and legal level of the family as the best means of strengthening it. The realization of any of these desiderata will inevitably bring about improvement in the position of women in the family and the routine of the household, enabling women to engage in independent and more creative activity even within the home.

THE SOCIAL POSITION OF WOMEN

While the social position of women varies in the different countries, one can state generally that there is everywhere an increasing tendency to improve it, but that it is palpably inferior to that of men.

Within each country, the social position of the urban woman is superior to that of her rural sister, who has much more limited work and cultural opportunities. Again, the position of the woman of immigrant stock is higher than that of the native woman of the same socioeconomic level; the former is, as a rule, better equipped to take her place in the more active segment of the working population. This can be observed most clearly in the large capital cities in which much of the population is of European descent, and where the native women who come up from the provinces to find work, without training and without even knowing how to read and write, stand a poor chance of obtaining a job that could mean social advancement. In almost all cases, such women must work as live-in maids; the current housing shortage in most big cities is another difficulty that impedes their efforts to improve their situation.

In Argentina, in 1956, a Domestic Service Law was enacted that regulated the maids' wages, provided for their paid vacations, and obliged employers to respect their night's rest. It also introduced compulsory affiliation with the National Institute of Social Welfare, which provides retirement pay. This law is calculated to introduce considerable improvements in the circumstances of domestic workers, but unfortunately, it is not yet generally observed.

In some cases, the native rural women, after arriving in the city, find work in suburban factories. The housing shortage forces these women to live in boarding houses and to spend almost their entire salary on room and board.

These three groups of women: the rural ones who live on a subsistence level within their families, and the domestic and factory workers who live in the cities in somewhat better or worse circumstances, constitute the overwhelming majority of the female half of the population in Spanish-American countries. In addition, and in contrast to them, there is a small but growing group of outstanding women who have succeeded in gaining access to culture, in acquiring professional skills, or in finding a place for themselves in the sciences or the arts; and there are others, more numerous, who, without having reached such distinctions, have yet managed to free themselves from the shackles of backwardness, ignorance, and destitution, have forged ahead through their own efforts, and today occupy positions of greater or lesser importance within the social spectrum of their country.

The social and historic responsibility of these women in view of the generally backward position of their sisters in Spanish America is grave indeed. It is with a sense of deep satisfaction that one can state that, far from being satisfied with their individual achievements, most of these women participate, in one way or another, in the struggle for the emancipation and the betterment of the economic, social, and cultural position of all members of their sex.

As a result of their work, and of other circumstances that cannot be detailed here, all Spanish-American countries have witnessed in recent times substantial movements for the encouragement of women to fill important jobs and functions.

In Mexico, women have energetically surged forward on all social and cultural fronts. They occupy today important public positions and are active members of unions and all kinds of social-welfare organizations, at times in directorial capacity. The last national elections in Mexico returned eight women as federal deputies, two as substitute senators, sixteen as local deputies, thirty-five as municipal presidents, and one hundred and ten as councilwomen. In Panama, in the last elections, forty-three councilwomen and two women deputies were elected, and at present, there are fifty-one women in the diplomatic corps, some of them in important posts.

In Argentina, women are mainly engaged in teaching, public administration, the professions, and all spheres of work in which labor legislation protects them; as well as in political parties, unions, and social-welfare institutions. Their devotion to work, sense of responsibility, understanding, and enthusiasm are generally recognized. Similar developments are taking place in all other Spanish-American countries.

Nevertheless, the women of the continent are still far from having achieved all that their ability merits. This is indicated by the disproportion between the number of women who actually occupy outstanding positions in any country, and the number of positions they would be capable of occupying. Thus in Argentina, in 1951, women constituted 48.9 per cent of the electorate and six women senators, twenty-three deputies and four women territorial delegates were elected to the National Congress. In 1960, although women constituted 50 per cent of the electorate and several women ran for office, no single woman was elected.

In Ecuador, the discrepancy between the letter of the law and the actual situation moved the women members of the political parties to meet and demand that the women be enabled actually to exercise the rights granted them by law.

Similar protests are taking place throughout the continent. This is one more indication that Spanish-American women have become aware of their situation and have understood the role they can play in society.

WOMEN'S OCCUPATIONS

The occupations of women, as all other activities, vary in the different zones of development of each country. As is to be expected, there is a definite correlation between the occupations of women and the degree of development attained by the economy of which they and their families form a part.

In general, in both city and country, the great female masses devote most of their time and energy to domestic tasks. The woman of the rural zones raises animals, dries fruits, prepares candies, spins and weaves, sews articles of clothing, and makes accessories. Mexico, Peru, Argentina, Bolivia, Colombia, among others, are outstanding for the quality of the domestic craftsmanship which constitutes one of the main occupations of the women in certain regions.

The native women show rare skill in the art of spinning, invented, according to ancient Peruvian tradition, by Mama Ocllo, the wife of Manco Capac, the first Inca and Son of the Sun. But today the work as well as the marketing of the product is carried out in a primitive way and is paid very poorly.

In the cities and suburban areas, most married women do not work outside the home, but many of them take in paid work. The poorest sew clothes for wholesale dress houses; they are extremely poorly paid since, like all home workers, they enjoy no effective legal protection. To make her work worthwhile, such a seamstress must devote more than twelve hours a day to it, including Sundays and holidays; and with all this effort her wages still remain the lowest even in the poor milieu in which she lives.

Women who work outside the home—most of these are single—do so either in business firms as office workers, sales ladies, telephone operators, secretaries, and the like, or in an industry such as textiles, food, metallurgy, clothing, meat, chemistry. Some work in public administration, and of course a great many in domestic employment. Such, at least, is the situation in Argentina.

Housewives, to the extent to which they find time, make clothes for their children, their husband and themselves, and economize in this manner. Many women, and increasingly more of the middle class, at least in Argentina, find in knitting—especially by machine—another possibility to increase their income; as a rule, they make articles of clothing to the order of individual customers or merchants.

All over Spanish America women are turning with increasing interest to the professions. In countries like Argentina, Mexico, and Uruguay, among others, they have access to all professional careers, although economic and social circumstances limit their actual participation in them. Not all women who wish to study can do so; fewer job possibilities are open to women than to men; and many women, even if qualified, become absorbed in their household tasks.

Among the professions, teaching is the one to which most women devote themselves, for which they show great natural aptitude, and whose daily schedule and long vacations make it easier than other occupations to combine with taking care of their own children and home. In Argentina, more than 90 per cent of the primary-school teachers and 50 per cent of the secondary-school teachers are women. In Mexico, women make up more than 60 per cent of the teachers.

Among the other professions that attract women in Argentina are biochemistry, pharmacy, and dentistry; in choosing the latter, which is the favorite of the three, the fact that they can set up an office in their own homes is an important consideration. Next in popularity are philosophy and letters—most of the students taking these studies are women—law, economics, medicine, sciences, psychology, and sociology.

Women are outstanding in literature and the arts; some of them enjoy an international reputation. Pilar de Lusarreta, Victoria Ocampo, Maria Alicia Dominguez, are among the best-known Argentinian writers. Women are found among the devoted technicians and researchers of the important scientific and technical-research centers, such as those of the Scientific and Technical Research Council of Argentina.

In Uruguay, women excel in medicine and social welfare. In Mexico, they show growing interest in political and social-science careers and do important work as socially conscious writers and journalists.

In Honduras, the greatest percentage of female students is attracted to the economic sciences.

In general, in all Spanish-American countries, the number of women in the professions increases steadily, although the rates of increase vary from place to place. So do the possibilities of effectively practicing their careers, depending on the economic, social and cultural level of the environment.

WOMEN'S ORGANIZATIONS

There are numerous women's associations in Spanish America; their importance and quantity increase in direct relation to the democratic development of each country. In general, these associations are devoted to social welfare and to professional, cultural, and civic activities.

Of the numerous women's associations in Argentina, mention can be made of the Association of Business and Professional Women; the Argentine Association for the United Nations; the Association for Fight Against Infantile Paralysis; the Christian Feminine Association; the Feminine Center of Civic Culture; the National Council of Women; the Argentine Council of Jewish Women; the Argentine Women's Club; the Argentine Federation of University Women; the League of Housewives.

In Mexico, the Mexican Women's Atheneum; the Society of Friends of Gabriela Mistral; the International Women's Club; the Association of Mexican University Women do important work.

In Colombia, the Women Citizens' Union, a non-party institution, carries out an extensive citizens' education program throughout the country.

A growing tendency can be observed among these women's organizations to establish working relations and cooperation both nationally and continent wide. Examples are the collaboration of 784 women's organizations in the Seminar on the Participation of Woman in Public Life (Argentina, 1960); the National Federation of Women's Institutions of La Paz, Bolivia, which includes twenty-three organizations; and the Feminine Civic Interchange of Argentina which unites seventeen institutions.

On the inter-American scene, great promise is held out by exchange with United States women's organizations whose high level of achievement sets an example of what such organizations can do for the benefit of society as a whole.

In the national and inter-American cooperation between women's organizations, fundamental is the role of the Inter-American Commission of Women, which carries out, in areas of special interest to women, the type of cooperative work done by the Organization of American States for the economic and social development of all countries of the Western Hemisphere.

THE OUTLOOK

The Spanish-American woman manifests a growing eagerness to acquire an increasingly responsible social position. This attitude is evinced in particular by her interested response to the possibilities that are opening up to her in the areas of work, study, the arts; in the civic, cultural and social-welfare organizations; in politics, public functions and other public life.

But the high positions achieved by some women are only samples of what the Spanish-American woman is capable of doing. For her to realize her abilities fully, the economic, social, and political conditions must first be changed for the better. The most urgent tasks, therefore, are to raise the living standard of the millions of men, women and children who live on the continent; to increase their working and training opportunities; to augment their income; to balance their cost of living; to provide them with adequate housing; to reorganize the transportation system by constructing railroads and highways; and to increase the number of schools, hospitals, clinics. In other words, only within the framework of a complete socio-economic development can the Spanish-American woman give to her family, society and nation all that is in her, and become a full partner and equal of man.

Brazil

By Levy Cruz

*F*ollowing *South America's colonization* by Spaniards and Portuguese, the bulk of the continent was split into two language areas, a Spanish and a Portuguese, the latter comprising Brazil. Since the two colonizing nations were not only neighbors in Europe but also possessed very similar cultures, they introduced many common elements throughout South America. Differences in the physical environment, in historical development and in the influences of diverse native cultures, however, resulted in differently textured societies and cultures, including aspects relative to the situation of women. It is these factors that both justify and necessitate the treatment of Brazil apart from the Spanish-American countries in an analysis of the situation of women in the Western world.

Translated from the Portuguese by Sylvia Fisher.

THE TRADITIONAL SITUATION

In the initial phases of colonization the situation of women could not be other than the one brought to this part of the American continent by the Portuguese: one of dependence and inferiority in relation to men. Basically, society was patriarchal with the wife and children confined to the farm house and, later, the two-story urban house, and allowed to go out only to attend Mass on the four annual holidays. And even within the house, when male visitors arrived, the girls and married women had to withdraw to the most secluded rooms. Well-to-do women passed the time sewing, swinging on the hammock, tasting sweets and preserves, calling for their servants, playing with parakeets, peeking at strange men through doors not completely closed, smoking cigarettes and sometimes cigars, and bearing children. This remained the situation to the end of the nineteenth century.

Although, generally, the women seem to have adjusted to this way of life, it would often happen that the wife or the daughter of the house would give vent to her hostility toward husband or father by punishing slaves with unnecessary severity.

Women were in charge of matters connected with religion—they kept the chapel in order, took care of the children's baptism and first communion, arranged the slaves' religious wedding, and so on—and would practice their religion much more assiduously than the men.

Very rarely did the women of colonial times know how to read and write. Education did not exist for them and the arts were not cultivated either. As far as music was concerned, most landowners were satisfied with the singing of birds kept in cages all over the house.

A woman could have no close relationship with persons of the opposite sex other than her husband, while a married man frequently had sexual relations with other women, including European governesses and slaves. It is quite probable that it was due to this fact that many landowners' wives conceived a strong hostility against beautiful or seductive mulatto women.

Apart from their domestic activities, no leadership whatsoever was exercised by women in society as a whole. By the same token, they participated neither in political nor in artistic affairs. One should bear in mind, though, that some women throughout this patriarchal era, and especially landowners' widows, exhibited a tremendous amount of social energy, administered farms, directed the family's affairs, and filled man's tasks sometimes with a greater ability than their deceased husbands.

TOWN AND COUNTRY

When the patriarchal system of society crumbled under the impact of new social influences, the ensuing changes affected first and foremost the women. These changes originated in towns which still continue to radiate them out into their hinterlands. At any particular time, the town always represented the more advanced stage, that is, a situation in which the changes were both larger in number and greater in extent.

Among other things, women began to appear on the streets, a deportment considered scandalous by a great many conservatives. Young girls began to take an interest in reading books; women started to cultivate music to the point where piano lessons were almost compulsory in well-to-do families; later, country girls followed the same procedure. Through the windows of the two-story buildings in the cities one could frequently hear a young girl singing to a piano accompaniment.

At the end of the nineteenth century girls were first admitted to schools; the first two girls who ventured to join a belles-lettres course graduated from it in 1907. Prior to 1930, very few women went to high schools and practically none attended college. After that year, the number of girls in the new high schools all over the country began to approximate that of boys.

To the present time, the peasant families in the rural areas exhibit largely traditional behavior patterns, differing considerably from well-to-do families in the towns with their intensive social and cultural changes. This does not mean that no changes have occurred in the social structure of rural families. In the past, all marriages were arranged; often the bride and groom met the first time at the foot of the altar. Nowadays, even though the choice is made by the boy, the girl's father still has the decisive say. Most families have accepted flirting and even occasional dates, which the conservatives still regard as scandalous.

Generally speaking, Brazil is a country with a high rate of fertility. In this respect, differences between town and country became pronounced when contraceptive methods were adopted by the urban communities. According to the 1950 census, in urban groups there were 78.41 children aged up to nine for every 100 women aged fifteen to forty-nine; in the suburbs (which, from a sociological standpoint, are urban centers in their majority), the corresponding figure was 105.35; and in rural groups, 143.85. Thus, the fertility of women in the rural areas was almost twice as high as in the urban areas. The National Statistics Board comments upon this data that "in rural areas birth control by preventative measures and voluntary abortion seems rather rare, but such methods have been rapidly spreading in certain urban centers, such as Rio de Janeiro and São Paulo." Also the number of illegitimate children is greater in rural areas: for instance, in the State of Maranhão, which is essentially agricultural, 56.39 per cent of the single girls twenty years or older had borne children, with an average of four children per woman.

THE LEGAL STATUS

Brazil's present Civil Code, dating from 1916 and amended in 1919 and later, rules that at twenty-one both men and women become of age, thereby becoming capable of performing all civil acts. However, the legal rights of married women are severely curtailed: certain legal acts performed by them can be voided, if they were carried out without the express consent of the husband.

The Civil Code also provides that a husband can file suit against his wife in order to have their marriage annulled if she was found to have been "previously deflowered," and he can contest the legitimacy of his wife's child.

The minimum age for legal matrimony is sixteen for girls and eighteen for boys. Underage marriages are subject to annulment, unless the wife has become pregnant. Those under the age of twenty-one must obtain their parents' consent to be able to marry. If the parents disagree, the father's will prevails; if the parents are legally separated, or their marriage has been annulled, the will of whoever has custody of the children prevails.

The husband is the head of the conjugal family; he is legally empowered to represent the family and to administer the family's assets, as well as his wife's private property, which he is enabled to do under the matrimonial regime adopted, or under a prenuptial pact to select and change the family's place of residence. If the wife wishes to engage in an occupation, or to take up residence away from home, she can do so only with the husband's consent. The husband must provide for the family's maintenance except if there is a separation of property, in which case the wife is "obliged to contribute to the couple's expenditures in the same proportion in which her estate's revenues relate to her husband's unless a different disposition is provided for in the prenuptial contract."

What are the things a husband cannot do without his wife's consent? He cannot "alienate, mortgage or encumber the couple's real property or equitable titles to other people's properties," "plead, as either plaintiff or defendant as to such assets and titles"; "be part in a suretyship contract," or "give unprofitable or small value donations" using income derived from community property.

With reference to women, the Civil Code establishes that "by marriage a woman assumes . . . the condition of a man's companion, consort and helper with the family's burdens." Therefore she cannot "carry out. without her husband's consent, the same acts which he cannot carry out without his wife's consent." Therefore, the wife cannot alienate or encumber her real property which is under her private management; cannot alienate her equitable titles to other persons' properties; cannot accept or repudiate heritage or legacy; cannot accept guardianship over minors or incompetents or accept any other public duties; cannot plead in civil or commercial courts, except in cases prescribed by law; cannot practice a profession, acquire obligations that might jeopardize the couple's assets, or accept legal mandates—without the husband's consent.

Only a few modifications have been introduced into this law in recent years, endowing married women with somewhat greater rights. At present, a completely revised new code is being prepared which will result in considerable improvements in the legal position of women.

There is no divorce in Brazil, only judicial separation from bed and board. Spouses thus separated remain legally married to each other.

Under the 1943 consolidation of labor laws, provisions were made for special working conditions for woman, including prohibition of night work, that is, between 10 and 5, except in special occupations such as nursing. The law also provides for an uninterrupted rest period of at least eleven hours between every two working periods and prohibits women's employment in working places detrimental to their health. Pregnant women are forbidden to work six weeks before and after childbirth, during which time they must be fully paid. Upon their return to work they are given two extra daily rest breaks of half-an-hour each, to enable them to feed their babies.

The right to vote was granted to women over eighteen years of age by legislation passed in 1950; however, voting is not compulsory for any woman who is not engaged in a profitable profession.

EDUCATION

Brazil's illiteracy rate amounted in 1950 to 57.2 per cent. It was higher among women, of whom only 39.33 per cent knew how to read and write as against 46.04 per cent of the men. The 1950 average represented an improvement compared to 1940, when the percentage of literate women was only 34.11. In the rural areas illiteracy is greater, and there, too, it is higher among women than among men.

In the big cities, the situation is improving. More and more girls attend schools, and the percentage of those going on to high schools and colleges is on the increase.

It is an interesting fact that for three decades, although somewhat more boys than girls have been admitted to elementary schools, somewhat more girls than boys graduated.

The percentages for three selected years are as follows:

	1936		1946		1956	
	Boys	Girls	Boys	Girls	Boys	Girls
General registration	51.3	48.7	50.7	49.3	51.1	48.9
Effective registration	51.1	48.8	50.5	49.4	50.9	49.1
Graduated	49.7	50.3	48.0	25.0	48.9	51.1

As to secondary education, at the beginning of the 1950 school year there were, in all of Brazil, 554.089 girl students and 623,333 boy students —88.9 girls for every 100 boys. The relationship between the number of boys and girls varies with the type of secondary education. In normal schools (teachers' training schools) there were 147.7 girls for every 100 boys; in regular high schools, 88.8; in commercial schools, 44.4; in industrial schools, 27.2; and in agricultural schools, 5.5. While women thus predominate in normal schools, they represent a minority in all other types of secondary schools. Their number in the agricultural schools (only 348 girls in the whole country) and industrial schools (5,542) is very small.

By and large, the seven years of secondary education are regarded as a preparation for a superior course. The last three years of high school (called college) comprise two trends: one with a scientific and the other with a classical curriculum. In the latter, most pupils are girls in most of the states (except Bahia, Paranã, and Santa Catarina), averaging 173.4 for every 100 boys in the whole country.

In 1957, 4,792 girls and 10,173 boys graduated from the universities of Brazil, or 47.1 girls for every 100 boys. The initial registration in 1958 showed an even greater disproportion between sexes: 21,875 girls as against 62,606 boys, or 34.9 for every 100 boys. The greatest number of women registered in 1958 for courses in fine arts in general, music, librarianship, domestic relations (only women), nursing, social sciences, geography, history, natural history, belles-lettres (except classics), pedagogy, didactics, museology and social service.

The graduates of 1957 showed a similar preference for the same courses, except for those graduating in social sciences in which the boys exceeded the girls; on the other hand, more girls than boys graduated in philosophy.

What subjects did girls *not study* at the beginning of 1958? Aeronautics, criminology, electronics, civil engineering, and naval engineering. There were, however, a few girls in all other engineering fields; and in 1958 girls registered in all other courses in higher education. An interesting observation is that the percentage of girl students in the colleges increases steadily from year to year. Of students registered in 1958 for their first year of study, there were 47.5 girls for every 100 boys; in the second year, 40.3; in the third, 35.6; in the fourth, 17.7; in the fifth, 11.5; and in the sixth, 15.7. In other words, the earlier the class started to study (the sixth year of the 1958 class started in 1953) the smaller the ratio of women to men.

SEX MORES

Insofar as sex mores are concerned, the differences between the attitudes of men and women are impressive in Brazil. Practically everything is permitted to men, while almost everything is forbidden to women. The conduct of men and women is based on three disparate and, to some extent, incompatible complexes.

The *complex of virility* is the incentive for men to seek maximum satisfaction in sexual activity as early as possible. When a boy reaches puberty, his parents and relatives encourage him to have sexual relations. Male virginity is ridiculed.

The *complex of virginity*, on the other hand, imposes upon girls the strictest prohibition of sexual relations before marriage. Girls who deviate from this rule live in contempt of society, because even the most liberal men shy away from the possibility of marrying a woman with premarital sex experience. If the fiancé learns the truth while he is still engaged, he breaks off the engagement; if the bridegroom discovers that his bride was not a virgin, he will probably try to have the marriage annulled. Deprived of the chance to get married, a woman has to choose between the undesirable situation of living as a spinster in a relative's household, or the equally undesirable alternative of becoming a concubine or a prostitute. A boy's sexual initiation usually occurs with a prostitute. Contact with prostitutes, as a rule, persists throughout a man's life, and is motivated by the unceasing drive to satisfy his sexual desire. There are, of course, differences according to social classes, which means that there are also differences between town and country. With reference to the lower social classes, it has been observed that in them there seems to be no perceptible discrimination between sexually inexperienced and experienced women, that virginity is not considered a prerequisite for marriage, and that consequently the rules of vigilance and segregation as to sex are much less intricate than in the middle and upper classes.

The *complex of matrimonial fidelity* requires that a woman avoid any act that might be regarded by a jealous husband as a threat to his sexual monopoly of her. In other words, she must carefully avoid all situations in which any man might find an opportunity to court her. If a married woman is caught *in flagranti*, both she and her paramour will be murdered by the enraged husband. Inability to commit this "crime of honor" results in loss of status in society. Recent surveys indicate that the same complex is operative not only in the upper and middle, but also in the lower classes, including the poor rural population. Since World War II, a certain change has begun to show its signs in the upper class, with the effect of allowing married women a somewhat greater liberty; in the middle and lower classes, however, female sexual behavior is still under strict control.

As to the wives' attitude to their husbands' extramarital affairs, their general tendency is to tolerate them, if discreetly carried on. A wife will usually resign herself to the situation rather than react vehemently; she has practically no other alternative. More permanent extramarital unions are rare in either the upper or the lower classes. Once in a while one hears of a man with two families, living in *de facto* bigamy.

THE MARRIAGE PATTERN

As has been indicated the parents (mainly the father) used to have a rather active role, if not an exclusive one, in choosing their daughters' spouses. Flirting was not allowed, or consisted only of furtive glances or the exchange of gestures.

In rural areas, much of this traditional situation still prevails. However, it has been observed, for instance, in the State of São Paulo that flirting with discretion is now accepted by the family. It still starts usually with the universal language of the eyes, but it soon leads to actual meetings. On these occasional dates the couples as a rule only converse. Even at parties, or at a ball, when a boy dances with a girl, it is done almost at arm's length. Many parents do not yet allow their daughters to participate in such social occasions.

In cities, towns and, to a lesser degree, rural areas, flirtation still constitutes only an innocent pastime or, in a more optimistic mood, it represents attempts to find a future spouse. Occasionally, it is actually the first phase of a process of getting to know each other, and culminates in marriage. In the course of the entire process, however, the family's vigilance over the daughter never relaxes (the same applies to the son, but less intensively), not by directly selecting the daughter's future groom, but by vetoing her precipitate choices. It is obvious that in a few cases flirtation helps the girl become better acquainted with the boy, thus giving her an opportunity to make up her mind with regard to him. In large urban centers, the choice of spouses is almost exclusively made by the youngsters themselves who meet on dates, go to the movies, attend parties, either in a twosome or under the supervision of a chaperon. In the small towns, too, matrimony is preceded to some extent by flirting and a period of engagement.

Engagement begins when the young man pays a special visit to the girl's father to ask for her hand. Occasionally, the girl's father gives a negative answer, mainly because during the preceding phase of flirting he has decided to use his powers of veto. While engaged, the future spouses get to know each other better, making use of the freedom the family grants the girl, such as being left alone with her fiancé in the living room or on the balcony meeting somewhere in the city, going for walks or to the movies, and so on. Nevertheless, on dates which might lead to closer contacts, the girl's parents, aware of the standards of their society, provide for a friend (such as her sister, or, less frequently, the boy's sister) to chaperon them. Again, in rural areas there is a different standard. Engagement there is sometimes a period with much less freedom than during preliminary flirting.

Marriage in Brazil is of two principal types: civil and religious. The former is governed by the country's laws which regard it as the only legal one; the latter is not legally binding, except in the form of "religious wedding with civil effects." This, in effect, is a religious ceremony, performed by a religious representative, and combining the two types of marriages, after the legal requisites have been fulfilled. In the majority of Brazil's rural communities only the religious wedding is performed.

The civil marriage is, as a rule, very simple, with a few guests invited to attend the ceremony. The presence of these guests is necessary in order to comply with the laws and folkways that require witnesses to the act. On the other hand, a religious wedding is more elaborate; it is the real marriage, to the extent that whenever one says that one goes to a wedding, the religious ceremony is invariably meant. For this occasion the bride wears a special white floor-length gown (this feature has been changed by recent fashion to somewhat shorter gowns) and a full veil, and carries a bouquet of flowers. At upper-middle- and upper-class weddings, music is played by the church organ or even an orchestra. Following the religious wedding, there is a banquet with cocktails, given by the bride's father, in accordance with his financial position. In well-to-do families the couple takes a honeymoon trip, to Rio de Janeiro or São Paulo, or even abroad. If they belong to the middle class, they sometimes go to the nearest resort. No trip at all follows the wedding in the lower classes, and, to a certain extent, in the rural communities, irrespective of the spouses' social status.

WOMEN'S POSITION IN THE FAMILY

Due to the common preference for boys, the inferior position of the Brazilian woman in the family commences with her birth; the desire that the couple's first child be a boy is especially pronounced. Also, a male child gets far better treatment than a girl.

Even after getting married, a woman's position of inferiority with respect to her husband continues. The authority over the daughter formerly exercised by the father now passes to the husband, the head of the house. While the wife's authority is much less than her husband's, she is the one responsible for practically all domestic activities, including those demanding outside errands. Present standards inflict greater hardships on wives and demand greater sacrifices from them. This is particularly true in rural communities, where the women are largely confined to subservient positions. If, for instance, an outdoor party is given by a man, his wife would entertain the guests by serving them coffee, bread, and alcoholic beverages, but she would remain indoors most of the time, preparing the food and fulfilling the guests' requests. Women participate in folk dances only on rare occasions. When the family goes to town, if only one horse is available, the husband will ride, and the wife will follow him on foot, carrying their youngest child. To the man, on the other hand, marriage brings only advantages. This is standard throughout Brazil's rural areas according to several independent surveys.

As one ascends the social hierarchy, one finds that the differences between man and wife become less pronounced. Women in the middle and upper classes in small country towns do less work, and whatever work they do is not as hard as in the poor classes. In the upper class, a major departure from the old family traditions is the increasing equality of women, their greater participation in both home life and activities outside the home, and the fact that decisions and actions are made jointly by the married partners.

As far as the other classes are concerned, one does well to keep in mind the warning of several scholarly analysts who emphasize the difference that can frequently be observed between the ideal picture of intrafamily relationships and the actual reality. The ideal of the dominant husband and subservient wife may influence the spouses' behavior when strangers are present. In reality, however, the woman is quite often the central figure of the household.

THE HOME ROUTINE

There are considerable differences in home routine between Brazil's rural and urban communities. Rural areas lack modern facilities, such as electricity and piped water. Consequently, the women are kept busy with such daily chores as fetching water and firewood, cooking, washing and ironing clothes, cleaning the house, caring for the children and training them in proper conduct, helping care for domestic animals, working in the fields when needed, sewing, embroidering, knitting, crocheting, and making *broglio* (lace fringe on flour sacks). These activities are conducted in a primitive manner: cooking is done on a wood-burning mud stove; clothes are washed at a river bank or sometimes in basins, and pressed with a coal-burning iron; a pestle is used to pound the coffee, husk the rice and grind the corn. All this requires much effort and expenditure of physical energy. Nevertheless, since these activities are part of the traditional culture, some women who have become used to them say that they enjoy them.

A complementary side of this picture is that the women participate in social gatherings to an even lesser extent than the men. The sons can at least enjoy themselves in summer, going swimming, riding, playing ball. The daughters, on the other hand, must spend their time at home with their mothers, and all they can do is to pay an occasional visit to a married girl friend or sister.

In the towns, the situation is different. During the last few years some facilities have been developed which have made home routine easier for middle-class married women. The number of refrigerators has increased (only fifteen years ago they were relatively rare); kerosene or paraffin oil stoves (more common within the lower classes) and bottled gas stoves (now in even greater demand than refrigerators and used mostly in middle- and upper-class homes) have almost completely replaced the old coal-burning stoves; electric irons, and, very recently, washing machines have been introduced. The importance of these new appliances for the home routine of Brazilian women becomes evident if one considers that Brazilian men do not help their wives in home duties at all. A further easing of the women's home routine was brought about by the increasing availability of ready-made clothes, as a result of which the work of sewing clothes at home for their own use has been greatly reduced or completely eliminated.

The middle-class woman's routine in the city consists of instructing her maid as to the food she wishes to have cooked for the different meals, of having her clean the house, getting the children ready for school (in many cases the maid takes them to school), etcetera. There is little social life; going to movies is the most common type of amusement. Books and newspapers are seldom read. Nevertheless, to judge from the great increase in the circulation of women's magazines, which contain mostly love stories, reading has become customary for women of the lower-middle and lower classes. In the latter, though, the habit is stronger among working girls than among housewives. The same applies to the romantic serials broadcast over the radio, which have become very popular in the last fifteen years.

THE SOCIAL POSITION

It is more or less obvious from all of this that the social position of Brazilian women has evolved from absolute inferiority and dependence in relation to men to her present status of apparent and relative inferiority. To this day, in Brazilian society as a whole, the highest positions are held by men. Women, moreover, receive lower salaries, even if they do the same work as men. As far as the family is concerned, as already pointed out, a woman spends all her life in dependence; first her father, later her husband makes all the decisions for her. The law itself does not treat men and women equally.

A widespread concept among men—and also among quite a few women—is that women are incapable of carrying on many activities, which, consequently, are the exclusive domain of men. On the other hand, certain biological female incapacities, either permanent or temporary, are taken into account by the law which provides special labor conditions for women, in general, and for pregnant and nursing women in particular.

Important nationwide affairs, such as industry and commerce in general, as well as politics, are practically out of bounds for women. In the former, no woman has so far played an outstanding role; in the latter, only a few hold offices, and only of local scope, for instance as municipal councillors. There are extremely few state congresswomen, one in the federal Congress, none in the Senate. As to executive positions, there are only two or three women mayors in the whole country, in small towns of the interior; and no woman has as yet served as state governor. State secretaries' offices have always been held by men, even those dealing with education and social service. Only in the last two or three years has a woman occupied the position of State Secretary for Education in the State of Pernambuco, while another woman was State Secretary for Social Services in the State of Guanabara.

Several inquiries and researches carried out in rural communities show that there are no women among the local leaders. A survey on leadership in a community in the State of Minas Gerais showed that both urban and rural leadership was exclusively male and that not even a single female leader existed in any section in the community. The author's own studies in a community in the State of Pernambuco have led him to the same conclusion.

WOMEN'S OCCUPATIONS

Until a few years ago, Brazilian women lived exclusively for their families and homes; only in recent years have they started to take outside jobs. Even those who study or work would usually neither give up marriage nor postpone it for the sake of their professions.

The occupation preferred by girls and married women is that of teaching in elementary schools. This is considered by men to be essentially feminine work. The countrywide average in 1936 was 706.8 women teachers in grade schools for every 100 men; in 1946, 1,421.4, and in 1956, 1,347.1. In some of the states of Brazil practically all elementary school teachers are women. In Paraiba, Pernambuco, Sergipe, Rio de Janeiro there are, respectively 5,184.3, 4,831.6, 4,328.2, and 4,264.7 women elementary school teachers for every 100 men. It is interesting to note the relative paucity of women among the high school and college teachers. In 1950, there were only 76.7 women high school teachers for every 100 men. College teachers are mostly men.

The constantly increasing economic pressures induce many middle-class husbands (as well as men in other classes) to let their wives take jobs other than teaching. As to unmarried daughters, they not only are permitted to work, but sometimes even expected to.

The percentage of working women in Brazil varies from area to area While in the country as a whole only 9.6 per cent of the women are economically active, this average hides a wide range varying from a minimum of 3.2 per cent in the middle west to a maximum of 23.1 per cent in the State of São Paulo. These data clearly show how limited is the role of women in Brazil's economically active population, in comparison with other countries.

The largest number of women throughout Brazil are engaged in services, including social-service careers. Next come agriculture, cattle raising, and forestry. Smaller contingents of women workers are employed in national defense and public security, in real-estate brokerage, agencies, credit, insurance and investment firms, as well as in liberal professions.

WOMEN IN LEADERSHIP

There are certain areas in Brazilian life in which women have become outstanding, although it is not quite sure that the term leadership can be applied to these cases.

Although social-service careers are an exclusively feminine domain, the top administrative positions in all the national and regional social-service organizations are held mostly by men. Only the principals' positions in social-service schools are held by women, since the law provides that these positions must be filled by experienced social workers who are predominantly women. For similar reasons, all the principals and teachers in schools of nursing are women. Since almost all nurses are women, nursing teachers are also women, although occasionally male professors of medicine are invited to lecture on special subjects.

In elementary education women predominate. They fill the posts of principals as well. Although there are presently no women Secretaries of Education in any state of the federation (these positions, in any event, are of a political rather than professional character) the offices immediately under the Secretaries are quite often held by women.

The participation of women in theatrical life is significant. There are several leading actresses on the Brazilian stage and groups of them have formed their own schools of dramatic arts in Rio de Janeiro and São Paulo.

Libraries and archives are another field in which women exceed men in numbers and in which they exercise effective leadership through their participation in conferences and seminars at home and abroad, teaching and managing schools or courses for librarians and archivists. Recently, three female archives' experts founded a private enterprise to help in the organization and maintenance of documentation services for commercial and industrial concerns.

In the social sciences, especially in sociology, a few women have achieved prominence in teaching and research. Others, who recently graduated, show promise as future social scientists. However, this intellectual movement is practically limited to São Paulo which is the center for the social sciences in Brazil.

In colleges, the girls actively participate, together with their male colleagues, in efforts to improve Brazilian college education, in plans for modifying the country's social structure, and in religious activities. Both sexes are represented in the Juventude Universitaria Católica (Catholic College Youth) and the Associação Cristã de Acadêmicos (College Christian Association) which is Protestant.

Finally, one must not overlook the leadership exercised by women in philanthropy by either sponsoring or actually directing the work of social-assistance institutions, or by promoting special fund-raising campaigns for such institutions.

Women as Cultural Transmitters

In a society such as the Brazilian, in which the family was and still is the most important social unit and a woman's life is largely restricted to family activities, women would inevitably have outstanding roles as cultural transmitters. The fact that 93 per cent of the grade-school teachers and 68 per cent of the normal-school teachers, that is, of the teachers of future teachers, are women also point in the same direction. As mothers, they spend much more time with the children than the fathers; also, the cultural and social activities that take place in the home are considered essentially feminine.

As mothers and grade-school teachers, women have influenced generation after generation of Brazilians. The education of each new generation starts with what the mother teaches her children. She takes care of her child in the first months of life, when it starts to form first habits. She is there when the child pronounces its first words and starts the first steps. Somewhat later, it is again the mother who is in charge of teaching her child "good manners," hygienic habits, and proper speech. For a daughter it is extremely important to learn the manners characteristic of her sex; the mother, therefore, teaches her to behave better than the boy, to have "better manners," to sit down, walk, take care of her clothes, her hair, to adorn herself in the proper, accepted manner.

The children's recreation is almost always provided by the mother. Usually, she is the one who tells them tales of folklore, or stories that have been lately published in children's books.

Religion is transmitted to children practically by women (mother and teacher) only; the first prayers are taught to the child by the mother, almost never by the father. It is the mother who checks whether the prayers, once duly learned by the child, are said at the appointed times (such as before going to bed). In the case of Catholic families (the great majority in Brazil), the mother is the one who takes care of every detail of the child's preparation for the holy sacraments, such as first communion, and the daughter's wedding. Finally, the mother has a most active role in choosing her children's first friends, and preventing undesirable contacts (in this selection she takes into account not only the morals of the friends' families, but frequently their social rank as well).

Generally speaking, sexual education is not given in Brazil; only in recent years has it begun to interest a few educators, but not the parents.

Paradoxically, sex is a cultural aspect in which parents have no important role at all, not even a mother in relation to her daughter. The first knowledge a child obtains in this area comes from other children; the sexual initiation of teen-agers takes place without the parents' knowledge. Even the daughter's menarche occurs without the mother having prepared her for such an important event, and only thereafter does the mother try to explain things to her and teach her the hygienic steps to be taken. By the same token, the mother gives no sexual instruction to her daughter, not even preparatory to marriage, but lets her learn the significance of matrimony from schoolmates, office colleagues, and others.

By and large, women do not seem to have much influence in choosing their sons' careers; this is under the fathers' jurisdiction. The mother limits herself to opposing the son's choice of "dangerous" careers, such as military professions, or flying, or any other occupation which requires his prolonged absence from home. As women do not participate in politics, the young generation is not influenced in this area by its mothers or teachers.

THE OUTLOOK

Due to Brazil's vast territory and the differential pace of economic and social development in its diverse regions, the Brazilian communities of today are distributed along a continuum. At the one end, there are primitive or folk communities; at the other, highly urbanized communities, with a more developed and entirely different social and cultural life. This means that the social position of women, their behavior, attitudes and feelings, necessarily vary from one extreme to the other. The most obvious consequence of this situation is that the outlook for the women in Brazil points toward a shift in the folk communities in the direction of the changes which have already occurred in the urban centers.

What other, more specific prospects do Brazilian women face? The large families are in the process of vanishing, and their place is taken by the small, well-knit family, in which the distance between husband and wife, as well as between father and children, is smaller. The women will thus have a less disadvantageous position in relation to men. To this can be added that the growing number of women who hold remunerative jobs, the growing number of girls attending high schools and colleges, the prolongation of the boys' education for certain careers, are all factors helpful in strengthening the independence of women. The same factors influence the average age at which girls get married; this is now somewhat higher than it used to be.

The development of transportation and traveling facilities in regions which not long ago were completely isolated also contributes to the acceleration of changes in the position of women.

A bill proposing the establishment of divorce in Brazil has been more than once vetoed by Congress. If the increase in the number of affirmative votes it has been receiving is an indication of future trends, it is quite probable that divorce will be instituted in Brazil in the near future. This, in turn, will increase the independence of women and strengthen their position in the family.

As far as the work situation is concerned, no substantial changes can be foreseen, since, in spite of the increasing number of girls attending college, many of them do not really intend to pursue a career. Going to school may increasingly serve as a pretext to leading a freer life, and to meeting boys among whom a girl might find her future husband. It is also probable that the complex of virginity will weaken and disappear, beginning with the upper classes, through the middle and lower classes. First indications of this tendency are already apparent in Brazil's largest urban centers.

BIBLIOGRAPHY

Azevedo, Fernando de, A Cultura Brasileira: Introdução ao Estudo da Cultura no Brasil, Tomo Terceiro, "A Transmissão da Cultura," São Paulo: Edições Melhoramentos.
Barros, Edgard de Vasconcelos, O Problema de Liderança, Rio de Janeiro: Serviço Social Rural, 1960.
Cãndido, Antonio, "A Vida Familial do Caipira," Sociologia XVI (4), 341–367, Oct. 1954.
Conselho Nacional de Estatística, Pesquisas sôbre as Populacões Urbanas e Rurais do Brasil, Rio de Janeiro: Conselho Nacional de Estatística (IBGE), 1954.
Fontenelle, L. F., Raposo, A dinâmica dos Grupos Domésticos no Arraial do Cabo, Rio de Janeiro: Serviço Social Rural, 1960.
Freyre, Gilberto, Sobrados 3 Mucambos: Decadência do Patriarcado Rural e Desenvolvimento do Urbano, Rio de Janeiro: Livraria José Olympio Editora, 1961.
——, The Masters and the Slaves, New York: Alfred A. Knopf, 1946.
Hamburger, Adelaide, "A Familiá numa Pequena Comunidade Paulista." Sociologia XVI (3), 284–292, Aug., 1954.

Hutchinson, Harry William, *Village and Plantation Life in Northeastern Brazil*, Seattle : University of Washington Press, 1957.

Pereira, Luiz, "Mulher e Trabalho," *Educacão e Ciencias Sociais*, 8 (15) : 143–158, Sept. 1960.

Pierson, Donald, *Cruz das Almas: A Brazilian Village*, Washington : Smithsonian Institution, 1951.

Revista Brasiliense, "Cacilda Becker—Nídia Lícia," No. 33, Jan.–Feb. 1961.

Wagley, Charles, *Amazon Town: A Study of Man in the Tropics*, New York : The Macmillan Co., 1953.

Willems, Emilio, *O Problema Rural Brasileiro do Ponto de Vista Antropológico*, São Paulo : Secretaria da Agricultura, Indústria e Comércio, 1944.

——, "The Structure of the Brazilian Family," *Social Forces* XXXXI (4), May 1953.

IV

Between Old and New

FRANCE, WEST GERMANY,
ISRAEL, AND JAPAN

The four, otherwise greatly disparate, countries discussed in this section resemble those of the preceding group, but with one significant difference: the balance between tradition and modernism has definitely shifted in the latter's direction. Yet the power of tradition must still be taken into account: its influence is felt in the legal position of women in France, in the vestiges of male authoritarianism in Germany, in the restrictive Jewish attitude to women in Israel (especially in the Middle Eastern half of her population), and in the formal deference to men that is expected of women in Japan.

France

By Andrée Lehmann

THE TRADITIONAL POSITION

*T*he *traditional situation* of French women up to the
time of World War I was comparable to that of women throughout
Western Europe, especially those in the Latin countries. The ideal occupation for young girls of the middle class was preparation for marriage. This
training included instruction in the art of making pleasant conversation,
and thus concentrated on history, modern literature, and the arts. Girls
usually pursued their studies only until their sixteenth or eighteenth year.
At the same time, they studied painting, drawing, music, the applied arts,
and sewing. Great attention was paid to the acquisition of good manners,
and the art of discreet flirtation. At the beginning of the twentieth century,
young girls were usually still chaperoned when they went out, and their

---

Translated from the French by Ann Patai.

correspondence and friendships were strictly supervised. Preparation for marriage did not yet include sex education, nor training in household management and child care, all of which are taught today. In these areas, the mother's example substituted for formal instruction. Religion, too, played an important part in a girl's upbringing. Tradition, handed down from one generation to the next, usually turned the young woman into a good housekeeper and an excellent mother.

Married women of the middle class rarely worked outside the home, although the wives of shopkeepers with small to medium-sized businesses assisted their husbands and worked as hard as did the employees. For a married woman of this class to seek and accept a paid job constituted something of a step down in the world both for her and her husband, it being considered the latter's responsibility to support the family by means of his earnings and the careful management of his wife's dowry. Thus, the married woman devoted herself exclusively to her household, to the care and training of her children, and to entertaining, mainly in order to further her husband's interests. Her own amusements consisted solely of visits to stores, or to tea salons (never to cafés!) either alone or in the company of women friends, and the exchange of social visits.

Although legally the husband alone took charge of all the family business, his wife's assets as well as his own, the French woman always had considerable influence over her husband, and the welfare of the family often depended on her wise management, intelligence, and foresight.

The unmarried woman was held in pathetically low esteem; after the age of twenty-five, she was considered an old maid. Women over the age of forty or so were considered old. The unmarried mother, who to this day is all too often called *fille-mère* (girl-mother), was treated with scorn and contempt.

In the working class, the woman's situation was hardly enviable. From the time she left school, at the age of about twelve or thirteen, the young girl began to perform hard physical labor, dividing her daily sixteen to eighteen hours of work between a paid job and household chores, an arduous regime because of low wages (women's wages averaged only half of those paid to men) and primitive household equipment.

The female wage-earner, from 1892 to 1918, put in eleven hours of work a day at factory or workshop. When she returned to her modest quarters in the evening, she continued the day's work by preparing meals, caring for her children, and waiting on her husband who, at that time, never helped with the housework. Rising early in the morning, she tidied the house and prepared breakfast for her family before leaving for the factory or workshop.

The situation of the large number of women employed by business firms was scarcely easier. The working hours were approximately the same as in the factory, the salaries generally lower, and to make the situation even worse, these women were expected to maintain a smart appearance on their meager earnings, especially those who worked as saleswomen or cashiers.

At this time, many women worked in the lesser jobs of the civil service. With salaries as low as those of women working for business firms, they were burdened in the same way by having to present an attractive, well-groomed appearance.

In the latter two occupations, the working day was often longer than in factories, and the women had to perform the same household chores, under the same conditions, as the female manual laborers. Their housework was possibly even more arduous, for their standard of living was higher than that of working-class women, and consequently required additional effort on their part.

The situation of working women with very young children was made even more difficult at this time because of the insufficient number of nurseries and the absence of kindergartens. Such nurseries as did exist often operated under unsanitary conditions.

A law of November 2, 1892, gave the first legal protection to women workers, limiting their work day to eleven hours, guaranteeing them a weekly day of rest, and forbidding them night work, or work hazardous to their health.

Town and Country

It is impossible to describe in general terms the situation of the French woman living in the country, for the conditions of life vary enormously from region to region. In times past, these regions were autonomous provinces, and they have, in most cases, retained their own traditions. Thus, whatever will be said in this section must be modified when one focusses attention on one particular province, in view of its own specific mores.

Traditionally, France was an agricultural country and more than half of the population were peasants. The life of the country woman was, and still is, harder than that of her urban sister, for all women living in the country, rich and poor alike, were obliged to work.

The life of the peasant woman took place almost entirely within the confines of the farm. Indeed, she seldom went anywhere, except to take the farm produce to market. The city woman, in contrast, divided her time between two distinct spheres: her household and her outside work, whether her activities in the latter were undertaken for payment or simply for her own amusement. The farmer's wife, whether her husband owned the farm or merely rented the land, and whether the farm was large or small, rich or poor, had to follow an exhausting routine seven days a week. Having risen at four in the morning, she would always be the last one to bed, rarely before eleven in the evening. This long day was divided between the farm work entrusted to her (milking, caring for the animals, gardening, drawing water, supervision of the farm hands if any, and so on) and household tasks (care of the children, preparation of meals for the family and farm hands, and keeping the account books). In addition, when necessary, she shared with her husband the arduous labor of the fields. In a farm economy, the role of the farmer's wife is indispensable. She is her husband's helpmeet in many respects, and sustains him morally as well.

The daughters of a peasant family helped their parents from a very early age with the various farm chores; they did not always attend primary school regularly up to their twelfth year, and, at about that age, were obliged to terminate their schooling altogether.

The situation of the hired girl on a farm was nearly always deplorable. She was required to perform hard labor of every kind, lived in unsanitary conditions, and was often promiscuous.

The rapid changes in agriculture which have come about since World War II have caused the living conditions of country women, at least those living on large farms, to approximate much closer the way of life of urban women. On large farms, which are almost entirely mechanized, the woman today no longer works in the fields, and she is freed from the heavy burden of preparing meals for innumerable farm hands, since the latter now live outside the confines of the farm. Although the chores traditionally reserved to her still remain her responsibility, she no longer actually performs the physical work herself, but only supervises it.

The household conveniences of the country woman have become identical with those of urban women. The automobile, which is part of the equipment of a large farm, enables the woman to go into town quite frequently, and radio and television also allow her to escape from her former isolation.

On the other hand, the simple bookkeeping of the farm, always the woman's responsibility, has become more complicated. It is still she who has charge of the administrative and financial management of the farm.

On small farms, still the most numerous in France, the woman's situation remains quite different from that of the city woman. It has scarcely changed at all during the last twenty years, although certain improvements can be noted. She no longer works in the fields, and her house is equipped with modern comforts more or less like those of urban houses. Still, her work remains excessively heavy and demanding, leaving scarcely a moment's freedom.

There is yet another transformation accompanying the mechanization of farming that has made the situation of country women more comparable to that of city women: many girls from farming families, freed by the machine, now work in factories which have sprung up in nearly all regions of France since the end of World War II. These women lead almost the same life, under the same conditions, as working-class women in the city, and, like the latter, are unionized.

Considerable improvements have taken place in the educational field as well. Today, almost all country girls go to school until they are sixteen or seventeen, and many of them graduate from high school.

On the whole, the situation of women in town and country has become remarkably similar. Regional costumes have almost totally disappeared, and are worn only on holidays. The style of dress of country women when they go out has become nearly identical with that of urban women. Nevertheless, in certain parts of the country the inferior status of women still manifests itself in symbolic forms. In these places one can see women serving their husbands and the men of the farm at the table, and taking their own meals later, alone, or together with the female servants.

EDUCATION

The evolution that has taken place in France relative to the education of women began in 1886 when obligatory primary education for both sexes was introduced. This was preceded in 1882 by the opening of the first *lycées* for girls. These institutions gave instruction at the secondary-school level, which led to a diploma. This was not, however, the equivalent of the baccalaureate given to boys at the end of their secondary schooling. Thus, women could not hope to enter any liberal profession, nor any university, to which the baccaleureate alone gave access.

The middle class soon realized the disadvantages of this situation and demanded that its daughters be allowed to prepare for the baccalaureate. Gradually, beginning in 1907, the requisite courses were offered to girls. Male professors began to teach Latin in the girls' lycées as an optional subject only, but nevertheless more and more girls succeeded in passing the baccalaureate examination after only three years of Latin studies instead of the six years devoted to the subject in the boys' lycées.

The social evolution of women was precipitated by World War I (1914–1918). During the four years of the war women had to replace men in almost all occupations on the home front, notably in the educational field, where many of them became teachers in the boys' lycées. Once the war was over, many families recognized the necessity of opening up professional careers to their daughters. It was evident that many of them would not find a husband, since 1,500,000 Frenchmen had been killed in the war. Moreover, changing economic conditions had resulted in the diminishing of many a private fortune and consequently of the dowries as well. The young girl's profession, in many cases, had to replace the dowry.

Since cultural equality was a precondition of advancement in all other fields, it was felt that one of the most urgent tasks was the elimination of differences between the programs of secondary education of boys and girls. The unification of the school curriculum for boys and girls was initiated in 1924, beginning with the sixth grade. From 1931 on, it was extended to all grade levels. Simultaneously, a unification was effected in the teacher training programs of both sexes, beginning with 1922. By 1938, all special degrees for women had disappeared.

Since the end of World War II, the number of girls in the lycées has increased; at the present time, it is larger than the number of male students. With regard to instruction in the technical fields, the situation is less favorable. Although the number of girls doubled during the last ten years, while the number of boys increased by only one third during the same period, girls still account for only one third of the total.

The results of the annual competitive examinations, open to the best students in all lycées throughout the country, are significant. Girls regularly win many first and second prizes in literature, Greek, Latin, French, modern foreign languages, and history. They are less brilliant in the sciences, being as a rule oriented toward the humanities. Recently, however, the opposite tendency is beginning to manifest itself, in response to the urgent need for engineers.

In higher education, the number of women students is increasing rapidly. At the present time, they account for about 42 per cent of the total enrollment. The number of women professors has more than doubled during the last ten years, and women are to be found in many scientific fields including electronics, mechanics, and engineering. Several highly specialized schools, closed to women until recently, have now opened their doors to them, for example, the School of *Ponts et Chaussées* (Civil Engineering). A few are still open only to men, such as the military schools, the *Ecole Supérieure de Commerce* in Paris, the *Ecole Supérieure de Céramique* (Ceramics) at Sèvres, and the Mining School. However, these rules are but the relics of a period that has reached its end.

Sex Mores

The progressive liberation of the French woman, which began at the end of the nineteenth century and has almost reached completion today, has naturally resulted in a profound modification of mores.

The physical, moral, and intellectual submission of the woman to her husband has almost disappeared. This development received legal approval by a law of 1938 which suppressed from the Civil Code the article stating "The woman must obey her husband."

The relations between men and women have become freer and franker. This freedom, however, is by no means a sign of greater license. Nor by any means has the traditional French gallantry disappeared. In the totality of the relationship between the two sexes, the man's behavior remains characterized by discretion, respect, reserve, and refinement. The conquest of the French woman is a much more difficult thing to accomplish than that of women in many other countries, notwithstanding the contrary opinion shared by many foreigners which is based on misinformation derived from second-rate literature and exported motion pictures. The number of divorces on the grounds of adultery has not increased. The married woman of today retains her respect for her conjugal duties and her dignity as a wife. However, she is not considered to compromise her reputation if she goes out alone with men other than her husband to the theater, sports events, and the like. Although formerly it was not thought suitable for women to go alone to public places, they are now seen unescorted in almost as large numbers as men at cafés, public meetings, the cinema, and museums.

The change in the way of life of young girls is even more significant. The development of coeducation (although many families continue to send their girls and boys to separate lycées); dating without chaperonage; the participation of both sexes in many sports and cultural activities; their meeting at vacation camps, and the freedom to read whatever they please, all permit most young girls to know and understand the young man they go out with much better than was formerly the case.

The relationship between young men and girls has become more direct. However, while this situation undoubtedly has many advantages, it is fraught with dangers. Virginity on the part of the girl no longer constitutes an essential condition for marriage. The number of children born out of wedlock is large, although, among the middle class, such births are nearly always legitimatized by subsequent marriage.

Prostitution still serves its traditional function in France, and prostitutes are quite numerous, but their condition has greatly improved. Although only yesterday they were considered the dregs of humanity, scarcely to be mentioned by an "honest" woman, today it is generally recognized that they are but the victims of a faulty social structure. Regulation of prostitution has almost entirely disappeared. Having ratified the International Convention on the Repression of Trade in Human Beings, France has put her own legislation in harmony with its principles. The officially recognized houses of prostitution have been closed and prostitutes are no longer required to submit to periodic sanitary inspection. Thus, they are not hounded by the police, who, until very recently, could arrest and detain them by reason of their means of livelihood alone. On the other hand, hotel keepers who illegally harbor prostitutes are relentlessly tracked down and prosecuted.

The question of the evolution of manners and morals in France, and their state at the present time, may be summarized by saying that they are neither better nor worse than formerly, although the public behavior of French women might be misleading to the uninformed observer. The fact is that there has been no degeneration in morals, but the hypocritical modesty which pretended to guarantee the purity of women has become a thing of the past.

MARRIAGE

Marriage agreements and the laws applying to them had undergone only very minor changes from the publication of the Civil Code (Napoleonic Code) in 1804 until the promulgation of the new law of July 1965. Since 1804, marriage can take place only publicly, solemnized by an authorized official, before whom the two spouses must proclaim their free consent.

A girl cannot enter into matrimony without her parents' consent before she is fifteen years and three months of age; a young man cannot do so before the age of eighteen. Since 1924, the father and mother of a couple wishing to marry have equal rights with regard to giving their consent.

A couple intending to wed, may have a marriage contract drawn up and sworn to by a Notary Public, but 80 per cent of the couples in France marry without such a contract. The law contains a set of provisions concerning matrimony called Rules of Community Property, and it is principally the modification of these regulations which forms the object of the new law. Previously the husband was entitled to oppose the pursuance of a separate occupation by his wife, and had the right of disposal of almost all the household assets, including those of his wife, if she was not gainfully employed. According to the new law, the husband remains the head of the family and he alone decides where the couple should live. But the wife can now engage in an occupation of her own without the husband's consent, and she can open a bank account of her own. The new regulations of community property limit the rights of the husband. They give the wife the right to dispose freely of her own assets. However, the husband alone administers the community property, and has the right to dispose of it. Although his freedom to do so is limited by certain rules, he retains complete liberty to dispose of all mobile assets. The wife has lost the right, which she possessed in the past, of disclaiming responsibility for a joint debt if her husband dies or in the case of divorce, while retaining the assets she acquired as a result of her personal work.

Those 20 per cent of the couples, who prior to their marriage have a contract drawn up, have the choice among several possible systems which either augment or restrict the powers of the husband. Among these conventional systems is the "separation of assets" which gives the wife the same rights enjoyed by the husband.

The Position of Women in the Family

The position of women in the family has scarcely been changed either. Although legally, the family name of a married woman remains that of her father and must be used, for example in signing official documents, with certain rare exceptions she bears the name of her husband during marriage and after she becomes a widow, if that occurs. She frequently uses even the first name of her husband. In case of divorce, the husband may object to his ex-wife's continuing to use his name, in which case she again takes the name of her father. This, of course, may be quite prejudicial to her, since she may have become known by her husband's name.

Normally, the married woman has her legal residence only with her husband. Since 1938, however, she may legally establish another residence, if it is in the interests of her family to do so.

The mother has no legal rights over her children. It is the husband alone who wields parental power, and only he may decide how his children shall be cared for, supported, and educated. This legal incapacity of the married woman should not be exaggerated, however. In actual practice, it becomes important only in cases where the spouses do not get along well. Under normal circumstances, the woman's position within the family is predominant. Although she has few legal rights, her influence is, and has always been, considerable. Decisions are almost always reached jointly by both spouses who discuss matters between themselves before taking action. When the two are not in complete agreement, one or the other usually compromises.

The woman is and always has been queen in her home. She alone organizes and manages it, with the tacit assent of her husband. It is she who supervises the children's upbringing, their moral and intellectual training. The father participates only to a very minor degree. When there is a discussion between the parents concerning the future of the children, it is generally the mother's wishes which prevail. No wonder that one often hears it said in France that a man is what his mother made him.

As we have seen, relations between husband and wife are no longer characterized by the woman's subjection to the man; nearly always they become good and equal companions. Although respect of children for their parents has, in nearly all families, been replaced by camaraderie, affection tinged with deep respect remains the relationship of sons and daughters to their mother.

The Woman at Home

With regard to home life, French women can be divided into two rather distinct categories: those who devote themselves entirely to their household and children, and those who, in addition to performing their household tasks, hold down paid jobs.

The everyday home life of the woman in the first category has been transformed by social changes and technical developments. The great majority of middle-class families no longer have domestic servants (general maid, cooks, chamber maids, nurses) as they did before World War I. Some are able to get help only for heavy cleaning a few hours a day. The result is that household schedules everywhere have been greatly simplified. In many well-to-do families, the daily meals are no longer served in the dining room, but in an attractively decorated kitchen. And the husband and children are beginning to share various household chores. However, the mother in a middle-class family must now perform herself nearly all the chores which formerly were done by servants. Although her work is heavier, it does not take all her time, because of the great advances in home appliances that have been made since World War I. Today, one finds almost everywhere washing machines, refrigerators, hot and cold running water, gas or electric ranges, vacuum cleaners, and electric irons. The increase in household work is thus to some degree compensated for by better organized households. However, the woman must still perform all the traditional duties of wife and housekeeper. It is she who cooks all three meals which the family usually takes at home (the practice of taking the midday meal outside is still not general). And she must still take care of her children, fetch the youngest ones from school, and supervise the homework of the older ones.

Radio and television, found in nearly all homes today, permit the woman to feel less acutely the isolation and boredom of her daily routine. They provide not only entertainment, but sometimes actual enrichment of the brief moments of leisure.

The everyday home life of the woman who also holds a paid job, and who is necessarily away from home at least nine to ten hours a day, is much more arduous. To make her life tolerable, such a woman must make the most of her resources of organization, courage and energy.

In principle, she must perform during the few hours she is at home almost all the tasks that are incumbent upon the woman who does not work at an outside job. For her especially, improved household appliances and good organization are invaluable, and she must economize her time and avoid overexertion. The sharing of household chores by the husband and children has largely come about since World War II.

THE SOCIAL POSITION OF WOMEN

The preceding sections have shown that the social position of French women in general has altered profoundly since World War I. Among the upper-middle class, however, the women's situation has remained quite stable. A woman remains the unobtrusive helpmeet of her husband; her life depends entirely on his position. The only activities considered appropriate for her are participation in various social and cultural affairs and charity projects.

In all other classes, the woman makes her own place in society, and it is a place which more and more closely approximates that of men. She enjoys esteem and affection, or submits to indifference or scorn, depending upon the responses which her personality evokes in those around her. Her participation in social and political life varies as between town and country, and from region to region.

She is interested in politics to only a minor degree as yet (women did not acquire the franchise until 1944). It is only when she considers the possibility of holding public office, such as that of municipal councillor or deputy, that she really takes part in political life. Women vote, however, in as great numbers as men.

In the labor unions, the number of women has increased but still remains relatively small. The same is true of political parties and clubs of all kinds. French women are, for the most part, hostile to the idea of clubs. Women's clubs, where one goes to take meals, relax, meet friends, and enjoy recreational activities, are almost unknown in France, although a few women's associations and women's sections of political parties do exist, with limited memberships.

On the other hand, the development of French social legislation, considered today as among the most advanced in the world, has brought advantages of all kinds to women. They are now entitled to a weekly rest period of one and a half to two days, which allows them a fuller social life. Their health and that of their families is better protected and they are freer from worry. Various benefits have brought a greater degree of comfort into their lives than ever before. The existence of homes for old people, and old-age insurance, allow them much greater freedom from concern about the future than formerly.

WOMEN'S OCCUPATIONS

Under this heading, paid occupations must be distinguished from those which are not paid. Unpaid housekeeping duties and raising children remain the woman's primary activities. For all women these tasks consume a major part of each day.

The character of social work done by individual women has changed somewhat so that the effort formerly devoted directly to charity work is now given to various social institutions.

With regard to paid occupations, contrary to what one would expect, the number of working women has remained almost constant over half a century. Since 1900, there has been even a slight decrease in the number of women who work outside the home. Following World War II, the workers' wages increased and married men became better able to support their families on their earnings alone, so the number of working wives dropped.

The change which makes it appear that the number of working women has increased involves the types of jobs held by them. While at the beginning of the century almost all working women were manual laborers, employees, white-collar workers, or domestic servants, by the middle of the century, more and more women were taking positions in the liberal professions, in higher government employment, as business executives, and in politics. One may say that, with few exceptions, one finds women in all trades and professions in France. In 1965 there were in France 6,589,260 women working at paid jobs. This means that one out of every three workers in the country was a woman. Of these working women, about one half were married, which means that the great majority of gainfully employed women had given up their jobs upon getting married.

Teaching—Since the beginning of the century, teaching has attracted a great number of women. However, the number of teachers has grown since World War I, and since World War II it has increased even more rapidly. Today, the total number of women teachers is larger than that of men teachers. In the primary grades, more than twice as many women teach as men. As for the secondary schools, although few women were teaching in them before World War II, their number now exceeds by 2,000 that of men. In universities, although there were practically no women faculty members before 1939, there were 198 in 1946, and 580 in 1954, as against 3,460 men. In 1962, there were 1,120 women university teachers, or 20 per cent of the total. The results of recent qualifying examinations increased the last figures, and undoubtedly also the proportion of women professors will soon be greater. At the present time, many women are teaching in university departments of arts, literature, the sciences, medicine, pharmacy, and law, some of them as full professors.

The Sciences—At the beginning of the century, women had not yet entered the various scientific fields. Today, they attract many women. In 1954, there were 1,280 women as against 3,480 men devoting themselves full time to one or another of the sciences. Today, the number of women scientists is 3,580, or 27 per cent of the total. The number of women working at the National Center for Scientific Research leaped from 70 in 1950 to 1,115 in 1960, out of a total of 3,311 research workers. In 1965, there were 1,480 women out of a total of 4,594.

Literature constitutes in France, as in all other countries, a field which attracts many women. In 1954, there were 840 women in literary occupations as compared with 2,280 men. In 1962, there were 940 women, or 33.6 per cent of the total number.

The Arts have always been considered a field appropriate to women, but until the beginning of this century, women practiced them in a non-professional way. They have really competed with men only since 1896, the date at which the *Ecole Nationale Supérieure des Beaux-Arts* (National School of Fine Arts) in Paris was opened to them.

Librarians and Museum Curators are for the most part women at the present time. Although after World War I only a few women were graduated from the *Ecole de Chartes*, which offers training for these occupations, the number of women candidates admitted today far exceeds that of men.

Translators also are women in the majority of cases, although, their proportion is slightly smaller. In 1954, out of a total of 3,980 translators, 2,440, or 61.3 per cent, were women. In 1962, there were 2,900, or 69.3 per cent of the total.

Public Administration—The admission of a large number of women to almost all levels of public administration goes back to World War I. At that time, women replaced men called into military service, and, when the war was over, they continued to fill the vacancies left by men who did not come back. Most of the examinations for admission to high-level administrative positions have been gradually opened to women since 1920.

Between the two World Wars, many women were employed as clerks in the civil service in Paris, in various Ministries, the police, public welfare offices, and so on. Two women have been appointed as department heads. In 1946, fifty women were department heads in the central offices of various Ministries. Since 1950, they have the title of Administrator. Examinations for admission to the new School of Administration, designed to train higher personnel for administrative work, is open, on the same conditions, to members of both sexes, and women graduates are more numerous each year. In 1954, out of a total of 1,154,540 officials 406,920 were women. In 1962, there were 775,260 women officials, and their proportion in the total has increased from 34 to 37 per cent. The percentage of women officials as against men is inversely proportionate to the importance of the positions they occupy.

Religious Occupations have always been attractive to many women. There are today in France 103,120 women out of a total religious personnel of 154,840. Only the Protestant churches admit women to the ministry (since 1949).

Health and Social Welfare activities also have always interested large numbers of women. Qualified technical workers of the female sex are more and more frequently encountered in these fields since World War II. Today, women form a majority of 63 per cent in these occupations.

Accounting is a profession, which has recently been regulated by law, and it attracts more women each day. Results of the last examinations indicate an even more rapid increase in the future. The number of women certified public accountants has tripled in the past nine years.

Business and Commerce—The number of women working for business firms, either as employees or as executives in their own companies, has always been high, and is now almost half of the total number of persons so employed.

Domestic Service, which includes household help, waitresses, laundresses, and so on, has always been the almost exclusive domain of women. Today one finds 836,400 women, constituting 88.8 per cent of all domestic workers, although fewer women are engaged in domestic service than formerly.

Industry and Trade—The place of women in these occupations has scarcely changed during the last fifty years. There are and always have been women workers in all trades and industries, almost without exception. At the present time, one seventh of all heads of industrial firms are women. For the past ten years, female labor has been very much in demand in fine mechanics, electrical manufacturing, electronics, television and radio.

Agriculture continues to occupy a large number of women. Although their number has decreased, because of a general reduction in the number of agricultural workers, they still number 1,264,120, constituting 32 per cent of the total agricultural labor force. As to administrative positions connected with large-scale cultivation projects, women are able to obtain only a very few of them. There are in all only 20 women directors of agricultural works, as compared with 9,760 men, and only 40 women function as husbandry chiefs, as compared with 10,160 men.

WOMEN IN LEADERSHIP

Politics—Up to the time of World War II, despite energetic campaigns led by feminists and the efforts of many members of Parliament, women in France had no political rights. It was only after the liberation from German occupation that the right to vote and eligibility for election to both chambers of the French bicameral legislature were accorded to women, by virtue of an ordinance initiated in Algiers and proclaimed by General de Gaulle the very evening he arrived in Paris.

Immediately women began to enter municipal councils. They were nominated, as were men, because of their participation in the Resistance. By the end of September 1944 there were more than 100 municipal councillors of the female sex in the Paris region, most of them simple working-class women. Several of them were named Deputy-Mayor. From the moment they took over, these women councillors became involved in such problems as augmenting food supplies, distribution of milk to infants, distribution of reserves left by the Germans, and reorganization of the schools.

At the same time, women entered the Provisional Consultative Assembly, composed of 248 members, which included representatives of the Resistance, as well as former parliamentarians. A dozen women were named for seats because of their Resistance activities. This Assembly was given consultative powers. From the time it started functioning, women took a very active part in its work. They participated frequently in the debates, and proposed numerous amendments and resolutions. They demanded, naturally, equal rights for the two sexes, and the admission of women to the magistracy.

On April 29, 1945, French women voted for the first time in municipal elections. Nine women were then elected to the Municipal Council of Paris, and many more to those of other large cities and towns. On October 21, 1945, following the Liberation, women took part in the first general elections for the National Constituent Assembly. They voted in as large numbers as did men, and the result of the balloting was a feminine victory, for the Assembly included, among its 545 members, 33 women — more than those in the British Parliament, although women in Great Britain had been voting for twenty-six years. A woman was elected Secretary of the Assembly. The role of the women deputies was important: in addition to all general questions, they were especially concerned with those relating to public health, education, the relation between mother and child, and women's rights. They served on almost all the important committees: those on National Education, the Family (seven women members on each), Food Supply (five women, including the chairman), and Constitution (three women).

During the ensuing twelve years of the Fourth Republic, in spite of the progressive reduction of their number, women continued to play in both National Assemblies a role comparable to that of their masculine colleagues. Although they continued to be involved primarily with matters of a social nature, all questions pertaining to the general welfare of the country held their attention. A major factor in the reduction of the number of women deputies has been the almost total disappearance of the Communist Party. In the First Assembly of the Fifth Republic, the number of Communist Party members was reduced from 138 to 10, and among those not returned were 15 women. However, there is a more important reason for the diminishing number of women. Although they have obtained the franchise, they have not acquired the talent for getting themselves elected, which is due no doubt to their lack of serious interest and active participation in political life. Thus the Second National Assembly of the Fifth Republic, elected in November 1962, which was still in session in 1965, included only nine women. Its executive included only one woman: the vice-president. However, there are only two large committees on which women do not serve.

Three women are on the committee for culture, family and social work; three on the committee for foreign affairs; one on the committee for national defense; one on the committee for industry and trade.

In the course of the first seven years of the Fifth Republic, the women parliamentarians interested themselves in particular in problems of children, mothers, the family, the aged, health, education, war victims, the equality of the rights of the two sexes; however, all the questions relative to the general interest of the country also received their attention.

Cabinet Posts—During the past twenty years, women have held several cabinet positions. Madame André Vienot became Under-Secretary for Youth and Sports in June 1946 in George Bidault's cabinet. The following year, under Schuman, Madame Poinsot-Chapuis received the first full cabinet post ever held by a woman, that of Minister of Public Health. Her important achievements included the fight against alcoholism. She also became one of the Vice Presidents of the National Assembly.

Following General de Gaulle's election as President, the first Government of the Fifth Republic, formed in January 1959, included one woman, Mademoiselle Nafissa Sid Cara, an Algerian Muslim who became Secretary for Algerian Affairs. Her appointment symbolized the highest hope of the cloistered women of Algeria. The second government of General de Gaulle, formed in April 1962, did not include any woman of cabinet rank.

The Municipal Councils—There are 11,145 women sitting in the municipal councils of towns and cities, large and small, throughout the country. Some of these women, more numerous each day, fulfill the functions of mayor or deputy-mayor. (Of the deputy-mayors of Paris, appointed by the government, 11 were women in 1946; 7 from 1950 to 1952; 10 in 1959, and 16 in 1965.) In Paris, where the Municipal Council consists of 90 members, the proportion of women has decreased as in Parliament, and for the same reasons. In 1947, there were 13 women in the Municipal Council of Paris; in 1953, nine; and the municipal elections of 1965 returned only 12 women to the Council. Since the Liberation, one Vice-Presidency of the Municipal Council of Paris has always been given to a woman.

All of the women serving as councillors for the 37,962 "communes" of France cannot be listed here. The results of the elections of March 19, 1965, in the nine cities with more than 120,000 inhabitants returned six women municipal councillors in Lyon, five in Havre and Lille, three in Nice, two each in Bordeaux, Nancy, Toulon and Toulouse, and one in Nantes.

Diplomatic Service—Up to date, France has had no woman Ambassadors. Several women, however, currently hold the rank of Chancellor, Vice Consul, and Consul. In 1955, a woman was appointed Vice Consul, heading the Chancellory at Sofia. In 1958, another was named Vice Consul to the French Embassy in Madrid. In 1959, a third was named Vice Consul to head the Chancellery of the French Consulate General in São Paulo.

The Magistracy — A law of August 5, 1946, opened the magistrate's career to women. In 1952, women first entered the Council of State, the highest administrative body in the country. Today, eight of the 180 members of this court are women. A woman professor with a law degree sits in the Court of Cassation, the highest civil and criminal court in the country. One woman, after having been appointed in 1961 as the first counselor in the Court of Appeal at Douai, has subsequently become vice-president of the Tribunal of the Seine. In 1965, there were 148 women judges in Superior Courts (or 5 per cent of all judges), and the number grows each year. Several women have served in the provincial courts as Substitute District Attorneys of the Republic and as Arraigning Magistrates.

There were 84 women among the judges of the courts of first instance, formerly justices of the peace, constituting 10 per cent of the total. This proportion too is rapidly on the increase.

The law of March 20, 1948, opened the function of judicial auxiliaries to women. There are today 31 women notaries public in France, and 12 women solicitors.

Other Professions — The liberal professions have been open to women for more than half a century. Women could become lawyers since 1900. Today, out of 6,639 lawyers in the Court of Appeals, 1,408 are women; in Paris, there are 845 women lawyers out of a total of 2,946.

The first women physicians in the world received their degrees in France in 1870. Today, out of 50,529 practicing doctors, 4,418 are women. Up to the present time, two women have been elected members of the Academy of Medicine, the first being Madame Curie.

In 1964, there were only 96 women architects. In 1951, a woman presented the plan of urban development for the city of Bangui in French Equatorial Africa.

In 1954, 2,000 women were practicing engineers, out of a total of 100,000. By 1962, their number reached 5,160, or 3.7 per cent of the total. At present, about 8 per cent of all chemical engineers are women. Women are numerous in the offices of the Atomic Energy Commission. In 1959, the Center for Nuclear Studies at Saclay employed a total of 950 engineers and scientists, including 110 women. Forty women engineers are employed in Public Works. In 1959, the first girl was admitted to the *Ecole des Ponts et Chaussées* ("School of Bridges and Roads," i.e. School of Civil Engineering).

Women are contributing a great deal to the advancement of the sciences. In 1950, there were already 70 in the National Center for Scientific Research, and their number is growing. By 1965 they constituted a third of the personnel of the Center, or 1,480 in absolute figures.

Numerous prizes, of which several are offered by the Académie Francaise, are won by women each year. In 1911, the first *Grand Prix de Rome* was given to a woman, and since that time women have won sixteen at various times. Many works of art by women are included in the collections of the national museums, as well as in the private museums both in France and abroad.

Of the eighty theaters in Paris, fifteen are headed by women directors, and six by women in association with men directors.

WOMEN AS CULTURAL TRANSMITTERS

As we have seen, women participate in the development, maintenance, and transmission of all aspects of culture. Their role as cultural transmitters, however, transcends the numerical proportions in which they are represented in the various fields of cultural endeavor. In their capacity as mothers and teachers it is they who decisively influence the cultural orientation of the children and adolescents. Thus the responsibility of transmitting French culture to future generations rests primarily with the women.

Apart from this general role fulfilled by them, French women are responsible for a number of special cultural developments in which France has the uncontested leadership. French fashions, perfumes and cosmetics, produced, it is true, mostly by male experts, but in the service of the French woman, are recognized all over the world as the finest. The culture of no other nation contains comparable woman-centered features admired, used, and imitated everywhere.

OUTLOOK

It is difficult, if not impossible, to make predictions about the future condition of women in France. The changes which may expand women's position are manifold and complex, involving economic, social, geographic, and political factors. It seems almost certain, however, that French women, having acquired almost total autonomy, will insist on retaining and inereasing their gains until they achieve equal rights with men.

West Germany[1]

By Helge Pross

*W*est Germany today is a modern society indeed.
Highly industrialized, about 85 per cent of her population of 53 million live
in smaller or larger towns, and only 15 per cent reside in villages and semi-
rural communities. Little more than one tenth of all gainfully employed do
agricultural work while approximately nine tenths are occupied in industry,
private and public administration, handicraft, commerce, cultural institutions, or other nonagricultural jobs. During the last three or four decades
the German social structure has undergone fundamental changes resulting
in a society chiefly middle class in character. After World War II, the

---

1. This article deals only with women in the Federal Republic of Germany. Since
the political, social, and economic setup of the communist German Democratic
Republic is fundamentally different, the position of women there will not be
discussed.

landed aristocracy, powerful for many a century, disappeared, while the industrial proletariat, exploited and underprivileged in the past, achieved a greatly improved economic position. Since the turn of the century a large and still growing new middle class of white-collar workers and civil servants emerged. To be sure, class distinctions have not been leveled out. They are marked, as far as property, income, social prestige, and educational opportunities are concerned. There is a small upper stratum consisting of a few extremely wealthy capitalists, the top executives of large industrial firms, high government officials, and the decision makers in the major political parties and pressure groups. However, this upper class, strong as its influence may be, has ceased to be a homogeneous ruling caste. On the other hand, no class of paupers is left at the bottom of the social pyramid. Working in an economy which for nearly a decade and a half has known no unemployment; enjoying a large measure of leisure (the workweek has been reduced to forty to forty-two hours); protected by an elaborate system of social security against the financial pitfalls of illness and age; and supplied with numerous opportunities for education and amusement, most Germans are citizens of quite an "affluent society" indeed.

Modern as the Federal Republic may be in her economic and social structure, she has not as yet broken with all traditions of an authoritarian and patriarchal past. The democratization of the state after World War II has not made for an egalitarian society. Although all men are equal before the law, society does not offer all of them equal opportunities. Some groups are still underprivileged in various ways. This holds true particularly for women. Remnants of age-old traditions regarding them as the intellectually weaker sex, less able to shoulder responsibilities in politics or the professions, stand in the way of true equality. Although the struggle for emancipation has been won, women are still discriminated against in the world outside the family and the home. Generally speaking, women in West Germany are confronted with social and psychological problems that, to a large degree, arise out of the disharmony between a demanding present and an unmastered past, and the conflict between preindustrial roles and the demands of modern life.

THE LEGAL POSITION

Women in West Germany have nothing to complain about in regard to their legal position. The Basic Law, the Federal Republic's constitution, adopted in 1949, endows both sexes with equal rights. Women have the franchise, and enjoy the right of equal pay for equal performance. In 1957, the Federal Parliament took the last and decisive step towards the implementation of full legal equality. By a special bill all civil law was adapted to the constitutional principle. Among the many provisions of the new law, most important are those revising property and inheritance rights of husband and wife.

Under the old civil law, formulated at the end of the nineteenth century, the husband had remarkable privileges: he had the usufruct of his wife's estate and acted as her trustee. He managed their common property, and could dispose of it even against her will. At his death, the wife inherited only one quarter of his estate unless the couple had concluded a special contract in her favor.

All this has now been changed. The management and disposition of the wife's property is solely her affair. The husband is no longer allowed to handle their common estate without her consent. All decisions about common goods must be made by both. If the husband dies, the wife inherits one half of the property. In case of divorce, regardless of which of them is the guilty party, she not only retains what she brought into marriage, but receives in addition half of the possessions acquired by the couple while married. Even if the husband accumulated a fortune from his earnings, while the wife had no income of her own, she gets 50 per cent. This provision is meant to protect the housewife whose work the law considers indispensable for the creation and preservation of the estate. Formerly, if divorced, she had no legal claim to her husband's savings, she now suffers no financial loss if, instead of seeking gainful employment, she devotes herself to the family and the home.

In addition to the provisions mentioned, the new law parts in all other respects as well from the old principle of the husband's right to decide in controversial family affairs. Formerly the decision about the children's education—whether they should or should not be sent to a *gymnasium* (academic high school), or to a university—was left to him, now both parents must agree. Also, the wife now has legal claim to regular payments of household expenses and pocket money for her personal needs.

The implementation of the principle of equality also affects the wife's claim to maintenance after divorce. According to the marriage law the guilty partner has to maintain the other one if the latter is unable to do so "adequately." The definition of what is adequate support varies, and is left to the courts. A woman with children is usually deemed incapable of earning an adequate living. If the woman is not guilty, yet able to take a job, she cannot claim regular payments. On the other hand, if she is guilty, and her husband is unable to support himself, she must make payments to him. This regulation, though sometimes criticized, is perfectly in keeping with the doctrine of equality. Based on the assumption that both partners have equal responsibilities for each other, it protects the institution of marriage as such. The husband cannot get rid of his wife without financial loss, nor is the wife allowed to sell her consent for the price of large alimony payments. On the whole, divorce against the will of the innocent party has become a rather difficult affair.

Finally, one more outcome of the doctrine of equality is worth mentioning. A woman marrying a foreigner used to lose her German citizenship on the day of marriage. The new regulations allow her to keep it.

TOWN AND COUNTRY

In many respects West German agriculture lags behind the urban and industrial sectors of society. While some villages have taken great steps toward the modernization of their economic and social life, in others people still cling to more traditional patterns. Generally speaking, the rural population is also passing through a period of transition. Struggling to adapt to the requirements of a market economy, a large number of farmers surrendered and took up industrial jobs. In fact, from 1949 to 1959 about 50 per cent of the agricultural laborers, and one third (1.5 million) of the independent peasants quit agriculture. Many, if not most, of those who stayed cannot keep up economically with the urban population. Though all of them, male and female alike, work harder than the average city dweller, their standard of living is lower. So is their level of education. Of course, there are no illiterates in the rural regions, and much is being done to improve the farmers' general and vocational training. Many villages have centers for adult education or community houses offering regular lectures on agricultural techniques, home economics, baby care and sociopolitical subjects. Since these community houses frequently provide certain facilities, such as washing machines or deep freezers, for common use, they act as agencies of modernization also for those who could not be reached by mere theoretical instruction. In addition, radio and television, popular all over the country, are links to the non-rural world. Nevertheless, the average villager still seems to be less informed on national events. Nor is information about modern child-rearing techniques disseminated among them. In many places, children are looked after only until they are four years old. Afterwards, mothers leave them to themselves, rarely having the time to supervise and to guide them. Child labor is widespread, almost all village youngsters being obliged to help in the home, to look after cattle and poultry, or assist their parents in the fields.

Within the last two or three decades the rural family too has undergone some change. As to size, it does not differ much from its urban counterpart. Since the end of World War II the nuclear family has emerged as the representative and most widespread rural type. The number of children is small, almost never larger than two. This change indicates that the rural population has also turned to a more rational, calculating attitude toward life. The internal family structure is, however, somewhat different from the urban one. With respect to the position of mother and wife, roughly three types can be distinguished, each representing a different stage of adaptation to more democratic ways.

First, there is the traditional patriarchal family, dominated by the father, with wife and children still subordinates rather than partners. In these families, practically all decisions are left to the oldest male. He manages the family budget, decides matters concerning the farm, and has the final word in controversies about the children. It is interesting that the patriarchal family's economic behavior also follows more traditional lines. Rarely are economic ends and means linked in a rational way. Neither do such families adopt a sensible scheme of division of labor, nor are there conscious efforts at better management. One result is an overload of work for the women. Responsible for the house, the poultry and the garden, they also work in the fields and have to step in wherever and whenever additional hands are needed.

In general, the working hours of peasant women in all types of families are long, from 60 to 80 hours per week. In spite of this heavy contribution, women are little respected. Most villagers show only a modest appreciation of female work, and the women themselves are too much resigned to their lot to object. Being overworked, they often are in a poor state of health and thus lack the physical energy as well as the time to search for improvements.

While according to the estimates of some sociologists a decade ago this traditional patriarchal family was the most widespread type in rural regions, more recently a different type has developed, the so-called partnership family (*Partnerschaftsfamilie*). In it, economic and personal matters are discussed between husband and wife, and decisions reached by mutual agreement. Again, family pattern and economic behavior are intimately linked, both evincing a certain open-mindedness and a more enlightened philosophy of life. On the whole, the partnership family seems to be quite efficient, oriented toward the market, and eager to introduce modern methods in production, work, organization and financial administration.

Finally, there is the family in transition, apparently the most unhappy one. Wives in such families, though they no longer unquestioningly accept the authority of the males, have not yet entirely emancipated themselves from their traditional role of subordination. Being the dominated party, they resent their responsibilities, and are as unable to collaborate reasonably as are the husbands. In these families (but not only in these) the conflict between traditional and modern norms makes itself felt also in the relation between older and younger generation. Regular pay and regular leisure, and even the claim to both, being denied to them, the hard-working boys and girls often leave family and village, though they may be heirs to the farm. Girls in particular want to get away so that they need not lead the miserable life of their mothers.

On the whole, the lot of rural women is difficult, particularly on medium-size and small farms (that is, in the majority of all farms): too much work, bad health, insufficient education, and too little help from outside. What is needed is a large-scale effort of government and private groups to educate both husband and wife, and teach the women how to better organize their work, recognize and defend their rights. (Further mechanization, still badly needed in the household, will not lead to the expected results unless rural women become more efficient in the organization and planning of their jobs.) However, the improvement of village life depends not only on education and individual intelligence. In the long run education, even when coupled with much needed mechanization, can bear fruit only if also the property structure of the entire rural sector is thoroughly reorganized.

WORKING WOMEN

As in most industrial countries, the life of women in West Germany is influenced above all by the necessity to combine what is usually referred to as "women's two roles." [2] One role is that of wife and mother, and the other that of the working woman employed outside of her home. A young girl who leaves school or finishes her vocational training has to find a job, but most girls also want to get married and a good many of them do. However, in the older age groups there are some exceptions to this general rule. There are those women who devote their lives solely to the traditional female tasks. They belong exclusively to the older generation (from fifty-five years upward), in which there are still quite a few, particularly among the bourgeois women, who have never been anything but housewives and mothers. On the other hand, there is a large group of about two million women, now roughly between thirty-eight and fifty years of age, who never have been and never will be anything but working women. They too would certainly like to marry, but have no chance to do so as a result of the fact that their potential husbands were slain during the war or died in Nazi concentration camps. In 1965 there were 27.9 million men and 30.9 million women in the Federal Republic, a surplus of 3 million women.

While many women give up their jobs after getting married, or, more frequently, after the birth of their first child, quite a number of wives and mothers continue to work. To do so has become more popular in recent years, particularly among young wives. Although in 1950 only 28 per cent

2. Alva Myrdal and Viola Klein, *Women's Two Roles*, London, 1956.

of all married women from twenty to twenty-five years retained their jobs, the percentage rose to approximately 50 in 1957. In 1962 nearly one third (4.7 million) of all married women, and a little less than one third of those married mothers who lived together with husband and children (mothers in complete families) were working. In addition, there were in 1957 nearly 1.8 million working mothers of incomplete families, that is wives separated from their husbands, widows, divorced women, and mothers of illegitimate children, all with children living with them in the same house.

Large as the number of working mothers was, of all mothers who lived (1957) in complete families only a minority of 12 per cent (or one million) worked outside of the home. The majority, about 18 per cent (1.45 million) were occupied mostly in small family enterprises in or next to the home. These women, the wives of peasants, independent artisans or small business men, did not need to leave their children alone while at work. Though frequently overburdened, they can move freely between workshop and home. Neither of the two worlds these mothers live in, the family and their business world, is antagonistic to the other, and rarely do the tasks in the first conflict heavily with the duties in the second.

As compared with this group (the so-called *Mithelfende Familienange-hörige*), the 1.2 million married and unmarried mothers who worked (1957) in factory or office, and whose children (under eighteen years) lived with them, had a more difficult time. These constituted 16 per cent of all mothers (married and unmarried) with children under eighteen years. It is these women who have to leave the children alone or under the supervision of somebody else, usually a relative and very rarely a neighbor.

The demands on working mothers being high, why do they consent to the twofold task? The motives vary chiefly according to social class, and change with time. A decade ago almost any German family still suffered from the damages of war, having lost home, furniture and clothing, or being refugees from the eastern provinces of the former German Reich. Very often, families could be founded and the household rebuilt only with supplementary income produced by the mother and wife. Once this emergency passed, the motives changed. Today, it is primarily, though not solely, the desire to improve the household equipment, to buy an apartment, or to build a house which makes mothers seek employment. This is true particularly of women in the lower-income classes. While the wages of industrial workers and of the rank and file in civil service and private offices are usually sufficient to cover current expenses, they very often do not allow for additional expenditure. If the family wants to maintain what is nowadays considered a decent standard of living, the mother must step in.

It would be too simple to call these women (as is often done) materialistic. Normally, it is not for luxury that they work. Of course, the definition of luxury varies. According to present standards in West Germany, a private car, an electric refrigerator, perhaps also a television set, but certainly not a radio, are deemed by many families to be luxuries. On the other hand, the working women, like practically everybody else, are victims of the "hidden persuaders" of advertising. In this context, moral criticism is not only useless but unjust as well. It usually overlooks the fact that many industrial workers and small business men can rise above the level of mere subsistence only by the additional labor of the wife. For the first time in German history these classes have a chance to keep up with the bourgeois families, and thus become more self-assured. They believe that it is more important to get ahead and to secure for their children a materially better life than for the mother to be present in the home all day during the early phases of her child's life. Psychoanalytic theory not being popular with Germans, and practically unknown among workers and in the lower-middle class, mothers think it more essential to stay at home when the children reach school age than to be available for the babies.

There is a small fraction of mothers who go on working primarily for the sake of personal independence or because they just love their jobs. Almost exclusively they are wives who went to college, women physicians, lawyers, economists, high school and university teachers. While the majority of working mothers would prefer to remain at home, and while many are likely to do so as soon as the family can afford it, quite a number of the women university graduates would not voluntarily withdraw.

The German public, being conservative in many respects, is ambiguous about working mothers. Among their most ardent opponents are the women themselves: two thirds advocate a law forbidding mothers with children under ten years to accept gainful employment. In general, however, the agitation against working mothers is of no avail. Manpower being in extremely short supply in Germany, wives and mothers are the only labor reserve left. Barring a recession in the near future, more and more mothers will be absorbed in the productive process. Society could and should help the mothers and their children in counteracting this trend not by outlawing work for them, but by a revision of the tax and wage system in favor of low-income groups. If special rebates were given to large families, making it more attractive for mothers to stay at home, probably quite a number would do so. It was the working mothers and their families who, by shouldering additional burdens, made a large contribution to the so-called "economic miracle" in West Germany. The country having been rebuilt, with the wealth of the nation greater than ever before, it is now time for society to repay them in such a manner that no mother with small children need seek employment solely because otherwise the family could not rise above the level of mere subsistence.

THE WOMEN IN THE FAMILY

Surprisingly little is known about family structure in the Federal Republic. Aside from some sociological studies carried out soon after the war, almost no empirical research was done in the field. Relevant questions as to the internal structure of the family, the balance of power between husband and wife, the relations of parents and children, and the emotional climate of the group, have not yet found satisfactory answers.

Even without adequate research it is evident that the authoritarian family, long representative in Germany, has vanished. No longer is the urban family ruled by a powerful father, and no longer are wife and children willing just to obey. Although it is clear that the traditional structure is broken, and that especially in families of the younger generation hardly any trait of it is left, there is no reliable information as to what has taken its place. While according to some authors the relationship between husband and wife is now more that of partners who arrive at decisions by discussion and compromise, others insist that no such democratic family pattern has evolved, and that an atmosphere of indifference prevails in which neither authoritarianism nor individualistic attitudes can thrive.

Generally speaking, the family in Germany shows all the traits characteristic of fully developed industrial societies. Girls and boys decide themselves, almost without exception, whom they are going to marry and get married at the average age of 23.7 and 26 years respectively. Arranged marriages are entirely unknown. The future partners meet on the job, in the youth groups, or at parties. They want to marry chiefly for love. There are other motives, too, for instance, to escape the sense of loneliness and to gain security. Also, quite a number of them feel obliged to legalize an actual relationship because the first child is on its way.

To what degree women are content in marriage is generally unknown. A study carried out as far back as 1949 does not give too rosy a picture. At that time only half of a representative sample of wives thought it necessary for a woman's happiness for her to be married, thus pointing indirectly to some sort of dissatisfaction with their own marriages. One in six confessed frankly to being unhappy, and one in four did not believe their sex life harmonious. On the other hand, men gave the impression of being emotionally and sexually more contented, thinking marriage more rewarding than did the wives.

The habit of having but two children is a novelty, and to some degree an amazing one. This is not so much because in the past children used to be numerous, particularly in the lower social strata, and now it is exactly these strata which adhere to the new pattern (while in the upper classes there is a slight tendency towards larger numbers of children). Rather, the almost universal adoption of planned parenthood and of having few children is surprising for another reason. From its advent to power until its collapse in 1945, the Nazi government strongly favored a population increase. By propaganda, by prohibiting the sale of contraceptives, and by making special allowances for large families, it tried to induce parents to have many children. The result was a relatively high birth rate in the 1930's. However, after the war a change set in without ever having been publicly recommended. On the contrary, since 1949 all national governments have been formed by the Christian Democratic Union, the majority party which was strongly influenced by Catholics. Also Protestants had, until very recently, reservations about birth control. Nor were there powerful private agencies spreading information. In fact, the Planned Parenthood Association is little known, and the subject of family planning is seldom discussed in public. Yet people do plan—primarily for economic reasons. Realizing that at present they cannot have both large families and a high standard of living, they cut down on the number of offspring. This might change again, if material conditions continue to improve. Then Germany may witness a baby boom. Whether this would be desirable for women is open to question. It could easily lead to a revival of concepts defining the family as the only legitimate domain of women, and to public agitation to confine them to it once again.

How stable marriages are in this country is difficult to assess. Figures on divorce—83 per 1000 marriages in 1960 as against 75 in 1938—reveal little as long as other data, such as the number of couples living separately, remains unknown. It may well be that under the strain of war, and in the misery of the postwar period, families proved more stable than might have been expected. However, with the return to normality since the 1950's, this may have changed. Whatever the case may be, German experiences of the last three decades allow for the hypothesis that a national crisis does not necessarily become also a familial crisis, while, on the other hand, stability of broader social structures does not inevitably make for the internal stability of the family. Rather, it can be suspected that in the present relatively stable social order destructive impulses of the inidvidual, having few outlets, turn against the family, upsetting its peace, without, however, destroying the unit.

SEX MORES

Aside from the few data about marital happiness and unhappiness, there is practically no reliable information available on sex mores, and one can only speculate. Casual observations seem to indicate that German young people follow liberal patterns, though not in excess. Nearly half of all first-born children were conceived before their parents were married.

Furthermore, abortion seems to be resorted to very frequently, in spite of the Catholic-inspired laws prohibiting it.

While these facts indicate the prevalence of premarital sexual experience among young people, they do not reveal how frequently boys and girls change partners before they settle down to marriage. We may safely conclude that girls tend to disregard the traditional rules which insist on premarital virginity and to experiment sexually with their fiancés and probably with other men as well. The men accept this practice readily, no longer demanding chastity of their future wives.

Although nowadays young men as well as young women are strongly inclined to idealize the family and marriage as an escape from loneliness and lack of parental understanding, there is no doubt that adultery has become rather a common practice, particularly for men after several years of marriage. For men over thirty or so, there are abundant opportunities, since many women between thirty-five and forty-five are unmarried and quite willing to consent to a love affair with a married man. Prostitution is well established in all of the larger cities. Thus, the conditions prevailing since the end of World War II invite adultery and extramarital relations on the part of men, while women, both married and unmarried, are in a vulnerable position, and must compete with each other because of their larger numbers.

THE HOME ROUTINE

From mere observation it seems that young wives with children are not too satisfied. Though probably all of them wanted to get married and to have babies, some find it difficult to adjust to the traditional roles. In the first place, they are frequently overburdened. Maids and cleaning women are in extremely short supply, and usually there are no relatives around so that housework is entirely left to them. Of course, technical facilities ease the job. However, many of the labor-saving devices, like dishwashers, washing machines, automatic electric stoves, and so forth, are still too expensive to afford. So far the average German household is far from being as well equipped with major and minor appliances as is the American one. Furthermore, German husbands are not yet quite used to helping their wives in the home. Thus, mothers are continuously busy, and do not always like their work. Some of them feel lonely, too. Used to working in the company of adults, to having more leisure and money of their own, they resent their isolation during the day.

This dissatisfaction, evinced especially by young women, has its roots not just in individual failure or simply in egotism. It is the result partly of the necessity to combine women's two roles, partly of inadequate preparation. The conflict between the new demands and the traditional attitude makes for trouble also among those who need not take a job after marriage.

EDUCATION

However, many of those who resent matrimonial life could easily spare more time for activities linking them closer to the outer world if they only knew better how to organize their work. Lacking adequate training either for the homemaking job or for her other tasks, the average woman is unable to find her way out of drudgery and isolation.

A definite deficiency in the principles of education makes itself felt here. While schools at all levels provide rather thorough training in many fields, they fail as far as social and psychological preparation for the future task of women is concerned. First, schools do not supply the information about women's position in modern society needed to make girls more aware of what lies ahead. Discussions in class about the changes in family structure and the female role in the family are rare indeed. Also, instruction in child psychology is entirely neglected. Consequently, many young women, not properly prepared by their parents either, underrate the importance of their duties as the prime socializing agent of their children and of their responsibility for the home. Such misapprehension might be one cause of frustration, of the woman feeling cut off from the stream of life. Obviously, abstract ideological tribute which is abundantly paid to mothers by the public at large will not do. Rather, the future mothers need to be prepared more realistically for their job, gain more self-confidence and pride in it.

Moreover, while at school girls are not sufficiently made aware that they themselves will be responsible for their lives, and that they have to take the initiative in introducing desired changes. Thus after marriage they rarely seize the opportunities to improve their condition. Neither the school nor the average parent imparts that rational attitude toward everyday problems which is a precondition of mastering them. The capacity to plan and to organize one's work is also insufficiently developed, as is the ability to grasp the limits of such endeavors. What women ought to learn, and schools to teach, is, therefore, a better awareness of ends, and the faculty to select means accordingly.

Once again it is evident that women in Germany are in a state of transition, confronted with new tasks while still searching more or less unsuccessfully for exemplars to guide them. For those married women who could manage to find spare time it would be helpful if some of their energies were channeled into voluntary work with political and social associations. More active participation of such women in local government, school administration, adult education and the like would certainly be to great advantage. However, such activities have so far gained little popularity, partly because the public is not used to them, and partly because the women themselves either do not recognize the opportunities or shy away from responsibility. This reluctance is not confined to women. Rather, it is a consequence of the specifically German political atmosphere. In contrast to the British and American tradition, the participation of individual citizens in local affairs and private initiative in public matters were never encouraged. Getting away from such patterns is more difficult for women. However, most men too still have to learn that lesson.

WOMEN'S OCCUPATIONS

In 1962, West Germany had a female labor force of 9.4 million, roughly one third of all gainfully employed. Seventy per cent (6.7 million) were salary and wage earners, the remaining 2.7 million either independent business women, themselves owners and managers of small or medium-size firms, or assistants in some family enterprise. Two fifths of the wage and salary earners work in industry; one fifth in commerce, banking, and insurance companies; the rest in agriculture, traffic, and construction. Female labor is of course nothing new in Germany. Common among farmers, and in the handicrafts of preindustrial times, modern industry made use of it almost from its very beginning. Since the 1840's, proletarian women have entered the shops, and later on, also, bourgeois women came to the fore, chiefly in lower clerical and teaching posts. Ever since, a large army of females has been on paid jobs—some 15 million during World War I, and somewhat fewer during World War II. After 1945 many withdrew, only to return in the 1950's. Under the pressure of an extreme shortage of labor, the trend is towards further increase, which, however, may have reached its natural limits by now.

In West Germany, as in any industrial country, female labor is no transitory phenomenon. Women have entered the productive process to stay. Even the most conservative minds realize that without female cooperation practically no branch of the economy could function efficiently. If all working women went on strike, a national catastrophe would result. Thus the public debate about women's rights to gainful employment, carried on for many a decade, has come to an end.

Though entirely indispensable, working women are somewhat underprivileged in several ways. Subtle discrimination begins early with the selection of future training and job. In 1960, twice as many boys as girls of the lower and lower-middle classes, upon leaving school at the age of fourteen or fifteen, began vocational training. Young girls of the same strata have a narrower choice as far as training and vocation are concerned. In industry, there are some three hundred categories of skilled jobs, yet most girls, on the advice of parents or teachers, stick to only half a dozen, which are traditionally considered better suited for them. Others take a job without special training, attending, in addition, schools for home economics until they are eighteen. These unskilled or semiskilled women make up 90 per cent of all the female labor in industry as against 10 per cent who went through apprenticeships. On the other hand, among men, the ratio of skilled to unskilled or semiskilled workers is 50:50.

To be sure, the majority of girls would prefer to receive further education after high school. Formerly, almost all unskilled women hoped to enter a qualified trade, yet were refused the opportunity by their parents. Many parents, particularly in the lower strata, consider additional schooling for daughters a mere luxury. Trusting the girl will marry, they want her to earn money immediately after finishing school and to acquire a trousseau. Rarely are they aware that additional training would open better jobs to her, let alone that she has the right to have her talents awakened and developed. The girls themselves, being too young to stand up against parents and relatives, after a brief period on the job become indifferent, and profoundly resigned. Realizing that without additional training they have no chance to get ahead, they now cherish the dream of marriage, expecting it to bring salvation from factory life. In recent years, however, there has been some improvement. In 1960 twice as many girls became apprentices in qualified trades as in 1950. Also, the number of lower-class girl students in vocational schools has increased.

Girls of the upper-middle and upper classes who want to attend a university are also confronted with special problems unknown to boys. However, their number has risen too. While in 1951 girls constituted only one fifth of the student body, the percentage rose to 23 in 1964. Nevertheless, the fact remains that in universities and *Hochschulen* women cluster in the so-called typically female disciplines such as teaching and medicine. Only a few dare enter the fields traditionally reserved for men. In law only 5.5 per cent, and in economics and social sciences only 7.8 per cent of the students are girls.

Adult women too, are at a disadvantage in several respects. First, some of them still do not get equal pay for equal performance. While this situation might change in the near future under the pressure of the (not too energetic) trade unions and some sections of the general public, optimism is less justified with regard to women's careers and their chances of promotion in industry, public administration, and the professions. Among top executives of private corporations there are almost no women, with the exception of those whose inherited property gave them access to positions of control. Nor can they easily rise to the middle-managerial level. According to sociological studies carried out in recent years, the vast majority of female white-collar workers in business concerns is employed in the lowest ranks. Thus, in the administrative sector of corporations, women are, so to speak, privates led by an almost exclusively male officer corps. Or, as a group of sociologists has put it: "With regard to norms and stereotypes, the entire white-collar sector is dominated by conservative attitudes. To have a woman in a leading or otherwise highly qualified position seems in many places to be as revolutionary a thought as it was decades ago."

Also in the academic ranks of public or semi-public bureaucracies it is difficult for women to get ahead. While studying in the universities girls enjoy practically full equality with men, but upon graduation their situation becomes different. In the higher echelons of the German civil service, exclusively manned by university graduates, the proportion of women is between 2 and 3 per cent. Of all judges in the Federal Republic somewhat less than 3 per cent are females. One woman is a member of the Federal Supreme Court. The percentage of female university teachers is also low, not more than three. In the academic year of 1958–1959, of 2,328 full professors in the universities and technical universities of West Germany and Berlin, only eight were women. In the lower faculty ranks there were 3,558 men as against 111 women. There are almost no women among engineers, only a few in the diplomatic service (none of whom has achieved ambassadorial rank), and certainly not many in the legal profession. On the other hand, women are numerous in professions traditionally considered female. Thus they constitute roughly one third of the teachers in high schools (*Gymnasium*), two thirds of the teachers in elementary and secondary schools, and slightly less than one fifth of the physicians.

In politics, the picture is not much different. Of all adults entitled to vote some 55 per cent are women, and about one quarter of all members of political parties; but in state assemblies they are represented by only 6 to 8 per cent, and in the Federal Parliament by no more than 9 to 10. In 1961, for the first time in German history, a woman became the head of a national ministry, that of health.

Several factors explain why the number of women in higher and highest ranks is, and perhaps always will be, smaller than that of men. Many women do not really seek a career. Some of them, particularly young girls and married women, prefer to stay in lower positions with little or no responsibility involved. Many quit the job after marriage or after the birth of the first child. A further explanation is to be found in the fact, already mentioned, that on all levels the number of trained females is comparatively low. Some women work only temporarily to help out in a family emergency or to earn money for some other purpose. Finally, in a number of jobs such as civil service and teaching, it is difficult to promote married women, because promotion would demand that they move to another city. Since their husbands are usually tied to the place by their jobs, wives often turn down offers of promotion. It follows that even if they enjoyed fully equal opportunities, women would not be as numerous in the advanced positions as men.

All these factors, however, do not explain why the percentage of women in responsible ranks is so extremely small. The ultimate reason must be sought, not in the women themselves, but in the resistance of the environment. In conformity with the general ideological and intellectual conditions prevailing in Germany today, employers' attitudes and thinking are frequently dominated by old-fashioned prejudice, a general dislike of change, and possibly also by some fear of disturbance. Therefore, with rare exceptions, they hesitate to promote women. Many men in positions of authority are convinced that to remain in subordinate posts is to the good of the women themselves and of the community at large.

Generally speaking, the female role in Germany is still defined along traditional lines. The majority of men, and many women as well, hold with the old concept according to which the nature of women disqualifies them from shouldering responsibility outside of the home, acting as superiors, or performing intellectual tasks, let alone scholarly work. All the elements of the traditional definition of female character are still there: women are believed to be passive and emotional, and, due to their innate and unalterable disposition, incapable of abstract thinking. Nature, it can still be heard over and over again, has created them to serve in the family and the home, not in the world of men. Such arguments serve a twofold purpose: on the one hand, they restrain female ambition, on the other, they provide men with a justification for acting as they do.

When questioned as to their opinion about the promotion of women in business firms, employers usually point to these so-called innate deficiencies of women and to what they believe is woman's natural lack of technical interest, stamina, and psychological stability. On the other hand, they are believed to have an inborn talent for monotonous, dependent work, and should therefore be kept in dependence. It is interesting to note that those entrepreneurs who, in spite of widespread disapproval, promoted their women employees, gave excellent reports. Also, those women who did make their way up did not confirm the stereotyped expectation that they would not be accepted by subordinates.

To deem women principally incapable of qualified work is, however, not confined to businessmen. Leaders of institutions of higher learning cling to the same belief. University professors, usually considered more enlightened, would not like to have women on the faculties, either. First, so the learned men argue, women can have no authority with students, and second, they are mentally and physically unsuited for scholarly work. As one of them put it: "Intellectual creativity is a privilege of men," meaning that it should remain a male privilege. Ironically enough, none of those who were strongly opposed to having women on the teaching staff—and such is the attitude of the vast majority of those questioned—deemed the performance of girl students inferior to that of the men. The fact remains that the overwhelming majority of the men who hold the power of decision either hesitate or altogether refuse to let women get ahead. At best they do not encourage them.

The question arises why the considerable minority of women who want a career do not fight more energetically for it, and why in general women in and out of jobs do not strive more energetically for their rights. In many instances, such endeavors are likely to succeed, since the shortage of labor on all levels, including schools and universities, compels employers to hire even those deemed less fit. Although in recent years there may have been some progress, the number of women making use of such opportunities is still small. Obviously, the vast majority is not actively engaged in the strife. As mentioned above, there are some two million women now in their thirties and forties who realize that they have no chance to marry, simply because of lack of men. The self-respect of these women depends primarily on the appreciation of their work by superiors, colleagues and friends. However, even they do not rebel. Rather, they believe that the situation is unalterable. Why should this be so?

Again the answer must be sought mainly in the force of tradition which influences women no less than men. Growing up in a world which directly and even more indirectly tells women that they are unsuited for intellectual and technical work, for executive or other superior jobs, and for political activity, many actually become incapable. They have no chance to develop that kind of self-confidence which is a precondition of success. Further, they fear being considered unfeminine. If political activity, interest in a career, and professional ambition are considered unfeminine, then, of course, many women will behave "femininely" and avoid deviating from the commonly-accepted pattern. Instead of emancipating themselves from the outdated concepts, they adjust. Being afraid of society's criticism, and of becoming outsiders to their reference groups, they surrender, suppressing whatever fighting spirit might once have been in them.

One more cause for the resignation of many German women should be mentioned. Many accept things as they are from sheer physical and psychic exhaustion. The women of this country have for decades known no stability of national life, and hence none in their personal existence. Brought up in the misery of wars, thwarted by the experience of the vast unemployment in the late 1920's, witnesses to a totalitarian dictatorship, intimately acquainted with the horrors of refugee life—no wonder that they are exhausted, drained. Also, too many have lost their husbands, and devoted themselves entirely to bringing up the children without help. How could there be much energy left in them?

There are undoubtedly exceptions. It is on them, their activity, stamina and work performance that the future position of working women in Germany depends, to a considerable extent.

OUTLOOK

Modern society grants many privileges to all its members, male and female alike. It gives them freedom from poverty and from ruinous physical labor; it prolongs the average individual's life; it makes free education available to all. In the democracies, each citizen enjoys a measure of political and personal freedom which was formerly unknown even to the ruling classes.

At the same time, society puts high demands on everyone, above all on women. They must act responsibly, not only in the family but also in the business world. More than ever before, the functioning and efficiency of the productive process depend on their cooperation; but, again more than ever before, also the functioning of the family depends on them. Whether the family will be able to realize its new possibilities: to be a humanizing agency, a haven for the individual where he can relax from, and shake off, the regimentation and discipline of his work, all this, almost entirely, depends on women. It is they who, more than men, will determine the future personalities of their children.

Moreover, women have to fill a third role as well, that of a citizen capable of forming judgments of her own and arriving at rational political decisions. In the political sphere, too, women have become indispensable. Western society, with all the economic well-being and social security it grants its members, is in constant danger not only from threats of war, but from domestic perils. The dangers of rightist or leftist totalitarianisms, with their tendency to transform men into masses, to deprive the individual of his own identity, to dehumanize the human being, threaten women no less than men. Thus, the political fight against them is of concern to both sexes. If women want to preserve their privileges they must become citizens not only formally but in substance.

Thus far, women in Germany are as ill-equipped for these tasks as for securing their rights. They still have a long way to go in order to become mentally and psychologically independent, and able to judge for themselves. Too many of them are still shaped in the traditional image of femininity. What is needed is to abandon the old model and to replace the former virtues of passivity, unconcerned subordination, and adaptation, with the virtues of reflection, critical thinking, and the courage to resist domination.

In Germany there are few historical models for such a change. For many generations the country has idealized the pious woman, subservient to husband, church, and throne. To this, the Nazis added a special note, degrading women to biological machines whose primary function was to give birth to as many children—future soldiers—as possible. Undoubtedly, there is today some awareness that these norms do not suffice, and certainly only a tiny lunatic fringe still pays homage to the Nazi idea. The lack of sensible historical models at least partly explains why the majority of women has no clear idea of what they should be. Nor has the public at large. Both male and female shuttle, so to speak, uneasily between present and past. This insecurity makes itself felt everywhere: in the ambivalent attitude towards working mothers; in taking for granted female labor while excluding women from the higher ranks; in granting them suffrage but discouraging them from political activity; in the overburdening of rural women and housewives; in granting personal freedom, while maintaining the traditional type of femininity as the ideal.

It will take a long time until the majority of German women arrive at a better understanding of their new position and of the new demands. Much depends on education, for which, however, the educators themselves still have to be educated. Some people have begun to formulate progressive programs. The goal is to make female students and teachers alike more intimately acquainted with the society they live in, and, above all, as has been pointed out by Marianne Grewe, to help them "get rid of their own prejudice as regards their inferiority . . . to give them better criteria for the evaluation of men, and for the social order in general."

BIBLIOGRAPHY

Baumert, G., *Deutsche Familien nach dem Kriege*, Darmstadt: 1954.
Bremme, Gabriele, *Die politische Rolle der Frau in Deutschland*, Göttingen: 1956.
DGB Frauenarbeit, No. 2. *Gewerkschaftliche Beiträge zur Frauenerwerbsarbeit*, Düsseldorf: 1959.
——, No. 3. *Ergebnisse einer Befragung über die Belastung der erwerbstätigen Frauen durch Beruf, Haushalt und Familie*, Köln: 1961.
——, No. 5. *Das Verhältnis der Frauenlohne zu den Lohnen männlicher Arbeitskräfte*, Köln: 1962.
Dillmann, Erika, "Die Frau in der Landwirtschaft." In *Gegenwartskunde: Zeitschrift für Wirtschaft und Schule*, No. 2, 1962.
Friedeburg, L. V., *Die Umfrage in der Intimsphäre*, Stuttgart, 1952.
Grewe, Marianne, "Aspekte einer politischen Bildung der Frau." In *Die deutsche Berufs und Fachschule*, vol. 57, June 1961.
Hampe, Asta, "Die Lage der habilitierten weiblichen Hochschullehrer im Bundesgebiet 1958/59." In *Informationen für die Frau*, No. 11/12, 1960.
Hinze, E. and Knospe, E., *Lage und Leistung erwerbstätiger Mütter*, Berlin-Köln: 1960.
Hofmann, A. Ch. and Kersten, D., *Frauen zwischen Familie und Fabrik*, München: 1958.

Hohn, Elfriede, *Das berufliche Fortkommen von Frauen.* Zusammenfassender Schlussbericht. (No date. Unpublished manuscript.) Rationalisierungs-Kuratorium der deutschen Wirtschaft, Frankfurt a.M.

Karsten, Dorothea, "Die Frau." In *Deutschland Heute.* Ed. Presse und Informationsamt der Bundesregierung, 5th rev. ed., 1959.

Lorenz, Charlotte, *Entwicklung und Lage der weiblichen Lehrkäfte an den wissenschaftlichen Hochschulen Deutschlands,* Berlin : 1953.

Mayntz, Renate, *Die moderne Familie,* Stuttgart : 1955.

Pfeil, Elisabeth, *Die Berufstätigkeit von Müttern. Eine empirisch-soziologische Erhebung an 900 Müttern aus vollständigen Familien,* Tübingen : 1961.

Rationalisierungs-Kuratorium der deutschen Wirtschaft, Dept. Frauenarbeit. *Ergebnisse einer Befragung,* Berlin-Frankfurt-Köln : 1959.

Schelsky, H., *Wandlungen der deutschen Familie in der Gegenwart,* Dortmund : 1953.

Schmucker, Helga, et al., *Die ökonomische Lage der Familie in der Bundesrepublik Deutschland. Tatbestande und Zusammenhänge,* Stuttgart : 1961.

Wurzbacher, G., *Leitbilder gegenwartigen deutschen Familienlebens,* Dortmund : 1951.

———, and R. Pflaum, *Das Dorf im Spannungsfeld industrieller Entwicklung. Untersuchung an den 45 Dörfern und Weilern einer westdeutschen landlichen Gemeinde,* Stuttgart : 1954.

Israel

By Zena Harman

BACKGROUNDS AND BEGINNINGS

Woman's part in any society is governed by many factors, not least of which is the nature of the society in which she lives, her historical and cultural heritage, her legal rights, and the place accorded to her by tradition and custom. The women of Israel are mostly immigrants, and few of them are more than third- or fourth-generation settlers. The society in which they live is still changing by virtue of new immigration: it is a society in transition. While the majority are Jews, their countries of origin are so varied, their education and experience so different, that it is impossible to view them as a homogeneous whole.

Israeli women are undoubtedly much influenced by the environment from which they came. The early Jewish settlers, the pioneers of the first and second *Aliyoth* or immigrant waves, came, for the most part, from Eastern Europe, from good middle-class homes. They were idealists, influenced by the revolutionary socialist movement in Russia, determined to dedicate their lives to laying the foundations of a Jewish homeland where their persecuted and hard-driven kinsfolk could find a haven in a more equitable society, and every individual would be protected and afforded equality of opportunity and treatment. They were intellectuals and came to Palestine, which was then stagnant under the restrictive rule of the Ottoman Turks, with every intention of transforming the country into a thriving new Utopia. They translated their views into a new idiom of everyday living through their own labors and what they called personal self-fulfilment. There were women in their ranks, fired with the same enthusiasm and hopes.

Fifty years ago, these women pioneers, *Halutzot*, as they were called, held their first rally in the small village of Merhavia. "What we want," said one of the small assembly of earnest participants, "is that women should have the right to live their own lives and to develop as equal partners with the men in the new society being created in Israel." They demanded equal rights and responsibilities; they fought doggedly for the right to work alongside their menfolk, irrespective of the hard physical nature of the work. They wanted to share in building roads, clearing the rocky soil, draining the swamps, taking their turn at guard duties. Conditions were grim and rough, but they were undaunted as the grandeur of their objective inspired them to find within themselves the strength to tackle the most formidable obstacles. Their situation did not require suffragette tactics; there was no government to bombard with requests for political recognition and enfranchisement. Philosophically, their demands were acknowledged, but in practice the men were loath to accept them as working partners, preferring them to engage in domestic chores. Their struggle for equality of status, pursued with all the fervor of the suffragette, and spiced with the same aggressiveness, was concentrated on the struggle for the right to share in the assumption of duties.

These early pioneers set standards and precedents which have remained valid for hundreds of thousands of women today. There were two girls with the ten men who in 1911 founded the first *Kibbutz* or collective settlement, Degania, which gave women full membership in a unique new form of society, where everyone shared equally in the proceeds of the work in which each had invested according to his ability. Domestic chores were shared by all, so that the women were free to work together with the men in all branches of the farm's work. As these communities grew, some of the members concentrated on child care so that the children, living in Children's Houses, were cared for by women, for the most part, who opted for special training for this purpose. Originally, as long as the women were committed to full partnership with the men in all the hard tasks of pioneering, the Children's Houses were a convenient, even essential arrangement. Without them, the women could never have persisted in their determination to share equally with their menfolk all the grueling tasks of sinking firm foundations in the soil of their historic homeland. They still serve the same important purpose, freeing the women for all kinds of work, although they are regarded now as one of the more interesting if controversial aspects of the *Kibbutz* way of life.

Other forms of rural cooperative settlement have followed the *Kibbutz*, modifying the original pattern in certain aspects. Some settlers preferred more privacy, with the mother running her own household and caring for her own children. Even under this arrangement, the woman continued to contribute her labor to income-producing branches of work and to take part fully in all aspects of the village's life and development. In the *Moshav* she worked outside the home for an average of two hours daily, while in the *Moshav Shitufi*, closest in organizational structure to the *Kibbutz*, she worked five hours. Her part in the life of the village has remained one of unquestionable participation on equal terms with the men.

As the years passed and the villages blossomed, the mood of the women mellowed and a tendency developed among them to assume more of the responsibilities that traditionally belonged to their sex. The oldtimers of today, many of whom have risen to positions of highest responsibility in the government and national bodies, feel that the younger generation may have compromised somewhat with its principles and that some of the old fighting spirit has faded, which is perhaps natural. Nowadays, women are rarely asked to engage in hard physical labor nor do they want to. Few of them hold positions of central importance in the village hierarchy or even seek leadership roles. They are, for the most part, content in the knowledge that they are serving their community competently in work which is suited to them both by temperament and capacity. They are by no means confined to the kitchens, the sewing rooms, the Children's Houses, or the laundry. They work in the dairy, vegetable gardens, poultry houses, in field, workshop, and factory. While there is evidence of some discontent among the younger women themselves over spending too much time on traditional women's tasks, many of them appear to prefer the more feminine role which their predecessors scorned. "The graces and beauty aids of womanhood are becoming more desirable and attractive to them," as one report described it. The frugal, bare forms of living, the starkness and simplicity, dictated by necessity and converted into a philosophy, have given way to a greater interest in clothes, interior decoration, landscape gardening, and more gracious living generally, despite the hard, often arduous, work which is demanded of them particularly in the areas of new settlement.

The pre-State foundations of Israel were built on solid pillars of democracy. The pioneering settlement was and has remained the quintessence of the democratic form of group living. The individual consciously and freely subordinates himself to the best interests of the group, at the same time finding happiness and fulfilment for himself. Not everyone has the strength of character required for this type of life, but it remains an influential pattern. It has infused a spirit into public life and institutions which affects all facets of life in the country. The President, the Prime Minister and many members of his Cabinet, were, and many still are, members of *Kibbutzim* which are their homes. The women fought for their place in the *Kibbutz;* their full partnership in the national endeavor is never questioned. Their equality is recognized in law and in fact. The State of Israel is a fully functioning democracy and the woman, vocal, active, and able, is an integral part of its fabric.

When the State of Israel came into existence in May 1948, the women as well as the men had acquired varied experience in conducting the manifold affairs of state in the Jewish national institutions which gave a large measure of autonomy to the Jewish community under the British Mandatory regime. The Declaration of Independence, issued on May 14, 1948, assured full equality for women: ". . . it will ensure complete equality of social and political rights to all its inhabitants irrespective of religion, race or sex." This simply confirmed what had already been acknowledged in practice for many years. There was no aspect of the national struggle in which the women had not taken part; they had fought with distinction in the underground and in the British Army during World War II; they had dedicated themselves, often with heroism, to the work of rescuing refugees from the terror of Hitler's Nazi Europe; through their women's organizations they had established a network of social-welfare institutions and training centers. Women with specialized knowledge and professional skills were working in all branches of the country's life. Their ability, reliability, and competence were recognized as an important national asset and taken for granted. The acquisition of statehood meant giving legal recognition to a status which no one denied them. Prime Minister Ben-Gurion, in a statement of government policy at the opening of the First *Knesset* (parliament) said that there was to be "full and complete equality for women, Jewish, Christian, and Muslim, in their rights and duties as citizens, workers, members of the community."

THE LEGAL STATUS

However, to ensure a measure of stability and continuity, the new state had carried over the whole body of law applied under the British Mandatory regime, much of which had been inherited by the British from the Turkish Empire. During the rule of the Ottoman Sultans, the three communities living in Palestine—Jewish, Muslim, and Christian—had been granted religious autonomy. Each had its own religious courts through which it exercised exclusive jurisdiction in all matters pertaining to personal status, namely, marriage, divorce, births and deaths, guardianship, and inheritance. Under the religious law the woman is discriminated against and suffers certain disabilities. The law is ancient but it might be interesting to note that by comparison with the attitude to women in other ancient civilizations, the Jewish woman occupied a position of honor and respect. The statement in Genesis that "male and female created He them, in the image of God created He them," is the basis of the concept of equality as expressed in the modern approach to human rights. Although the woman in Biblical law is subservient to man she is not a chattel; even if a father could marry off his daughter at will, she had certain rights—food, clothing, conjugal rights. Abraham, Isaac, and Jacob had wives who were wise, strong, and energetic, exercising a great influence on their husbands. Deborah emerged as an inspired leader of her people. In the Ten Commandments, both the father and the mother are to be honored. The implication is clear; both parents were to be revered equally. Throughout Jewish history the mother was the pivot of the family's welfare. She was immortalized in poetry and prose for her intelligence and wit, her virtue and courage, her beauty and patience. The *Eshet Hayil*, the Woman of Valor in the Book of Proverbs, is the prototype of the Jewish woman and mother. "She is clothed with strength and dignity,"

> And she laughs at the days to come.
> She opens her mouth in wisdom,
> And kindly counsel is on her tongue.
> She looks well after her household,
> And eats not the bread of idleness.
> Her children rise up and bless her—
> Her husband also, and praise her:
> "Many women have done well
> But you have excelled them all."

In the vicissitudes of Jewish history, if the people have remained virile, lashed as they have been by persecution and suffering, if they have shown great resilience in the face of cruelty and vituperation, if they have manifested creative genius despite discrimination and despair, if the moral fabric of their family life has remained sturdy and steady, it has been due in no small measure to the traditional role, the ideal of the mother and wife, handed down and proudly perpetuated from generation to generation.

The fact remained, however, that the law maintained a number of disabilities in relation to women. Questions of personal status still are within the jurisdiction of the religious courts. According to Rabbinical law, women are not permitted to own property; all income derived from the dowry goes to the husband. If a man dies leaving no will, the male heirs have precedence over the female. A woman is not regarded as the natural guardian of her children. In the event of her husband's death, custody of the children goes to his relatives. The father is given custody of the sons of a separated couple. A woman's testimony is not accepted in a Rabbinical Court. Only the husband may sue before the Rabbis for divorce, although either party may apply to the court, and divorce is always possible by mutual consent. As far as marriage is concerned, as early as the sixteenth century the code known as the *Shulhan Arukh* by Rabbi Josef Caro states that "a woman cannot be married unless with her free will. A marriage against her will is null and void." Custom decreed arranged marriages, which included a financial arrangement; only the latter was binding. The marriage agreement or *Ketubah* is still used at Jewish weddings today. It dates back to the second century B.C. In this document the groom agrees to pay his wife a fixed sum out of his estate in the event of his death or a divorce. This provided some degree of protection for the wife in that the husband would be expected to think twice before seeking a divorce, which would mean his making a cash payment.

In the modern state of Israel a subordinate position for women was inconceivable. If, for a number of reasons bound up with the unusual composition of the population and internal considerations, a change in the prerogatives of the Rabbinical Courts regarding matters of personal status is not likely to occur for some time, the position of women, at least in secular law, could be laid down clearly. In 1951, therefore, the Women's Equal Rights Law was passed. It specified, *inter alia*, that "a man and woman shall have equal status with regard to any legal proceedings; any provision of the law which discriminates with regard to any legal proceeding against women as women shall be of no effect." It went on to abolish disabilities with regard to women's property and inheritance rights, and acknowledged both parents as natural guardians of their children, so that in the event of the death of one parent, guardianship was automatically assumed by the other. Paragraph 7 laid down that "All courts shall act in accordance with this law; a tribunal competent to deal with matters of personal status shall likewise act in accordance therewith unless all parties are eighteen years of age or over and have consented before the tribunal of their own free will to have their case tried according to the laws of their community."

The equal status of men and women includes, of course, the right of women to vote (both men and women acquire this right on their eighteenth birthday), and their eligibility to hold office in all elective bodies, national and local.

NATIONAL SERVICE

In 1952, women were acknowledged as citizens of the state in their own right. This implied the assumption of all the duties of citizenship as well as the rights, including service in the Armed Forces. Girls as well as boys enter the army between the ages of eighteen and twenty-six, the girls for two years compulsory service as against the boys' two and a half years. Women had fought to be permitted to share in guard duties in the early days of the pioneer settlers. They were members of the Self-Defense Organization (*Haganah*) set up to protect the Jewish community against periodic Arab riots; they took part in the fierce fighting that accompanied the British withdrawal from its Mandatory responsibilities, and then in the War of Liberation that followed when the Arab armies invaded the country. Many gave their lives in the War of Liberation and the names of women are interspersed with those of men on simple war memorials scattered throughout the country and dedicated to "Our Children Who Died That the Nation Might Live."

During World War II some 3,000 girls joined the auxiliary units of the British Army, where many of the women, later to become high-ranking officers in the Israel Women's Army, received valuable training and experience. There were three women among thirty-two Palestinian parachutists who were dropped on a dangerous mission behind enemy lines in Europe. Two were captured, tortured, and executed by the Gestapo. One of them, Hanna Szenes, wrote poetry, patriotic and stirring. These are heroines of modern Israel, courageous, fearless, and proud, to be emulated and revered. To have excluded girls from service in the Israel Defense Forces would have been inconceivable. Important precedents had already been established. Women had proved themselves apt and brave. The only exemptions granted are for married women or conscientious objectors on religious grounds. The women are a fine asset to the army—smart, intelligent, and reliable. They are not trained for combat duties, although they are taught to handle defensive weapons and have proved adept, among other things, at rifle shooting. For the most part, they undertake jobs that release the men for more active fighting roles, although a female soldier may volunteer for a fighting assignment and occasionally will be accepted if considered competent. They provide land services for air and sea forces; they are clerks, supply workers, communications officers, undertake vehicle and munitions repairs, draw maps, drive cars, do psychological testing, work in kitchens and canteens.

Israel's population comprises close to a hundred groups of different ethnic origin. Its dominant characteristic is diversity. These people of varied backgrounds must be welded into a homogeneous national unit committed to the aims and ideals of the state, willing and able to serve the best interests of the nation as adjusted, mature citizens. The special role of the woman is self-evident; she has to be prepared physically, mentally, and morally for a possible dual role in the home and outside it, in an environment of rapid change, crises, and dangers from without, often very different in every respect from what she had been accustomed to in her country of origin.

Uprooted, frequently a victim of oppression and discrimination, having left a situation that threatened her security and made her life intolerable, she requires special understanding and assistance as she settles down in her new country. Developing roots may take considerably more than one generation, and her children, too, may need special help in bridging the gap between the semi-assimilated home and the immediate environment of school and neighborhood.

Army service for girls against this background is a first-rate educational process. The opportunity afforded of living together in close proximity, girls from every kind of home and background being trained together, studying together, playing together, helps to break down barriers and reduce prejudices to a minimum. The army authorities envisage their responsibility toward their soldiers as being that of teacher, instructor, and youth leader. A girl who has personal assurance, pride in her appearance and achievement, toleration for her companions, a sense of loyalty and discipline, has the makings of a good and worthy citizen and a good soldier. The major purpose of the state is peaceful development; an army dedicated to peaceful objectives will have the inner strength and morale equal to any challenge if called upon to defend the homeland.

EDUCATION

The Jewish people are known as the "People of the Book," and traditionally have put much store on learning and intellectual achievement. One of the first legislative acts of the state, within the first year of its existence, was to introduce compulsory, free, primary education for all children between the ages of five and fourteen. Immigrants were pouring into the country: there was a shortage of teachers, buildings, and equipment, but a place was found for every child, often in makeshift, primitive surroundings, with semi-qualified staffs. Many parents, particularly the illiterate, saw no purpose in education for their daughters, and would happily have kept them at home to help with the domestic chores and to care for the younger children. But the law was inescapable and the girls went to school. In the early years, absenteeism had to be dealt with severely, as well as attempts to withdraw children before they completed the curriculum. Resistance has not entirely disappeared, but as the years go by school attendance for girls, as well as boys, is being taken for granted. In the Arab community, where education for girls was rare, at least among the *fellahin* in the villages, the percentage now attending school is increasing annually. Schooling in the Jewish sector is coeducational, except in the case of the ultra-Orthodox group which continues to regard separation of the sexes as a religious imperative. Coeducation is gaining acceptance among the Arabs as well, although there are special government-approved classes and schools for girls only, where the community is not ready for the mixed school. Coeducation has done much to facilitate a natural attitude of acceptance of both sexes by educators and teachers, as it has encouraged a healthy attitude of friendship and mutual recognition between the boys and girls themselves.

The Hebrew language is the major unifying force in knitting together the different ethnic and cultural groups. It is not only the medium of everyday communication, it is the repository of accumulated human and spiritual experience. Hebrew, as a living language, was the language of the Bible, and this is the classical text-book used for its teaching. All the ethnic groups, irrespective of the countries of origin, have been familiar with the Bible as a source of religious teaching. The richness of the language, its beauty and subtle depth, inevitably influence the mode of thought and idiom of expression of those who master it.

The importance of learning the language and being able adequately to use it is obvious. It is imperative for the newcomer who must be absorbed in employment as soon as possible. Special intensive courses are provided by the government and voluntary bodies, which have been singularly successful in enabling the average man and woman to acquire a good working knowledge of the language in a relatively short period of time. For the housewife, who has no intention of working, or for the woman who is not dependent upon language for the kind of employment she seeks, the problem is more difficult. It is fully realized that these women will be hampered in their efforts to become fully integrated in the country until they know the language. Some never master more than the minimum required for shopping or other simple needs related to housekeeping, which means that they are virtually excluded from taking an active part in life outside their homes. It is a further cause for friction between the mother and her children who have grown up with Hebrew as their mother tongue.

The women's organizations have done yeoman service in arranging Hebrew classes for women, often combined with the teaching of civics and instruction in home economics. In many instances, tours are arranged to enable the women to become familiar with life and conditions in different parts of the country. These visits to town and settlement, their encounters with other women, who are busy and happy in their pursuits, is an added incentive to learning to read and write, to becoming active in the women's organizations, and to contributing in their own way to the life around them. By degrees, the newest women immigrants, many of whom were totally unprepared for the dynamic conditions of the new Israel, are being slowly absorbed into the country's established pattern of life modelled on the idealistic concepts of pioneering and service to which the feminists of the Second *Aliyah* (1903–1914) dedicated themselves. The example of the wife of Israel's second President, Mrs. Rachel Ben-Zvi, who devoted many years to developing agricultural education for girls and encouraging them to find their place alongside the men in the farm settlements, is still an inspiring and dominant influence, as is that of Mrs. Rachel Shazar, the wife of the present President, who for many years edited a magazine for women.

In another sphere, when the newcomers were taught nutrition and how to prepare well-balanced meals, women volunteers actually went into their homes to teach them how to cook. Food habits are stubborn, but the mothers gradually mastered the preparation of new dishes, both healthful and tasteful, and the teacher on her part took recipes home which were new to her. There are today in Israel many Middle Eastern restaurants and the heavy aroma of spices has begun to permeate the Western kitchen as well. The *pita* and *falafel* take their place with potato chips and hot dogs in the corner refreshment stands. The Middle Eastern mother can set a table with food well appreciated by the friend whose parents hail from Poland or Germany.

Its strong cultural and spiritual traditions and its reverence for learning are ingrained in the character of the Jewish people. The Government's purpose in introducing compulsory education as a first legislative act was motivated by considerations basic to the ideals of the new state, which envisaged a society built on principles of equality and social justice. The successful implementation of the democratic process depended upon a literate population able to function as responsible citizens who, on their own merits and as a result of their own efforts, would determine the rate and measure of progress achieved. A young country, poor in natural resources, surrounded by enemies, with its doors wide open to immigration, needed a conscious, educated electorate. Its greatest asset was its people. The state was not an end in itself, but existed as a political entity in order to serve the needs of the people, so many of whom had sought an escape from injustice and discrimination, when they left, or fled from, their countries of origin. Each individual, irrespective of sex, was equally precious, to be afforded every opportunity to develop to his or her fullest capacity. The state's preoccupation with people and their needs, with human welfare, is understandable since this was the foremost reason for its existence.

Education is the pivot of democracy. Not only formal education, commencing with the kindergarten and proceeding through high school to university or vocational schools and technical institutes, but education in the broader sense of over-all preparation for the vicissitudes and demands of life in a rapidly expanding modern technological society. Women in Israel can be admitted by law to all institutions of learning, all professions and all offices, the only criteria being personal qualifications, fitness, competence, and merit.

MARRIAGE

In the eleventh century, the great Jewish Rabbi and leader, Rabbenu Gershom, issued an ordinance forbidding polygamy. The *Ashkenazi*, or European, Jewish communities have conformed with this decree ever since, but the *Sephardi* (or Mediterranean) and the Middle Eastern communities continued to practice polygamy, although not to any large extent. In 1951 polygamy was outlawed in Israel. Child marriages were also forbidden. The Age of Marriage Law (1950) prescribed that a girl may not marry under the age of seventeen. Eighteen is considered the normal minimum for men, although under Rabbinical law it is thirteen, the age of maturity. The courts permit the marriage of girls under the age of seventeen only with the parents' consent under special circumstances, such as the pregnancy of the girl. Penalties for violating the Child Marriage Act are heavy, up to two years imprisonment plus a fine of up to six hundred pounds. Problems arise with new immigrants from the Middle East, old men bringing young wives. The girls can sometimes be released by the payment of a refund to the husband, but obviously the law cannot be implemented retroactively. No new polygamous or child marriages have been permitted since the law was passed, so these marriages are virtually past history.

The Marriage and Divorce Law of 1953, which confirmed the continued jurisdiction of the Religious Courts in these matters, included certain stipulations favoring the woman. In the Hebrew language the word *ba'al* or husband also means owner or master. The law, therefore, replaced the word *ba'al* wherever it appeared, with *ish* or man, to eliminate entirely any implication of the woman's inferior status. A woman can retain her maiden name after marriage if she wishes to. Married women can opt to retain their own citizenship or adopt that of their husbands; the children are permitted double nationality if their parents are of different nationality. The mother is the natural guardian of the children in case of the father's death, whereas previously it may have been the father's kin. In the event of separation, the father remains responsible for the support of the mother and children; daughters remain with the mother but boys stay only until they are six; afterwards the father has custody unless the courts find that it is in the boy's best interest to remain with his mother. No change has been introduced in the Rabbinical law, which gives the child the mother's religion in the event of a mixed marriage. Property disabilities have also been removed. Married women have the right to own property acquired before or during marriage, as well as to share in the common property of their spouses.

And, finally, the 1936 Communal Law Ordinance was amended so that "where the husband dissolves the marriage against the will of the wife without a judgment of a competent court or tribunal ordering the wife to dissolve the marriage, the husband is guilty of a felony and shall be liable to imprisonment for a term not exceeding five years." This very important stipulation meant that no divorce was possible without the consent of both parties. Men who leave their wives without mutual agreement or without the consent of the court are subject to imprisonment of up to five years. If the husband leaves the jurisdiction of the court, the court itself may issue the actual bill of divorcement. While this constitutes a marked improvement, the fact remains that there is no secular marriage in Israel and questions of marriage and divorce still remain to all intents and purposes within the exclusive jurisdiction of the religious courts.

There is considerable public pressure for the introduction of civil marriage. As the years go by, the religious courts show more willingness to accept the recommendations of trained social workers and probation officers with whom they consult. They are, for the most part, guided by the overriding principle of what is best for the child. They will rarely permit a divorce unless they are assured by the social worker that the children will be adequately cared for. As regards the illegitimate child, the Rabbis rule that where paternity is known, a child born out of wedlock is considered legal and must be supported. If the father dies, the child inherits equally with other children born in wedlock.

There exists in Israel a dichotomy between the liberal approach of the governmental authorities as incorporated in a series of progressive legislative measures and the conservatism of Rabbinical law, steeped in ancient traditions and concepts. The fact that there is no civil marriage in Israel is a thorn in the flesh of many people, and a number of women's groups are clamoring for a change. As long as those who favor a change are unable (for a number of reasons which have no bearing on the status of women) to bring this about, the government, committed to supporting equality for women, has tried to offset the possible discriminatory effects of religious (canonical) law by introducing a comprehensive body of legislation to protect these rights. This includes The Law of Guardianship 1962, The Law of Adoption 1960, The Law of Maintenance 1959 and The National Insurance Law 1953 with subsequent amendments. Almost every year sees the passage of new measures with direct or indirect significance for the woman, which have the effect of safeguarding her full equality before the law, and ensuring her interests. There is considerable vocal support in Israel against the compulsion still implicit in the authority of the Religious Courts and in favor of civil marriage and exclusive civil jurisdiction.

BETWEEN THE HOME AND SOCIETY

The state has made provision for compulsory schooling; it also provides a network of comprehensive health and social services. The pioneering efforts of the women's organizations in many instances paved the way for governmental action, and many pre-state projects initiated, financed, and run by voluntary effort were incorporated in government services. The newcomers, many of whom came from countries where no such services existed, had to be assisted to understand the value of these services and how they would contribute to their welfare. Compulsory medical examination, immunizations, prenatal care, hospitalization for childbirth, dental and medical care in schools, among other services, were available to them for the first time. The effectiveness of these measures depended primarily upon the wife's and the mother's ability to follow advice and apply basic principles of personal hygiene, cleanliness, nutrition, and child care in her own home. Would she stand up to the new demands made upon her, the additional effort required in order to conform to standards which were strange and sometimes incomprehensible to her? Could she cope with the growing disaffection of her husband, as his traditional role of master of the family, his absolute authority, no longer remained valid? Could she discipline her children who rapidly absorbed new ideas, acquired new horizons, and demanded a different routine of living? Could she retain their respect as they became aware of her inadequacy as compared with the educated mothers of their Western schoolmates? Could she cushion the almost inevitable crisis arising from the clash between the rigorous demands of the patriarchal tradition and the relative permissiveness in child rearing practiced in the Western family?

Experience showed that the Middle Eastern immigrant woman generally was not slow to grasp the value of the maternal and child welfare clinic, the public-health nurse, and the local sanitation, once she began availing herself of these services. It was not long before she began to attend sewing classes at the clinic, and demonstrations arranged by the women's organizations in cooking, making preserves, or canning the fruits and vegetables she was growing for the first time. Her misery, confusion, and feeling of insecurity gradually gave way to a new self-respect and a growing self-confidence. Sometimes slowly, sometimes with accelerating speed, she put behind her the docility of the past and joined the ranks of the women who had become, in their own right, full-fledged citizens of the state, taking an active part in community affairs. The illiterate flocked to evening classes to learn to read and write, joined clubs, attended political meetings, became members of the P.T.A. In all this the women's organizations played an outstanding role. It is perhaps of special interest that one of the tasks assigned to girl soldiers in the course of their training was to work, especially in the villages, with the woman and the family as a kind of multi-purpose amateur social worker and public-health nurse, who entered the home as a friend and adviser.

However, not all the women were willing to be wooed into a changed pattern of living by the benign assistance they received, however sincere and well-meaning. There were those who remained suspicious of the innovations and resented all efforts to change their age-old routine. Some were incapable of understanding what was being demanded of them; others were unwilling to face the almost inevitable clash with their husbands, who refused to contemplate changes that affected their traditional prerogatives. The most susceptible to change were those with young children, who rapidly recognized the advantages of the health and social services. The kindergarten was used as a means of educating the mother along with the child, by imposing upon her certain duties and involving her in the child's activities. The influence of the school inevitably extended to the home, often resulting in added tensions. Where the gap between home and school was irreconcilable, the household was beset with difficult educational, social, and psychological problems which had serious consequences for both children and parents, and occasionally disrupted the family. For the most part, though, the stimulation and encouragement introduced into the home through the school child became one of the most important factors in the modernization of the family, provided the mother was receptive and understanding.

Where the woman leaves her home to work, as is frequently the case especially in urban areas or in villages close to them, the process of adaptation to the new life tends to be speeded up. Again, the women's organizations, in some instances jointly with the local authorities, have provided a network of well-run day nurseries, creches, and children's homes for the convenience of working mothers. Many women prefer part-time employment, the unskilled in domestic service, although the Day Care Centers keep the children from 7 A.M. until 4 or 4.30 P.M. which coincides with the working hours in most factories and farms. Shop assistants and restaurant workers find it more difficult to manage, as do office workers whose hours are staggered and often arranged differently. Generally speaking, though, unless the family budget is hopelessly inadequate, the Middle Eastern woman will not work outside the home. The Western woman, whether skilled or unskilled, is far more amenable to outside work, and does not look askance at manual labor as does the Middle Eastern woman accustomed to a society in which only the lower strata engage in physical labor. As she becomes better educated, acquires some understanding of the importance of all types of work, and sees her Western neighbor wielding a pick on the roads, returning from the factory in oily overalls, or tending her fields, the old prejudices die a natural death and the idea becomes more acceptable.

The new generation of girls and women, thoroughly at home in their environment, has every opportunity to take its place in society fully with men. Admittedly, there still remain some disabilities, but they do not affect the life of the average girl or woman. The daughter of illiterate Middle Eastern parents will graduate from school, and become a competent and skilled worker in any of a number of trades and professions. Her parents might attempt to arrange her marriage, but she will insist on marrying "for love," accustomed as she is to free association with boys at school and in her recreational activities. Married, she will find advice readily available on how to limit the size of her family, even though her religion exhorts her to "be fruitful and multiply." She will be more education-conscious and seek expanded educational facilities for herself and her offspring. The mores of the parental home, deeply rooted in the ancient cultural traditions of Middle Eastern or North African lands, may be shed in one generation, partially or even totally.

If the home remains reasonably intact despite the shattering effects of all the changes encountered in the process of moving and resettling, the probabilities are that the children will make a relatively smooth adjustment and the girls will grow to maturity capable of fulfilling themselves as women and as individuals to the extent of their ability and aspirations. Where the resilience has been less marked and the parent child relationship marred by conflict engendered by the complex forces of socio-cultural change, the children will rarely escape unscathed. In such situations a girl may seek consolation in early marriage far from the parental fold, or in sexual promiscuity, or even in outright delinquent behavior. She may fling herself headlong into the foray of modern life as a revolt against the restrictiveness of the old traditional codes of conduct. This is true of all ethnic groups in a period of transition, but the dangers are intensified among immigrants who in Israel find themselves in a different century. It is remarkable that the juvenile-delinquency rates for girls in Israel are comparatively low, an indication, among other things, of the strength of Jewish moral and ethical teachings which have fortified the Jewish family throughout its tortuous history.

WOMEN'S OCCUPATIONS

There is almost no facet of life in Israel in which women have not played a part. There is nothing to prevent them from pursuing any vocation, undertaking any kind of work and aspiring to the highest public office. Mrs. Golda Meir served her country as Minister for Foreign Affairs with exceptional brilliance and distinction. She has ten colleagues in the

Knesset or Parliament, representing some eight per cent of the membership. Four of the eight Deputy Speakers of the Sixth *Knesset*, elected in November, 1965, were women. A woman heads the Building Research Department at the Haifa Technion and was responsible for building one of the busiest bridges in the country, over the River Yarkon, on the main Haifa–Tel Aviv highway. The Chief Chemist at the Bureau of Standards is a woman, and women have distinguished themselves in research and teaching on the staff of the Weizmann Institute of Science. There are women judges and magistrates, lawyers and doctors, diplomats, economists, and civil servants. There are women archaeologists and nuclear physicists, teachers, nurses, social workers. There are women in industry, architecture, and agriculture.

Women have left their mark on the intellectual and cultural life of the new Hebrew society. They have contributed much to the arts, music, literature, the theater. There are talented women poets, novelists, and critics; there are excellent women journalists who have recorded with fervor the pathos and the heroism, the sufferings and the exaltations of Israel's diverse population. They have given expression to the variegated nuances of life in town and village, captured the spiritual and emotional experience, interpreted the yearnings and the frustrations. There are the great and the less great among them, but they all express their creative genius in an atmosphere of complete intellectual freedom. The quality of their output is all the more remarkable because they write in the Hebrew language, revived and transformed into a modern medium, which they have mostly acquired as a second language. In the past, Hebrew authors wrote on religious themes — they were philosophers and theologians who could not be women. It was only towards the latter part of the nineteenth century that the language began to be used for secular writing by a group of enthusiasts who recognized its importance in the context of the Jewish national movement and the Zionist objective. Today, at the country's universities, there are women lecturing on the Hebrew language, composition, even on Jewish philosophy, mysticism, and religious movements. There are many women musicians, fine instrumentalists, and one of the outstanding conductors is a woman.

The working women in Israel are protected by special labor legislation. The 1954 Employment of Women Law prohibits night work and occupations injurious to a woman's health, and therefore, to her potential motherhood. A pregnant woman cannot be dismissed without special consent from the Minister of Labor, and is entitled to three months' maternity leave with seventy-five per cent pay. She may extend this leave for an additional nine months without pay and the employer must keep her job open for her. A nursing mother has the right to take two periods of half an hour each during the day to feed her baby. This law supplements the 1953 National

Insurance Act, which provided for maternity benefits to cover the cost of hospitalization and a layette. Old-age pensions are paid to women over the age of sixty, while men receive them at sixty-five. Widows of fifty also receive the pension, with smaller pensions for younger widows.

A woman may also expect to receive the same remuneration for her work as her male colleague. Government and municipal services make no distinction, and the great majority of undertakings and enterprises follow the government's lead. Although there is no "equal pay for equal work" law, some 90 per cent of all women workers are paid the same as men for similar work. The exceptions occur in certain industries and workshops where employers argue that the productivity of women is below that of men, particularly where heavy machinery is utilized. They contend that there is no intention of discriminating against women, that the wage scale is based on objective evaluation and the results of job analyses. There may well be some justification for this approach, but there is no doubt that a certain measure of exploitation is current.

There are trades and professions in which women predominate, as in many other countries—nursing, social work, teaching, the needle trades, textiles, some light industries, among others. Nevertheless, there are employers who have reservations about women workers on the grounds that they are less reliable and frequently leave in response to domestic and family calls, after considerable investment has been made in them in terms of their training. On the other hand, as a result of collective bargaining, many public institutions have agreed to special conditions for mothers with two or more children under the age of fourteen. They may receive the same pay and be permitted to work an hour less than the daily norm.

The concern manifested by the state for women workers is in line with its philosophy, its recognition of women's ability, and its acknowledgement of their importance in an expanding economy. It is not without significance, however, that despite official blessing, the labor force is only 27 per cent feminine; lower than the percentage employed in the United States, Great Britain, France, and other countries. There are good economic reasons why women should want to work, as few families find it easy to make ends meet on the husband's income alone. Israel prides itself on being one of the most egalitarian societies in the world. The wage differential between the lowest- and highest-paid worker is approximately five to one gross, three to one net. Its people are also among the most highly taxed. The average salary in most professions and trades covers little more than what is needed to meet the cost of basic necessities of rent, food, clothing, recreation, and culture. Furthermore, a woman's status is, if anything, enhanced if she works. Many of the newcomers, particularly from the Middle Eastern countries, are unskilled and unschooled. They have large families, and while they may need desperately to supplement the family income, there is little they can do except domestic work and that they tend to shy away from. As the new generation becomes better educated and more capable of filling jobs requiring a measure of skill and training, it can be anticipated that the number of women seeking employment will increase. In the situation of full employment which the country is experiencing, married women are being urged and encouraged to return to work. In the stimulating atmosphere of rapid growth, when within a few years almost everyone has experienced the impact of improved conditions, the incentive to be a useful cog in the fast-moving machine becomes more attractive.

The statistics are, however, deceptive. The new immigrant women may not only be untrained but entirely unaccustomed to the very idea of women working for compensation. They had been kept more than busy in their homes tending to the needs of a large brood and what went with the homestead, perhaps a store, some home craft, feeding chickens and goats. Many of them were not even permitted to do the marketing. In the patriarchal family group, the father controlled all the reins of family life, handled the money, did the shopping. Disputes are not infrequent in immigrant families where the wife, returning from work with her earnings, is expected to hand them over to her husband, who is possibly without employment or only partially employed. Her new role as wage earner and the influence of her changed environment have made her no longer willing to submit to the strict rule and domination of her husband. Fundamental changes are inevitable in the traditional pattern and patriarchal structure of the Middle Eastern family in Israel. The break-up of the old system, the rapidity with which it occurs, and the strains it evokes, are among the many problems which challenge the authorities as they seek to minimize the pains and stresses of integration.

The Middle Eastern woman immigrant, faced with the problem of settling in a new home in totally different conditions, the whole idiom of her daily life suddenly changed, unfamiliar with the language, pressured by various public services to conform to standards about which she knows nothing, is unlikely to be a willing or apt addition to the country's labor force. The married woman is frequently forced by circumstances to seek paid employment to supplement, or even to provide, the family income. She then turns mainly to domestic service, or unskilled factory work, which she dislikes and regards as being degrading, but which can be fitted without too much difficulty into her daily routine of work at home.

Many older women, among the settled population, also need to work for economic reasons. Tuition fees in high schools are quite exorbitant in relation to the level of salaries, and few men are able to earn enough to provide their families with adequate comforts and also pay for their children's secondary schooling. Thus some women look for work when their children leave elementary school in order to help bear the financial burden. The labor market can easily absorb most women with skills and training. Unskilled women, however, must compete with an abnormal number of unskilled men, new immigrants, who may have been small traders or shop-keepers in their countries of origin and must be retrained before they can be absorbed in lucrative work. There are numerous retraining projects, vocational training courses for both men and women, run by both governmental and voluntary agencies, many of them initiated by the women's organizations.

As the more experienced and often better educated older settlers became familiar with the traditions and customs of the more recent arrivals, they acquired a growing respect for their values, their serenity, the cohesiveness of the family unit among them, the practical wisdom and native good sense of the mother, the discipline of the home. In helping the mother to reach out beyond her home and exercise her rights of citizenship, they became aware of the need to bolster her ego and encourage her instead of adding to her growing sense of incompetence and incapacity to deal with the new problems confronting her. Efforts were made to help her continue in the practice of her native skills. Many of the women were skilled in embroidery, basketwork, carpet making, weaving on hand looms. These crafts, handed down from mother to daughter through many generations, were admired and made the basis for a thriving home industry, an obvious means of supplementing the family income. The products are marketed through special shops in the cities and have become popular with tourists. They have, moreover, influenced the whole gamut of arts and crafts in the country.

The Middle Eastern immigrants also brought with them their folk music and dances, which too have had a strong influence in Israel. The Yemenites founded, for instance, the Inbal Dance Troupe, well known today for its performances of Biblical ballet in a unique style. A number of Israel's leading singers, mostly women, are drawn from this community, and many new songs show the influence of Middle Eastern music. This encouragement of native arts has also helped the younger generation to appreciate its own family or "tribal" traditions instead of rejecting them as out of harmony with the new society.

WOMEN'S ORGANIZATIONS

The women's organizations in Israel have made a vitally important contribution to every facet of life in the country. The needs of the woman, in all their ramifications, her position in the home, the family, the community, and all aspects of the national endeavor, have come within their purview. Some 450,000 women are members of these organizations, which have given them a new and deeper understanding of their role and function in society and enriched the content of their lives. The organizations, many of them having affiliates throughout the world, have established and supported a network of services benefiting primarily the mother and child. In the pre-state days, they assumed responsibilities which should normally have been carried by government. They pioneered in day care, agricultural education for girls, child-welfare institutions, vocational training, adult education, social and medical services. They fought for women's rights and were constantly alert to any attempts to infringe upon or whittle down those rights. They have been vocal on national issues and active in politics. In times of danger—and the history of modern settlement in Palestine and Israel has been riddled with such periods—they were among the first to volunteer for service, always efficient, disciplined, and loyal. Their major contribution has been in the area of immigrant absorption, the central purpose for the state's existence, to provide a haven and a homeland for those driven in despair from conditions ranging from terror and persecution to discrimination and insecurity.

The immigrant family of today comprises the citizens of tomorrow. Its welfare, its well-being, its health and state of mind, its capacity to support itself and find contentment, will be the measure of the success of the state. The statistics of growth and progress are valid only insofar as they represent an increase in happiness and human satisfaction. These are the considerations that have motivated most of the women's organizations as they approached the tasks which they set themselves. Their strength and their achievement have been a central factor in reducing to a minimum the inevitable tensions and strains implicit in a situation compounded of mass immigration, new statehood, lacking the traditions of an old and established government, an infant economy, paucity of means and natural resources, with enemy states waiting to pounce on every border.

The early women pioneer settlers set much of the tone and the standards for the women's organizations. They founded the Working Mothers' Organization, which today has a membership of 315,000 in town and village. Each organization tends to serve and be served by its own membership, representing a number of different ideological and religious points of view. The seven largest are organized in the Council of Women's Organizations, in which they join forces on a number of noncontroversial issues and coordinate their international representation. Irrespective of viewpoint, they concentrate their attention on the new immigrant family, whether it came from Europe with an educational and cultural background similar to that of the earlier settlers, or from the Middle East with ancient customs and habits little influenced by the trends of modern civilization. This latter group representing an ever-increasing proportion among the immigrants, has posed a great challenge to some of the women's organizations dominated by Western settlers and dedicated to the most liberal and progressive interpretation of women's role in modern society.

The Orthodox religious women's organizations are spiritually closer to the religious Middle Eastern immigrants since they too adhere to the Rabbinical laws and support without question the jurisdiction of the religious courts on matters affecting the family, marriage and divorce; but the Orthodox *Ashkenazi* is still centuries ahead in terms of educational, cultural, and material values. This refers, of course, to the large majority of the Middle Easterners who comprise the poorest and most neglected elements, not the educated minority. While the integration process taking place in Israel represents an interesting synthesis of east and west, a merging of the new and the old, the situation is fraught with much of the same strain and stress found in other countries where the women are in the process of emancipating themselves from the shackles of an obsolete world. Even where the law has recognized her new stature, and her rights are legally assured, the traditions of centuries do not crumble overnight by virtue of statutory decisions. The process of change is slow and halting as it penetrates the crusted layers of custom and inertia.

Women's role is particularly difficult in those groups which live according to the strictest Orthodox tradition, yet are fully exposed to the requirements and pressures of the technological era. These include leading scientists and mathematicians who find no irreconciliability between their Orthodox beliefs and the rationale of modern life. In the 1920's, these groups were not prepared to include women in their ranks. Determined women would listen outside the windows when they convened to discuss political issues (the Orthodox groups have their own political parties). Today, they have a woman representative in the Knesset, although the most extreme groups, who verge on the fanatical and are small in number, still exclude them. The women conform to the requirements of the ritual and accept without hesitation the derogations dictated by religious law, yet a growing flexibility towards those aspects that hinder their full participation in the life of the country is discernible. The Mizrachi Women's Organization supports a fine group of child-welfare services comparable in efficiency and scope to those of the other women's organizations, with the difference of greater stress on religious instruction. They are active in politics and vocal on many issues, and are an important factor to be reckoned with in the ranks of their own political parties. It is significant that today they participate freely in educational discussions and in Talmud and Jewish philosophy study-groups, which would have been unthinkable for their mothers and grandmothers. Yet, the Orthodox way of life continues to be adhered to in all its essentials. Its rejection by some girls, who find even this modern version onerous, leads to problems not dissimilar to those encountered among the Middle Eastern immigrant communities where revolt against the old tradition is a frequent occurrence. The refusal to accept parental discipline and the rejection of the moral prop of religious teaching lead to some floundering as they grope for a new self-confidence.

CHALLENGE AND OUTLOOK

East and West, traditionalism and modernism, Orthodoxy and secularism, illiteracy and the highest scientific attainment, all are present in the Israel mosaic. The women are everywhere, making up the colorful, intricate pattern which reflects the realities of a state still in the making. The lines are firm, the outline bold and clear, their place assured. The contribution they are making in every field of the nation's life has earned them respect and acceptance as full partners, working together for the nation's good. Yet, women still have not emerged sufficiently as leaders or important factors in the determination of national policies at the topmost level. Only few hold pivotal public positions. Even in the *Kibbutz* there is a tendency to delegate them to duties associated traditionally with women and the household. Intensive discussions in the columns of women's journals and newspapers, as well as in the general press, revolve around the question as to whether women, in fact, desire major leadership roles or seek to any extent the opportunity for larger participation in government and policy-making. The importance of the motherhood role is being emphasized as the need to reinforce and strengthen the family unit becomes more urgent and traditional practices give way to new norms in a society still in a state of flux. The older feminists are beginning to lose ground to those who would upgrade femininity.

This has not meant any relaxation in the efforts of the vocal women's groups as they seek redress of their remaining grievances. The sensitive matters pertaining to personal status, marriage, and divorce, the demand for civil marriage still remain bones of contention. They want family property automatically registered in the names of both husband and wife and seek income-tax regulations that would permit working wives to deduct from their earnings the sums they spend on domestic help. They would like to have state legislation assuring equal pay for equal work without having to rely on the goodwill of some employers who could defy what has become more or less accepted practice.

Women in Israel today are confronted with the challenge of realizing to the full the opportunities which they have and making the most of the favorable situation in which they find themselves. As the country develops and standards of living rise, some women, experiencing relative comfort for the first time, are content to bury themselves in household activities and resent attempts to draw them into outside affairs. In times of emergency, when there are serious challenges from without and within, they are ready and prepared to do their part, but many are apathetic when no crises and dangers threaten. Others are faced with problems as they seek to reconcile the demands of home and outside work, and resent the burden of responsibilities on so many fronts. On the whole, however, Israel's women are alert and highly conscious of the part they can and do play in building their country. Their position fully established, their lives enriched by new dimensions, they can fulfil their natural role of wife and mother in harmony with the developing community around them.

Japan

By Takashi Koyama,
Hachiro Nakamura,
and Masako Hiramatsu

The Traditional Situation

*I*t *was not* until the end of World War II that women in Japan attained legal equality with men. Since that time, with wider scope for their abilities, they have made a very satisfactory adjustment to their new position. Social changes, however, do not always parallel legal changes, and this has been the case with Japanese women: even prior to their legal liberation, they had improved their social position to some extent beyond the legal framework; today, traditional concepts about inequality between the sexes still survive in some circles of Japanese society, lagging behind the legal achievements.

According to the traditional social pattern, women were required to be completely submissive to men. This pattern became so firmly established during the era of the Tokugawa Shogunate (1564–1867) that contemporary Japanese society still cannot eradicate it entirely. The success of the stable, feudalistic regime that endured for three centuries was attributed to its rigid distinction of four classes—warriors, farmers, craftsmen, and merchants, in that order of importance—and to the isolation of Japan from most foreign countries. It was of paramount importance in the social order of the Shogunate to know one's place, which depended on the estate or class into which one was born; but for a woman it was equally important to know her place in relation to men.

The institution of *ie*, the family system peculiar to Japan, was calculated to maintain strict status distinction on the basis of sex, and made women accept their subordinate position as a matter of course. The family was not merely a group of related people living under one roof, but a social entity transcending each of them, continuing from generation to generation, and expressing itself in such tangible forms as the ancestral tomb, Buddhist and Shintoist family shrines, the family house and other property, the warriors' hereditary stipend, the farmers' land, the craftsmen's traditional trade, the merchants' *noren*, reputation or good will, and so on. Moreover, the *ie* prescribed norms (*kafu*, or family traditions), by which the family members had to abide. Each individual was required by the norms of the *ie* to know his or her family status and behave accordingly. The patriarch was the representative and head of his *ie*; the eldest son was the prospective patriarch, and other sons were considered as reserve candidates for the position in case of the eldest son's death or incapacity. The norms required that male members be valued more highly than female ones.

This inequality was exemplified by the inheritance laws. Even if a family lacked male descendants, no female descendants were entitled to share in the family property. In such a case, the husband of the eldest daughter inherited the *ie* as an adoptive heir. In order to ensure the birth of a male descendant and thus guarantee the succession of the *ie*, the patriarch was allowed concubines. His wife had no claim upon him, although strict fidelity was required of her, and she had to obey him under all circumstances, not reluctantly, but willingly and graciously. That she should initiate, or even wish for a divorce, was unthinkable. Romantic love was strictly forbidden as a threat to the *ie*.

The inequality of the sexes was essential to feudal society, and the Shogunate tried to justify it and give a moral basis to all its social distinctions by attributing them to official recommendations of Confucianism. Thus, the system came to be accepted as the only morally proper one. One of the famous injunctions of Confucianism, "Boy and girl aged seven do not sit together," was strictly adhered to. A woman's respect for whatever the system prescribed was highly praised as a special feminine virtue. *Onna Daigaku*, a moral code for woman, written by Ogyu Sorai, a prominent Confucianist of the seventeenth century, was widely used until the turn of the present century as a textbook for the moral education of young women. It contains specific moral directives, a typical example of which are the

Shichikyo no sei, or seven rules of divorce, and the *Sanju no oshie,* or three rules of obedience. A wife is to be divorced if she is (1) barren, (2) licentious, (3) disobedient to her parents-in-law, (4) argumentative with her husband, (5) thievish, (6) jealous, or (7) incurably ill. The three rules state, "A woman must obey (1) her parents when she is young, (2) her husband, when she becomes an adult, and (3) her sons, when she is old. In brief, what was meant by a woman's virtue was the complete subordination of her will to that of the men of her family.

The attitude of contempt for women is expressed in many old Japanese proverbs, such as "A woman's womb is a borrowed vessel to beget a child"; and "The newer, the better is a wedded couple."

The ideal described above was, in reality, only approximated to varying degrees, but was cherished for so long during the history of Tokugawa feudalism that it carried over into the modern age, and was given up only after World War II. Vestiges of it survive to this day.

Town and Country

The Meiji Restoration of 1868 marked the end of the feudal regime and the beginning of modern Japan under the reign of Emperor Tenno. One of the principal measures of social reform was the abolition of the distinction between the four classes. The *ie,* however, was retained, because it was regarded as crucial for the maintenance of the Emperor's absolute sovereignty. Japanese nationalism regards the Imperial Household as being descended directly from the common ancestor of the entire Japanese people; that is, the Imperial Household is the main family, and all the *ies* throughout the country are branches of it. Loyalty of members of the *ie* to its patriarch is, therefore, synonymous with loyalty to the Emperor. This being so, women's status in the family remained subordinate, and in society at large, women retained the inferior position they had held prior to the Restoration.

However, certain variations in the behavior of women did exist, depending upon their social class and the region in which they lived. These differences can best be illustrated by a comparison of the position of town and country women.

Most of the towns during the Tokugawa era were fortress communities, with warriors constituting about one half of the population and merchants and craftsmen the other half. Since feudalistic morality existed to justify the feudalistic rule based on the hierarchic social order among the four estates, and warriors constituted the ruling class, it was among them that the feudalistic mores were most strictly observed, and women most rigidly denied all human rights. Women of this estate tried anxiously to live up to the ideal of female virtue. Merchants, who officially ranked lowest in the social scale, but wielded economic power which often forced warriors to defer to them, tried to imitate the warriors and adopted many of their customs, including the relegation of women to a very inferior position. In the case of the poorer townspeople, craftsmen for the most part, whose *ie* involved neither prestige nor property, the status of women was somewhat better. Concubinage was not practiced among them, and love marriages were frequent and often condoned.

Among the country people, who accounted for 80 per cent of the total population of Japan at that time, women's position was considerably better, although the small proportion of village officials and upper-class farmers observed sex inequality as strictly as did the warriors and rich merchants. The economy of the ordinary farmers was poor, and half or more of their meager produce had to be paid to the feudal lords as tribute. Under such circumstances, in order to subsist, all family members were obliged to work together, and the contribution of the women was as important as that of the men. Outside the family, in the village, a wife could not represent her *ie*, although she could act for the patriarch. But within the family, she was responsible for managing the household and trying to make ends meet. For this purpose, she was vested with *shufuken* (housewife's authority) to which even the patriarch deferred. Marriage, endogamous within a village, often took the form of *tsumadoi*, or "visiting marriage." A bride, instead of entering the household of her husband's family, continued to live with her own parents for some time. Such marriages were the outcome of free association between the young men and women of the village, romantic love, and free choice of a spouse.

When the Meiji Government was in the process of drafting a civil code, heated debates ensued among opposing jurists. The winning group objected to both the Western individualistic principle, as foreign to the national structure of Japan, and to the customs of family life practiced among the peasants, as coarse and debased. The result was a civil code permeated by Confucianism. Its spirit was incorporated into the education which the Tenno regime made compulsory for both boys and girls, and in which obedience of women to men was stressed as the greatest female virtue. With the spread of compulsory education, the inequality of the sexes appeared to grow even stronger, especially in the rural areas, than it had been in the Tokugawa era.

Towards the end of the nineteenth century, when the textile industry emerged in Japan as a forerunner of modern industries, daughters of poor farmers were recruited in large numbers to work in the urban factories. These girls worked extremely hard for a number of years before returning home to marry. They greatly contributed to the rise of Japanese industry, but were, nevertheless, viewed with scorn because, according to the prevailing notion of the time, young women were supposed to stay at home and train themselves to become good wives and mothers. The girls gave most of their meager earnings to their parents, mainly to supplement and maintain their *ie*.

To this day, the simple, earth-bound life of the peasants lags far behind that of urban populations in social and attitudinal changes. Although a new civil code based on individualism and sex equality was adopted in 1947, it still has not greatly altered the way of life of rural people.

In contrast, in urban areas, influences undermining the concept of *ie* had been growing side by side with the rise of modern industrialization and the acceleration of village-to-town migration of young people. Ancestral family traditions, anchored in village life, were not binding on families which established themselves in the cities. The descendants of old urban families lost most of the hereditary sources of family income, mainly as a result of the impact of modern industry, and became wage and salary earners. The concept of *ie* continued to be preserved by law and supported by official policies, but the new social and economic conditions of the cities militated against it.

Furthermore, as individualistic thinking was gradually introduced from the West, around the turn of the century, pioneering women began to demand the emancipation of women. The movement reached its peak with the surprisingly rapid development of modern industries resulting from World War I. Women worked side by side with men in labor and other social movements to attain the feminist goals.

During World War II, nationalistic political and military leaders suppressed the feminist movements and stressed instead the need to reinforce the traditional concepts of women's place and virtues. However, the increasing urgent need for women in armament plants helped to eradicate the contemptuous attitude towards women working outside their homes. After the war, democracy dealt a fatal blow to militant nationalism, the new civil code removed the traditional fetters of the *ie*, and coeducation was initiated. With these social reforms, the equality of the sexes became a reality, at least in major sectors of the urban population. Today, if a woman, after finishing school, does not take a job at least until she married, she is in a somewhat awkward position.

Young women in rural areas, who are being raised in the democratic atmosphere of postwar days, are making constant efforts to eliminate, or at least modify, the traditional concept of submissiveness. Their efforts, combined with the social and economic improvements of rural life, are gradually bearing fruit. The authority of the *ie* is diminishing, little by little, and although the process is slow, one can anticipate that by the time these young women become the mothers of a new generation, the rural-urban differences in the social position of women will be almost negligible.

THE LEGAL STATUS

During the reorganization of Japan following the Meiji Restoration—a reformation from a feudal state to a modern one—it was natural that a number of pioneering leaders should emerge to fight for women's rights. Among them were women who championed a movement for women's suffrage and tried to awaken Japanese women to the need for improving their position both within the home and on the job. Their efforts fell far short of a nation-wide movement, however, because most Japanese women lacked both material means and education. Then, almost overnight, democratic social reforms following World War II brought about legal equality for women.

The 1946 Constitution guaranteed all Japanese men and women equality under the law:

All people are equal under the law and there shall be no discrimination in political, economic or social relations because of race, creed, sex, social status or family origin.

In connection with family relations, too, the new Constitution recognized the rights of women:

Marriage shall be based only on the mutual consent of both sexes and it shall be maintained through mutual cooperation, with the equal rights of husband and wife as a basis.

Underlying such definite prescriptions for marriage and family relations is the notion that the replacement of the patriarchal family system by the conjugal one is fundamental to the democratic reformation of the nation. (One should keep in mind that the patriarchal family system in Japan had been an integral part of its totalitarian nationalism.)

The Constitution also states, concerning the qualifications for members of both houses of the National Diet and the electors:

. . There shall be no discrimination because of race, creed, sex, social status, family origin, education, property, or income.

Since the first session of the National Diet in 1890, under the Meiji Government, women's political activities had been prohibited, women's suffrage had not been recognized, and women political leaders had been frowned upon. With the above provision, however, women were at last guaranteed equal political rights with men.

On the basis of these constitutional principles, detailed laws covering women's political, educational, family, and occupational rights were successively revised. Since the legal recognition of their political rights, women have been taking an increasingly active part in politics, as is reflected in voting statistics. At the present time, there are almost as many women voters as men.

Following World War II, a series of changes along democratic lines were effected within the educational system, and, along with legal provisions, the new educational doctrines contributed greatly to the diffusion of the idea of sex equality throughout society. In 1957, the Fundamental Law of Education was promulgated, which states:

All people shall be given equal opportunities for receiving education according to their ability, and they shall not be subject to educational discrimination on account of race, creed, sex, social status, economic position, or family origin.

And again:

Men and women shall respect and cooperate with each other. Co-education shall be recognized.

Thus, Japanese education underwent fundamental reforms based on co-educational principles.

No less important was the revision of laws governing family life. The new Constitution abolished the institution of the *ie*. Laws governing family life were revised, accordingly, almost in their entirety. Important points in the revision with regard to the position of women may be summarized as follows:

1 The stipulation disqualifying the wife from representing the family was eliminated; the wife is now legally as qualified as her husband.

2 An adult man and woman need the consent of no other person in order to marry and divorce.

3 Judicial causes for divorce apply equally to husband and wife.

4 Equal rights of inheritance are recognized, with no discrimination on the basis of sex.

Underlying all specific details is the principle of sex equality.

Although the new family laws reflect a profound change in the attitude toward women, the power and authority so long vested in the family head (parents or husband) have not disappeared abruptly or easily. In addition, as one might imagine, the degree of conformity to the new family laws varies according to region, occupation, age, and social class. Conformity at all levels still seems far in the future. Many problems dealt with by the family court at present stem from confusion in interpreting the new laws, and from varying attitudes toward them as compared with the old ones.

The Labor Standards Law was enacted to provide equality for women in connection with working conditions. It stipulates:

The employer shall not discriminate between women and men in the matter of wages.

With particular concern for the physical condition of women, the law provides for menstruation leaves, prohibits night work, and forbids the hiring of women for hazardous work such as mining. A period of leave before and after childbirth and free hours for nursing a child are also provided by the law.

Thus, discrimination against women has been eliminated in all spheres of Japanese society, from the legal standpoint. Nevertheless, traditional concepts and customs restricting women to a submissive position still persist in quite a few circles. It will be interesting to see how Japanese women will overcome these subtle barriers that still stand in the way of their equality.

EDUCATION

In the evolution of women's position since World War II, three factors have been particularly important: legal reforms, education, and the mass-communications media. What the laws established as new goals to aim at have been supported and publicized by the mass media. In the meantime, education has served to indoctrinate the new generation with the idea of sex equality.

It has been noted already that the Fundamental Law of Education set forth the principles of equal educational opportunities. Coeducation was viewed as the most crucial and effective means through which women might improve their social and economic position. All levels of the compulsory school system (primary and junior high school) were made completely coeducational as early as 1947. In 1950, the coeducational system was adopted by the vast majority of senior high schools and subsequently by colleges and universities, with a few exceptions. There was, of course, much opposition to coeducation on the part of traditionalists, especially in connection with the senior high schools. But it is now commonly recognized as a merit of the coeducational system that boys and girls associate with each other naturally in an unstrained and friendly atmosphere, that the tendency toward mutual understanding and cooperation between boys and girls is growing, and that girls have developed greater academic ambitions and been able to fulfill them. Coeducation has contributed remarkably to the growth of the proportion of girl students receiving higher education. In senior high schools, the number of girls now approximates that of boys. Only on the college level do men students greatly outnumber girls, and even here the proportion of girls has grown tremendously. Between 1950 and 1963, the ratio of girl to boy students in senior high schools and colleges and universities changed as follows:

	Senior High Schools		Colleges and Universities	
	Boys	Girls	Boys	Girls
1950	1,203,749	733,766	364,642	40,668
1960	1,756,205	1,483,211	569,127	142,491
1963	2,079,798	1,825,444	710,305	208,399

This rapid increase in the number of girl students tells us not only that the highest levels of education, once limited almost entirely to men, are now open to a growing number of women, but also that the former unfavorable public attitude toward educated women is fast disappearing.

The increased number of educated women implies also, of course, a higher general level of culture for women, and leads inevitably to their more active participation in occupations and social activities. In the past, the vast majority of working women came from poor families receiving only the minimum education and were forced to work outside their homes for economic reasons. Partly because of this, the public attitude toward "working women" was not favorable. Today, however, more than 60 per cent of all women graduates of senior high schools, colleges, and universities hold paid positions, most of them clerical or professional. Thus, the improvement in women's education has led to the improvement of their economic position.

Position in the Family

The family is a primary social group into which one is born, and it remains the most important one throughout the individual's life, but the relationships between its members are conditioned by the relationships and values of society at large. Women's position within the family is therefore related to their general situation, as illustrated by the traditional position of women under the authority of a patriarch.

An opinion survey on the present family system, conducted by the Prime Minister's Office in 1956, showed that the ratio of supporters of authoritarian and equalitarian family systems varies with differences in sex, age, education, and region. The difference is not so clearly marked between men and women, but older people were found to be more likely to support the authoritarian system, as were the less highly educated. As for rural-urban differences, the largest number of supporters for the authoritarian family system were in small towns and villages, the smallest number in large cities. This may be interpreted as showing a difference between agricultural and nonagricultural workers. At any rate, it is evident that there is still a large proportion of Japanese people whose attitudes do not accord with the principle of the equalitarian conjugal family system, although it is supported by the new laws governing the family life of the nation.

It is not surprising, then, to find some instances of women still occupying a subordinate position in the family. The new inheritance law is based on the principle of equality, but recognizes the right of an individual to give up his or her inheritance. Table 1 shows the distribution of men and women who, in 1961, registered in the domestic court their desire not to inherit, and the reasons stated.

TABLE 1—Men and Women Relinquishing Inheritance Rights, for Reasons Stated (1961)

Reason	Children		Spouses	
	Sons	Daughters	Husbands	Wives
Property was already received as a gift during lifetime of family head	2,113	3,541	2	176
Living conditions satisfactory so that inheritance is not needed	10,239	17,998	27	1,092
Property involved is too insignificant	5,021	6,428	16	913
Wish to avoid small subdivisions of property	3,166	3,758	8	728
Prefer that children or oldest son or mother inherit the property, or because heir has married or has been adopted, or other reasons	18,836	34,743	173	12,117
Reasons unknown	718	924	4	207
Total	40,093	67,390	230	15,233

From the children's total, we see that 1.7 times as many daughters as sons gave up their inheritance. Twice as many daughters as sons gave it up in order to enable another heir to inherit (especially the eldest son). Some 66 times as many wives as husbands gave up their inheritance mostly in favor of their children. One may assume that the idea of a woman's inferior position may be a factor in these acts of relinquishing property.

The existing inheritance customs are thought to reveal the most backward aspect of women's position in the family, but compared to prewar days, family life has been greatly modernized, as reflected in figures showing recent changes in the composition of families. By 1960, the percentage of nuclear families (consisting of husband, wife, and unmarried children only) had increased to 65.2 per cent, while that of extended families (including, besides unmarried children, direct ascendants and/or descendants, and/or other relations) had been reduced to 34.8 per cent. In 1964, nuclear families constituted 69 per cent and extended families only 31 per cent. Rural-urban comparisons indicate that the proportion of nuclear families is higher in large cities (80.1 per cent in 1964) than in medium-sized cities (68.8 per cent), and higher in medium-sized cities than in towns and villages (62.4 per cent). This indicates a recent, steadily increasing tendency for young husbands and wives to live separately from their parents. Needless to say, this tendency is almost invariably favorable to the woman's position.

Marriage Pattern and Sex Mores

Women's position within the family becomes even clearer when one examines the marriage pattern.

Concerning the choice of one's spouse, the new civil code provides that marriage shall be based upon the sole consent of the man and woman concerned, whereas the old civil code stipulated, "For marriage, a son or daughter should obtain the consent of the parents with whom he or she lives." In practice, too, the consent of parents was a prerequisite to marriage in prewar days, and this custom still has great influence today, in spite of the law. An opinion survey reveals that 26 per cent of the Japanese people believe that a choice made by the parents is preferable to one's own choice. Such a reply reveals again persistent traditional tendencies.

There are two main types of marriages in Japan: the love marriage, initiated by romantic attraction between a man and woman, and the *miai* marriage. *Miai*, which means "to see each other," is the first step leading to the traditional, arranged marriage. According to this system, a *Nakodo* (go-between) arranges the first opportunity for a man and woman to see each other formally, together with their parents. When a *miai* ends favorably, the engagement is announced. A survey of married women, conducted by the Women's and Minors' Bureau of the Ministry of Labor to discover which type of marriage is most prevalent, showed that the overwhelming majority had been married by means of the *miai* system. It is reported that, whereas in large cities *miai* marriages account for 75 per cent of all marriages, as against 25 per cent love marriages, the proportion of the former rises to 86 per cent in rural areas, with love marriages constituting only 13 per cent. In this area, then, we find a dominant trend towards the traditional pattern, but the higher proportion of love marriages in urban as compared with rural areas may imply that a modern pattern is gradually emerging in the cities. Another finding of the above survey—that 47 per cent of the women respondents aged twenty to thirty had married as the result of a romantic attachment—reveals how rapidly the modern pattern is replacing the traditional one.

Concerning the marriage proposal, research carried out by the author and his associates in Tokyo and its environs revealed that 60 per cent and 83 per cent of all marriages in an urban and a rural area, respectively, were initiated by a proposal on the part of the man.

As indicated by the figures above, most marriages in the past were initiated by a woman's parents or prospective husband. The old, inferior position of women with regard to marriage may, in part, be attributed to the traditional disapproval of free association between men and women, but it reflects, also, the traditional position of a woman under the institution of *ie*: she became not just the wife of her husband, but the bride of his *ie*.

Marriage is legally recognized, for the purpose of subsequent protection, when it is registered under the prescribed laws. This kind of "complete" marriage was rather rare in the past. In many cases, the husband and wife did not register their marriage until the birth of their first child. Recently, under urging by the authorities, there has been an increase in the number of couples registering their marriage shortly after the wedding ceremony. The proportion of marriages registered within one year after the ceremony now constitutes 85 per cent of all marriages, while 10 per cent are registered within two years of the ceremony; only 5 per cent are not registered even after two years. Some instances of delayed registration are caused by carelessness or ignorance of the law, but the persistence of traditional doctrines and practices also plays a part. There are, in addition, many cases of extra-marital unions, of both long and short duration. Such relationships vary according to region, social class, and age, and it is difficult to generalize about them.

The old patriarchal family system required the eldest son and his wife to live with his parents, an arrangement known as *yomeiri-kon* (literally, "marriage having a bride move in") or patrilocal. Only if a family lacked a male heir did a husband move into the house of his wife and live with his parents-in-law—an arrangement called *mukoiri-kon* ("marriage having bridegroom move in") or matrilocal. With urbanization, these traditional arrangements have gradually given way to neolocal marriage, that is, one in which the married couple settle in a residence of their own, separate from the parents of either spouse. The result of this tendency is an increase in nuclear families.

With regard to sex mores from the woman's standpoint, mention must be made of the problem of prostitution which has been debated for long and only recently seems to be nearing solution. Prostitution in Japan began about a thousand years ago, and the literature of olden days attaches certain romantic and aesthetic values to it. After the Meiji Restoration, the government gave official approval to the practice by licensing prostitutes. However, since the Meiji Restoration (or for about 100 years), feminists and Christian social reformers had been constantly fighting to suppress prostitution until the outbreak of World War II.

During the postwar period, with its poor economy, social turmoil, and influx of foreigners, the number of prostitutes, many of them simply street walkers, rapidly increased. As social concern about these women mounted, the movement for the abolition of prostitution was revived, and finally succeeded in forcing the Diet to repeal its official approval of 1950 and pass a bill for the prevention of prostitution (1956). This legal action was interpreted as a prohibition of all kinds of prostitution, and more than 130,000 prostitutes in cities, resorts, watering places, and small towns where occupation forces were based were forced to disguise or discontinue their activities. But since the vast majority of them (80 per cent) had become prostitutes from economic necessity, they were unable to give up their "profession," and a considerable number of them are still active. Measures for their protection have been taken by the authorities, and a dedicated group of volunteer women social workers devote themselves to their problems.

Concubinage, which is regarded as a kind of polygamy, is another type of union not legally recognized. The government ceased to sanction it legally around the close of the last century, but in spite of this, some upper-class men continue to keep concubines as an old-fashioned demonstration of their status. However, under the present democratic social regime, criticism of the practice is very severe and the function it formerly fulfilled has lost all significance.

In the past, in many rural areas, free association and even sexual intercourse, between young men and women was permitted, but this freedom has been disappearing recently. In urban areas, on the contrary, among the upper and middle classes, free association and, of course, sexual intercourse, were strictly prohibited, but recently a more liberal attitude has been growing. Love marriages are gradually replacing *miai* marriages, as previously noted, and the free association of men and women during the engagement period is common practice. Even in the case of *miai* marriage, the prevailing pattern is to allow a considerable time to elapse between the *miai* and the wedding ceremony, during which the man and woman see each other frequently and become well acquainted. The engagement may be cancelled if the relationship does not prove satisfactory.

Dating has become a common practice among young people. As in Western countries, they meet in tea shops, at the theater, in parks, and so on. Information regarding patterns of physical contact in connection with dating is very limited, but seems to indicate that passionate behavior, such as necking and petting, is rare. About half of all dating couples probably do not go beyond what might be termed affectionate embraces.

During the war, the government urged people to have as many children as possible, so that Japan could increase her manpower; but since the war, the desired number of children has been decreasing each year, according to a survey. This tendency has been coupled with a growing concern for family planning. About half of all couples in Japan are now practicing, or have at some time practiced, birth control (see Table 2). This is attributed not only to economic conditions, but to a desire to improve the quality of family life, and concern for the mothers' health. The number of couples practicing birth control doubled between 1950 and 1957.

TABLE 2—Couples Practicing Birth Control, By Husband's Occupation (1957)

	Per Cent			
Occupation of husband	now practicing	have once practiced	have never practiced	unknown
Farmers and fishermen	31.0	14.8	45.2	9.0
Factory workers	34.4	18.4	41.5	5.4
Shop keepers and factory owners	37.1	19.7	39.7	3.5
Salaried workers	48.8	17.8	31.0	2.7
Professionals	48.9	17.8	33.3	—

Source: Survey by the Population Research Association of the Mainichi Newspaper Company

The Home Routine

As one may suppose, women of families in traditional occupations (farming, shopkeeping) perform different functions from those whose husbands are engaged in modern occupations and earn wages and salaries. The most concise summary of this difference comes from a survey on "Class Differences in Housewives' Time Allocation in Daily Life." This study shows that there is no appreciable class difference with regard to the time one can or does spend sleeping, bathing, taking meals, and so on. The time spent in working for pay is minimal for the wives of wage and salary earners (when they do work, it is usually on piecework at home). On the average, wives in the white-collar and blue-collar classes devote only ten and forty minutes per day, respectively, to this activity. As for self-employed workers' families, the wife of a farmer spends more than three hours, and the wife of a shopkeeper more than six hours a day working for pay. Such a difference in the time devoted to paid work is, of course, reflected in a considerable difference in the time spent in housekeeping and the care of children. Whereas housewives of both the white-collar class and blue-collar class can allocate nine hours or more a day for housekeeping and the care of children, this time must be reduced to less than seven hours and only about five hours by the wives of shopkeepers and farmers, respectively. A difference in time allocation is also observed in leisure-time activities: self-improvement, hobbies, entertainment, etcetera. The wife of a shopkeeper has only two and a half hours of leisure a day, as against the four and a half hours at the disposal of the white-collar worker's wife. The wife of a farmer is a little better off in this respect, for as the result of the shorter time spent in earning income, she can reserve more hours for leisure—in fact, her leisure may be very close to that of women in the blue-collar class. Presumably, this reflects the trend towards more efficient organization of housework and the mechanization of farming, which has been growing remarkably in recent years.

Of particular interest is the home routine of wives who work outside the home. Their number is still rather small, but the proportion of such women to the total number of working women has been steadily increasing. Since much of their time is taken up by their jobs, they are likely to be excessively tired, although the time given to housekeeping and the care of children is greatly curtailed. Of great help to these women is the changing attitude toward housework on the part of men: in the past, housework was scorned by men as beneath their dignity, but today a growing number of husbands help their wives around the house as a matter of course.

The activities of women at home vary considerably according to the size of the family and its social standing, but, generally speaking, the basic housekeeping chores and the care of children are the same for all.

The difference between the housekeeping activities of rural and urban women is one of the most clearly marked. According to a survey conducted by the Ministry of Labor, daily expenditures are controlled by the husband in 91 per cent of all farming households, whereas in the households of workers employed in small and medium-sized factories, 86 per cent of the husbands hand over their entire salaries to their wives. Thus, exactly the opposite situation exists in rural and urban households with respect to household budgeting. Generally speaking, control of the household expenditures by the wife is also more common in nuclear than in extended families.

The same pattern is found regarding family property. Only a very small proportion of wives in rural areas have full knowledge of their family property, but more than 80 per cent of all urban wives are consulted in connection with family property transactions. A noteworthy recent trend in this regard is the striking increase of urban wives who invest in the stock market, in real estate, etcetera, entirely on their own judgment.

In the past, a family's social activities centering around children's coming of age, marriages, funerals, holidays, and the like were entirely controlled by the patriarch, or by the oldest son if the patriarch were absent. But recently these functions have gradually been handed over to women.

From the above, one may see the recent trend of the changing position of women at home. Although the tasks of women at home traditionally included all activities pertaining to the maintenance of family life, the planning and decisions were handled by the patriarch, while women only carried out instructions. Nowadays, however, such matters are becoming more and more the equal responsibility of husband and wife. The following paragraphs, written by a celebrated author, summarize the changing mores of Japanese family relations.

My mother was married in 1886. From her wedding day on, she obediently served my father, who was given to violent outbursts of rage over trifles. For forty years, until the death of her husband, my mother managed to live with him without quarreling. I never saw her taking a drink with my father, nor even demanding anything of him, yet, apparently, she got what she wanted. Perhaps her freedom and happiness were of a very different sort from ours.

The freedom and happiness of my sons and their wives are quite "modern." Both husbands and wives hold paid jobs and share the housekeeping. In all respects they have equal responsibility and obligations. They travel together, enjoy sports and concerts together and entertain their friends together. Hand in hand, they attend the May Day celebrations. The wives drink beer and whiskey just as their husbands do, and the husbands wash dishes and cook rice, side by side with their wives. This concept of freedom and happiness is considerably different from what prewar Japanese people meant by these terms.

As for my own generation, my wife and I went through our adolescence during the pre-war days. When the two of us take a drink together, my wife often gets a bit tipsy, but it is I who often get really drunk and I count on my wife to look out for me. She never participates in political demonstrations, and I, too, am reluctant to be involved in group activities. It would seem that I have somewhat more freedom and enjoy life a bit more than she . . .

WOMEN'S OCCUPATIONS

Census data of 1960 reveal that of the 33,774,300 Japanese women aged fifteen and over, about half, or 17,081,300 work at paid jobs. The following table shows the distribution of women in various types of occupation.

TABLE 3—Working Women Aged 15 and over, by Occupation (1960)

Occupation	Number of Women Working	Per cent of Total
Agriculture	7,158,900	41.9
Manufacturing	3,090,400	18.1
Wholesale & Retail Trade	2,899,300	17.0
Domestic Service	2,515,400	14.7
Other	1,417,300	8.3
Total	17,081,300	100.0

It should be noted that 84 per cent of women working in agriculture are unpaid family workers, while 62 per cent of the women working in manufacturing, wholesale and retail trades and domestic service are paid employees. In view of this difference, it seems advisable to treat these two groups of women separately in the subsequent discussion.

It is customary for women agricultural workers to work both before and after marriage as unpaid family workers. In Japan, the major agricultural product is rice, cultivated in water, which requires scrupulous care and perseverence. Women have always fulfilled these requirements very well, and are regarded as capable and indispensable farm workers. Female labor has been especially important in the planting of the rice sprouts, an essential part of aquatic rice cultivation. Of course, this has placed a heavy work load on women. Until the turn of this century, when a self-sustaining economy prevailed in rural areas, women had a much heavier work load, because not only the production of raw materials and foodstuffs but the processing of them were women's tasks. In comparison with those days, women have a considerably easier time, for they now buy food and clothes produced in factories and sold in shops.

On the other hand, farming has become exclusively a woman's occupation. During the last war, adult male members of farming families were mobilized as soldiers or factory workers, leaving the women alone to work the farms. Recently, farm work has become considerably easier due to the introduction of agricultural machinery, high-quality fertilizers, and new diffusion techniques in using insecticides and fungicides. The result of the improvements is an increasing number of part-time farming households, called "housewife farming families," in which the adult male members are engaged in nonagricultural work, and the farm work is carried out by the women, most of them married, with the help of elderly men. Under such conditions, the women allocate a considerable amount of time per day to working for pay.

In discussing the position of these working women, one must examine much more than the nature of the farm work from a technical standpoint, because in Japan agriculture is undertaken as a family enterprise, and farm work is inseparably linked with family life. But in respect to their family life, the position of rural women is no better than it ever was, for they are harassed by the old patriarchal family pattern which still persists in spite of the legal changes calling for a democratic family pattern. In the patriarchal family, a husband and wife, their sons, and their sons' wives all live under one roof. Such a family is still considered the best suited to carry out small-scale farming, the most common type in Japan. It should be mentioned here, in connection with the decline of the patriarchal family system, that it is becoming more and more difficult for two couples of different generations, brought up under different social circumstances, to live together in the same house. Young women in rural areas are reluctant to marry into farming families and wait on the parents of their husbands. Because of this fact, migration to the cities is the goal of many more young women than young men, over twice as many. Thus the farmers experience difficulty in finding wives.

The history of working women in urban areas begins with the exodus of rural young women to the cities; in other words, it is a recent phenomenon. The capitalistic system and mass production appeared in Japan around the turn of this century and attained a peak during World War I. At that time, the majority of working women (60 to 70 per cent) was employed in spinning factories. Most of them were the daughters of farm families who had received a minimum of education. This was one of the reasons why the term "working women" had a pejorative connotation. Then, during World War II, it became imperative to employ all available women in offices and factories, and their job performance resulted in the opening up of new occupational fields to them, and an increased respect for their capacities. This was the background for their employment after the war when they were obliged to work for economic reasons during a period of great social turmoil. The number of women working in secondary and tertiary industries gradually surpassed the number working in primary industries.[1] In 1950, working women in primary industries constituted 62.3 per cent of all working women, but in 1960, women in secondary and tertiary industries constituted 57 per cent of the total, as against 43 per cent in primary industries. By 1963 a further shift had taken place: only 36.6 per cent of the working women were engaged in primary industries, as against 63.4 per cent in secondary and tertiary industries.

The pattern of women working in factories, offices and shops has been too complex and fluid to be described briefly, for it has reflected industrial developments and changing economic and social conditions since the end of the war. But one may say that the vast majority of all employed women are young and unmarried, and that, on the average, after only four years, they quit their jobs to be replaced by newcomers fresh out of school. Such a situation means that, for the time being, women cannot expect too much in the way of improved working conditions and opportunities.

However, the number of women who continue working outside the home after marriage has gradually been increasing, year by year: it accounted for 15 per cent of all paid women employees in 1955, 19.6 per

---

1. Primary industries comprise agriculture (in which are employed 98 per cent of the workers in this category) and forestry, hunting, fishing and aquaculture (2 per cent). Secondary industries comprise mining, construction and manufacturing; tertiary industries are wholesale and retail trade, finance, insurance, real estate, transportation, communication, electricity, gas and water supply, services and government.

cent in 1960, and 25.3 per cent in 1963. The increase of married women employees may indicate a higher degree of stability in the field of women's occupations, but in view of the present working conditions, especially for working mothers, the picture should not be interpreted as altogether favorable to women. New laws for the protection of working mothers and their children are now under consideration. With nuclear families increasing in number, it is hoped that a situation will evolve in which women can work before marriage and until the onset of their child-bearing period afterwards, then stop working to care for their children, and resume work during middle age when the children no longer need constant attention.

Social Position and Women's Organizations

The most important factor contributing to the improved position of women was the reformation of the legal and educational systems along democratic lines, which did away with the notion of female submissiveness. But almost equally important has been the influence of the mass-communications media, which have taken the lead in changing public opinion regarding women. These media have not always been favorable to women, for they have sometimes supported prejudiced views and sometimes flattered the female public to no good purpose. Yet, on the whole, the newspapers, the radio, and television have been calling the attention of the public to new trends and concepts regarding women's position, expressing definite opinions, and suggesting suitable policies toward them. Since almost all Japanese people are reached by one or another of these media, one can conclude that their influence has been considerable. For example, an analysis of editorial articles appearing since the war shows that, shortly after the cessation of hostilities, most articles were urging women to make the most of their capabilities and trying to orient them towards conformity with the newly revised laws. Following the conclusion of the Peace Treaty, when the foreign powers allied with the democratic reformation of Japan retreated, and a possible regression of women's position to the status of prewar days was feared, the editorials contributed much toward alleviating such fears in the minds of Japanese women. Later, as Japan resumed her social stability some ten years after the war, the articles began to reexamine the position of women and urged the public not to remain content with discussing abstract principles of sex equality.

But have Japanese women relied entirely on such external forces as legal reforms, and the influence of the mass media and foreign powers for the improvement of their social position? They did not, but made effective efforts of their own.

Soon after the end of World War I, a feminist social movement, the *Shinfujin Kyoka* (New Women's Association), was initiated. This was the first feminist movement organized by women themselves. It was soon dissolved because of a number of internal difficulties, but it acted as a stimulus for a variety of liberal and socialist organizations and movements which culminated in the demand for women's suffrage. Although the franchise for women was denied, the movement continued until the military government suppressed it.

Apart from this, local women's organizations were established in all municipalities of Japan, with the support of government officials, as part of a national movement. Two of these nationwide organizations were the *Aikoku Fujinkai* (Women's Patriotic Society), organized in 1901, with the stated aim of helping Japanese women to educate and improve themselves at home, and the *Dai-Nihon Rengo Fujin Kai* (Great Japanese Federation of Women's Associations), organized in 1930. During World War II, the *Kokubo Fujin Kai* (Society for the National Defense of Women) was established for the purpose of supporting the home-front activities of women. These organizations, though each had its own specific and limited purpose, laid a broad foundation for the social activities of women in general, and directly or indirectly contributed to the elevation of their position in society.

These government-sponsored organizations were dissolved soon after the war, but as the democratic reform of Japan was gradually realized, new local women's organizations sprang up for the purpose of awakening women and improving their position. In 1952, the *Zenkoku Chiiki Jujin Dantai Renraku Kyogikai* (National Council of Women's Organizations) was set up as an agency to integrate the local groups on a national basis. The Council has since been holding a national meeting every year to advance movements for the improvement of women's position, the welfare of local communities, and world peace. Regarding the social activities of rural women, the *Nogyo Kyodo Kumiai* (Agricultural Cooperative Union) first established after the war on a national basis as a farmer's organization, came to include women's sections in its local branches, in order to help rural women solve the problems peculiar to them. Subsequently, in 1951, these women's sections organized their own national council. PTA is an educational organization established in every school district of Japan after the war. Its membership consists of the parents and teachers of school children, but since it is primarily mothers who attend its meetings and participate in its activities, it has served as an agency for promoting social activities and the training of women in democratic principles and procedures. Other voluntary organizations for women have appeared during the postwar period, including the following:

1) The *Nihon Fujin Yukensha Domei* (Japanese Women Voters' League). The aim of this organization is to awaken the political consciousness of women and promote political participation on their part.

2) The *Shufu Rengo-kai* (Housewives Federation). Based on the principle that house-wives should solve the problems peculiar to them, through their own efforts, the organization has developed a very active movement. Its activities are well known because of the aprons worn by the members and the large diapers they hold up at parades as symbols of the housewife's tasks.
3) The *Nihon Daigaku Fujin Kyokai* (Japanese Association of University Women). Its stated purpose is to promote women's education and social life, as well as international good will.
4) The *Nihon Fujin Yushokusha Domei* (Japanese Working Women's League). Its aim is to alleviate the burdens of working women.

The activities of these voluntary women's organizations have had wide appeal for the public, under the democratic social regime of Japan. One must applaud their efforts to solve various problems, and the role they have played in the elevation of women's social position.

Recently, organized activities of Japanese women have expanded on the international scene, as indicated by the Japanese National Women's Commission, established as an unofficial body under the sponsorship of the United Nations; the Asiatic Women's Conference of the YWCA; and the Pan-Pacific and South-East Asiatic Women's Conferences, both held in Japan. Thus, outstanding women are found examining their social position from the international standpoint.

WOMEN IN LEADERSHIP

In the past, under the pervasive notion of male superiority, women were required to develop those virtues involving submissiveness to husbands and parents within the family, and modesty in society at large. Under such circumstances, a woman who held a position of leadership was not looked upon with favor, either by her family or by society. A woman who happened to hold a dominant position within the family was scorned as a "hen crying cock-adoodle at dawn." Women's involvement in political affairs was criticized as a source of confusion. This attitude persisted even after Japan had reorganized herself into a modern state. But after the last war, the situation radically changed. Under the newly created democratic social forms, women were encouraged to express their own opinions, both within the family and outside the home. With the improvement of their education and the broadened social fields open to them, a rapidly growing number of women took over positions of leadership.

Beginning with the enforcement of universal male suffrage in 1925, the demand for women's suffrage was enthusiastically pushed by a number of prominent women, and finally, after twenty years, the National Diet passed the bill granting them suffrage, in 1945. In the general election of Diet members held the following year, no less than thirty-seven women were elected to the House of Representatives. But this overwhelming success was the result of what proved to be a passing popularity of women candidates. After this trend subsided, women members in each House continued to number about ten. With this steady political advance, it was not surprising that a woman received a cabinet post in 1960.

Meanwhile, women were advancing in local politics; ever since 1947, the year of the first local elections after the war, a steadily growing proportion of women have been elected to assembly seats in prefectures, cities, wards, towns, and villages. In 1952, seven women were elected to the position of town or village mayor. This remarkable showing has not been maintained, however, indicating, perhaps, how few women even today are eligible for such positions.

As for various appointive public offices, such as member of a board of education, district welfare commissioner, domestic court mediator, and civil liberties commissioner, women have been making strides here, also. For example, the total number of women holding the office of domestic court mediator is now 5,000, or 20 per cent of all occupants of the position, indicating the recognition given to women's aptitudes for dealing with complicated and subtle domestic problems. And there are now more than 1,000 women on boards of education throughout Japan. Women are increasingly being recognized as well qualified to deal with matters pertaining to educational and cultural fields.

In various other fields, too, women have assumed positions of leadership. Thirty women were appointed at one time as principals of public elementary and junior high schools. Subsequently, the position of director, section chief, and other senior offices in the Women's and Minors' Bureau of the Ministry of Labor were occupied by women. A woman section chief was appointed in the Ministry of Education. Young women, too, have begun to assume leadership, as indicated by the fact that thirty of them passed the first examination for appointments in the National Public Service, while others have become magistrates, attorneys and diplomats. Their number is still small, but they have successfully pioneered in opening new fields for women. In the academic fields, too, women have achieved a high degree of success, and obtained teaching positions in the universities. Many women are now pursuing their studies in graduate schools throughout Japan and abroad. One may predict an even greater leadership on the part of women in the future.

WOMEN AS CULTURAL TRANSMITTERS

In the past, not all Japanese women were content to be good wives and mothers. After the Meiji Restoration, a number of women achieved unusual recognition in the fields of literature, the drama, and the fine arts, inspiring young women to prepare for careers in these fields. With the general improvement of women's education, the removal of social norms confining them to the family, and the officially stated policy of sex equality after the war, an increasing number of women have been winning fame for their cultural achievements, and the areas in which they can compete with men have broadened.

Especially remarkable, too, has been the trend to popularize culture, and here again, the mass media, especially television, have been influential. Cultural fields, not formerly accessible to women of the lower classes, are now enjoyed and appreciated by large numbers of women of all social classes. This phenomenon is particularly important from another standpoint: the thousands upon thousands of women to whom culture is now available constitute a responsive audience for women of talent and make it possible for them to achieve outstanding success. It should be noted, too, that a growing number of women are engaged in the radio and television industry as producers, directors, masters of ceremonies or announcers.

Traditionally, Japanese culture comprised features particularly suited to women's talents, such as the tea ceremony and flower arrangement. In the past, these arts were the exclusive province of women of the upper and upper-middle classes, who learned them within the confines of their own homes under the supervision of strict parents. Today, with the popularization of culture, these arts are taught not only in the home, but also in places of business, and are available to women of all classes. Thus the everyday life of the average woman has been greatly enriched.

In addition, the women of today, whether students, factory workers or middle-aged housewives, often go out with friends to visit art exhibitions, listen to concerts or attend the theater. Excursions for the purpose of studying classical architecture, landscape gardening and sculpture are common

THE OUTLOOK

Supported by legal reforms, education, and mass media, Japanese women have achieved a new status for themselves since the war. When the Ministry of Labor conducted a survey on women's position in 1949, 84 per cent of the respondents were already able to report a very real improvement in their position. In 1955, the Ministry again conducted a similar survey and found that 70 per cent of the respondents recognized the necessity for further improvement of their position. The older the respondent and the higher the level of her education, the more apt she was to make this reply. Thus women realized that they had achieved much, but were still not satisfied with their position.

What are the obstacles standing in the way of further improvement? The previously mentioned survey by the Ministry of Labor in 1949 included a question on this point, and reported that the largest proportion (42 per cent) of the respondents mentioned as an obstacle the survival of feudalistic institutions and practices. Other obstacles mentioned were lack of understanding on the part of men and the public in general (35 per cent); unfair family arrangements (30 per cent); lack of awareness and passivity on the part of women themselves (27 per cent); economic insecurity (14 per cent) and low level of education (9 per cent). The 1955 survey showed similar results.[1]

These findings suggest possible steps to be taken for the future improvement of women's position, but these suggestions are of a general nature. In practical situations, women confront complicated networks of human relations, involving social, economic, and emotional factors, which often call for professional analysis and treatment. For instance, one runs across male egos that still cling to the notion of male superiority and are at a loss without legal sanction for their attitude; or different generations living under the same roof but acting in accordance with disparate value systems; or a clash between rural and urban cultures; or a gap between everyday life and officially sanctioned doctrines. There are men who concede too much to women, and women who assert themselves too aggressively, both misunderstanding the meaning of sex equality. In short, the passage of ten years seems insufficient to have created a coordinated system for the relations between men and women, although a good start has been made.

What is needed for the further improvement of women's position is an examination of the actual problems which women encounter in everyday life, and continued efforts for their practical solution. Only in this way can the ideal norms be translated into practical terms. We stress this, because we feel that the fundamental principle of sex equality has been put into practice without consideration for the many specific problems involved, and without sufficient preparation for handling them.

BIBLIOGRAPHY

Baber, Ray E., *Youth Looks at Marriage and the Family—A Study of Changing Japanese Attitudes*. Tokyo, International Christian University (1958).

Isomura, E., Kawashima, T., and Koyama, T. (ed.); *Kekkon eno Michi—Gendai-Kazoku Kôza* II (The Road to Marriage—The Modern Family Series II) Tokyo, Kawade Shobô (1956).

Kawashima, Takeyoshi, *Ideologii to shite no Kazoku-seido* (Ideologically Defined Family System) Tokyo, Iwanami Shoten (1957).

---

1. No data more recent than 1955 are available. In the opinion of the authors, confirmed by the Women's and Minors' Bureau of the Ministry of Labor, the very fact that this type of information was no longer gathered after 1955 indicates a shift in concern from the ideological conflict between the traditional and the modern views on the status of women, to the concrete obstacles which still stand in the way of further improvements in their position. Instead of studying the issue in general terms, as did the 1949 and 1955 surveys, the more recent inquiries examine concrete obstacles one by one.

Koyama, Takashi, *The Changing Social Position of Women in Japan*. Paris, UNESCO (1961).
—— (ed), *Gendai Nihon no Josei* (Contemporary Women in Japan), Tokyo, Kokudosha (1962).
—— (ed.), *Gendai Kazoku no Kenkyû — Jittai to Chôsei* (A Study of the Contemporary Japanese Family — Its Actual Manifestations and Problem Solution) Tokyo, Kôbundô (1960).
Rôdôsho, *Nihon Fujin no Hosei-jô no Chii to Genjô* (The Legal Position of Women in Japan) Tokyo : Ministry of Labor (1952).
——, *Fujin no Chii no Henka* (The Position of Women in Transition) Tokyo : Ministry of Labor (1962).
Segawa, Kiyoko, *Konin Oboegaki* (Papers on Marriage) Tokyo, Kôdansha (1957).
Takamure, Itsue, *Nihon Josei Shakai-shi* (Social History of Women in Japan) Tokyo, Shinnihonsha (1947).

V

Afro-Asian Traditional Freedom

SUB-SAHARAN AFRICA, BURMA
AND SOUTH-EAST ASIA, INDONESIA

The three world areas discussed in this section comprise a large variety of cultural traditions. These cultures have traditionally included freedoms which, in other parts of the world women have only recently begun to enjoy or aspire to. Outstanding among these is the sexual liberty of women in certain African societies, and the important roles women play in commercial activities in both Africa and Southeast Asia. Thus the base line of the change is very different here from what it was in most other countries of the world, and the outcome of the transformation taking place in them at present can also be expected to be different.

Sub-Saharan Africa

By Elizabeth Hunting Wheeler

INTRODUCTION

*E*uropeans and Africans first met in the 1430's when Portuguese traders touched the Guinea coast. Dutch, English, and French merchants soon followed, and within two centuries missionaries joined the busy communities surrounding the trading posts along the coast. By the latter half of the nineteenth century, Dutch and Portuguese power had waned, but Britain, France, and Germany competed vigorously for the extension of their empires. Coastal trading posts became staging areas for European expeditions to the interior. At the turn of the century resistance had been subdued and colonial boundaries set.

The new colonies covered an area twice the size of the United States so that no power could hope to administer them directly through its own officials. Instead, the colonial governments ruled indirectly through the traditional or appointed chiefs. Once turned into civil servants, however, the chiefs' authority was irrevocably undermined, and the way was cleared for even deeper changes. Missionary evangelists, supported by the colonial administration, attacked the foundations of the traditional kinship system through unceasing opposition to polygamy. New foreign trade opportunities, demands for manufactured goods and skilled services, and the imposition of taxes helped transform a barter economy into a money economy with cash crops.

These corrosive forces precipitated the social disorganization of the countryside, and contributed to the growth of the towns which were better able to provide the synthesis of a new society. Tribesman first took jobs in towns to buy the goods they desired, and then to pay the taxes enforced by the colonial government. When they earned sufficient funds, they returned to their villages. Gradually, young men settled in towns leaving their wives and families behind. They returned home regularly, and relatives visited them often. But this arrangement proved too great a strain upon the family, and so more and more women followed their husbands to town, and as the ratio of men to women equalized, family life settled down.

However, it took a different form from the traditional family which included grandparents, aunts, uncles, cousins, half-sisters and brothers, and even servants or boarders. Urban families fragmented under the pressures of housing shortages and new social values, and the nuclear family —husband, wife, and children—became commonplace. The wife, who would ordinarily be under the direct authority and responsibility of her husband's family, was now on her own. She, therefore, tended to strengthen her blood ties through frequent visits, kinship associations, and mutual self-help societies. She looked not to her husband's family for security and support, but to her own family.

The city opened other new avenues of self-expression to her. Girls married at older ages because they wanted to finish school, and when they did marry, they chose husbands who were willing to be companions and able to provide the full family income. Some preferred to be concubines until they found the best catch from among their suitors. Still others took jobs which they maintained during their marriages, and as widows preferred to support themselves through their trades rather than remarry.

Dramatic changes are apparent in any contrast of the modern urban and the traditional rural life. But it must be remembered that all African women live ambivalent lives that fluctuate between traditional and contemporary patterns. Muslim women, veiled and restricted by purdah, are nonetheless learning to read and write. The family of a village girl still expects the traditional symbols and gifts sealing the marriage contract, but plan for their daughter a Christian wedding complete with bridesmaids and bouquets. West Africa's famous traders congregate in the traditional market places, but now their customers demand enamel pots, bicycles, cigarettes, and aspirin. University graduates, eager to educate their own children, willingly dip into the family savings to buy medicine for a grandmother or pay school fees for a second cousin.

Americans tend to think of the educated elite as the modern African women. But taking a somewhat broader view we will soon see that all those African women who, in the exercise of the daily lives, successfully blend the old and the new comprise the modern African woman. It is to her that this article is dedicated.

SOCIAL POSITION AND FAMILY LIFE

"Traditionally in Africa women had very little social standing and were regarded mainly as the chattel of men, to work and have children." "Speaking generally, the women of Nigeria are seldom of the chattel type and correspond little to the widely-held idea of the downtrodden slave or unregarded beast of burden."

These two statements, the first made by J. Aduke Moore, a Nigerian woman, and the second quoted by F. Adetowun Ogunsheye, another Nigerian woman, to express her point of view, illustrate the difficulty of generalizations about the social position of African women. But neither point of view describes adequately the status of the woman in the home and family. An excellent analysis was prepared by Guy Kouassigan, a Togolaise lawyer, and Madame Marie Sivomey, Chief of the Office of Social Affairs, for the UN Seminar on the Status of Women in Family Law. For them the woman's role is defined by the idea of the family. Thus in Africa family applies not only to persons linked to a common ancestor, but also to servants, dependents, freed slaves, or alien workers. This extended family system is, in effect, the community cemented by relationships which carry with them well defined rights and duties.

In this community the rights and duties of the unmarried girl are dominated by the idea that she cannot contribute to the maintenance or continuity of the family group. Her rights and duties are defined in relation to her future role as wife and mother in another family. She cannot, for instance, inherit property, for the unity and strength of the family rest on its collective heritage of the land. To allow a girl to inherit land is tantamount to weakening the family. Furthermore, the girl is restricted from taking personal action on her own account.

The family organization is dominated by the clan head. He is responsible not only for acts done on behalf of the family but also for those performed by members on their own account which, regardless how minor, affect the family itself. Thus, he can commit a girl to marriage because marriage is essentially a family affair or a social contract joining two groups. Since the family represents a social, economic, and often political unit, its strength depends not only on its numbers but also on its internal cohesion.

Every member has his or her place and designated rights and duties. Marriage, which removes a female member from the family, therefore, weakens it and upsets its internal equilibrium. Hence, marriage payments are both compensation to the family for this loss, and a seal that solidifies the alliance between the contracting families.

Because the clan is the basic social unit, marriage does not presuppose the formation of a new household. Instead the structures of the contracting clans are altered by the woman leaving her own family and being absorbed into that of her husband. Though she is still subject to the will of the clan head, as a married woman her rights have expanded. She can inherit personal property; she can farm a plot of land designated to her use, and employ the product of her efforts as she sees fit. She can divorce her husband on a number of grounds, such as impotency, neglect, excessive abuse, chronic illness, and violent dislike. However, these rights are still limited and there is relatively little formal protection against abuse.

Within the family system there are two social characteristics which influence the position of women and demonstrate the variations within the system: purdah and matrilineage.

Purdah is generally associated with Islam. But the general condition of wife seclusion among the Nigerian Hausa, for instance, is more accurately understood in terms of the economic position of the husband and the role of Hausa wives.

Living in complete seclusion, a woman may never leave the women's quarters except to visit her family once a year. Less strict observance allows her to quit the compound only after dark to visit family and friends or collect water and firewood. However, the peasant women, lowest on the social scale, can move freely about the village, help in the farming, and visit kin at will. In short, only wealthy men can afford to remove their women from productive activity and use enforced seclusion as a symbol of their own prestige.

But confinement was not always the rule even in Muslim Africa. Ibn Batuta, when he entered the frontiers of the Melle Kingdom in 1352, complained that the Muslim women were not confined to the harem and traveled unveiled mixing freely with men. He also noted that the Muslim Berbers, who occupied the Melle capital at the time, had adopted the practice of tracing the family through the female line "as with native dynasties in the pre-Mohammedan days." This practice continues today among some West Coast societies and gives women a status not permitted in patrilineal systems.

The Akan, for instance, determine kinship and succession through the mother. That is, the clan is united in the belief of descent from a common woman ancestor. Each child is said to inherit his mother's "blood" and his father's "spirit." Like other matrilineal societies, the Akan have male chiefs but they also have a female head who wields high moral authority based on the maternal ties and her closeness to the family ancestors.

DAILY ROUTINE

Whether or not purdah or matrilineage are part of the social fabric, all African women share the tasks of daily living. Most of their time is spent collecting firewood and water, cooking meals and keeping the house clean, farming, and caring for children. The following accounts, though written by persons thousands of miles apart, show marked similarity, and could easily be interchanged with one another.

In Southern Nigeria — "When I was five, all those things which used to be childish play turned into real and earnest activities," wrote a "Nigerian Teacher," a girl from the south. "My mother would make me draw two or more potfuls of water every morning from a river about half a mile from home. She would make me sweep the inside rooms and the house premises, make fire to warm the soup and to prepare the breakfast of either cooked yams eaten with palm-oil or porridge eaten with beans or soup. After this, I might start to weave clothes, or spin cotton wool into thread, or draw water for my mother to mix her dyeing materials. While mother was busy mixing them, I sometimes carried my younger brother or sister on my back or on my shoulders, far away from mother to allow her to get on with her work. By this time I had learned a good many of our native songs and dances, and these proved very useful when younger children were carried away by their elder sisters to play. We usually formed circles and squares with the children from other houses and we played native games, sang songs, beat drums, and danced a lot.

"My mother had one special trade which provided for our needs more than any other, and that was *gari* making, which is still today one of the staple foods at home. . . . I liked very much to carry it out to sell because of the money we got for it and because it was really a good opportunity for me to walk far from home, have free discussions with my customers and friends.

"I was useful, too, to my father. I sometimes helped him plant his new crops, like cotton, beans and yams. When crops were ripe, I often joined my other sisters and their mothers to help him harvest them and carry some to the market to sell. Always we had great joy on coming back from the market to hand over our one shilling or one shilling and sixpence to our father to add to his wealth, because all took him to be a rich and big man. At times we went as a group to the farm to make palm-oil for father. . . . Each time we went to help our father harvest crops, small quantities were given to us at the close of the work as our reward for the faithful work done. With the exception of these rewards from our father, he no longer undertook any other responsibilities for us girls. Each woman had to bring up her children single-handed from her own scanty resources. The grandfathers and grandmothers usually told us folklores in the evening, especially when the moon was shining. We often sat round the storyteller. He or she usually led the song in the story but all joined in to sing the choruses. Moral lessons to teach the cultural beliefs were given to both boys and girls."

In Buganda—"The main occupation of women in Buganda was the growing of food and its preparation," is the recollection of M. B. Nsimbi, a man from that area. This "included fetching water and collecting firewood from forests or bushes. . . . A woman, even if she was the only wife in a house, was expected to feed all the people in her home. . . . In Buganda it is considered ill-bred for a woman to say in front of her husband that she is hungry. The other major occupations of the woman were to look after the children; to make baskets used for food and other things; and to cut grass for thatching new and old houses. They also cut a different kind of grass known as *tteete* for spreading on the floors of houses. . . .

"Wives of the ordinary peasants spent any spare time they had during the day in visiting and talking to their women friends in their neighborhood. The best time for the women was at night after supper about 7 : 00. They would collect in one home with the children and start telling traditional stories and legends and they would play riddles. Some of these stories required the group to move to and from one friend to another. Storytelling by women and children lasted until late in the night. This is how the children learned about the traditions, customs and fables of their country."

In Northern Nigeria—"In the morning when the sun got up, our mothers would rise and start cooking bean cakes and we would go round the village selling them," recalls Baba of Karo, a Muslim woman from northern Nigeria. "When we had sold them we came back and mother gave us some grain to grind. She did a lot and we did a little. We sang our songs at the door of her hut; as we were grinding away, one would start the song and the others would answer.

"We brothers and sisters all lived in our mother's hut and at night we would tell stories and talk. When day came we got up and washed our faces, we made porridge and we made millet balls. When we were able to make porridge and pound grain in the mortar and grind it on the stone, we used to tell mother to sit down and we would do it for her. My mother and her co-wife spun thread for sale, made millet balls, brancakes, groundnut cakes, roasted salted groundnuts, fried groundnuts and groundnut oil—they sold them all. The wives used to make porridge and stew for their husbands, they made it very tasty with meat. Boys follow their fathers, they learn to farm and recite the Koran; girls follow their mothers, they spin and cook. . . . After the morning meal, if mother had things to sell we went to market and sold them for her. When you had sold everything you went back home with your cowries and your mother counted them — that's all till tomorrow! She hid them in a cooking pot and if you saw something you wanted she would buy it and give it to you. My mother was a secluded wife. She didn't leave the compound. If we sold our wares quickly we came back home at once; if they didn't sell we brought them home at night and gave them to the children to eat. When we came home they would be making millet balls or porridge or bean cakes steamed in leaves or whatever was wanted for the evening meal. We were given a little grinding to do, we were learning. Then at night we would play and dance and sing our song."

In Guinea—"In the morning, when, after some persuasion, we rose, we would find breakfast all ready. My mother used to get up at dawn to prepare it," a Guinean man, Camara Laye, recollects. "We would squat round the great steaming platters: my parents, sisters, brothers, and the apprentices, those who shared my bed as well as those who had their own hut. There would be one dish for the men and another for my mother and my sisters.

"My father presided over the meal. Nevertheless, it was my mother's presence that made itself felt first of all. Was that because she had prepared the food? Maybe. But there was something else: my mother, by the mere fact of her presence, and even though she was not seated immediately in front of the men's dish, saw to it that everything was done according to her own set of rules: and those rules were strict. . . .

"In our country, the woman's role is one of fundamental independence; she has great personal pride. We despise only those who allow themselves to be despised; and our women very seldom give cause for that. My father would never have dreamed of despising anyone, least of all my mother. He had the greatest respect for her, and so did our friends and neighbors."

Whether Ibo, Hausa, Buganda or Mandingo, the daily routines of these women were governed by common social patterns: the subordinate position of the woman in caring for her husband and her children; the distinct duties assigned to every member of the household beginning at a very early age; the responsibility of the woman for the good conduct and early teaching of her children; the specific education of girls in domestic duties by their mothers; the closeness between mother and child. Even in urbanized and apparently Westernized societies African women still suffer from shyness and show the reserve expected of them in traditional settings. Hugh and Mabel Smythe note that wives of prominent men have little preparation for the new and strange functions they must perform. "Foreign visitors in the home marvel at the speed with which wives fade into the background after being introduced, leaving refreshments to be served by stewards.

"The wives of the non-Muslim elite at the very top may be better educated, somewhat traveled, and more experienced; thus, they are better able to adapt themselves to their husbands' new positions."

But in general, "the wife in the elite home leads a relatively traditional personal life with her husband. She attends the children, remains outwardly reserved, and (except in the North) goes out to social affairs because her husband's work requires it, through it all remaining a shadow beside her husband, rather than a person of substance in her own right."

Need for Change—Educated African women believe the mental and social restrictions under which their sisters live are not acceptable in today's world. At the First Congress of West African Women, in 1959, the delegates who are the pace setters for women throughout the continent supported Mali's Minister of Commerce when he said:

"The independent African woman should not be only for the purpose of giving birth and keeping the house; she should be the companion of men in all instances, she should share our efforts and our sorrows, and create with us the true conditions for our emancipation."

And the delegate from Senegal concluded, "The woman's place has always been in the background. Forgotten, of much less standing in the concert of nations than men, women carry with them the tradition and the future of the country. In a revolutionary Africa we women must become aware of our responsibilities, both with the family and socially. For this, we ask the reevaluation of our position and our participation in the life and progress of our people in a free, united and happy Africa."

Less militantly but with the same conviction, the Uganda Council of Women expressed the change in the African women's outlook on life and her place in it. "Nowadays, women are more conscious of themselves as people who have needs and ideas of their own that they wish to express; they want to become true partners in marriage; they hope for more equal companionship with their husband; they hope to share in making plans for the family; they want to bring up their child to be a happy and responsible member of the community; they want to live in good houses, cook good food; send their children to school, they want to improve their own knowledge by going to clubs and classes."

It is unlikely that the African woman will ever need to engage in emancipation movements like those experienced in the United States and Europe. The strength of social movements which embrace her may ultimately make the African woman's participation in community life more genuine, complete, and influential than anything her American counterpart has yet achieved.

Marriage and Sex Life

Despite endless variations in tribal custom, four characteristics are common to all traditional African marriages: they are polygamous; they are sealed by a marriage payment; they constitute social contracts between two kinship groups; and their chief aim is procreation.

Polygamy—Polygamy has its roots in the social and economic demands of African societies. More wives mean a more bountiful harvest. And the surplus wealth from the harvest is "invested" in additional wives. Since rich and poor live much alike, a man's success is judged by the number of his wives. The wives share the benefits of his prestige, and enjoy the security of his household.

The "Bride Price"—The terms of the bride price vary, but traditionally the bridegroom offers goods and/or services to the bride's kin. Some scholars suggest that the bride price constitutes compensation to the bride's family for losing one of its members. More likely it seals the alliance between the two contracting families and acts as insurance for the protection of the wife as well as for the stability of the marriage.

Marriage as a Family Alliance—The traditional African marriage is basically an alliance between families and only secondarily a union of two individuals. Marriage is a business transaction, a contract with assumed specific rights and obligations of the parties. It is a major means of strengthening the clan and the clan's relationships with other groups. Once married, a woman remains with her husband's tribe and even as a widow she expects to marry her husband's kin. The single woman is so foreign to some tribes that their language has no word for her.

Childbearing—To bear children, many children, is not merely a joy but also a duty of a woman. One reason for the great emphasis on many children is that of every ten babies born, three to five die in infancy, and of those who survive no more than half reach adulthood. Therefore, a barren woman is a misfortune and her clan is obliged to supply a new wife, or, in some cases, she is given a relative's child to rear as her own.

Premarital Standards—Traditionally, therefore, marriage is the goal of every young girl and her entire education is focused on preparing for it. Some tribes have institutionalized premarital relations designed to educate both partners or serve as trial marriages. But even where virginity is not considered important, there is often a strong feeling against unsanctioned conception—that is to say, conception which occurs before marriage, or, alternatively, before the appropriate puberty rites have been performed. The latter case is often regarded as more serious. The rules of premarital relations seldom allow complete freedom, but provide, instead, a clearly circumscribed pattern of sex behavior.

Extramarital Relations—Restrictions against extramarital relations are rare, perhaps because under the traditional polygamous marriage system there was no need for them. Some tribes even regard adultery as a way of providing a legal issue to an impotent husband; whereas in others a woman may have a lover if he abides by the rule of offering his services to her husband. Where prostitution does occur, particularly among the women traders who travel long distances from market to market, the money gained is considered a legitimate supplement to their commercial earnings.

Divorce—Running away seems a favorite female technique for initiating a divorce. Without breach of the law, a woman can leave a man she no longer loves or of whom she is genuinely afraid. In some instances, she may provoke him to take the initiative by refusing to cook and clean and by quarreling with him. He will then send her home, the usual method of terminating a union.

Generally, however, marriages are expected to last, and families will try to patch up difficulties especially if the break is not sanctioned. Termination of the marriage is official and final when the woman's family returns the marriage payment. Sanctioned reasons for divorce on either side are: the wife is barren or chronically ill; the wife commits adultery regularly and outside the customary rules; the wife is quarrelsome and neglects her duties; the husband is impotent; the husband beats his wife excessively; the husband is too old; either partner has leprosy; either partner is mentally deranged; or, there is a violent dislike on either side.

THE BEGINNING OF CHANGE

Christianity—With the arrival of Christian missionaries the traditional system sustained its first direct attack. Polygamy was immediately and vehemently denounced. Official action in promoting the Christian ideal of marriage has never waivered even though the missionaries understood the function of polygamy in indigenous marriage systems. Therefore, when conversions might otherwise have been rapid and sincere, Christian opposition to polygamy created a difficult obstacle. No early missionary could fancy polygamy as anything but an uncivilized institution, and he often regarded himself as the primary civilizing agent. In 1910, the World Missionary Conference at Edinburgh termed polygamy "one of the gross evils of heathen societies which, like habitual murder and slavery, must at all costs be ended."

This policy of destroying the old cultural pattern and substituting a new one irrespective of whether it could be woven into the remainder of the social fabric or harmonized with existing beliefs and institutions, gradually gave way in the twentieth century to a new policy of reinforcing those customs which were compatible with the Christian ideal. But neither posture could solve the problems of plural marriage, an institution which many converts wished to continue, or of church membership for converts living in polygamous households. Missions tried to substitute the Christian ideal of purity and individualism for tribal morality and solidarity. However, religious sanctions remained ineffective against illegitimacy, infidelity, and excess marriage payments, because there were no effective social sanctions, no outraged public opinion, to support them. Thoughtful church-men agree that the Christian concept of marriage will be accepted only when industrialization and urbanization impose supporting values on the society. Unfortunately, urbanization and the change it stimulates also create social arrangements that are still contrary to the Christian ideal.

Polygamy and its alternatives—Polygamy remains a durable institution in spite of the resistance of the Christian Church. Among the Central Lagos families of Nigeria, one half of the Muslim men, and one fifth of those who described themselves as Christian, have more than one wife. In both groups, the number of wives tends to increase in relation to income. The men also claim that polygamy has a practical and moral advantage. Because it is traditionally wrong to have sexual relations with a woman from the onset of pregnancy until the child is weaned at two years, the husband should not be expected to remain celibate for such a long time. Furthermore, the wife might go home to wean the baby or she may be a trader and away from home for a long period, and thus, without a second wife the man would have no one to keep house for him.

Men, who prefer to maintain monogamous marriages, or single men can now find alternative sexual relationships with concubines or prostitutes. The unmarried men in Sierra Leone's capital of Freetown often have "sweethearts" who live with them temporarily and fill the role of wife. These women, like those who live in the Kisenyi district of Kampala, Uganda, may have relations with a group of men and can change these relationships as they please. In the Poto-Poto section of Brazzaville (Congo), women are scarce and well aware of their value. Most of the unmarried young girls prefer concubinage. They will prepare meals and give sexual service in return for an agreed sum of money and occasional gifts. Men who cannot afford this arrangement resort to prostitutes.

Sometimes the reputation for high living scares marriageable men away from the concubines and prostitutes, and there has been an increasing number of unmarried mothers. But marriage is possible for them if they appear to be good homemakers.

Most educated women resent polygamy and male philandering. One Nigerian woman, Mrs. A. Manuwa, was provoked to remark, "Polygamy is a thing that is taken for granted in our part of the world. But, of course, not with educated people. The husbands of all the Nigerian ladies that you see here have only one wife. Of course, men are naughty, but you are not sup-posed to see that." It is this sense of moral outrage which will undermine polygamy and help institutionalize new standards of behavior.

Attack Upon Marriage As Group-Alliance—Nowhere is the change more apparent than among young people. Couples prefer a partnership where the husband helps with the household tasks and the wife contributes to the family budget. Peter Marris reports that "in the households interviewed,

many young husbands not only provided their wives with a means of livelihood, but gave or lent them additional capital, bought them clothes, added
pocket money to their incomes. They helped with the housework, cleaning
or washing, cooking or looking after the children when their wives were
busy. . . . The wives, in return, helped to meet the housekeeping bills, lent
money to their husbands, or even maintained them altogether when their
business was going badly. In marriages like this, husbands and wives are
partners, rather than parties to a contract where each limits responsibility
for the affairs of the household."

Other women have gone further than just looking for partners, and
have elected to marry men outside their tribe. In the social survey of
Sekondi-Takoradi (Ghana), 30 per cent of the marriages sampled were intertribal. This percentage occurred in Lagos, Nigeria, too. Furthermore, many
older women, notably those who have found employment, prefer not to remarry within the tribe after their husbands' deaths, but maintain themselves
on their own income.

The endeavor to attain greater independence from family authority has
manifested itself in other ways. Young men want to choose their spouses
and consequently have accepted the responsibility of raising their own
marriage payments. Fathers, on the other hand, have recognized a weakening of the alliance system and demand sometimes excessive rates for their
daughters. Add to this the expense of wedding costs, and the groom's family
must either go into debt or the young man must postpone the marriage.

Marriage Ordinances—Some countries have passed legal limits on the
amount of the marriage payment, but only Mali has legislated a comprehensive marriage law binding for all marriages. However, the new law enacted
by the Mali National Assembly in February 1962, caused such confusion
and alarm that the President had to hold a series of public meetings to
explain the law and its social significance. The Minister of Justice also went
to the public with the following points: under the former system a girl
could be abused by parents, or a wife by her husband; the new law was
enacted to correct this; the Code, although a civil ordinance, is generally
inspired by the Koran and Muslim jurisprudence. It sets a low legal limit on
the marriage payments. It allows a girl to marry at fifteen years with the
consent of her parents and at nineteen without their consent. It provides
that both parties sign a contract before marriage which binds them to either
a monogamous or polygamous union, but the husband can change the
monogamous contract with the consent of his wife. He is, as in traditional
Muslim law, limited to four wives, each of whom must be properly cared
for. The marriage can only be dissolved by a legal divorce, and the grounds
for divorce are contained in the Code.

A government action of this kind, missionary resistance to polygamy
and the marriage payment, urbanization, and industrialization each con-

tributes to the decline of traditional marriage customs. The emphasis on procreation still survives almost intact, but parents increasingly face the choice between a higher standard of living and many children. Polygamy has withstood the frontal attacks upon it, but in urban areas it tends to take the form of illicit unions. The marriage payment is fast losing its traditional significance as a seal between two families, and the inflated prices have only brought disrepute on it. With these basic components under attack, marriage as a bond between two kinship groups has greatly weakened, and with it the very basis of the traditional social system has begun to crumble.

EDUCATION

Traditional African education emphasized the preparation of girls for womanhood. This kind of training had a strong sexual content and also stressed the skills that would make a girl a better wife and housekeeper.

Content of Traditional Training—Teaching covered child care, cooking, the art of trading, as well as proper conduct, and the lore of the clan. Much of this training was an informal, day-to-day process, although some of the women's societies undertook to instruct their junior members when they reached marriageable age.

Sister Marie-André du Sacré Coeur, who spent nineteen years in West Africa, says, "African mothers teach their daughters how to grow the staple foods and the indispensable ingredients that go with them. . . . The woman who makes millet beer, vegetable butter, soap, or pottery, teaches her daughter the technique of these crafts, takes her along to the different markets, and entrusts to her care her little brothers and sisters. These responsibilities, assumed at a tender age, plus the example of courage, endurance and devotion she sees and admires in her mother, all go to fashion the mentality of the young African girl and form the basis of her moral training. Meanwhile, she is also being taught the rules of good breeding, the social customs of the tribe, and respect for the chiefs and older people, whom she must obey on all occasions."

Initiation Ceremonies and Schools—In the initiation ceremonies girls demonstrate their fitness to assume the role of wives and mothers. "What is taught in the initiation schools," according to George H. T. Kimble, "is, in most cases, less important than the manner of teaching. By the age of puberty there is probably not much that any cult-school teacher can tell the initiates, boys or girls, about the customs of their tribe or its history. What is deemed important is that the initiates should come to look back upon their days and nights of testing in the cult school as the climactic experience of their adolescence. To this end, everything that wit and cunning contrivance can do to heighten the drama of the occasion is done."

Secret societies among the Mende, as reported by the Ottenbergs, fulfill four functions: they provide a general education in social and vocational training, the regulation of sexual conduct, the supervision of political and economic affairs, and the operation of various social services. The schools of the Sande societies for girls are the most vivid and intensive educational examples that are recognized as such in the community. Training is imparted through symbolism, endurance tests, and practical instruction in sex matters, homemaking, crafts, child care, and social attitudes and virtues. During the graduation procession a special medicine is carried to foster womanly character and virtue and to cleanse and purify old members who have fallen short of the society's goals.

The Humoi society is as important as the Sande, for it regulates sexual conduct and personal hygiene for the community at large. The head of the Humoi is traditionally a woman and the senior positions in it are held by hereditary right by members of certain families. Women who led the Humoi were often in positions of great influence in the community.

Because life in traditional societies was centered in the struggle for livelihood and in a web of family relationships, the training through the age sets, cult groups and parents emphasized obedience, endurance, and cooperation in a recognized unit; correct behavior toward equals, superiors, and inferiors; and the acquisition of farming, housekeeping, and craft skills. The periodic rituals came to a climax with the initiation rite at puberty when a child received instruction in sexual intercourse, sex hygiene, and sexual behavior in general.

Modern Education for Girls—Until recently modern education eliminated all sexual education, and with it education in social behavior. The praise songs, fables, dances, and music of all kinds are now being reintroduced into school curriculums. But the lore and legends of the clan, its history and genealogy and the relationships among the various social groupings have no place in a school system that must unite all tribes.

Instead, modern education emphasizes ideas of individual choice and responsibility, loyalty to country before clan, and technical skills which have no relation to the maintenance of the clan. African parents regarded these ideas as dangerous and the skills useless for girls.

Problems of Female Education—Indeed, the subordinate status of women and the preoccupation with their homemaking and childbearing roles have been the two factors most hindering the acceptance of modern education for girls in traditional societies.

In Uganda, according to L. A. J. Maleche, "Many ignorant parents neither understand nor appreciate the meaning of or the need for education. They argue that school will make girls discontented and immoral, and, therefore, less willing to undergo the heavy labour in the field or the domestic drudgery which is their normal lot in life. Where the custom of bride wealth is strong, and this is so in most parts of Uganda, parents prefer marriage to schooling for their daughters.

"Ignorance and outright poverty in many homes combine to hamper the education of girls. Evidence of this is seen in the demand made on the child's time. For example, children are still withdrawn from school to help in the garden and the home as mother substitutes to nurse babies, clean the house, fetch firewood and water, cook food, and milk cows. Many girls, already exhausted from early morning work, leave for school on empty stomachs and may walk up to ten miles to school. At school there is often no midday meal. After school the girl has to walk back home, do her daily duties in the home before she gets her evening meal. . . ."

This attitude is not limited to Ugandan parents. The percentage of female primary school enrollment varies from as low as 8.0 in Mauritania to 35.9 in Nigeria, although in the Lagos area the percentage is as high as 46.4. Secondary-school percentages of female enrollment range from zero, according to United Nations figures, to 33.3 in Senegal.

Other reasons for this disparity between education for boys and for girls are lack of money; lack of buildings, equipment, and women teachers; curriculums unsuited to the needs of girls, particularly those who begin late; lack of employment opportunities, and a shortage of women teachers whose presence will reassure parents of the moral safety of their adolescent daughters.

Even in those countries where education is free, sending children to school often involves the purchase of textbooks, exercise books, pencils and uniforms. Other costs involve transportation, or room and board in distant schools. The biggest cost, however, is tuition, which runs between $25 and $100 a school year at the secondary level. If parents cannot meet these expenses, it is usually the girl, regardless of her ability, who is sacrificed for the sake of the boys' education.

Finally, most curriculums are designed for young children, but many girls enter school as late as at the age of ten. Moreover, the curriculum is not geared to the interests and the future of either the older students or of those students who will complete only eight years of education. A more practical and less classical approach might be more useful. All these reasons limit the enrollment of girls and add to the high attrition on the secondary level.

Trends in Adult Education—There are, on the other hand, factors bringing girls into the educational stream. Not the least of these are the adult education programs aimed at mothers. Generally, the curriculum includes reading, writing, simple arithmetic, child care, nutrition, homemaking skills, farming methods and instruction in the government's development goals.

Most of these mass education schemes are initiated through Departments of Social Welfare or Community Development. In some cases, the departments have worked through traditional women's societies. Sierra Leone reports that the natural leaders, such as women chiefs and heads of women's secret societies, are showing growing interest in family and child-welfare services and now include in their initiation camps some teachings in modern child-care methods and home improvement techniques. Sierra Leone works also through clubs formed by the Social Welfare Department. By 1954, there were nineteen branches of the Women's Institute, all but one initiated and financed by the Department. These clubs often take on a life of their own and are able to engage in the joint purchase of sewing materials, acquisition of equipment, sale of products, and the operation of bank accounts. They also become a recognized part of the community's social life and function as a group in local ceremonies and collective community efforts.

In Uganda, where there were no traditional women's societies, the Ministry of Community Development formed its own rural women's clubs. The Economic Commission for Africa reported that by 1960 the club membership numbered over 24,000. Eleven full-time officers and assistant officers with a junior staff, assisted by approximately 200 leaders, served over 1,000 clubs whose motto is: Good wives, good mothers, good citizens.

To trace the evolution of these clubs is an instructive exercise. For they can become powerful instruments not only for the emancipation of women, but also for the successful execution of government development plans. Ghana's program provides a typical example.

Beginning in 1948, the program emphasized literacy in the vernacular. Classes were organized entirely on a voluntary basis, and backstopped by voluntary leaders and village literacy committees. During this first stage, wherever a staff of women was available, village groups were formed to receive regular instruction in sewing, nutrition, child care, and hygiene, These women's groups were invariably involved in the literacy classes.

The second stage occurred when the community, encouraged by the staff, wanted to improve its environment. The voluntary leaders began to enjoy their new status, and the two groups, the literacy class and the women's group decided to institutionalize themselves. The literacy committee then expanded its functions and became the development committee. This committee was responsible, with staff guidance, for the organization of communal labor. The women's group either worked with the men or, if they had a dynamic leader, they worked as a group with special responsibilities, such as collecting sand and stones.

During the third phase, the program concentrated on the election and training of voluntary village leaders who could continue the work in the absence of the staff officer. Efforts were made to select dynamic and committed women for a three month training period given at a national center under a senior training officer.

Trends in Formal Education—This concerted effort to change the attitudes and aspirations of adults has meant expanding educational opportunities for daughters. Many parents now regard the education of their daughters as an investment in the advancement of the family. Many working girls are contributing to the school fees of younger brothers and sisters as well as to the general support of the family. Other parents see education as a means of raising the marital prospects of their daughters and of receiving higher marriage payments. The latter may range from £5 for an illiterate, to £150 for a literate, girl. Educated young men prefer girls who can be companions to them, can entertain their friends and appear with them at social gatherings. The ambitious man knows that a wife with social poise is an asset to his career, and the parents know that an education is the best insurance for their daughter and the family.

Demands on African educational systems are, therefore, increasing. For many countries education is the largest single public expenditure frequently reaching 25 per cent of the national budget. Some of this money will go for curriculum revisions, which more adequately reflect the needs of girls, and staffing and housing arrangements more acceptable to African parents. Governments are well aware that the female half of their human resources has been underutilized, and they are now taking steps to train women and girls for their modern roles. The Final Report (1961) of the United Nations Conference on the Development of Education in Africa, signed by thirty-nine states, stated: "The need is urgent for the increased use of educated 'women power' in the working life of the community in such callings as nursing, social work and teaching. Increasing attention in school curricula and in adult education must be given to child care and domestic science. Most urgent is the need to develop a new conception of the role of women in the life of the community—to improve their condition as homemakers, to expand their opportunities of employment, to encourage a greater participation and leadership by women in community affairs and public life. To meet this goal an expansion and reform of education for girls is required."

EMPLOYMENT AND PROPERTY

Under traditional conditions, the occupations of men and women are clearly defined. Women engage in those activities most essential to the maintenance of the home, and, except for farming, these activities are by and large controlled by them. Three features characterize the economic life of women: to a greater or lesser degree all women are agriculturists; many of them practice some craft or trade; and they sell the produce of their labor or their services in the marketplace.

Women in Agriculture—Agriculture is Africa's wealth and her poverty. In no other sector of the economy is there such room for growth, and yet 80 per cent of the continent's agriculture is subsistence. Generally, men perform the more arduous tasks of bush clearing, fence building, tree felling, and plowing, while the women sow, cultivate, and harvest the crops. Their tool is a short-handled hoe that requires backbreaking work. Millet, most root crops, and sometimes corn are grown by the women. Any small amount left over from home consumption is hers to sell.

In Southern Nigeria, where yams are the staple crop, the woman cultivator has a special interest in such subsidiary crops as pumpkins, cassava, groundnuts, beans, and pepper. These are planted to provide the relish dishes into which mush or porridge is dipped. A wife's success is measured by her ability to vary the diet from her garden. There is, in the African bush, a variety of edible wild plants, roots, mushrooms, and fruits. Parties of women collecting these in the appropriate seasons are a familiar sight. Women also keep livestock—goats, chickens, cattle, pigs—except among the pastoral tribes, where wealth is determined by livestock and belongs exclusively to the men. Pastoral women, therefore, exercise relatively less influence than farm women. The severity of the farm labor is a mark of their importance in the economic system, and their ability to market surplus crops provides an opportunity for them to acquire property of their own.

Sale of Handicrafts—Property can also be acquired through the sale of handicrafts. A craft is handed down from mother to child and its secrets are jealously guarded by the family. All the crafts are associated with the home-making activities of the women, but girls are taught the family skill primarily to give them a source of income. Often the sale of handicrafts is combined with farming, but in the case of the many urbanized Yoruba (Nigeria), the women spend most of their time in town trading and only travel to the farms at harvest.

In traditional Yoruba society the upbringing of a girl is calculated to give her a means of earning her livelihood. She is considered fit to marry only after she has acquired a craft or learned to trade. She starts her apprenticeship very early, either with her mother or with a guardian. Usually she is taught the family craft—weaving, potting, mat-making, or trading—as well as cooking and farming. Emphasis is laid on her ability to produce cash. The woman without a craft or trade, who is wholly dependent on the husband, is rare and often regarded with contempt.

Midwifery, Hairdressing and the Sale of Beer—Two other traditional occupations are hairdressing and midwifery. Hairdressing can be an elaborate process involving conditioners, straightening irons, and difficult styles to set. There is good money in the business, but nothing near the prestige enjoyed by midwives, whose authority stems from the importance of pro-creation in African society and their knowledge of matters of hygiene.

The sale and brewing of many varieties of alcoholic drink has always been a popular occupation of women. In the Kisenyi district of Kampala, Uganda, three quarters of the beer sellers are women. Those successful enough are often able to build houses for themselves and to increase their wealth by letting rooms. No other occupation there rivals beer-selling for income, but women also sell mats, plaintains, buns, or charcoal in the marketplace.

Women as Traders—Market places in Africa are like department stores in the United States. They are a woman's world, the center of communica-tions, the hub of society. In smaller communities the marketplaces open twice a week in a clearing around a prominent tree or in a location con-venient to the surrounding villages. In the large daily markets women display their wares from permanent stalls, before their houses, or from atop their heads as they hawk trays of goods through the streets. Here traders sell foodstuffs, cooked and raw, textiles, pottery and utensils, canned goods, provisions. Except for the economic contribution they make as cultivators, the African women's most significant economic impact has been in trade. In Nigeria, for example, market women control 66 per cent of the country's trade, and, as the 1960 census indicated, 77 per cent of the work-ing women listed themselves as traders. Of those in Central Lagos, about one-half work at home and an additional 20 per cent hawk their wares as well. Some women are wholesalers and exporters, but most depend on the small sales from their stalls and stands set up in front of their houses. Profits generally run between 2 and 5 per cent. To attract and keep steady customers, everyone extends credit and time payments. Even the large traders, who may turn over £5,000 of business a month, have little cash available, and their chief asset is access to short-term credit. Therefore, most stocks have to be sold quickly.

The chain of middlemen is probably the most efficient means of dis-tributing goods in such a highly competitive market. The market is like a pyramid with a few importers at the top who sell to the wholesalers on credit. The latter sell to retailers who in turn may sell to petty traders. This means that a single item may pass through four or five hands. The system will change only when more dealers can afford to tie up their capital in stocks for longer times.

Since a woman's trade is so important to her, it often gets more atten-tion than her home. She may be away from home for weeks and months at a time buying and selling. Women coming from smaller towns to major market centers will usually collect several orders before they make the trip. They will purchase for their clients on commission, and also buy other goods they can sell at home.

Reasons for Trading—The marketplace is never dull, and the opportunity of meeting people and getting out of the house proves attractive even to those women who work to make ends meet. Others work because they value the economic independence which has been traditionally theirs. But many women prefer trading to farming and will buy food for themselves and their children rather than grow it. Otherwise they spend their income on clothes, jewelry, and other luxuries, on a house or other real estate, and the more prosperous, on a trip to Mecca. A few West African women are wealthy enough to invest in a bus or truck, and occasionally they parlay their business into a fleet.

Even in the Muslim areas women are expected to trade. In Zaria, Northern Nigeria, women are responsible for their daughters' dowries, make their contribution to their sons' marriage payments, provide their own cooking utensils, the children's clothes, and their own ornaments. Trading is carried on through the men of the family or the unmarried daughters. But Hausa women may leave purdah after menopause to trade in the marketplace. Here trade usually takes the form of exchanging agricultural goods harvested from their own plots or from a specified portion of the husband's plot. Some women sell special delicacies they cook, or the household utensils and furnishings crafted by their household.

Women's Property Rights. A Hausa woman's purchases from her own resources, and the items produced by her own hand, are hers. Although the man may dispose of her property, he would not do so without her consent, and some men may be financially dependent on their wives.

Among the Yoruba, the man will give his bride a lump sum of money to capitalize her business. In theory, if she grows rich he can claim a share. In fact, however, the money belongs to her and she can use it to acquire property, expand her business, or assist her husband as she chooses. Hausa custom makes a clear distinction between the property of man and wife, and in some households members buy and sell goods even among themselves. Some wives will not lend to husbands without a definite arrangement for repayment. Although generally African women cannot acquire farm land except by allocation from the husband, land systems among the Ganda in Uganda and the Akan in Ghana allow women to acquire and hold land in their own right. However, women do not generally share equally in the succession of property, although specific items, such as household utensils, are customarily reserved for them.

Women do suffer economic and legal disabilities, but it would be incorrect to conclude that their importance in the economic life of the community is overlooked. Traditionally, African women are expected by men and by themselves to work as part of their contribution to the maintenance of the household and family. Labor is shared between man and wife, and generally the income from her trade and the produce of her plot are recognized as her own.

Changing Economic Role of Women—However, the traditional partnership between man and wife has been subject to considerable strain under present-day urban conditions. When women, whose primary occupation had been farming, followed their husbands to the city, their traditional role altered. Their lack of education barred them from the urban labor market, and the lack of land prevented their customary economic activity. They were, therefore, forced to depend on their husbands for support and thus lost their independence. Even when unskilled jobs, such as those of shop assistants and domestics, were open to them, husbands were reluctant to have their wives work for a strange man.

In Kisenyi, Gutkind and Southall observed that "since African wage employment began on the basis of migrant male labor, the towns have always been full of men, and the first women to town were inevitably the prostitutes. This has colored the African attitude toward women in town ever since. Town women, it is felt, are bad women, and they are to be used for pleasure but not to be married. All women who work for wages tend to be put into this category. The good woman, according to this set of ideas, is the one who stays at home in her husband's room, refuses to speak to strangers and remains unprofitably idle except for the performance of the domestic chores which, in view of African eating habits and the paucity of housing accommodations in town, are extremely light. There is practically no cultivation, no collection and carrying of firewood, and water is often reasonably near. Yet rarely has anything more profitable taken the place of this 'toil.' "

This description is less true of West African towns where the habit of trading is an integral part of a woman's life. But even in West Africa village parents strongly object to their unmarried daughters living in towns. There are few housing facilities for single girls, so most live with relatives. But urban housing is already overcrowded and hardly satisfactory for even the closest relatives.

Even married women face barriers which retard their employment opportunities. Girls tend to marry young and have many babies. An employer willing to train a worker and advance her according to the normal criteria is hampered in doing so by her frequent absences. For this reason, some employers will not hire women under twenty-five.

These women, by then responsible for a family, are concerned about adequate day care centers for the children. Traditionally, a mother took her children with her to the field or left them in the communal care of the village. But in the cities, the relatives of working women may also work, and even if they do not, they may live too far away.

Mainly, the employment of African women is hindered by their lack of education. There is a growing shortage of skilled workers particularly in schools, hospitals, institutions, transport, and government service, all job categories that require some formal education. Governments are trying to fill the shortage by establishing vocational training centers to teach dress-making, typing, and stenography, domestic service and hotel service (chambermaids and waitresses).

New Employment Opportunities for Women—Unskilled work under-taken by women wage earners is mainly seasonal. In the Ivory Coast cocoa, and Uganda cotton plantations, women work as weeders and help harvest the crop. They are usually paid by the day and are often wives of men em-ployed in nonagricultural work, particularly manufacturing industries. The number of women employed in manufacturing or service activities is com-paratively greater in areas where economic expansion and city growth have gone the farthest. Factory work, however, does not appeal to women and many of the unskilled operations are mechanized. Furthermore, trade is often much more remunerative and will be even more so as their marketing cooperatives get established. There are dyers' cooperatives in Dahomey, dry cleaning, launderette, and refrigeration cooperatives in Nigeria and Ghana.

As civil service and business posts are "Africanized," men move to posi-tions heretofore unavailable to them. Opportunities for greater upward mobility make men less concerned with lower job categories, and women are moving into positions of office workers, domestic servants, shop assis-tants, and laboratory assistants. They are found also in other skilled and semiskilled jobs, such as radio announcers and program assistants, X-ray technicians, hairdressers and beauticians, agricultural officers, journalists, social workers, policewomen, librarians, and pharmacists. In Ghana nearly all the telephone operators are women, and every West African paper has its women's editor. The few girls who reach the university are attracted to social work, the legal and medical professions, and, above all, teaching and nursing.

PUBLIC LIFE

One of the most fascinating tales to come out of Africa is that of a remote interior kingdom ruled by a queen whose chief ambition was the destruction of all men. She commanded an immense army of Amazons who were so ferocious and skilled in arms that no enemy could withstand them. Her kingdom, although never located, was reported to be extensive and ever growing under her ruthless rule. She killed most of her enemies, except those of great physical excellence, who were allowed to live and breed new warriors for her ranks. The female offspring were nurtured carefully, but the male children were either cooked and eaten, or crushed and their dried remains converted into amulets.

The Legendary Amazons—The single element of truth in this gruesome story is that a corps of women warriors did exist in an African country. The Amazon Corps of Dahomey may have been organized as early as the 1700's and was well established by the middle of the nineteenth century. Following the French occupation, however, it dwindled and disappeared, although women still have dances commemorating Amazon exploits.

The women in the King's household were divided into four groups: wives, Amazons, female slaves, and older women. Legally, the Amazons were considered the king's wives but he did not use them as such because they were unattractive. They were expected to remain virgin, and men were punished by death if caught with an Amazon. The Amazons spoke of themselves as men and under the military organization they were paired with males of equal rank. They took pride in competing with men and did so skillfully. Recruits for the corps were selected from among the young girls, and the king chose the officers from the most promising of these. The rest were soldiers or were returned to their parents. Estimates of their number ranged from 4,000 to 10,000.

Women as Chiefs, Administrators and Arbiters—Nor were the Amazons the only women in the kingdom's public life. The system of internal taxation was based on control exercised by the king through the women of his household. Each ranking functionary was "controlled" by a woman in the palace. That is, she was charged with keeping track of his accounts and with checking her independent reports with his. She acted as the king's personal advisor on matters affecting the functionary she "controlled." These women were themselves "controlled" by other women, eight of whom were always with the king and present to hear all the accounts and reports. In case of a dispute on any testimony, their judgment was final. Two other groups fulfilled the same function before lesser chiefs and priests.

The authority of the chiefs and priests rested on their role as intermediaries between the living and the dead. This was a role not unlike that of the Queen Mother among the Akan tribes. Although she was called "mother" and she was constitutionally regarded as the chief's mother, she was usually his sister. Her official title was "Ihemma" or female monarch. She had the right and the obligation to scold the chief and was responsible for his good conduct. She was consulted in matrimonial matters of the royal family and she had her own "stool," elders, and spokesmen. She used to be a member of the chief's court and received a share of the court fines and fees. She did not control all the women of the state (each lineage had its own senior women), but when the men went to war, she, as head of the royal lineage, superintended rites of the women in praying for victory and their safe return.

A number of societies even permit women chiefs. Women from leading Mende families in Sierra Leone are to this day eligible to hold public offices such as that of Town Chief. They are responsible for settling local disputes, finding housing for strangers, and collecting taxes or tributes for the Section Chief. The head wife or sister of a Paramount Chief may be made a Section Chief, and in a number of instances women have become Paramount Chiefs. The Paramount Chief leads a state with a population of 5,000 to 20,000. Elevation is by recommendation of the old chief and approval of the people.

Elsewhere in Senegal, among the Wolof, a woman could succeed the chief. Otherwise, the head of the women in the kingdom was usually the chief's mother or sister. She had a number of dependent villages which cultivated her farms and paid tribute to her. She had her personal entourage and her own court concerned with women's matters.

Women's Associations—Women also engaged in public life through various associations. Yoruba women held positions in the governing bodies of their communities by virtue of their leadership in craft guilds. All the crafts were organized into guilds with a recognized head. These guilds were often represented in the State Council, the highest judicial body of the chiefdom. Other women's organizations existed for social reasons yet their strength made them potent political forces. One prime example was the Aba rioting instigated by Eastern Nigeria's Ibo women in 1923.

The main cause of the riots was the belief that the government intended to tax the women. The trouble began in Owerri Province where a warrant chief under instruction from the District Commissioner was making a re-assessment of the taxable wealth of the people. In doing so he attempted a census of the women and children, and a count of their domestic animals as well as those belonging to the men. Rumor spread, and after one of the women was asked to count her goats and sheep, a meeting of all the women was immediately called. By the time the women arrived at the District Commissioner's, the group had grown to 10,000. The women were not convinced by his reassurances, and by the second week in December the disturbances had spread to Aba. Here a crowd of equal size looted European shops and released prisoners from the jail. After two days the crowds were dispersed but unrest spread again to the Calabar region. In the two days of demonstrations there, fifty persons were killed and fifty wounded. Throughout the entire disturbance the solidarity of the women never wavered, and a subsequent inquiry revealed the vigor and conviction with which they organized their opposition.

The success of this operation was undoubtedly due in no small measure to the existence of the women's associations among the Ibo. They were organized by towns and led by women chosen for their wisdom rather than seniority or wealth. The association existed to solve women's problems and where no formal means were available for them to gain their ends, the members would resort to strikes, ridicule, and cursing. On the other hand, members were subject to the discipline of the association and decisions of the group were enforced by ridicule, ostracism, and even destruction of property.

Right of Suffrage and to Hold Public Office — Although these examples suggest that women were not altogether barred from participation in public life, and indeed held positions of considerable responsibility in several societies, they were at a disadvantage in comparison with men. And they still are. Today, however, few serious public officials or politicians would deny women equal rights. The nationalist slogan of "One Man, One Vote" has been interpreted to mean women too.

Sekou Touré, President of Guinea, spoke of the emancipation of women as essential to the realization of the revolution and of independence: "If we question ourselves objectively about what was the hardest thing for us to bear under foreign domination, we must give pride of place to the permanent constraint, the perpetual subordination . . . the constant disrespect. . . . Can we now bring the same subordination to bear on our sisters, our wives, our daughters? Can we now treat them with the same contempt?" His position is a matter of public policy in nearly every African state. Universal adult suffrage and the right to hold public office were written into the constitutions of all the West African independent states, even the predominantly Muslim ones, except for Niger, Mali, and the Northern Region of Nigeria. The Ghana government has gone a step further by reserving ten seats for women in the National Assembly which were filled on June 27, 1960. Such an unusual provision is in keeping with Ghana's pioneering position. As early as 1954, Mabel Dove became the first woman to be elected to the Gold Coast Legislative Council.

Influence of Church Associations — Women in high public office are still few, however. But many able women are associated with voluntary organizations and constitute a reservoir for the future. In Sekondi-Takoradi, Ghana, about one third of the population are members of religious organizations, most of which represent a branch of the Christian faith. Although they have been attracted by the social and educational aspects of membership, the Christian church in Africa has placed great stress on Christian obligations to the community. Every parish has its mothers' guild, and most women begin their voluntary activities through association with church mothers' clubs. For this reason, and because of their freedom from purdah, it is the Christian women in Northern Nigeria who are active in community affairs and voluntary associations like the Girl Guides and the Red Cross. Muslim women have not had the same encouragement, but several organizations now exist among them in Southern Nigeria.

Types of Voluntary Associations — Voluntary associations can be divided into five categories: village women's clubs, often under the direction of Departments of Social Welfare; community-initiated self-help and self-improvement societies; trade associations; international organizations; and national umbrella organizations which attempt to include all the women's groups in their membership.

In Uganda, where village women's clubs have had a substantial impact on community improvement, A. R. G. Prosser noted, "It is a common thing now to see a house on a shamba complete with proper ventilation, bathroom, deep-pit latrine, plastered walls and floors, sun tables for the drying of kitchen equipment and an efficient mud stove in the kitchen; the farm itself well laid out with banana plantations, properly mulched, and a flourishing vegetable garden, the front of the house probably adorned by flowering shrubs and a flower garden. The results are indeed impressive; up to date thousands of shambas have been improved in this manner, and when the women put into effect the lessons learnt at the clubs, then a tremendous leap forward in family living is observed."

Trade Associations—Trade Associations are organized by craft or product and apparently united by their common market place. Besides being organized for purely economic reasons, the market women belong to benevolent societies that are primarily money-saving plans. If one member is in trouble, others help her out. They have regular meetings and collections. And, occasionally, these groups contribute to a community institution such as a hospital. Little is known of the market women's organizations, but their importance in West African societies warrants thorough study.

Community Groups—Self-help and community-improvement groups are usually organized around common interests. Nigeria, for example, has been a fertile soil for such groups. The Lagos Women's League, organized in 1936, petitioned the governor to increase the number of openings for women in the civil service. Over twenty years ago the Ladies Progressive Club, open to women who had completed secondary school, began its long career of community service by raising money for worthy causes and scholarships for outstanding girls. Recently the Kaduna Women's Club, the Ibadan Women's Improvement Society, and the Isa Ba Deen Muslim Women's Society were organized. The first is interested in home and family improvement, the second in running a day nursery, and the third in building a Muslim girls secondary school in Ibadan. A recent count of the National Council of Nigerian Women listed over 500 voluntary women's groups.

International Organizations—The most active international voluntary women's organizations in Africa are the Young Women's Christian Association, the Girl Guides, and various church-related groups. Other organizations (such as the Business and Professional Women's Clubs, Associations of University Women) are embryonic. The World Association of Girl Guides and Girl Scouts has chapters in the Central African Republic, Chad, Congo (Brazzaville), Dahomey, Gabon, Gambia, Ghana, Ivory Coast, Liberia, Mauritania, Nigeria, Senegal, Sierra Leone, Togo, Uganda, Upper Volta, and thirteen other African countries, with a membership of nearly 20,000. Through the Brownie and Guide system these branches train girls in good character and citizenship. But the community as opposed to family orientation of the Scout pledge, the basis for all Guiding, has caused some conflicts for the members. At the All Africa Conference held in Uganda in 1961, delegates pointed out the difficulties of adapting foreign institutions to the African scene, but were nonetheless firm in their support of the Guide Principles.

This difficulty is less severe for the Young Women's Christian Associations. The YWCA has tried to remain nonracial and nonsectarian and to some extent has succeeded. Indeed, one of its organizing secretaries in Eastern Nigeria is a Muslim. The YWCA program includes homemaking and first-aid classes, agricultural and typewriting classes, and the setting up of residences for single girls in urban areas. The first YWCA activity began in Sierra Leone in 1855. Today, through the Mutual Service program of the World YWCA, there are Association activities in Ghana, Nigeria, Liberia, Uganda, Cameroons, Dahomey, Ivory Coast, Senegal, Togo, Rhodesia, Zambia, Kenya, Tanzania, Ethiopia, and Malagasy.

Role of Voluntary Groups in Public Life—The contributions of voluntary organizations like the YWCA and the Girl Guides were recognized by the 1960 Seminar on the Participation of Women in Public Life held in Addis Ababa, Ethiopia. At the end of the debate on the role of the voluntary organization in expanding the participation of African Women in public life, the *rapporteur* drew the following conclusions:

1) The activities of voluntary organizations are important factors in increasing the participation of women in public life. Among such activities, which promote the welfare of the community are:
   a) financial and other assistance to the poor, the aged, the physically handicapped, and the mentally retarded;
   b) establishment of shelters for unmarried mothers and abandoned children;
   c) establishment of social centers to provide mental and physical recreation for women;
   d) establishment of day nurseries for children of working mothers;
   e) establishment of centers for family and child guidance;
   f) action to overcome racial, cultural, and language barriers which impede the unity of the community.
2) National voluntary associations should attempt to meet the standards required for affiliation with international organizations. The information, experience, and technical assistance given by international organizations are valuable aids in carrying out effective programs on a national basis.

3) Voluntary organizations should co-ordinate their programs in order to avoid wasteful duplication of efforts.
4) Voluntary associations can promote international goodwill and understanding by initiating regional and international study programs, exchange tours, and regional conferences.

Women's Federations—Finally, the national umbrella organizations, those which incorporate all women's groups into a single federation, are of two kinds: those which are dominated by the controlling, national political party, and those which have managed to retain their independence. Generally, these organizations are the ones which represent the women at official international conferences. Since African unity is a major public issue, the different points of view inherent in the two positions have caused some difficulty. Party-controlled organizations are inclined to be more political in orientation, independent organizations more concerned with social services.

The choice facing African women today is whether to keep their organizations free from politics and concerned with social problems and the status of women, or to take advantage of government support to achieve their social goals and at the same time function as part of the political structure. The tradition of independent organization and international affiliation and the prevalence of diverse political views within each African country are important factors in determining the decisions African women will make. No clear trend is yet visible, partly because African women's organizations are still embryonic, and partly because the women themselves are still debating this issue.

Conclusion

Even this cursory survey should reinforce the notion that general statements about African women are unwise and usually inaccurate, for they cannot faithfully describe the varied situations in which African women find themselves. The African way of life ranges through the whole spectrum of social change—from societies of ancient origin to a contemporary blending of this traditional culture and modern technology. To speak of the illiterate villager without speaking of the young university graduate would be to ignore the dynamics of the continent today. Even when discussing the traditional way of life, the widely travelled market woman and the queen mother are as much a part of the total picture as the Muslim woman living secluded behind her compound wall, and the girl-child who is betrothed before she reaches puberty.

Because Africa contains such a variety of contrary experiences, today's feminine elite have a substantial foundation from which to influence those customary practices which they regard as discriminatory and unjust. In their efforts they are aided by a revitalized Christian church, urbanization and industrialization, and the penetrating political philosophy of nationalism. The mainstream of world events no longer bypasses Africa, and she is the single underdeveloped continent most pre-occupied with the present and most optimistic about the future.

BIBLIOGRAPHY

Baba of Karo, see Smith, Mary.

Economic Commission for Africa, *Uganda Statement on Family and Child Care Services*, Accra: International Conference of Social Work (1960).

Gutkind, Peter and Aiden Southall, *Townsmen in the Making*, Kampala: East African Institute of Social Research (1957), p. 60.

Kimble, George H. T., *Tropical Africa*, Vol. II, New York: The Twentieth Century Fund (1960), p. 16.

Kouassigan, Guy, and Marie Sivomey, *Background Paper* U.N. Lomé, Togo: Seminar on the Status of Women in Family Law. Aug. 18–31 (1964).

Laye, Camara, *The African Child*, London: Fontana Books (1954), pp. 56–58.

Maleche, A. J., *Sociological and Psychological Factors Favouring and Hindering the Education of African Women in Uganda*. Kampala, Uganda: East African Institute of Social Research (1962), pp. 5–6.

Manuwa, Mrs. A., "The Family in Nigeria." Tel Aviv: International Seminar on the Role of Women in a Developing Society, Ministry of Foreign Affairs, p. 156.

Marie-André du Sacré Coeur, in *African Women Speak*, Maryknoll, New York: Office of UN Affairs, National Catholic Welfare Conference, Report No. 26, World Horizon Reports (1960), pp. 11 12.

Marris, Peter, *Family and Social Change in an African City*, Evanston: Northwestern University Press (1960), pp. 48, 54–55.

Moore, J. Aduke, "The Sphere and Influence of Women in Africa," *Journal of Human Relations*, Spring and Summer (1960).

"Nigerian Teacher," "Growing Up in Nigeria," in *African Women*, June 1958, pp. 73–75.

Nsimbi, M. B., "Village Life and Customs in Buganda," *African Women*, Dec. 1956, pp. 4–5.

Ogunsheye, Adetowun F., "The Women of Nigeria," *Presence Africaine*, Vols. 4–5, p. 39.

Ottenberg, Simon and Phoebe, *Cultures and Societies of Africa*, New York: Random House (1961), p. 200.

Prosser, A. R. G., *The Role of Women in Community Development with Particular Reference to West and East Africa* (mimeographed), New York: Economic Commission for Africa (1960), p. 14.

Seminar on the Participation of Women in Public Life, New York: United Nations (1960), p. 25.

Smith, Mary, *Baba of Karo*, London: Faber and Faber (1954), p. 24.

Smythe, Hugh and Mabel, *The New Nigerian Elite*, Stanford: Stanford University Press (1960), pp. 95–96.

Touré, Sekou, "Toward Full Re-Africanization," *Présence Africaine*, Paris (1959), pp. 70–73.

United Nations Economic Commission for Africa, *Final Report: Conference of African States on the Development of Education in Africa*. Paris: UNESCO (1961), p. 6.

Burma and South-East Asia

By Mi Mi Khaing

THE TRADITIONAL SITUATION

*W*omen *have long been* as active as men (often more active) in the economic life of the community, acquiring property, retaining their claim to it in marriage, sure of legal redress if marriage arrangements proved unfair, and inheriting family property equally with men.

These traditional female rights were an integral part of the old local Buddhist culture, but how they were exercised was determined by a basic concept of that culture; namely, that man is endowed with greater spiritual potential than is woman. This view does not hamper any of the woman's material or financial interests, but it does limit her in other areas.

Restraints are not rigid. For example, there are no places to which a woman cannot go—pagodas, monasteries, bazaars, theaters, law courts— she visits them all. But once inside a pagoda, although worshipping as men do, with no line of demarcation, every woman knows that in placing her offerings at the shrine, she should keep from brushing the image quite as closely as her male companions. Yet, if a service needed to be rendered for the image, and no male were present, a woman would not be transgressing if she performed it.

TOWN AND COUNTRY

Southeast Asia is predominantly a rural society, and even the towns-people are slow to alter the fabric of their village background or change their customary behavior. Nevertheless, urban life has successfully thrust one or two wedges between the townswoman and the village woman.

First, the number of communal festivities is greatly reduced in the towns. This has made women more self-conscious in their manner toward men, in contrast to the traditional free behavior in the villages. This is as true of Thailand as of Burma.

Second, women's occupations are a differentiating factor. In the villages, women's activities make them partners in the family fields, oil press, or cottage crafts. They drive the bullock cart, plant the rice paddy, help to reap it, winnow the grain, and sell the produce, sharing the necessary tasks as strength or convenience dictated.

In the town, however, the woman does not share in the man's salaried job. In Thailand especially, the townswoman is far more restricted to her household affairs than her village counterpart. But in Burma, where women engage in more economic activity, she merely shifts occupations. The urban wife engages in independent work, such as cheroot rolling and food hawk-ing in the poorer sections, or brokerage or shopkeeping in the richer ones. This does not, however, alter the relationship between man and wife, mother and children, which remains the same as among the village people.

LEGAL STATUS

In Burma, as the outcome of its development as an independent nation, women's traditional claims to equal legal consideration with men were formally incorporated in the Constitution which marked Burma's emer-gence as a modern state and which affirms: "All citizens, irrespective of birth, religion, sex or race, are equal before the law. . . . Women shall be entitled to the same pay as that received by men in respect to similar work."

In South Vietnam, however, until the Family Law Bill was passed in 1958, woman was classed, in Madame Ngo Dinh Nhu's words, "in the category of infants and the insane; she was a minor—an incompetent." From that deplorable position she has advanced legally further than any other Southeast Asian woman, for, to quote Madame Nhu again, "today she enjoys all the rights until now reserved for her husband, and this equality of rights carries with it no loopholes or tricks as it does in other countries." Marriage, concubinage, legitimacy of children, financial matters, including even bank accounts, are provided for.

In Thailand, the changeover from an absolute to a constitutional monarchy in 1931 was accompanied by an exhibition of broadmindedness regarding women's rights which, as Madame Pibul Songram declared in a public address, "I cannot help admiring." The new Thai Constitution provides for equality in all respects between men and women.

EDUCATION

In Burma, greater educational opportunities for women came about not because of a drive to raise feminine standards in particular, but because the change in national conditions automatically offered greater opportunities to all. Formerly, schools were rare in rural areas. Monasteries filled the need, but their basic educational aim was the preparation of boys for their novitiate, and the teachers were the monks themselves. The 1931 census showed, not surprisingly, only 3,356 female to 175,506 male pupils in "private primary institutions," which then meant mostly monastic schools. In "public primary" schools in the same year, however, girls numbered 136,553 and boys 165,649. Since independence, the government has opened several thousand new schools all over the country. By 1953, females constituted 37.9 per cent of the total literate population. The gap which this figure still shows should be further narrowed as public schools reach the remoter rural areas.

In the postwar period throughout Southeast Asia, the number of women studying in institutions of higher learning has greatly increased as well as those in educational extension programs. This, too, is due, not so much to a sudden emancipation of women as to a general quickening of the people's interest subsequent to obtaining nationhood, to the throwing open of windows to the modern world after long years of colonial seclusion, and, not least, to the rise in the cost of living which makes women eager to equip themselves to earn a regular income should the need arise.

SOCIAL LIFE AND DRESS

In the midst of new intellectual and professional pursuits Burmese women have retained their traditional dress and their manner toward men. This behavior pattern is part of the traditional elder-younger, man-woman, parent-child, pupil-teacher, monk-donor relationships. But while the circumstances of modern life have loosened the other relationships, toned down deferences, modified acceptances, they have had very little effect on the concept of desirable feminine behavior.

Girls, for example, attend coeducational schools as a matter of course, but they do not play with the boys during recess. They do not go out alone at any time. Although those who are so inclined wear shorts, participate in school sports, and may even play football, no sooner do they change back into ordinary clothes than they resume the modest demeanor which allows no lounging, no thrusting out of feet, no getting close to male friends, no touching even their own male relatives familiarly.

Among adults, too, although there is much mixing and a high degree of social ease between male and female members of friendly families in their outings, segregation is still the rule at any public gathering. It is a light rule, with no strict boundaries between male and female sections; men and women group themselves in two ends of the same room perhaps, and a few of both sexes feel free to mix in small groups. This traditional pattern has survived into the present, transplanted from the community's religio-social feasts to official parties with international guests.

Thai women at first sight present a very different picture from the Burmese with their rapid adoption in recent times of the "highest" Western fashions—short, narrow skirts, high-heeled pointed shoes, and waved hair. But in actual fact, their manners and relationships with men in their own lives, away from the presence of Westerners, are very much in keeping with Thai traditions. These require more deference and graceful attentiveness toward men than does the traditional Burmese etiquette.

For some years, groups of people in numerous small towns of Burma were swept by a fervor for one highly publicized institution of the West —the beauty contest. Hardly a day passed but newspapers carried, to the annoyance of many, pictures of Miss Gangaw, perhaps, or Miss Yamethin, in swimsuit and high clogs, mounted on a stand with the ribbon of victory. Following the revolution of March 2, 1962, however, despite urgent problems of rebels and of blackmarket operators, and while hastening measures of national urgency, the government paused to take care of one trifling task. It banned these contests, with the terse explanation that they offended Burmese tradition.

MARRIAGE

Burmese Buddhist law, though not actually Buddhist, is so called because it is observed by the people of Burma who are Buddhists. Since about the fifth century A.D., Indian Buddhists entering Burma as a golden land to settle in brought over their modifications of Hindu law. Buddhism was embraced by the people of Burma, and the law, further modified by influences from the customary laws of the Burmese people, came to be the law of the land, whose rules govern marriage, inheritance, and property rights for more than 85 per cent of the people.

A Civil Contract—Marriage for Burmese Buddhists has no religious character. It is a purely civil contract between two parties. For the marriage to be valid, these two parties must, first of all, be of age, which means that the man needs only to have attained puberty, but the girl, unless she has the consent of her parents or guardians, must be twenty years old. A widow or divorcee, however, may marry at any age. The two parties must also be mentally competent to contract; their kinship to each other must be such that their union does not offend the sentiment of the community; they must give their mutual and free consent to becoming man and wife; and there must be consummation. As for "dowry," true Burmese tradition, still adhered to in the rural and hill regions where Buddhist influence is stronger, requires the groom or his parents to offer gold, jewelry, or a set of clothing when asking for the bride's hand.

Though parental consent is necessary, a minor cannot be forced into a marriage against his or her will. Prohibited degrees of relationship are left to the sentiment of the community, which as a rule, frowns upon marriage between cousins born of two siblings of the same sex. Marriage between a man and his deceased wife's younger sister is common, but marriage with a deceased brother's widow or a deceased wife's elder sister is disapproved of.

Arranged Marriages — As marriage approaches, any time after a girl is seventeen, Burmese parents remember one of the five basic duties of parenthood — settling the child into a suitable matrimonial arrangement. In carrying out this duty, more and more parents are relying on the greater fluidity of modern life and the greater opportunities their daughters have in colleges or at work to meet desirable partners. Where, in spite of such facilities, a girl still fails to find a suitable partner in time, the traditional method of arranging is resorted to, even among the most modernized families, not only by parents but by friends and solicitous elder sisters, without the girl herself having any sense of failure.

Elopement — Parents rarely impose a harsh decision upon an unwilling girl. This was true even in former times. A girl who was unwilling to follow the parental lead did so usually because she had her own preference. Elopements are extremely common, not because parents are unyielding, but because the observance of filial obedience in this matter is still too customary to bear public flouting by a marriage contracted in cool deliberation without parental approval. It is rare that an elopement is not soon followed by a reconciliation which makes everything proper. Recognition by parents and a few reputable elders before whom the couple bow down in respect constitutes an established marriage.

The Marriage Ceremony — As to the marriage ceremony, though in some cases it is not regarded as essential to the validity of marriage, it is customary between parties marrying for the first time to have an assembly of elders and some sort of entertainment of friends as evidence of the wedding, which usually takes place in the bride's house. It is customary also for the newly-wed couple to go to pagodas together, and to visit and receive friends together. As for choice of residence, the law rules that when the husband is able to live separately from his parents, the wife is not bound to live in the same house with them; convenience decides the rest.

Plurality of Wives—Polyandry is never permitted, but polygyny is. But though this right of the man is recognized by the old law books and still prevails here and there in Burma, there is a strong feeling against the practice. On the whole, Burmese Buddhists are monogamous, rather than polygamous, by inclination.

In cases where more than one wife is taken, the law clarifies their positions. A man may give his wives equal status, and they will then be known as superior wives or wives proper. He may, on the other hand, differentiate between them. In that case, the wife who lives on terms of equality with him is endowed with proprietary and personal rights, takes part in the husband's business and contributes to the acquisition of property, and is considered the superior wife; the other, an inferior wife. Clandestine relations do not constitute marriage. A marriage is established by reputation, and there must be some body of neighbors to witness that a man and his lesser wife live regularly together in a manner that will cause the community to treat them as man and wife.

Having taken a second wife, a man cannot force his chief wife to live in the same house with her. A woman, however, who marries a man knowing that he already has a wife cannot refuse to live in the same house with her. Actually, it is extremely rare for two or more wives to live with the husband in the same house.

Divorce—Marriage is easily dissolved between Burmese Buddhists if there is mutual consent, yet divorces are rarer in Burma than in many other countries. A divorce based on mutual consent must have some formal expression; angry letters and hasty rejoinders will not suffice to establish it. If there is no mutual consent, neither party can divorce the other without some matrimonial fault on the latter's part, even if he or she is willing to surrender joint property or to pay compensation.

Matrimonial faults include misconduct, cruelty, desertion, and misrepresentation. Misconduct usually means adultery. Adultery on a wife's part entitles a husband to sue for divorce; but if the husband takes another wife without her consent, she has the right, except in certain cases, to divorce, if she does so within a couple of months after her husband's new marriage. She cannot object to her husband's second marriage if she has produced no children after eight years of married life; she has given birth to eight daughters in succession and has no son; her children died in infancy; she is suffering from a severe disease, such as leprosy, insanity, or epilepsy; and she breaks the customary rules of conduct and shows no love for her husband. Cruelty as grounds for divorce includes mental as well as physical mistreatment. Desertion as defined differs for a man and a woman. A wife who has no affection for her husband and deserts him for one year, during which time she receives no maintenance from him, is considered as having deserted her husband. Before a wife can sue for desertion, however, the husband must be shown to have deserted her for three years without supporting her or communicating with her. Misrepresentation as grounds for divorce means that one of the parties was induced by misrepresentation to marry.

THE WOMAN'S POSITION IN THE FAMILY

Property Rights—In Burma it has long been customary for the wife to acquire property, and Burmese wives have definite property rights.

During marriage, property is regarded as belonging equally to husband and wife, though the husband is deemed to be the manager of the family. The names of husband and wife (the wife does not change her name on marrying) are often coupled in business affairs; documents are often drawn up in their joint names; they sue jointly; and they are in turn often sued together by their adversaries. When the husband's and the wife's wishes about the disposal of property do not coincide, or if a marriage is being dissolved, the types of property owned by the couple must be differentiated.

First, there is the *payin*, or property of either spouse before marriage, which he or she continues to control. A husband must not dispose of his wife's payin property without her consent. And though he can so dispose of his own payin property, he cannot give it to his concubine. Then there is *lettetpwa*, or joint property, which accrues from the exertions of one spouse alone, or is inherited by one spouse alone after marriage. Of this, the spouse who acquires or inherits it is entitled to two thirds and the other to one third. There is also *hnapazon*, property which accrues during marriage by common efforts or from produce of property already held. This belongs to both, and neither party can confiscate the other's share.

Effect of Divorce upon Property—In a divorce, division of property is based on (1) whether the divorce is by mutual consent or for some matrimonial fault; (2) whether the parties have both been married before, or whether only one or neither has been previously married; (3) whether one party brought much property into the marriage and the other little or none, or one alone acquired or inherited property during marriage.

When division is by mutual consent, the husband and wife each takes back his or her payin property and they divide the joint property equally. But where they stand in supporter and dependent relationship, the supporter gets only two thirds of his original payin property, and the dependent gets one third; and the same applies to the joint property acquired during marriage.

When there is a matrimonial fault on the part of one party, however, cases are judged on their merits, and the guilty spouse may either get the shares as described, or may have to forfeit his share in joint property, or even his or her own original payin property.

In a divorce by mutual consent, the children are generally given to the parent of the same sex, but decisions are often modified to safeguard their interests.

Inheritance—A Burmese Buddhist cannot make a will. His property must be inherited according to Burmese Buddhist laws. The general principle behind these laws is that inheritance shall not ascend when it can descend, and that the nearer by blood shall exclude the more remote. These principles establish the following order of priority of inheritance:

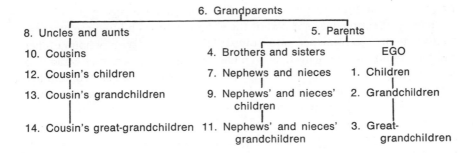

The table does not contain Ego's spouse. If there are no children, or if the children are all minors at the time of Ego's death, the spouse, whether male or female, succeeds to the whole estate including the right of the deceased to a share in an undivided ancestral estate. This, however, does not apply if there is among the children one whom the law calls an *orasa*, a first-born, legitimate child, either son or daughter, who has attained majority and is competent to undertake the responsibilities of a parent of the same sex. If the first born dies or becomes incompetent before attaining majority, the next eldest son or daughter becomes orasa. The orasa's privilege is that he or she may, upon the death of the parent of the same sex, claim a quarter share of the parental estate from the surviving parent of the opposite sex. If, however, the orasa is of the sex of the surviving parent he or she cannot press the claim as long as the widowed parent does not remarry. When both parents are dead, all children get equal shares regardless of sex or age. An adopted child has claims if he or she can be shown on community evidence to have been adopted with a view to receiving inheritance rights along with the other care which parents usually give their own children.

It will be seen from the foregoing that the laws of marital rights recognize very little difference between men and woman, while the laws governing property rights are equal for both sexes.

HOME LIFE

The wife, rather than her mother-in-law, has always been the main source of inspiration in the home. Although ultimate authority resides unquestionably in the man, it is she who most often handles the finances, all earnings being handed over to her. Modern life, however, has tended to decrease the number of families where this is still true. The growth of urbanism, with its shops, cafés, clubs, and cinemas, makes it increasingly necessary for a man to handle money constantly.

In the moral sphere of the family, despite her lesser spiritual status, a woman has full authority over sons and younger male relations, age taking precedence over sex in this respect. She can command them unhesitatingly, only taking care not to insult their manhood in doing it.

Family affection does not permit the widow, whose children are married, to live alone. Convenience and compatibility decide with whom of her married children she will live. Whichever home she chooses, tradition defines the contribution she makes there, for she is considered to have attained, by this time, the status of one who has by good fortune arrived at the third stage in human life.

The Three Stages of Life—Every person's life is thought of as divided into three stages. The first, from birth to about the age of twenty-five, is that of learning and is spent in a receptive attitude toward parents and teachers. The second stage is that of striving to acquire sufficient property to enable one to discharge adequately one's duties as a parent and as a Buddhist. The third stage comes when one can, and indeed should, cease from preoccupation with acquisition, and give ample time to religious works and to meditation on the peace that comes with detachment from a world which one must soon leave.

The time an older woman spends in such spiritual exercises, in preoccupation with the family altar, or in giving religious instruction to the children, is an active contribution to the household of her daughter or son. In a land where the practice of religion is so strong that not even the gayest young couple feels easy if altar duties are skimped, the presence of the older woman with her beneficent aura of meritorious old age is welcome indeed. "You are lucky having an old person in the house" is as common a compliment as "You are fortunate in having such a nice view" would be elsewhere. Tradition ensures, at the same time, that this older person should not wish to join in activities where consideration for her might mar the boisterousness of the occasion.

The Home Routine—For full feminine existence, one might envy the life led by the well-to-do Burmese wife. She rises early, and makes offerings to the altar with fruit and rice cooked by a servant who has risen before her. After a light breakfast with the family, she changes the altar flowers and water, or going into the kitchen, looks through the basket of the cook just returned from the bazaar. She might mix a dish or two to keep her hand in, and do light kitchen tasks while someone else does the heavy work. The children are sent off to school after a meal which includes one cooked dish. Then husband and wife will have their full curry and rice meal in time for him to go to the office.

She can, after this, potter around making pickles or picking the chaff from a tray of dried shrimp. She can read or visit or rest until about noon, when she will bathe and dress to look her best. Then she might go out to do some casual business, selling gems or handloomed materials, or visit the cheroot-rolling unit she has set up, either on the grounds of her house or close by. One afternoon she might attend some neighborhood affair (described later).

She will be back, replenished in spirit or in pocket, by the time her husband returns home. She attends to his needs and those of the children, does some gardening, or sees that a fresh pot of soup, rice, and a new lot of vegetables are prepared to supplement the main dishes from the morning meal. Dinner is early. Visitors might drop in later to chat, with the children listening and cuddling close.

By nine o'clock she will have said her prayers, meditated in front of the altar, seen her children to bed, and locked up her house. Then she is able to sleep, looking forward to another such day. This is the pattern of life also for the average poorer woman, except that she usually has relatives to help, not servants, and she engages in other occupations to earn money.

WOMEN'S OCCUPATIONS

Education was predicated upon the assumption that should it become necessary for a woman to earn a living, she would take one of the few fixed types of jobs for which this education was a training. It was assumed that the small bits of business, carried out with such enterprise and enjoyment in time spared from homemaking, were only for those women who have not had the benefit of education or professional training.

Even less fortunate are those women who, too poor to save up any capital and too insecure to chance living from the yield of the fields, work as unskilled labor on buildings or in small factory jobs which, in the last two decades, have offered steady though small wages.

For these two groups of women, the described home routine is largely lost. They must compress their early morning duties at altar and kitchen (they rarely omit them altogether) and give up their community work to a large extent. But their evenings still follow the same pattern, and their marital relationship is not thrown out of balance by being earning partners, for this was the old way too. There is no question of the husband's sharing household duties; the wife carries on with the help of an extra relative or servant, or shoulders the additional workload herself.

Home versus Career—The earning activity of a wife is still so new in many countries that women's papers often dwell on the effects of their work on home life. In Burma, too, a magazine modeled on the women's journals of the modern world recently debated the same questions, such as: Should women choose one hundred per cent home without career? Which should come first, home or career? Does a career, by offering a woman outside interests, interfere with her role as wife and mother?

The author's reply follows, in part. "Most of the problems are, fortunately, not ones Burmese women usually have to face. They are, no doubt being raised in view of the transition to a modern society that we are undergoing, still in its very early stages. But let us look at our lucky compatriots who are still following the old Burmese style for a wife.

"Here, in my town, Mrs. A is making extra money and finding interests outside the house by selling Mogok gems in tiny packets which, when she goes visiting, she extracts from her bodice pocket, tight against her waist. Mrs. B is achieving the same results with a small knitting machine on which she makes sweaters for sale. Mrs. C makes mango pickles and marian preserves, also wrapped *Kyaukchaw* jelly which she sends to the local schools by modest hundreds. Mrs. D, with a more aesthetic touch, sells cut gerberas, rare rose plants, and delicious ice cream to people who call at her house for them.

"But these are the activities of ladies interested only in small exertions. Mrs. E, on the other hand, has built a smithy beside her house and finances her goldsmith cousin and two apprentices. Mrs. F lends money at 30 per cent interest per annum while holding gold or land deeds (nothing less sure will do) as security for her loans. Mrs. G has a *longyi* shop in her sitting room because her cousins in the village twenty miles away have looms and send her regular stocks of *longyis*. Mrs. H has a thriving timber business in the downstairs of her house. In the downstairs of Mrs. I's house, on the other hand, a bevy of cheroot rollers roll away like mad because she pays by the thousand cheroots rolled. In none of these activities are the husbands of the good ladies involved, having office or other jobs that keep them busy enough.

"But the real point about all these ladies is that while you and I are rushing off to get to that desk or beat that schoolbell, they are placidly tidying their clothes, supervising aromatic meals in the kitchen, or preparing offerings to their altars. While we are still hard at work with perhaps a slight headache or a consuming hunger for lunch, they have brunched, rested, bathed, put *thanakha* cream on their faces, and emerged fresh and ready for their smithy, their cheroot rollers, or their gem clientele. And on the day following, they might well decide to let such venal things lie, and instead, emerge, equally fresh and good, to contribute toward some worthy community project for which they win much esteem.

"That is the real Burmese way, and in this progressive town of present-day Burma with its population of 40,000 a large majority of wives still carry on in this way, only differing in the scale of operations. We poor 10 per cent or so not only have the worse life; we pay carefully calculated income tax on the pittances we earn.

"Another aspect of women's earning activities at this particular stage in Burmese society occurs to me. Our nation has awakened only since Independence to trade and manufacture. This means that, unlike established urban societies with factories and chain stores filled with enticing mass-produced cheap goods, it is still open to anyone with enterprise, energy, and imagination to make money in commerce of some sort or another. And in all this surge of economic activity, women, with their ancient genius and experience in broking gems, silk, cheroots, and pickles, have played a large part, naturally. In a report on Joint Venture Corporations some-time ago, the corporation which made the highest profit was the one with an all-woman Board of Directors!

"But is not all such big business absorbing all a woman's energies, taking her away from home, husband, etcetera? Well, you know the generous attitude of our men to which I referred when I spoke of the advantages of according them a revered place, of deferring to their higher spiritual status. The generosity extends to this sphere, too.

"But our deference to men's spiritual superiority is not the only factor making for tolerance on their part. This being Burma, with no such things as budgets, savings accounts, or set allowances for this and that expenditure within the family, the wife usually takes the easy line and runs the house out of her earnings. She might sometimes ask for all of her husband's pay to buy jewelry (which is still our biggest form of investment, and as such desired by both husband and wife), but if she does not do so, then the husband has all his pay to spend.

"How often have I seen such a fond husband, on his way to the office, leaning against a shelf in the shop, showing an interest in the family's money mine! Big officials some of them, they don't mind a bit helping with rush orders, or chasing around in their spare time to push through their wives' applications and other paper work. And then there are our nice easy ways which don't make any shop or office strictly a place of business. If a wife's job takes her all day and she has to lunch out, it will be behind the showcase, on that big divan, and if the husband comes along, the meal will be laid out with his favorite dishes, and he can even stretch out after it, instead of driving back to the residential suburbs for his lunch-hour rest. Such a husband doesn't need to regard the business as a rival; it is an extension of his home and comforts."

Working Women in Thailand — In Thailand, the effect on the home of women going out to work is greater because Thai women, more than Burmese, have made an art of homekeeping. They take pride in the artistic preparation of fruits and flowers for altar and table, and scrub their homes incessantly, while Burmese women have made a prosaic job of the home and gone forth more to participate in outside life.

Occupational Choices — In all these countries, especially in Burma, marriage is still the first career aimed at. Hence, though there has been a woman ambassador, and women have occupied positions in all walks of life, including high academic posts, the armed forces, politics, journalism, company administration, and the like, very little regard is paid to this as a point of pride. The particular women holding high posts are worthy of them as individuals; it is a coincidence that they are free from marital ties and thus can fill these posts, and their success is not necessarily a victory of feminism.

While postwar developments in the economy and in society have widened the number of occupations open to women, there has been no change in the principles governing their choice, with primary emphasis on the more pleasant and physically lighter jobs. In 1931, for every 1,000 men there were 2,794 women in textiles; 1,915 women hawkers of food; 1,064 women raising small animals; and 962 women working in hotels and cafés. But in tanning hides, for example, there were only 197, and in mining ore 48 women to 1,000 men. Recent statistics still show the same proportions. Among transport workers in the rural areas there were only 4 men to 1 woman (probably driving carts), but in town there were 108 men to 1 woman (driving motors, too). Although retail sales and related occupations show more women than men, managerial and administrative occupations still show far more men. It is the traditionally "higher" spiritual status of men which qualifies them for such jobs of prestige and authority as government administration, whereas the inclination of women is to shrink from such onerous calls on their strength.

SOCIAL LIFE

Burmese families do little Western-style formal entertaining. Social occasions are either totally intimate and unplanned, or communal in spirit, embracing social enjoyment, religious observance, and community welfare all in one. Such get-togethers include all the people in the neighborhood, without discrimination, even if having a party on such a scale means that one can have it only rarely. Each household plays host in turn, the poorer ones joining resources. On these occasions, monks are feasted and given offerings, while they, in turn, give sermons or recite sacred verses. In such a celebration, a great many people must help the host and hostess to buy, cook, serve, decorate, and receive. This is real community work performed by women, because these parties mean a great deal of free entertainment for the poor, who mingle on equal terms with the others, join in with the chores, eat their fill, and share in the sense of well-being and merit acquired.

Some women's duties toward society include attendance at divorce arbitrations and at bethrothal and marriage ceremonies, not merely as social functions, but in order to give the event a recognized status for which the presence of elders is both necessary and sufficient.

Organized Social Work — This large force of busy women playing a prominent part in Burmese society is a traditional development; it is not organized, but stems from the structure of society itself. As to deliberate and highly organized social work done by women, Burma has nothing to compare to women's efforts in South Vietnam, for example. Having secured for women all the rights needed to make them equal citizens with men, these women founded a nationwide organization called the Women's Solidarity Movement. This organization aimed at penetrating to the hamlet level in order to contact all women living within the area and bring them assistance as needed. It set up kindergartens, dispensaries, orphanages, home economics courses, and other such much needed institutions, besides making monthly house calls.

In Thailand, in addition to such organizations as the Thai Red Cross and discussion clubs in the capital, the Club of the Bureau of Women's Culture has some 64 branches in various provincial centers. Their activities include lectures, music, homemaking, English lessons, and public charities. In Malaysia, the Women's Institutes modeled on the British pattern also have similar activities in up-country centers.

Burma does have a highly organized system of maternity and infant welfare, sponsored and aided by the government and run by the voluntary labor of women in every small town and big village. This work was given great impetus by Madame Aung San, widow of the national leader, General Aung San, and is now firmly established. There were also able and active social-welfare workers employed by the government, though the most outstanding leader in this area, Daw Tee Tee Luce, the recipient of a Magsaysay award, began the work completely on her own. Despite such leaders, there is no nationwide organization of women as such, and no movement to promote their activities or improve their status.

Women as Cultural Transmitters

For all this, Burmese women play a specific role in maintaining the national culture and passing it on to future generations. The stability of the Burmese nation rests on the values and attitudes bred by its Buddhist culture. Lighthearted though the people seem normally, in times when they feel the need to stop and take account of their reverses or perplexities, the doctrine of Buddhism is still the sustaining strength for their spirit.

The repository of this doctrine is the Buddhist clergy, the monks, who form 3.3 per cent of the adult male population. In traditional villages, the monastery is still the focal point of activities, where the men of the family, still closest to the monks, frequently gather. Modern conditions have caused many men to discontinue visits to the monastery, but there are few who do not hold fast to Buddhist doctrine in their hearts and expect the Buddhist offices to go on functioning as a base to which their life is anchored.

These offices, however, have nothing mystical about them. The monks are in close touch with the people, who often assemble to listen to them, and who supply the monasteries with their material requirements. The main occasions for these activities are the community gatherings, like the ones described earlier. And it is this essential element of the nation's culture that women carry squarely on their shoulders. All their centuries-old experience in raising money and handling it, in buying and cooking, stands them in good stead here.

The Burmese nation, like others undergoing a metamorphosis at present and striving toward a materially richer future, must take into account its past growth and development in order to obtain real and lasting benefits. As long as the women continue in their present role, one can count on the persistence of the traditional Burmese community life, stable and spiritually satisfying, which can serve as the solid basis for that revolutionary intensification of life and work which the easygoing Burmese people so greatly need to have urged upon them. Perhaps the energy of the Burmese women will be channeled by the present forward-looking government into more timely community projects which will raise economic and physical standards as well as promote spiritual well-being.

This could be true of most of Southeast Asia where the primary interest of women is focused firmly where it should be, on the home.

Indonesia

By Cora Vreede-de Stuers

*T*he *archipelago* of Indonesia consists of some three thousand islands, strewn in a mighty crescent on either side of the equator and from 95° to 141° eastern longitude—a span greater than that of the United States from coast to coast. The land area of more than 735,000 square miles contains a population of 96 million.

The heart of this humid tropical archipelago is Java, a slender island 600 miles long. Only 8 per cent of the total area of Indonesia, Java holds over two thirds of the population, over 1,000 people per square mile. To the northwest of Java lies Sumatra, four times as large but much less densely populated, with only 75 inhabitants per square mile. Even more thinly populated—18 per square mile—is Kalimantan to the northeast, the Indonesian portion of Borneo, largest island in the chain. The wide Strait of Makasar divides Kalimantan from mountainous Sulawesi (Celebes), where there are about 90 persons to the square mile, and still further east lies the lightly populated island group of Maluku (the Moluccas), the famous Spice Islands, which in the sixteenth century attracted the first ships from the West. To the east of Java and its neighboring island of Madura stretches the chain of Nusa Tenggara (Lesser Sunda Islands): Bali, Lombok, Sumbawa, Sumba, Flores, Timor, and a host of other islands, with an average population density of just over 200 per square mile.

Although officially the inhabitants of all these islands are today called Indonesians, their regional appellations remain of importance in so far as local customs are concerned. The Atjinese, Bataks, and Minangkabaus on Sumatra; the Dayaks and coastal Malays on Kalimantan; the Minahasans, Toraja, Bugi, and Makasars on Sulawesi; the Sundanese, Javanese, and Madurese on Java and Madura—each of these and of the countless other regional groups has its own ethnic and cultural characteristics, its own language, its own type of dwelling. But a unity exists in this diversity, as is proudly proclaimed in the national motto of the Republic of Indonesia, and because of this unity it is possible to attempt to describe "the Indonesian woman."

THE TRADITIONAL SITUATION

There is abundant historical evidence attesting to the high place occupied by women in traditional Indonesian society from early times down to the present. The ancient *Pararaton*, or book of the kings of Tumapel and Majapahit, lists several women who ruled in Java during the medieval Hindu period; in the sixteenth century there were reigning princesses at Japara and Gresik on the same island; from 1641 to 1699 the throne of Atjeh on Sumatra was occupied by women; and in the little kingdoms of southern Sulawesi so many women have reigned through the years that one would be hard put to list them all. Moreover, the records abound with examples of the active part taken by matrons in the family councils of Minangkabau and Minahasa and in the village and religious councils of the Batak country and the island of Ambon. It is indeed at the levels of family and community life, and in rural areas away from the courts and cities, that the basic character of the Indonesian woman has been formed and manifested.

Many customs and traditions, collectively known as *adat*, regulate rural society throughout Indonesia. Though its origins are clouded in the mists of history and its forms vary from region to region, adat has shown a remarkable ability to adapt itself to religious, political, and social change. Under it the individual is subordinate to the group, yet each individual has a distinctive place in the pattern of family and community relationships.

There are, in the main, three traditional types of genealogical organization: the patrilineal/patrilocal, found, among other places, in the Batak country of northern Sumatra and on Nias, Bali, Lombok, and several islands of Maluku; the matrilineal/matrilocal, occurring chiefly among the Minangkabaus of central Sumatra, as well as elsewhere in the archipelago; and the parental, found in Java and Bali, among the Toraja of central and the Mina-hasans of northern Sulawesi, the Dayaks of Kalimantan, and in other areas.

Some scholars ascribe the existence of such differing social organizations in various parts of Indonesia and the role of women in them to the rural environment in which they evolved. Through the ages, agriculture has been the principal occupation and source of revenue in the entire archipelago. At present more than 80 per cent of the population are employed in agricul-tural pursuits which vary according to local conditions. In sparsely settled islands like Sumatra, where large tracts of forest and grassland are available, shifting cultivation and cattle breeding are more common than in heavily populated Java, where people long ago settled down in fixed localities amid rice fields. These permanent settlements developed into the Javanese and Balinese *desa*, villages surrounded by their wet and dry fields and "mixed" or kitchen gardens. These mixed gardens, however, are typical not only of the Javanese and Balinese village communities, but occur throughout Indonesia wherever people have become sedentary and are engaged in cultivation.

Usually planted around the house, the mixed gardens contain all that is needed for the kitchen — vegetables and fruits, herbs and spices. They are invariably worked by the women, who often inherit them with the house and are free to sell the surplus in the market. The prevalence of a matri-lineal/matrilocal kinship organization, as among the Minangkabaus, or of a parental system, as in Java and Minahasa, seems to be linked up with the existence of such gardens. In areas where a patrilineal/patrilocal system prevails, as in the Batak country and on the islands of Nusa Tenggara, these mixed gardens are absent, and the chief occupation is the breeding of cattle on extensive pasture-lands — an occupation from which women are excluded.

In agricultural communities, large or small and fixed or shifting, tradi-tion governs every action from the sowing and harvesting of crops to con-duct between the sexes. Matters of marriage and child-rearing, of the disso-lution of marriage by death or divorce, of property settlement and succession rights — all are ruled by adat. The variations of custom within the three genealogical systems are of great influence in the lives of Indonesian women.

The patrilineal/patrilocal Batak communities, for instance, are spread over wide areas, each clan or subclan (called *marga*) occupying its own territory and bound in a particular relationship to every other clan. By inviolable marriage custom one clan, designated as the *hula hula marga*, supplies the women for another, women-receiving, clan, called *boru marga*. A hula hula marga will never take women from its boru marga; the latter becomes the hula hula marga of a third group, and so on. In this way closed circles of three or more clans are formed, with the brides rotating constantly in the same direction. As the girl passes from her own group of kinsmen to her bridegroom's group, a compensation in the form of a bride price is collected by the bridegroom's relatives and offered to her family. They, in turn, prepare a dowry, equal in value to the bride price; this they send with the girl when she goes to make her new home in the family house of her husband's marga. The two clans thus establish a cognate relationship, of which the bride is the binding link: her relation with her own marga is not broken, and her place in her husband's marga is secured when she becomes a mother. This bridging of two kinship groups through the marriage of two of their respective members is illustrated by a Batak couplet:

> One person builds the bridge, all walk over it;
> One person forms the link, all are thereby joined.

In the matrilineal/matrilocal community of the Minangkabau country, the girl does not leave her family house when she marries. Instead, her husband comes to live with her. "Where the she goat is, the he goat should be," as the local folk-saying puts it. Since she is not lost to her family in the sense that the Batak woman is lost to her kinsmen upon marrying, and since she continues to be entitled to her customary right in the family estate, there is no need for compensation in the form of a bride price or equivalent dowry. On the contrary, the custom is that the marriage proposal comes from the girl's family and that the bridegroom is presented with gifts in cash or kind. The wife and her children belong to her own clan, and neither her father nor her husband will ever be one of them to the same degree that her mother's brothers and her own brothers are. Her eldest brother automatically becomes responsible for the well-being of her children, whose mamak or protector he is, and her husband, although he may be the mamak for his own sister's children, in his own household is ("like cinders on the stump,") of least importance and least authority.

Varying widely in so many ways, these two kinship systems nevertheless agree in considering marriage a family concern rather than a matter of individual choice. The welfare and continuation of the group is held to be more important than personal happiness. Marriage outside the community is of course not countenanced. "If you marry a stranger," says a Minangkabau mother to her son in an Indonesian novel, "I will not be able to call it my grandchild." "Come now, Mother. Imagine not being able to call him your grandson!" "It is not that, Jalil, but my grandson would not have the right to marry a girl from our kampung [group]. He would have to stay in strange parts. That is our adat: a man from another region has no right to marry one of our girls." Then she quotes to her son the proverb: "The adat of Minangkabau, the law of our ancestors, does not get moldy in the damp and does not melt in the heat." In the unilateral descent systems, the wedding represents a junction of two large kinship groups.

The situation is different in the bilateral parental system (as it is found, for example, in Java), where the wedding marks a new autonomous nuclear family, which separates itself from the parental families on both sides. Although a bride price is customarily paid to the girl's family, it does not have the same significance as that which changes hands in patrilineal societies. To enhance his own prestige, a prosperous villager may sometimes make handsome dispensation to his bride's family, but in general the bride gift is nothing more than a small amount of money "to buy the salt which flavors the food for the wedding feast."

Despite the fact that, if a bride price is given, it goes to the parents and not to the girl herself, the consequences for the young woman deviate significantly according to whether the price is large (Batak), small (Java), or nonexistent (Minangkabau). Whereas the Batak woman is seldom divorced, for the good and sufficient reason that the high bride price would be a total loss to her family-in-law should she be sent back to her own family, the women of Java and Minangkabau are frequently cast aside. But the situation of the divorced Minangkabau woman again differs from that of her Javanese counterpart: because she still belongs to her family and has her place in the family house, her share in the family estate, and her children's education is provided for by her brother who is their mamak, she is physically and economically secure. The Javanese divorcée, on the other hand, may, or may not have private property or a part in the property acquired together with her husband; nor does she belong to an extended family group to which she may automatically return.

These hindrances do not mean that the Javanese divorcée is always left entirely destitute. Under the parental system, the cultivable land as well as the mixed gardens are inherited by the children of both sexes. Whatever personal property a woman may possess at her marriage or acquire after marriage through gifts or inheritance, she may retain in case of divorce or the death of her husband. The possessions obtained in common by the couple during marriage, are divided between them upon divorce. Even among the upper-class Javanese families, where until recently custom did not permit a married woman to take up gainful employment, the idea is widespread that, by running the home, a wife helps her husband to earn his living and is consequently entitled to her share of the family income.

In the Minangkabau kinship organization, the undivided family property belongs to the women jointly. The share of the married woman, consisting mainly of agricultural land, is transmitted to her daughters, for they belong to her *suku*. Moreover, at the death of her husband or in the case of divorce, she is entitled to her share of the goods acquired through common effort during marriage. The custom governing the partition of property when the marriage bond is dissolved by divorce is expressed in the following saying:

> The goods acquired together are divided,
> the bond is dissolved;
> the goods brought into marriage by the husband are returned
>   [to his family],
> the goods brought by the wife remain [in her family].

Although the Batak woman, like the Minangkabau woman, is a member of a joint family and therefore able to return to her family house should her marriage break up, her situation in other respects varies considerably. The Batak estate is inherited jointly by the male members; daughters inherit nothing. A divorced woman would be wholly dependent on her own family were it not for the substantial dowry which she took with her at her marriage and which returns with her. Part of this dowry is usually a piece of land, which she is free to manage at her will, but not to dispose of. She may cultivate it and use or sell the products herself. Further, any personal gifts she may have received after her marriage remain her exclusive property.

In none of the three Indonesian kinship organizations is the woman entirely dependent economically on her family, nor is she entirely independent of them. There is freedom within bounds, the bounds being always the larger interests of the group as determined by adat. And the subordination of the individual to the group applies equally to men and to women.

Within the framework of communal life, many opportunities are seized to counterbalance the diminution of individuality. For the woman the possibility of owning property, out of which she may derive some personal profit, affords a measure of independence. In areas where there are mixed gardens she has the right, as has been noted, of marketing her surplus fruits and vegetables. Where such gardens do not exist, she busies herself with spinning and weaving, the plaiting of baskets, or pottery-making, and again she is free to sell her products. To anyone traveling about Indonesia, the marketplace thronged with women buying and selling is a vivid and lively reminder of the economic importance of these women in their communities.

Moreover, the woman's role in the family as manager of the household and as first educator of her children assures her a place in the communal organization. Many women have exercised a determining influence, open or concealed, on the public affairs of their villages or districts. Conspicuous or not, the woman is pivotal in Indonesian society: it is she, and not the man, who is the permanent and essential element.

That the woman has been accorded an elevated position in the social and economic life of Indonesia may therefore be said to rest on firm traditional grounds. The question then becomes: how has her role within the adat structure been affected by other factors, most notably by the influence of Islam (the dominant religion in Indonesia), by Christianity, and by the long existence of a colonial government?

At the outset it must be recognized that adat and Islam are inextricably interwoven in social life, like the woof and the warp of one and the same piece of material whose contrasting colors are harmoniously blended.

THE MUSLIM INFLUENCE

Islam reached Indonesia as early as the thirteenth century by way of the trade routes which led first to Maluku and then to Java, the center for many centuries of a mighty Hindu-Javanese empire. Christianity was introduced by the Portuguese and the Dutch. Throughout the seventeenth century the Dutch East India Company extended its hold over a large part of the archipelago, driving out the Portuguese and coming into frequent conflict with local princes and adat chiefs. To gain the support of their subjects, against the foreign encroachment, many of the native rulers embraced Islam, which had earlier been adopted by great numbers of the common people. The new religion spread widely and steadily, exercising a unifying effect. In the long run, indeed, the sense of solidarity it created beyond the frontiers of tribal and regional particularities weakened the power of the princes and customary chiefs and helped to forge the bonds of nationalism.

Christianity was hindered in its spread by the obstacles commonly encountered in the rise of colonial empires. As the faith of the foreign conquerors, introduced with the help of arms, it alienated the native peoples instead of winning them. To be sure, it succeeded in establishing footholds here and there, and many inhabitants of the Spice Islands, the first to come into contact with Christianity, became converted to it for reasons that had perhaps less to do with conviction than with a desire to achieve equal status with the dominating Europeans.

Today, of ninety-six million Indonesians, eighty-six million are Muslim, and about four and a half million, Christians. On Bali are to be found one and a half million Hindus, the remainder are non-Christian Chinese citizens, resident aliens, and animistic peoples living mainly in the interiors of Sulawesi and Kalimantan.

Islam brought to Indonesia a fixed set of prescriptions, called *hukum*, regulating the behavior of each individual toward God and his fellow men. Ever able to adjust to new conditions, adat absorbed to a great extent those parts of Islamic law that pertained to matrimonial and religious life. In this way elements of hukum, completely integrated in the old adat, came to be felt by the Indonesians themselves as part of that adat and not alien to it. And conversely, certain adat customs were merged with hukum.

The counterinfluence of the two is observable in many matters affecting the life of women. For example, the high position of the woman in the original adat has prevented her from being segregated and veiled, as custom requires her to be in various other Islamic countries. The same high status has also worked to her advantage in the practice concerning repudiation, by which most Islamic marriages can be arbitrarily dissolved at the wish of the husband. Within the three adat kinship systems, repudiation (and polygamy) had long been permitted under certain specific and strictly limited circumstances, such as the barrenness of the woman. Early in its adjustment to the far greater latitude allowed the man under hukum, adat succeeded in preserving some of the traditional freedom of the woman by adopting one of the several Islamic forms of divorce (*talak*), that of the suspended repudiation, or *talik at talak*. To explain the operation of the Indonesian talik and its importance to the individual woman, the jurist and future prime minister Ali Sastroamidjojo gave this definition of it at the first Indonesian Women's Congress in 1928:

In our country the talik has a special meaning which is not usual in Muslim law. According to Indonesian customary law, this talik is pronounced at each wedding immediately after the contract of marriage. . . . This rule formulates a condition which protects the woman's position, for, by means of this talik, the husband declares that his wife will be definitely freed if he fails (by deserting, maltreating, or not supporting her) to keep the terms pronounced at the time of the marriage. . . . This talik does not come into force until after the wife has notified the judge.

The last clause, granting the wife the right to decide whether or not she will place the repudiation in the hands of the judge, is typically Indonesian and prevents the husband from acting in such a way as to obtain automatically the dissolution of the marriage.

In principle Islam regards marriage as a contract between two consenting individuals, a concept that should bring hukum into conflict with adat. In actual practice, an Islamic marriage is as much the family's business as it is under adat. Because Islam permits the marriage of minors and prescribes that the bride must be represented by her mandatory or *wali*, hukum like adat throws upon the parents the responsibility for, and the main right of deciding about, the marriage of their children, especially of their daughters. After marriage, the Muslim husband is bound to support his wife and children. The married woman, having a legal status of her own, retains complete freedom in the handling of her goods and may dispose of them without the approval of her husband. Fidelity is not required of the man, but if the wife is unfaithful, she runs the risk of repudiation.

The stability of marriage within the three traditional kinship systems may be correlated with the respective customs concerning the bride price. Islam does not recognize any payment to the family. A bridal gift, *maskawin* (Arabic *mahr*), of little importance is presented by the bridegroom to his bride through the medium of her *wali*, who acts on her behalf at the marriage ceremony. For Islamic marriages within the framework of either matrilineal or parental kinship groups, the insignificance of the maskawin proves little deterrent to later repudiation, and the divorce rate remains high. In the patrilineal system, the small amount of the maskawin is effectively counterbalanced by the important bride price, which continues to serve as a brake on divorce.

More conflicts between adat and hukum might be expected in matters of inheritance than in other fields of family law. For, according to adat, inherited goods may remain undivided, as is the case with the joint family property of Minangkabau and Batak areas. In many other regions property may be shared, but custom decrees no uniform rule for its division. In one community, adat may allow equal parts to sons and daughters; elsewhere, daughters are favored above sons; in many places, daughters inherit less than sons. Hukum, on the contrary, demands that all property be divided under a system of partition that is minutely regulated and strictly individual. It invariably permits a daughter to inherit precisely half of that which goes to a son.

Quite often this apportionment according to hukum has been so thoroughly integrated into customary life, appearing as part and parcel of traditional thinking, that it is difficult to determine what is the original adat, and what is the Islamic adat. The following sayings, the first from central Java, the second from Bantam in western Java, both typical of rural life, give expression at once to the hukum division of inheritance and to the traditional idea that the son bears greater responsibilities than the daughter:

The son carries on his shoulders, the daughter on her head [that is, half the weight borne by the son].
The man bears a *pikul* [pair of baskets] on his shoulder pole, the woman one basket slung on her hip.

Islam also provides alternative interpretations of adat as the situation demands. If it has been customary to retain the family property undivided, the Islamic institution of *wakap* (Arabic *wakf*), or property held in trust, is utilized to reconcile the old and the new concepts. For the disposition of the property acquired in common by husband and wife—a form unknown to Islam, which recognizes only individual property—a solution acceptable to hukum is found in the Islamic *sarikat* (Arabic *sharkat*), or business partnership. If a father, in the matrilineal Minangkabau society, wishes to leave all he has gained to his own rather than to his sister's children, whose mamak he is, his action can be legalized with the help of the Islamic *hiba*, which permits a man to give away, unconditionally and irrevocably, all of his personal property during his lifetime.

Despite the generally successful synthesis of ancestral custom with the institutions of Islam, the process has not been, nor is yet, without conflict. In their attempt to develop a viable society, Indonesians sought the support of universal Islam to further their attacks on the various regional traditions which they had come to regard through their contact with Western ideas as obstacles to this goal.

Early Stirrings

At the end of the eighteenth century, the Dutch government took over the administration of the Indonesian islands from the bankrupt East India Company. For the next hundred years, colonization continued apace, marred now and then by regional disturbances—some serious and long lasting, such as the rebellion in Java from 1825 to 1830, the intermittent Padri uprisings in Minangkabau, and the war in Atjeh from 1873 to 1907. On the whole, however, the period brought prosperity to the foreign plantation owners and merchants. Consequences of this Western penetration included the introduction of a money economy, the construction of roads and railways, and the promotion of hygienic measures, which resulted in a rapid increase in population, especially on Java. The development of plantations on tracts leased from local farmers, though of value agriculturally, had the deleterious effects of weakening native ownership of land and of dislocating traditional rural life. At the beginning of the twentieth century the expanding activities of the colonial government and of private enterprise made it necessary to train native personnel; then, for the first time outside of a few missionary schools, public education on Western lines was made available for a select number of Indonesians. And it was this education that acquainted a new generation with ideas of democracy and individual liberty.

The opening up of the country through roads and improved methods of communication served to efface regional boundaries and local authority and to give scope to the wider authority of the Islamic faith. Under its expanding and unifying force, its adherents came to feel that they belonged to a common nation. The growing consciousness of the Indonesian that he was responsible for his own life and actions made him distrust the authoritarianism of both the family and the colonial government.

Nationalism and a desire to reform society were thus closely related ideals for the new generation at the beginning of the new century. In the realization of the goals of individual, social, and national emancipation, the woman had an important role of her own to play. "Women's emancipation." wrote an Indonesian author in the late thirties, "was born in the twentieth century as the younger full sister of Indonesian nationalism."

In 1901 a change in the Dutch colonial policy was announced by Queen

Wilhelmina in her annual speech at the opening of Parliament. The *laissez-faire* policy in effect during the latter part of the nineteenth century was to be transformed into a program of guided initiation of the native population into modern culture and Western technical knowledge. Furthermore, the government pledged to appoint a commission of investigation to look into the causes of, and to recommend ways of ameliorating, the declining welfare of the peoples of Java and Madura, where rapidly increasing population and decreasing availability of arable land had created serious problems.

Part of the resulting inquiry, which took years to complete, was published in 1914 under the title *Verheffing van de inlandsche vrouw* (Improvement of the Position of the Native Woman). Containing many facts and statistics, this report also includes the statements of nine Javanese women consulted by the commission. Their declarations were among the first signs of a revolt inevitable for a people desiring and bound to progress in order to survive. At the same time, they were the first rules of conduct to come from the Indonesian woman herself.

A little earlier, in 1911, another book had been published that was to have profound effect on the feminist movement in Indonesia. Edited by J. H. Abendanon, one-time director of the colonial government's Department of Education, and entitled *Door duisternis tot licht* (Through Darkness into Light), the small volume was a collection of the letters of a young Javanese girl named Kartini, daughter of the Regent of Japara in central Java. Kartini wrote her letters in Dutch and mainly to Dutch correspondents, between 1899 and 1904. In them she vividly portrays the life of the *priyayi* or upper-class Javanese family of that period. That she wrote in Dutch is illuminative of this class, which had been the first to enjoy Western education and to be influenced by Western culture.

If the women cited in the commission's report indicated incipient revolt, Kartini does so even more. With youthful vehemence she rebels against the seclusion of marriageable girls (though the seclusion of women was far less stringent in Indonesia than in other Muslim countries) and against forced marriages. Regarding polygamy as practiced among the upper classes to which she belonged, she expresses the greatest repugnance—a reaction explained in part by the fact that she herself was the daughter of a secondary wife of the Regent. Although in priyayi society the children of the principal wife customarily ranked higher, the children of the cowives were treated equally within the bounds of conventions regarding sex, education, familial duties, and so on—which meant, of course, that the boys had far greater freedom than the girls. Of the wives themselves, the principal wife received preferential treatment, living in the main building and sharing in the social life of her husband. To a sensitive girl like Kartini, fiercely desirous of independence, the double standard applied to men and women and the inequalities of polygamy must have been particularly distressing.

Polygamy, to be sure, implies a well-to-do society. It and the concomitant bane of repudiation are found mainly among the upper classes and the residents of the larger towns, rarely among the peasants and laborers of rural areas, who for economic and other reasons remain monogamous. Among those unable to afford the luxury of polygamy, a form of disguised polygamy was often resorted to: a man could repudiate one wife after another, and marry again and again. Since the marriage gift was very small on Java and nonexistent in Minangkabau, he ran little risk of serious economic consequences and enjoyed in effect the pleasures of serial polygamy. The fact that nearly half of the marriages contracted were terminated by repudiation would be an indication of this practice.

Up to Kartini's time, girls had always been brought up in accordance with tradition, which taught them to submit in silence to the decisions of their families and the whims of their husbands. A mother instructing her daughters in their conjugal responsibilities might well have expressed herself thusly:

> If you are not the only wife,
> or he is invited for another,
>
> . . . . .
>
> that is the practice of the adat
> and is commanded by religion.
> Let him go ungrudgingly,
> let him go with a smile,
> and have no ill-feeling.
> The Holy Book forbids this.

Though they may have been taught to put up with polygamy, the women of Indonesia have given all indications that they suffer under the system. They regard the appearance of a second wife as one of the worst calamities that can befall them, and bemoan the uncertainty and wretched lot of women under polygamy, the frustration of family life, the unhealthy atmosphere for children.

Kartini and the nine women of the commission's report were in complete agreement about the most effective way to combat this and other evils of their society and to bring about the emancipation of women. Education was their answer — the education of both boys and girls, in accordance with the best tenets of Western teaching. In October, 1902, Kartini wrote to Professor and Mme G. K. Anton of Jena, whom she had met when they visited Java:

If we demand education and instruction for girls . . . it is not that we want them to compete with men . . . but . . . to render them more capable of fulfilling the great task which Nature has entrusted to them: that of mother — the first teacher. . . . It is to the mother, center of the family, that the important task falls of bringing up her children . . . for the large family of which they will one day be a part—the giant family called society. It is for this purpose that we demand education and instruction for girls.

Before her death in childbirth in 1904, when she was only twenty-five, Kartini started a little school in her own home; but her great hopes for a career as a teacher remained tragically unfulfilled.

Other women, less well known outside Indonesia because they did not write, showed by example the path to freedom through education. As the founders of the first schools for Javanese girls, they fought indomitably against great odds to bring their pupils into the light of modern times. Slowly they succeeded, and from their schools emerged the organizers of the women's movement who were to make education one of the rallying points of all their activities.

Though of greatest importance in breaking down the barriers against feminine education, the schools in Java were not the first to which Indonesian girls had access. In regions such as Minahasa in northern Sulawesi, Christianity took root in a parental kinship organization long before the period of colonial government. There, monogamous family life and the absence of any form of female seclusion made possible a harmonious balance between the sexes in their social and educational rights. Many years before Kartini was born, Christian missions in Minahasa opened primary schools. Girls attended these schools side by side with boys. And at a time when elsewhere in Indonesia the first primary schools for girls were yet to be started, the Minahasa missions had progressed to vocational schools, including the household school at Tomohon, founded in 1901. Not until after the First World War were similar household schools established on Java and Sumatra.

The early and equable emancipation of the Minahasa girl, whose position has never been as subordinate as that of the Javanese girl of certain social classes or of the Batak girl under the patrilineal kinship system, may help to explain the absence of a vigorous women's movement in this region. Apart from nationalistic aspirations, to which the Minahasans subscribed with the same ardor as did other Indonesians, the principal goals of the women's organizations could be of little interest, because not applicable, to the Minahasan woman.

WOMEN'S ORGANIZATIONS

The women's movement in Indonesia was not long in organizing its activities as part of a general nationalist movement that aimed first at social emancipation, and eventually (though for the time being not openly) at a free and sovereign state. Even before 1920, any number of women's associations were functioning in Java and Sumatra. The goal of all these groups was improvement in the position of the woman, particularly in matrimonial matters, by means of education. Their initial merit was that they opened doors to the women of the middle and upper classes, freeing them from their lives of secluded idleness and impelling them to meet their fellow-women on grounds of common interest.

At the various women's congresses that began to be held during the twenties in Java and Sumatra, the members—mostly women from those higher social classes who had benefited from the new educational opportunities—formulated in no uncertain terms their increasing dissatisfaction with matrimonial conditions. As a remedy, they proposed adequate legislation based on a valid and thorough understanding of the relevant Koranic prescriptions.

Simultaneously with the energetic early activities of the women's organizations and other groups, there arose a literary movement typified by what might be called "problem" novels. Since the problems with which the writers were concerned were those troubling countless other young Indonesians, these books were of considerable effect in articulating basic social conflicts. While their literary quality on the whole is not high, it is significant that all of them were written in the Indonesian language (which is based on Malay, the *lingua franca* of the archipelago) and not in the vernaculars of the regional communities to which the authors belonged. Significant, too, is the fact that a number of the novelists were women and women play major roles in all the stories.

The themes reflect the revolt of youth against suffocating tradition: the contrast of the marriage arranged by the family and the marriage based on mutual affection; the misery of polygamy; the desire for independent parenthood, with full responsibility for one's own children. Nearly all these books are melodramatic in plot and tragic in ending, for they were written by a generation torn by the conflict between the old concept of the clan's joint responsibility and modern ideas of marriage. In the strife between generations, the young people of the period between the two world wars scarcely ever won.

Though losing must have seemed to them inevitable, the youth remained heroically idealistic. As an effective means of attaining their goal of social and national liberation, they devised practical programs for extending education. In the women's movement the conviction grew that, in order to be treated as equals, they had to achieve economic independence. And for this, vocational training was necessary. Kartini and her contemporaries had wanted to become teachers so that they might educate the next generation. Now women began to claim the right to be trained in the professions and, if necessary or because they so desired, to stand on their own. This evolution in the women's movement is clearly noticeable in the concurrent development of the problem novels. Whereas in the first of these books to be published the reformers strive only to overcome the local adat, in the later novels the scope is considerably widened. Here is the heroine of one of the later books discussing the aspirations of her sex:

We must point the way in order that the new woman may be born, a liberated woman who will have the courage to stand up for all she does and all she thinks. . . . It will no longer be possible to confine her to the house; the whole world will become her domain. Marriage will not be her one and only destiny. She will be free to study for a scientific or social career or dedicate herself to art. . . . no longer the man's slave but his equal; no longer appealing to his feeling of pity.

During the first four decades of the twentieth century, the traditional structure of Indonesian society underwent many alterations. Of the factors leading to change, Western education was not the least. Also of importance was a deterioration of rural conditions brought about by overpopulation and lack of appropriate industrialization to absorb the ever-increasing numbers of the unemployed who migrated to urban areas in search of work. Once there, they succeeded for a while in preserving their rural pattern of life, but gradually urban customs took over, exercising an individualizing influence that contributed to the disintegration of communal life. Nationalism initially took root among the new urban middle class of small traders and the new intelligentsia in government service. The women of these two groups were among the first to benefit from Western schooling. For the great masses in the rural countryside, such opportunities did not yet exist.

The women's movement between the two world wars should be seen mainly as a striving by the members of the urban middle and upper classes to improve their own position. By demanding education for themselves, they became literate on a wider scale than ever before. Yet at the beginning of the war in the Pacific, the bulk of the female population of Indonesia was still illiterate. Little by little, however, and in imperceptible ways, new ideas and new modes of life were making their way into rural areas. The old kinship bonds were undergoing subtle transformation, affording women greater opportunity as individuals and making them increasingly aware of their larger social relationships in a nation newly aroused.

POST-WAR DEVELOPMENTS

The Japanese occupation of Indonesia from 1942 to 1945 caused great suffering, but the privations endured in common brought the women of various social groups into closer union. Moreover, the enemy made much wider use of the initiative and energy of women both in offices and in the field of social welfare than had been the case before. During the revolution for national independence from the Dutch, which followed upon the heels of the Pacific war, the bonds between women were further strengthened.

Religious, social, and regional barriers were lifted as women helped their men carry on the struggle, fighting beside them in Java and Sumatra and in their own battalion in Minahasa, nursing the wounded and feeding the hungry behind the combat lines, working the land and managing the home in the absence of their husbands.

Typical of the harmony among the women of this period was the Pemusharawatan Wanita Indonesia (Indonesian Women's Conference), which took place a few months before the transfer of sovereignty on December 27, 1949. From all parts of the archipelago, and representing eighty-two different associations, women traveled to Jogjakarta in central Java, heart of the nationalist resistance force, to prepare their program for united action once the Republic was established. A year later a federation of the women's organizations, the Kongres Wanita Indonesia (Indonesian Women's Congress), was founded. Through it the activities of the member groups are coordinated and specific objectives promoted.

In 1941 the colonial government had granted Indonesian women the right to vote and to hold elective office. This right and others, including increased public education, access to all trades and professions, and medical and hygienic care, were reaffirmed and guaranteed by the provisional constitution drawn up by the revolutionary government in 1945. Of importance on the agendas of the various women's conferences during the late forties and fifties were discussions regarding the more precise formulation in the forthcoming constitution of the rights already given them and an extension of legislation into fields not yet covered, particularly matrimony.

In all circles, masculine as well as feminine, education was considered one of the most important items on the program for national development in the new Republic. To be effective, compulsory education, as anticipated in the provisional constitution, had to be prepared for by a vigorous policy of increasing the teaching staff. The problem of illiteracy was energetically tackled by the Ministry of Education, to which the women's associations gave their full support by arranging courses for women. The efforts were successful: before World War II the illiteracy rate for the total population of ten years and older was about 90 per cent; the 1961 census figures show an illiteracy rate of 53.3 per cent (65.9 per cent for women and 40.2 per cent for men).

From the start, vocational training was stressed. The need for teachers at all levels led to the establishment of normal schools. In the cities, many young women felt attracted to the medical profession and directed their studies toward it, while in rural areas, many others chose the humbler but no less necessary career of midwife. Indonesian society has always known the *dukun*, the older married woman, with her broad knowledge of medicinal herbs, called upon to treat illnesses of all sorts and come to the aid of women in childbirth. To offset the acute shortage of doctors, midwifery schools were started in order to train the dukun in modern hygienic and medical procedures. Mother and child welfare centers have also been opened in large numbers in rural districts. These centers, as well as the training courses for nurses and midwives, are inundated by women.

Instruction leading to the job of home visitor, which is supplemental to the work done by the health centers, is included in the national educational curriculum. Social work, however, though admirably adapted to the talents and capacities of women, lacks prestige in Indonesian public opinion, and this attitude discourages girls from taking it up as a profession.

Higher education in general is quite new in Indonesia. The first colleges were started in the 1920's. Shortly before the Japanese occupation, the Dutch government united the various schools of higher education in Jakarta into one university, afterwards called the Universitas Indonesia. During the revolution, the Universitas Gadjah Mada was founded at Jogjakarta, and many regional universities have been opened throughout the whole country since the establishment of the Republic. The number of girls completing their studies at these institutions is still very small. Of those who have finished, the great majority now occupy responsible positions in government service or the professions; they also play an important part in the women's movement.

The contribution of peasant and working-class women to the economic life of the country continues to be considerable. Many country women do not work full time in the fields, but merely lend their husbands a helping hand at sowing and harvest time. Part-time industrial work, or at least a job that can be done at home along with other household tasks, is also often preferred by women. Employment of this kind, perhaps best exemplified by the making of batik cloth on a piecework basis for fabric manufacturers, is a typical feature of rural areas. Not infrequently it results in a considerable divergence between the wages of male and female workers, although in theory a woman's pay is on the same scale as that of a man for work of equal value.

Economic independence for women of all classes of society is a principal aim of the women's movement not only because it will advance the nation's over-all prosperity, but also because it is hoped in this way to bring an element of security into marriage. An often-remarked side effect of the general instability of marriage ties in Indonesia is the inordinate fondness of the women for jewelry. This is not so much a matter of desire for personal adornment as it is one of investment. Because of their precarious financial position in case of divorce or widowhood, women are apt to spend whatever money they can save on jewelry, which is easily negotiable, in order to support themselves and their children should they be left alone. The disadvantages of such a solution are obvious. Greater security is offered by membership in cooperative societies.

Nearly all women's associations have a section dealing with economics and cooperative enterprises. The sharing of labor and responsibility is no stranger to the Indonesian woman, who well knows what joint effort means to the well-being of large families. For this reason the rotating credit associations and other cooperative endeavors have met with considerable success in both rural and urban areas, especially among women. Further, women's savings banks, founded and managed by women, have played an increasingly helpful part in protecting women from moneylenders and in inculcating into them the habit of saving for important occasions and rainy days. Planned, rather than whimsical, management of their earnings, it is felt, is essential to the achievement of economic independence and the preservation of stable homes.

It is impossible to empasize strongly enough the distress the women of Indonesia suffer by the instability of marriage. Time after time in conversations I have had with them, they have reverted to this theme, and it has remained the *leitmotiv* of the various postwar congresses of the women's organizations. The divorce rate, already very high in prewar Indonesia, has risen disconcertingly since the war. The general social unrest that prevailed under the Japanese occupation and continued during the revolution has apparently not yet run its course and is certainly responsible in part for the alarming statistics on repudiations. Although recent figures are not available, the situation has not changed appreciably since 1954, when 55 per cent of all marriages contracted on Java were dissolved by divorce. On the other islands the percentages were lower: for example, 31 per cent for Sumatra and 19 per cent for Sulawesi. Yet these high rates are surpassed only by those of nearby Malaya, where over the nine-year period from 1945 to 1953, the divorce rates for the Muslim population ranged from 40 per cent in Malacca to 59 per cent in Negri Sembilan, with 56 per cent in urban Singapore.

It has been maintained that Islam is the principal cause of this high frequency of divorce. This view, however, is counter-indicated by the much lower frequencies of divorce in the Muslim Middle Eastern countries.

Another correlation has been sought between the instability of marriage and the type of kinship organization. But the bilateral peoples of Java and Singapore have much the same high divorce rates as the unilateral matrilineal societies of Minangkabau (where the rate in the 1950's was 40 per cent) and Negri Sembilan. As was pointed out earlier, the triviality of the bridal gift in Java and its absence in Minangkabau, where the husband also remains more or less a stranger in his wife's family, without question encourage repudiation.

It is difficult to determine the exact causes of divorce. From discussions I had with the heads of two official marriage councils in Jakarta and Bandung, it became clear that more than one factor was often involved and that sometimes the ostensible reason concealed the real one. The main grounds given in applications for divorce are unjustified polygamy, insufficient financial support which Islamic law requires the husband to give to the wife, and incompatibility of temperament. Unjustified or "unhealthy" polygamy to Indonesians means a polygamous marriage that cannot satisfy the conditions laid down by Islam. One of these conditions is that the polygamous man must have an income sufficient to support more than one wife with her children. Many cases of incompatibility of temperament today also seem to stem from financial problems. While the conception of incompatibility as a motive for divorce is not new, this economic aspect of it is unknown in traditional society.

In some parts of Indonesia, notably on Java, the instability of the marriage tie is attributed to the persistence, in a rapidly changing society, of forced marriages and to the "triangle problem." Unlike the Western "eternal triangle" of husband/wife/lover, the Indonesian triangle consists of husband/wife/family. All the complications and difficulties that can develop through the interference of the family in the lives of their married, or marriageable, children are comprised in this graphic concept. Forced marriage, which is frequently given as a cause of divorce, represents one form of interference against which the new generation steadfastly puts up resistance.

Recognition of the insecurity of the married woman in social life, coupled with the growing disintegration of the family and neglect of children especially in cities, has led to the unanimous conviction among the women's organizations that appropriate marriage legislation is needed. Mme. Nani Soewondo, one of Indonesia's leading women trained in the law, declared in 1955, "Today's deplorable situation will never show signs of any definite improvement until marriage bills to protect woman against polygamy and repudiation are passed." Under the sponsorship of the women's groups and some of the men's, various projects for an all-Indonesian matrimonial code have been submitted to the government. After having shelved these projects for years, the Ministry of Religious Affairs at last placed them before the Cabinet in 1956. To date, however, the proposals have not been decided in Parliament.

Despite the uncertain future facing her after wedlock, the average Indonesian woman of course does marry. To become a mother means fulfilling her destiny as a woman. Traditionally, the mother was solely responsible for the nurture of her children during their early years. Among joint families this meant a pyramidal structure of child-rearing, with the children forming the base, looked over by all the mothers of the community, and topped by the grandmother, wife of the head of the group. In such an environment little girls were trained to the duties of good housekeeping, taught how to receive guests and to serve them, and given the job of looking after their younger siblings. The relationship between mothers and daughters was close and affectionate.

As late as the beginning of the twentieth century, and at some social and regional levels even later, the young girl looked like a miniature woman. With her hair arranged in a bun, and clad in her long-sleeved jacket and her sarong reaching down to her ankles, she was the replica of her mother. As she grew older she grew quieter, never raising her voice, remaining modestly in the background, walking with tiny, neat steps. Upon entering adolescence she would become even more restrained in behavior, and her parents would start looking for a suitable husband for her. Soon after her first menstruation, she would be married, frequently to a man she had never seen before.

Today, not only in the towns but in the villages as well, this miniature woman has disappeared. Children are dressed as children, their clothes home- or ready-made of manufactured materials. The remotest communities have been invaded by the traveling salesman, who arrives across the rice fields carrying two baskets on a pole over his shoulder. These contain a wealth of cotton, silk, and nylon prints for the women's jacket, gay frocks for the girls, bright plastic hairclips, dainty handbags. When he is gone, the women get busy with their sewing machines.

With the disappearance of regional costumes from daily use, it has become popular to display the traditional garments at fashion shows during meetings of the women's associations. Handed down from mother to daughter for generations, this apparel delights the eye in its color and workmanship: heavy indigo-blue or red hand-woven cottons from Batak and Minangkabau regions, the cloth of the latter stiff with gold thread and worn under gorgeous silk tunics; transparent blood-red tunics of the women of southern Sulawesi; hand-dyed Javanese batiks in a thousand intricate designs and subtle colors. The Javanese daily dress consisting of a jacket worn over a batik sarong, has become the Indonesian national costume, which all the women wear for official or formal occasions. For everday use, both girls and married women now often wear Western-style clothes. The old regional costumes, carefully preserved, are used only at wedding ceremonies, which are still performed according to the customs of the community to which the bride belongs.

Marriage today is generally delayed until after the girl has finished her primary schooling, which means rarely before her sixteenth birthday. Among the middle and upper classes it is often much later, after she has completed a college or university education. And in the patrilineal societies it is also frequently delayed, owing to the amount of time it takes to collect the stipulated bride price. Where early marriage is still the rule, the parents choose the husband, guided by considerations that local custom demands. Girls who marry at a later age, after having mixed freely with boys in college or university, usually discuss with their parents the choice of their future mate. Love marriages are increasing in the predominantly urban circles.

Opposition on the part of young people to the family's prerogatives in deciding about a marriage partner existed in the past. Some couples took matters into their own hands by choosing to elope; others formed "illicit" relationships. Adat, which takes individual insubordination into account in its regulation of social behavior, has sanctioned but discouraged marriage by elopement in certain areas. It has also made provision for the unmarried pregnant woman by having her married in time to a man, not necessarily the father of the child to be born, "to cover the shame."

By stressing the irregular character of impetuous behavior, adat is not well suited to help the modern girl, who would prefer to make her own choice and yet at the same time avoid conflict with, or even gain the support of, her family and community.

Although the traditional high respect shown to the older generation —noticeable in the use of special terms of address—continues to prevail throughout Indonesia, the authority of the parents and elders of the family is constantly questioned by the young people of today, a generation which, although born during and after the struggle against colonialism, feels no longer bound to the revolutionary ethics of national solidarity. Recent events have shown that—independence no longer being an aim in itself— various internal political and social problems occupy their minds to the point that both boys and girls go into action where they think their elders fail.

THE NEW INDONESIAN WOMAN

In the past the Indonesian woman was valued as an important asset to the economy of the family and as the continuer of the lineage. She emerges today as an autonomous individual, capable of sharing with her male counterpart the responsibilities of citizenship in the new sovereign Republic.

Accustomed through the ages to work hard at home and in the fields, to organize all that belonged to her own realm in family and community life, and to contribute to the family income, which she managed, she found little difficulty in adapting herself to the conditions of a modern state. She took to heart the words of President Sukarno: "Do not lag behind in our revolution of today, or in our effort to build up a just and prosperous society. In this society you will become happy; you will be independent women."

As part of her heritage, and with a keen sense of duty, the Indonesian woman in the past learned to suffer without question the authority of the family head and the adversities of fate. She encounters today a greatly altered scale of values. Battles about the right of family authority have been waged between the old and the new generations. To those formed by modern education, foremost in the conflict, the right of authority has passed from the family to that much larger group, the nation, in which, as it is expressed by the contemporary Indonesian poet Rivai Apin,

> We are the children of the same father,
> We are the children of the same mother.

The "unyielding arms of tradition," so hateful to Kartini, were definitely forced apart by the national and revolutionary struggle, when men and women fought as equal members of a united people for one single fatherland.

Once the revolution was over, the woman, having proved herself as an indispensable and independent worker both at home and in public life, was accorded full civil rights within the framework of modern legislation. Entrusted with responsibilities no less than those of the man, she entered into the professions and government service, office and factory work, and a hundred other careers. Simultaneously she managed her home and cared for her children. Under ideal circumstances, the home itself became the center of family life, and the father and mother partners in the rearing of their children.

But ideals are difficult of achievement. Having attained social, economic, and political equality, it is not surprising that the modern Indonesian woman today claims her right to emotional equality as well. However, public opinion—that is to say, masculine opinion—has proved reluctant to admit her right to equal treatment in the matter of personal feelings.

One token of this masculine disinclination is found in the continual postponement of parliamentary discussion of the marriage-law proposals. Another is the encouragement given to polygamy by the notorious Act 19 of 1952, which granted widow's pensions to the several wives of a polygamous man, a measure vigorously opposed by all the women's organizations. The fact remains that until the terror of easy repudiation and illegal polygamy has ceased to haunt the thoughts of the woman, she will be unable to fulfill satisfactorily her new tasks as marriage partner and as mother.

Although the outlook is bleak for constructive action regarding the marriage laws, in other respects the well-being of the woman is receiving greater consideration than before. Her health and that of her children, rather than the problem of an ever-increasing population, has led to discussion of family planning. So far the government, though concerned about the rapid growth of the population, has not officially endorsed birth control, but an Indonesian branch of the Planned Parenthood Association was started in 1957. Furthermore, in a speech given in 1958 to a group of university students, Nasaruddin Latif, a Muslim member of Parliament, declared that Islamic teachings contained no prohibition of birth control, and that the spacing of births is necessary for the mother's health.

Such statements on the part of men — men who are, moreover, strict followers of the Faith — have been of considerable support to those women, doctors and midwives, who in numerous urban and rural medical consultation bureaus give advice on the spacing of conceptions. The planning of families, it is hoped, will not only contribute to reducing the high rate of infant and child mortality (some 60 per cent of the total death rate) but also have a beneficial effect on the physical and mental health of the mother.

The outlook of the contemporary Indonesian woman has changed to fit the times she lives in, yet echoes of the past linger in her ears: "Work for you is a law of life." "Judge the rise and fall of prices." "Use your brain and be wise." In her life today these old sayings have the same validity they have always had, but her work is different, and to learn wisdom she has the help of education. When guarantees of a more stable conjugal life and more tolerable child-bearing are added to the rights that legislation and public opinion already have granted her, she will again be able to utilize to the full her overflowing energy, her powers of endurance, and her organizing genius. Even now, as she fulfills her destiny of motherhood and the making of a home, she is, as from time immemorial, the pivot around which all life in Indonesia turns.

BIBLIOGRAPHY

The page numbers following some titles indicate the passages referred to in the foregoing article.

G. J. A. Terra, "Some Sociological Aspects of Agriculture in S.E. Asia," *Indonesië*, VI, 1952–53, pp. 297–316.

M. H. Nasoetion, *De plaats van de vrouw in de Bataksche maatschappij* (The Place of Woman in Batak Society), Utrecht: 1943, p. 23.

Kedjora, *Karam dalam gelombang pertjintaan* (Wrecked on the Waves of Love), Jakarta: 1926, p. 50.

K. M. Koentjaraningrat, "The Javanese of South Central Java," in G. P. Murdock (ed.), *Social Structure in Southeast Asia*, Chicago: 1960, p. 101.

P. E. de Josselin de Jong, *Minangkabau and Negeri Sembilan: Socio-political Structure in Indonesia*, Leiden: 1951, p. 56.

J. Prins, *Adat en Islamietische plichtenleer in Indonesië* (*Adat* and Islamic Law in Indonesia), The Hague: 1954, p. 154.

Ali Sastroamidjojo, "Tentang hak nikah dalam hukum Islam" (Marriage in Islamic law), *Wasita* (Indonesian women's magazine), 1928, pp. 14–15.

A. Boerenbeker, *De vrouw in het Indonesisch Adatrecht* (Women in Indonesian Customary Law), The Hague: 1931, p. 141.

Adi Negoro, "Soal ibu" (Woman's Problem), *Keutamaan Isteri* (Indonesian women's magazine), April 21, 1939.

Agnes L. Symmers, *Letters of a Javanese Princess*. London: 1921.

A. H. Johns, *Rantjak diLabueh: A Minangkabau Kaba*, New York: 1958, p. 62, 64.

H. T. Chabot, *Verwantschap, stand en sexe in Zuid-Celebes* (Kinship, Status and Sex in South Celebes), Groningen: 1950, p. 168.

Takdir Alisjahbana, *Lajar terkembang* (Under Full Sail), Jakarta: 1936, Fifth edition, 1955, p. 51.

Aboebakar, *Sedjarah mesdjid dan amal ibadah dalamnja* (A History of the Mosque and Its Religious Ceremonials), Bandjarmasin: 1955, p. 473.

Judith Djamour, *Malay Kinship and Marriage in Singapore*, London: 1959, p. 137.

Nani Soewondo, *Kedudukan wanita Indonesia dalam hukum dan masjarakat* (The Position of the Indonesian Woman in Law and Society), Jakarta: 1955, p. 162.

Sukarno, *Sarinah: kewadjiban wanita dalam perdjoangan Republik Indonesia* (Sarinah: Women's Duties in the National Struggle of the Indonesian Republic), 2nd ed., Jakarta: 1951, pp. 328–29.

Rivai Apins poem "Élégie," in French translation, was published in Ilen Surianegara (ed.), *Poèmes et Nouvelles*, Paris: 1958 (A Selection of modern Indonesian literature).

S. M. Nasaruddin Latif, *Ilmu perkawinan* (Guide for Marriage Affairs), Jakarta: 1956, p. 51.

Lettres de Raden Adjeng Kartini: Java en 1900. Selected and translated by L. C. Damais, with an excellent introduction by Jeanne Cuisinier, Paris: 1960.

Hurustiati Subandrio, *Kartini, wanita Indonesia* (Kartini, the Indonesian woman), Sixth edition; Jakarta: 1955.

——, *Speeches and Lectures*. A bound, mimeographed collection of speeches delivered in England by Mme. Subandrio during the years when her husband was the Indonesian Ambassador to Great Britain. London: Indonesian Embassy, 1955.

Cora Vreede-de Stuers, *The Indonesian Woman: Struggles and Achievements*, The Hague: 1961.

VI

The Communist East

THE SOVIET UNION
AND MAINLAND CHINA

The common factor in the two countries discussed in this section, so different in their traditional culture, is the ruthlessly executed legal and administrative equalization of the positions of men and women in all areas, but especially in that of employment. Another common factor is the purposeful playing down of the importance of family life and the gamut of emotions centering around it, in line with the general tenet of subordinating the individual to the people and the party.

The Soviet Union

By Vera Alexandrova

IN OLD RUSSIA

There is at present a widely held opinion to the effect that women in prerevolutionary Russia had no legal rights whatsoever and had the status of family slaves. That is both true and untrue, but more untrue than true. The condition of women in old Russia was indeed very often onerous, but there was no question of a total absence of rights. On the contrary, a characteristic trait in the development of Russian law was the recognition—dating back to ancient times—of a far-reaching formal equality between men and women in almost everything that involved everyday life, the family, and conditions of life, and, in particular, in the right to dispose of property and in questions of family law. In these spheres, the position of women in Russia was formally often better than that of women in many countries of Western Europe. It was only and mainly

Translated from the Russian by George Reavey.

in questions of inheritance that men enjoyed significant advantages, but even here the limitations on women's rights were to a great extent removed shortly before the beginning of World War I.

Nevertheless, even in Russia before the Revolution there was a widespread notion that women enjoyed no rights at all; this notion was founded not so much on formal and legal limitations as on the facts of the environment which, because of the primitive conditions and the extreme poverty of the vast majority of the population, proved especially disadvantageous for women. It was a matter not so much of the absence of equal rights as of the absence of equality in daily practice despite a wide range of equality from the formal standpoint.

But there was also lack of equal rights, and this had stimulated a strong movement in favor of equality for women. Fundamentally, this movement had as its aim not so much the attainment of equal rights in everyday life, in the sphere of civil rights, as in the attainment by women of equal rights to education, especially higher education, to the liberal professions, and to state and social services. In these spheres there were many limitations, but also some notable achievements, and in several of them Russian women had achieved success before the women of a number of Western countries. This success was due to the sympathy with which many circles of Russian educated society regarded these strivings. However, there was a very long way still to go until equality of rights was attained in these spheres, and here wide possibilities opened up with the Revolution.

The February Revolution of 1917 put an end to all formal limitations on the rights of women. In general, women were now admitted to state and social service and to the only profession still closed to them—the legal profession; higher education was now opened widely to women; and, of course, women were allowed to take part in democratic elections. Already in the early pre-October period of the Revolution, no limitation remained on women's rights except some small inequalities in the sphere of civil law.

What remained, however, was inequality in practice. A long social process is required to overcome this, and it is still incomplete although a great deal has already been achieved.

THE NUMERICAL SUPERIORITY OF WOMEN

Before proceeding to analyze this process and its results, it is essential to examine one trait of Russian life that, especially in the period after World War II, has had an unfavorable effect in many ways on the position of women; but has at the same time helped to develop in them a feeling of independence. This trait is unconnected either with the special structure or the level of economic development of the country, and it sharply distinguishes the Soviet Union from any other large state: it is the vast numerical superiority of women.

The census of 1897, the only general census of the population before the Revolution, revealed that there were 101.1 women to every 100 men. A similar proportion is observable in normal conditions in all countries. But the census of 1926, the first in the Soviet Union, revealed a far less favorable proportion: there were then 107 women to every 100 men. Here were manifest the heavy consequences of both World War I and the Civil War. In these wars the mortality rate was particularly high. The second Soviet census, that of 1939, showed a further deterioration: there were then 108.7 women to every 100 men. These figures remind one of the dread years of collectivization, during which millions of people perished, the majority of them men. The "big liquidation" in the second half of the 1930's must have pointed in the same direction.

The last Soviet census of 1959 revealed a really tragic situation. In January 1959, the total population was 208,800,000, composed of 94,000,000 men and 114,800,000 women. Thus, there were then 20,800,000 more women than men, or 122.1 women for very 100 men, an almost unheard of ratio in international population statistics. But even this figure does not fully reflect the whole situation as it has developed since the war. The tremendous quantitative difference between men and women, as shown in the 1959 census, applies entirely to the middle-aged and older groups. It was noted in the official census report that, out of the total population up to the age of 31, there were 62,729,000 men and 62,489,000 women. The men of this age (the eldest of whom were seventeen at the end of the war) had taken no direct part in the war, and in these age groups the proportion between the sexes remained normal. But in the age group of thirty-two and over there were 31,317,000 men and 52,284,000 women, or 166 women to every 100 men. Even if it is assumed that the mortality among mature men was somewhat higher in the postwar years than that among women, which is very likely, yet the ratio between adult (eighteen and over) men and women immediately after the war reached the staggering figure of no less than a 100 to 150!

The proportion of men to women in the population of the country as a whole, approaches nearer to the normal with each year. The older generations are dying out, and the influence of the war no longer has any bearing on the numerical proportion between the sexes among the younger generations. However, a good quarter of a century—without war—must pass before the numerical proportion between the sexes will reach the prewar Soviet figure. Almost a half century—again without war—must pass before it reaches the level attained on the eve of World War I.

The process of change that has taken place in the position of women during the entire period of the Revolution might be characterized on the whole as a process of social amelioration for women. But this amelioration has often developed in an unhealthy manner, and women have frequently had to pay a high price for their achievement.

THE CRISIS IN SEXUAL MORALITY

In the first decade following October 1917, women experienced a very painful weakening of family ties. In everyday life, as well as in literature, this trend has usually been described—though somewhat exaggeratedly—as "the disintegration of the family." There were several causes for this. Certain signs of it could already be observed in the war years before the Revolution. But the process was greatly speeded up by the rapid collapse of the old way of life and by the inauguration of a new order following the October Revolution. During the years of the New Economic Policy (from 1921) this development assumed a menacing character. In this period, following the collapse of the moral foundations of the old society, the majority of the adherents of the new moral criteria suffered a shock. Family life was affected very unfavorably by the widespread propaganda of the new sexual morality, implied in the formula of "free love" and expressed in the half-ironic and soon very popular slogan of *"Without Birdcherry"* (after the title of Panteleion Romanov's story written in 1927).

The extremes of *"Without Birdcherry"* began very soon to provoke a reaction from Soviet society, but the fundamental support given to "free love" remained unshaken until almost the middle 1930's. Boris Pilnyak's story, *"The Birth of a Man"* (1935) may serve as an interesting illustration of these attitudes, for this story mirrored the approaching collapse of the concept of "free love":

In the diary, which Antonova, a woman prosecutor and the heroine of the story, keeps during her pregnancy, she confesses to casual relations with men in the past: "I never thought of having a child. I knew I could not have one. I could not waste time on a child. A child was outside my sensations. That was an axiom. Twice I had an abortion. That was just an ordinary three-day indisposition. . . ."

The child she was now expecting owed its life to sheer chance. Antonova had delayed her abortion too long, for she felt herself pregnant for the first time only when the child stirred within her, but the doctors informed her that an abortion might now prove dangerous. Her pregnancy and the birth pangs produced a profound moral revolution in Antonova. The title of Pilnyak's story applies both to the act of giving birth and to the moral renewal of the heroine.

It would, of course, be an exaggeration to maintain that this form of sexual morality entirely defined the character of the Soviet family in the period of 1921–1935; but there is no doubt that it often helped to weaken family ties, and contributed to the disintegration of many families. It was only in the mid-1930's that a cautious campaign and then a more decisive one was directed against the "theory" of free love. It was only during World War II and the years following that the family was fully rehabilitated.

THE WEAKENING OF FAMILY TIES

But another factor was also involved in the disintegration of the family in the 1920's—a factor of a very different nature. It was the growth of woman herself and her emergence from the frame of family existence. This is very patently illustrated in Fedor Gladkov's novel *Cement* (1925), in its day one of the post popular works of Soviet literature.

The plot of the novel is simple. Gleb Chumalov, a worker-bolshevik, returns to his native town at the end of the Civil War. His wife Dasha, with whom he had lived very happily, meets him with joy, but something about her has changed. In his absence she had been arrested by the Whites but, on being released, she had associated with the Red underground. After the town had been liberated by the Red Army, Dasha continued her new associations. She had placed her daughter in a children's home where the child died. The child's death had snapped the last thread uniting Dasha with her former life as a wife and mother. One day Gleb found a note informing him that Dasha wished for a time to lead an "independent life." In Gladkov's other novel, *Energy*, written twenty-five years later, the reader learns that Dasha never did return to her husband.

The impact of this factor—the growth of an independent woman—was felt in later years, as well as at present following the renewed recognition of the significance of the family in strengthening society. In his novel *Maria* (1946), Grigory Medynsky launched the theme which has since become almost a commonplace of the difficulties that can arise in collective farm-families as a result of the active part played by the wives during the war, when they became presidents of the collective farms and found social work to their liking, whereas the husband, just returned from the war, preferred to have his wife go back to domestic work.

CIVIL MARRIAGE AND DIVORCE

The collapse of traditional sexual morality and the semi-official approval given to the theory of "free love" created conditions in which the development of the new family legislation of the early years of the Revolution, which was fundamentally progressive, was often turned against women. In 1917, up to the October Revolution, the reform of family legislation never emerged from the preparatory stage. It was only under the Soviets

—on December 18, 1917—that the first decrees relative to civil marriage and divorce were published. Until the Revolution, marriages had been concluded and dissolved by the ecclesiastic authorities according to the ecclesiastic laws (distinct for each religion), which were particularly repressive in the matter of divorce. Civil marriage did not exist at all, and the term "civil marriage" in everyday life was used to denote permanent *de facto* cohabitation, which did not involve any legal consequences.

The decree of December 18 put an end to all this. A system was introduced for the registration of marriages by specially created government organs (the departments for registering acts of citizenship status). These became widely known under their abbreviated name of ZAGS, and henceforth registered marriage became the only recognized form of wedlock. *De facto* marriage—known in the United States as common law marriage—was, as previously, not recognized. No registration—no marriage. This severe attitude toward *de facto* marriage was motivated in part in the interests of the struggle being waged against the custom of religious marriage. Persons living in a state of *de facto* marriage were now asked to register their marriage and to state the length of time they had been so married, and this statement was given legal validity. All religious marriages concluded prior to the civil marriage decree were recognized as being in force. As for the future, religious marriages were not prohibited, but they were regarded as merely "the private affair of the marrying couple."

The nonrecognition of *de facto* marriage was a heavy blow to the women and the children. It took nine years before Soviet lawgivers decided to recognize *de facto* marriage side by side with registered marriage. This was done by promulgating the code of laws of November 19, 1926, concerning marriage and the family. From then on even the terminology changed. The registration of a marriage in the ZAGS was now called a "formulation" rather than a "conclusion." This development was later reversed.

Corresponding with the simplified concept of unlimited freedom between the sexes, which gave rise to the theory of free love, the authors of the new Soviet laws concerning the family and marriage proclaimed total freedom and an extremely simplified form of divorce. The Decree of December 18, 1917, laid down that a marriage could be dissolved at the request not only of both parties, but also of one party without the necessity of presenting any arguments to justify this request. If the request for divorce emanated from both parties, it would be presented directly to the ZAGS, which then registered the divorce. If only one party made the request, it was taken to court and the judge in person, without examining the substance of the matter, pronounced the decree. In either case, whether the matter was brought before a court or before ZAGS, it proved a mere formality. Later, in 1926, court procedure was entirely abolished, and ZAGS could register a divorce at the request of one party only. The other party need not know anything about it until he or she received the decree of divorce.

This order of things lasted until 1936, when a change was introduced — unfortunately for the worse. But before attempting to define it, we must consider another very important question without which we cannot evaluate correctly the position of the Soviet woman in the first twenty years of the Soviet regime. That is the question of abortion.

From Legal to Illegal Abortion, and Back Again

Russian legislation prior to the Revolution applied strictly the principle of criminal penalties for "aborting the fruit." At the beginning of the Revolution these penalties were not applied in the majority of cases, but they were only rescinded formally on November 18, 1920. The new legislation permitted abortion under hospital conditions, free of charge. Abortion had to be carried out by qualified doctors. This ordinance was warmly received by the broad masses of the population. A heavy burden seemed to have fallen from the shoulders of millions of women, whom the old legislation had pushed on the path of secret abortion with all its dangerous consequences. True, the population as a whole, and young women in particular, were insufficiently informed of the possibly unpleasant consequences of abortion. Likewise, insufficient attention was paid to questions of preventing pregnancy at a time, in the early years of Communism, when a very casual attitude to sex and the problem of abortion was current. As a result, free abortion led in practice to a vast increase in irresponsible abortions, for which many thousands of women had to pay a heavy price in the years to come. Even worse was the fact that secret abortions were still being practiced after the law of 1920 had come into force. This was due to various causes, such as the bureaucratic methods of granting a certificate of abortion, the overcrowded hospitals, and the desire sometimes on the part of women to conceal their pregnancy. In 1936, when the question of abolishing free abortion was raised, many items in the press referred to the widespread practice of secret abortion and even to secret "abortion clinics." Nevertheless, the ordinance promulgating free abortion had done much of positive significance.

Legal abortion had, it seemed, become a Communist tradition. But in 1936 the Soviet government decisively broke with it. The Law of June 27, 1936 reestablished penalties for abortion. Some exceptions were admitted "exclusively in those cases when continued pregnancy represented some danger to life or threatened serious damage to the health of a pregnant woman, and also where serious hereditary diseases might be transmitted

by the parents, and then only on the premises of hospitals and birth clinics."
In this respect, the new law could compare with the legislation of the most
"pious" countries, since few countries forbid abortion where continued
pregnancy threatens life or creates the threat of severe damage to the
mother's health.

The prohibition of abortion was a means of increasing the birthrate
which had begun to fall rapidly in the second half of the 1920's. It was no
accident that a multitude of articles in the Soviet journals and papers commented on and praised the prohibition of abortion while at the same time
carefully avoiding any suggestion of popularizing any birth-control measures. The Law of June 27 had been propounded as an active measure in
population politics, and Stalin himself appears to have taken the initiative.
This supposition is borne out by the following strange incident which took
place at the beginning of 1936 at a Kremlin conference between the leaders
of the Communist Party and a numerous Buryat-Mongol delegation. When
speaking of her life, one of the delegates, a woman collective farm worker,
said: "I have a family of seven children." Stalin interrupted her approvingly:
"Another seven, that would be good!" The delegate was confused for a
moment and failed to reply to the comment from on high, and this comment, contrary to custom, was not repeated anywhere in the press. But
Stalin's new attitude to woman as a generative machine was here expressed
with all precision, and it was soon to be formulated in legislation.

The serious consequences of the prohibition of abortion very soon came
to light but almost two decades had to pass, and Stalin himself had to
disappear from the historical scene, before this prohibition was removed
and the Soviet Union returned, with the decree of November 23, 1955, to
the position that had existed prior to the 1936 Law. M. D. Kovrigina,
Minister of Health of the USSR, referred to this fact in her report "On the
System of National Health Preservation and State Protection of Mothers and
Children in the Soviet Union" presented at the International Women's
Seminar in Moscow in September 1956.

In the first two years after the promulgation of the law prohibiting
abortion, the number of illegal abortions was small. But from 1938 on
their number began to increase. As a rule, the women who had recourse
to illegal abortion entered medical institutes with hemorrhages. Many of
them already had serious complications, and it was not always possible to
save the victims. These "outside" abortions not infrequently resulted in
serious gynecological illnesses and sterility.

With a view to preserving the health and life of women, the Praesidium
of the Supreme Soviet of the USSR had issued, in 1955, a decree withdrawing
the prohibition of abortion. Now a woman desiring to interrupt her pregnancy has no need to seek the services of ignorant persons and to expose
her health and life to danger.

This is a severe *ex-post-facto* judgment of the law of 1936, and even more of the stubborness with which it was kept alive for almost twenty years despite the damaging consequences which had immediately become obvious.

THE YEAR 1936: THE BEGINNING OF THE REACTION

The year 1936 marked not only the beginning of a reaction in the attitude to abortion, but also the beginning of the reconstruction of the whole system of Soviet family legislation. But although this reconstruction was clearly permeated with a reactionary spirit, the concrete measures promulgated showed at times some improvement in the situation as it existed till then. In part, some procedural improvements were introduced in matters of divorce: it was made obligatory for both parties to be present at ZAGS; the divorce decree was registered in the passport; and fees in the case of a second and third divorce were increased.

However, formally everything remained unchanged in the matter of concluding and dissolving marriage. Only in 1944 did divorce legislation undergo any significant changes. By the Law of July 8, 1944, court procedure was introduced; the court had to acquaint itself with the motives which induced the man and wife (or one of them) to plead for divorce and also to attempt in the first instance to reconcile the parties. Except for the needlessly complex procedure for examining divorce cases, all this might have proved of positive significance. But this was not the most important element in the new procedure; it was rather a striving to hinder divorce by charging very high court fees and imposing additional taxes to a considerable amount—fines in fact—chargeable to either one of the parties or both. It is not surprising that Maurice Hindus, who was at the time correspondent of *The New York Herald Tribune* in Moscow, summed up the situation in a despatch that passed the censor: "The financial and the formal demands (of the new law) make divorce almost impossible except for people of very high income and remarkable patience."

The hostility to divorce displayed by the authors of the Law of July 8 was also reflected in the proviso that divorce cases must be heard in public. Only as an exception, but not a mandatory one, could the court decree, at the plea of either party or both, that the examination of the case might be held in closed session.

THE DENIAL OF RIGHTS TO CHILDREN BORN OUT OF WEDLOCK

The break with the past was even more drastically evident in another innovation introduced by the law of July 8, 1944. This law returned to the concept found in earlier Soviet legislation (prior to 1926) which recognized as valid only a formally registered marriage. This was tolerable only as long

as it was still easy to obtain a divorce. It might often have grave consequences when the right to divorce was restricted. But the main difference
between the earlier position and that operative after the law of 1944 did
not lie in this. In the early years of the Revolution, the question of the
recognition or nonrecognition of a *de facto* marriage had been merely a
question of the mutual relations between the *de facto* couple. This did not
affect their children. The recognition or not of a *de facto* marriage had no
influence on the relations between the *de facto* parents and their children;
and the parents' obligation to care for their children bore an independent
character.

The law of 1944 turned this upside down. The nonrecognition of *de
facto* marriage now became the basis for completely denying any rights
to children born out of wedlock. Article 20 of the law of 1944 made this
outright statement:

"To abolish the existing right of a mother to seek to establish through
the courts a case of paternity and to demand alimony for the upkeep of a
child from a man to whom she is not legally married (in a duly registered
marriage)."

This famous clause of *La recherche de la paternité est interdite* (Article
340 of The Napoleonic Code of 1804) had now been revived in 1944 in
the Soviet Union. In France it had already been abolished by the Law of
November 16, 1912, after a century of unceasing protests. In Belgium it
had been abolished earlier, in April 26, 1908. The practical significance of
this ordinance was, it is true, somewhat softened by the simultaneous
introduction of government allowances, motivated by demographic politics,
for the upkeep and education of children born out of wedlock. But the
destructive impact of this ordinance on public morality could not be
diminished by the fact that the government now assumed responsibility for
the fathers of illegitimate children.

Although at one time the Law of 1944 was greeted in the Soviet press
with unanimous praise, what is especially noteworthy is the fact that it
has subsequently received an entirely different appraisal. Thus Boris
Grushin wrote in the June–July issue of the *Moldaya Guardia:* "With
reference to the position of the legitimate and illegitimate children, the law
(of 1944) was a large step backwards as far as the legal position of the
woman is concerned."

The law has proved especially distressing for those children who, upon
entering school, learn that a mere stroke has replaced the name of the
father in their matriculation forms. This is the "stroke" (*procherk*), which
has assumed such a wide, sad notoriety. This stroke cannot be removed
even if both parents insist on mentioning the father's name and surname
in the matriculation form. *The Literary Gazette* of January 23, 1962, stated
that it had published some eight years earlier a letter-article by the writer

Helen Serebrovskaya, in which she had sharply raised the question of this stroke. Her article had stimulated a very wide response. Since that time the editors had received thousands of letters and articles on this question and the flow has not ceased. These letters were written by ordinary Soviet citizens and men of public standing, such as Samuel Marshak, Ilya Ehrenburg, Dmitry Shostakovich, Valentin Katayev, and others. Many of these letters and articles had been printed in *The Literary Gazette*. The unanimous consensus in all of them was that the stroke should be abolished. But these expressions of public opinion have had no effect until now. The editors expressed the hope that, in view of the intended revision of legislation respecting marriage and the family, this ugly aspect of the law will be rescinded.

ALLOWANCES TO MOTHERS OF LARGE FAMILIES

The new Soviet legislation respecting the family (in the wider sense), which was begun by the law of 1936, did not stop at the prohibition of abortion and paternity claims, and the change in the regulations governing marriage and divorce. It also contained progressive elements, such as large-scale development of birth clinics and children's homes as well as an extension in the regulations protecting maternity. Positive traits are also to be found in the "state assistance to large families." But the system of allowances to large families, which had been dictated by motives of demographical rather than social politics, assumed a distorted form from the beginning.

Allowances to mothers of large families were introduced by the law of 1936. They began with the seventh child; 2,000 rubles per annum was allowed for each child from the age of seven to that of ten; 5,000 rubles for the eleventh and any subsequent child in its first year, and 3,000 rubles in subsequent years during a five-year term from the birth of the child. This allowance was clearly in the nature of a premium for high fertility rather than a state subsidy for the upkeep of a child (such an allowance should have been given no later than at the appearance of the fourth or fifth child, and the amount might have been lower). It is sufficient to compare the amount of this allowance with the sum of 10 rubles a month provided by social insurance for the nursing of an infant, in order to realize that the chief aim of these subsidies to large families consisted in encouraging mothers of three, four, or five children to undertake a "mass production" of children in the pursuit of premiums.

This was a sort of monstrous "assault" on the birthrate "front." This aspect of the allowance system is strongly confirmed by the restrictions imposed by the five-year term. During this term the family will become accustomed to an increased budget, and the prospect of having the allowance cut off will thus act as an additional stimulus for the timely "production" of a new child.

The Law of 1944 had considerably expanded the system of these allowances, preserving in full measure and strengthening its specific populationist character. Since then allowances to mothers of large families have been paid as follows (after the monetary reform of 1961 all these figures lose a nought):

	First Year	Monthly Allowances for the Next Four Years
For 3rd child	400	—
4th ,,	1,300	80
5th ,,	1,700	120
6th ,,	2,000	140
7th ,,	2,500	200
8th ,,	2,500	200
9th ,,	3,500	250
10th ,,	3,500	250
11th and every subsequent child	5,000	300

It is characteristic that the allowance is increased with each succeeding child, even though extra expenditure probably tends to diminish rather than to increase with the birth of each new child.

Mothers of large families are also granted awards. The Maternity Medal is awarded to mothers of five and six children; the order of Maternal Glory to mothers of seven, eight, and nine children; and the honorable title and order of Mother-Heroine to mothers of ten or more children.

ALLOWANCES TO UNMARRIED MOTHERS

The Law of 1944 likewise stipulates allowances for unmarried mothers. That is one side of the medal; the other proclaims that no claims of paternity should be made! Here the state appears to be taking upon itself the responsibility for the upkeep of an illegitimate child. The allowance disbursed in such cases amounts to 100 rubles a month for one child, 150 rubles for two children, and 200 rubles for three or more children. The allowance is operative until the children reach the age of twelve. Here, incidentally, everything seems to stress the misshapen nature of the general system of allowances to mothers of large families.

To understand the position of women more fully, it is essential, after examining their status as wives and mothers, to clarify also their role as workers and as social entities. This is especially true of Soviet women.

THE PART OF FEMALE LABOR IN THE NATIONAL ECONOMY

The early participation of women in factory work is a characteristic feature of Russian development. This was connected with the predominance of female labor in the textile industry and with the large role which this industry played in the early history of Russian industry. By contrast, the role of female labor was insignificant, almost even nil, in metallurgy, machine factories, the coal industry and like industries which began to develop very rapidly in the last quarter of the nineteenth century.

But neither the textile industry, nor industry as a whole, could absorb the majority of women seeking employment. Thus, at the opening of the century, the majority of employable women were working as servants (or baby nurses) and in agriculture. It should perhaps be noted that, until the Revolution, and especially in the heart of Russia, female labor found no outlet in trade.

When, after a decline during the civil war, industry was rebuilt and further developed in the first half of the 1920's, women again played their part in the textile industry. In 1913, the number of women in the textile industry reached 360,000 out of a total number of 636,000 women industrial workers. By 1928, at the start of the first Five Year Plan, the total number of women in factories and mills had already exceeded the 1913 level, but in growth the textile industry outdistanced industry as a whole. The percentage of women in industry rose from 24.5 in 1913 to 28.6 in 1928; and the total number of women in industry rose to 769,000. Of these, 425,000 were textile workers.

The year 1928 marked a breakthrough not only in the Soviet economy, but also in the life of a vast number of women. The beginning of enforced industrialization required a great increase in the total number of industrial workers, and produced not only a vast movement of the population from the villages to the towns, but also an energetic involvement of the town workers' wives and daughters in industrial plants and to the so-called "activization of (town) labor reserves." Female labor now began to penetrate into all branches of industry, including those where it had never before been employed. Already at the beginning of 1933, towards the end of the first Five Year Plan, the total number of female industrial workers had reached 1,826,000—an increase of almost two-and-a-half times since 1928—although the number of women in the textile industry (434,000 as against 425,000 in 1928) showed only a small increase. Women now accounted for more than a third (35.5 per cent) of the total number of industrial workers. The process was continued energetically and by 1941 women already formed more than 40 per cent of factory and mill workers; and in 1942 they were already in the majority with 52 per cent. The same could be observed very often in an even more marked form in other branches of labor. According to the data in *The War Economy of the USSR in the Period of the Fatherland War* (1947) by N. Voznesensky, the chairman of the Gosplan, the number of women laborers and employees increased between 1940 and 1942 as follows:

	Per Cent of All Workers	
	1940	1942
Railway Transport	25	36
Communications	48	67
Communal Economy	42	64
Trade	37	55
Public Food Services	67	83
Education	58	73
Health	76	83
State Service	35	55

Particularly remarkable was the increase in the number of women engaged in skilled industrial work, which had almost been closed to them until then. Thus, still according to Voznesensky, as steam-engine operators, the percentage of women increased from 6 in 1941 to 33 at the end of 1942; as boiler stokers, their percentage increased from 6 to 27; as metal turners, from 16 to 33 per cent; as welders, from 17 to 31 per cent; as hand molders, from 12 to 32 per cent; as electricians in power stations, from 32 to 50 per cent; as loaders, from 17 to 40 per cent. The same could be noted in mechanized agriculture: the number of women tractorists in the Machine-Tractor Stations jumped from 4 to 42 per cent in the same period; from 6 to 43 per cent in MTS combines; from 5 to 36 per cent as drivers of the MTS; and from 1 to 10 per cent as brigadiers of tractor brigades.

That was in 1942. During the war years this process was continued, though at a reduced tempo, in all branches of labor. After the war, of course, an opposite trend set in. But after the enormous loss of manpower in the war and the resulting numerical preponderance of women in the adult population, the percentage of women employed as laborers and employees in general, and industrial workers in particular, never again dropped to the prewar level; and in recent years it has become stabilized at a level of about 45 per cent in industry and 47 per cent for the national economy as a whole.

This percentage has been preserved despite the gradual leveling out of the numerical disproportion between adult men and women. Thus the percentage of young women who have grown up in the postwar years and who seek employment is markedly higher than before the war.

These data refer only to hired labor. They do not include the labor of collective farmers, who even now comprise no less than a third of the total labor force of the country. In the collective-farm villages all this appears in even sharper relief. In wartime, the preponderant mass of labor, of elementary physical labor in particular, was carried out by women, and this remained basically true of the postwar years. In his sketches, *The Village Diary* (1956), Yefim Dorosh describes the life of a present-day village in the northern part of the central, non-black-earth region as follows: "The local peasant woman works hard here, far harder than the man. . . . Almost all the male labor, such as plowing, sowing, hay mowing, harvesting, is mechanized. But women still use rakes to turn over the hay and pitch-forks to pile up haystacks at the same hay mowing where the men use mowing machines. . . ." In addition, the women have to work on their garden plots, look after the cattle, prepare food, do the washing and the sewing for the whole family. "So by forty she looks like an old woman."

There is a multitude of such observations scattered through the most recent literature and the daily press. Not only do the men almost always occupy the leading positions on the collective farms or do better paid and less strenuous mechanized work, but they are also to be found in the easier administrative positions, which are likewise usually better paid than physical labor. There has even developed an original sort of folklore round this theme. In his book of sketches, *A Difficult Spring* (1956), Valentin Ovechkin quotes a *chastushka*, which he had heard sung on a collective farm by village maidens working in the fields:

> In connection with the harvest,
> I'd like to speak a little of the men.
> Bitterly I'll take them all to task—
> Not for nothing, not without a cause.

> Like good fellows, they all flock to meetings,
> (And especially to the tea-room bar!)
> But when it's time to do the work
> You won't find them in the workshop . . .

> .   .   .   .

> There goes the registrar, a handsome fellow,
> With his yardstick strolling all day long;
> There, too, an orator, a club manager,
> And one that sits in a garden like a tree stump.

> But we're in the fields, by the machine.
> They're all for sleeping and for eating.
> What sort of men are these, I ask?
> They're women—that's what they really are!

The "mechanized women" of the war years have apparently been for-gotten and have taken up other work. But of recent years—as a result of some "unhealthy publicity"—the idea has been advanced that young women and girls, who had been hand-picking cotton, should be put on cotton-harvesting machines. This initiative has apparently been having some success.

PROTECTION OF FEMALE LABOR

The widespread use of female labor in the Soviet Union has made necessary a corresponding development in measures to protect female labor. Apart from the general measures for labor protection, the Soviet labor code stipulates a series of special guarantees for women. These apply almost exclusively to cases of pregnancy, childbirth and child nursing, in brief, to maternity cases. But there are also several general norms of protection for female labor that have been established independently of cases of pregnancy or childbirth. These prohibit the use of female labor in types of work that would be too hard or injurious to the health, establish given norms for carrying and moving heavy loads by women, and partly prohibit the use of female labor under ground.

But the controls and prohibitions relative to carrying heavy loads and doing especially heavy labor are very badly observed. Women doing heavy labor and carrying great loads are such a widespread phenomenon in the Soviet Union that it has more than once attracted the attention of visiting foreigners, who have watched with astonishment women acting as stevedores and longshoremen, as well as carriers of heavy loads on construction sites, and as sanitation workers in the cities — work almost exclusively done by women. Soviet papers have often commented with critical reserve about this back-breaking work and the violation of the regulations governing women's work.

The problem of prohibiting female labor under ground is more complex. Initially, by the Code of the Labor Laws of 1918, female labor under ground was unequivocally forbidden, and this prohibition was formally preserved until 1940. But, in practice, it had been violated ever more frequently since the early 1930's, and this state of affairs was finally legalized by a decree of the Soviet of People's Commissars on October 25, 1940. This decree abolished the general prohibition against female labor under ground, but retained the prohibition against the heaviest and most dangerous types of work enumerated in the decree. But even these restrictions were constantly violated especially during the war years. In the Urals, in Kopeisk near Chelyabinsk for example, one coal mine in particular gained a lot of notoriety because all the work in it was done by women. In a number of Coal Trusts in the Donbass the proportion of women in the coal mines reached 50 and 60 per cent. After the war the situation began to improve, but not immediately. It was not until the Decree of the Soviet of Ministers of July 13, 1957 that female labor under ground was again prohibited, with a few exceptions applying to labor that did not require any great physical exertion. But unexpectedly long terms were laid down for the application of this decree—until January 1, 1959, for the coal industry. By way of illustration, one can refer to a painting by M. P. Trufanov entitled "Donbass Miner Girls," which was exhibited in the 1961 All-Union Exhibition in Moscow. A colored photograph of this painting was also included in the March 1962 issue of the monthly magazine, *Young Guard* *(Molodaya Guardia)*. The painting shows two pretty young women wearing miners' overalls and carrying miners' lamps.

The more detailed and the more strictly applied regulations for protecting female labor are those governing maternity. Of a more general character are the prohibition of night labor by pregnant women and nursing mothers and the prohibition of overtime work for these women (the prohibition of night labor applies as from the fifth month of pregnancy). It is essential to note that, contrary to a widespread opinion, the Soviet labor code has not admitted for a long time the general prohibition of night labor for women as it had been originally laid down in the code of 1918.

The law provides guarantees against any discrimination by employers against pregnant or nursing women; against pregnant and unmarried women with children up to one year of age when being dismissed; against any lowering of the wages of pregnant women and nursing mothers when they are transferred—on doctor's orders—to lighter work, and so on.

The regulations dealing with maternity leave are more important and more strictly observed: pregnancy leave for women is eight weeks before and eight weeks after childbirth with a social-insurance allowance in most cases equivalent to their average earnings for the past six months up to the date of their leave. In addition, the woman is entitled to her normal (paid) vacation at her discretion either before or after the pregnancy leave. Moreover, after her pregnancy leave and general vacation with pay, a woman may, at her discretion, obtain three months' additional unpaid vacation, without loss of her job, and taking into account both her additional paid vacation and the duration of her employment.

The special measures for the protection of female labor, including the measures to protect maternity, resolve only partially the problem arising in connection with widespread employment of women. To estimate correctly the position of a woman laborer and employee, it is essential, even briefly, to consider also those measures which have as their aim to improve the position of women and which often just make it possible to attract them to outside work. These include the development of children's institutions, such as nurseries, kindergartens, playgrounds, pioneer camps.

This development is significant in an absolute sense. But it is also very modest in comparison with the demand. The total number of children up to the age of three has reached, according to the last census of 1959, about 16,000,000 or more.[1] But the total number of places available in permanent nurseries in the same year was no more than 1,208,000, or about seven-and-a-half per cent of the total number of children up to the age of three. Of course, not all of these children needed nursing care, but the dispro-portion between the number of children and the number of nursery places available is so considerable that it leaves no doubt as to the extreme lag in the development of the nurseries in comparison with the demand.

The kindergartens are also far behind the demand.

Women as "Specialists" and their Place in the State and Party Apparatus

Soviet "specialists" are people who have received a "special" education, that is, a university or a specialized higher school education. The American term "profession" corresponds to it best of all. What distinguishes the Soviet Union is that all the specialists there are state employees. But this is the formal aspect of the question when we examine the role played by women as specialists engaged in public work. It is far more important to clarify the proportion of women in the various branches of professional work and their role in a particular hierarchy.

There is a tremendous number of women specialists in the Soviet Union. Before the war, women already had won for themselves a secure position as students in universities and high schools. It is astonishing to note that the postwar percentage of women students at these educational institutions has even shown a tendency to fall.[2] This can be explained apparently by a big increase in the male student specialists rather than by any decline of interest in specialized education on the part of young women.

The varied attraction which the higher professional educational estab-lishments have for women is also characteristic. Women are only 26 per cent of those attending the higher agricultural institutions; only 31 per cent in the higher educational establishments which train industrial, con-struction, transport, and communication workers (unfortunately Soviet annual statistics do not provide more differentiated data). But, according

---

1. The census only provides summary data as to the age groups of the population: the total number of children up to and including the age of nine in 1959 reached 46,363,000; there were, therefore, on an average over 5,000,000 in each year-group, and a little more in the youngest groups.

2. For the four years 1956–60 the percentage of women among students at higher educational institutions reached the following yearly percentage: 51-49-47-45; and in the middle specialized schools: 52-48-47-46.

to the latest data, women form 59 per cent of the students in the higher training centers, of health, physical culture, and sport (the percentage would undoubtedly be higher for health alone). And women make up 63 per cent of educational, art and cinema workers.

To be a doctor or teacher is the most popular profession for women. Before the Revolution only 10 per cent of doctors were women (excluding dentists), but there were already 50 per cent by the end of the 1920's. At the beginning of the war the figures rose to 60 per cent, and after the war to 75 per cent or more. The percentage became stabilized at 75. The percentage of women is higher in the ranks of the average medical personnel (which, in the Soviet Union include the dentists). By the end of 1959, 92 per cent in this category were women.

In teaching the picture is more complex. The number of women in the primary and junior schools is enormous. The lower the school grade, the greater the percentage of women teachers. In 1959–1960, the number of women teachers in the general, non-specialized primary and junior schools reached 1,270,000, or 70 per cent of the total number of teachers. But, in the first four grades, women constituted 88 per cent of the total; in the grades five to seven, 76 per cent; and in grades eight to eleven, 67 per cent. Women formed 69 per cent of the principals in primary schools, and 20 per cent of directors in the junior schools.

In 1957, women represented 39 per cent of teachers and other specialists in educational establishments and organizations training personnel, that is, in higher and special junior educational institutions. But as directors, rectors, principals, and deputies of these institutions, women only numbered 15 per cent. There were only 41 per cent of women professors, readers, teachers, and instructors; and 61 per cent of laboratory assistants.

The fact that women are lagging behind in the hierarchy of specialists can be observed in all branches of specialized work. To some extent this is natural in many spheres where the flow of women into the ranks of the specialists is a comparatively new phenomenon (this does not apply to health or the primary school). But, in practice, this lag is everywhere in excess of what might be explained by the difference in the time-period of a specialist's work in a given sphere. This is a problem that still awaits resolution.

The sharp increase in women as engineers in factories in the postwar period deserves attention. The woman engineer in the factory has now become a daily occurrence. Already prior to the war a significant number of women students in the higher educational establishments were being trained as engineers, but the woman engineer was still an exception in the factory. During the war a great deal of work had to be done by women engineers and, after the war, the woman engineer stayed on in the factory as a common phenomenon, not infrequently in the capacity of foreman, but rarely—except in the traditionally female textile industry—in the capacity of a director and even more infrequently in the role of chief engineer. This has also found its reflection in literature: in the most recent Soviet novels, short stories, and plays, we constantly meet women working as engineers in factories; and the authors of these works usually do not even stress the new phenomenon. The woman engineer has now solidly entrenched herself in the life of the factory.

In the light of such widespread use of female labor in all branches of professional life, it is all the more surprising to note the relatively weak influence exercised by women on the life of the State and the Party. It is true, women are elected, for the most part, into the Soviets (both lower and higher) from the village Soviets in which according to the data for 1958 and 1959 (in the special statistical volume of the Central Statistical Institution *Woman in the USSR*, 1960) the percentage of women deputies is around 38, to the Supreme Soviets of the Union Republics, where the percentage of women is about 32, and the Supreme Soviet of the USSR, where they number about 27 per cent. But these figures reflect their real influence only to a very small degree.

In the postwar years local Soviets have often displayed notable activity, not so much as representative bodies but rather as organs which, through their departments and commissions, serve many cultural, social, and economic necessities of the population. Here women, both deputies and non-deputies, often find a field for the application of their public energy. But leadership in this work, even on the lower rungs of the Soviet system, almost always remains in the hands of men. The number of women occupying the position of chairmen of the executive committees (*ispolkoms*) of local Soviets is quite insignificant; and in the regions (*oblast*), there appears to be no executive committee which has a woman president.

If nevertheless the percentage of women in the regional Soviets, in the Supreme Soviets of the Union Republics, and in the Supreme Soviet of the USSR, remains considerable (even though far less than their percentage in the population as a whole and especially in the adult population), these figures do not represent the real influence of women. Their aim is not so much to insure such influence as to be demonstrative. This has, of course, a certain significance, since it accustoms the population to the idea of the social equality of women. But this is far from actual equality.

It is no accident that only an insignificant number of women, in secondary positions and mainly for demonstrative purposes, form part of the governments of the Union Republics. The government of the USSR contains only one woman, Yekaterina Furtzeva, who is Minister of Culture also mainly for demonstrative purposes.

The only exception to the limited participation of women in state officialdom is their role in the law courts and people's courts in which one often meets women not only as members of the court, but also as assessors. In the Supreme Court of the USSR, elected in April 1962, there was one woman among sixteen justices, and of its forty-five assessors there were twelve women. It is interesting to note that five of these latter were Muslims, although Islam denies women the right to participate in public life.

The role of women is still weaker in the party apparatus, which is more influential than the state (Soviet) apparatus. Very rarely are women to be found in the lower rungs of the party apparatus—those of secretaries of district committees (*raicoms*). There is not a single woman among the first secretaries of the regional and town committees (*obkoms* and *gorkoms*). As an exception, one may note that Yekaterina Furtzeva had been first secretary of the Moscow town committee (*gorkom*) since 1954, then a member of the Praesidium of the Central Committee and, finally, Minister of Culture. But the new Central Committee, which was elected at the Twenty-second Congress in October 1961, did not reelect Furtzeva to the Praesidium; and in the Supreme Soviet elections of the spring of 1962, she was not elected as a member either.

The data of the Twenty-second Party Congress bear witness to the insignificant role played by women in the party apparatus. The number of women in the party up to the time of the Congress was relatively modest (20.7 per cent). Among the delegates at the Congress, corresponding to the directive about the election of at least one woman to each regional delegation, the percentage of women turned out to be somewhat higher, namely, 22.3 per cent. But women played a very modest part in the work of the Congress. There were only three women among the 68 delegates who commented on Khrushchev's report on the activities of the Central Committee and on his report about the project of a new party program. And only ten women out of 330 members and candidates for membership on the Central Committee of the Party were elected at the Congress. And finally, when the new Central Committee had formed its Praesidium and its Secretariat, there was not a single woman among either the sixteen members and candidates of the former, or among the five members of the latter.

Khrushchev was right when, at the Twentieth Congress of the Communist Party, he declared (in his report about the activities of the Central Committee) that women are rarely promoted to leading positions in a number of party and Soviet organs. There are very few women in executive positions in either party or Soviet work, or as the secretaries of party committees, chairmen of executive committees of the workers' Soviets, directors of industry, of collective farms and state farms. The situation has in no way changed since.

THE NEW ASPECT OF WOMAN

After the serious crisis which it suffered in the early period of the Revolution, the idea of the family was revived in the middle 1930's. But the woman's position in and her attitude to the family was now different from what it had been before the crisis. Of course there are still many families of the old, prerevolutionary type in the Soviet Union. But many new traits can also be observed in the family and, if we attempted to generalize about them, we sohuld be confronted with the image of a new Soviet woman and a new Soviet family.

Girls and young women still want to have a family, but not in order to gain financial support or freedom from the necessity of working outside the home (although, of course, there are some who marry for this reason); rather, they want to lead a fuller life and to have children. Nor do they identify the notion of a fuller life with that of a much fuller sexual life. On the contrary, there is the recrudescence in the relations between the sexes of a certain trait of reserve, of "puritanism" even, characteristic of the heroes of Russian classical literature. To a certain extent this may be a reaction against "the excesses" of the early Revolution.

Life is hard, and the earnings of a husband or father may often be insufficient to support a family. The woman must often of necessity seek additional means of livelihood. But necessity is not the only reason for her seeking it. In large families, especially workers' families, in which a great deal of work falls on the woman, it is considered normal for a woman not to seek outside employment; and, as the mother of a family, she enjoys respect and authority. But in small families, and particularly in those of the intelligentsia, all this often turns out very differently. If a woman remains a housewife and does not engage in outside work when the family is in relatively good circumstances, she usually becomes the object of silent and sometimes of open condemnation on the part of her neighbors, and thus remains, and at times feels herself, socially and to some extent morally at a disadvantage.

This, it would seem, is the general trend. But it would be a mistake to suppose that the process is already far advanced. Quite on the contrary, in the literature of the last few years there has been a noticeable change in the attitude toward the desirability of women engaging in work outside the home. Arkadi Pervenzov's novel, *A Branch of Olives*, published in 1965 in the magazine *October*, can serve as an illustration. Pervenzov describes the life of progressive workers in a factory, headed by Engineer Pavel Karej, one of those who in the 1930's built up the industry of the new state. Karej's daughter, Ludmilla, is a worker in the Scientific Research Institute. Karej, after having lived for many years as a widower, falls in love with his daughter's girlfriend, Varya Okatova, who also works in the

Research Institute. One one occasion Ludmilla admits to her father that she would enjoy cooking a tasty meal. "What? You want to return to the kitchen?" asks the father. "Why not?" answers the daughter. "Ask Varya, she would vote for this with both hands. And if you want to know, as soon as husbands will be a little better off, the wives will leave the machines, nor will they continue in their scientific professions, except perhaps in the easiest work."

This passage expresses frankly the desire of the women of the Soviet elite to give up their hard, professional work for an easier and more quiet life. The same subject is handled even more seriously in a story by Vitali Vasilevski, entitled *The Knot* (1959). The scene is a village inhabited by workers of a large textile factory. The secretary of the local committee, Tatiana Kirsanova, a woman engineer, young, beautiful and full of energy, converses with a younger girl, Elena Saltikova, a pilot by profession, and at the moment hospitalized as a result of a crash. Elena wants to get married, and while she does not yet know what she will do once she can leave the hospital, it is clear to her that she no longer wants to be a pilot.

"Am I obliged to work?" she asks Tatiana.

"To work?" Tatiana answers. "A woman does not have to work all her life, unless she must support herself. She must have children, must bring them up. Although, to do nothing at all is also wrong and a shame."

The widespread participation of women in outside work, and the higher regard paid to women's domestic work in large families, have developed in women a feeling of equality and independence. This is not only a feeling of independence from the husband. Soviet literature and the daily press very often afford us striking examples of their great independence on collective farms, at workers' meetings and plants; but this is more rarely observable at party and komsomol meetings. And even more remarkable is the relatively small part women play in the activities of the Party apparatus, especially on the higher rungs.

The radical change in women's social status and her sharply increased independence are perhaps best illustrated by the radical change of attitude toward unmarried mothers. A young unmarried woman who has a child does not feel any sense of social condemnation; sometimes she is even treated with greater consideration. This is all the more noteworthy because there exists at present, generally speaking, a negative attitude toward casual affairs.

All the factors just discussed are already solidly established traits of the Soviet woman's situation. Further development can only lead to greater social and economic equality.

Mainland China *

By Ai-li S. Chin

INTRODUCTION

*T*he women of China have come a long way from the olden days of bound feet and seclusion within the family compound of the well-to-do, or the illiteracy of the farm wife with a mental horizon limited by boundaries of the village and marketplace. The modern Chinese women enjoy the same educational opportunities as men, and can be found literally in every walk of life. In the Republic of Free China, married professional women work under their maiden names, while girls compete on an equal basis for admission to the top national university. In Communist China, vast numbers of women turn their small children over to day nurseries, and work in steel mills and mines, on the railroad, highways, and steamships, as well as in offices, communes, shops, and government posts. What is the story of this transformation, and what is the cost of this newly won freedom?

* Parts of the data for this article were gathered under the auspices of the East Asian Research Center, Harvard University.

The 1949 political splitting of the country into Nationalist and Communist China has meant two separate lines of development in the continued forward thrust of the women of China. While both streams are of equal historical significance, we shall discuss predominantly the women in Communist China because the situation is less well known there and data are relatively inaccessible to the general public outside. But the true meaning of recent developments cannot be appreciated without reviewing the position of women in the stable, traditional China of past centuries, and tracing the beginnings of change in the turbulent, exciting period of transition during the early Republic. This main historical stream is now carried on by women in Free China on the island of Formosa, while on the Communist Mainland, the formerly spontaneous feminist movement has come under the control of the state, and is channelled and redirected to serve national goals as conceived by the leaders of the regime.

TRADITIONAL SITUATION

Traditional Chinese society was dominated by the patrilineal family system. A daughter was considered a temporary member of her parents' household, to be "lost" to the husband's family at marriage. After marriage even her individuality was sacrificed; she dropped her personal name and became known by the husband's surname followed by her own. After the birth of children she was referred to indirectly by her children's name. Upon her death, only her family surname was recorded in her husband's genealogy, and her personal identity was lost to history.

The Extended Family—A second feature of the Chinese family was the solidarity and mutual obligation of all male descendants of the name line throughout their lifetime. Mature sons were obligated to maintain a position submissive to their fathers, and married brothers were expected to continue their mutual loyalty and support. These familial obligations overshadowed all other social obligations and were to the traditional family and society a major source of strength and stability. The perfect Confucian ideal was the extended family, five generations living under one roof and ruled by the eldest male. (The actual prevalence of the large household and of alternative patterns will be discussed later.)

Within this large household there was a definite hierarchy of authority and deference, governed by the principal of seniority of generation and male dominance. The women occupied a specified status with well-defined duties. These duties were succinctly stated in the classics and upheld by generations of Confucian scholars: A woman must serve her parents when young, serve her husband's parents and her husband when married, and after the death of her husband, remain a widow and serve her sons. Between husband and wife there must be a clear separation of functions and a distinct division of labor.

A Girl's Place in the Family — As a child in her parents' family, a girl learned early to adjust herself to life in a group with a definite structure and hierarchy of authority. The small family unit of her own parents and immature siblings constituted but one part within the extended family and had to be submerged in importance to the larger group. A child in her everyday activities learned to obey her grandparents, parents, aunts, uncles, older siblings, and cousins. She learned that her place was secondary to male children of the same generation. Thus her early years prepared her for the much more difficult adjustment upon marriage. In such a milieu, the spirit of independence and self-assertion in the young people was not fostered, especially in girls. Instead, individuality was subordinated to the higher value of group harmony essential to the survival of the large family.

The Bride's Place in the Family — After marriage, the traditional Chinese woman had to submit herself first and foremost to the authority of her parents-in-law, and secondarily to that of her husband and all other elders in the large family. Her place in this new family was far different from that in her parental family. Although a daughter was not formally valued as a permanent member of the parental family, actually her position there was often cushioned by bonds of natural affection and indulgence. In her husband's family, she was constantly on trial; she was judged on her adequacy as a daughter-in-law and put in a competitive position with the other daughters-in-law. She also had to win the acceptance and affection of the unmarried daughters. It was customary for the bride to prepare and serve some food to the parents-in-law, even if symbolically, to demonstrate her abilities in the kitchen. Her handiwork was examined and evaluated for excellence; and, above all, she had to be a model of deportment at all times.

In this critical phase of her life, she had the support and comfort of no one nearby, not even her husband, whose first duty and loyalty was to his parents. She could not return home for visits before a prescribed time interval, and in any case she could not do so too frequently. Her own family was for all purposes cut off from her new life. In cases of complaints of maltreatment, the wife's family usually counseled patience and forbearance, or even sided with the husband's family in order to prevent an open feud between the two family units. Grounds for divorce initiated by the wife were so stringent and the social disgrace and isolation for the divorced woman so serious a problem as to make divorce practically impossible.

There remained one last recourse for the unhappy daughter-in-law: suicide. That was an ultimate avenue of escape and weapon of revenge, a means of bringing disgrace to the husband's family and public censure.

Thus the bride had few institutionalized means of protection for her interests and welfare, while all the pressures were lined up on the other side: the subjugation and incorporation of a new member into an ongoing social unit. This is why Chinese folklore abounds with tales of the cruel mother-in-law. However, there were mitigating factors. In many families, the daughter-in-law was genuinely welcomed with affection and esteem. Parents with no daughters of their own often treated a congenial daughter-in-law as if she were their own flesh and blood.

Furthermore, there were many facets of life in a large household which compensated for the uncertainties and subservience of married life for a woman. Though women's activities in a family of the gentry were confined to the home, there were many family celebrations and traditional festivals which called for the preparation of special foods, decorations, and festive clothes. All this broke up the day-to-day routine and provided an atmosphere of group cooperation toward a common goal. Also, the extended family provided a readymade community of women. After her initial period of adjustment, the daughter-in-law could choose someone from among several women of her generation to be her friend and ally. Among the daughters-in-law, there often existed a feeling of sympathy and mutual protection superseding the spirit of competition for the esteem and approval of elders. Certainly in the crises of an ordinary life, the married women had the unquestioned support and assistance of a large family group.

The Mother's Place in the Family — A woman's power became greatly heightened and her position much more secure after the birth of a child, especially a male heir. Her authority increased steadily as the years passed. Through her son and on his behalf, she entered into more and more of the major decisions of the family. Without a male child, her position as wife could be jeopardized by the family's decision to bring in a secondary wife or concubine, justified in traditional times in the interest of continuity of the male line. By the time a woman's own sons married and brought in brides to be placed under her tutelage and control, she could occupy an envied position in the hierarchy of women, which paralleled and followed the male hierarchy in every extended family.

Although the traditional woman led a circumscribed life, she might achieve not only respect but power. This was far from rare, partly because the power of the male head could not be too arbitrary or absolute; he was subject to check by his own male peers in the clan. In practice, some of the decision-making processes affecting the family were informally shared by the oldest woman. And in domestic affairs, she reigned supreme. Many families, including some famous ones, were in fact ruled by strong women whose husbands had no inclination for the exercise of power or whose official duties called for long absences from home.

The large family of several generations living under one roof remained the unshaken goal throughout the centuries, but only a minority of the gentry and well-to-do merchant families could realize it. The great majority of Chinese lived in much smaller family units averaging four to six persons.

However, the Chinese family system is still described as the large-family system and the life of women under it as typical in principle for all of China. There are two reasons for this. One is that, as far as possible, the people strove to approximate this goal; and the other, that the smaller units were broken segments of the large family: parents were expected to remain with one of the married sons if the sons for economic or other reasons had to divide the property and scatter to different localities. Therefore, a young woman expected to be married according to arrangement by the family elders and to live as a bride under the dominance of the surviving elder of the husband's family or at least under the surveillance of the nearest relative. Only if her parents-in-law were both dead, would she be the uncontested mistress of her own family unit.

Variations of the ideal family prevailed among the peasants whose small plots of land could not support a large family, among the small shopkeepers, and the urban poor. The prosperous farmers and well-to-do merchants typically bought more land and kept all male branches living under one roof, or moved into town and emulated the life of the gentry. Among the peasants and the urban poor, the women were less dominated by the hierarchy of family elders. For economic reasons they also had to take a much more active part in the family enterprise, whether farming or shopkeeping. In many peasant families, the wives worked as maids in town to augment the cash income at home. The over-all effect of this economic necessity was that women from the low socioeconomic level had a greater voice in family affairs and greater freedom for social contacts in the village or trading places. Nevertheless, these women had to play a secondary role to surviving male elders, especially in formal and public matters outside the family.

Class Mobility—China was an open-class society. In theory, any person with ability could climb the social ladder, usually by way of the examination system of officialdom, although this avenue was in practice beset by difficulties for the economically handicapped. Then through commerce one could accumulate money, buy land and, at certain periods and in a minority of cases, even buy an imperial degree or an official appointment. A woman's social status, therefore, was by no means fixed at birth or even at marriage, but rose or fell with the fortunes of her parental family. She could also change her class status through marriage or through the later academic success of her husband. Normally, marriage was arranged between two families of equal status because it cemented relations between two name lines. Marriage of the conventional type occasionally also occurred across class lines.

Special instances of upward social mobility were the concubines, who were taken into well-to-do gentry or merchant families from among the poor. The status of the concubines remained secondary to that of the wife, but in cases where she bore the only male heir to the line she could rise in position and power to be a threat to the main wife. However, mobility was slow in a society with a large family system because the successful individual was obligated to raise the social and economic standards of his parents and brothers and contribute to the support of other needy relatives. Moreover, concubinage was restricted chiefly to well-to-do families who could afford the luxury of large households. Among the peasants and urban workers, and in most families of moderate means, monogamy was the rule. Other than through marriage, avenues of individual mobility were, for practical purposes, closed to women.

Separation of Sexes in Religion and Ritual—In matters of religion and public ceremonies, there was a clear segregation of function between men and women, Confucian ancestral rites belonged exclusively in the male province. Women observed many Buddhist rituals of worship and food abstinences, and frequented Buddhist temples and shrines. In addition, women of lower economic groups also took part in a mixture of animistic Buddhist, and corrupt Taoist practices.

Women of Distinction—While careers outside the home were inconceivable for the traditional woman, she could still achieve a measure of social distinction and cultural contribution besides receiving public honor for being a virtuous wife or mother. Some women became well educated in the Confucian classics at home. There were noted women poets, historians, and scholars in the classics. The most famous was Pan Chao who in the first century distinguished herself as a court historian and has ranked through the centuries among China's foremost scholars of traditional learning. She was chosen by an emperor of Han, the first dynasty to rule a unified China, to be historian to the Imperial Court, though she had no formal title. She wrote a treatise on the education of women which remained a classic. In subsequent centuries, not a few women made a name for themselves through literary and artistic accomplishments. Thus, women in traditional China were not prevented from engaging in intellectual pursuits, or, in the case of merchant families, from developing their managerial skills.

Under the Republic

Life for women in China remained essentially unchanged from the time of Confucius (ca. 500 B.C.) up to the beginning of the twentieth century. When Western impact began to be felt late in the nineteenth century, the entire traditional social structure started to crumble. Western ideas of science and democracy destroyed the airtight system of Confucian thought that had guided the ruling group of China for so long. Western industrial advances and military might shattered the primacy of the land-based gentry.

Politically, the 1911 revolution of Sun Yat-sen succeeded in overthrowing the Manchu dynasty and establishing the Republic of China. In the following quarter of a century, ideas about modernizing China, which arose during the declining years of the Ching dynasty, culminated in wave after wave of social movements which manifested the rising nationalist consciousness of the nation and which in turn roused the people of a stable, ethnocentric civilization to a restless search for a modern way of life.

Women's Demands—In towns and cities women began demanding a chance for formal education, a greater voice in marriage, and freedom to broaden their horizons beyond the strict confines of the Confucian Code. In the early decades of the twentieth century, while the nation was struggling with the formation of a stable, democratic government, women fought for and won new outlets. They took part in actual revolutionary battles and long military marches alongside their male compatriots in the fight for political and social rights. Ch'iu Chin was only one of the famous girl martyrs of the 1911 revolution. In the ensuing ideological, intellectual, and cultural movements known as the Renaissance or New Culture Movement of 1917, and the May 4th Movement of 1919, women, though in the minority, became equal partners with men.

In this cultural renaissance, which encompassed language reform as well as experimentation with Western forms of literary and psychological self-expression, sentiments of a national and social reappraisal came to the fore. Perhaps nowhere else can we find a more cogent and passionate plea by young men and women for individual development and freedom from familial and traditional restraints than in the "New Literature" of the 1920's and 1930's.

Several of the nationally known writers, both essayists and storywriters, were women, who wrote not only about the special problems of becoming modern women, but about issues of national scope and concern. Women also had their own publications. Among the earliest were *Women's Journal*, *Women's Messenger*, *Young Women*, and *Women's Miscellany*. In addition, women joined young men seeking guidance in the adjustment to social change by writing to the "letters-to-the-editor" columns of magazines and newspapers, a respected outlet of expression which was taken seriously by both readers and editors interested in the cause of modernization.

Pressure for Freedom from Family Control—Young people in urban centers began to demand freedom from parental control. In fact, the family became the favorite target of attack for all kinds of social evils. Under these circumstances, parents no longer served as role models for young people. Nor was the traditional parental prerogative of match-making acceptable for the younger generation. What took its place was not a complete transplanting of the Western idea of romantic love, but a demand for individual determination based on a mixture of rational criteria and personal compatibility. A boy's ideal girl was described in one advice column as having these qualities: "gentle nature," "good health," "not too ugly," and some degree of education. Girls during these years were looking for husbands not with good family background but with personal abilities and educational training sufficient to achieve independent occupational status. Compatible mental outlook and common interests became important qualities. In short, equal status and mutual companionship were, above all, desired by the newly emancipated women. Living in an age when the cultural horizon seemed to be expanding without limits, women entered into the struggle for independence and self-determination with confidence, indeed, with the zeal of crusaders. They felt that in their efforts to shake off centuries of inequality, they were helping to build a strong and modern nation.

Freedom of Education for Girls—During this Republican period, women fought for and attained the freedom to receive an education outside the home. As modern schools were opened first in cities and towns and gradually in rural areas, girls flocked to them, as well as boys. At the secondary level, separate schools for girls were opened, many of which concentrated on the training of teachers. However, in the general movement to erase illiteracy, women's progress still lagged behind that of men. In a sample survey of nine counties in South China, in 1942 and 1943, only 19 per cent of the women were literate as compared to 48 per cent of the men.

In colleges and universities, women began attending classes with men students and receiving an equal education, though, of course, women students remained in the minority, often concentrating in a few preferred fields, such as teaching and nursing (the first professional fields to receive women in large numbers), literature, history, and the arts. However, the sciences and other professional fields attracted adventurous and able women. A few among them also followed the first men in going abroad for advanced training. In professional fields, pioneer feminists became doctors, lawyers, teachers, and writers as soon as opportunities opened up, or entrance was individually fought for and won. All-women banks, staffed by women and serving women, YWCA's, and other associations for professional and artistic self-expression were soon formed.

Educational Role of Missionaries—In opening up educational opportunities for women in the early Republican years, missionaries played an important role. In fact, the position of women in general played a part in rousing the missionaries' indignation, and motivated the more socially minded among them to work in China. In higher education, Ginling College for women was well known. At the secondary level, missionary boarding schools in the cities gave many girls from well-to-do families a modern, Western-oriented education and social contact with foreigners; while in provincial towns, mission-supported schools provided a much needed avenue of educational mobility for ambitious girls from villages and small towns otherwise relatively isolated from modern influences. A less dramatic contribution of the missionary to freeing the woman from her tradition-bound status was the creation of the "Bible woman," one of the first modern semi-professional roles open to women who remained in the countryside.

Perhaps due to the selective educational efforts of missionaries, and because of the basic fact that women's roles were less firmly imbedded in the occupational and political structures of society, women in modern China have been more easily, and in some quarters more thoroughly, "Westernized" than men in comparable social strata. In sheer size, though, the process of modernization has probably affected a smaller number of women than men.

New Work Opportunities—For the vast majority of uneducated women both from the villages and in new urban industrial centers, change in status followed other avenues. Some copied the educationally better prepared women in first freeing themselves from bound feet, an early symbol of emancipation. This gave them greater freedom of movement both in and out of the home and opened up possible outside employment. The economically less-privileged women sought chances to enter the industrial job market: the cotton mills, hosiery and knitting mills, and tobacco factories. Here, in the early years of industrialization, women worked under the labor-contract system, with long working hours and under substandard working conditions.

The plight of these early women laborers brought forth efforts of reform by missionary groups and by some educated Chinese women. Not much has been written on the lives of these women factory workers of this period. It is known that they had to live in dormitories, where, in their loneliness and bewilderment, women formed pseudo-familial groups, with older women acting as "fathers" and "mothers." Other women workers in some of the urban centers, especially in Shanghai and in South China cities, formed sororities in which lifelong loyalties were pledged for mutual protection against the vast impersonal forces of the industrial metropolis.

Results of Freedom in Wider Marriage Choice—One consequence of the new-found freedom and opportunities was a widening of women's mental horizon from the confines of domestic affairs to social, cultural, national, and indeed international matters. For the few able and ambitious women, opportunities for education and a career had few unsurmountable obstacles. For the vast majority, emancipation meant freedom to choose their marriage partners and to have a much stronger voice in determining their own life course. Within the family, it meant that modern women were liberated from the ever-present and sometimes overwhelming pressure of tradition and parental authority. Outside the home, it meant a chance, within limits, to hold jobs and take part in group activities and maintain social contacts. For a minority of modern women, unfortunately, sex equality and freedom from traditional duties and obligations was not accompanied by a new code of familial and social responsibility. With the small family system as the new norm, bearing sons to carry on the family line did not have to be the primary duty and source of satisfaction for women, though it might well remain her important role from the husband's point of view even in more or less modern families. The new education was not always adequate for training women to regard life in the home, now shrunken in size and functions, as a creative job, neither did it always prepare women for practical employment outside. The result was a new leisure class among women, to be taken into account along with the many real contributions made by women of this transition period.

For the lower socio-economic groups, women's liberation meant their release for the industrial labor market and the weakening of male authority in the home. Increasingly, working women brought in cash incomes substantial enough to give them a claim to power and authority in the home and outside. However, economic gains for the less privileged women were not accompanied by any basic changes in outlook or way of life.

The Sino-Japanese war (1937–1945), with its increased demand for labor power and dislocation of families, intensified the trend toward independence and responsibility among women.

Women In Taiwan

When the National Government moved to Taiwan (the Island of Formosa), it carried the mainstream of the social-cultural tradition of China. The trend of spontaneous, gradual change in women's status also continues in Taiwan. Here, with a stable administration and under the guidance of Sun Yat-sen's political doctrine and Western ideas of democracy, women continue their steady, though unspectacular, development toward a greater part in national and social affairs. Leading in prestige is of course Madame Chiang Kai-shek, who in her travels abroad often represents her government officially or in a symbolic capacity. Women in Free China participate in political as well as professional and business activities. By law, women are guaranteed one tenth of the elective offices. In the Taiwan Provincial Assembly, for example, there were ten women to sixty-four men during the 1963–1964 session. In the city and county councils in the same period, women had ninety-five seats while men occupied 834, or a rough ratio of 1:8.

Women can be found in nearly all the modern occupations in Free China. A high proportion of married women continue to hold paid jobs to raise the family income or to find outlets for their professional, artistic, or managerial abilities. To give but one example, in the postal and telecommunications sector alone, there are nearly 3,000 female employees. The prolification of personal service industries provides many jobs for large numbers of girls from rural areas and the less privileged urban families, thus giving the young graduates of primary or junior high schools a measure of personal and economic independence from their families before entering into marriage. In the traditional style shops and on farms, women continue to have a share in productive responsibilities.

Today, universal education provides girls as well as boys with a minimum of six years of primary school education. Beyond that, nearly 40 per cent of junior high school pupils are girls, while in senior high schools there is one girl to every two boys. In colleges and universities the ratio of girls to boys becomes one to three, but this figure does not include students enrolled in teachers training schools, where girls slightly exceed boys. Thus, while girls are underrepresented among high school and college graduates, educational opportunities are open to the more ambitious ones. And since educational advancement is governed by a strictly guarded, universalistic, national examination system, girls compete equally with boys for educational attainments, subject to personal preference and some degree of differential treatment in the family.

For the majority of women in Free China, marriage and the family is still the main life goal. But family living for an increasing number means the small, separate household of husband-wife and unmarried children. The wife is no longer under the unquestioned authority of the mother-in-law. This is increasingly the pattern with young people who choose their own marriage partners. A recent study showed that high school students preferred to choose their own marriage mates over parental choice by four to one, though the ratio of their parents' own marriage choice was the reverse. The younger generation is also planning to have smaller families. The same study revealed that high school students now wish to have three to four children, while their parents actually have five to six. The trend toward smaller families is intimately tied to the increasing independence of women. Even in rural areas, family planning is making inroads, while the farmer's wife is enjoying a rising standard of living. It is a common sight to find the sewing machine and radio as standard equipment in the rural home.

Besides home and work, the contemporary women in Free China may also join a variety of voluntary associations for patriotic, professional, recreational, or social activities. The Government-sponsored Chinese Women's Anti-Aggression League had a membership of 230,000 in 1962–1963. Some of the more prominent professional associations are the Society of Women Doctors, the Society of Nurses, the Union of Midwives, and the Taiwan Provincial Women Writers' Society. The Taiwan Provincial Women's Association is an organization devoted to the protection of women's rights, and the promotion of their interests, education, and welfare. Other women's organizations have international affiliations, such as the Women's Association for the Study of Asian Problems or the International Women's Club. Many of the associations engage in social welfare work aimed at bettering the lot of women. Training classes in homemaking or maternity and child care are ever popular, though vocational training is rapidly gaining ground. Other services rendered to women by these associations include legal counselling, mediation in family disputes, aid to the aged and disabled, and even matchmaking.

While voluntary associations of many kinds can be found, the contemporary woman of Free China is typically not a "joiner." Without advanced mechanical equipment in the home, the Chinese woman has little leisure or resources for forming the manifold club or community service organizations familiar on the American scene. The daily life of the average woman is largely confined to her home or job, a small circle of friends and relatives, and a certain amount of physical mobility. Her mental horizon, though, is infinitely extended by the educational opportunities and the wider network of intellectual and social contacts.

The Communist Regime

After the Communist revolution, changes in women's position and activities that had started as part of a spontaneous social movement became incorporated into government policy. The labor potential of women was put to the fullest use because of the vast need for manpower in the rapid program of industrial and agricultural expansion. Moreover, equality and the duty of every able-bodied person to be economically productive are part of the Marxist doctrine. The result has been a nationwide program of enforced liberation of women from familial bonds and duties and other social restrictions in order to work outside the home. Government-sponsored movements of various sorts encourage to the utmost women's participation in "socialist reconstruction."

Although this discussion on women in Communist China has had to be based on whatever published material has come out from behind the iron curtain, such information must not be dismissed as mere propaganda. With methodological safeguards, one can glean much from Communist writings, especially from mass-communications material intended for internal consumption. In fact, we can construct a substantial picture of what Communist leaders, utilizing all the apparatus of the party and the state, are trying to develop. There is, unfortunately, little information on how people actually behave, think and feel.

New Marriage Law — The first and perhaps the most basic step of the Communist authorities to further women's liberation was the new marriage law of May 1, 1950. This law, in preparation since 1948, before the establishment of the People's Republic, occupied an important place in the early planning of the Communist leaders. Its essentials are as follows:

1. Marriage shall be based on the free choice of husband and wife. Interference in this freedom by any third person is prohibited. The obtaining of money or goods by a third party, functioning as an intermediary marriage broker, is likewise prohibited.

2. A marriage must be registered with the local organ of the People's Government, which shall issue a certificate of marriage after all regulations have been complied with.

3. There shall be complete equality between husband and wife, each having the right to keep his own surname after marriage, to choose his occupation, to join in outside activities, to own and manage property, and to inherit the other's property.

4. Parents have the duty of raising and educating their children. Children have the duty of supporting and helping their parents. Neither is permitted to oppress or abandon the other. Parents and children have the right to inherit one another's property.

5. Children born outside of legal marriage shall enjoy the same rights as children born of legal wedlock. No one may discriminiate against them. When paternity is proved by the mother or other witnesses, the father has the duty to assume all or part of the child's support and education till the child reaches eighteen years of age. If the natural mother agrees, the child may live with his father.

6. Divorce shall be granted upon mutual agreement between husband and wife. It shall also be granted if only one party insists upon divorce, and the local People's Government and judicial organ fail to dissuade the person. After divorce, if husband and wife both wish to resume married life, they must register their intention to remarry with the local People's Government.

7. While the wife is pregnant, the husband may not petition for divorce, but must wait one year after the birth of the child. If the wife wishes to initiate divorce, she is not limited by this condition.

8. After divorce, parents still have the duty of supporting and educating their children. Babies of nursing age live with the mother. After nursing age, if both parents want to keep the children and cannot settle the question, the People's Court will decide in the best interest of the children. If the children live with their mother, the father must assume all or part of the cost of their support. If the mother remarries and her new husband wishes to support the children of her previous marriage, her former husband's contribution may be reduced or discontinued.

9. At the time of divorce, the wife retains the property which belonged to her before marriage. Common property which belongs to both husband and wife is to be disposed of according to mutual agreement.

If they cannot agree on its disposal, the People's Court shall decide according to the welfare of the children.

10. Upon divorce, debts incurred while husband and wife were living together shall be paid out of their common property. If their common property is not sufficient to repay such debt, the husband shall assume it.

New Law Breaks Traditional Patrilineal Stress—The significance of the New Marriage Law must be examined in light of the past. Equality of the sexes, partially and unevenly won in the Republican period, is now made legally almost complete. In the eyes of the law, the wife is, with minor exceptions, a fully equal partner with her husband in name, in property rights, and in the choice of jobs and outside activities. Patrilineal emphasis has all but disappeared, except that a father's duty to support children under different circumstances is greater than that of a mother. In both traditional and Republican days, the husband's property went to his sons upon his death, but now a wife can inherit her husband's or even her children's property, or own and dispose of her own property without her husband's consent. Women did enjoy limited property rights in pre-Communist days, but that right was not widely exercised. Similarly, concubinage was declared illegal by the Republican government, but this regulation was not universally enforced.

Besides establishing sex equality, the new marriage regulations destroyed the traditional stress on the father-son relationship and paternal authority. Since the son in traditional days occupied a position subordinate to his father during the latter's lifetime, he remained with the father in the event of divorce. Even in Republican days, minors in a divorce case went with the father as a rule, in recognition of the age-old emphasis on the male line of descent. Now the father-son relationship is greatly weakened. Although the father still has the primary duty of supporting minor children, many legal decisions are to be made in the interest of the children without the past regard to family continuity.

Results of Easy Divorce—Divorce itself, which in the past was theoretically possible but in practice almost unobtainable for women and which was given limited legal support in Republican days, now has become an easy, almost casual step. No legal grounds are necessary for divorce, no lawyers and court fees, merely the wish of one or both parties. This and the simplicity of the marriage procedure may lead to some instability of the family unit. One Communist newspaper reported in 1953 that in four cities alone (Shanghai, Peking, Tientsin, and Wuhan) divorce affected an annual two million people, including children and parents of involved parties. This high figure is undoubtedly the temporary result of the new law, a sudden dissolution of many accumulated cases of unstable marriages held together only by convention. We have no information that would lead us to the

conclusion that the divorce rate is excessively high at present. A high proportion of these divorces are initiated by women, according to a judicial
report of 1957, especially in rural districts, for men stand to lose more in
divorce action.

The Communist legal policy on marriage did more than free women for
productive work outside the home; it had some profound consequences for
the relationship between man and woman, parent and child. The sudden
rise of women in town and villages alike demanding divorce from their
husbands and release from the oppressive environment of large families,
brought forth violent reactions not only from husbands but, paradoxically
enough, also from some party activists who, because of other alignment
with vested male interests on the village level, lent their new political
power and prestige to discouraging and shaming of women who asked for
divorce. The Communist Minister of Justice herself pointed out that prejudice against divorce resulted in many instances of humiliation and intimida-
tion of women. A period of general confusion and restlessness followed
during which some cases of murder and suicide were reported. Unfortunately, we have no way to assess the true extent or duration of this
temporary period of confusion.

This freedom of divorce, together with the freedom of marriage, however difficult it might be for individual women to take full advantage of,
is something new in the lives of rural women. In the Republican period,
modern influences on women's rights only penetrated urban centers, and
even there the effects were largely restricted to the educated minority.
Now, with political backing, indeed, with deliberate propaganda pressure,
women even in remote areas have been exposed to their new rights and
their obligations to follow the current wave of equality and freedom in
marriage and divorce. The devaluation of the family and the emphasis on
productive employment in the new industrialization drive have not, however, brought a decline in the birth rate. The campaign on birth control in
1956 and 1957 was short-lived. By 1957 the government census reported a
total population of 656½ million (340 million men and 316½ million
women). The rate of population increase is officially stated to be 2 per cent
annually. At present, government efforts to slow down the population explosion have taken the shape of a concerted campaign for late marriages.
Though birth control is no longer an officially sponsored or even approved
program, contraceptive devices, both traditional and modern, are said to be
available.

Political Control through Registration of Marriages — As soon as the
women of China freed themselves from traditional shackles they became
subject to a new external force controlling their destiny. Because of the
requirement to register all marriage and divorce cases with the local government organ, its political representative has the potential power to approve

or disapprove marriages. The criteria for marriage choice now has to include political acceptability. After marriage, a woman's duties in the home are likewise under constant public scrutiny; her home life has to be subordinated to her duties as a citizen and a productive member of the Communist society. Contemporary fiction, which is rigidly controlled by the state and therefore represents a propaganda channel for transmitting politically sponsored ideals and morals, abounds with heroes and heroines who sacrifice personal or familial considerations in the interest of socialist goals.

A new avenue of mobility is now open to women with ambition. To marry a Party member is obviously one way of achieving distinction and obtaining certain privileges. The cost, however, is high, a fact which may be a serious deterrent for many women. The life of an activist is supposed to be completely dedicated to the Party. Unquestioned obedience is expected of him in all matters, including temporary separation from his family for distant missions, and demands on his time and energy at all times. The prospect of any predictable family life when one cadre member marries another is not very promising.

Restrictions on Social Relationships — Similarly under political scrutiny are the new mores governing social intercourse between men and women. Traditional sex mores were stringent for women but nevertheless explicit. Emancipated women in the Republican era, who enjoyed limited freedom of social contact with men, were hampered largely by lack of established norms of behavior and by uncertainties over the changing nature of social situations. Now, a new factor has been introduced. Communist ideology with its underlying puritanism and asceticism, has placed an intangible but definitely felt overriding restriction on the relationship between the sexes.

Romantic love is considered to be bourgeois, ideologically incorrect, a decadent habit which takes time away from politically more important and economically productive pursuits. "Real love" can come only out of "class friendship," "collective friendship." One wonders, if a girl is approached by a politically advanced cadre or activist for "friendship," does she dare refuse?

"Indiscriminate pairing off" or dating, if it interferes with production and especially if there are romantic overtones, can be suspected and open to criticism, either in routine criticism meetings or periodic, state-sponsored campaigns on Communist morality. "Questionable" behavior in mixed company may even lead to political investigation. Women of the Republican period merely groped for new patterns of behavior between the sexes; for the liberated women of Communist China there is always the possibility that disapproved behavior could be questioned on political grounds. An article in a prominent Communist newspaper complained that some young people whose attitude toward love affairs was judged indecent by the organization they worked for were castigated in general. There were other organizations, the article continued, which refused to objectively analyze cases of alleged corrupt and debased conduct, but censured the parties on irrelevant grounds. As a result, the article concluded, "no one knew what should be right and what is wrong," and "there is fear in the hearts of people that something dirty may be smeared on them." In properly defined work situations, relations between the sexes are apparently free and equal, and undoubtedly quite matter-of-fact. Whatever tensions may exist in the work situation would logically arise in many instances from the necessity for some men to be in subordinate positions to women.

Changes in Dress and Appearance—Another area of a woman's life affected by public policy is her physical appearance. In the early years of the Communist revolution, women in "liberated areas" wore a drab, shapeless uniform and short-hair style which made them almost indistinguishable from men. As cities and towns were taken over by the advancing Red Army, out of fear, women hid their wardrobes and wore the sexless garment. By the mid 1950's the dark tunic and trousers had become almost a national mark. But in 1955 a shift in government policy was reflected in speeches and newspaper articles on the desirability of introducing color and gaiety into women's clothing. Within a short period the women of this regimented society complied—flowered prints appeared on blouses, ribbons decorated the ubiquitous braids, a slight variety appeared in styles. Now to be feminine, within very narrow limits, was allowed, indeed encouraged.

But the glamour-girl type is definitely eliminated. Absent also are the Western types of smart club women or informal suburban matrons. A large number of the wealthy, Westernized women from metropolitan centers like Shanghai left the mainland along with politically-motivated and freedom-seeking women leaders in various fields. Many, however, remained for a variety of reasons, not necessarily out of political conviction. But, whatever their former social class or cultural types, they have largely been reduced to a mass type of "native" women perhaps distinguishable now mainly as urban rather than rural. The visible class distinctions in dress, appearance, and style of home life have all disappeared, except for a small number of politically privileged women in high positions. Western, "bourgeois" influences have been systematically eradicated.

Thus the family revolution that started half a century ago has now been brought to an extreme if logical end. The small biological family is now the national norm as well as the reality. Marriage and divorce are free, and women's position is legally and theoretically equal to that of men. Under a government policy of treating women of all ages as productive labor outside the home, the woman's economic independence is now forced upon her, and her status within the family is raised to a level supposedly equal with that of her husband. The fact that women work gainfully outside the home is of course nothing new in an industrialized society. What is of significance in Communist China is compulsory work for many women in industry and agriculture and required participation in organized activities.

Effects Upon the Home Routine—It remains to discuss the effects upon the home routine and what is left of the woman's functions as wife and mother.

Before the communes further revolutionized the lives of women, sex equality could mean equal rights but did not abolish the daily routines, and homemaking functions which fell to women even in a socialistic society. Outside employment and political meetings were merely burdens added to her regular duties at home. These multiple demands on women must have been a constant harassment. Possibly as a consequence of the resulting confusion, there was a move in 1956 to restore the importance of women's place in the home, subject, of course, to her higher duties to the state. The *wu-hao*, or "Five Good," program became a national campaign. Women were told to (1) arrange their homes in a proper way; (2) help and unite with neighbors; (3) encourage their husbands to work and study well; (4) educate their children in the proper way; and (5) study hard.

Economic Regimentation of Women Through Commune Movement—The Big Leap program of 1957–1958 paved the way for more drastic measures of the commune program. The emphasis in 1957 was largely economic. Women were urged, along with able-bodied men, and including those past their normally productive years, to take part in production. One and one half million urban housewives who did not already hold regular jobs reportedly set up small workshops, knitting mills, and primitive foundries. Day nurseries and kindergartens run by factories and other organizations took over the care and indoctrination of young children.

It was the commune movement, however, which fundamentally changed the home life of women. In urban centers, the communal mess halls, nurseries, and household service centers reduce the home to a mere shell of what it was. These centers, which may serve 500 to 1,000 families in an urban neighborhood, do such necessary chores as household cleaning, laundering, mending, shopping, paying bills, and caring for the aged, the infirm, and pregnant women, wherever working couples or families with special circumstances are in need of such services. The work is done by committees of resident "volunteers" who receive no pay and no rewards, but who are expected to be satisfied with the idea of serving the people and helping the socialist society. Some young mothers have to pay nursery care out of their own pockets in order to "contribute" services to such neighborhood centers. The regimentation of a woman's life must be thorough and unrelenting, penetrating the very center of intimate home life.

However, the urban commune movement never became as extensive or as pervasive as the rural communes. By 1960, the majority of urban families were resuming part or all of their familial functions. But the role of women in the neighborhood district and lane associations is an important Communist innovation. This role as intermediary between the residents and the city administration is crucial in the leadership structure.

In the large, rural communes, which range from 2,000 to 10,000 persons, the individual is the economic unit. The individual rather than the family is the unit for accounting, for political indoctrination, for organization of group activities. Husband, wife, and young people are assigned individual jobs, with equal pay for equal work. Hence, what the peasant woman in the past did for her family now gets public recognition, with pay. This gives her a degree of independent status in the community and some voice of authority within the family. Since the early 1960's, the effective working unit in the commune has been reduced in size. More responsibility has been delegated from the central organ of the commune, to, first, the production brigade and then the production team. At the same time, greater freedom is granted the family to grow supplementary food in small family plots. Hence some family functions in rural households have also been restored.

Sometimes family units are separated according to job needs. Young mothers with infants may be housed in working girls' dormitories that lack provision for the most primitive baby-care facilities. One remarkable interview with such a working mother, reported in a national Communist magazine during the Great Leap period, listed detailed complaints and pleas for a separate dormitory for working mothers so that they could have a heating stove for washing and drying diapers and help one another in times of need. For example, the article pointed out, mothers could care for sick infants without fear of disturbing the sleep of single girls who did not understand such difficulties.

Reduction of Woman's Function in the Home—The woman's central function as unifying force in the home is now greatly reduced especially since, in Communist morality, it is the political duty of children to inform on "backward" parents, and husband and wife to criticize each other's political standing. The moral unity of the home, the women's vital function, is made extremely difficult to maintain in the face of constant political intrusions. Religion, which is an important foundation for moral unity, has, of course, no place in Communist society. Recently, there has been a nationwide concern with moral education for the younger generation. However, there is as yet no sign that the responsibility for this has been placed in the home or added to the duties of the wife or mother. In time, the party or state may find it expedient to strengthen the home and enlist its aid in building up the moral fiber of the younger generation.

Educational Opportunities—Outside the home, the woman's educational and occupational opportunities have been increased and placed on the same basis as those of men. Women in the Republican period, though in theory equal with men in these respects, often lagged behind. Now, all prejudices and restrictions are supposedly removed. Even in rural areas, peasant schools, spare-time schools, and winter schools supplement regular educational opportunities for women. Back in the Yenan days (1940's) before the establishment of the People's Republic, a China Women's College was established primarily for the purpose of training women cadres or party activists. By 1957, it was claimed that 100,000 women were in various institutions of higher learning, constituting 23.2 per cent of the total student body in these institutions, as compared to 19.8 per cent in 1949. There is no doubt that the general level of literacy throughout the country has risen. The total number of women with primary, secondary, and college education is also higher. But due to the restricted curriculum of many academic disciplines, there is less freedom of choice for women in the fields of higher education in spite of the opening of traditionally male fields of study to them.

Women in Male Occupations — In many occupational fields, the early pioneers are now followed by women in masses. Even conventionally male occupations boast of "forward-looking representatives of socialist women." The first batch of railroad engineers, train despatchers, tractor drivers, mining engineers, harbor pilots, and so on, have all been duly reported and made subjects of mass propaganda. There is even a woman major general, a Madame Li Chen, with several decades of military service.

The proportion of women in the professions in general has been increasing. One recent source claims that 40 per cent of medical students are women. In Tsing-hua University, now a polytechnic institute, 20 per cent of the students enrolled in its engineering college were girls. Women teachers in schools of all levels total 440,000. In addition, a new class of women administrators has arisen. Beginning with early women leaders of agricultural mutual-aid teams and farm cooperatives, women continued to join men working in the next stage of rural collectives. Communes boast of 5,000 women chairmen and vice-chairmen. A great proportion of these administrators are young women, whose job demands undoubtedly cut into the time and energy available for homemaking.

Women Required to Give Labor — To turn women out of their homes for the massive job of building a socialist economy overnight, the Communist government uses both coercion and incentives. We shall never know the true extent of subtle, day-to-day pressure on women to contribute labor to the state. We do know that housewives "voluntarily" built and operated backyard furnaces, ran neighborhood "factories" and household service centers.

Besides neighborhood associations from which no one could escape, women for the first time in history are nationally organized into the All-China Democratic Women's Federation, an organ which can transmit state policy affecting women all the way down to the remotest village. This federation, whose membership is composed of women's organizations of all kinds, reached a total of 76 million or more women.

The incentives held out to women include equal pay for equal work, maternity leave, health benefits, retirement pensions, Homes of Respect for the aged, and so on. An integral part of government propaganda policy is the wide dissemination of popular hero literature—men and women war heroes, model workers, industrial inventors, agricultural innovators, and persons outstanding for some specific heroic act. This gives a measure of public recognition to substantial numbers of rank-and-file women.

International Contacts—One consequence of the centralized organization of women is an increase in contact with other organized bodies of women: minority groups, such as Tibetans and less well-known tribal representatives from the South West, send their political delegates and cultural missions to Peking. Women's groups from Communist-bloc countries as well as some neutral countries have paid visits to Communist China and made contact with their Chinese counterparts. In the first decade of the regime alone, some 787 official women visitors came from 71 countries. These new contacts, though highly controlled and managed by the state, give the women of the mainland a sense of wider horizons and national and even international participation.

Women in Political Prominence—As to leadership on the higher political levels, the Communist government has from its Yenan days onward seen to it that women are represented, symbolically or otherwise, in various branches of the administration. At the top is of course Madame Soong Ching-ling, vice chairman of the People's Republic, widow of Sun Yat-sen and eldest sister of Madame Chiang Kai-shek. She is also honorary chairman of the All China Democratic Women's Federation. On the State Council, according to an official statement in 1959, there are two women ministers and four vice ministers. The Standing Committee of the National People's Congress has a woman vice chairman and four women members. In the National People's Congress itself, women occupy 150 seats, or 12 per cent of the total. An earlier report stated that, at the primary level, women deputies make up 20 per cent of all people's deputies. Women have also become mayors and magistrates (2.8 per cent), and government functionaries on the level of department heads and bureau directors (3 per cent).

In the Communist Party itself, which in a real sense is the seat of ideological and political control and at the same time the chief instrument for implementing policy, the proportion of women is only 10 per cent. Thus the much-advertised equality of the sexes perhaps does not really spread to matters of central importance.

Merging of Sex Roles—Since women's activities have been moving toward an approximation of those of men, they are losing some of their unique cultural-transmitting functions. The fields of literature and art were traditionally male-dominated, not only in the creative aspects but also in the transmission of the arts, though women were never barred from participation. Academic teaching was likewise a man's occupation in traditional days, leaving the transmission of household arts and skills the exclusive domain of women. Buddhism as an organized religion was staffed almost exclusively by men, while popular Buddhism as a household religious activity was carried out predominantly by women. Thus, women's role as cultural transmitters in classical China was largely found in popular religious practices and household arts and crafts. Women's creative role in the fine and performing arts was negligible.

The twentieth century has seen a gradual merging of sex roles in all these respects. Women have been increasingly sharing with men in the transmission of learning and of the arts. In present-day Communist ideology, women, being equal with men, carry no unique functions in society aside from that of childbearing. Even the rearing of children and the integration of moral values have been partially removed from the realm of women's activities. The authority for defining moral values resides not with the men of the family who traditionally interpreted universally accepted Confucian values, but with the state which, because of the need for periodic definitions of orthodoxy, reserves ultimate moral authority for itself.

Inadequate Information on Reaction to Regime — Before estimating the future status of women in Communist China, some cautions must be expressed. We know only some of the reported conditions on the mainland. True, we have had occasional eyewitness accounts by a handful of travelers. But China is vast, complex, and fast-changing, and what these observers were able to see, granted a minimum of bias, is necessarily sketchy. We lack adequate studies on the social structure of Communist China against which to evaluate these fragmentary reports. The best we can do is to infer from what the regime chooses to publish and to carefully evaluate every source of information.

Aside from isolated indications of reactions in the internal press, we have no comprehensive impression of how different sectors of the population actually feel in response to administrative policies. Clearly, the peasant women who experienced periodic food shortages in the past and were victims of forces beyond their understanding and control would have a different set of attitudes toward, and anxieties about, the communal mess hall than the urban well-to-do women with memories of servants and a varied and self-determined family menu. Similarly, nurseries and kindergartens would answer different needs or elicit different fears depending upon the past experiences and present resources of the working mother. In all these questions we lack, first, access to sufficient necessary information, and, second, methods for making generalizations to cover conditions in a

country as vast as China. With all the regional, rural–urban, and social–
class differences, one must expect many and great variations in patterns of
behavior. Furthermore, due to the rapidity of social change and the periodic
introduction of large-scale social experiments, little can be said that applies
to the permanent social structure. Women constitute but one sector of the
population which the government is attempting to remold in the light of
ideological and political-economic requirements.

Generalization on the Status of Women Today—With these qualifications in mind, one can, nevertheless, make a general statement on the probable situation of women in Communist China. First, the extended family
which was in the process of breaking up in the urban centers during the
Republican years is now fast disappearing, probably irrevocably so, both in
rural and urban centers. The small family unit, consisting of father, mother,
and young children, remains. Despite inroads into some of the family
functions, there is no evidence that the basic family unit is being broken up.
But the primacy of political authority overrides all other types of authority,
including that of the family. The result is that whenever there is a conflict,
the interests of the state take precedence. Thus women are mobilized for
industrial and agricultural production when labor power is needed. Families
are separated temporarily when different job locations call for such a move.
Children are placed in day-care centers to free mothers for work. A large
proportion of women work outside the home and will probably continue
to do so. As long as the government's present ideology is in the ascendancy,
the enforced political and social participation of women will be expected
and inescapable.

Some of the alternative roles filled in the past by many women receive
no official approval: the completely home-oriented woman, the politically
passive and economically inactive woman, the woman oriented toward
conspicuous consumption, and so forth. No longer is adjustment to a well-
defined large family group the goal and moral ideal for a young woman.
Instead, a premium is placed on the training of a generation of assertive,
independent-minded, achievement-oriented women. Outside rewards await
the women who are outstanding in various fields of work, who can be
inventive, and who can without feelings of undue modesty surpass male
competitors. Only time can tell what permanent structural results will
emerge from such a deliberate redirection of social forces on a massive
scale. For changes in the position of women will come about not only with
each new policy affecting women as such but also indirectly as a consequence of sweeping changes in other parts of the social system.

To summarize, after weakening the authority of the family and many
of the home functions of women, the government has released or forced
open a vast source of female labor power. However, despite the provision
of substitute services for the home, it remains a question whether women

are adequately motivated to perform their newly defined tasks both in and out of the home. After all, the integration of women's role with new institutional setups on the one hand and deep-seated human needs and satisfactions on the other is not a simple matter. It cannot be easily accomplished by mere legislation or administrative policy.

BIBLIOGRAPHY

The page numbers following some of the bibliographic references indicate the pages referred to in the preceding article.

Nancy Lee Swann, *Pan Chao, the Foremost Woman Scholar of China*. New York: Century Co., 1932. A study of the personal and intellectual life of a remarkable woman.

C. K. Yang, *The Chinese Family in the Communist Revolution*, Technology Press, 1959. P. 112.

Ai-li S. Chin, "Some Problems of Chinese Youth in Transition," *American Journal of Sociology*, July, 1948. Pp. 1–9.

Shih Kuo-heng, *China Enters the Machine Age*. Transl. by Fei Hsiao-tung and Francis L. K. Hsu. Cambridge, Mass.: Harvard University Press, 1944.

Chao Feng-Chieh, *Chung-kuo fu-nü tsai fa-li-shang chih ti-wei* (Women's Position in Chinese Law). Shanghai: Commercial Press, 1928.

Ch'en Shu-fang, *Chung-kung ti hsin-hun-yin-fa* (New Marriage Law of the Chinese Communists). Kowloon: Yu-lien Publishing Co., 1953.

China Yearbook 1963–64. Taipei: China Publishing Co., 1964.

Kao Jen-lan, *Chung-kung hsin hun-yin-fa p'i-p'ing* (A Critique of Communist China's New Marriage Law). Kowloon: Freedom Publishing Co., 1954.

Chao Chung and Yang I-fang, *Students in Mainland China*, Hongkong: Union Research Institute, 1956. P. 77 (quoting *Jen-min-jih-pao* (People's Daily) of Apr. 28, 1955.

Chin Feng, "Good Housewife Campaign Sweeps the Country," in *Women of China* (organ of the All-China Democratic Women's Federation), Peking, Nov. 3, 1957.

Chung-kuo ch'ing-nien (China's Youth), Peking, Sept. 1, 1958; *Kung-jen jih-pao* (Workers' Daily), Peking, Nov. 13, 1960. (Descriptions of two household service centers).

Hsin kuan-ch'a (The New Observer), Peking, 1957, No. 1, pp. 6–9. (Interview with a working mother.)

Lord Boyd Orr and Peter Townsend, *What's Happening in China*, New York: Doubleday, 1959. P. 83.

Women of China (organ of the All-China Democratic Women's Federation), Peking. Issues No. 1, 1956, pp. 11–12; No. 2, 1957, pp. 8–10; No. 4, 1959, pp. 14–17; No. 5, 1959, pp. 3, 13.

VII

The Western Spearhead

SCANDINAVIA, GREAT BRITAIN,
AND THE UNITED STATES

This last section deals with those countries in which women have fought for and achieved the fullest measure of equality with men. By and large it can be said that in these countries the equality of the sexes is an accomplished fact in all areas that count: law, social life, economic opportunities, cultural achievements, and so forth. And precisely because this is the case, it is most significant that the women of these countries have come to realize more and more that the primary satisfactions life holds for them are found in the home whence they started out on their feminist crusade only two or three generations ago.

Scandinavia

By Harriet Holter

INTRODUCTION

*F*ew *Western countries* exhibit today such a lively public interest in the status of women as Scandinavia. The governments, the political parties, the church, as well as representatives of a number of large organizations, express themselves in the matter, and on the ideological level there is obviously a move towards more radical attitudes concerning women's role. This is true especially in Sweden, where the more advanced debate no longer focuses on the status of women but on the whole complex pattern of men's and women's social roles.

The situation is characterized by ambiguity. Having been oppressed and discriminated against in the past, Scandinavian women have at present achieved a high degree of legal and theoretical equality with men. At the same time, the traditional concepts of male and female roles still have a strong influence on behavior. Thus, two sets of ideas, norms and values concerning sex roles guide the actual practices and modes of conduct in various spheres of society.

437

This article will describe the situation precisely in this frame of reference: How the traditional status of women developed into one of legal equality through the efforts of pioneering men and women; and how their visions and ideals have left their mark on present ideologies. Then the patterns of reality will be discussed, including the actual modes of behavior of women as compared to men, in various spheres of life. In addition, some implications and mechanisms of the discrepancy between ideology and reality will be brought to attention.

The four Scandinavian countries, Norway, Sweden, Denmark and Finland,[1] resemble each other in many respects, but differ in others. They all strive to be, although with varying degrees of emphasis, modern welfare states with well-developed systems of state insurance and support of weaker social groups. Sweden and Denmark are more industrialized than are Norway and Finland. Sweden, Denmark, and Finland share more continental traditions and contacts as against the Anglo-American orientation of Norway. Neither Sweden, Norway, nor Finland had the feudal structure which long characterized Denmark. In Finland, the question of national liberation has had overwhelming importance, and as an indirect result Finnish women were the first in Europe to obtain the right to vote. Also, Finland's special position between East and West should be appreciated; the last World War left Finland with an excess of women which was not the case in the other Scandinavian countries.

It may well be that these national differences are reflected in the position of women in the four countries. The differences are, however, not significant enough to warrant inclusion in a brief presentation of the general situation.

THE TRADITIONAL SITUATION

The old peasant society in the Scandinavian countries was patriarchal. Men had the political power and were heads of the families. Although women figure prominently in Nordic sagas and mythology, the same sources also present them as objects to be bought and sold by men. The introduction of Christianity strengthened the patriarchal elements in the Nordic countries, although canon law improved women's position in certain respects, as compared to the old Germanic law. Protestantism, introduced into Scandinavia about 1550, did not provide the same institutionalized opportunities for unmarried women as did the Catholic Church.

The industrial revolution found Scandinavian women in the same position as women elsewhere in the Western world: as wives of peasants and artisans, they bore their burden of heavy work, although occasionally they

---

1. Iceland, also a Scandinavian country, could not be included in this limited article.

were influential and respected in family affairs, including business transactions. Among the upper classes, their tasks and responsibilities were quite restricted. In all groups, the prestige of a woman reflected the status of her husband or other male relatives. In no social class was there any room for women outside the family sphere.

With the onset of industrialization, the wives and children of the new working class were recruited into factories. Only gradually did these women limit their sphere of activities to housekeeping. As the bourgeois class became stronger, their wives became ladies of leisure responding to the feminine ideal of the protected and refined woman whose main tasks were embroidery and gracious entertaining.

In the pre-industrial society, unmarried women were supported by their fathers or other male relatives, in exchange for which they helped with the household chores. With the change in the organization of work and family structure, these women gradually had to find a means of livelihood outside the home. This presented severe difficulties, because women were under the guardianship of men and had no right to conduct businesses or to own property. Furthermore, no crafts were open to women. Under the pressure of the increasing economic difficulties of unmarried women in the growing middle class, new laws were introduced in Scandinavia in the 1850's: unmarried and widowed women became legally independent and were permitted to qualify for business certificates and to practice certain crafts. Daughters were also given equal rights of inheritance with sons, except in connection with landed property.

In the late nineteenth century, these legal reforms opened up new opportunities for women, and they took various types of clerical jobs in private business firms, as well as in government offices. At an early date, women had been accepted as teachers in elementary schools. But, in general, only the lowest-paid and most modest positions were open to women, and very often the vocational training institutions were closed to them. The poverty-stricken seamstress, as depicted in the Norwegian literature of the time, seemed to symbolize these women. The introduction of women into vocational and professional training was a very slow process, but, in many ways, prejudice was easiest to fight in the educational field.

THE EMANCIPATION MOVEMENTS

The forerunners of an organized movement for women's rights were small clubs and groups with various social, religious, and educational aims. But a long period of latent unrest passed before a strong, effective movement could be formed. In Norway, a central figure in the struggle was the authoress Camilla Collet (1813–1895), who, like Sweden's well-known Fredrika Bremer, belonged to an old, cultured family, and whose books and pamphlets were shocking to the majority. Both women expressed the latent dissatisfaction with the legal, political and economic situation of women. During the latter part of the nineteenth century, a number of able and determined women continued the fight for women's rights. At the same time, many members of the literary elite of Norway spoke out concerning the position of women. Henrik Ibsen's *A Doll's House* started a Norwegian literary tradition of support to women, which has lasted to the present time. (However, the great Swedish author, Strindberg, took the opposite stand: he despised and constantly fought the new movement for the emancipation of women.)

The first emancipationist organization in Europe was started in Sweden by Fredrika Bremer, in 1845. The Norwegian National Association for the Rights of Women was formed in 1884. The Scandinavian women's movements had as their ideological basis the Declaration of Independence of 1789, and the Declaration of Human Rights of the French Revolution. The new theories in the field of biology, and especially in genetics, as well as the rational attitude of the natural sciences, in general, contributed effectively to the new doctrine on women's position.

As in most other countries, equal political rights for women was a main purpose of the Scandinavian emancipationist movements and a number of prominent and gifted men and women led the long struggle for women's right to vote. Finland reached this goal first (1906), Norway (1913), then Denmark (1915) followed, and finally Sweden (1921).

The high hopes which carried the fight through to victory have perhaps not been completely fulfilled in the decades that have passed since women received the franchise, for women's participation in certain types of political activity is still considerably less than that of men. Nevertheless, the formal recognition of women as politically equal members of society symbolized the introduction of a new and important value into Scandinavian society.

Although women's right to vote was considered the most important issue of the emancipationist movement, it was not viewed as the only means of securing equality between men and women. While the struggle for suffrage was being waged, reforms in the fields of women's education and occupations were being pressed forward.

Sweden and Finland were pioneer countries with respect to women's professional education. In 1870 Swedish women were allowed to study medicine and to become physicians, and, in 1873, all academic fields except law and theology were opened to them. A few years later, the same thing happened in Denmark, and in the 1880's, Norwegian women achieved the right to take all academic degrees.

From this time on, civil-service posts were gradually opened to women. In Norway, women were admitted to the bar in 1904. In 1905, the first woman civil servant was appointed. In 1912, parliament decided that all government posts should be open to women, with the exception of cabinet, clerical, diplomatic, and military positions. By 1938, only the position of clergyman was closed to women, and a law of 1956 dropped this last formal barrier to women's equal rights to governmental and civil-service posts.

Throughout the nineteenth century, women of the lower class were restricted to the most menial jobs. Women of the working class, both married and single, were employed to a large extent in factories, under miserable conditions, and for considerably lower pay than men received. Later, the rapidly growing labor movement encouraged women workers to organize trade unions, and one of the first extensive strikes in Norway was that of the match workers (1889), most of whom were women. This strike was supported by the Norwegian Association for Women's Rights. The Women's Social Democratic Society was a leading exponent of the rights and interests of working-class women, and various improvements in the working conditions of women were gained through the efforts of the labor movement.

Equality of wages for men and women had for many years been part of the ideology of Scandinavian labor unions, and the four countries have signed the Geneva convention about equal pay.

THE SEXUAL REVOLUTION

The drive for equality left its marks on various other spheres as well. For example, the development from the Victorian sex mores, prevalent during the nineteenth century, toward the modern attitude about sexual relations is closely tied up with the question of women's status. In Norway, the first well-known opponents of the Victorian norms were a group of authors and artists commonly known in the 1880's as the Bohemians of Christiania. Many authors of works later to be considered classics were among the Bohemians, who opposed the double standard, prostitution, negative attitudes toward sex in general, and the view that sexual drives were sinful, and even more so in women than in men.

These new ideas on sex were opposed by various camps, foremost among whom was the conservative bourgeoisie. They joined forces with groups of especially pious Christians, whose presence had long been a peculiar manifestation of Norwegian culture.

During the 1920's, a group emerged headed by a young, enthusiastic physician, Karl Evang, who transformed the radical ideas about sex behavior into a practical program of action: information about sex hygiene and birth control should be disseminated to the entire population; the concept of sin should be eliminated from sexual mores, both in and outside of marriage; abortions should be legalized. In Sweden, the same practical work of disseminating information and promoting open discussion was encouraged by the well-known Elise Ottesen Jensen. These two people started what might be termed a revolution in sex attitudes, by means of lectures, magazine articles, books, and field work throughout Norway and Sweden.

These changes had great implications, especially for women, of course. First of all, the general acceptance of birth control relieved the poorer classes of women of their burden of bearing many children. Second, the new ideas encouraged more tolerant attitudes toward unwed mothers and premarital pregnancy, attitudes that were not foreign to the traditions of the old Norwegian peasant society, in which premarital sexual intercourse was customary and often had the specific function of proving the bride's ability to bear children. Third, the new theories weakened to a considerable extent the sex norms usually referred to as the "double standard." "Single standard" meant that the idea of equal rights and responsibilities for men and women should be extended also to the sphere of sexual relations.

Important participants in the development of the new ideas about sex were a number of outstanding women who distinguished themselves by working for social reforms, especially in connection with mothers and children. In 1915, the Norwegian Castberg's Children's Act, providing a pattern for other countries, secured equal rights for children born in and out of wedlock, and made it possible for illegitimate children to bear the name and inherit the property of their father.

A more liberal view on abortion was also advocated, and the two questions—birth control and *abortus provocatus*—were eagerly debated in the first part of this century.

THE OFFICIAL IDEOLOGY

The depression of the 1930's showed that the economic position of women was not on a level with their legal and political status. Strong voices demanded that jobs should be reserved for men, and that the unemployment crisis should be met by sending women employees back to domestic work. In the beginning, this demand concerned only married women, but, nourished by various other ideological streams, it was gradually extended to working women in general.

This situation was met by vigorous opposition from adherents of equality both within and outside political parties. The Norwegian Association for the Rights of Women was reorganized and once more became a militant force. The parliamentary elections of 1935 brought labor into the government, which resulted in considerable support for the principle of equality in the labor market. By the time of the business upturn at the end of the 1930's, the attacks on women's rights had largely been suppressed.

During the German occupation of Norway and Denmark, the role played by women in the resistance movements contributed to an increasing respect for them. The rebuilding of Norway began in a climate of political and social reform, an atmosphere which seemed favorable to continued advances in the position of women.

Scandinavian women today are generally considered to occupy a fairly strong position, to be independent and equal partners of men in most spheres of life. On the theoretical level, this is close to the truth. Norwegian law, for example, expresses this official philosophy very clearly. In almost all respects, it stipulates equal rights for men and women. Both come of age at twenty-one, both may marry at that age without parental consent. Neither men nor women lose their citizenship upon marrying foreigners. Men and women are granted equal political rights. Both must be twenty-one years of age to vote in national or local elections, and they are equally eligible for election to all divisions of national and local government. Women as well as men may serve on juries or be appointed to the bench. All civil-service posts, except those of the military service, are open to women, and women may become ministers of the church, if the local ecclesiastic council approves. Openings in public administration must be advertised in the newspapers under the heading "Vacancies for Men and Women," rather than, as before, under "Vacancies for Men." The law also requires that certain public positions, such as that of work inspectors, must partly be filled by women.

Throughout Scandinavia, men and women have equal rights to own and conduct businesses and to set up their own enterprises. All schools and universities are open to women, as well as to men. Indirectly, the law may be interpreted as granting daughters and sons equal education. A paragraph relating to family law in Norway states that parents are obliged to give their children an education corresponding to the financial means of the parents and the abilities of the children. Although the law does not specifically say so, most authorities agree that this means equal educational rights for boys and girls.

The principle of equal wages in industry has recently gained new support in Scandinavia. In addition to signing the international convention about equal pay, the Norwegian government appointed in 1959 a permanent Council of Equal Pay for Men and Women.

The law offers certain privileges to women in industry: pregnant women have the right to stop work six weeks before delivery, and to remain away until six weeks afterwards; the law also protects the mother from being dismissed during this period. An employee who is nursing a child is entitled to take time off for this purpose. Marriage cannot be used as an excuse for dismissing a female employee.

With regard to the inheritance of landed property, some traditional inequalities still exist in Norway. Whereas sons and daughters are treated alike in all other respects, only sons have certain freehold privileges. Sons have precedence in relatives' rights concerning the repurchase of farms that have been out of the family for a certain number of years. And the closest male descendant of a landowner has the right, upon the owner's death, to take over the land undivided at a fixed and reasonable price. Certain inequalities also prevail with regard to women's rights in various pension systems, but generally, women have equal rights in connection with governmental insurance systems and welfare measures.

Norwegian family laws stipulate equal rights and responsibilities for husband and wife: both spouses should contribute to their household according to their ability, that is, by work outside or within the home. The domestic work of a wife, in principle and according to the law, is counted as economically equal to the husband's work. The law implies not only that the husband is duty bound to maintain his wife, but that a wife is under obligation to maintain her husband, according to her ability. This implies that a wife, who takes care of the household and thus has no cash resources, is entitled to a certain share of her husband's income. The money is considered as having been earned by her.

Moreover, each partner in a marriage has the right to a certain amount of cash for his or her own personal use. In contrast to the situation in many European countries, Scandinavian women dispose of their own income and property after marriage. Furthermore, both spouses have the right to act on behalf of the other in financial matters, and the wife has certain special privileges in this respect. Husband and wife have the same responsibilities with regard to the children, and the law provides for joint parental authority.

Until recently, women who wanted to keep their own maiden name had to apply to the government. According to the newly revised Law of Personal Names, she may now keep her own name after notifying the authorities. The revised law also gives children the choice between the last name of the father and that of the mother. The present law underlines the principle of women's separate and individual social identity.

We thus find that there are only a very few and insignificant exceptions to the principles of legal equality in the sphere of marriage. The same is true in education, business and politics. Scandinavian legal systems emphasize the equality of the sexes.

PATTERNS OF REALITY

Political Participation and Leadership—The actual pattern of women's participation in political life is somewhat different from that envisioned by the suffragists, even though the pessimistic prophesies of their antagonists have not been fulfilled. Women have played, and still play, a modest role in Scandinavian politics, relative to their number.

Women now vote in Norway, almost as extensively as do men: in the parliamentary election of 1961, 77.3 per cent of the women electors voted, as compared with 80.9 per cent of the men. This is a considerable improvement over the first election in which women voted in 1915, when 54 per cent of the female and 70 per cent of the male electors voted. Women's voting behavior is, to a certain extent, similar to that of men's: the married vote more often than the unmarried, urban women vote more frequently than rural women. The change in the voting behavior of women is found mainly in urban districts. Age and education seem to be more determining forces for women's voting pattern than in the case of the men's.

In general, the introduction of women voters has not changed the balance of power between political parties, but may to some extent have modified their programs. If anything, women voters have strengthened the conservative elements in politics in most countries. At the same time, we usually find — as in Norway — that about 90 per cent of all married women vote for the same party as their husbands. The conservative element, therefore, is mainly comprised of unmarried women (unmarried men do not seem to be as conservative as unmarried women). One should note, however, that the analysis of the poll results also shows an agreement between men and women in regard to a wide range of concrete national and international political questions.

With respect to other political activities, women are much less active than men. In a poll of 1950, 41 per cent of the women, as compared to 13 per cent of the men, answered that they were not interested in world politics, and in 1953, one third of the women as against one fifth of the men stated that they had no political or social interests whatsoever. But polls from 1946 to 1953 seem to show that in questions of religion, morality and personal relationship, women are as interested and informed as men.

In 1953, none of the Norwegian political parties estimated their women members at higher than 25 per cent of their total membership. On the basis of data on voting behavior, it seems reasonable to suppose that the conservative parties — the Right, the Center and the Christian People's Party — have a higher percentage of women members than do the Leftist and Socialist parties.

The greatest discrepancy between men and women, and also between ideology and reality, is found in the field of political leadership. A few women representatives are usually found in or near the top circle in all political parties, but these circles are almost invariably dominated by men. Furthermore, in all the Scandinavian countries, few women are nominated and elected to political office. Some Norwegian figures are illustrative: in the municipal elections of 1963, 6.3 per cent of all the elected representatives were women. This represents an increase compared with the 1930's. Only two women have been municipal mayors in Norway. Compared to

Norway, female representation is more extensive in Sweden; in Denmark, less.

In the 1953 Norwegian parliamentary elections, about 18 per cent of all the candidates nominated were women, as against 9 per cent in Germany and France. Usually, the female candidates are put in the middle of the slate, and rarely have a real chance of being elected. Today, 8 per cent of the members of the Norwegian parliament are women, most of them from the Social-Democratic party.

Denmark was the first Scandinavian country to have a woman cabinet member (Minister of Education, 1924–1926). But it was only after World War II that it became customary to have at least one woman member in the cabinets in Scandinavian countries. Today, Norway has one woman cabinet member (Department of Family and Consumer Affairs). The Swedish, Danish and Finnish cabinets have had more women members than the Norwegian ones.

The cabinet posts occupied by women show very clearly that in politics the traditional division of labor between the sexes still prevails. With some exceptions, the female members of the cabinet are in charge of social welfare, education, health, family relations, or religious activities, spheres traditionally considered suitable for women. Such fields as economics, industry, agriculture, trade, and international relations are reserved for men.

We may safely conclude, then, that in political life, the actual situation does not accord with the visions of those who pioneered in the struggle for women's rights, nor with the present official policy of the Scandinavian countries. Advances are being made, though at a very slow pace.

EDUCATION

In Scandinavia, the educational area is perhaps the one in which equality of the sexes is most thoroughly realized. Although, as we shall see, there is a sex difference in school attendance from the end of elementary school on, the standards and values dominating the institutions themselves seem to allow for more equality between the sexes than does any other sphere of social life. It should be noted, too, that women seem to perform better in the educational field than they do in others.

The Scandinavian public schools, to which most children go, are co-educational. Because elementary school (which, according to a new system now covers nine years) is compulsory, this means that until the age of fifteen or sixteen, girls and boys receive the same instruction in practically all fields. In Norway, until lately, girls received more training in home economics and boys took more algebra, but boys and girls are now given the same amount of instruction in all subjects, except for carpentry and sewing, which are taught exclusively to boys and girls, respectively.

Until the 1950's, Norwegian girls continued their education after elementary school less frequently than boys. Present statistics show, however, that this is no longer the case, but that the level of the girls' education in general is lower. Boys, more frequently than girls, attend secondary schools which prepare students for the universities, while girls more often go to folk high schools [2] and continuation schools. The proportion of women students has increased in the Norwegian universities from 15–16 per cent in 1950 to 23 per cent in 1963/64. Norway is, however, behind the other Scandinavian countries in this respect. In Sweden the figure is about 32 per cent, and the situation in Finland is remarkable: about half of the Finnish students taking a university degree are women.

On the secondary-school level, a clearcut difference between the sexes can be noted with regard to the subjects chosen. Girls favor languages, whereas the overwhelming majority of boys concentrate on science. This sex difference is clearly marked in the vocational schools and universities, as well.

The implication is that more boys than girls attend vocational schools, technical schools of all kinds, and agricultural schools, whereas a majority of the students in the commercial schools, and schools of applied arts, nursing and home economics are girls. In the state teachers' college, there is also a slight majority of women.

In academic work, the usual division of interests may be observed: women students more frequently than men enroll in the fields of language, pharmacy, psychology, and more rarely go into theoretical sciences, law, and economics. In Finland the pattern appears to be somewhat different, and the majority of physicians and dentists are women.

It is not known exactly how many women in the Scandinavian countries make use of their education in full or part-time jobs. In Norway, the 1960 census data show that 55 per cent of the married women with a university degree work outside the home, as against 22 per cent of those with only elementary school education. The figures probably are somewhat higher in the other Scandinavian countries. It appears certain, however, that a considerable number of academically-trained women leave their careers at an early stage to become housewives. This practice has often been viewed as a problem, involving frustration for the women and a loss to society which bears the expense of their education.[3] Others maintain that this is a privilege that women in a welfare state should have: to receive an education without

2. The purpose of the folk high schools is to provide further education in general subjects for older adolescents. Upon its completion, graduates are entitled to enter a "county grammar school," a teachers' training college or a vocational training school.
3. In Scandinavia, university education is practically free, and a large number of students obtain loans from the government to cover their living expenses during their years of study.

using it in gainful employment, if they so wish. Granting this right, however, does not solve the psychological and ethical problems that may be involved. An academic education is a process of socialization toward occupational participation, and the goals and standards learned during this process cannot easily be dismissed as belonging to a temporary stage of the individual's life. Thus, as far as the individual woman is concerned, a long-term education often implies difficult choices and stresses which can only be lessened by considerable changes in the present patterns of sex roles.

Norwegian studies show that, upon leaving elementary school, girls, on the average, get somewhat better grades than boys, a pattern which is reversed on the higher educational levels.

Boys who continue their education beyond the elementary level have a more varied social background than the girls, who, on the whole, come from wealthier families. The implication of this is that girls start at each educational level with better previous performance than boys. It seems, however, that girls perform progressively less well on each higher level, after the conclusion of their elementary studies. In the final examinations preceding the university, the average grades of girls are lower than those of boys. And at the university level, too, it is the male students who usually excell in most fields at the final examinations.

Various explanations may be advanced for this peculiar pattern. The likeliest seems to be that as a girl grows older, her academic performance becomes increasingly influenced by the image of her role in family and society, which may be somewhat discouraging to high intellectual achievement.

OCCUPATIONS

The official viewpoint concerning women's occupations is quite clear in Scandinavia: women have the same rights and obligations as men. In spite of this, women do not hold paid jobs to the same extent, nor do they have the same attitudes toward occupational activity.

The proportion of women in the labor-force varies between the four Scandinavian countries.

**TABLE 1—Percentage of women in the labor force. Census data 1960
(Total labor force = 100)**

	Per Cent
Norway	22.9
Sweden	29.7
Denmark	30.9
Finland	39.0

As shown in Table 1, the percentage of women in the labor force is rather low in Norway, whereas the Finnish figure is remarkably high, compared to many other Western countries. Behind these differences lies a marked difference in the extent to which married women work outside the home. In Finland 25.9 per cent of the married women are working outside their home, in Norway this percentage is only 9.5. In both Denmark and Sweden the comparable figure is 23 per cent (1960).

The difference between Norway on the one hand and Sweden and Denmark on the other may be explained by the higher degree of industrialization and urbanization in the last two countries. In the more isolated parts of Norway there are few possibilities for employment for women, and the percentage of working wives varies as much as from 21 per cent to 3 per cent in different administrative areas. But the rather large Finnish-Norwegian difference in the proportion of working married women requires special attention. Both countries are sparsely populated, both are somewhat less urbanized than Denmark and Sweden. Furthermore, the Norwegian tax system is more favorable to working wives than is the Finnish. Thus it seems natural to ask whether there exist certain differences between the two countries in women's basic attitudes toward work outside the home. No data are available, however, which could answer this question.

It should be noted that the proportion of married women seeking employment seems to be increasing in the Scandinavian countries, and will probably continue to do so under conditions of full- and over-employment. It may also be significant that Norway provides kindergartens for only 7 to 8 per cent of all children, whereas the percentage is about 40 in Sweden and Denmark.

The female section of the labor force differs in Scandinavia, as in most countries, from the male contingent. Women workers are to a larger extent than the men unmarried, young, and unskilled. (These are generalizations which may not apply to various small groups.)

The Scandinavian labor picture is furthermore characterized by a sharply marked sexual division of work, especially at the low and very high occupational levels. Certain jobs are considered suitable only for women, others only for men. Nursing, domestic service, social work, and many types of clerical work are fields restricted to women. Heavy manual work, technical and mechanical jobs, and certain handicrafts are men's occupations. Although changes are taking place (in Norway, men are taking up nursing and social work, and women a few handicrafts), the over-all picture remains very much the same. In industrial establishments, the production departments are usually divided into "women's" and "men's" sections, and almost all jobs are designated "male" or "female." Much the same is true in service occupations, office work, and commerce. Almost everywhere women occupy subordinate positions, the foremen and

superiors being men. In the professions and the civil service, the divisions
are less rigid, although some government establishments, such as the telegraph and telephone services, are almost wholly staffed by women. In
posts requiring academic training, men and women do the same types of
work (as physicians, dentists, high school teachers). Law was for a long
time considered the domain of men, but a fair number of women now
practice it. Although women's best chances for promotion lie in public
administration and the professions requiring academic training, relatively
few women choose careers in these fields.

In spite of the official policy favoring equal pay for equal work, women
still receive lower wages and salaries than men, in all the Scandinavian
countries, except in public administration and the academic professions,
although, following World War II, a trend to increase women's pay was
evidenced. From 1944 to 1952, the wages of female industrial workers in
Norway increased from 59 to 69 per cent of those of men. In 1960, women
with the same level of training, of the same age, and doing the same jobs
as men, received 70 to 85 per cent of the men's wages. In Sweden and
Denmark, the corresponding figures are 80 to 90 per cent. A similar comparison for office workers shows that women earn 82 to 87 per cent of
what men earn in similar positions. The last five years have witnessed some
lessening of this inequality in wages, but on the whole, women's total
earnings in Norway have gone down in relation to men's because men's
employment in the better-paid jobs has increased.

In 1961, the main organizations of employers and employees in Norway
agreed to a program of equal pay for equal work to be realized over a
period of six years. This, however, will not result in a marked improvement
for women employees in general, since the concentration of women in the
poorly paid jobs will not be affected by the rule of "equal wages." As long
as the division of labor according to sex continues, women will probably
receive less than men.

Scandinavian employers maintain that, generally speaking, women
should be paid less than men, because their work performance is poorer.
Women, they say, have higher rates of absenteeism, which must be balanced
by lower wages. It is also contended that women do not work as many
years as men, which makes the average training expenses higher for women
in industrial jobs. Employers also consider women to be less generally
useful on the job: they sometimes refuse to do certain tasks which men
accept readily (cleaning and repairing machinery, for instance), and are
less flexible than men, more resistant to change, all of which in the modern
factory are serious drawbacks.

Norwegian and Swedish research confirms the existence of fairly widespread beliefs about sex differences in work behavior. The results, somewhat similar to those presented by the British economist Ferdynand Zweig,

show that women are thought to be unstable employees, more resistant to change, less interested in their work, less identified with fellow-workers and with the enterprise, more apt to be emotionally upset about small matters and to develop conflicts within their work groups, more submissive and less ambitious than their male co-workers. On the other hand, they are considered more punctual, exact, patient, and conscientious than men.

Whether or not these images of men's and women's behavior in the work situation are true remains to be seen when more extensive research data can be presented. So far, Norwegian sociological research indicates that they may apply to some but not all categories of employees in factory and office work.

It seems to be a fact, however, that female employees are more reluctant than are male ones to organize and fight for their interest. They are, in general, less interested in trade unions than men, and participate to a somewhat lesser extent in union work. In industry and in business offices, most male employees are organized. The percentage of organized female employees is lower in almost all fields. Women, especially the younger ones, usually look upon their work as temporary, expecting to marry and give up their jobs, and they see no reason to struggle for the sake of a larger group, or for future employment advantages. Middle-aged and older women employees also seem to be less inclined than men to think in group terms: they appear to be in a sense more individualistic than men and often refuse to take a long-range view of the consequences of their actions.

When attempts are made to explain such patterns as those described above, it should be noted that, in most Western countries, the occupational sector of society has adopted quite fully the traditional sex role prescriptions. Thus, the factors contributing to differences between men's and women's behavior in the work situation probably include lack of the possibility of promotion (which implies, among other things, lack of superior role models); conflicting demands of the job and the family; and conflicting demands between the traditional concepts of femininity and the attributes necessary for occupational success. In addition, the ideal of the woman of leisure, presented with considerable vigor through the mass media, competes with the norms implied in education and training for careers. Conflicts such as these are apt to produce frustrated and deviant behavior, for example rigidity, emotional instability, passivity, and lack of interest.

However, in spite of the practical and psychological stresses involved, an increasing number of women are occupationally active in the Scandinavian countries. One gains the impression that there is a tendency toward more acceptance of women in positions hitherto reserved for men, and also a greater willingness on the part of women to accept responsible and demanding positions.

Sex Mores and Marriage Patterns

How do the actual behavior patterns compare with women's official status, in the area of sex mores, marriage, and family living? Lack of statistical data compels us to rely on casual observation and speculation in arriving at an answer.

The standards and attitudes, governing the relationship between young boys and girls prior to marriage, set the stage, to some extent, for the relationship between husbands and wives. In many countries, Scandinavia is viewed as a place where the norms for sexual behavior are more relaxed than in the rest of the Western world. Sweden, in particular, has long been in the spotlight for those interested in free sexual behavior, although there is no reason to believe that either Denmark or Norway differs greatly from Sweden in this respect.

An American observer has this to say about Norway: "The newspapers, the arts and the beaches are far more candid but more relaxed about sex . . . [than in the U.S.]." In Sweden, an illustration of the prevailing attitude is given in the responses to a poll regarding the sexual intimacy of unmarried persons: a little over half of those polled found such intimacy to be proper. The usual pattern of sexual behavior among young people can be described as follows: from the ages of sixteen to twenty, most youngsters have some casual sexual experiences with various partners. In their early twenties, they establish more stable relationships with the intention of getting married within a few years. During this time, which may or may not be marked by a formal engagement, the partners have fairly regular sexual intercourse, sometimes acknowledged publicly, but more often kept private as a matter of discretion. Parents often close their eyes, or declare the affair to be the private business of the young couple. Variations can, of course, still be found in different parts of the country.

Although casual observation seems to indicate considerable similarity between the sex mores of men and women, significant differences do exist. Scandinavian children of both sexes are accustomed to playing together on fairly equal terms, yet adolescent girls are usually encouraged to turn their attention toward marriage and family matters, whereas boys are urged to concentrate on their studies and preparation for earning a living. At the same time, girls often are given to understand that in their relations with boys, they should be relatively passive, leaving the initiative of making overtures to the boys. And, it is the women who are expected to set the limits to sexual intimacy. Thus, the burden of responsibility falls on the partner who is denied the initiative, a rather curious combination of rights and obligations, but one which is characteristic of most of the Western world, and not just Scandinavia.

It should be noted that certain changes seem to be taking place in the mores of the present generation. For example, the custom that the young man pays for any entertainment enjoyed by the couple seems about to vanish among students. This could be highly significant, since the question of "who pays" and "for what" is basic to all aspects of the relationship between the sexes, including initiative and responsibility for decision-making.

How is the position of women affected by the changes in sex mores? Does this more relaxed sexual pattern give them more of an advantage than the traditional one? Suffice it to mention here that opinions are divergent in this matter. Adherents of tolerant sex mores maintain that such norms strengthen the position of women by affording them greater possibilities for wholesome development and natural sexual satisfaction. Others stress the desirability of equality and the necessity for eliminating the double standard. Opponents of the freer sex mores point to the disadvantageous position in which young girls will be placed, with the risk of premature sexual experience and unwanted pregnancies. A Norwegian study of the attitudes of adolescents toward sexual matters indicates that girls felt undue pressure to enter into sexual intimacy with boys. Additional research is needed, however, before any definite conclusions can be drawn.

Another change of attitude which seems to have taken place following World War II is attested by the marriage rates. In 1901–1905 there were 6.08 marriages per 1,000 inhabitants in Norway; in 1951–1955, the comparable figure was 8.02. With better economic conditions, people find marriage easier, and the desire to marry seems to have become more widespread throughout the population. This pattern appears to be accompanied by an increased idealization of marriage and family life.

Research in other countries confirms the notion that success for women is judged mainly in terms of their marital status, while that of men is measured in terms of occupational performance. This expresses one of the most significant differences between the social and psychological situation of the two sexes. The two life-goals require different personality traits and represent two different social systems. Adjusting to the life-goal of marriage implies the cultivation of one's appearance, charm, social relations, and "feminine" qualities, in short, one's attractiveness to the opposite sex. Occupational fitness and abilities come second. Marriage as the life-goal also implies a satisfactory orientation toward the culturally-defined concept of "love"—in our society often viewed as a somewhat mysterious, irrational, and highly individualistic affair. In a society that stresses rationality, technical advances, and "universal" values, extreme involvement with so-called romantic love can present difficulties, both social and psychological. The conflict which may arise has been studied in the United States, where it was found that girls often have difficulties in adjusting to the feminine ideal and the educational ideal at the same time. For example, they feel that they must pretend to be non-intellectual, if they want to attract boyfriends, whereas their teachers demand the opposite type of attitude. This conflict is probably not unknown to Scandinavian girls either, and can be expected to increase in intensity unless the incompatibility of the ideals to which young girls are exposed is eliminated.

The average age for marriage has been decreasing since World War II. Before the war, in Norway, the average age of bridegrooms was 29.39, and that of brides, 26.38. In 1959, these figures fell to 27.54 and 24.29, respectively. The fact that the age difference between brides and grooms has remained the same indicates that the traditional idea that the husband should be older than the wife still prevails.

Regardless of legal stipulations, vestiges of a patriarchal family type still exist throughout all the Scandinavian countries. The wife and children usually take the name of the husband. The husband is, in some connection, still regarded as the head of the family, although this has no legal implications. Many people still feel that the husband should decide the most important family matters. According to Swedish data, many wives do not know how much their husbands earn, and are ignorant also of their own economic legal rights. But, in general, it seems safe to conclude that in family matters, the influence and authority of the modern wife have increased considerably over the last decades.

The democratic family in which decisions are shared and the children, too, have their say in matters of common interest, is held up as the ideal one by official ideology, by the law, and by various educational philosophies. On the other hand, mass media, advertising, and informal sources of influence often idealize the strong, determined, aggressive man and the protected, passive, dependent woman. More recently, the increasing influence of American culture has probably tended to reinforce this pattern.

THE HOME ROUTINE

The majority of women in Scandinavian countries do their own household chores. In Norway, in 1960, about 50 per cent of all adult women were housewives working only at home. Since this is the case, there is reason for asking, what are the main social characteristics of this group, what is their social, economic, and psychological situation, and what are their main problems and worries?

One of the greatest changes that have taken place in the lives of housewives during the last twenty-five years is the general increase in employment outside the home and in personal earnings and standard of living. Together with a steady decrease in the number of children, the change from the depressed economy of the 1930's to an economy of full employment since World War II has had a great impact on the situation of the housewife. In Norway, the average number of children per couple was 2.28 in 1960, the number of children being higher in rural than in urban families. But the variations are small enough so that the typical family can be termed small. This obviously means that a relatively shorter period of a housewife's life is filled with child care. Also, less domestic work in general is implied and technical improvements both in and outside the home have reduced the burden of housework. The young married woman of today has a far easier life than had her mother or grandmother, and her problems tend to be psychological or social rather than economic.

Thus, the social isolation of the urban housewife is nowadays often mentioned as a problem in Scandinavia. The suburban residential areas are usually drained of men during the day, and a community of women and children is believed to produce a drab and unstimulating atmosphere. Housewives are isolated by the distances of a modern city from their relatives and friends, and often there seems to be no natural basis for cooperation and social intercourse between neighbors. Swedish studies indicate that a majority of mothers have only limited contact with neighbors throughout the day. It is not shown clearly whether the housewives feel isolated, but very often the desire to be with other people was mentiond as a main motive for taking work outside the home. The same finding was made in a more recent Norwegian study. Equally important though is another result from Norway: a majority of the housewives feel that they enjoy too little prestige in society in general.

The difficulties involved in conceiving of the work of the housewife as a regular occupational role are obvious, and the housewives' basis for identification with one another is narrow. The housewives' institutional or integrative framework is the family, not groups of housewives. They constitute a social category more than a group. Nevertheless, in Scandinavia the attempts to organize the housewives have met with success. There exist fairly large and important housewives' associations, which are active in a number of fields and also act as pressure groups toward government and administration. In particular, education and information concerning household and family care have been in focus of their work.

The heterogeneity of the category housewives, however, is marked, and in Norway, for example, three different organizations represent the interests of housewives.

A recent dividing line among housewives in modern societies appears to be that between married women who work outside the home and those who do not. In Norway, Sweden, and Denmark, an antagonism between these two groups is sensed. The problems and general situation of wives who work outside the home are often under public discussion. Occasionally, they are referred to as trouble-makers for the family institution and contributors to juvenile delinquency, divorce, and a general disintegration of the family. At the same time, the housewife who does not hold a paid outside job is sometimes accused of being unenterprising, lazy, and dull.

Comparisons between families with working mothers and those in which the mother stays at home are interesting. Swedish data indicate that the similarities in the home routine between the two types of families are in many respects greater than the differences. Naturally, the working mother spends less time on various household tasks than the mother who remains at home. Women of the first group clean less often, prepare fewer meals, use more canned goods and collective services, and very often eliminate such tasks as baking and sewing. In families where the mother works, husbands, relatives, children, and paid domestic servants do a greater part of the housework than in families where the mother does not have an outside job. The wife is the chief housekeeper, however, whether or not she has another job. Assistance from husbands is limited, although newer data show some changes in this pattern. Thus a recent Norwegian study indicates considerable differences in the division of labor in the two types of families, the husband participating far more actively in "working-wife families." Extensive studies show that both groups of housewives organize their work similarly and use about the same appliances. If anything, the women who stay at home have more household appliances than those who hold jobs.

Swedish statistics indicate that a number of husbands prefer their wives not to work outside the home, and this seems to be of great importance in the decision of married women to stay at home. It has been suggested that the husband's dislike of domestic chores is a main factor in their negative attitude toward their wives' work. Other motives have also been suggested. It is often held that a working wife is more independent and free in relation to her husband, and that her career brings about changes in the traditional patriarchal structure of the family. Swedish and Norwegian studies, like those in the U.S., offer no clear evidence for the hypothesis that wives with careers exert more authority and influence than those who remain at home. In the American reports this is suggested to indicate that the average family, in which the wife stays at home, has already become so much of a democratic institution that having her own income does not increase the wife's power, already equal to that of her husband's.

DIVORCE

It is often maintained in oral discussions and popular magazines that those marriages where the wife works outside the home are more susceptible to marital unhappiness and divorce than are the marriages with a "domestic" wife. Scandinavian research data give contradictory results on this point. Some Swedish and Norwegian investigations show tendencies that support the common belief; whereas Danish material indicates significantly *fewer* divorces in the families of working wives.

The divorce rates show a wide range in the Scandinavian countries. Although Norway has one of the lowest divorce rates in the Western world, Finland, Sweden, and Denmark have higher rates, Denmark's, in particular, being twice the Norwegian. In Norway, the number of divorces was .7 per 1000 inhabitants in 1961, the corresponding figure in both Finland and Sweden was 1.2, in Denmark 1.4, and in the U.S. 2.2. These differences may be partially explained by the variations in degree of industrialization of the four countries. Furthermore, Norwegian life is in some parts of the country more marked by pietistic and strict religious traditions than is life in the other Scandinavian countries.

Whatever the causes for the differences in divorce rates, the trend is similar in all Scandinavian countries. Divorce rates have been increasing steadily over a time, and we may discuss briefly the implications of this phenomenon for women in general.

The fact that a person is divorced is usually not considered relevant in politics, professional life, or public affairs. Nevertheless, although a divorce is generally accepted in most circles, there are groups, mostly religious ones, that take a strong stand against divorce. Also, behind surface acceptance antagonism and uncertainty are often found in relation to a divorced couple. The negative consequences of a divorce, for example social isolation, seem to hit women more than men. This is especially true of women with children who have not kept in touch with work life.

Scandinavian divorce laws, which are among the most liberal in Europe, are largely based on the philosophy of equality between the spouses. The obligation to maintain a former spouse covers in principle both partners to a marriage. Divorce is usually granted by administrative decision, and very few divorces are brought before the court. In neither case are divorces or divorce proceedings open to the public or commented upon by the press. Either spouse can apply for and get a divorce, although the time of legal separation may vary from one to three years. The question of guilt is considered irrelevant in granting a divorce, and is regarded relevant only in special cases with reference to the economic settlements between the spouses or to the question of custody of the children.

The only sex differentiation—although an important one—admitted in the divorce law concerns the right to bring up the children. As a rule, the mother is given this right and obligation; only very grave offenses can deprive a divorced mother of the right to keep her children. The possibility that this principle constitutes an injustice toward fathers has recently been given much consideration in Norway. The rules are felt to imply discrimination, giving women special privileges.

WELFARE MEASURES

For divorced mothers a system of state guarantee has been established for the children's support. If the father does not pay, the state advances the money and then claims a refund from the father. Some limited help from the government is also offered to women who are in the category of lone providers. They enjoy some tax reductions; they get a state allowance for each child, and additional allowances in some communities. Such mothers have priority in getting their children admitted to kindergartens. Kindergartens are, however, scarce in all Scandinavia, and this is even more true of institutions taking care of small children throughout the working day.

Since the 1930's there has been considerable interest in the Scandinavian countries in state-controlled family welfare measures. The impetus behind the movement, which is linked with the names of Alva and Gunnar Myrdal, stemmed from concern about the declining birth rate and a desire to redistribute national wealth in favor of families with children. Today, in Denmark, Sweden, and Norway, various direct and indirect benefits contribute to the improvement of the living standard of families with children, such as cash allowances for children, mothers' allowances, housing subsidies, vacation allowances for housewives, school meals, free education, and health insurance. In Norway, since the end of World War II, an annual allowance, max. kr. 500 ($71.00) for the second and each subsequent child is now being paid by the government. Single providers receive this allowance for the first child as well. Various local allowances are given to unwed mothers. Such a social system tends to strengthen the position of the mother and housewife and to make life easier for her. This may be increasingly desirable in societies in which the ties to a wide circle of relatives have been severed, community contacts weakened, and the stress on technical efficiency has become more and more important.

IDEOLOGY AND REALITY

We have seen that the actual practices and modes of behavior reflect a more traditional concept of women's position in society than the one underlying the legal and official doctrines. An informal set of norms seems to intervene between ideology and reality. Various aspects of these norm systems have been studied by Scandinavian social scientists. Psychological investigations of Norwegian children and adolescents indicate that the learning of differential norms for males and females begins in early childhood.

According to these studies, the degree of difference between the prescriptions for girls and those for boys is more marked than has been commonly assumed. In various spheres—work, personal relations, and religious behavior—the children maintain that different modes of behavior are appropriate for boys and girls. Both boys and girls believe that it is appropriate for boys, but not for girls, to fight and to use harsh language. It is believed to be more suitable for girls than for boys to say evening prayers, go to church, and help sick people and small children. Wood chopping, driving and repairing cars, and seeing "tough" movies were considered boys' activities, and reading love stories and helping with the dishes were girls' activities. Mothers, when asked in one study whether they thought boys and girls should be treated alike, responded positively. But when the question was applied to concrete activities, such as helping with housework or getting an education, the principle of equality gave way to more traditional, sex-differentiated views. An investigation of adult blue- and white-collar employees in the Oslo area confirmed the notion of an egalitarian ideology of sex roles. Certain differences between men and women were, however, revealed, women holding more egalitarian attitudes than men. Only slight differences were found among persons of different socioeconomic backgrounds.

How does it come about that principles of equality, which have been officially maintained and believed in for about forty to fifty years, have not been able to break through the informal sex role prescriptions? And how is it possible to maintain a considerable gap between the formal and the informal standards?

One answer to the first question lies in the fact that the learning of sex roles begins very early in a child's life. It is intimately tied up with processes of identification and the shaping of a self-image, mechanisms that cannot, because of their deep psychological roots, be easily changed by ideologies encountered later in life. One implication of this is that both men and women may need the traditional concept of sex roles to bolster their ego and sense of security. And obviously, the presently existing situation contains privileges and rewards for many women: freedom from certain types of worry and a large degree of protection and comfort.

Furthermore, the informal norms regulate certain spheres of social life that are not easily controlled by law. They apply largely to private modes of conduct, are transmitted by the family, and are anchored in early childhood experiences. Legal, economic and administrative rules, educational, policies, etcetera, may bring about only indirectly and over a long period of time, changes in cultural images and private conduct. Also, the generality and vagueness of the principles of equality make them unfit for application to everyday situations. "Equality between the sexes" may be interpreted in a number of different ways and thus leave a broad margin for diverse practices. Finally, overemployment and the steadily increasing standard of living sometimes cover up more subtle social and psychological problems.

One of the peculiarities of the present situation is the fact that patterns of behavior exhibited by men and women often seem to reflect neither the official equality norms, *nor* the traditional norms. Studies in various types of deviant behavior show strongly marked patterns of sex-differentiation. Thus, in the Scandinavian countries, only about 10 per cent of all convicted criminals are women (1933–1952), a figure approximating those of other European countries. In Norway, the number of female alcoholics is only between 5 and 6 per cent of the total. Furthermore, about twice as many men as women die as the result of accidents; among Norwegian children aged ten to fourteen, only 15 per cent of those who suffered accidents in 1946–1947 were girls. One hypothesis for explaining the sex ratio with regard to crime is that the masculine role is closer to the criminal role, and that criminal behavior may be an extension, or an exaggerated form, of the daring behavior often resorted to in order to assure the boy or man of his masculinity. Similar arguments might be valid in connection with the sex differences exhibited in the incidence of mental illness: women seem to be more prone to the less violent or dramatic types of mental disorder (neuroses), men to the more severe types (psychoses). Similarly, women apparently suffer more often, whereas men die earlier. Perhaps the role of the patient is more suited for women's present make-up. And finally, in Scandinavia, as in most other countries, the suicide rate is significantly higher for men than for women.

It may be asked whether such sex differences are symptomatic of greater mental and emotional stress inherent in the social role of the man, and whether this is the price men must pay for their greater influence, power and prestige. At least, it seems evident that the qualities involved in "male-ness" require more drastic and dramatic expression. The stresses of fulfilling the female role appear less striking, but are probably as profoundly felt. The studies of work behavior, previously mentioned, seem to show, for example, frustration and conflicts that women holding paid jobs exhibit more often than men.

The Outlook

We have presented the situation of Scandinavian women as one marked by a conflict between new principles of equality and the principles of an old, traditional culture. It is pertinent to ask: will the future increase or decrease the ambivalence of women's situation? Which forces will triumph?

The efforts to follow the principle of sex equality in the legal domain are continuing, although at a slower pace than earlier. The recent interest in the problem on the part of the governments and the political parties have brought to the fore viewpoints and proposals which may lead to elimina-tions of the last remnants of formal inequality (the national insurance systems, the alodial privileges of sons). Also the question of taxation of married women working outside the home is being discussed. Measures are taken to attract more women to vocational training and higher education.

Moderate emancipationists stress that women must prepare, psychologically and academically, for an alternation between the family role and the job role, and that everything should be done to facilitate their adjustment to both areas. The more radical — and leading — emancipationists advocate abandoning the idea of "women's two roles" in favor of a system whereby women would devote themselves to occupations and careers in the same way as men do. Such a system would entail a complete revision of the home routine, with a different division of labor in housekeeping tasks. Collective housing and an extensive network of institutions for taking care of children, actively supported by national and local governments, are envisioned as parts of the scheme. The grand old lady of the Norwegian emancipationists, Margarete Bonnevie and her young Swedish disciple, Eva Moberg, are strong advocates of this system. The rapid increase in educational standards in general would seem to favor the latter point of view.

The outlook for the position of women cannot, however, be seen in isolation from the prospects for women in other parts of the world. Increasing contact with other cultures will undoubtedly affect the situation. Some Scandinavian women have expressed fears that increased contact with continental Europe may hamper the development toward equality, since their position is better than that of women in many other places. Others feel that these fears are groundless, for developments everywhere seem to be taking a direction favorable to equality. At any rate, the future will almost certainly be characterized by a continuation of the rapid technical and social changes that have hitherto influenced women's position in various, often incompatible, ways.

Technical development may, in itself, make possible the elimination of certain sex differences: for example, the concept of heavy work being restricted to men may disappear, since everybody can push a button. Technical improvements may also eliminate much housework and thus leave women free to create new roles for themselves. On the other hand, it is precisely the world of technology that has traditionally been closed to women, on the grounds that it is incompatible with their interests and abilities. If this pattern prevails, and it seems surprisingly tenacious, women run the risk of continuing to be left out of one of the dominant forces of our culture. Women have traditionally been more interested in religion, morality, and personal relations. But even these areas are being increasingly subjected to technical analysis and professionalization. Experts are taking over many of women's traditional tasks, applying new standards and values to them. An important question, therefore, is whether women can adjust themselves to this world of technology and specialization, or whether they will prefer to keep their traditional orientations and bring them to bear upon the world of technology. We may conclude that the present situation of Scandinavian women displays the same confusing, yet promising, trends exhibited by the situation of women throughout the Western world.

BIBLIOGRAPHY

Aubert, V., "Kvinner i akademiske yrker." *Tidsskrift for Samfunnsforskning*. Nr. 4, 1961. ("Women in Academic Professions." *Journal of Social Research*, No. 4, 1961.)

Bonnevie, Margarete, *Fra Mannssamfunn til menneskesamfunn* (From a Man's Society to a Human Society), Oslo: 1955.

Brun-Gulbrandsen, S., *Kjönnsroller og ungdomskriminalitet* (Sex Roles and Juvenile Delinquency). With a summary in English, Oslo, 1958.

——, & Ås, B., "Kjönnsroller og ulykker." *Tidsskrift for Samfunnsforskning*. Nr. 2, Oslo: 1960 ("Sex Roles and Accidents," *Journal of Social Research*, No. 2, Oslo: 1960).

——, *Kjönnsrolle og asosialitet* (Sex Roles and Asocial Behavior), Mimeo, Oslo: Institute for Social Research, 1958.

Dahlström, E., Holter, H. and others, *Kvinners liv og arbeid* (Women's Life and Work), Stockholm: 1962.

Eliot, Th., Hilman, A. and others, *Norway's Families*, Philadelphia: 1960.

Grönseth, E., "The Political Role of Women in Norway," in Duverger, M. (ed.), *The Political Role of Women*, Paris: UNESCO, 1955.

Holter, Harriet, "Kjönnsforskjeller i skole og arbeidsprestasjoner." *Tidsskrift for Samfunnsforskning* ("Sex Differences in Performances at School and Work," Oslo: *Journal of Social Research*), Sept. 1961.

——, *Work Behavior and Sex Roles*, Unpubl. ms., Oslo: 1965.

Jensen, Johannes V., *Kvinner i Sagatiden* (Women in the Sagas), Köbenhavn, 1942.

The Norwegian Joint Committee on International Social Policy, *Facts about Women in Norway*, Oslo: 1960.

Quist, Gunnar, *Kvinnofragan i Sverige 1809–1846* (Women's Position in Sweden 1809–1846), with a summary in English, Göteborg: 1960.

Rokkan, S. & Valen, H., "Mobilization of the Perifery," *Acta Sociologica*, Vol. VI. Fasc. 1–2, 1962.

Sysiharju, Anna-Liisa, *Home, Work and Equality*, Helsinki: 1960.

Zweig, F., *Women's Life and Labour*, London: 1952.

Great Britain

By Viola Klein

THE TRADITIONAL SITUATION

*T*he *mistake is sometimes made* to speak of women as if they formed one, more or less homogeneous, social class. "The Status of Women" is indeed a popular subject of doctoral theses and learned treatises. Yet it is no less a fallacy to treat all women as having the same social status than it would be to make such an assumption about men.

Women, to be sure, have suffered from many disabilities. These have, however, not affected all women in the same manner or to the same degree; nor have all inequalities applied to a majority of the female sex.

The disqualification of married women from administering their own property, for instance, which was the subject of a heated controversy and a prolonged parliamentary struggle during the second half of the nineteenth century—and which resulted in the Married Women's Property Acts of 1870, 1882, and 1893—primarily concerned the prosperous minority of upper- and middle-class women, even though the legislation eventually passed to redress this wrong also secured for working wives the right to their own earnings.

The absence of vocational opportunities, which prompted the earlier feminists to claim for women the "Right to Work," was also primarily a middle-class affliction. There was no lack of work, albeit few vocational opportunities, among the women of the poorer classes. On the contrary, they suffered from a surfeit of labor, in particular as, to quote a Factory Inspector's Report of 1843, "the small amount of wages paid to women acts as a strong inducement to employ them instead of men, and in power-loom shops this has been the case to a great extent." The same exploitation of women as cheap casual workers was practiced in agriculture no less than in industry.

As a result of this situation, protective legislation had to be introduced to reduce excessive working hours and set certain minimum standards of health (abolishing night work, for instance, in 1802, prohibiting the employment underground of women in coal mines in 1842, and introducing, in 1892, women factory inspectors to see that the regulations were obeyed). Factory legislation, by definition, affected only women of the working classes.

When the issue of votes for women was first raised, the working-class men were still disenfranchised. During the debates on the Reform Bill of 1867, John Stuart Mill put forward a motion for the enfranchisement of women together with suggestions for the adoption of proportional representation, neither of which was accepted. In achieving the right to vote in parliamentary elections, which women over the age of thirty received in 1918 and women over twenty-one in 1928, they were some thirty years behind the generality of men. Seen against the background of the British governing classes, however, women—excepting the monarch—were centuries behind men in achieving political rights.

These instances are quoted to illustrate the fact, obvious enough, that the class structure of society affects women no less than men. The social position of women cannot, therefore, be usefully discussed without reference to the social class of which women form a part.

My reason for stating this so explicitly is that in thinking about the traditional situation of women one is faced with a general assumption that woman's place used to be the home and that this definition sufficiently describes women's former role in society.

It is by now well enough known that in pre-industrial times the home was the center of many, if not most, productive activities and that, therefore, woman's place therein involved her in a multitude of important economic functions. It is less frequently appreciated that even after the Industrial Revolution thousands of women were employed in the new centers of production. Yet, the population census of 1851 shows that, at a time when Britain's industrialization was already in full swing, one married woman out of every four was engaged in some extraneous occupation, that is, was referred to by a professional category other than housewife. This does not take into account the wives of farmers, small shopkeepers, innkeepers, butchers, shoemakers, and others, who helped in their husbands' businesses but were registered as housewives. Among the widows of that time two in three were gainfully employed.

The maldistribution of the newly created, unprecedented wealth which characterized the early stages of industrialization was clearly reflected in the lives of women. At the one extreme, there was poverty and sweated labor in overcrowded slums, at the other, a growing and increasingly prosperous middle class.

"The proportion of mothers employed," stated a Report on the Condition of Children in Receipt of Relief submitted as evidence to the Royal Commission on the Poor Law in 1909, "varies from 92 per cent in Lambeth to 59 per cent in Paddington. . . . The children as a rule do not get suitably fed unless special arrangements can be made for them . . ." which, the report estimated, was the case in 40 per cent of the families investigated. This was London; but conditions in other industrial centers, the Lancashire cotton areas or the Staffordshire potteries, for example, were no better. Numerous mothers of large families, and young girls from the age of nine upwards, worked in factories from 6 A.M. to 6 P.M. every day; their working week was limited by a statute of 1850 to fifty-eight-and-a-half hours, excluding meal breaks.

At the other end of the scale, there was now, in addition to the landed gentry, a growing urban middle class whose wealth derived from the expansion of trade and industry. One of the status symbols of this class was the idleness of their women. Daughters were brought up to be decorous, modest, and chaste and they were closely guarded and chaperoned so as not to stray from the path of virtue. Knowledge and initiative, intelligence and experience were equally discouraged. The education of ladies was aimed at producing accomplishments—a smattering of music, art and needlework, as well as social manners; but did not include serious training in any subject. "Nobody dreamed," wrote Francis Power Cobbe, the social reformer, in 1904, "that any of us could in later life be more or less than an ornament to society. That a pupil in that school should become an artist or authoress would have been regarded as a deplorable dereliction. Not that which was good and useful to the community, or even that which would be delightful to ourselves, but that which would make us admired in society was the *raison d'être* of such requirement. The education of women was probably at its lowest ebb about half a century ago. It was at that period more pretentious than it had ever been before, and infinitely more costly, and it was likewise more shallow and senseless than can easily be believed."

As this milieu was the setting of nearly all literary works of the time and, moreover, provided the model for those aspiring to climb the social ladder, it is not surprising that middle-class women were the brand image of nineteenth-century womanhood: leisured yet impotent, severely restricted in their freedom of movement, placed on a pedestal but fenced off from all positions of power and sources of learning by a barrier of rigid social taboos.

It borders on the miraculous that, nevertheless, the period produced a score or more of outstanding women—writers, social reformers, administrators—whose names have become part of Britain's cultural heritage and who would be the pride of any country.

It is remarkable, too, that so many women, living in the gilded cage of bourgeois comfort, should have begun to revolt against their situation. They were induced to do so by the climate of opinion of the age which combined a general belief in the values of education with an increasing emphasis on opportunity for all talents; they were prompted, moreover, by the more immediate and practical necessity of making provisions for the future in case they were unable to find a husband. The emigration of many able-bodied young men, because of the expansion of the colonial empire, increased the fear that many daughters of middle-class families might have to live by their own resources.[1] Lacking any other equipment, they had but two alternatives: either to become governesses or else to live as maiden aunts on the charity of relatives. Either prospect was sufficiently humiliating to convince at least the more enlightened parents that investing in a systematic education and, possibly, even a professional training, of their daughters was safer than speculating on their marriage chances.

The existence of shining examples, referred to earlier, such as Annie Besant, Josephine Butler, George Eliot, Octavia Hill, Harriet Martineau, Florence Nightingale, Beatrice Webb, to name but a few, encouraged pioneering spirits to follow suit. Once the doors were opened, women ventured out of the confines of their homes in increasing numbers.

What had started as a trickle at the turn of the century became a flood within less than fifty years. But in the meantime two world wars and a technological, scientific, and social revolution had transformed the structure of society, altered its economic basis, and thrown overboard a good many traditional ideas that had outlived their usefulness.

---

1. According to the 1875 edition of the *Yearbook of Women's Work*, there were in 1861 over half a million more women than men in Great Britain, or 106.2 females to every 100 males. "Few women," the Yearbook goes on to say, "much above the servant class emigrate, and the postponement of marriage by the higher classes till a later age than used to be the practice of our grandmothers, strengthens the explanation we are offering of the existence of a large body of adult single women wanting employment in the middle and upper ranks of society."

Town and Country

Differences between town and country in Britain are striking by their absence. Britain, with 571 persons per square mile, is one of the most densely populated countries in the world; distances between town and country are therefore never very great. Mobility between rural and urban areas is so high that an indigenous rural population, in the sense of families having cultivated their land for many generations without ever leaving it, hardly exists. The country is highly motorized and has a network of excellent roads even in the depth of the countryside. Thus communications between outlying farms and villages, and between villages and towns are easy. Television is available to 98 per cent of the population and three-quarters of all households own their TV set. This, combined with an even wider use of radio and the existence of a national press, has contributed to the increasing uniformity of standards between town and country.

This uniformity is not, however, as recent as the reference to TV and sound broadcasting would seem to imply. Britain is not only one of the most highly industrialized countries in the world but was also the first to be industrialized. Coal and tin mines were discovered, and industries developed, in the midst of agricultural areas in the last century. Migration from country into towns and the decline of agriculture therefore set in earlier than elsewhere.

The latter became a serious problem especially during the two world wars, and successive governments have tried to stem the flight from the land by giving financial assistance to farmers in the form of subsidies and guaranteed prices and by other means. Technical and advisory services were set up, agricultural research was developed, marketing boards for farm produce were created, minimum wages for agricultural workers were raised and the amenities of the countryside were improved, including also a postwar program of rural housing. Farming today is one of Britain's most highly organized industries and is one of the most mechanized agricultures in the world.

As the mainstay of British agriculture is the breeding of livestock (cattle and sheep) rather than the growing of crops, a very large proportion of the land is under grass. Pastures, separated by hedges and interspersed with old trees, cover large areas and give the impression of England as one huge park—the unending "golf course" of travellers' tales. It is, indeed, astonishing in a country of so high a population density to find that vast stretches of land appear rural in character: green fields, crossed by narrow streams and littered with grazing lambs; scattered old villages; and occasional large houses standing on their own in enormous gardens.

This brings up another reason why there is little conflict between town and country in England: The rapprochement between the two has not been a onesided adjustment of rural to urban standards. The emotional home of Englishmen and women is the countryside. Only very recently and reluctantly have they begun to live in apartment houses. The vast majority prefer one-family houses with gardens even in the towns. Hence the outward movement from the center of cities, the never-ending encroachment of suburbia on the countryside.

The house in the country—if possible, in addition to a flat in London—is the ideal of the upper strata of society. Many an ex-civil servant, or a former company director, retires into the country; professional men and women, writers and artists, often live in country cottages, even if their work necessitates a daily journey into town. Acquiring, modernizing and running a farm, as a "gentleman farmer," has seemed to many a businessman a more attractive way of spending surplus money than paying high taxes. Retired army officers run country inns; middle-class ladies supplement their incomes by keeping antique shops or serving tea in their front parlor or garden. Charming old thatched-roof cottages in immaculate condition are likely to be inhabited by architects, barristers, or the widows of colonial civil servants rather than by "countryfolk" proper. Farmers discovered a long time ago that they can profit by letting rooms to visitors from the cities during summer vacations.

Life in the countryside, naturally, proceeds at a slower pace; the opportunities for education and for work are smaller; and the choice of goods available in the shops is more limited, hence the movement from the country, especially of the younger generation.

This movement is even more marked among women than among men. Factories and offices offer them a wide range of employment and they are attracted to the cities not only by better earnings but also by more varied social contacts.

If statistics were available, they would probably show that the consumption of nail varnish per head—or hand—of the female population is somewhat smaller, the production of home-made jam somewhat larger in rural than in urban areas. But in their dress, use of cosmetics, bearing, and manners, countrywomen in England hardly differ from their town-cousins. They drive cars, and sometimes tractors and vans; they ride on horseback or bicycle; they belong to a Women's Institute (while housewives in town meet at the Townswomen's Guilds) and possibly will also be members of one or another women's organization. If they live in outlying areas, they will have their bread and other provisions—standardized, mass-produced, and prepacked—delivered to their doorstep by motorvan. Their work and leisure pursuits, their furniture and household equipment, their role in the family, the number of their children, their status, and their general outlook on life will be the same or, rather, will show the same individual differences as if they lived in the suburb of any big town.

THE LEGAL STATUS

In law, women's position is virtually equal to men's. This is now so generally accepted that it seems strange to remember of how recent a date this equality is.

Its major instrument was the Sex Disqualification (Removal) Act of 1919 which provided that women should not be disqualified by their sex from holding any office or post, profession or vocation, nor should they be excluded from jury service. The only exceptions to this rule were membership in the House of Lords, which was granted in 1958, and the taking of Holy Orders.

By a series of acts passed from 1870 on, the disabilities of married women to hold and dispose of their own property were abolished. Women can make business contracts independently of their husbands, can sue and be sued, and have a right to their own earnings.

Only in two respects is women's position in regard to property rights still subordinate to their husbands': savings which a wife makes from her housekeeping money belong to her husband; and the proceeds from joint efforts go to the husband, unless he contracts to share them with his wife. That is to say, if a couple should write books together the royalties would belong to the husband, unless otherwise agreed upon.

On the other hand, a husband is liable to support his wife, an obligation that is not reciprocal. Nor can he pledge her credit, no matter how rich she is or how much she earns. The husband is also liable to pay tax on his wife's as well as his own income, unless the couple applies for separate assessments.

A husband has no right to deprive his wife of her liberty or to use force against her. But as recently as 1946, when a wife sued her husband for divorce on the grounds of cruelty, a court decided that the husband was not guilty of the offense because, if the wife had not disobeyed him, he would not have hit her. This decision was, however, reversed by the Court of Appeal.

A husband can still claim compensation from a corespondent in a divorce suit for the loss of his wife's services or sue him for enticement. A wife can do neither, if her husband runs away with another woman. On the other hand, women still do occasionally sue a man for breach of promise, although such cases are out of harmony with current sentiment and have therefore become very rare.

In relation to their children, the father has no longer any superior right to the mother. The factor which carries most weight in any judicial decision is the welfare of the children and for this reason courts tend to favor the women. Family allowances, paid by the National Insurance for second and subsequent children, are paid to the mother.

Wives can sue for divorce on equal grounds with men. There is no divorce by agreement (on the contrary, a petition may be refused on the ground of collusion between the parties). The grounds for divorce, widened by the Herbert Act of 1937, are limited to adultery, desertion, cruelty, and incurable insanity (under certain conditions); a wife can also obtain a divorce if the husband commits certain criminal sexual offenses. In addition, a marriage can be declared void for a number of specified reasons, but nullity proceedings are much less extended in scope than they are in some Catholic countries.

In cases of divorce the courts have wide powers to enforce maintenance of wife and children, and will do so if the wife is judged to be the innocent party; they will, as a rule, also order the husband to pay the costs of the proceedings. There has been an increasing tendency in the courts to award the matrimonial home to the wife, even if it is registered in the husband's name.

Access to divorce facilities has been much widened by the introduction after the war of legal aid, free—or almost free—to persons who do not possess a certain minimum income. For this reason, and as a result of war-time conditions, the divorce rate rose steeply during the years immediately following the war: from 7,111 divorces in 1940 to 52,249 divorces in 1947. Since its peak in 1947 the number of divorces has, however, steadily declined and is now roughly 1:18 new, or 2 per 1000 existing, marriages.

As a result of a report submitted by a committee under the chairmanship of Sir John Wolfenden, soliciting in the streets has been prohibited and is severely penalized. Prostitutes have therefore been driven "underground" and use various devious means to secure customers. Living on the immoral earnings of a woman is an offense that carries severe penalties. Another recommendation of the Wolfenden Report, that homosexual relations between consenting male adults should no longer be illegal (about which controversy is still raging), has not been carried out and prosecutions for this offense are still frequent. Homosexual relations between women, however, are ignored by the law and the public.

To sum up: Apart from a few and, on the whole, insignificant survivals from bygone days, the legal status of women is equal to men's, except where the law takes into account some weaknesses in women's social position and their special role in the family. In regard to these, women enjoy the legislators' protection.

EDUCATION

If schools are the cradles of future society, they are also products of the contemporary social situation and reflect its stresses and current needs. The British educational system is in a state of ferment because British society is in transformation.

The basis of the present educational system in Britain is the Education Act of 1944. Its principal achievements were the introduction of free secondary-school education for all and the expansion of existing facilities for voluntary further education. Independent schools—among which the public schools are the most widely known and carry most social *cachet*—continue to exist and are attended by about 6 per cent of the boys and less than 2 per cent of the girls; but whether a child, boy or girl, goes to a school that will qualify him for a university or another type of higher education, now depends, in principle, on intellectual ability shown at the age of eleven rather than on the income of parents.

Not all provisions of the 1944 Act have yet been put into force. In particular, the extension of compulsory full-time education up to the age of sixteen and the introduction of compulsory part-time education for young people between sixteen and eighteen have not, so far, been implemented.

Meanwhile, the shortage of teachers at all levels has become acute, mainly because of the increase in the birthrate immediately after the war (the so-called "bulge" which until recently swelled the classrooms of secondary schools and has now begun to overspill into the universities) and, after a return to normal, another steep rise in the birthrate, from 1956 onwards, has taken place.

At present, education is in a state of flux. Technological progress and social changes equally exert pressures on the existing system and demand readjustments. Various official and other bodies have in recent years examined whether the educational system is adequately fulfilling its functions. The Central Advisory Council of Education, headed by Sir Geoffrey Crowther, has published a report on "Early Leaving" and two further volumes on the education of boys and girls during their immediate postschool years (generally known as the Crowther Report, HMSO, 1959); a committee, appointed by the Prime Minister under the chairmanship of Lord Robbins, investigated higher education in Great Britain in 1961–1963, and published its report in 1963 (HMSO, Cmnd. 2154), followed by several volumes of Appendices; and another committee, set up by the Central Advisory Council under the chairmanship of Sir John Newsom reported on the education of less gifted children in a volume entitled *Half Our Future* (HMSO, 1963).

It will be gathered from this brief summary that many postwar changes in the educational system affect both sexes. This has to be borne in mind when the educational opportunities for girls are discussed. The emphasis on more and better education for as many young people as are capable of benefiting from it is a general trend.

Girls have, relatively speaking, derived greater advantage from this development because they were lagging further behind and thus had an opportunity to catch up. Their equal right to education is now not only officially recognized but also widely accepted by parents who, up to a point, will try to give their children of either sex the best education they can afford. This is evidenced by the fact that the proportion of girls in full-time education beyond the minimum school-leaving age is roughly the same as that of boys, namely about one quarter of those aged fifteen to seventeen. At the age of eighteen, however, 7.8 per cent of the boys are still at school compared with 5.4 per cent of the girls; at university level 2.5 per cent of women in their age group compare with 5.6 per cent of men in full-time education. If all types of higher education are put together, that is, if teacher-training colleges are included, the comparison is between 7.3 per cent of women and 9.8 per cent of men in full-time courses. Roughly one quarter of the students in British universities and about two thirds in training colleges are women. The most notable difference between the sexes in higher education is among those pursuing part-time and private study: the proportion of women taking courses of this kind is almost negligible (0.6 per cent of their age group), while 12.6 per cent of men (that is a higher percentage than in full-time courses) entered higher education through part-time study in day or evening classes or through correspondence courses.

Some differences between the education of boys and girls exist even at the secondary-school level. Although coeducation, almost general in the elementary schools, has increased in the newer types of secondary schools, less than 30 per cent of the grammar schools are coeducational, and the curricula in girls' schools usually differ from that of boys' schools. Girls' education is, as a rule, more general than boys'; more time is given to non-academic subjects, such as art and music; less importance is attached to mathematics and science; if science is taught, it tends to be biology rather than physics and chemistry, although efforts have recently been made to amend this situation.

There is a consensus that the purpose of education transcends mere preparation for future employment. "The primary concern of the schools," as the Crowther Report so aptly put it, "should not be with the living they will earn but with the life they will lead." There can be little doubt, however, that the nature of the school curriculum is, quite naturally, influenced by future career prospects. This is one of the reasons for the less academic character of girls' education even in grammar schools. There are many openings for women that require further education, beyond the secondary school level but not of university standard, for instance in nursing, teaching, secretarial work, and others. This does not apply to men to anything like the same extent.

To take the teaching profession as an example, three quarters of all teachers in elementary schools are women. Nearly twice as many girls go to teachers' training colleges as go to universities; *vice versa*, nearly five times as many boys go to universities as go to teachers' training colleges.

Another consideration which is never far from the minds of those responsible for women's education is that most girls marry—today at an earlier age than before—and that, for this reason, their career prospects are uncertain. Even if it is thought desirable, in their own interest and in the interest of the community, to give them the best general education they are capable of absorbing, there is less inclination to provide them with the long and specialized training which a professional career requires.

Many girls, for the same reason, are willing to forego their chances of making the best of their mental abilities and prefer to take jobs instead —sometimes even in menial occupations—which will bring them immediate financial independence. During a period of full employment, with fairly high wages, there are strong incentives for many young people to start earning a living as soon as possible rather than to submit to a lengthy training that will bring its rewards only in the distant future. For obvious reasons, girls are more easily tempted by such short-term considerations than boys.

The same reasons operate, even more forcefully, against university education for women. In British universities generally, as said earlier, there are at present three men students for every one woman undergraduate; at Oxford it is six to one, at Cambridge ten to one.

Yet, set against prewar figures this represents an enormous advance. In view of the great need for highly qualified personnel in many professions —notably in those which have by now largely become feminine domains, such as social work, teaching, and the health services—one would be inclined to assume that women have secured a strong and permanent foot-hold in the places of higher learning and are in a good position to expand it.

This can, however, by no means yet be taken for granted. The great demand for their services itself and the necessary limitations to university expansion, have rendered the women's position somewhat precarious in these areas. It has been calculated that the average expectation of active service of a woman teacher—after a training period that has recently been raised from two to three years—is two and a half years; and it is estimated that over two thirds of women doctors are not in medical employment.

Universities, as Mary Stocks, ex-Principal of Westfield College, once said, "deal with a kind of education which aims, not so much at producing a professionally trained human being for the upper ranges of employability, as at cultivating and expanding mental capacity to an extent which enables its possessor to see fields of knowledge in relation to one another, to evaluate fine shades of meaning, and to acquire some sense of the magnitude and (through affectionate intimacy with some parts of it) the quality of the world's cultural inheritance."

Many people will concur with this view which, ideally, is probably correct. Society may well be in urgent need of men and women whose minds have been cultivated in the sense here indicated. However, it is to be feared that more ultilitarian considerations may prevail and this involves the risk that the limited number of university places may be allotted primarily to candidates who are most likely to excel in purely professional achievement.

Sex Mores

The present survey of changes in the position of women has been confined to the post-World War II period largely for reasons of convenience. The line had to be drawn somewhere; and in times of swift social changes a period such as has elapsed since 1945 is long enough to show significant modifications in social attitudes and practices. The war itself has precipitated some social changes and has hastened the disappearance of many old traditions. While it was thus a milestone on the road of development, it must not be mistaken for its mainspring.

This *caveat* is particularly appropriate in the present context when current sex mores are being discussed, for there is a tendency in many circles to blame the war for the relaxation of taboos on premarital sexual relations — the "loosening of morals," as it usually is called. This is a gross oversimplification. The more permissive attitude in matters of sex has developed slowly over a long time. It is the combined result of improved contraceptive methods, modern means of transport (the motorcar, especially), the decline of religion, the development of and the widespread interest in depth psychology and, last but not least, the emancipation of women. It is obviously more difficult to lock up your daughters when they work alongside of men than it was when they sat at home waiting to be wooed.

In this limited sense the war has accelerated the process that had already been in progress for other reasons. Girls who were drafted into the armed forces and were posted to the far corners of the globe could not, at the end of hostilities, be expected to submit once more to close parental supervision.

It has, in fact, become customary for young unmarried women to live alone and to entertain men and women friends with no chaperonage nor questions being asked. This is now so accepted a practice that the British Council, in a recent guidebook for foreign students on "How to Live in Britain," thought it necessary specifically to mention it — with the rider that this freedom should not be taken for licence.

The outcome of the various influences mentioned is a peculiarly ambivalent state of affairs. The old codes of sexual ethics have quietly been abandoned, but new rules of conduct which take account of the changed social conditions have as yet hardly been developed.

This situation causes much bewilderment, especially among young people. Their need for guidance is thwarted, not only by their natural disinclination to accept the advice of their elders, but also by the inability of the older generation, because of their own uncertainty, to give it. A kind of double standard of morality exists, no longer in the traditional sense of different sets of values applying to men and women; but as a contrast between an "official" point of view and the sex mores actually practiced. (It will be gathered from the context that the term "official point of view" does not refer to precepts—there is nothing new in a conflict between precept and practice—but rather to a set of assumptions about reality untinged by evidence.) Its exponents—judges, ministers of religion, editors of women's journals, and others—feign to ignore the change in morality and regard those deviating from the traditional path of virtue as sinners deserving of their self-inflicted suffering.

Regardless of this "official" attitude, young girls will tell you frankly and without a trace of self-consciousness that they have spent their holiday with a boy friend or are going away for weekends with their fiancé. Whatever may be said about the sex mores of the postwar generation, hypocrisy is less rampant than it used to be.

Illegitimacy rates bear witness to the widespread practice of premarital intercourse.[2] On the evidence of the Registrar General's published returns, 7 per cent of live births in 1963 were illegitimate; the chance of a married couple having a baby within eight months of their wedding-day is one to four.

Birth-control clinics—now called "Family Planning Clinics"—have until recently not been allowed to offer advice to unmarried girls. Under the pressure of changing mores a few of them now give advice to "engaged couples." Their avowed aim is to counsel married people on spacing their families, as well as to help unfertile ones to have babies. Birth-control propaganda and the advertisement of contraceptives are excluded from the press and other mass media on the ground of "good taste."

Abortion is illegal and severely punished, except if undertaken by doctors in good faith for the purpose of preserving the life or health of a pregnant woman. No figures are available as to how many pregnancies are therapeutically terminated on these grounds; but Kenneth Robinson, M.P., who unsuccessfully introduced a bill to alter the existing abortion law,

---

2. A survey on *The Sexual Behaviour of Young People*, undertaken by a research team headed by Michael Schofield under the sponsorship of the Central Council of Health Education (Longmans, 1965) found that 17 per cent of girls and 34 per cent of boys have experienced premarital sexual relations by the time they reach the age of eighteen and that about half of them "have very little interest in birth control and will be slow to profit from instruction in the use of contraceptives."

estimated that the number of criminal abortions carried out each year is between 50,000 and 100,000 — not all, of course, performed on unmarried women.

It is widely asserted that the present generation of girls mature younger, physically as well as mentally and emotionally. However this may be, they are certainly given greater freedom and encouraged to make their own decisions at an earlier age. They often are financially independent when they are still in their teens and therefore form a special target for the "hidden persuaders"; and films, television and press present them with adult models to imitate whose main attraction is their "sex appeal."

THE MARRIAGE PATTERN

One of the salient features of the postwar marriage pattern is that women tend to marry at younger ages. The marriage age of women declined from 25.38 years (for first marriages) in the years preceding the war to 23.49 during 1956–1960. More than 25 per cent of spinster brides were under the age of twenty in 1960, compared with 11 per cent in 1938.

At the same time, the proportion of women entering matrimony has been rising. If present trends continue, within the next ten years three quarters of all women under the age of twenty-five, and one quarter of all women under the age of twenty will be married. The proportion of women remaining single is expected by 1972 to fall to 5 per cent, compared with 15 per cent of the women born about 1900, and under 10 per cent of the women born 1915–1920.[3]

Earlier marriage has been made possible not only by full employment and better earnings, and by the freer association of the sexes mentioned earlier, but to a considerable extent also by the gainful employment of women. Setting up a home, and providing the substantial capital outlay this entails, are obviously easier on two incomes than one. It has therefore become a widespread practice, not only in the working classes in which it is an old tradition but also among the middle and professional classes, for young women to continue in their occupation after marriage, as far as possible. Very frequently they give up their jobs only a short time before the arrival of their first baby, in many instances even later.

Among the various social changes so far discussed the large-scale employment of married women is the only genuinely new phenomenon. In all other respects — whether urbanization, education, the emancipation of women, sex mores, or the lowering of the marriage age — postwar develop-

3. These projections were made by C. M. Stewart of the Government Actuary's Department in a paper read to a conference of the British Sociological Association in March 1960 and published as "Future Trends in the Employment of Married Women" in the *British Journal of Sociology*, Vol. XII, No. 1, 1961.

ments were the continuation and amplification of processes going back over many decades.

In some ways, of course, the gainful employment of married women, too, has a history at least as old as the Industrial Revolution; but the spread of this practice from the neediest of the poor into all strata of society is new, and both the scale and the speed of this expansion have been so great as to amount to a qualitative as well as a quantitative social change.

Shortly after the end of World War II (during which married women up to the age of fifty were conscripted for National Service unless they had young children) there were some 1,500,000 married women in employment; by 1963 this figure had risen to over 4,300,000. The measure of this increase will be more fully appreciated if seen in perspective: in 1947 roughly 18 per cent of all married women were working outside their homes, in 1951 just under 25 per cent, and in 1961 over 32 per cent. This compares with about 12 per cent before the war.

It is worth noting that the rise in the employment of married women coincides with an increase in the birthrate. The number of annual live births per 1,000 of the population rose from 15.0 in 1955 to 17.4 in 1961.

The gainful occupation of a large section of married women is the outcome of a number of apparently disparate developments. Foremost among them are full employment, accompanied by acute labor shortages in many spheres, particularly in the more feminine types of occupations; rising standards of living and, with them, an abundance of consumer goods which are not only alluring but accessible to large sections of the population in return for an extra effort; growing use of labor-saving devices in the home; earlier marriages; small families; increased expectation of life, especially among women; improved training facilities for young women; and, finally, the well-nigh universal practice of female employment prior to marriage.

All these trends are likely to continue. They have, moreover, created a climate of opinion in which the employment of married women is increasingly taken for granted. As the practice has been growing it has developed into a behavior pattern that acts as a model for others to emulate. In the decade between 1950 and 1960 alone the number of married women in employment increased by 44 per cent. During the same period the total female labor force grew by only 12.7 per cent; that is to say, the number of single women available for work has actually diminished and they are now outnumbered by married women. This illustrates the statements made earlier that more women get married, that this occurs at an earlier age and that many of them stay on in their jobs. But an increasing number also return to employment when they have brought up their families. The vast majority of working wives are older than thirty-five.

Not all of this employment is full time. A substantial proportion of working wives—possibly as many as 50 per cent—are in part-time jobs in a wide range of fields, from office cleaning to journalism, from serving canteen meals to adult education. Because of the shortage of female staff, part-time employment, despite its unpopularity with managements, has been increasing in recent years in factories, offices, shops, hospitals, and schools.

Ideally, the work pattern to which a very large proportion of women now aspire is first a period of full employment at the beginning of married life, a second phase during which they devote themselves entirely to raising a family, and, finally, resumption of outside work, preferably part time, when their children no longer require full attention.

This rhythm of work and family care is achieved only by a minority; but it is a sizable minority, considering that one third of all married women are in employment, and, at any given time, just over one half of all households with married heads have no children under sixteen.

Apart from the financial reward and all it entails in terms of higher living standards and personal independence, one of the strongest incentives for married women to seek work outside their homes is the contact this brings with other people. For there can be no doubt that the modern housewife, whose husband is away at work all day, whose children are at school or have already left the parental home, and who as a rule lives at some distance from near-relatives and close friends, feels isolated and "left out." In many instances she will also feel underemployed because of the greater ease with which housework now can be done and the consequent sense of guilt many women experience for "not fully pulling their weight."

This situation is today so widely appreciated that the gainful employment of a married woman no longer involves a loss of status either to herself or her family but is accepted as one of the facts of modern life.

WOMAN'S POSITION IN THE FAMILY

Husbands have adjusted themselves remarkably well to this new situation; the middle and professional classes even more so than the working classes among whom a wife's going out to work is sometimes felt to reflect on the husband's earning capacities. However, among the younger generation of workers the new pattern has also come to be accepted as the natural order of things, always with the proviso that mothers of young children should stay at home wherever possible. The material advantages of wives' working are too obvious to be ignored, and there are the more intangible benefits of better chances of harmony due to less friction over money matters and the greater feeling of partnership. "There is more to talk about," and "it's making my wife a more interesting (or more contented) person," are typical reactions, in addition to: "we are able to do things which we couldn't otherwise afford."

In return, husbands have to take a greater share in domestic work. "If the wife is not to get so tired that she is no longer a companion to her husband," advises a booklet of commonsense rules issued by the National Marriage Guidance Council, "it is essential that her husband should be willing to lend a hand." The pamphlet then goes on to give concrete instances of the division of labor required: "First thing in the morning get him to make the bed whilst you get the breakfast and whoever is the last person to leave the house can wash up the breakfast things."

The husband's cooperation in household chores is widely accepted and not confined to families where the wife goes out to work. It is part of the prevailing partnership pattern of marriage and is even more widespread among the classes who before the war were able to employ domestic servants. The adjournment of the House of Lords to enable "Their Lord-ships" to help their wives washing-up is a standing joke; but there are innumerable civil servants, barristers, university teachers, or bank clerks who, at the end of a day's work, rush to their suburban homes to do just that or to bathe the baby.

No matter how much assistance she may get from her husband or adolescent children, and irrespective of whether or not she also has a job, household management remains the wife's responsibility. In addition to doing most of the routine work, her task will, foremost, be one of organization and of creating the home atmosphere. This has assumed much greater importance than before because, with growing prosperity and better housing conditions among the majority of the population, the emphasis on domestic comfort has increased and husbands as well as wives tend to spend much more time at home than was customary in pre-television days.

The change is so marked that Mark Abrams, a sociologist working in the field of consumer research, contends that "home-centredness" is a major characteristic of our present society. "For the first time in modern British history," he says, "the working-class home, as well as the middle-class home, has become a place that is warm, comfortable, and able to provide its own fireside entertainment—in fact, pleasant to live in. The outcome is a working-class way of life which is decreasingly concerned with activities outside the house or with values wider than those of the family. The good husband is now the domesticated husband—the man who, when he has finished his work at the factory or the office, spends his evenings and his weekends not with his workmates but at home with his family, enjoying common fireside relaxations with them, or else 'pottering' round the house maintaining its comfort and appearance." Even the motorcar, he asserts, has made little difference to this home-centered pattern, for most owners treat their car as "a small mobile room that can be taken to the seaside or the country and in which they can sit in isolation when they have arrived at their destination."[4]

The major part of household expenditure goes through women's hands, not only for day-to-day catering and clothes, but also for the many durable household goods which form a substantial proportion of most family budgets.

From what has been said before it will be seen that in the present order of things women hold key positions. They have, with less recognition, of course, always done so. Their status in the family has increased not only because they are better educated, more widely interested and hence more equal companions, but also because they can, if necessary, contribute toward the support of the family. Their status has risen also because of a revaluation of their traditional functions as administrators of the home, guardians and educators of their children, and as the active link between the generations, upholding the bond with aged parents as well as with children and grand-children.

This rise in women's status has not, in Britain, led to a matriarchal, or quasi-matriarchal, family system. The overbearing and oppressive "Mom" — the subject matter of so many American novels and plays — is here relatively rare. This may be due to a fairly old tradition of "live-and-let-live" in human relations, and also to the allied fact that the British, emotionally as well as geographically, live in a more moderate climate.

HOUSEHOLD ROUTINE

Two opposite developments have, in conjunction, considerably altered the normal household routine.

On the one hand, the Industrial Revolution has, at long last, now reached the home. Electrically operated labor-saving appliances of one kind or another are used in a growing number of homes. Nearly three quarters of all households now own vacuum-cleaners; more than 40 per cent have washing machines; about one quarter own refrigerators. (So as not to give too glossy a picture of contemporary Britain, it must be added hastily that, in 1958, 29 per cent of households still were without bathrooms.)

Apart from these and a great variety of other gadgets which lighten the burden of domestic labor without actually taking it off women's shoulders, much assistance in reducing the work load comes from sources outside the home. The consumption of frozen food has spread enormously, not only in the big cities. Together with dehydrated soups, vegetables and sauces, canned fruit and similar products, they have considerably reduced the time spent on preparing meals and washing up. Supermarkets are mushrooming

---

4. In his study *The Worker in an Affluent Society* (Heinemann, 1961), F. Zweig made very similar observations on the family life of British industrial workers.

all over the country in big and small towns alike and, although often sneered at, simplify catering in large measure.

Children who, from the age of five, are kept at school both mornings and afternoons get their midmorning milk and midday meal there. This is a relief to housewives who, unless they have an infant or invalid at home, are saved the trouble of cooking lunch and can content themselves with a light midday snack.

On the other hand, more time is spent at home by the family and more pains are taken to make it not only a comfortable but also an attractive, modern, and efficient place to live in. Owing to the high cost of labor, the industrial production of semi-finished consumer goods and easy-to-apply materials has been developed, thus encouraging many variations on the do-it-yourself theme. People are busy decorating their homes, papering their walls, modernizing old or assembling new furniture, laying floor coverings, giving the paintwork a new coat, tiling their bathrooms, and so on. These activities, mostly shared between husband and wife, aim not only at improving the appearance of the home but also at making it more easy to run.

To the normal and more traditional household routine a number of new domestic activities have thus been added which take up a large part of the increased leisure time.

Moreover, the labor-saving machines need a good deal of cleaning; the shining kitchen and bathroom floors, "supersealed" to reduce the amount of scrubbing and polishing, show every speck of dust; the white enamel surfaces of stoves, refrigerators, and washing machines call for constant attention to look their spotless best.

Thus, what has been saved on the swing is largely lost on the roundabout. In total working hours the modern housewife has not gained very much, particularly because a psychological need will impel her to make up for any time saved by widening the range of domestic activities. The work can, however, be done more easily, with less sweat and backache; much of it can be done jointly, with the husband's or children's assistance; and part of it can, if necessary, be put off for a more convenient time. That is to say, there is no longer that relentless pressure of never-ending chores that used to characterize housework, nor is there the same need for a rigid timetable unless there are young children in the family or the housewife goes out to work.

Infants are, of course, as they have always been, an exhausting full-time job, and they tend to get better care and more attention than was customary when families were larger. Free medical care for everyone, including prenatal clinics, hospital or home confinement, welfare centers for young babies, the free provision of vitamins and orange juice, Health Visitors who call at home during the period following childbirth, a Maternity Grant

—by which the National Insurance contributes to the cost of having a baby, and a weekly Maternity Benefit over a period of eighteen weeks—all these are means by which the Welfare State tries to ease the lot of young mothers.

Domestic help is scarce and resident maids, in particular, have almost disappeared. The few who still exist are mostly serving rich old ladies or wealthy bachelors. The nearest substitute families can get in the way of home help are "dailies"—more likely to call for a few hours once or twice a week—or foreign girls who come here, for a year at a time, to learn English. Their conditions of work are regulated by the Home Office which issues their permit; students have to be allowed time off to attend language classes in addition to spare time for leisure, and they are normally treated as members of the family. They are employed mainly by the professional classes; but present living and housing conditions are such that many families prefer to do their own housework with the assistance of mechanical aids, and to rely on babysitters when they want to have an evening out, rather than to have a stranger in their midst.

It is in times of emergency that the absence of domestic help or living-in relatives makes itself felt painfully. Relatives or neighbors have to be called to the rescue; but where everything else fails, resort can again be taken to the social services: so-called "Home Helps" will come in, if necessary at public expense, to keep the home going during a crisis.

Occupations

These brief hints at some of the social services available to families in the event of ill health, pregnancy, confinement, and various emergencies may already have indicated that a wide and growing field of occupations has been opened to women in recent years.

The comprehensive system of social security which came into force in July, 1948, has brought with it an enormous expansion of health and social-welfare services both of which largely depend on qualified female staff. Hand in hand with the extension of these services went their professionalization. Although voluntary organizations still exist and play an important part in social welfare (notably the ubiquitous Women's Voluntary Service, the British Red Cross, the Family Welfare Association, the National Marriage Guidance Council, and many other bodies), social work is increasingly done by professionally trained, salaried workers, most of whom are women and all of whom are in short supply.

Similarly, the expansion and improvement of the health services has led to a growing and, so far, never fully satisfied demand for nurses, midwives, physiotherapists, dietitians, radiologists, occupational therapists, and other personnel auxiliary to medicine.

Finally, the growing number of children born in recent years has led to an acute shortage of school teachers at all levels, and emergency measures are being taken to use partly trained personnel, to bring married women teachers back to work and to increase the number of training colleges.

In addition to the above, women are, in varying numbers, practicing in nearly all professions; they have recently, and reluctantly, even been admitted to the pulpit. It is simpler, therefore, to state the few fields from which they are still excluded.

The first woman to become a High Court Judge was appointed in 1965 and there have been, so far, only two women "Recorders," that is, barristers who as part-time judges preside in so-called Quarter Sessions (criminal courts sitting periodically); many women, however, sit as unpaid lay magistrates and justices of peace in Magistrate Courts.

Women are barred by trade-union policy from being trained as printers and compositors. Nor are women admitted to the Stock Exchange. There are only a few women in the diplomatic service, none of whom is of ambassadorial or ministerial rank. (One woman, Miss Barbara Salt, actually was appointed Ambassador to Israel but died between her appointment and assumption of office.)

All other professions have a fair sprinkling of women. Relatively few are accountants or lawyers (they are some 3.5 per cent of the legal profession), but they are nearly one-in-six of all doctors and slightly under one-in-five in the middle and higher grades of the Civil Service (taking all grades of the nonindustrial civil servants together, however, women form roughly one third of the staff). Women are on all ranks of the academic ladder in the universities, as scientists, historians, teachers of literature, the social sciences, and numerous women work for publishers, the press, TV, and radio, in market research, advertising, and many other fields.

In fact, there is no bar on women entering any profession; but it is still more difficult for them to get into the higher ranks than it is for men, and only quite exceptional women reach the top. Only three women ever reached the highest post of Permanent Secretaries, that is, permanent Heads of Ministries (Education, Housing and Labor, respectively); all three have since retired. With the virtual disappearance of the generation of educated spinsters, able and willing to devote their lives to their careers, it is a moot point whether women will ever again reach such exalted positions. There are, however, a few dozen women in the higher echelons of the Civil Service, for instance as Assistant Secretaries (that is, Heads of Departments) in various Ministries. Their small number is not surprising if it is recalled that the marriage bar for women civil servants was only abolished during World War II.

Conditions of pay and service are the same for women and men in

nearly all professions. Equal pay was gradually introduced, after a prolonged parliamentary struggle, in seven annual stages between 1955 and
1961, in the teaching profession, the national and local government services,
the national health service, and the nationalized industries.

Equal pay does not, however, apply to manual workers in industry.
A comparison between the average weekly incomes of men and women
industrial workers, published by the Ministry of Labor, reveals a very wide
discrepancy between the two: In April 1961, women full-time manual
workers earned 152s 7d (or $21.36) per week, while men's average wage
amounted to 301s 4d (or $42.18) per week. Outside industry, too, there are
still many occupations—nonmanual as well as manual—where women are
paid at a lower rate than men even when they are doing the same job.

Generally speaking, there has been a movement away from domestic and
industrial work toward the nonmanual occupations which have increased
in number and variety.

The economic expansion that has characterized the postwar era, not in
Britain alone, has created an increasing need for skilled workers of many
kinds. It has produced, at the same time, the development of numerous
service industries, the growth of sales organizations and an increasingly
complex administrative machinery. Consequently, the need for office and
sales personnel of all descriptions has grown by leaps and bounds. Add to
this the expanding tourist and entertainment industries and it will be
clear that never before have women been so much in demand nor have
they had as good a chance of finding occupations to suit their personal
abilities and interests.

LEADERSHIP ROLES

For the woman of average competence and moderate ambitions the
prospects are, relatively speaking, excellent. The able woman with ample
energy can rise to a good middle position on the social ladder by her own
efforts, irrespective of her feminine charms. But ambitious women must
not set their aims too high, however gifted they may be; no woman has
yet entered the inner sanctum of Big Business or Finance, and very few
have held high government office.

In the history of British Government five women have, so far, been
Ministers of Cabinet rank. The first was Margaret Bondfield who served as
Minister of Labor in MacDonald's Government, 1929–1931. Four others
followed since the last war: Ellen Wilkinson and Florence Horsborough
were Ministers of Education—the former in a Labor, the latter in a Conservative Government; Dr. Edith Summerskill was Minister of Pensions
and National Insurance and Barbara Castle is a member of Mr. Wilson's

Cabinet as Minister of Transport (previously as Minister of Overseas Development).

In addition, the Labor Government of 1966 includes seven other women of ministerial rank: Miss Margaret Herbison as Minister of Pensions and National Insurance; Miss Alice Bacon as Minister of State, Home Office; Miss Judith Hart, Minister of State, Foreign Office; Miss Jennie Lee (widow of Aneurin Bevan), Joint Under-Secretary of State, Ministry of Education and Science, with special responsibility for the arts (the nearest approach to a Minister of Culture Britain has ever known); Miss Harriet Slater, Lord Commissioner for the Treasury; and Miss Shirley Williams, Parliamentary Secretary, Ministry of Labor.

The 1966 Parliament includes twenty-six women Members of whom 19 are Labor and seven Conservative. The Liberal Party has a woman, Miss Nancy Seear, as its chairman, although none of its women candidates were elected among its small number of parliamentary representatives.

Women were only admitted to the House of Lords in 1958 with the introduction of a system of Life Peerage. The Upper Chamber now includes fifteen Life Peeresses and three Hereditary Peeresses.

On the organizational side of politics, there are some hundred qualified women election agents, including the National Agent of the Labor Party, and many more "professionals" in senior positions of responsibility.

In local government women play a more substantial part. There are some 10,000 women councillors in the country as a whole, even if they form only small minorities on each local council, and towns of various sizes and importance have women mayors. The powerful London County Council (now replaced by the Greater London Authority) had six women chairmen in the course of its history.

Eighteen women have been party chairmen since the first one was elected in 1926; eight Conservative, eight Labor and two Liberal (including the 1965 President, Miss Nancy Seear).

In trade-union affairs women play an active part and hold a variety of offices, including that of President of the Trade Union Congress, but "it is still almost as hard for a woman to become general secretary of a trade union as for a camel to go through the eye of a needle," commented *The Guardian* in a leading article on the occasion of the appointment, in 1962, of a woman doctor as General Secretary of the Medical Practitioners' Union.

For many years serious English newspapers have published profiles of outstanding women on their women's pages. Reading these one gets a fair picture of the contemporary feminine ideal with which intelligent women wish to identify themselves. It is clear that the blue-stocking is as much out of fashion as the hard-working domestic drudge. The modern heroine is a young-looking woman in her thirties or forties, immaculately dressed, happily married, mother of three or four children, who runs a business, works in a newspaper office, acts as management consultant, or practices any other profession; in addition she sits on a number of committees for various public causes, keeps an open house for her own and her children's friends, and in her "spare time" writes books.

Surprisingly many women seem to have the boundless energy and drive required to fulfil such combinations of multifarious roles. Each one of them, individually, is a cause for marvel. Even leaving the inevitable domestic responsibilities aside, one only has to think of the women hours that go into being "well-groomed"—choosing clothes, sitting at the hair-dressers, making up, and so on, to realize how encumbered women are in the handicap race to the top.

Collectively, the existence of this new type of universal woman goes a long way toward explaining why, despite their new opportunities, women are found in the second rather than the first rank of most professions: Star positions are hardly ever reached without a singleness of mind and purpose which most modern women, with their scattered commitments, are unable to achieve.

Having said this, it is not to be denied that prejudices against women still exist in many walks of life and that in professions open to both sexes a woman usually has to be twice as able as her male competitor to be considered for the same appointment.

If women have had little or no say in policy-making decisions of State, Church, and Army, many of them have made distinguished contributions to art, science, and literature. No attempt will be made here to give names of outstanding women writers, painters, sculptors, musicians, or scientists. The list would be tediously long. A few isolated facts may, however, be worth mentioning.

The 1964 Nobel Prize for Chemistry was awarded to Professor Dorothy Crowfoot Hodgkin of Oxford for her "exceptional skill" in determining the structures of important biochemical compounds, notably penicillin and vitamin B–12. (Professor Hodgkin, aged fifty-four, is mother of three children and a grandmother of three.)

A Society of Women Artists holds a regular annual exhibition which art critics have increasingly declared to be anachronistic and superfluous. The general standard of exhibits is so high and individual styles are so varied that there is no longer any point in sex segregation. The work is judged, and can stand, on its own merit.

If women want to lobby the Prime Minister about an issue on which, they feel, feminine views carry special weight, they have no difficulty in recruiting from their ranks a deputation of formidable collective brain-power. Women Fellows of the Royal Society (the highest distinction for scientists in Britain), of the Royal College of Physicians, and well-known authors can be included in any delegation.

There is no branch of literature—biography, fiction, crime, history, poetry, or travel—in which women are not among the best. Of a literature which includes Jane Austen, George Eliot, and the Brontës among its classics this hardly needs saying, nor is it news. Only among playwrights are women relative newcomers. There are on the London stage some half-a-dozen plays by women authors, one, by Agatha Christie, having had a run of over five years, and one of the outstanding theatrical producers is a woman, Joan Littlewood.

WOMEN AS CULTURAL TRANSMITTERS

Whether women have made a distinctive, as opposed to a distinguished, contribution to the arts is a moot question. The adjective feminine, if used by critics, normally has a derogatory connotation, and one is glad it has, on the whole, been dropped. To the evaluation of a work of art or literature the sex of its creator is as irrelevant as his, or her, age. What counts is creative ability, artistic integrity and professional competence. These are neither the prerogative of one sex nor the other.

Moreover, as Virginia Woolf said, for a writer "it is fatal to be a man or woman pure and simple; one must be woman-manly or man-womanly some collaboration has to take place in the mind between the woman and the man before the act of creation can be accomplished. Some marriage of opposites has to be consummated."[5] This, surely, applies to all art.

Whether or not there are any aspects of culture especially transmitted by women is a question of opinion rather than fact. My own view is that culture—irrespective of whether the term is used in its narrow sense of intellectual and artistic production or in its wider meaning embracing all social values, beliefs, ideas, customs, and manners—is our common human heritage.

It might be said that, with regard to culture in this widest sense, women occupy certain vantage points: they are in charge of infants at their earliest age and impress on them some basic standards of behavior—"don't lie," "say 'thank you'," etcetera. But these values are common to humanity and not properties of its female segment alone. Furthermore, each person learns from father as well as mother, and from numerous other people as well, through personal contact and books. Each individual mind is nourished by the wisdom and knowledge of past generations of men and women and enriched by the thoughts and experiences of innumerable contemporaries. It is difficult to see—difficult, that is, for midtwentieth-century citizens—

---

5. *A Room of One's Own*, Hogarth Press, 1931, p. 157.

how our joint inheritance could be split up in a way which makes women
—or, for that matter, men—the transmitters of any special part of it.

Women used to be excluded from many aspects of culture by being
kept in ignorance and denied access to a wide range of experiences.
Important sectors where therefore the exclusive property of men. This, however, is no longer the case. Women share with men their ideas, beliefs
and experiences. Short of turning the table and dispossessing men, which
they have no intention of doing, even if they had the means, they cannot
annex particular aspects of culture.

It is not to be assumed that a new specialization of roles between the
sexes will occur. The development has, on the contrary, been in the
direction toward greater equality and, as we have seen, still has quite a
good way to go. It is unlikely to change its course because it is not based
on a temporary climate of opinion or a mere ideological fashion, but is the
outcome of a long technological, economic and social evolution which
—barring a cataclysm of such unprecedented horror as to throw all
human calculations overboard—can never again be undone.

United States

By Margaret G. Benz

*I*t is in the lives of women that many of the most profound economic, social, and cultural changes come to focus. This is true all over the world, whether in ancient, once static societies now in process of radical reconstruction or in societies like our own that are habituated to change but where the pace has been immensely accelerated. The specific impact is obviously different in countries where women's lives have been defined in terms of the extended family, primitive technology, limited education, and rigidity of status and in our society which has long been characterized by individualism, advancing technology, mass education, flexibility of status and social mobility.

THE TRADITIONAL SITUATION

The American family heritage was based on the older patriarchal European traditions of the early settlers in New England and the Southern colonies. Following the European custom, marriage was considered an arrangement between families rather than a bond based on romantic attraction. Because of the Protestant Reformation, marriage and divorce were considered to be civil contracts under the civil authority rather than sacraments under church authority.

Because of the rugged conditions under which the early colonists lived, some of the European customs had to be adapted to new situations. There was a marked shortage of women in all of the early colonies, which gave individual women much greater choice of a husband; and no longer was a dowry needed to secure a husband. With no centralized church and very few clergymen, many colonists had no formal religious guidance. Common-law marriage came to have special significance at this time.

During this early period, the husband-wife-child teams prevailed over almost unbelievable hardships, forming the basis for a more democratic form of family life than that from which they had come. Parental consent was required for marriage, but because of poor transportation there was little likelihood of marrying someone who was unknown to the family. Colonial marriage was based on economic necessity, but courtships which involved romantic love were by no means uncommon. As time went on, love marriages became more and more frequent. Where there is a shortage of women and they are allowed a hand in choosing their husbands, the climate is ripe for romanticism.

With the English and European background of the colonists, it was to be expected that women and children would have inferior social status. Justification for this stemmed from Biblical sources. With few exceptions, the common law of the American colonies was patterned after English common law. This placed women under the control of their husbands; property, possessions, earnings, even the clothing they wore belonged legally to the husband.

However, women did have some very real legal rights and protections, even with the many restrictions which were placed on their activities. Husbands were responsible for the support of their wives and for any debts incurred by them. Women also had certain inheritance rights with regard to their husband's property. As time went on, women gradually achieved more independence and a more satisfactory personal identity.

The Protestant ethic was firmly established by the early colonists. Work was something to be done for its own sake, something that it was good to do; and too much leisure was somehow wrong and not to be encouraged. All segments of the population, whether Catholic, Protestant, or Jewish, were imbued with this idea. The prevailing technology, together with the determination to rise in the social economic scale, perpetuated long hours of work.

The later waves of immigration from Ireland, Central, Southern, and Eastern Europe reinforced the subordinate position of women in the home and in outside work. Because the population grew by immigration as well as natural increase, and immigrants were predominantly young males, there was always a scarcity of women.

TOWN AND COUNTRY

Differences between the marital roles in the rural farm family and the urban family were very striking, but grew less so with the increase of technology and communication. In 1790, only 5 per cent of the population were living in urban communities and 95 per cent lived in rural areas. In 1960, about 70 per cent of the population was living in urban communities, about 23 per cent in rural nonfarm areas, and about 7 per cent in rural farm areas. Of the total number of households, about three out of four were composed of families with a husband and wife present in the home.

The rural home is still the center for the roles of both husband and wife, whereas in the urban community most economic activity occurs outside the home. The members of the farm family work together as a unit, which results in greater family solidarity than is the case in urban families. The role of the farm wife centers about such traditional activities as cooking, mending, sewing, housekeeping, and child-rearing. The wife of the upper-middle-class businessman conversely is expected to be companion, hostess, and representative of the family. The farmer's wife is still occupied largely with manipulating things, as she performs the physical activity of housekeeping. The businessman's wife, on the other hand, is more concerned with manipulating people (entertaining) and symbols (conversation).

In addition to the rural-urban differentiation, considerable differences in marital roles exist between occupational groups. The husband's occupation, whether he is doctor, lawyer, businessman, clerk, salesman, farmer, or manual laborer, sets the specifications for the wife's role. The ultimate goal of the middle- and upper-middle class wife is to enhance her husband's professional and social status and thus further the family goal of upward mobility. For the lower-class urban worker, the role of the wife is still oriented about the home. She is expected to take care of the children, keep the house in order, and provide an emotional haven for the husband. Lower-class families do not, by and large, stress upward mobility as much as do middle-class families. Hence the wives have different roles.

In recent decades, more and more young women have left the farms for jobs in small towns or urban centers. Consequently the sex ratio shows a surplus of young women in cities and of young men in the farm areas.

With improved communications due to automobiles and paved roads, there is little isolation of the women in the rural areas. The centralized schools provide good education through the secondary level, and many young people go on for specialized training. Radio and television programs have further tended to break down the differences between rural and urban families.

Many of the joys and sorrows of marriage arise from the comparative ability or inability of the participants to measure up to the role behavior expected of them. Men who are good providers, faithful husbands, and loving fathers fulfill the major role expectations of society. Women who are good mothers, responsive wives, and affectionate companions likewise live up to their reciprocal responsibilities. Failure in any one of these roles may bring frustration and unhappiness.

The wife has the traditional right to be supported by the husband, and he assumes this obligation when he marries. In a traditional society, rights and obligations connected with different roles are clear and well defined. Everyone knows what is expected of him and is equally clear about his obligations in return. If he is not able to support a wife and family through his own efforts, he is supposed to postpone marriage until he is able to do so.

These assurances have gone with many of the other "eternal verities" of a traditional order. No longer are husbands exactly sure of what they are expected to do when their wives are gainfully employed. When the latter contribute to the support of the family, they may question their subordination to the husband. Many of the insecurities of modern marriage arise from this decline of the old role expectations before rising urbanism, industrialism, and education. In the rush of social change, new roles have not yet emerged to take the place of the old. In order to protect the young man's self-esteem, instead of proclaiming that man is the natural provider, the young husband might be reminded that wives have always made an important contribution to the home. It is not the fault of the husband that this contribution must now take the form of earning money outside the home, rather than weaving cloth within it. As a matter of fact, the early nineteenth century pioneer wife made a greater economic contribution to the operation of the home than the young wife working in offices, factories or service operations with her cash income.

Rather than postpone marrying the young man of her choice who may still be in school, getting started in business, or in military service, today's young woman expects to be gainfully employed outside the home at the beginning of her marriage.

THE LEGAL STATUS OF WOMEN

In the nineteenth century, the woman's rights movement aimed at legal rights and privileges; it was primarily status-oriented. Women were literally second-class citizens. They suffered many legal disabilities both outside and inside the family. They were disenfranchised. Their legal existence, as Kephart put it, was "suspended during the marriage, or at least incorporated and consolidated into that of the husband." A militant woman's rights movement together with many technological inventions, most important of which was the typewriter, created a tremendous change in the status of women. The nineteenth Amendment to the Constitution extended the right to vote to all women over twenty-one in the United States. At the present time, there are few status differences between the sexes embodied in legislation. Women have attained the first objective of the social movement for the emancipation of women—entry into the world of activities formerly monopolized by men. World War II, like World War I, accentuated the trend toward equality of vocational opportunities and equality of pay. The mores that are undermined by this economic emancipation of women are those associated with the subservience of women to the "head of the house." Readjustment of familial patterns in the direction of companionship and mutual affection is promoted by women's actual or potential economic independence and by their educational and social equality.

Whatever status differences now prevail are likely to be embodied in crescive—customary or traditional or moral—sanctions rather than in statutory ones. This does not make the problem any easier. It is often harder to fight customs, traditions, and mores than it is to attack laws. A husband's attitude or employer's prejudices may be more effective than a law in determining status.

Between 1900 and 1940, before the impact of World War II, divorces increased considerably more rapidly than did either marriages or the population as a whole. In the years 1945–1947, the peak of divorce was reached in this country. The ratio of divorces to marriages contracted in those two years was one in three. This was when large numbers of hastily contracted war marriages broke under the strain of the realities of reunion and living together.

More often than not the woman initiates the legal action for the divorce, whether she is actually desirous of securing one or not. It is felt that this will make the readjustment following divorce easier for her. Alimony is granted by the judge less frequently now than in the past when women did not customarily work at paid employment.

In the United States as a whole, annulments constitute only a small proportion of legal dissolutions. In 1946, they represented only 3.5 per cent of the total. But they were much more important in the states of California and New York. In some of the New York counties, the number of annulments exceeded that of absolute divorces. New York had this high annulment rate because it granted divorce only for adultery, but gave annulments for any one of eight different grounds, many of which were ill-defined. The Roman Catholic influence is clear. A liberal change in the divorce laws was introduced in New York State in 1966.

A generation ago, blood tests as a legal requirement for marriage were unknown in the United States. It was not until after World War II that the idea became generally acceptable. Today all but a few states have the blood-test provision. Even where the blood test is a requirement, there are legal ways of getting around the provision. Because of medical advances in the control of syphilis, as well as for other reasons, at least some of the public health officials feel that premarital blood tests are currently serving little purpose.

In order to prevent hasty, spur-of-the-moment marriages, more and more states have instituted a waiting period between the time of application and the actual issuance of the license. This is customarily a three-day waiting period. A few states have stricter waiting requirements for non-residents than for residents.

The minimum legal age for girls to be permitted to marry with or without parental consent is customarily two to three years below that required for boys.

THE EDUCATION OF WOMEN

Formal schooling was started in the seventeenth century but was available only to boys. In Massachusetts, some girls were permitted to go to school in the summer time when the boys were not using the schools. However, with the development of the free public schools and the land grant colleges in the middle of the nineteenth century, women were expected to attend. With compulsory school attendance, the number of boys and girls graduating from secondary schools is now about equal.

These advances in education have further complicated the role conflict of the modern wife. Education for women is one of the great glories of the democratic system because it increasingly places women on an equal plane with men. The democratic ideal of maximum self-realization presumably applies equally to both sexes, and the educated girl can hardly be blamed if she takes this ideal literally. These attempts at self expression have not, however, met with the unqualified acceptance of the community, the husband, or even the wife herself. The democratic ideal of equal education for both sexes comes into direct conflict with the traditional role of the wife. This role emerged from a society based upon patriarchal relationships since the dawn of history. The wife was expected to remain in the home, to receive a minimum of formal education, and to play a subservient role in most of the "serious" aspects of life.

The educated woman is often frankly bewildered as to her role. Although her education has encouraged her to play both the domestic and the working role, traditional social expectations interfere with this performance. This conflict of expectations is most acute among college and university graduates. Education for women is an extremely complex problem, viewed very differently by those who firmly believe in the "practical" or "vocational" and those who are equally insistent upon the liberal arts.

Advocates of a vocational curriculum for women argue that because the great majority of women college graduates become housewives and mothers, they should be educated for their principal roles, specifically in such fields as home economics, child care, marketing, budgeting, food preparation, and nursing. They should, in addition, receive courses in cosmetics, table-setting, interior decoration, and entertaining, so that they can adequately perform their roles as companions, hostesses, and home makers. Many parental homes fail to train for these skills and formal education should fill this gap. After all, say these advocates, women will always be wives and mothers and they should be educated as such.

This point of view assumes that the qualities now considered as feminine are biologically determined and have been the same for all time. As against this biological determinism, however, one should stress that, in reality, the roles of the sexes are socially and culturally defined. "Throughout history," observes Margaret Mead, "the more complex activities have been defined and redefined, now as male and now as female, now as neither, sometimes drawing equally on the gifts of both sexes, sometimes as drawing differentially on both sexes."

The increasing awareness of cultural expectations in forming personality has seriously shaken this biological determinism and with it the assumption that certain personality traits are instinctive and unchangeable. Many characteristics formerly considered biologically feminine reflect the role expectations that have dominated Western culture since Biblical times. Any system of education based upon the unalterable qualities of men or women therefore ignores modern knowledge of human behavior. The behavior of women responds partially to social conditions, not entirely to biological heritage.

Higher education for women is still oriented toward the liberal arts. The democratic assumption is that women are citizens first and homemakers second, and should be so educated. Men and women have equal rights under the law and should have equal educational opportunities.

As the activities of women range into business, industry, politics, civic affairs, social welfare, and the creative arts, they should be educated for these emerging roles. The liberal arts curriculum teaches women the principles of economics before home economics; the principles of biology before the care of children; and the principles of sociology before the art of interpersonal relationships.

It is manifestly impossible to solve completely the problem of the educated, gainfully employed wife. It has been suggested, however, that higher education for women should reflect three general considerations. The first comprises the fields of study (mathematics, for example) which are obviously the same, irrespective of sex. The second stresses the contemporary world and training for responsible citizenship. Roles of men and women are growing closer together in this field, and their educational opportunities are tending to coincide. The third consideration concerns the needs of women as women, and the special problems they meet and will meet as wives and homemakers. Whether in college or in adult education, special training should be available for these special roles. The best answer would appear to be, as Jessie Bernard put it, "an education which would give the possibility of differentiation within a broad framework which would be the same for men and women."

Studies of women in two coeducational colleges showed that the girls preferred marriage to a career, although they also wished to prepare for a productive occupation and practice it for some time before their marriage. Practically all women prefer marriage and homemaking, but not on the limited basis that a one-income family provides.

The working wife is therefore faced with a dilemma not of her own making. She is responding to the demands of her environment in working outside the home. She is reacting to her immediate situation, which is the only way she can react.

SEX MORES

The culture of the United States is one of extreme disapproval toward sex expression. It is impossible to understand the American family without recognizing that it incorporates a distinctly repressive attitude toward sex. The repressiveness is evidenced, however, more by shame and guilt feelings than by successful methods of repression. There is a vast gap between rule and practice. Sex stimuli are ever present in advertising and the mass media.

It is expected that husbands and wives will be sexually faithful to one another. It is known, through various research studies, that a significant proportion of our married couples—though still a minority—does not live up to this expectation, but this does not mean that they are not expected to do so.

Dating is a pattern of social interaction that is unique to American society, both in extent and intensity. No other society has a similar type of behavior. Many primitive societies have a licensed period of sexual experimentation before marriage, whereby adolescents are permitted considerable heterosexual experimentation. Advanced societies have a formal and ritualized pattern of courtship, whose expectations are fully understood by the participants and where the steps lead to marriage. Both of these patterns are very different from dating. Sexual impulses play a part in dating, but the most important goal is the self-esteem derived from success in a group-sponsored activity. Furthermore, sexual behavior in dating, in contrast to the premarital copulations of many primitive youths, is aim inhibited. Lovemaking in dating is supposed to stop short of complete sexual union. Dating may also develop into "true" courtship, but it is not intended to do so, especially in the early years.

Dating is viewed as an end in itself and is highly esteemed in a pleasure-conscious society, where even the serious institutions of marriage and the family are pleasure-yielding relationships. Dating also performs certain functions for a heterogeneous society, where marital choice is made almost entirely by the participants. It confers status, offers emotional assurance, provides a variety of experience before marriage, and gives a measure of maturity. Dating is not supposed to end either in sexual intercourse or in marriage, but is regarded instead as a dalliance relationship. When engaged in dating, adolescents are always playing with fire, in that one may be hurt, rejected or otherwise emotionally injured. In theory, each plays the game according to the rules and is not seriously hurt. In practice, things do not always work out that way, especially in intercultural relationships, where the same behavior has different meanings.

Although our society seems to favor complete equality of the sexes, judging by the legal code, this is far from true in courtship. Although the church, the school, and the family maintain that premarital coitus is immoral, sinful, and dangerous, a certain latitude has been tacitly given the man. He is permitted to have sexual intercourse with women of a lower social class, or, if a lower-class person himself, with women outside of his immediate social environment. Women of all social levels, on the other hand, have been permitted very little latitude, and any lapse has been met with strong moral condemnation.

This situation has changed in recent decades, especially with regard to the premarital sexual behaviour of women. The Terman study in the 1930's indicated a definite trend toward increasing premarital intercourse by women. Of those born in the decade 1900 to 1909, only 51.2 per cent were virgins at marriage, as compared to 86.5 per cent of those born before 1890. A large part of this decrease in virginity involved relations with the fiance only.

The Kinsey study indicated the same general trend. Among the 5,940 white females in this study, approximately 50 per cent had had premarital coitus. Less than half as many women born before 1900 had premarital intercourse as did those born after 1900. Subsequent generations, says Kinsey, appear to have accepted the new pattern and maintained or extended it.

In the Burgess and Wallin study, 32.2 per cent of the men and 53 per cent of the women reported no premarital intercourse. Some 17.4 per cent of the men and 35.6 per cent of the women reported coitus with the future spouse only, whereas 27.8 per cent of the men and 9.8 per cent of the women had it with the intended spouse and others. The same general pattern is apparent in the Terman and Kinsey reports—namely, a considerable proportion of middle-class persons have premarital coitus with their intended spouses. This is a pronounced change from an earlier day, but it does not indicate widespread premarital promiscuity. It does indicate, however, an increased freedom in engagement.

Premarital coitus violates the traditional norms. The reasons for this violation reflect basic changes in society. Large numbers of engaged people have a strong desire for premarital sex relations with their future mates. In earlier decades, similar desires were likewise present, but the social values were different. Moral imperatives were then presumably stronger, and young people were more restrained by religious, ethical and familial prohibitions. Such evidence as we have indicates that middle-class couples did not even consider premarital intercourse a possibility. For most of them, such behavior was unthinkable. Today this is no longer the case.

Given the desire and the possibility, other factors have contributed to this change in behavior. Engaged couples have more privacy than ever before and find ample opportunity for sexual intercourse. Methods of contraception have improved and information on their use has been widely disseminated. The fear of pregnancy has been largely (although not entirely) removed. The new drugs for the treatment of venereal disease are an additional reason for this greater freedom, although this fear is negligible for most engaged couples.

Psychological factors, rather than merely sexual contact, are important in this behavior. The reaction to the sexual act, whether before or during marriage, is crucial to the woman's sexual adjustment.

The affectional role is undergoing a basic change in our society. This change may be summed up as one from action to interaction. The traditional role has largely involved sexual action by the husband and passive reaction by the wife. The husband has traditionally taken the initiative and the wife has responded as best she could. Insofar as coitus was supposed to involve pleasure, apart from its procreative function, that pleasure was expected to be experienced by the husband, not by the wife. Recent developments are the acceptance, gradually but increasingly, that "nice" women can and do enjoy sex and the man's discovery that he himself enjoys sex more when the woman enjoys it too. Husbands and wives are only beginning to realize the improved basis which this attitude toward sex as a process makes possible within their marriage. This change is somewhat more marked among middle-class and upper-middle-class women than with lower-class women. The latter are more conservative in their sexual relationships and continue the traditionally more passive female role.

THE MARRIAGE PATTERN

At a time when people have more choice about what they are going to do and the way they are going to do it than they have ever had before —what do they do? They get married, and at a somewhat earlier age than their parents or their grandparents did. Today, more than half of our young women are married by the time they are twenty years old, and more than half of our young men by the time they are twenty-two and a half years old. Those young people who attend college, of whom there are constantly increasing numbers, tend to marry two years later than the general average for both young men and young women, making the average age at marriage for college women twenty-two, and for college men, twenty-four. At this age, they can look forward to forty-five or fifty years of marriage, as their life expectancy is that much greater.

The choice of marriage partner is primarily the responsibility of the young couple themselves. Parents do not impose definite authority over their sons' or daughters' selection of a mate. Dating is the process of helping young people make a satisfactory selection. The parents' influence upon dating comes through the earlier training of their children in choice of friends and marriage ideals. With the increased emphasis on marriage as an intimate, personal relationship instead of an arrangement to gain social status or wealth, dating increases in importance. It is helpful to date a number of persons of the opposite sex, in order to find out what one really wants in a personal relationship and what one is able to give.

Most people marry someone with a background similar to their own. Catholics tend to marry Catholics, Jews tend to marry Jews, and Protestants tend to marry Protestants. Whites tend to marry whites. Orientals marry other Orientals, and Negroes tend to marry Negroes. Those of similar socio-economic background and of similar schooling tend to marry one another. Like tends to marry like. However, due to increased mobility, there is an increase in interfaith, intercultural and interracial marriages, many of which are as successful as any other kind. The rate of breakup of such marriages is higher than the general average, but there are many couples able to overcome the increased difficulties and make a satisfying relationship.

When it comes to personality characteristics, there seems to be a tendency to marry someone who complements one's own personality needs, who builds up one's feelings of adequacy, and who is not competitive in interpersonal relationships.

More than three quarters of the marriages take place with some religious officiant rather than in a civil ceremony alone. It is customary for the bride's family to arrange and finance the wedding ceremony, with some help from the groom's family. In recent years, weddings have become increasingly formalized and expensive. The bridal showers and the gifts associated with a large wedding help the bride assemble equipment for her new home. Dowries as such are no longer a part of the marriage contract. Various studies show that persons who have a religious affiliation have a better chance of a successful marriage than those without such affiliation.

Newly married couples tend to live separately from either set of parents in this urbanized, industrialized society. With the mobility associated with military service and beginning jobs they tend to rent living quarters for the first few years. This preference for independent living represents a sacrifice of solidarity, mutual protection, and continuity of family experience. If there were more concern with the transmission of real property, such as landed estates, there would be more incentive to establish extended, residential families. When the family fortune is in a bank or negotiable securities, there is less need for adult children to maintain contact with their parents through joint living arrangements.

Six out of ten families own their own homes, more than half of these homes have a mortgage. About three quarters of the families own an automobile and some 10 per cent have more than one car. In 1962, more than 90 per cent of the families had at least one television set, with 13 per cent having two or more sets. About 60 per cent of the families have electric refrigeration, either electric or gas cooking stoves, and powered washing machines. Not all of their equipment has been paid for, and there is sometimes strain in meeting the monthly payments.

Most young couples would like to have three or four children and are making a good start toward achieving their goal. They would like children of both sexes, and girls are as welcome as boys. Childbirth is safer for both mother and child than it has ever been. Means and knowledge for planning and spacing babies is available to most families, yet the birth rate has never been so high. Parenthood is an attractive status to our young people, even though in our industrial economy children are not an economic asset—quite the contrary.

No longer is the rearing of children an exclusive responsibility of mothers. Young husbands are considered important during the pregnancy, and are sharing what the psychologists call the most important early years of a child's life, in which his basic personality patterns are laid down, and his concepts of the sex roles are established. The shorter work week on most jobs makes such association a possibility.

With the very high rate of marriage, the diverse backgrounds from which couples come, the early age at which choice of marriage partner takes place, and the not-always-helpful-attitude of families and schools, it is to be expected that an increasing number of marriages will not be able to endure the strains of unemployment, illness, financial stress, and emotional immaturity. With or without counseling, many couples decide after a few years that their marriage is an intolerable burden to them. The bonds of love, loyalty, and interdependence break. Husband and wife not only do not look to each other for satisfaction of personal needs, but one or both begin to look to friends, parents, or new lovers for emotional satisfactions. Usually they separate and live apart, sometimes returning for another try at marriage and separating again. Eventually, the decision is made to part permanently and end the marriage. It is estimated that approximately one fourth of the marriages made around 1960 will be terminated voluntarily by the couple through divorce.

Some couples are ready to call a halt after only a few months of marriage. Forty per cent of all divorces occur during the first four years of marriage. After that period, rates gradually decline, as couples are inclined to stay together for the sake of the children. This is not always a wise decision to make. People in middle and old age, who have been married for many years, sometimes secure divorces.

There is less and less rejection of divorced persons as prospects for second and third marriages. Sometimes the same situations that caused the breakup of the first marriage cause the breakup of the second. But many such marriages seem to have benefited from the increasing maturity of the partners and their improved and stabilized economic conditions.

THE WOMAN'S POSITION IN THE FAMILY

The most important economic role of the woman remains that of housewife. The current emphasis upon the employment of married women outside the home may obscure the fact that most wives devote most of their time to domestic activities. Seventy per cent or almost 30,000,000 wives continue to make their chief economic contribution in the home.

In general terms, the behavior of most wives still coincides with their traditional role. Whether they like it or not, do it well or not, most women, rural and urban alike, devote a large portion of their time to the homemaking role. In performing her domestic role, one of the wife's main functions has been the maintenance of the home as a harmonious place for her husband, herself, and her children.

This is a difficult and intangible task, combining as it does the physical skills of homemaking and the interpersonal skills of group interaction. The success or failure of the wife is not as obvious as that of the husband nor has her performance been open to comparison with others as long as she remained in the home. For better or worse, the wife has been unique in her own family group. However, the woman is often discontented with the behavior expected of her as housewife and mother. This disenchantment arises from her higher level of aspiration. In the old days, she was occupied from morning to night in backbreaking drudgery. Combined with continual child-bearing, this toil made her an old woman at thirty and put her in her grave at forty. In physical terms, the role of the modern housewife is much less burdensome than that of her great-great-grandmother. At the same time, society no longer places as high a value on the role of housewife. The contrast between expectation and realization generates much of the wife's discontent with her role.

Many housewives suffer from boredom, dissatisfaction, and rebellion against the implications of their domestic role. They feel that they have been educated for "other" ends than to act as unpaid and comparatively inefficient domestic servants. They complain of the lack of leisure, their inability to maintain their intellectual interests, and of the dearth of moments when they can be completely themselves. The modern wife is experiencing difficulty in adjusting her aspirations to the realities of her domestic role.

The domestic role has been modified by a succession of social and cultural changes. These changes have included a smaller number of children in the home, a decrease in the time necessary to prepare food, an increase in the number of personal services performed outside the home, a trend toward smaller and more compact houses, a related trend toward more labor-saving equipment for the home, and a decrease in many of the communicable diseases of childhood as a result of scientific advancement. Some of the physical drudgery in the performance of the domestic role has been eliminated or mitigated by these changes.

Despite these ameliorations, the domestic role continues to be very time-consuming. Studies of the work week of the urban housewife still show more than fifty hours a week expended in the actual mechanics of keeping house. For rural housewives, the total is several more hours a week. Activities connected with food form the largest single item, with approximately one half of the time of the farm wives and one third of the time of the urban wives spent in this way. The difference is in the meals "eaten out." The urban family spends more than 18 per cent of its total food bill in restaurants, whereas the rural farm family spends only 3 per cent.

Other activities that consume an appreciable part of the work week of the urban housewife are purchasing and management, care of family, care of house, laundering, mending and sewing, and "other" homemaking. The totals are only approximate, but about 20 per cent of the time involves care of the family, 15 per cent care of the house, and 10 per cent purchasing and management. The important point is not the exact allocation of time, but rather that the domestic role is a full-time job for most women.

The nature of the domestic role is also changing. The readymade clothing industry has lightened the load of the housewife. The nursery school has taken some of the burden of child care and training from the mother. The food industry prepares many types of food so that the wife has nothing to do but open a can or a package. These labor-saving mechanisms do not always provide a net saving of time. Shopping takes more time than before, because there are more things to buy and more choices to be made. Account-keeping takes some of the time of canning and preserving. Children must be driven to and from school and other activities, and much of the time otherwise saved by the mother is spent behind the wheel of the family car. Planning for the complex demands of the modern family calls for an additional expenditure of time. In a simpler society, planning of meals, purchases, and child care were virtually nonexistent. The mother had few choices in this earlier setting.

The standards of homemaking have also improved. The wife is more self-conscious about her domestic role and is expected to serve healthy and tastefully prepared meals. Advertisements in the women's magazines have made her more aware of gracious living and glamorous foods.

In consumer production, there is a tendency to use the time freed by labor-saving machinery, not for more leisure but for more goods or services of the same general character. The purchase of a washing machine often means more washing; a vacuum cleaner means more cleaning; and a dish-washer means more dishwashing. These new devices increase the efficiency of the operation, but the net increment of leisure is often not great. The modern house is probably the cleanest in history, but a great deal of time is still expended in cleaning. Standards have been raised, more work is done with fewer hands to do it, but the brave new world of leisure is still far from realization.

SOCIAL POSITION AND WOMEN'S OCCUPATION

The most important single change in the life of women is in their gainful employment outside the home. Today, millions of women partici-pate in the labor force before, during, and after marriage. Most women are gainfully employed outside the home at some time in their lives. Young women, marrying in the 1960's, can look forward to twenty-five years or more of such employment during their marriage. In some cases they work for a few years between school and marriage and then permanently drop out of the labor force. In others, they continue to work after marriage, only to withdraw from the labor force when they have children. In still other cases, they enter (or reenter) the labor market after divorce or the death of their husbands.

There is no clear cultural regulation of the sex division of labor at the present time. The census records have year by year shown an increasing number of women thronging into occupations and activities formerly regarded as masculine. Each war brings a further penetration of women into the so-called masculine spheres. In World War II, for example, women served in far greater numbers than in World War I, and undertook tasks that brought them closer to actual combat. It is true that an American husband is more likely to be an engineer, a professional baseball player, or a champion wrestler than his wife. On the other hand, women have no monopoly on washing dishes and it is not uncommon to see a woman clad in shorts mowing the lawn with a power lawn mower. One study showed that some 84 per cent of World War II husbands help their wives in household tasks.

In March 1963, there were in the labor force, 15,362,000 married women, of whom 14,061,000 were living with their husbands. This represents a spectacular increase in less than two decades, from the 4,200,000 gainfully employed married women in 1940, who comprised only about 15 per cent of all married women. In the space of twenty-three years, the percentage of gainfully employed women more than doubled, from 14.7 per cent in 1940 to 36.1 per cent in 1963. An increasing percentage of married women are thus attempting to play two economic roles—that of homemaker and that of earner. Such a division of energy between the home and the outside world is unprecedented in history.

The employment of married women has been part of a broader trend toward increasing the employment of women, regardless of marital status. In 1900, approximately 5,000,000 women over fourteen years of age were gainfully employed, a total equal to 21 per cent of all women of this age category. At the same time, only 5.6 per cent of the married women were included in this total. In 1963, the total number of employed women had increased to 24,675,000, representing 36 per cent of all women over fourteen years of age. In the period 1900–1963, the percentage of gainfully employed women approximately doubled, whereas the percentage of gainfully employed married women increased more than fivefold.

The economic role of women in general, and married women in particular, may be seen from the percentage of the total working force represented by women. In March 1963, the 24,675,000 employed women were divided as follows: 5,614,000 were single; 15,312,000 were married; and 3,699,000 were widowed or divorced. Women comprise about 32 per cent of all workers and married women far outnumber single women in the labor force. The absolute number of married women of working age is, of course, much larger than the number of employable single women. The 5,614,000 gainfully employed single women represent approximately 75 per cent of all single women between twenty and sixty-four years of age.

The increasing participation of women in the labor force reflects broad changes in the social and economic structure. As business becomes more complex, more records are needed and more people are needed to keep them. In 1964, the largest number of employed women were engaged in clerical occupations, with more than seven million out of a total of twenty-three million listed in this category. This is more than 30 per cent of all employed women. Clerical work is still largely done by women. With increasing automation in the office and the high skills required for automation specialists, it is highly probable that the monopoly of office jobs now held by women will be broken. More and more male specialists will come into offices to program and maintain automated equipment. The next two categories employing the greatest number of women workers are service workers (3,665,000) and private household workers (2,242,000), making a total of 5,907,000 women employed in service work; and professional and technical workers (3,193,000).

Science and engineering are traditionally male specializations. As opportunities for applied science and engineering open up in the office and factory, a major problem will be posed for women to retain jobs in their present areas of dominance.

Although the principle of equal pay for equal work is well established, it is still usual that the earnings of women are less than those of men. This is brought about more by a reclassification of jobs than a direct violation of the principle.

In 1960, of all married women in the labor force only 33 per cent worked at full-time jobs for the entire year. The contribution to the family budget by married women who worked was only about one fourth that of their husbands; the average income of wives was $1,260 and of husbands, $4,920. However, year-round, full-time working wives earned an average of $3,240. Despite their relatively small incomes, the wives' earnings were an important factor in the families' standard of living. In 1960 the wife worked in over half of all families with incomes of $7,000 to $15,000. By contrast, in families with incomes from $3,000 to $5,000 only about 40 per cent of the wives worked. Full-time work by the wife was about twice as prevalent in higher-income families as in lower.

Women are represented in all professional groups, but are predominant in the fields of teaching, nursing, and library work. There has not been any noticeable increase in the number of young women entering the fields of medicine, dentistry, and law. This is not because of any lack of fitness, but because of the prejudice against practice in those fields.

WOMEN AS CULTURAL TRANSMITTERS

After school and college, the large majority of girls become wives and mothers. During this phase of life miracles of modern medicine and surgery have removed many of the physical ills which formerly sapped so much of women's strength. The spacing of children has liberated them from the bondage of excessive child-bearing and the anxieties associated with it. Mothers are now able to regard nature not as an end in itself, but, as all intimate relations with life should be, as a means of spiritual growth through full experience.

American children are brought up by parents, not by nurses, servants, slaves, grandparents, or in large impersonal groups. Parents take the responsibility of punishing children either by active chastisement or by the withdrawal of love when they do wrong, thereby risking the children's hostility and hatred.

Modern psychological knowledge has added its force to the traditional conviction that the mother's role is basic in the early years of the child's life. All studies have tended to confirm the hypothesis that the security given by the mother figure during infancy can have a lifelong impact on the personality of the individual and his ability to cope with the demands of life.

The modern mother no longer considers that she has fulfilled her role as teacher when she has passed on to her daughter a series of household arts. In view of the range of possibilities opening to women today, the task of parents is to help their daughters explore and discover their interests and capabilities in new as well as traditional fields, and not to assume for them a limited stereotyped pattern of interest and behavior. The mother shares responsibility for helping both sons and daughters understand their world and develop their full potentialities in relation to it. These demands challenge the modern homemaker not only to make full use of her wisdom, her education and her capacities but to learn constantly in order to keep abreast of her family's needs.

The modern homemaker's sphere, moreover, cannot be limited to the home. Since much that her family needs cannot be supplied within the home, she must seek in the community the conditions for her family's well-being. Her job as homemaker forces upon her a concern for education, recreation, public health, safety and order, social welfare, and cultural enrichment.

Because of the father's preoccupation with his role as major provider, the mother has most of the responsibility for bringing up the children. Almost unconsciously, she makes the striving for success a very important part of this process. "The American sibling position," as Margaret Mead puts it, "is one of competition not for the mother's person, for her breast and soft arms, but rivalry for her approval and her approval has to be won by one's achievement. To win his mother's approval the two and a half year old must be dry, must feed himself, must go to sleep quietly with no one there; otherwise the loving approval vanishes from his mother's voice. Very well, he has learned, sometimes sorrowfully, sometimes eagerly, to do all these things, to take steps upward and outward toward greater independence of his mother's delicious care. And then along comes this small, insignificant interloper, who can't do any of the hard things for which he has been praised, for failing to do which he has been denied his mother's love—and the creature is petted and loved and not expected to do them at all. The betrayal, for so it seems, in which mother gives her love in one case and withholds it in another, is a seed out of which grows the bitterness toward all those 'who have it soft,' 'get by,' 'get away with murder,' a bitterness combined with envy. The initial condition inserted into the mother's simplest kiss, that 'I will love you only if you achieve as other people's babies. I can't love you, if you don't,' survives into every competitive situation in life. We can recognize that yearning for achievement which is planted in every American child's breast by his mother's conditional smile."

Whether or not one considers the inculcation of such an attitude into the child's psyche desirable, one is forced to recognize that this is one of the standard features of American upbringing. The mother who thus contributes to making her child achievement oriented, is herself torn between the wishes to achieve in two widely separated areas: those of the home and of outside work. In both she finds herself confronted by men, and the relationship between her and them is frequently competitive.

Yet competition between man and woman is not inevitable. It certainly is not a biologically determined condition. On the contrary. Men and women, shoulder to shoulder, can achieve real partnership, as two people of equal value who share in the enterprise of marriage and of living. Marriage must contain the fundamentals of satisfaction, for marriage forms the nurturing ground for the attitudes and behavior for future citizens. This is a vast challenge for women in particular, since they are the ones so closely involved in family upbringing.

Looking Toward the Future

If trends now in force continue, some changes in roles for the future may be predicted. The increasing number of married women who are employed is a fast-paced trend, now well established. At present, employment of women tends to fall into a cyclical pattern, with women working before and immediately after marriage, withdrawing wholly or partly while children are young, and then returning near middle age. At present certain forces favor increased employment of married women. Men and unmarried women are already employed almost to the maximum number that can be expected. Married women form the untapped labor pool, especially among trained teachers, nurses, occupational therapists, and social workers. Continued increase in production or the necessities of future national emergencies will place tremendous pressure on married women to work. In addition, the increased education of women prepares them in skills and psychologically for employment. The fact that their husbands may have well-paid jobs will probably not offset the trend toward increasing employment.

It will be better understood that a woman can be a distinguished chemist or pediatrician and at the same time a beautiful, feminine woman, just as we understand that a man can be a nuclear physicist and a handsome devotee of baseball or football. The insatiable demands of the next half century for intellectual activity cannot be satisfied by the male segment of the population alone, and, by one means or another, a higher percentage of the gifted women will have to find the means and the encouragement to work side by side with the men.

The chief obstacle to continuous employment of married women is the presence of young children. If the mother felt that she could leave her children in safe hands, she might return to work while the children were young or might not even stop work except for a short period at the time of each child's birth. The present method of substitute child care, arranged by each mother individually, is expensive and often results in incompetent care. Grandmothers are sometimes called upon, but fewer and fewer of them are going to be available, since they make up the middle-aged group of women who are returning to work in great numbers.

An alternative is care of children in nurseries, where expenses can be kept low and where those in charge will have training in child development. This plan is not widely used in the United States except for the children of mothers who work because of necessity or the children of upper-middle class families who believe that nursery schools promote the social development of their children. The great mass of middle-class children rarely have nursery school experience. If the pressures for married women to continue in employment increase, it seems probable that more child-care centers will be established than we now have, and that our philosophy of child care may also change (perhaps for the better).

The husband's roles may also continue to change. The need for children to have fathers in the flesh and not merely in absentia may be gratified by the continuous shortening of the work week. Employment of the mother may counterbalance the tendency of many men to take on a supplementary job to earn more money. Men will thus have more time to be fathers, while women, because of employment, will have less time to be mothers. The problem then will be one of creating a satisfying family life in the leisure hours shared by all when the father comes from his job, the mother from hers, and the children from the day care center. Some problems to be solved are fatigue from the day's work and managing necessary household work without permitting it to overbalance the shared activities, confidences, and emotional expression among family members that make for true family companionship. The shorter work week, together with the labor-saving devices in the home means that the couple will have more hours together than ever before.

In this country, women have won their equality with men. They can vote and run for office and take their places in business, the sciences, the arts, and every other field of endeavor. It is now up to them to manifest their special female attributes which spring not only from the capacity of motherhood but from all those traits of womanhood whose sum total is the true "feminine mystique." These female influences can help mankind achieve a gentler, less combative social order, revolving not solely around the concern with achievement, but around a second, equally important, focus: that of tender consideration for others. The possible evolution of woman intimates that in such a new, infinitely more satisfactory social order there will be a willingly accepted differentiation between the male and female roles within and without the home, and women will make their invaluable feminine contribution, far above child bearing and rearing and housekeeping, to many aspects of our modern ethos.

BIBLIOGRAPHY

Anderson, Nels, *The Urban Community*, Holt-Dryden (1959)
Bernard, Jessie, *Social Problems at Midcentury*, Dryden (1957)
——, *Dating, Mating and Marriage*, Howard Allen (1958)
Blood, Robt. O. Jr., *Marriage*, The Free Press (1962)
Bovet, Theodore, *A Handbook to Marriage*, Doubleday-Dolphin (1958)
Burgess, Locke Thomas, *The Family*, American Book Co. (1963)
Cavan, Ruth S., *American Marriage*, Thos. Y. Crowell (1959)
——, *A Book of Readings*, Thos. Y. Crowell (1960)
Christiansen, Harold T., *Marriage Analysis*, Ronald Press (1950)
Coolidge, Susannah, "Population vs People," *Population Bulletin* (October 1960)
Dubin, Robert, *The World of Work*, Prentice-Hall (1958)
Fishbein and Kennedy, *Marriage and Family Living*, Oxford Univ. Press (1957)
Glick, Paul C., *American Families*, John Wiley (1955)
Gutmacher, Alan F., *New Facts about Birth Control*, #136 Public Affairs Pamphlet (1959)
Kephart, Wm. M., *Family, Society, and the Individual*, Houghton-Mifflin (1961)
Kirkpatrick, Clifford, *The Family*, Ronald Press (1955)
Le Masters, E. E., *Modern Courtship and Marriage*, Macmillan (1957)
Martinson, Floyd M., *Marriage and the American Ideal*, Dodd-Mead (1960)
Mead, Margaret, *And Keep Your Powder Dry*, Wm. Morrow (1942)
Merrill, Francis E., *Courtship and Marriage*, Macmillan (1959)
Sussman, Marvin B., *Sourcebook in Marriage and the Family*, Houghton-Mifflin (1955)
Winch, Robert F., *The Modern Family*, Holt (1952)
Statistical Abstract of the United States (1964)

About the Editor
and the Contributors

PATAI, RAPHAEL was born in Budapest, Hungary and studied at the University of Budapest (Ph.D., 1933), the University of Breslau, Germany, and the Hebrew University of Jerusalem (Ph.D., 1936). From 1933 to 1947 he lived in Jerusalem, where he taught at the Hebrew University. In 1947 he came to the United States and subsequently has taught Anthropology at Columbia University, the University of Pennsylvania, the New School for Social Research, Dropsie College, Princeton University, New York University, and Ohio State University. In 1952 he prepared a report on social conditions in the Middle East for the United Nations, and in 1955–1956 directed the Lebanon-Syria-Jordan research project for the Human Relations Area Files, Inc., New Haven. Since 1956 he has been Director of Research of the Theodor Herzl Institute in New York City, and editor of the Herzl Press, and since 1966 Visiting Professor of Anthropology at Fairleigh Dickinson University. His published works include: *The Science of Man: An Introduction to Anthropology*, 2 vols., Tel Aviv (1947–1948); *Man and Temple in Ancient Jewish Myth and Ritual*. Edinburgh (1947); *On Culture Contact and Its Working in Modern Palestine*, American Anthropological Association, Memoir 67 (1947); *Israel Between East and West*, Philadelphia (1953); *The Republic of Lebanon* (ed.), 2 vols., New Haven (1956); *The Republic of Syria* (ed.), 2 vols., New Haven (1956); *The Kingdom of Jordan*, Princeton (1958): *Cultures in Conflict*, New York (1958) (2nd ed. 1961); *Sex and Family in the Bible and the Middle East*, New York (1959); *Golden River to Golden Road: Society, Culture and Change in the Middle East*, Philadelphia (1962); *Hebrew Myths* (with Robert Graves), New York (1964).

ABADAN, NERMIN, was born in Vienna of Turkish parents, studied in Izmir and graduated from the Faculty of Law of the University of Istanbul in 1944. Soon thereafter she was married to Dr. Yavuz Abadan. She began her professional career as a newspaper feature writer in Ankara. In 1949 she founded and became first president of the Turkish-American Women's Cultural Society. In 1952–1953 she studied in the United States on a Fulbright fellowship, and in 1955 received her Ph.D. at Ankara University for her thesis, *The Notion of Public Opinion* (published in Turkish). In the same year, she began to teach at the Faculty of Political Science of Ankara University. A Federal German governmental fellowship brought her to several German universities and research institutions where she worked on problems of bureaucracy. Her book on this subject was published in 1958, and that year she was appointed Associate Professor at the University of Ankara. Her third published book deals with the leisure-time activities of students in Ankara. She is vice-president of the Ankara branch of the Turkish University Women's Association.

AHMED, SHEREEN AZIZ, wife of the former Ambassador of Pakistan to the United States has an M.A. in English Literature and a bachelor's degree in education. She founded the Ramna Preparatory School at Dacca, East Pakistan, organized the East Pakistan branch of the All Pakistan Women's Association and of the Pakistan Women's National Guard, was vice-president of the Pakistan Federation of University Women, and a member of the Senate and Syndicate of the University of Karachi. She has represented Pakistan in various international conferences, was Pakistan's delegate to the Thirteenth Session of the U.N. Commission on the Status of Women, was a member of the Pakistan delegation to the fourteenth, fifteenth, and sixteenth sessions of the U.N. General Assembly, and represented the University of Karachi at the 1960 World Conference of Universities in Mexico City. She has contributed numerous articles on women's problems to magazines and newspapers. She is the mother of two daughters and two sons.

CHIN, AI-LI S., was born and educated in Shanghai. She came to the United States for her college studies and for graduate work in sociology (Wellesley, B.A., Radcliffe, M.A. and Ph.D.). Her main field of interest has been social change in modern Chinese society, and her research activities have centered on changing role structure, role conflict, and mass communications in modern China. Mrs. Chin is an Associate in Research, East Asian Research Center, Harvard University. Among her published works is an article, "Some Problems of Chinese Youth in Transition," in the *American Journal of Sociology*, 1948. She is married and has three children.

ALEXANDROVA, VERA, was born in Russia and lived, until her death in 1966, in New York with her husband, Dr. Solomon M. Schwarz. She studied at the

Universities of Odessa and Moscow and left Russia in 1922. She has contributed articles, mainly on Russian literary problems, to *The New Leader, American Mercury*, and *Saturday Review of Literature*, among others. From 1946 to 1948 and in 1950–1951, she was a member of the editorial board of the Russian language magazine *Amerika*, published by the U.S. State Department. From 1948 to 1950, as a research associate of the Columbia University Project for the Study of Contemporary Cultures (directed by Margaret Mead), she wrote a study on *The Non-Conformists in the Soviet Society* (still unpublished), and contributed to several published studies on Soviet society. From 1951 to 1956 she was editor-in-chief of the Ford Foundation's Chekhov Publishing House, in which capacity she edited over a hundred volumes of Russian writings, some forty of them with her own (unsigned) introductions. Her book, *History of Soviet Literature*, was published in New York in 1963. Yet another study of hers, *Control of Soviet Literature in the Post-Stalin Period*, awaits publication.

BENZ, MARGARET, was born in Yakima, Washington, and graduated from the University of Washington in 1922, having majored in sociology. She came to New York City to attend the New York School of Social Work and the Graduate School of Political Science at Columbia University. She received a diploma from the N.Y. School of Social Work in 1924, and went into professional social work with the American Red Cross in Florida, southern Illinois, Utah, San Francisco, and Los Angeles. In 1928, she married Luke Benz and moved with him to New York City, where he works as an investment counselor. She received her Master's Degree in child development at Columbia University in 1932, and her Ph.D. in sociology and child development, in 1940. Her dissertation, which was published, was *Family Counseling in a University Community*. The Benzes have a son and a daughter, both of whom are now married.

Dr. Benz was a research associate on the faculty of Columbia University from 1932 to 1939, and until her death at Mt. Kisco, New York in 1967, had been teaching in the undergraduate Sociology Department at Washington Square College, New York University, since 1939, where she was Associate Professor of Sociology.

She was a member of the American Association of Marriage Counselors, a certified social worker, a fellow of the American Sociological Society, and president of the Tri-State council on Family Relations.

CHURCHILL, CHARLES W., was born in Detroit, Michigan, and studied at Rutgers (B.A. in economics) and New York University (M.A. and Ph.D. in sociology and economics). He has taught at Cooper Union, Briarcliff College, San Diego State College, and, since 1951, at the American University of Beirut, Lebanon, where he is at present Associate Professor of Statistics and Sociology. Since 1951 he has been engaged in numerous projects in Lebanon, including social research into educational attitudes, public health, diet, and housing. His published writings include articles on Arab cities for the *Middle East Forum;* "New Techniques in Social Surveys," *The Near East*, January, 1955; *The City of Beirut, a Socio-Economic Survey*, Dar el-Kitab, Lebanon, 1954; "Village Life in the Central Baqa' Valley of Lebanon," *Middle East Economic Papers*, Dar el-Kitab, Lebanon, 1959; *Bibliography of Echinococcus with Selected Abstracts* (with Dr. L. Powers), American University of Beirut, 1959; "Field Research Problems in Public Health in the Arab World," *Proceedings of the Tenth Middle East Medical Assembly*, American University of Beirut, 1960.

CRUZ, LEVY, studied at the School of Sociology and Political Science of São Paolo, Brazil, and the University of Chicago. From 1948 to 1953 he was research assistant, and from 1953 to 1958, assistant professor, at the School of Sociology and Political Science at São Paolo; from 1958 to 1960, professor of sociology at the Catholic University of Pernambuco. Since 1960 he has been professor of sociology at the School of Social Work of Pernambuco and Director of the Division of Social Research and Studies, Regional Center for Research in Education, of Recife. In 1965 he obtained a three-year leave of absence from this institution to become an associate rural sociologist at the Interamerican Institute of Agricultural Sciences at Turrialba, Costa Rica. His published works include: "Aspectos da Formação e Desintegração da Família em Rio Rico," *Sociologia*, October, 1954; "Papel da Hipótese nos Estudos de Comunidade," *Anais do II Congresso Latino-Americano de Sociologia*, Rio de Janeiro, 1957; "Funçoões do Comportamento Político numa Comunidade do São Francisco," *Revista Brasileira de Estudos Políticos*, January, 1959; "Tendências de Mudança no Nordeste e a Educação," *Simpósio Educação para o Brasil*, Recife: Centro Regional de Pesquisas Educacionais, 1960; "Espaço, Tempo, Região e Educação," *Cadernos Região e Educação*, June, 1961; *Estudo de Caracterização Social dos I-migrantes do Recife*, to be published by the Instituto Joaquim Nabuco of Social Research; "Hipóteses e Sugestões sôbre o Ensino no Vale do São Francisco," *Revista Brasileira de Estudos Pedagógicos* with Donald Pierson and Octavio da Costa Eduardo, April–June, 1952.

FORMICA, MERCEDES, was born in Cadiz, Spain and lives with her husband and family in Madrid. She studied law at the Universities of Sevilla and Madrid, received her law degree in 1948, and embarked on a career of writing, lecturing, editing, and campaigning for women's rights. The inclusion of numerous articles pertaining to women's rights in the Spanish Civil Code of 1958 was to a great extent the result of Sra. Formica's work. Her report, "Women in the Professions," presented to the Ibero-American-Philippine Congress (Madrid, 1950), served as the basis for the Spanish law of July 22, 1961, which gives women access to various professions previously closed to them. While engaged in these campaigns, Sra. Formica also found time to write half-a-dozen novels and numerous articles, to practice law in Madrid, and to participate in frequent conferences discussing Spanish social problems.

HARMAN, ZENA, was born and educated in London where she studied economics at the London School of Economics and Political Science and sociology at Morley College. In 1939 she went to South Africa, and was married to Avraham Harman, at present Israel's Ambassador to the United States. In 1940 the Harmans settled in Jerusalem. There Mrs. Harman became head of the Children's Department in the Social Welfare section of the Jerusalem municipality, then served with the Youth Aliyah (the institution in charge of young immigrants), collected and edited the letters of Henrietta Szold, and edited a monthly bulletin. In the 1950's she was a member of the Permanent Delegation of Israel to the U.N., a representative of Israel on the Social, Cultural, and Humanitarian Committee and on UNICEF and was a member of the Commission on the Status of Women. From 1956 to 1959 she was director of the Division for International Organization in the Israel Ministry for Foreign Affairs. In 1960 she was elected a vice-president of the International Council of Women. Among her writings are numerous articles and studies on Israel, the U.N., and UNICEF, published in the *Middle East Journal* and other periodicals.

HIRAMATSU, MASAKO, was born in Japan, and received her M.A. in sociology at Tokyo Metropolitan University in 1959. In 1964 she earned her M.A. degree with a thesis on working women in the Japanese radio industry. She cooperated with Professor Takashi Koyama in the preparation of the volume *Changing Social Position of Women in Japan*, published by UNESCO, Paris, 1961, and contributed an article on women and their civic activities to the book *Contemporary Women in Japan*, edited by Prof. Koyama in 1962. Miss Hiramatsu has written extensively for Japanese periodicals, and is at present a reporter for the Radio Kanto.

HOLTER, HARRIET, was born in Norway, and lives in Oslo with her husband, who is a psychoanalyst, and their child. She studied at the University of Oslo where she received her Master's degree in economics in 1946. From 1946 to 1948 she worked as an economist for the Norwegian government which later sent her for a year's study to the United States. Here, and in London, she studied sociology and psychology. Since 1951 she has been associated with the Institute for Social Research at Oslo, where she is at present research leader. Miss Holter is also Lecturer in Sociology at the University of Oslo and at the Norwegian School of Social Work. Her research deals mainly with industrial and family relations. Her published works include : "Sex Differences in School and Work Performance" (in Norwegian), *Tidsskrift for Samfunnsforskning*, Oslo, September, 1961; "Rebellion against the Family" (in English), *Acta Sociologica*, Copenhagen, 1962; *The Life and Work of Women* (in Norwegian), with Prof. Edmund Dahlstrom, Stockholm, 1963.

KHAING, MI MI, who was born in Burma, studied there and for three years at London University. After serving briefly as a lecturer at the University of Rangoon and researcher for the British Ministry of Information, she was married in 1942 to Sao Saimong, son of the Chief of Kengtung, who was Principal Education Officer of the Shan State. In 1951 she founded Kambawsa College, a coeducational school, and served as its principal. She has been president of the Maternity and Infant Welfare Center in the city of Taunggyi and participated in several seminars on the status of women. Among her published works are *Burmese Family*, Bloomington, Ind., 1962; the chapter on Burma in the UNESCO volume *Men and Women in South-east Asia* (1962), and numerous articles in periodicals such as "The Citizen in Burma," "A Modern Review of the Shan State," "Burmese Character and Customs," "The Burmese Kinship System," and a series on "The Burmese Woman."

KLEIN, VIOLA, was born in Vienna, studied at the Universities of Paris, Vienna, Prague, and London; took a doctorate in modern languages at Prague in 1937, and in sociology (as student of Professor Karl Mannheim) at the London School of Economics in 1944. She arrived in London as a refugee in 1939, worked at the Foreign Office for about eleven years, and as a research officer at the London School of Economics for two years. She was a Simon Research Fellow and then senior research associate at the University of Manchester, and is now lecturer in sociology at the University of Reading (England). Dr. Klein's publications include : *The Feminine Character: History of an Ideology*,

London, 1946; Stockholm, 1948; New York, 1949; Buenos Aires, 1950; "The Emancipation of Women," *Ideas and Beliefs of the Victorians*, London, 1949; "The Stereotype of Femininity," *Journal of Social Issues*, Michigan, 1950; *Women's Two Roles* (in collaboration with Alva Myrdal), London and New York, 1956; Stockholm, 1957; Cologne, 1960; *Working Wives*, London, 1960; "Married Women in Employment," *International Journal of Comparative Sociology*, Leiden, 1960; *Employing Married Women*, London, 1961; *Britain's Married Women Workers*, London, 1965; *Working Women with Family Responsibilities*, O.E.C.D., Paris, 1965.

KOYAMA, TAKASHI, was born and educated in Japan, graduating in 1924 from Tokyo Imperial University, Department of Sociology. He was appointed Professor of Sociology at the Takaoka and Nagasaki Commercial Colleges, and subsequently superintendent of social education in the Japanese Ministry of Education. Following World War II he became Professor of Sociology at Osaka University, was chairman of the Department of Sociology, Tokyo Metropolitan University, and is at present Professor of Sociology at Toyo University and President of the Japan Sociological Society. Among his published works are: *The Contemporary Japanese Family* (ed., in Japanese), 1960; *Changing Social Position of Women in Japan* (in English), UNESCO, Paris, 1961; *Modern Women in Japan* (in Japanese), 1962; and over eighty articles in professional journals, mostly dealing with the family structure in Japan.

LEHMANN, ANDREE, was born in Paris, studied in Paris, and continues to live in Paris. In 1921 she received her *Licence en Droit*, and was admitted to the Paris Bar and to the Paris Court of Appeals. In 1924 she obtained her *Docteur en Droit* degree from the University of Paris. Most of the cases she has pleaded have been in the realm of family law. Dr. Lehmann's publications include (all in French): *The Legal Regulation of Women's Work* (doctoral thesis), Paris, 1924; *The Role of Women in the History of France; The Role of Women in the History of Gaul; The Role of French Women in the Twentieth Century* (3rd ed.), 1965. Mme. Lehmann is editor of the monthly revue, *Le Droit des Femmes*, president of the French League for Women's Rights, honorary vice-president of the International Alliance of Women, and prominently associated with other French and international women's organizations.

MARTI, ROSA SIGNORELLI DE, was born in Buenos Aires, Argentina, where she lives with her husband and two daughters. She studied at the University of Buenos Aires, in both the Faculty of Philosophy and Literature and the Faculty of Law and Social Sciences. After earning her Ph.D., she taught at high schools and at the University of Buenos Aires, and, at the same time, engaged in intensive work in various Argentinian women's organizations. She was awarded a fellowship by the U.S. State Department's Educational and Cultural Exchange Program, served as Argentine delegate to the seminar, "The Citizen in a Free Society," held in Washington in 1961 and sponsored by the Overseas Educational Fund of the League of Women Voters, and represented Argentina in international women's conferences. At present, she is technical director of the American Community School in Buenos Aires. Her published works include (all in Spanish): *Women in the Roman World* (a historical and juridical study); *Women in the Ancient World* (a social and political essay); *Civil and Political Rights of Women in the Argentina Republic; Civil and Political Rights of Women in the Modern World*.

NAKAMURA, HACHIRO, was born and educated in Japan, and graduated from Tokyo Metropolitan University, Department of Sociology (1957). He served as assistant in the Social Science Research Institute, International Christian University, Tokyo, and is at present Research Officer, Social Development Research Institute (a government-sponsored institute established in 1965). He cooperated with Professor Koyama in the preparation of the volume, *Changing Social Position of Women in Japan*, UNESCO, Paris, 1961, and has written several articles on urban problems.

NARAIN, VATSALA, was born in Madras, India, studied there and in Bombay, and received her M.A. and Ph.D. degrees in sociology from Bombay University. Her doctoral dissertation was a study on rural reactions to urbanization. For three years she taught and did research at the Gokhale Institute of Politics and Economics in Poona, and at the Institute of Economic Growth, Delhi University. Following her marriage to a lecturer in sociology at Bombay University, she moved to Bombay, and then came to the United States for a two-year stay with her husband, after which they both returned to India to continue their teaching and research.

PROSS, HELGE, was born in Düsseldorf, West Germany, and studied sociology, political science, and history at Heidelberg University, where she received, in 1950, her Ph.D. From 1952 to 1954, as a Fellow of the Commonwealth Fund, she studied at Stanford and Columbia Universities, and did research on German academic emigration to the United States. From 1954 to 1959 she was a member of the Institute of Social Research, and from 1956 to 1965 taught sociology, at Frankfort University. From 1959 to 1961 she was a research fellow of the *Deutsche Forschungsgemeinschaft*, for which she prepared a study on the separation of ownership and management in modern German industry. In 1965 she was appointed full Professor of Sociology and head of the Institute of Social Research of the University of Giessen. Among Miss Pross' published writings are: "A Romantic Socialist in Prussia," *The German Quarterly*, 1954; *Die deutsche akademische Emigration nach den Vereinigten Staaten, 1933–1941*, Berlin, 1955; "Soziologie, die unbekannte Wissenschaft," *Frankfurter Hefte*, October, 1955; "Soziale und ideologische Ursachen des Antisemitismus in Deutschland," *Gesellschaft, Staat, Erziehung*, Heft 3, 1957; "Die gesellschaftliche Stellung der Frau in Westdeutschland," *Deutsche Rundschau*, January, 1958; "Die soziale Schichtung in der Bundesrepublik," *Deutsche Rundschau*, October, 1958; *Die Frauenerwerbsarbeit und ihre Bedeutung in der Gegenwart*, Darmstadt, 1960; "Die Frau in der modernen Gesellschaft," *Gesellschaft, Staat, Erziehung*, Heft 2, 1961.

PSALTIS, EGLY, was born in Greece, studied in Athens, Paris, and Germany, and received her law degree and diploma in economics in Paris. She then engaged in postgraduate studies and research in international and public law in Paris, Brussels, and Berlin. Upon the outbreak of World War II, she returned to Greece where she served as private secretary to the Swedish president of the Swedish-Swiss Commission for Distribution of Assistance to Greece, as official interpreter for the U.N. Commission investigating the Greek frontier incidents, as chief of the Contracts Section of the Greek Recovery Program Coordinating Office, Ministry of Coordination, and, since 1951, as secretary-general of the Greek Refugee Service Committee. Miss Psaltis is also president of the Greek

Association for the Protection of Minors; president of the Greek League for Women's Rights; hon. secretary of the International Alliance of Women, and was awarded the Greek Golden Cross of Welfare.

TENTORI, TULLIO, is secretary-general of the Italian Association of Social Sciences, professor of anthropology at the University of Rome, and director of the National Museum for Folk Art and Traditions in Rome. His first interest was in the culture of the American Indians about whose religion, art and material culture he has written numerous studies. While in the United States in 1949, he decided to apply the anthropological methods to the problems of Italian society. Upon his return to Italy he studied Matera, a community in the south, and at the same time introduced anthropology into various Italian schools of social work. The results of his research into the life of working women in a suburban area near Rome and the impact of their experience upon family structure were published in 1960. His pocket book, *Cultural Anthropology*, discusses and evaluates recent trends and presents a new theory in the study of cultural processes. Among his other works are *La Pittura Precolombiana, Miti e Leggende degli Indiani dell' America Centrale e Meridionale* (with R. Pettazzoni), *Il Sistema di Vita della Communità Materana*.

VREEDE–DE STUERS, CORA, was born in Bodegraven, The Netherlands, and studied at the University of Paris from which she received the degrees of *Licenciée des Lettres, Diplômée de l'Institute d'Ethnologie, Brevetée de l'Ecole des Langues Orientales Vivantes* and *Docteur de l'Université* in Sociology. Following her marriage to Professor F. Vreede, she spent several years with her husband in Egypt and India. After the outbreak of World War II, she was interned on Java during the Japanese occupation. Following the war she was, until 1955, chief librarian of the Royal Batavian Society of Arts and Sciences and director of the first Library School of Indonesia at Djakarta. In 1959–1960 she held a traveling fellowship to India from the Ecole Pratique des Hautes Etudes of the Sorbonne. At present she is research associate at the Institute of History and Sociology of Southeast Asia, University of Amsterdam. Among her published works are: *L'Emancipation de la Femme Indonesienne*, Paris, 1959; *The Indonesian Woman: Struggles and Achievements*, The Hague, 1960; *The Hindu Woman of India* (in Dutch), Amsterdam, 1962; numerous articles (in Dutch) on the Hindu woman.

WHEELER, ELIZABETH HUNTING, was born in Brooklyn, N.Y., studied at Miami University, Ohio (B.A. in government), and did graduate work in African Studies at Boston University (1956–1957). From 1958 to 1960 she was engaged in free-lance research in African affairs, and undertook a six-month research trip to Africa concentrating on problems of education and women's activities. In 1960–1961 she served as executive secretary for the African Scholarship Program of American Universities, in which capacity she made a second trip of three months' duration to East and Central Africa. Currently, Miss Wheeler is program administrator for the Women's Africa Committee's experimental Leadership Program for African Women. Her published writings include *The Role of Women in Africa*, New York; African-American Institute, 1960; "Guideposts to African Aspirations," *Free World Forum*, Spring, 1960; "Southern Rhodesia at the Crossroads," *Journal of African Affairs*, Fall, 1961.

YARSHATER, LATIFEH (née Alvieh), was born in Iran, studied at the American School in Tehran, and received training in social work in the United States. Since 1953 she has been cultural adviser to the U.S. Information Service in Iran. In 1953 she helped establish the Iranian Youth Activities Organization, and organized and directed several summer camps for training camp counselors and club leaders. In 1954 she organized the progressive Shahnaz Girls Club, and in 1958 and 1959 she was one of the organizers and leaders of the Youth Conference in Iran. As a member of the Iranian High Council of Women, she represented Iran in several international women's conferences in Ceylon, Berlin, New Delhi, and Istanbul. Mrs. Yarshater has lectured widely, both in Iran and abroad, on the situation of Iranian women, has published numerous articles on the subject, and has contributed to Iranian school readers. Her Persian translation of a selection of Emily Dickinson's poems was published in 1963.